Evidence-Based Physical Examination

BEST PRACTICES FOR HEALTH AND WELL-BEING ASSESSMENT

Kate Sustersic Gawlik, DNP, APRN-CNP, FAANP, is an assistant professor of clinical nursing at The Ohio State University. She is certified by the American Nurses Credentialing Center as an adult and family nurse practitioner. She has extensive background in primary care, with experience in family practice, college health, urgent care, and reproductive care. Her clinical interests are evidence-based practice, population health, preventive medicine, clinician well-being, health professionals' education, wellness, and cardiovascular disease prevention. She has served as the project manager for the Million Hearts® initiatives at Ohio State's College of Nursing since 2013. She leads and serves on multiple state and national workgroups targeted at improving cardiovascular population health.

Dr. Gawlik started her nursing career in 2006 and completed her MSc in nursing with a specialization as an adult/geriatric nurse practitioner in 2009 from The Ohio State University. In 2015, she graduated with her DNP and a post-master's certificate as a family nurse practitioner from The Ohio State University. Dr. Gawlik was awarded the Outstanding Faculty Award in 2013 and the Outstanding Leadership Award in 2017 at The Ohio State University. She received an Abstract of Distinction at the Council for the Advancement of Nursing Science Conference in 2016 and the Editor's Pick for 2017 Paper of the Year by the *American Journal of Health Promotion* for "An Epidemiological Study of Population Health Reveals Social Smoking as a Major Cardiovascular Risk Factor." She was awarded the 2018 American Association of Nurse Practitioner State Award for Excellence for Ohio. She was inducted as a fellow into the American Association of Nurse Practitioners in June 2018.

Dr. Gawlik has been teaching nursing students since 2007. She has taught a variety of undergraduate, RN–BSN, and graduate nursing courses and serves as a clinical preceptor for advanced practice nursing students. Her passion lies in teaching in the online platform, both in synchronous and asynchronous classrooms. She has been teaching solely online since 2012. Dr. Gawlik developed an online educational module on cardiovascular population health that is used nationally and internationally. The educational module has led to the cardiovascular screening of over 75,000 people. Her educational interests include the development of new and innovative teaching modalities and pedagogies for online teaching with a focus on advanced assessment, evidence-based practice, and health promotion courses.

This is Dr. Gawlik's first book. She is hopeful that by integrating her three passions—advanced assessment, evidence-based practice, and health promotion—into one book, students will have the opportunity to apply and assimilate these three foundational skills in their journey to become expert clinicians.

Bernadette Mazurek Melnyk, PhD, APRN-CNP, FAANP, FNAP, FAAN, is the vice president for health promotion, university chief wellness officer, and professor and dean of the College of Nursing at The Ohio State University. She is also a professor of pediatrics and psychiatry at Ohio State's College of Medicine. In addition, she is the executive director of the Helene Fuld Health Trust National Institute for Evidence-Based Practice in Nursing and Healthcare. Dr. Melnyk earned her BSc in nursing from West Virginia University, her MSc with a specialization in nursing care of children and as a pediatric nurse practitioner from the University of Pittsburgh, and her PhD in clinical research from the University of Rochester where she also completed her post-master's certificate as a psychiatric mental health nurse practitioner.

She is a nationally/internationally recognized expert in evidence-based practice, intervention research, child and adolescent mental health, and health and wellness and is a frequent keynote speaker at national and international conferences on these topics. Dr. Melnyk has consulted with hundreds of healthcare systems and colleges throughout the nation and globe on how to improve quality of care and patient outcomes through implementing and sustaining evidence-based practice. Her record includes over $33 million of sponsored funding from federal agencies and foundations as principal investigator and over 400 publications.

Dr. Melnyk is coeditor of six other books: *Implementing the Evidence-Based Practice (EBP) Competencies in Healthcare: A Practical Guide for Improving Quality, Safety, and Outcomes*; *Evidence-Based Practice in Nursing & Healthcare: A Guide to Best Practice* (4th Edition), an *American Journal of Nursing Research* Book of the Year Award winner; *Implementing EBP: Real World Success Stories*; *A Practical Guide to Child and Adolescent Mental Health Screening, Early Intervention and Health Promotion* (2nd Edition); *Intervention Research and Evidence-Based Quality Improvement: Designing, Conducting, Analyzing and Funding* (2nd Edition), also an *American Journal of Nursing Research* Book of the Year Award winner; and *Evidence-Based Leadership, Innovation and Entrepreneurship in Nursing and Healthcare*.

Dr. Melnyk is an elected fellow of the National Academy of Medicine, the American Academy of Nursing, the National Academies of Practice, and the American Association of Nurse Practitioners. She served a 4-year term on the 16-member U.S. Preventive Services Task Force and the National Institutes of Health's National Advisory Council for Nursing Research and was a board member of the National Guideline Clearinghouse and the National Quality Measures Clearinghouse (NGC/NQMC). She currently serves as a member of the National Quality Forum's

(NQF) Behavioral Health Standing Committee. Dr. Melnyk also serves as editor of the journal *Worldviews on Evidence-Based Nursing* and is a member of the National Academy of Medicine's Action Collaborative on Clinician Well-Being and Resilience as well as an elected board member of the National Forum for Heart Disease & Stroke Prevention.

Dr. Melnyk has received numerous national and international awards, including the Audrey Hepburn Award, Mary Tolle Wright Excellence in Leadership Award, and the International Nursing Research Hall of Fame Award from Sigma Theta Tau International, the Jessie Scott Award from the American Nurses Association for the improvement of healthcare quality through the integration of research, education, and practice, the 2012 Midwest Nursing Research Society Senior Scientist Award, the NIH/National Institute of Nursing Research's inaugural Director's Lectureship Award, the AANP Sharp Cutting Edge Award, and the National Organization of Nurse Practitioner Faculties Lifetime Achievement Award. She has been recognized as an Edge Runner three times by the American Academy of Nursing for founding and directing the National Association of Pediatric Nurse Practitioners' KySS child and adolescent mental health program, her COPE Program for parents of critically ill children and preterm infants, and her Creating Opportunities for Personal Empowerment (COPE) cognitive-behavioral skills building program for depressed and anxious children, teens, and college students, which is being implemented in 45 states throughout the United States and five countries. She is also the founder of two companies that disseminate her evidence-based intervention programs.

Dr. Melnyk founded the National Interprofessional Education and Practice Consortium to Advance Million Hearts, which is a collaboration of over 170 organizations and academic institutions across the United States. She also created and chaired the first three National Summits on Building Healthy Academic Communities and is the founder of the National Consortium for Building Healthy Academic Communities, a collaborative organization to improve population health in the nation's institutions of higher learning, and served as its first president.

Alice M. Teall, DNP, APRN-CNP, FAANP, is director of graduate health and wellness programming, director of innovative telehealth services, and an assistant professor of clinical nursing at The Ohio State University College of Nursing. An expert in nursing education, Dr. Teall was honored with The Ohio State University Provost Award for Distinguished Teaching by a Lecturer and with the Wright State University Presidential Award for Faculty Excellence. While serving as director of the online Family Nurse Practitioner program, she was chosen as The Ohio State College of Nursing Graduate Educator of the Year for 4 consecutive years.

Alice M. Teall began her nursing career as a diploma graduate of Miami Valley Hospital School of Nursing in 1983. She earned her BSc in nursing from Capital University, her MSc with a specialization as a Family Nurse Practitioner from Wright State University, and her DNP from The Ohio State University. She has certifications as a Family and Pediatric Nurse Practitioner and as an Integrative Nurse Coach. Her clinical expertise and areas of interest include adolescent health, primary care of at-risk youth and families, college health, and recovery from substance use disorder. Dr. Teall has an extensive background in primary care, which includes addressing population health using telehealth technologies and improving access to care through statewide quality improvement initiatives. She has received leadership, alumni, and practice awards and is a Fellow of the American Academy of Nurse Practitioners.

An experienced educator, Alice M. Teall has taught assessment online and on campus for students across nursing programs, including LPN, traditional undergraduate, RN–BSN completion, accelerated graduate entry, traditional master's, BS-to-DNP, post-master's, and doctoral programs. Dr. Teall has published and presented nationally about the effective use of classrooms as engaged and collaborative communities of inquiry, where active learning, timely feedback, diversity of thought, and support for self-care and wellness are norms. Her contributions to advanced practice education include innovative use of synchronous web-conferencing, incorporation of health and wellness coaching techniques in clinical practice, and use of telehealth as an evaluation strategy for distance students. Her doctoral work included an evidence-based quality improvement initiative to improve clinician confidence in addressing health, wellness, and self-management of chronic disease using coaching strategies.

Dr. Teall has taught students nationally and internationally to provide evidence-based, patient-centered, collaborative care for individuals and families. This textbook includes best practice guidance gained from her experience in course and clinical teaching, program administration, and curriculum development. Her hope is that health science students will create authentic connection and partnerships with patients, peers, and faculty as they learn to implement the knowledge, skills, and attitudes required of evidence-based assessment.

Front Cover Photo Credits: (outer ring): ©Mike Liu/Shutterstock, (inner ring): ©Nigel Killeen/Moment Open/Getty Images, (c) ©Carrie Garcia/Houghton Mifflin Harcourt, (c overlay): ©Eyewire/Getty Images, (bc overlay): ©elenamiv/Shutterstock

Back Cover Photo Credits: (Units 1-6): ©Print Collector/Hulton Archive/Getty Images; ©Christophel Fine Art/Getty Images; ©A. Dagli Orti/De Agostini Editorial/Getty Images; ©Tonktiti/Shutterstock; ©jgorzynik/iStockphoto/Getty Images; ©Friedemann Vogel/Getty Images

Printed in the U.S.A.

ISBN 978-1-328-55679-0

2 3 4 5 6 7 8 9 10   0690   27 26 25 24 23 22 21 20 19

4500752966   B C D E F G

HMH | (into) **Literature**™

GRADE 12

Program Consultants:

Kylene Beers

Martha Hougen

Elena Izquierdo

Carol Jago

Erik Palmer

Robert E. Probst

Kylene Beers

Nationally known lecturer and author on reading and literacy; coauthor with Robert Probst of *Disrupting Thinking, Notice & Note: Strategies for Close Reading,* and *Reading Nonfiction;* former president of the National Council of Teachers of English. Dr. Beers is the author of *When Kids Can't Read: What Teachers Can Do* and coeditor of *Adolescent Literacy: Turning Promise into Practice,* as well as articles in the *Journal of Adolescent and Adult Literacy.* Former editor of *Voices from the Middle,* she is the 2001 recipient of NCTE's Richard W. Halle Award, given for outstanding contributions to middle school literacy. She recently served as Senior Reading Researcher at the Comer School Development Program at Yale University as well as Senior Reading Advisor to Secondary Schools for the Reading and Writing Project at Teachers College.

Martha Hougen

National consultant, presenter, researcher, and author. Areas of expertise include differentiating instruction for students with learning difficulties, including those with learning disabilities and dyslexia; and teacher and leader preparation improvement. Dr. Hougen has taught at the middle school through graduate levels. In addition to peer-reviewed articles, curricular documents, and presentations, Dr. Hougen has published two college textbooks: *The Fundamentals of Literacy Assessment and Instruction Pre-K–6* (2012) and *The Fundamentals of Literacy Assessment and Instruction 6–12* (2014). Dr. Hougen has supported Educator Preparation Program reforms while working at the Meadows Center for Preventing Educational Risk at The University of Texas at Austin and at the CEEDAR Center, University of Florida.

Elena Izquierdo

Nationally recognized teacher educator and advocate for English language learners. Dr. Izquierdo is a linguist by training, with a Ph.D. in Applied Linguistics and Bilingual Education from Georgetown University. She has served on various state and national boards working to close the achievement gaps for bilingual students and English language learners. Dr. Izquierdo is a member of the Hispanic Leadership Council, which supports Hispanic students and educators at both the state and federal levels. She served as Vice President on the Executive Board of the National Association of Bilingual Education and as Publications and Professional Development Chair.

Carol Jago

Teacher of English with 32 years of experience at Santa Monica High School in California; author and nationally known lecturer; former president of the National Council of Teachers of English. Ms. Jago currently serves as Associate Director of the California Reading and Literature Project at UCLA. With expertise in standards assessment and secondary education, Ms. Jago is the author of numerous books on education, including *With Rigor for All* and *Papers, Papers, Papers,* and is active with the California Association of Teachers of English, editing its scholarly journal *California English* since 1996. Ms. Jago also served on the planning committee for the 2009 NAEP Reading Framework and the 2011 NAEP Writing Framework.

Erik Palmer

Veteran teacher and education consultant based in Denver, Colorado. Author of *Well Spoken: Teaching Speaking to All Students* and *Digitally Speaking: How to Improve Student Presentations.* His areas of focus include improving oral communication, promoting technology in classroom presentations, and updating instruction through the use of digital tools. He holds a bachelor's degree from Oberlin College and a master's degree in curriculum and instruction from the University of Colorado.

Robert E. Probst

Nationally respected authority on the teaching of literature; Professor Emeritus of English Education at Georgia State University. Dr. Probst's publications include numerous articles in *English Journal* and *Voices from the Middle,* as well as professional texts including (as coeditor) *Adolescent Literacy: Turning Promise into Practice* and (as coauthor with Kylene Beers) *Disrupting Thinking, Notice & Note: Strategies for Close Reading,* and *Reading Nonfiction.* He regularly speaks at national and international conventions including those of the International Literacy Association, the National Council of Teachers of English, the Association of Supervisors and Curriculum Developers, and the National Association of Secondary School Principals. He has served NCTE in various leadership roles, including the Conference on English Leadership Board of Directors, the Commission on Reading, and column editor of the NCTE journal *Voices from the Middle.* He is also the 2004 recipient of the CEL Exemplary Leader Award.

UNIT ①

ORIGIN OF A NATION

PAGE 1

? ***ESSENTIAL QUESTIONS***

- What makes someone a hero?
- What is true chivalry?
- Can we control our fate?
- What happens when a society unravels?

UNIT **1**

COMPARE
THEMES

POEM
The Wanderer

POEM
Loneliness

UNIT 1

COMPARE THEMES

POEM
The Wanderer 110

by Anonymous, *translated by* Burton Raffel

POEM
Loneliness 118

by Fanny Howe

 INDEPENDENT READING 126

These selections can be accessed through the digital edition.

EPIC POEM
from **Beowulf**
by the Beowulf Poet, *translated by* Burton Raffel

Grendel's Mother   The Death of Beowulf
The Battle with Grendel's Mother   Mourning Beowulf
Beowulf's Last Battle

ARTICLE
Beowulf Is Back!
by James Parker

BALLAD
Barbara Allan
by Anonymous

ARTICLE
Journeymen Keep the Medieval Past Alive
by Melissa Eddy

Suggested Novel Connection

NOVEL
Grendel
by John Gardner

Unit ① **Tasks**
• Write a Short Story 128
• Create a Podcast 135

Reflect on the Unit 137

Key Learning Objectives

- Analyze characteristics of an epic poem
- Analyze Old English poetry
- Analyze narrator
- Analyze conflict
- Make predictions
- Analyze characterization
- Make inferences
- Analyze tone

 Visit the Interactive Student Edition for:

- Unit and Selection Videos
- Media Selections
- Selection Audio Recordings
- Enhanced Digital Instruction

Contents FM7

UNIT ②

A CELEBRATION OF HUMAN ACHIEVEMENT

PAGE 138

 ESSENTIAL QUESTIONS

- What can drive someone to seek revenge?
- How does time affect our feelings?
- What's the difference between love and passion?
- How do you defy expectations?

COLLABORATE & COMPARE

POEM
The Passionate Shepherd to His Love
by Christopher Marlowe

POEM
The Nymph's Reply to the Shepherd
by Sir Walter Raleigh

Suggested Drama Connection

DRAMA
Othello
by William Shakespeare

Key Learning Objectives

- Analyze dramatic plot
- Analyze conflict
- Analyze soliloquy
- Analyze arguments
- Analyze key ideas
- Analyze sonnets
- Analyze metaphysical conceits
- Interpret figurative language
- Analyze speaker
- Analyze rhetorical devices
- Analyze text features

Online **Visit the Interactive**
Ed **Student Edition for:**

- Unit and Selection Videos
- Media Selections
- Selection Audio Recordings
- Enhanced Digital Instruction

UNIT ③
TRADITION AND REASON
PAGE 360

? **ESSENTIAL QUESTIONS**

- How can satire change people's behavior?
- What is your most memorable experience?
- What keeps women from achieving equality with men?
- Why are plagues so horrifying?

© Houghton Mifflin Harcourt Publishing Company • Image Credits: ©A. Dagli Orti/De Agostini Editorial/Getty Images; ©Heritage Images/Getty Images; ©Time Life Pictures/Getty Images; ©Ridofranz/Getty Images; ©Mike Kipling Photography/Alamy; ©Hulton Archive/Getty Images; ©Picade LLC/Alamy

Key Learning Objectives

- Analyze satire
- Analyze mock epic
- Understand author's purpose
- Analyze tone
- Connect to history
- Evaluate arguments
- Analyze counterarguments
- Analyze graphic features
- Analyze historical setting
- Analyze narrator

Online Ed

Visit the Interactive Student Edition for:

- Unit and Selection Videos
- Media Selections
- Selection Audio Recordings
- Enhanced Digital Instruction

UNIT 4
EMOTION AND EXPERIMENTATION

PAGE 490

? ESSENTIAL QUESTIONS

- What can nature offer us?
- How do you define beauty?
- How can science go wrong?
- What shapes your outlook on life?

These selections can be accessed through the digital edition.

EXPLANATORY ESSAY

William Blake: Visions and Verses

by Rachel Galvin

POEM

Frost at Midnight

by Samuel Taylor Coleridge

PERSONAL NARRATIVE

Walking with Wordsworth

by Bruce Stutz

EXPLANATORY ESSAY

***from* A Defense of Poetry**

by Percy Bysshe Shelley

POEM

The Skylark

by John Clare

Suggested Novel Connection

NOVEL

Pride and Prejudice

by Jane Austen

© Houghton Mifflin Harcourt Publishing Company • Image Credits: ©Artokoloro Quint Lox Limited/Alamy; ©Culture Club/Getty Images; ©Jaroslaw Grudzinski/Shutterstock; ©sbozac/Shutterstock; ©Grezova Olga/Shutterstock; ©Wildlife World/Shutterstock; ©Redheadpictures/age fotostock

Key Learning Objectives

- Analyze Romantic poetry
- Analyze imagery
- Analyze stanza structure
- Analyze rhyme scheme
- Analyze science fiction
- Analyze motivation
- Evaluate essay
- Analyze form
- Analyze diction
- Analyze symbols

 Visit the Interactive Student Edition for:

- Unit and Selection Videos
- Media Selections
- Selection Audio Recordings
- Enhanced Digital Instruction

UNIT ⑤
AN ERA OF RAPID CHANGE
PAGE 586

? **ESSENTIAL QUESTIONS**

- What is a true benefactor?
- How do you view the world?
- What brings out cruelty in people?
- Which invention has had the greatest impact on your life?

INDEPENDENT READING 678

Online Ed

These selections can be accessed through the digital edition.

POEM
Sonnet 43
by Elizabeth Barrett Browning

POEM
Remembrance
by Emily Brontë

ARTICLE
The Great Exhibition
by Lara Kriegel

SHORT STORY
Christmas Storms and Sunshine
by Elizabeth Cleghorn Gaskell

ESSAY
Evidence of Progress
by Thomas Babington Macaulay

Suggested Drama Connection

DRAMA
A Doll's House
by Henrik Ibsen

Key Learning Objectives

- Analyze setting
- Analyze first-person point of view
- Evaluate documentaries
- Analyze allegory
- Analyze mood
- Analyze characterization
- Analyze compare-and-contrast essay
- Analyze sound devices
- Analyze imagery
- Draw conclusions about speakers

Online Ed **Visit the Interactive Student Edition for:**

- Unit and Selection Videos
- Media Selections
- Selection Audio Recordings
- Enhanced Digital Instruction

UNIT ⑥
NEW IDEAS, NEW VOICES
PAGE 690

? ESSENTIAL QUESTIONS

- What makes people feel insecure?
- Why is it hard to resist social pressure?
- What is the power of symbols?
- When should the government interfere in our decisions?

Key Learning Objectives

• Analyze third-person point of view
• Analyze stream of consciousness
• Analyze reflective essay
• Analyze irony
• Analyze setting
• Understand symbolism
• Analyze rhythmic patterns
• Evaluate persuasive techniques
• Analyze inductive reasoning

 Visit the Interactive Student Edition for:

• Unit and Selection Videos
• Media Selections
• Selection Audio Recordings
• Enhanced Digital Instruction

SELECTIONS BY GENRE

SELECTIONS BY GENRE

HMH
Into Literature Dashboard

Easy to use and personalized for your learning.

Monitor your progress in the course.

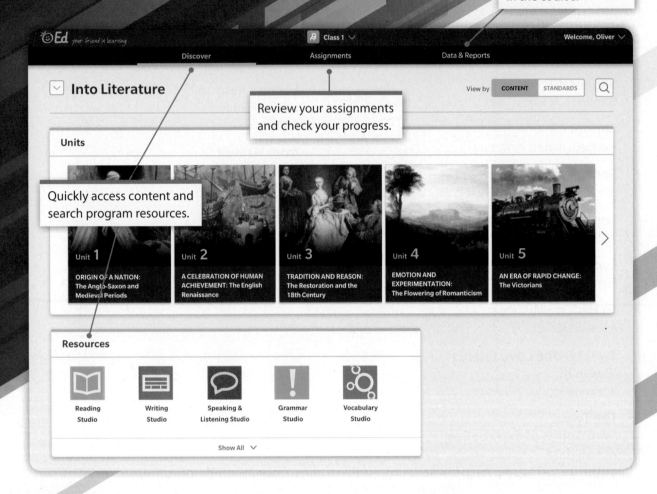

Review your assignments and check your progress.

Quickly access content and search program resources.

Explore Online to Experience the Power of HMH *Into Literature*

All in One Place

Readings and assignments are supported by a variety of resources to bring literature to life and give you the tools you need to succeed.

Supporting 21st-Century Skills

Whether you're working alone or collaborating with others, it takes effort to analyze the complex texts and competing ideas that bombard us in this fast-paced world. What will help you succeed? Staying engaged and organized. The digital tools in this program will help you take charge of your learning.

Ignite Your Investigation

You learn best when you're engaged. The **Stream to Start** videos at the beginning of every unit are designed to spark your interest before you read. Get curious and start reading!

Learn How to Close Read

Close reading effectively is all about examining the details. See how it's done by watching the **Close Read Screencasts** in your eBook. Hear modeled conversations on targeted passages.

Personalized Annotations

My Notes encourages you to take notes as you read and allows you to mark the text in your own customized way. You can easily access annotations to review later as you prepare for exams.

Interactive Graphic Organizers

Graphic organizers help you process, summarize, and keep track of your learning and prepare for end-of-unit writing tasks. **Word Networks** help you learn academic vocabulary, and **Response Logs** help you explore and deepen your understanding of the **Essential Questions** in each unit.

No Wi-Fi? No problem!

With HMH *Into Literature,* you always have access: download when you're online and access what you need when you're offline. Work offline and then upload when you're back online.

Communicate "Raise a Hand" to ask or answer questions without having to be in the same room as your teacher.

Collaborate Collaborate with your teacher via chat and work with a classmate to improve your writing.

HMH
Into Literature
STUDIOS

All the help you need to be successful in your literature class is one click away with the Studios. These digital-only lessons are here to tap into the skills that you already use and help you sharpen those skills for the future.

WRITING STUDIO

Ways to Organize Reasons and Evidence

Every argument must include reasons and evidence to support a claim. There are several effective ways you can organize that support. Check out some of those ways here.

Read the following techniques that will help you achieve cohesion, or coherence, in your writing.

Order of Importance

Least to most important

Claim: Homewood must switch from a volunteer fire department to a full-time fire department.

- Reason 1: The town is growing and getting more calls during they day when volunteers are at their full-time jobs
- Reason 2: Full-time firefighters can train daily instead of once a month, giving them more time to improve firefighting skills.

Easy-to-find resources, organized in five separate STUDIOS. On demand and on ED!

Look for links in each lesson to take you to the appropriate Studio.

READING STUDIO

Go beyond the book with the Reading Studio. With over 100 full-length downloadable titles to choose from, find the right story to continue your journey.

WRITING STUDIO

Being able to write clearly and effectively is a skill that will help you throughout life. The Writing Studio will help you become an expert communicator—in print or online.

SPEAKING & LISTENING STUDIO

Communication is more than just writing. The Speaking & Listening Studio will help you become an effective speaker and a focused listener.

GRAMMAR STUDIO

Go beyond traditional worksheets with the Grammar Studio. These engaging, interactive lessons will sharpen your grammar skills.

VOCABULARY STUDIO

Learn the skills you need to expand your vocabulary. The interactive lessons in the Vocabulary Studio will grow your vocabulary to improve your reading.

© Houghton Mifflin Harcourt Publishing Company • Image Credits : © VikaSuh/Shutterstock

ESSAY ON
Notice & Note

Dr. Kylene Beers and Dr. Robert E. Probst

In reading, as in almost everything else, paying attention is most important.

You wouldn't stand in the batter's box, facing a hard-throwing pitcher, with your mind wandering to what you may have for dinner that evening. The prospect of a fastball coming toward you at 80 miles an hour tends to focus the mind.

And you wouldn't attempt to sing a difficult song in front of a large crowd with your thoughts on what dress you're going to wear to the dance this coming weekend. The need to hit the high note, without cracking, in front of 500 people evokes concentration.

Paying attention is essential.

It's the same with reading. Of course, if you don't concentrate while reading, you won't suffer the pain of being knocked down by the fastball or the embarrassment of failing to hit the notes in front of the crowd, but you'll miss what the text offers. If you don't pay attention, there is barely any purpose in picking up the text at all.

But there is a purpose in reading. And that purpose, that point, is to enable us to change. The change may be slight, or it might be dramatic. We might, at one extreme, simply get a little more information that we need:

- Where is tonight's game?

- What time is band practice?

- What pages do we need to read for homework?

Reading for that sort of information doesn't dramatically change who we are, but it does change us slightly. Or, at least, it *might* change us slightly. Obviously, it is *we*, the readers, who must do the changing. The text doesn't do it for us. When we read that tonight's game is away, instead of at home, we have to change our plans to let us get to the other school. We have to take in the information and do something with it. If we don't, if we show up at the home field despite what we have read, the reading will have been pointless, a waste of time. And the evening will be wasted, as well. We have to pay attention to the book — what's on the page, and to our heads — what we thought before we read and what we now think. And we have to take it to heart — that is to say, we have to act on what we now know and think.

Other reading, however, might enable us to change more significantly. We might change our thinking about an important problem, or we might change our attitude about an important issue. We can't tell you which text will do that for you or how you might grow and change as a result of reading it. That's much too individual. It's hard to predict unless you know the reader well and know some of the texts that might matter to him or her:

- Some of us might read about child labor in foreign countries and change our minds about what we will buy and what we will boycott.

- You might read *To Kill a Mockingbird*, and change your thinking about race relations.

- You might read about climate change and wonder what you can do to help preserve the earth.

We can't know exactly what book will be powerful for which reader. But we can safely predict that if you don't notice what the text offers, think about it, and take what matters to you into your head and heart, then the reading probably won't mean much to you.

We're going to urge you to pay attention to three elements as you read:

- **The Book.** Or whatever text you have in your hand, whether it is a book, an article, a poem, or something else. We are going to urge you to listen carefully to what it tells you, and we're going to give you some strategies that we hope will make that easy for you to do.

- **Your Head.** We're going to ask you also to pay attention to your own thoughts. If it's an article you're reading, then keep in mind what you thought about the topic before you began, and then think seriously about how you might have changed your thinking as a result of what you've read. If it's a story or a poem or a movie, then think about what thoughts or feelings it brought to mind and how they might have shaped your reaction to the text.

- **Your Heart.** Finally, we encourage you to ask yourself what you want to carry away from the reading. What matters to you? How might you change your thinking? How might you have shifted your attitudes about something, even if only slightly? What do you take to heart?

It all begins with noticing.

But there's a lot in a book to notice, so it might help to keep in mind just a few things that you will probably see in almost any text (unless it is very short). We call these elements "signposts" because they serve readers just as signposts or street signs serve drivers — they alert them to something significant. The careless driver, who doesn't pay attention and misses a stop sign or a hairpin-curve sign, is likely to end up in trouble. The lazy reader, who doesn't notice the signposts, won't end up in trouble — he just isn't likely to know what's going on in the text.

THE FICTION SIGNPOSTS

We want to share 6 signposts that help you when reading fiction.

▶ CONTRASTS AND CONTRADICTIONS

Without a contrast or a contradiction, everything is just the same, just the usual, just what you would have expected. Boring.

But when some event occurs that contrasts vividly with what you would have expected, then you are likely — if you're paying attention — to notice it.

When a friend's behavior suddenly changes and contrasts with what you would expect, you will notice it and ask yourself why. Similarly, when a character in a story does something drastically different from what he has usually done, you should pause and wonder why. Or, when a writer gives you an idea that contradicts the thoughts you have always held, again you might slow down and ask yourself, "Is she right or am I? Should I accept those thoughts or reject them? Is the answer somewhere in between what I have read and what I used to think?" Keep in mind the general question "Why is the character doing or saying that?" and it will lead you to other questions you might ask about the moment of contrast and contradiction, that moment when you bump into something unexpected.

In Neil Gaiman's **"Chivalry,"** a student has noted a **CONTRAST AND CONTRADICTION** and asked this question: Why would the character act and feel this way?

Then she walked into her parlor and looked at the mantelpiece: at the little china basset hound, and the Holy Grail, and the photograph of her late husband Henry, shirtless, smiling and eating an ice cream in black and white, almost forty years away.

She went back into the kitchen. The kettle had begun to whistle. She poured a little steaming water into the teapot, swirled it around, and poured it out. Then she added two spoonfuls of tea and one for the pot and poured in the rest of the water. All this she did in silence.

She turned to Galaad then, and she looked at him. "Put that apple away," she told Galaad, firmly. "You shouldn't offer things like that to old ladies. It isn't proper."

> Mrs. Whitaker looks closely at the photograph of her late husband when he was young, as if she's thinking about him.

> Perhaps she refuses to take the apple, which could have restored her youth, because she misses him. Galaad's offer may not be "proper" because Mrs. Whitaker doesn't want to betray the memory of her husband.

AHA MOMENT

Sometimes too many days go by without one of those moments when you suddenly understand something. But when you have such a moment you recognize that it's important and you stop and think about it. One day you might suddenly say to yourself "I'm echoing everything my friends say, but I don't really believe any of it." That's an important moment that may lead to a change in what you do, or at least to some hard thinking about the choices you have made. You've had an insight — an Aha — and you have to ask yourself what it means.

In the same way, the character in the story will almost always come to some insight into his situation, some "Aha" moment in which he realizes, perhaps suddenly, something about himself, his situation, or his life. When you come to such a moment, ask yourself "How will this change things?" Because it almost always will. Aha Moments are usually indicated with phrases such as "I knew," "I understood," "He figured it out," "She slowly realized," or "She nodded, knowing what she had to do . . ."

In Katherine Mansfield's **"A Cup of Tea,"** a student has noted an **AHA MOMENT** and asked this question: How might this change things?

"Pretty?" Rosemary was so surprised that she blushed. "Do you think so? I—I hadn't thought about it."

"Good Lord!" Philip struck a match. "She's absolutely lovely. Look again, my child. I was bowled over when I came into your room just now. However . . . I think you're making a ghastly mistake. Sorry, darling, if I'm crude and all that. But let me know if Miss Smith is going to dine with us in time for me to look up *The Milliner's Gazette*."

"You absurd creature!" said Rosemary, and she went out of the library, but not back to her bedroom. She went to her writing-room and sat down at her desk. Pretty! Absolutely lovely! Bowled over! Her heart beat like a heavy bell. Pretty! Lovely!

Rosemary blushes, an Aha Moment, when she realizes that her husband thinks "Miss Smith" is pretty.

Then he says the girl is "absolutely lovely" and wonders if she's going to eat dinner with them.

I'll bet Rosemary's attitude changes. She sounds jealous enough to quit pitying the girl, and she might even try to keep her away from Philip.

TOUGH QUESTIONS

"Do you want pizza or spaghetti for dinner?" really isn't a tough question, even if you can't make up your mind. Your answer isn't going to change much of anything, and tomorrow you probably won't even remember that you made a choice. You aren't going to think about it for very long or very hard, and no one will ever write a book about the choice between pizza and spaghetti. If they do, we won't read it.

A tough question is one we struggle with, one that might change the course of our lives — one, at least, that will have some serious consequences for us. "Should I play football, as the coach wants me to, or should I join the band, as I want to?" "Should I follow the crowd, as everyone is pressing me to do, or should I respect my own thoughts and let the crowd condemn me for it?" These are tough questions, and how we might answer them will shape the days to come.

Often a story, even an entire book, is built around the tough question. If we ask ourselves "What does this make me wonder about?" we will probably be led into exploring the same issue the character or the writer is exploring. The writer probably wanted to see what would happen if his character answered the question in a certain way. If you notice the tough question, and ask yourself about it, you will probably be looking at the main issue of the book.

In Geoffrey Chaucer's **"The Wife of Bath's Tale,"** a student has noted a **TOUGH QUESTION** and asked this: What does this question make me wonder about?

"You have two choices; which one will you try?
To have me old and ugly till I die,
But still a loyal, true, and humble wife
That never will displease you all her life,
Or would you rather I were young and pretty
And chance your arm what happens in a city
Where friends will visit you because of me,
Yes, and in other places too, maybe.
Which would you have? The choice is all your own."

I wonder how I'd answer the same Tough Question. What leads to lasting happiness in a relationship? How important is appearance? Is it possible to ignore appearance, even if you know you'll be loved and supported forever?

WORDS OF THE WISER

You may think that you have heard too many of these in your own life.

You probably think there is always someone around who wants to offer you advice, teach you how things are, and tell you what to do and how to think. Sometimes these wise words are right, truly wise, and sometimes they are wrong. But they are almost always an effort to guide you, or the character, to teach something about living in the world.

In a story, we usually hear Words of the Wiser in a quiet moment, when two characters are in a serious conversation about a problem or a decision. Usually the one who is — or thinks she is — wiser, will offer a serious lesson about life. The story will be about the character struggling along, unwilling to learn that lesson until the end; or about the character accepting the lesson and following it to whatever adventures it leads; or perhaps, in rare cases, about the words of the wiser not being wise after all.

In any case, when you notice Words of the Wiser in the story you should ask the same question you are likely to ask in your own life — "What is the lesson, and how will it affect the character (or me)?"

In William Shakespeare's *The Tragedy of Hamlet*, a student has noted **WORDS OF THE WISER** and asked this question: What is the life lesson, and how might this affect the character?

Ophelia. No more but so?
Laertes.   Think it no more.
For nature, crescent, does not grow alone
In thews and bulk, but, as this temple waxes,
The inward service of the mind and soul
Grows wide withal. <u>Perhaps he loves you now</u>,
And now no soil nor cautel doth besmirch
The virtue of his will; <u>but you must fear</u>,
<u>His greatness weighed, his will is not his own</u>,
<u>For he himself is subject to his birth</u>.
He may not, as unvalued persons do,
Carve for himself, for <u>on his choice depends</u>
<u>The safety and the health of this whole state</u>.
<u>And therefore must his choice be circumscribed</u>
<u>Unto the voice and yielding of that body</u>
<u>Whereof he is the head</u>.

Laertes is trying to convince Ophelia that she shouldn't love Hamlet, no matter how they currently feel about each other.

His Words of the Wiser suggest that Hamlet will always do what's best for Denmark, even if it means marrying someone else.

Ophelia might reject Hamlet or pretend not to love him, despite her feelings.

AGAIN AND AGAIN

One teacher I had always called on the second or third person to raise a hand, or perhaps on some student who was looking out the window — never on the first hand in the sky.

It happened again and again. Until, of course, I got clever and decided to shoot my hand up quickly even though I didn't have the foggiest notion what the answer was. That must have been the day that the teacher recognized the lesson of Again and Again, and realized that he had established a pattern. Or perhaps he had been planning the switch all along. In any case, it was the day I shot my hand up first that he decided to change his routine. At my expense. . . .

Something that happens over and over, again and again, establishes a pattern. If we pay attention, we'll notice that pattern and ask ourselves, "Why does this happen over and over, again and again?" In our lives, the again and again moment probably teaches us something about our friends, or our teachers, or, perhaps, about the way the world works. And sometimes it alerts us to something that is likely to change.

In any case, whenever we notice something happening again and again, we should take note of it, and ask ourselves "Why does this keep happening repeatedly?" Our answer may be that it teaches us some consistent pattern that we can rely on. Or it may be that it is setting up expectations that we can predict will suddenly not be met. It may be leading us into a surprising Contrast and Contradiction. That, after all is what my teacher did to me. If I had thought more carefully about the Again and Again, and asked myself why he was always avoiding the first hand that waved, I might have guessed that he was preparing a trick and that one day he would call on that first hand.

In Sir Thomas Malory's *Le Morte D'Arthur*, a student has noted an instance of **AGAIN AND AGAIN** and asked this question: Why might the author bring this up again and again?

For three weeks, while Sir Gawain was recovering, the siege was relaxed and both sides skirmished only halfheartedly. But once recovered, Sir Gawain rode up to the castle walls and challenged Sir Launcelot again:

"Sir Launcelot, traitor! Come forth, it is Sir Gawain who challenges you."

"Sir Gawain, why these insults? I have the measure of your strength and you can do me but little harm."

"Come forth, traitor, and this time I shall make good my revenge!" Sir Gawain shouted.

"Sir Gawain, I have once spared your life; should you not beware of meddling with me again?"

Launcelot has been trying to end the conflict with Arthur, but Sir Gawain has resisted Again and Again, insisting that the kingdom's honor is at stake.

Malory might be bringing up Gawain's repeated attacks to show how a sense of lasting dishonor can prevent peace.

▶ MEMORY MOMENT

Sometimes, in a reflective moment, a memory will surprise you. You won't have been trying to remember that day, or that person, or that event. It will just pop up like an almost forgotten old friend who knocks at your door and surprises you.

But something called that memory up at that moment. Something that was happening right now reached into your distant past and pulled that memory into your thoughts. Figuring out why that happened will probably tell you something important. It may explain why you are feeling the way you are feeling. It may even explain why you are acting as you are at the moment.

In a story, the Memory Moment is an author's creation. She has decided to reach back into the past for something that she thinks you, as a reader, need to know. It's easy to skip over these moments. After all, you want to go forwards, not backwards, and the Memory Moment steps back into the past. But it's probably important to ask yourself "Why is this moment important?" Because you can assume that if the writer is any good at all, she thinks you should notice it and take note of it.

In the epic poem *Beowulf*, a student has noted a **MEMORY MOMENT** and asked this question: Why might this memory be important?

Hrothgar, the helmet of Shieldings, spoke:
"Beowulf, my friend, you have travelled here
to favour us with help and to fight for us.
There was a feud one time, begun by your father.
With his own hands he had killed Heatholaf,
who was a Wulfing; so war was looming
and his people, in fear of it, forced him to leave.
He came away then over rolling waves
to the South-Danes here, the sons of honour.
I was then in the first flush of kingship,
establishing my sway over all the rich strongholds
of this heroic land. Heorogar,
my older brother and the better man,
also a son of Halfdane's, had died.
Finally I healed the feud by paying:
I shipped a treasure-trove to the Wulfings
and Ecgtheow acknowledged me with oaths of allegiance."

Hrothgar relates the memory of his favor to Ecgtheow, explaining that Ecgtheow had sworn "oaths of allegiance" to him.

This Memory Moment explains why Beowulf feels obliged to assist the Danes in their fight: his family owes Hrothgar a debt for having ended the feud with the Wulfings.

NONFICTION SIGNPOSTS

Nonfiction has text clues as well. Just as in fiction, they invite you to stop and think about what's happening. These clues will help you focus on author's purpose — a critical issue to keep in mind when reading nonfiction. More importantly, these signposts will help you as you keep in mind what we call the Three Big Questions. These questions ought to guide all the reading we do, but especially the nonfiction reading. As you read, just keep asking yourself:

- What surprised me?
- What did the author think I already knew?
- What changed, challenged, or confirmed my thinking?

That first one will keep you thinking about the text. Just look for those parts that make you think, "Really!?!" and put an exclamation point there. The second one will be helpful when the language is tough, or the author is writing about something you don't know much about. Mark those points with a question mark and decide if you need more information. That final question, well, that question is why we read. Reading ought to change us. It ought to challenge our thinking. And sometimes it will confirm it. When you find those parts, just put a "C" in the margin. When you review your notes, you will decide if your thinking was changed, challenged, or confirmed.

As you're looking at what surprised you, or thinking about what is challenging you, or perhaps even as you find a part where it seems the author thinks you know something that you don't, you might discover that one of the following signposts appears right at that moment. So, these signposts help you think about the Three Big Questions. We have found five useful signposts for nonfiction.

CONTRASTS AND CONTRADICTIONS

The world is full of contrasts and contradictions — if it weren't, it would be a pretty dull place to live.

This is the same Contrast and Contradiction that you are familiar with from fiction. It's that moment when you encounter something you didn't expect, something that surprises you. It may be a fact that you find startling, a perspective that you had never heard before, or perhaps an argument that is new to you. We should welcome those moments, even though they may be disconcerting. They give us the opportunity to change our minds about things, to sharpen our thinking. The last person we want to become is that reader who reads only to confirm what he has already decided. That reader is committed to not learning, not growing, and standing absolutely still intellectually.

> In Marah's *My Syrian Diary*, a student has noted **CONTRASTS AND CONTRADICTIONS** and asked this question: What is the difference, and why does it matter?

My city was once magnificent. In spring, it bloomed. We used to wake up to the sound of birds chirping and to the fragrant scent of flowers. Today, spring is here again. But what kind of spring is this? We now wake up to the sound of falling bombs.

Every day, we open our eyes to our bleak reality: to the mortar shells that bring fear, death, disease and destruction. It has robbed us of our loved ones, destroyed our special places, hurt our close friends. Take my neighbor's daughter. At just seven years old, she has lost the ability to speak after a rocket landed close to our street.

Marah contrasts the past with current life in the city, which drives the point home: sights, sounds, and scents have been transformed by the conflict.

The beauties of spring and the city's magnificence have been lost.

EXTREME AND ABSOLUTE LANGUAGE

We are all guilty of overstatement all the time.

Well, that's an overstatement. We aren't all guilty, and those of us who are probably aren't guilty all of the time. When we hear "all," or "none," or "always," or "never," we can be absolutely certain — let's make that "almost certain" — that we are hearing absolute language. All it takes is one exception to make the claim false.

But we do tend to exaggerate and occasionally overstate our claims. Absolute language is easy to spot, and it's often harmless over-statement. Extreme language approaches absolute language but usually stops short. Much of the time, it's harmless, too. When you tell your buddy you're starving, you probably aren't. Or when you say you just heard the funniest joke in the world, even though that's probably not true, your comment causes no real harm.

Sometimes, however, an extreme statement is potentially dangerous. If, for example, someone in authority were to say something like, "I am 100% certain that the airline crash was caused by terrorists," and we had not yet even found the black box that would explain the cause of the accident, then gullible listeners might believe and form opinions based on that statement, even though the phrase "100% certain" shows us clearly that it is an extreme statement. After all, no one ever claims to be 100% certain unless he isn't. So the question becomes, "How certain is he?" 80%? 40%? 20%?

When we spot absolute or extreme language, we should ask ourselves "Why did the author say it this way?" Sometimes the answer will be revealing.

> In the Paston Family's *The Paston Letters*, a student has noted **EXTREME AND ABSOLUTE LANGUAGE** and asked this question: Why did the author use this language?

The duke's men ransacked the church, and carried off all the goods that were left there, both ours and the tenants, and left little behind; they stood on the high altar and ransacked the images, and took away everything they could find. They shut the parson out of the church until they had finished, and ransacked everyone's house in the town five or six times. The ringleaders in the thefts were the bailiff of Eye and the bailiff of Stradbroke, Thomas Slyford. And Slyford was the leader in robbing the church and, after the bailiff of Eye, it is he who has most of the proceeds of the robbery. As for the lead, brass, pewter, iron, doors, gates, and other household stuff, men from Costessey and Cawston have got it, and what they could not carry they hacked up in the most spiteful fashion. If possible, I would like some reputable men to be sent for from the king, to see how things are both there and at the lodge, before any snows come, so that they can report the truth. . . .

Throughout her letter, Paston uses both Extreme and Absolute Language.

Not only does her use of language stress the injustice of the attacks, but it also communicates how widespread and serious the attacks have been.

Paston's language emphasizes a distinct message to her husband: you need to come home, and you should bring help from the king when you do.

NUMBERS AND STATS

"If I've told you once, I've told you a million times. . . ."

Those are numbers — 1 (once) and 1,000,000 — though we prefer to see that as Extreme and Absolute Language. Still, it allows us to make the point, which is that numbers are used to make a point. In this case, they reveal that the speaker is annoyed at how often he has to repeat himself for you to get the message. You barely have to ask the anchor question "Why did the writer or speaker use those numbers or amounts?"

But that's the question you should ask when numbers or stats or amounts appear in something you are reading. Writers include them because they think those numbers, which look like hard, objective, indisputable data, will be persuasive. The questions are, "What are they trying to persuade you to think or believe?" And, "Are the numbers reliable?"

When a writer tells you, for instance, that 97–98% of scientists who have studied the issue think that humans are affecting the environment in damaging ways, we probably want to ask what those figures tell us, both about the situation and the writer's purpose. Our answer will probably be that the writer believes the scientists have reached a consensus that we are endangering the planet. The writer might have said "most of the scientists agree," but "most" is vague. It could mean anything from slightly more than half to almost all. But "97–98%" is much more precise. And it's very close to 100%, so it should be persuasive. Numbers and stats help us visualize what the author is trying to show; it's up to you to decide if there's more you need to know.

> In George Osborne's speech **"Budget 2016,"** a student has noted **NUMBERS AND STATS** and asked this question: Why did the author use these numbers or amounts?

Mr. Deputy Speaker, you cannot have a long term plan for the country unless you have a long term plan for our children's health care. Here are the facts we know.

- Five-year-old children are consuming their body weight in sugar every year.
- Experts predict that within a generation, over half of all boys and 70% of girls could be overweight or obese.

Here's another fact that we all know. Obesity drives disease. It increases the risk of cancer, diabetes and heart disease—and it costs our economy £27 billion a year. . . .

Osborne includes these startling Numbers and Stats because they clearly communicate a significant threat to children's health in the long term.

They also suggest that the extraordinary cost of obesity-related diseases will continue to rise, if children's health care is not addressed.

QUOTED WORDS

American writer Ambrose Bierce said that quotation is "The act of repeating erroneously the words of another." When writers use quotations they are probably doing one of two things. They may be giving you an individual example so that you can see what some person thought or felt about a certain situation, event, or idea. In that case, the writer is probably trying to help you see the human impact of what otherwise might be an abstract idea, difficult to imagine. A writer might, for instance, tell you about the massive damage Hurricane Harvey brought to the coast of Texas. A description of the widespread destruction will give you a picture of what happened; but the quoted words of someone who heard the hundred-mile-an-hour winds for hours when the storm came ashore or whose house was flooded by the rising waters will give you a feel for the impact of the storm on a real person.

Writers also use quoted words to lend authority to a claim they are making. Quoting the authority adds some credibility to the situation. The Houston meteorologist who has studied the data and reports, "Harvey dumped more water in a shorter period of time on Houston than any other storm in Houston's history" ought to be believed more than the guy on the street corner who announces, "This is the worst storm ever."

In Langdon Winner's "Frankenstein: Giving Voice to the Monster," a student has noted **QUOTED WORDS** and asked this question: Why is this person quoted or cited, and what did this add?

In a BBC interview last year, Stephen Hawking warned, "The development of full artificial intelligence could spell the end of the human race. . . . Humans, limited by slow biological evolution, couldn't compete and would be superseded by AI. . . . One can imagine such technology outsmarting financial markets, out-inventing human researchers, out-manipulating human leaders, and developing weapons we cannot even understand. Whereas the short-term impact of AI depends on who controls it, the long-term impact depends on whether it can be controlled at all."

I had no idea that a scientist as famous as the late Stephen Hawking saw danger in the development of artificial intelligence!

Winner includes Hawking's Quoted Words because Hawking is a trusted authority who poses concerns similar to those of Mary Shelley, supporting Winner's purpose.

▶ WORD GAPS

Unless we read such simple texts that we know everything there is to know about the subject, we will almost inevitably stumble into the gap between the writer's vocabulary and ours. Although that's occasionally frustrating, we might see it as an opportunity to sharpen our understanding. We might either learn a new word or learn how a word we already know might be used in a new way.

If we are in a hurry (and reading in a hurry is probably a bad idea because it doesn't give us time to think), then when we encounter a new word our first question might be, "Can I get by without knowing this word?" If you can, maybe you should make what sense you can of the sentence and move on. When we do that we lose the opportunity to learn something, but occasionally we just don't have the time. At the very least, you might jot down the word on the blank pages at the back of the book as a reminder to look it up later, so that the opportunity won't be completely lost.

A better way to approach the problem of the unknown word, however, might be to strategically ask several questions. Obviously the first step is to see if the word is at least partially explained by the context. For instance, if you read "hard, objective, indisputable data," and you don't know what "indisputable" means, you can easily figure out that it is something close to "hard" or "objective." Perhaps it means "definite," "not arguable," or something similar. Close enough. If you can get that far you can probably go on without losing much. You may want to ask someone later what the word "indisputable" means, or look it up in the dictionary, but at the moment you will be able to read on.

If that easy fix doesn't work, however, you might start with "Do I know this word from somewhere else?" If you do, then you have a place to begin. What the word meant in the context with which you are familiar might be a clue to what it means in this new context. For instance, you know what it means when someone says, "I'm depositing my paycheck in the bank." But then you hear your friend say, "You can bank on me." You know your friend isn't becoming a financial lending institution. But, if you'll give yourself a moment to think about what you know about banks, then you might be able to figure out that this means you can count on your friend.

Sometimes, the word is a technical word, a term used primarily by experts in the field, and if you don't know the language of that field, you'll simply need to look it up.

In Dr. Steven Hatch's *Inferno: A Doctor's Ebola Story*, a student has noted a **WORD GAP** and asked this question: Can I find clues in the sentence to help me understand the word?

But what was he concerned about? He was, after all, cured, possessing Ebola-specific antibodies and lymphocytes, which now made him immune to a repeat infection. But . . . did he know that? As I spoke with him, I sat there puzzling this over. Surely he knew at some intuitive level that he was not at risk of getting sick again while he spent day after day convalescing, although maybe he had thought a reset button had been pressed when he emerged from the decontamination shower. But how to explain a concept like acquired immunity to someone who probably had no formal education beyond grade school?

"Lymphocytes" is a technical word, but the sentence provides clues to its meaning. The word is related to curing George and to making him "immune to repeat infection."

READING AND WRITING ACROSS GENRES

by Carol Jago

Reading is a first-class ticket around the world. Not only can you explore other lands and cultures, but you can also travel to the past and future. That journey is sometimes a wild ride. Other books can feel like comfort food, enveloping you in an imaginative landscape full of friends and good times. Making time for reading is making time for life.

Genre

One of the first things readers do when we pick up something to read is notice its genre. You might not think of it exactly in those terms, but consider how you approach a word problem in math class compared to how you read a science fiction story. Readers go to different kinds of text for different purposes. When you need to know how to do or make something, you want a reliable, trusted source of information. When you're in the mood to spend some time in a world of fantasy, you happily suspend your normal disbelief in dragons.

In every unit of *Into Literature,* you'll find a diverse mix of genres all connected by a common theme, allowing you to explore a topic from many different angles.

GENRE: INFORMATIONAL TEXT

GENRE: SHORT STORY

GENRE: LITERARY NONFICTION

GENRE: POETRY

© Houghton Mifflin Harcourt Publishing Company • Image Credits: © Andrew Collings Photography

Writer's Craft

Learning how writers use genre to inform, to explain, to entertain, or to surprise readers will help you better understand—as well as enjoy—your reading. Imitating how professional writers employ the tools of their craft—descriptive language, repetition, sensory images, sentence structure, and a variety of other features—will give you many ideas for making your own writing more lively.

Into Literature provides you with the tools you need to understand the elements of all the critical genres and advice on how to learn from professional texts to improve your own writing in those genres.

**GENRE ELEMENTS:
SHORT STORY**
- is a work of short fiction that centers on a single idea and can be read in one sitting
- usually includes one main conflict that involves the characters and keeps [...] moving
- includes the basic ele[...] of fiction—plot, chara[...] setting, and theme
- may be based on real [...] and historical events [...]

**GENRE ELEMENTS:
INFORMATIONAL TEXT**
- provides factual information
- includes evidence to support ideas
- contains text features
- includes many forms, such as news articles and essays

**GENRE ELEMENTS:
LITERARY NONFICTION**
- shares factual information, ideas, or experiences
- develops a key insight about the topic that goes beyond the facts
- uses literary techni[...] such as figurative langu[...] narration
- reflects a persona[...] involvement in th[...]

GENRE ELEMENTS: POETRY
- may use figurative language, including personification
- often includes imagery that appeals to the five senses
- expresses a theme, or a "big idea" message about life

Reading with Independence

Finding a good book can sometimes be a challenge. Like every other reader, you have probably experienced "book desert" when nothing you pick up seems to have what you are looking for (not that it's easy to explain exactly what you are looking for, but whatever it is, "this" isn't it). If you find yourself in this kind of reading funk, bored by everything you pick up, give yourself permission to range more widely, exploring graphic novels, contemporary biographies, books of poetry, historical fiction. And remember that long doesn't necessarily mean boring. My favorite kind of book is one that I never want to end.

Mill on the Floss
George Eliot

A Tale of Two Cities
Charles Dickens

Take control over your own reading with *Into Literature's* Reader's Choice selections and the HMH Digital Library. And don't forget: your teacher, librarian, and friends can offer you many more suggestions.

SHORT STORY

Marriage Is a Private Affair
Chinua Achebe

Nnaemeka married for love, offending his father. Can he bridge the rift he created by choosing his own path?

EPIC POEM

from **Beowulf**
translated by Burton Raffel

Beowulf faces one last challenging enemy—a fiery dragon that threatens the safety of his people.

ARTICLE

Elizabeth I: The Reality Behind the Mask
Brenda Ralph Lewis

Discover the real Queen Elizabeth I, who exercised great skill to disguise her true personality.

ORIGIN OF A NATION

THE ANGLO-SAXON AND MEDIEVAL PERIODS

" It is chivalry that makes a true knight, not a sword. "

—George R. R. Martin

Discuss the **Essential Questions** with your whole class or in small groups. As you read Origin of a Nation, consider how the selections explore these questions.

? ESSENTIAL QUESTION:

What makes someone a hero?

As you read early British literature, you can see how ideas about heroes change over time. The Anglo-Saxon warrior Beowulf eagerly confronts monsters who test his strength and courage. For King Arthur and his knights, the challenges are more complicated. These heroes pledge themselves to uphold a code of honor, but conflicting loyalties and human flaws sometimes get in their way. How do people become heroes? What qualities do you most admire in a hero?

? ESSENTIAL QUESTION:

What is true chivalry?

During the medieval period, an honor code developed to govern behavior on the battlefield and at court. This code of chivalry presented an idealized view of brave, honest, loyal, and pious knights. They were expected to protect the weak, behave respectfully to women, and go on holy quests. Do you think anyone could fully live up to such ideals? What do we gain from reading about chivalry?

? ESSENTIAL QUESTION:

Can we control our fate?

Compared to most modern people, the Anglo-Saxons lived under very harsh conditions. They were constantly vulnerable to disease, natural disasters, and sudden acts of violence. The Anglo-Saxons believed that whatever good or bad happened to them was determined by fate. Do you think that people are generally in control of their lives, or does fate play an important role? How would a strong belief in fate affect a person's view of the future?

? ESSENTIAL QUESTION:

What happens when a society unravels?

Medieval England had a social system called feudalism, which was supposed to maintain peace and stability. However, civil war, popular uprisings, and deadly plagues often threatened the social order. What are the consequences to ordinary people when a society starts to fall apart?

THE ANGLO-SAXON AND MEDIEVAL PERIODS

When people think of the Middle Ages, they often think of elegant kings and queens in grand castles and shining knights on horseback. In reality, life was harsh, with diseases such as the Black Death taking their toll. The Middle Ages (or medieval period) in England lasted about 1,000 years, from the fall of the Roman Empire to the rise of the Renaissance. This was a time of religious, social, and political upheaval. Despite these challenges, it was also a time of cultural development. By the end of the Middle Ages (around 1485), England had established its own distinct literary tradition.

The Anglo-Saxons The Roman Empire had conquered all of the area now known as England (which they called Britannia) by the year 90. By the year 200, though, the Roman Empire was in decline. Areas on the edges of the empire, like Britannia, were under constant attack. One group of Germanic invaders, the Anglo-Saxons, began to conquer Britannia around 450.

The Anglo-Saxons did not originally have written literature. Instead, they had poems and songs that were passed down from generation to generation orally. These poems and songs were composed in various dialects of Old English. They usually had heroic themes related to important events of the past (such as *Beowulf*) or more recent battles and victories.

In 597, a monk, later known as St. Augustine, was sent to bring Christianity to the Anglo-Saxon rulers of England. Christianity spread, and with it, written literature. Some early texts were translated from Latin into Old English, and Anglo-Saxon poems and songs were written down for the first time. Very few examples of Old English poetry remain, but those that do give evidence of the rich oral tradition that preceded them. They also show the religious shift in Anglo-Saxon culture as Christian themes were incorporated into heroic tales that referenced an older pagan era.

The Norman Invasion In 1066, Normans led by William I "The Conqueror" defeated the Anglo-Saxons at the Battle of Hastings. Soon after, William I was crowned King of England. The Normans came from Northern France, and under William I much of the nobility of England now spoke French. With the introduction of French influence, the English language continued to evolve from its Germanic roots into Early Middle English.

COLLABORATIVE DISCUSSION
In a small group, review the timeline and discuss possible reasons why there are so few literary milestones recorded for the early years in Britain.

c. 450
Anglo-Saxon conquest of the Britons begins.

c. 787
Vikings begin raids on England.

c. 1000
The single surviving manuscript of *Beowulf* is copied.

400

597
St. Augustine arrives in Kent and begins conversion of the Anglo-Saxons to Christianity.

© Houghton Mifflin Harcourt Publishing Company

Literature, too, was influenced by the blending of the Briton, Anglo-Saxon, and French cultures that followed the invasion. Nobles in the court of William I and his successors were fascinated by tales of King Arthur. These tales, based on an earlier Briton oral tradition, had been recorded by historian Geoffrey of Monmouth in his Latin work *History of the Kings of Britain*. French poets of the 12th and 13th centuries expanded on these legends in works called romances that dealt with themes of chivalry and courtly love. Later, in the 15th century, the Arthurian romances written by the French poets were translated into English and used by Sir Thomas Malory as source material for his own versions of the legends, which remain popular to this day.

Turbulent Times Although William I's conquest of England had created ties between England and France, which had been strengthened by marriage alliances of later kings, these ties did not last. In 1337, war broke out as French and English rulers fought over control of lands on the European continent. The struggle continued on and off until roughly 1453, thereby earning the name the Hundred Years' War.

About the same time, a major event occurred that would forever change European society—the Black Death. Between 1347 and 1351, a pandemic broke out that killed an estimated one-third of Europe's total population. The sudden loss of so many lives created social instability. When combined with high taxes for the wars in France and oppression by the church and the nobility, there was widespread discontent in England's lower classes. In 1381, the Peasants' Revolt broke out. Rebels marched on London, killing several royal officials before the rebellion was put down.

© Houghton Mifflin Harcourt Publishing Company • Image Credits: © INTERFOTO/Alamy

RESEARCH
What about this historical period interests you? Choose a topic, event, or person to learn more about. Then add your own entry to the timeline.

1170
Archbishop Thomas Becket is murdered in Canterbury Cathedral.

c. 1387
Geoffrey Chaucer begins work on *The Canterbury Tales*.

1485
Henry Tudor defeats Richard III and becomes King Henry VII, ending the War of the Roses.

1500

1066
Norman conquest of England by William I "The Conqueror."

c.1136
Geoffrey of Monmouth writes *History of the Kings of Britain* in Latin.

1348
The Black Death spreads throughout Europe.

c. 1450
Johannes Gutenberg develops a printing press with movable type.

Although the Peasants' Revolt ultimately failed, it was against this backdrop of social unrest that many major works of Middle English literature were written. Chaucer, for instance, was likely living in London and employed by the court of King Richard II at the time. Later that same decade, he would begin writing his best-known works, including *The Canterbury Tales*.

The End of an Era In 1455 a civil war known as The War of the Roses broke out in England, as two branches of the royal family struggled for control. In 1485 Henry VII defeated Richard II to ascend to the throne. Some historians use this event to mark the end of the Middle Ages in England. Over the course of a millennium, English literature had developed from a small collection of Old English poems, based on an earlier oral tradition, to a much larger body of poetry and prose that reflected the political, cultural, and linguistic shifts in English society. As England moved from the Middle Ages into the Renaissance, the introduction of printing presses with movable type promised to revolutionize reading, writing, and literature in ways that could not yet be imagined.

CHECK YOUR UNDERSTANDING

Chose the best answer to each question.

1 Which event most directly affected the rise of written literature in England?

   A The conquest of the Britons by the Romans

   B The spread of Christianity

   C The conquest of the Anglo-Saxons by the Normans

   D The development of printing with movable type

2 Which was a result of the Norman conquest of England?

   F Written literature replacing the oral tradition

   G The death of one-third of the population

   H Blending of Anglo-Saxon and French cultures and languages

   J Widespread social unrest and revolt

3 Which factor did **not** contribute to unrest among the lower classes in the late Middle Ages?

   A Black Death

   B Hundred Years' War

   C Oppression by the church

   D Conquest by invading armies

ACADEMIC VOCABULARY

Academic Vocabulary words are words you use when you discuss and write about texts. In this unit, you will learn the following five words:

☑ collapse   ❑ displace   ❑ military   ❑ violate   ❑ visual

Study the Word Network to learn more about the word **collapse**.

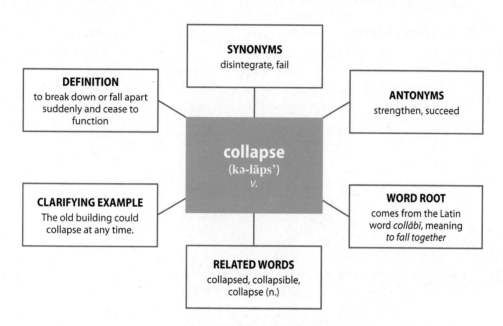

SYNONYMS
disintegrate, fail

DEFINITION
to break down or fall apart suddenly and cease to function

ANTONYMS
strengthen, succeed

collapse
(kə-lăps')
v.

CLARIFYING EXAMPLE
The old building could collapse at any time.

WORD ROOT
comes from the Latin word collābī, meaning to fall together

RELATED WORDS
collapsed, collapsible, collapse (n.)

Write and Discuss Discuss the completed Word Network with a partner, making sure to talk through all of the boxes until you both understand the word, its synonyms, antonyms, and related forms. Then, fill out a Word Network for the remaining four words. Use a dictionary or online resource to help you complete the activity.

Go online to access the Word Networks.

RESPOND TO THE ESSENTIAL QUESTIONS

In this unit, you will explore four different **Essential Questions** about English literature of the Middle Ages and other related texts. As you read each selection, you will gather your ideas about one of these questions and write about it in the **Response Log** that appears on page R1. At the end of the unit, you will have the opportunity to write a **short story** about what makes someone a hero. Filling out the Response Log after you read each text will help you prepare for this writing task.

You can also go online to access the Response Log.

from

BEOWULF

Epic Poem by the **Beowulf Poet**
translated by **Seamus Heaney**

? ***ESSENTIAL QUESTION:***

What makes someone a hero?

QUICK START

Think about one of your personal heroes. What characteristics does he or she possess? Write these characteristics in a list that can be shared with your class.

ANALYZE CHARACTERISTICS OF AN EPIC POEM

An **epic poem** is a long narrative poem that celebrates a hero's deeds. Traditional epics, such as *Beowulf*, began as oral poems retold over many generations before they were finally written down. Epic poems share certain characteristics and conventions, which are listed under Genre Elements. Use a chart like this one to help you analyze the characteristics of *Beowulf*.

QUESTIONS	ANSWERS FROM THE POEM
What qualities does the hero display?	
What obstacles must the hero overcome?	
What themes does the epic convey?	
What elements of epic style does the poem include?	

GENRE ELEMENTS: EPIC POETRY

- written about a hero, who is usually a strong, courageous person of nobility
- usually involves supernatural creatures, great deeds, and perilous journeys
- imbues the hero with traits that reflect the ideals of the larger culture
- conveys universal themes found in the literature of all time periods and cultures, such as good versus evil
- often features long speeches, as well as formal diction and a serious tone

ANALYZE OLD ENGLISH POETRY

Anglo-Saxon poets used techniques that made their verses easier to chant. This chart describes important techniques found in *Beowulf*.

TECHNIQUE	EXAMPLE
Alliteration is the repetition of consonant sounds at the beginning of words. This device helps unify the lines.	In **H**is **s**plendour **H**e **s**et the **s**un and the moon
The poem's strong **rhythm** is created by four stresses, or beats, in many lines.	′ ′ ′ ′ Sometimes at pagan shrines they vowed
A **caesura** is a pause that divides the line, with each part having two stresses. Usually, at least one stressed syllable in the first part alliterates with a stressed syllable in the second part.	′ ′ ′ ′ When he heard about Grendel // Hygelac's thane ′ ′ ′ ′ Was on home ground // over in Geatland.
Kennings are metaphorical compound words or phrases substituted for simple nouns.	The kenning "Hygelac's trusty retainer" is used in place of the name Beowulf, and "dread of the land" is used in place of the name Grendel.

CRITICAL VOCABULARY

aghast	unrelenting	affliction	plight
baleful	wail	loathsome	

To see how many Critical Vocabulary words you already know, use them to complete the sentences.

1. No matter what he tried, he couldn't make the _____ buzzing noise in his head go away.

2. The hero of the story defeated a murderous and _____ monster.

3. He was _____ at the number of casualties that occurred.

4. The village dogs began to _____ in unison at the full moon.

5. The tremors he experienced were side effects of a crippling _____.

6. Her _____ glance was brief, but it made the frightened child retreat.

7. After all of her good fortune in previous years, who could have predicted her unfortunate _____?

LANGUAGE CONVENTIONS

Mood Mood is the feeling or atmosphere that a writer creates for a reader. Poets may use imagery, alliteration, figurative language, descriptions, word order, and word choices to create this atmosphere. The use of these literary elements sets the mood by evoking feelings in the reader.

ANNOTATION MODEL

NOTICE & NOTE

As you read this epic poem out loud, you will recognize many examples of poetic techniques of Old English poetry. This model shows one reader's notes about this excerpt from *Beowulf*.

Then a powerful demon, a prowler through the dark,
nursed a hard grievance. It harrowed him
to hear the <u>din</u> of the <u>loud</u> <u>banquet</u>
every day in the hall, the <u>harp</u> being <u>struck</u>
and the clear <u>song</u> of a skilled poet
telling with mastery of man's beginnings,
how the Almighty had made the earth

These are examples of caesuras. I pause in the middle of each line, and each part has two stressed syllables.

Word choices create the mood of a crowded, noisy banquet hall.

BACKGROUND

In large gathering halls like the one featured in Beowulf, poet-singers provided entertainment to the Anglo-Saxon warriors. They told tales of courage and valor, celebrating great heroes. Sometime between the seventh and ninth centuries, an unknown poet consolidated the oral accounts of Beowulf, the hero who is the subject of this poem. This is the Anglo-Saxon epic that survives today, a testament to the belief that these great warriors would be remembered long after their society disintegrated. Though the poem is translated from Old English, the characteristics of the original poetry remain.

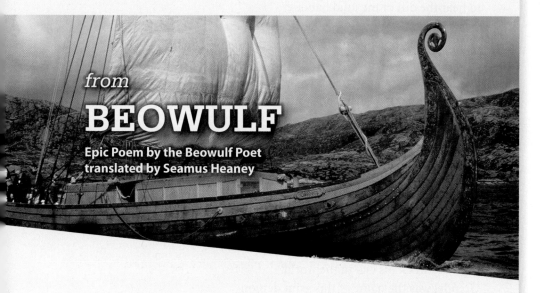

from

BEOWULF

Epic Poem by the Beowulf Poet
translated by Seamus Heaney

The Angles and the Saxons, as well as other Germanic tribes, came to England from northern Europe starting in the middle of the fifth century. Their culture became the basis for English culture, and their languages fused into Old English, the Anglo-Saxon language. They struggled to survive the challenges presented by nature and were frequently threatened by wars against new invaders. Anglo-Saxons lived communally for protection, loyal to their feudal lords and to their families. They believed in wyrd, or fate, rather than in an afterlife, but they hoped that acquiring fame and treasure through acts of valor would give them a kind of immortality. In this, they were aided by the highly valued poets, since their poems passed down the history of the Anglo-Saxon people and taught their values.

By the time the epic Beowulf was written down by a monk in the beginning of the eleventh century, the Anglo-Saxons had converted to Christianity. Thus, in the final version of the poem, Christian references are mingled with the original pagan beliefs.

In this excerpt, the warriors of the kingdom of the Danes are in constant mortal danger from the monster Grendel. Grendel comes out at night from his lair in the lowland, marshy areas to wreak destruction and ruin. In time, he meets his match in Beowulf, who fights the monster using an unexpected tactic.

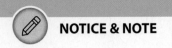

Notice & Note

Use the side margins to notice and note signposts in the text.

ANALYZE CHARACTERISTICS OF AN EPIC POEM

Annotate: Mark words and phrases in lines 14–29 that give clues about one of this epic poem's universal themes.

Analyze: What is the universal theme described by these lines?

18 marches: borders or boundaries of a country or an area of land.

18 heath: an extensive tract of uncultivated open land covered with herbage and low shrubs; a moor.

19 fens: areas of low wet land having peaty soil.

21 Cain: the eldest son of Adam and Eve. According to the Bible (Genesis 4), he murdered his younger brother, Abel.

SETTING A PURPOSE

As you read, pay attention to the ways the poet uses language and poetic techniques and elements to enhance the telling of Beowulf's heroic deeds.

Grendel

Then a powerful demon, a prowler through the dark,
nursed a hard grievance. It harrowed him
to hear the din of the loud banquet
every day in the hall, the harp being struck
5 and the clear song of a skilled poet
telling with mastery of man's beginnings,
how the Almighty had made the earth
a gleaming plain girdled with waters;
in His splendour He set the sun and the moon
10 to be earth's lamplight, lanterns for men,
and filled the broad lap of the world
with branches and leaves; and quickened life
in every other thing that moved.

So times were pleasant for the people there
15 until finally one, a fiend out of hell,
began to work his evil in the world.
Grendel was the name of this grim demon
haunting the marches, marauding round the heath
and the desolate fens; he had dwelt for a time
20 in misery among the banished monsters,
Cain's clan, whom the Creator had outlawed
and condemned as outcasts. For the killing of Abel
the Eternal Lord had exacted a price:
Cain got no good from committing that murder
25 because the Almighty made him anathema
and out of the curse of his exile there sprang
ogres and elves and evil phantoms
and the giants too who strove with God
time and again until He gave them their reward.

30 So, after nightfall, Grendel set out
for the lofty house, to see how the Ring-Danes
were settling into it after their drink,
and there he came upon them, a company of the best
asleep from their feasting, insensible to pain
35 and human sorrow. Suddenly then
the God-cursed brute was creating havoc:
greedy and grim, he grabbed thirty men
from their resting places and rushed to his lair,

flushed up and inflamed from the raid,
40 blundering back with the butchered corpses.

Then as dawn brightened and the day broke
Grendel's powers of destruction were plain:
their wassail was over, they wept to heaven
and mourned under morning. Their mighty prince,
45 the storied leader, sat stricken and helpless,
humiliated by the loss of his guard,
bewildered and stunned, staring **aghast**
at the demon's trail, in deep distress.
He was numb with grief, but got no respite
50 for one night later merciless Grendel
struck again with more gruesome murders.
Malignant by nature, he never showed remorse.
It was easy then to meet with a man
shifting himself to a safer distance
55 to bed in the bothies, for who could be blind
to the evidence of his eyes, the obviousness
of that hall-watcher's hate? Whoever escaped
kept a weather-eye open and moved away.

So Grendel ruled in defiance of right,
60 one against all, until the greatest house
in the world stood empty, a deserted wallstead.
For twelve winters, seasons of woe,
the lord of the Shieldings suffered under
his load of sorrow; and so, before long,
65 the news was known over the whole world.
Sad lays were sung about the beset king,
the vicious raids and ravages of Grendel,
his long and **unrelenting** feud,
nothing but war; how he would never
70 parley or make peace with any Dane
nor stop his death-dealing nor pay the death-price.
No counsellor could ever expect
fair reparation from those rabid hands.
All were endangered; young and old
75 were hunted down by that dark death-shadow
who lurked and swooped in the long nights
on the misty moors; nobody knows
where these reavers from hell roam on their errands.

So Grendel waged his lonely war,
80 inflicting constant cruelties on the people,
atrocious hurt. He took over Heorot,

aghast
(ə-găst´) *adj.* struck by shock, terror, or amazement.

ANALYZE OLD ENGLISH POETRY
Annotate: Kennings are often more descriptive than simple nouns. Mark the kenning in line 75.

Interpret: How does kenning help readers visualize Grendel?

unrelenting
(ŭn´rĭ-lĕn´tĭng) *adj.* having or exhibiting uncompromising determination; unyielding.

73 reparation: something done to make amends for loss or suffering. In Germanic society, someone who killed another person was generally expected to make a payment to the victim's family as a way of restoring peace.

© Houghton Mifflin Harcourt Publishing Company

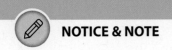

haunted the glittering hall after dark,
but the throne itself, the treasure-seat,
he was kept from approaching; he was the Lord's outcast.

85 These were hard times, heart-breaking
for the prince of the Shieldings; powerful counsellors,
the highest in the land, would lend advice,
plotting how best the bold defenders
might resist and beat off sudden attacks.
90 Sometimes at pagan shrines they vowed
offerings to idols, swore oaths
that the killer of souls might come to their aid
and save the people. That was their way,
their heathenish hope; deep in their hearts

95 The Almighty Judge: These references to God show the influence of Christianity on the Beowulf poet.

95 they remembered hell. The Almighty Judge
of good deeds and bad, the Lord God,
Head of the Heavens and High King of the World,
was unknown to them. Oh, cursed is he
who in time of trouble has to thrust his soul
100 in the fire's embrace, forfeiting help;
he has nowhere to turn. But blessed is he
who after death can approach the Lord
and find friendship in the Father's embrace.

affliction
(ə-flĭk´shən) *n.* something that causes suffering or pain.

So that troubled time continued, woe
105 that never stopped, steady **affliction**
for Halfdane's son, too hard an ordeal.
There was panic after dark, people endured
raids in the night, riven by the terror.

Beowulf

109 Hygelac's thane: a warrior loyal to Hygelac, king of the Geats (and Beowulf's uncle).

ANALYZE CHARACTERISTICS OF AN EPIC POEM

Annotate: Mark words and phrases in lines 109–124 that characterize Beowulf as a hero.

Infer: What is the hero's motivation to go on this quest?

When he heard about Grendel, Hygelac's thane
110 was on home ground, over in Geatland.
There was no one else like him alive.
In his day, he was the mightiest man on earth,
high-born and powerful. He ordered a boat
that would ply the waves. He announced his plan:
115 to sail the swan's road and search out that king,
the famous prince who needed defenders.
Nobody tried to keep him from going,
no elder denied him, dear as he was to them.
Instead, they inspected omens and spurred
120 his ambition to go, whilst he moved about
like the leader he was, enlisting men,
the best he could find; with fourteen others

the warrior boarded the boat as captain,
a canny pilot along coast and currents. . . .

                                     At the door of the hall,
125 Wulfgar duly delivered the message:
"My lord, the conquering king of the Danes,
bids me announce that he knows your ancestry;
also that he welcomes you here to Heorot
and salutes your arrival from across the sea.
130 You are free now to move forward
to meet Hrothgar, in helmets and armour,
but shields must stay here and spears be stacked
until the outcome of the audience is clear."

The hero arose, surrounded closely
135 by his powerful thanes. A party remained
under orders to keep watch on the arms;
the rest proceeded, led by their prince
under Heorot's roof. And standing on the hearth
in webbed links that the smith had woven,
140 the fine-forged mesh of his gleaming mail-shirt,
resolute in his helmet, Beowulf spoke:
"Greetings to Hrothgar. I am Hygelac's kinsman,
one of his hall-troop. When I was younger,
I had great triumphs. Then news of Grendel,
145 hard to ignore, reached me at home:
sailors brought stories of the **plight** you suffer
in this legendary hall, how it lies deserted,
empty and useless once the evening light
hides itself under heaven's dome.
150 So every elder and experienced councilman
among my people supported my resolve
to come here to you, King Hrothgar,
because all knew of my awesome strength.
They had seen me boltered in the blood of enemies
155 when I battled and bound five beasts,
raided a troll-nest and in the night-sea
slaughtered sea-brutes. I have suffered extremes
and avenged the Geats (their enemies brought it
upon themselves, I devastated them).
160 Now I mean to be a match for Grendel,
settle the outcome in single combat.
And so, my request, O king of Bright-Danes,
dear prince of the Shieldings, friend of the people
and their ring of defence, my one request
165 is that you won't refuse me, who have come this far,

LANGUAGE CONVENTIONS

Annotate: Mark the words or phrases in lines 134–141 describing Beowulf.

Analyze: What mood is created by the poet's word choice?

140 mail-shirt: flexible body armor made of metal links or overlapping metal scales.

plight
(plīt) *n.* a situation, especially a bad or unfortunate one.

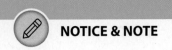

NOTICE & NOTE

the privilege of purifying Heorot,
with my own men to help me, and nobody else.
I have heard moreover that the monster scorns
in his reckless way to use weapons;
170 therefore, to heighten Hygelac's fame
and gladden his heart, I hereby renounce
sword and the shelter of the broad shield,
the heavy war-board: hand-to-hand
is how it will be, a life-and-death
175 fight with the fiend. Whichever one death fells
must deem it a just judgement by God.
If Grendel wins, it will be a gruesome day;
he will glut himself on the Geats in the war-hall,
swoop without fear on that flower of manhood
180 as on others before. Then my face won't be there
to be covered in death: he will carry me away
as he goes to ground, gorged and bloodied;
he will run gloating with my raw corpse
and feed on it alone, in a cruel frenzy,
185 fouling his moor-nest. No need then
to lament for long or lay out my body:
if the battle takes me, send back my mail-shirt,
this breast-webbing that Weland fashioned
and Hrethel gave me, to Lord Hygelac.
190 Fate goes ever as fate must."

188 Weland: a famous blacksmith and magician.

189 Hrethel (hrěth´əl): a former king of the Geats— Hygelac's father and Beowulf's grandfather.

Hrothgar, the helmet of Shieldings, spoke:
"Beowulf, my friend, you have travelled here
to favour us with help and to fight for us.
There was a feud one time, begun by your father.
195 With his own hands he had killed Heatholaf,
who was a Wulfing; so war was looming
and his people, in fear of it, forced him to leave.
He came away then over rolling waves
to the South-Danes here, the sons of honour.
200 I was then in the first flush of kingship,
establishing my sway over all the rich strongholds
of this heroic land. Heorogar,
my older brother and the better man,
also a son of Halfdane's, had died.
205 Finally I healed the feud by paying:
I shipped a treasure-trove to the Wulfings
and Ecgtheow acknowledged me with oaths of allegiance.

"It bothers me to have to burden anyone
with all the grief Grendel has caused

MEMORY MOMENT

Notice & Note: Mark the words or phrases in lines 191–207 highlighting the history between Hrothgar and Beowulf.

Infer: What can you infer from Hrothgar sharing this story of the relationship between himself and the poem's hero?

196 Wulfing: a member of another Germanic tribe.

© Houghton Mifflin Harcourt Publishing Company

14   Unit 1

210 and the havoc he has wreaked upon us in Heorot,
our humiliations. My household-guard
are on the wane, fate sweeps them away
into Grendel's clutches—

but God can easily

halt these raids and harrowing attacks!

215 "Time and again, when the goblets passed
and seasoned fighters got flushed with beer
they would pledge themselves to protect Heorot
and wait for Grendel with whetted swords.
But when dawn broke and day crept in
220 over each empty, blood-spattered bench,
the floor of the mead-hall where they had feasted
would be slick with slaughter. And so they died,
faithful retainers, and my following dwindled.

"Now take your place at the table, relish
225 the triumph of heroes to your heart's content."

Then a bench was cleared in that banquet hall
so the Geats could have room to be together
and the party sat, proud in their bearing,
strong and stalwart. An attendant stood by
230 with a decorated pitcher, pouring bright
helpings of mead. And the minstrel sang,
filling Heorot with his head-clearing voice,
gladdening that great rally of Geats and Danes. . . .

The Battle with Grendel

In off the moors, down through the mist bands
235 God-cursed Grendel came greedily loping.
The bane of the race of men roamed forth,
hunting for a prey in the high hall.
Under the cloud-murk he moved towards it
until it shone above him, a sheer keep
240 of fortified gold. Nor was that the first time
he had scouted the grounds of Hrothgar's dwelling—
although never in his life, before or since,
did he find harder fortune or hall-defenders.
Spurned and joyless, he journeyed on ahead
245 and arrived at the bawn. The iron-braced door
turned on its hinge when his hands touched it.
Then his rage boiled over, he ripped open
the mouth of the building, maddening for blood,

ANALYZE CHARACTERISTICS OF AN EPIC POEM
Annotate: Mark the words or phrases in lines 245–251 that illustrate Grendel's power.

Compare: How does Grendel's power compare to what you've read about Beowulf's abilities?

© Houghton Mifflin Harcourt Publishing Company

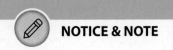

baleful
(bāl´fəl) *adj.* harmful or
malignant in intent or effect.

pacing the length of the patterned floor
250 with his loathsome tread, while a **baleful** light,
flame more than light, flared from his eyes.
He saw many men in the mansion, sleeping,
a ranked company of kinsmen and warriors
quartered together. And his glee was demonic,
255 picturing the mayhem: before morning
he would rip life from limb and devour them,
feed on their flesh; but his fate that night
was due to change, his days of ravening
had come to an end.

                                        Mighty and canny,
260 Hygelac's kinsman was keenly watching
for the first move the monster would make.
Nor did the creature keep him waiting
but struck suddenly and started in;
he grabbed and mauled a man on his bench,
265 bit into his bone-lappings, bolted down his blood
and gorged on him in lumps, leaving the body
utterly lifeless, eaten up
hand and foot. Venturing closer,
his talon was raised to attack Beowulf
270 where he lay on the bed; he was bearing in
with open claw when the alert hero's
comeback and armlock forestalled him utterly.
The captain of evil discovered himself
in a handgrip harder than anything
275 he had ever encountered in any man
on the face of the earth. Every bone in his body
quailed and recoiled, but he could not escape.
He was desperate to flee to his den and hide
with the devil's litter, for in all his days
280 he had never been clamped or cornered like this.
Then Hygelac's trusty retainer recalled
his bedtime speech, sprang to his feet
and got a firm hold. Fingers were bursting,
the monster back-tracking, the man overpowering.
285 The dread of the land was desperate to escape,
to take a roundabout road and flee
to his lair in the fens. The latching power
in his fingers weakened; it was the worst trip
the terror-monger had taken to Heorot.
290 And now the timbers trembled and sang,
a hall-session that harrowed every Dane
inside the stockade: stumbling in fury,

**ANALYZE OLD ENGLISH
POETRY**

Annotate: Poets often use a
caesura to create a dramatic
pause. Mark the caesuras in
lines 283–284.

Analyze: Which alliterative
words carry the stresses in
these two lines? How does the
poet use caesuras in these lines
to enhance the story?

© Houghton Mifflin Harcourt Publishing Company

the two contenders crashed through the building.
The hall clattered and hammered, but somehow
295 survived the onslaught and kept standing:
it was handsomely structured, a sturdy frame
braced with the best of blacksmith's work
inside and out. The story goes
that as the pair struggled, mead-benches were smashed
300 and sprung off the floor, gold fittings and all.
Before then, no Shielding elder would believe
there was any power or person upon earth
capable of wrecking their horn-rigged hall
unless the burning embrace of a fire
305 engulf it in flame. Then an extraordinary
wail arose, and bewildering fear
came over the Danes. Everyone felt it
who heard that cry as it echoed off the wall,
a God-cursed scream and strain of catastrophe,
310 the howl of the loser, the lament of the hell-serf
keening his wound. He was overwhelmed,
manacled tight by the man who of all men
was foremost and strongest in the days of this life.

But the earl-troop's leader was not inclined
315 to allow his caller to depart alive:
he did not consider that life of much account
to anyone anywhere. Time and again,
Beowulf's warriors worked to defend
their lord's life, laying about them
320 as best they could with their ancestral blades.
Stalwart in action, they kept striking out
on every side, seeking to cut
straight to the soul. When they joined the struggle
there was something they could not have known at the
    time,
325 that no blade on earth, no blacksmith's art
could ever damage their demon opponent.
He had conjured the harm from the cutting edge
of every weapon. But his going away
out of this world and the days of his life
330 would be agony to him, and his alien spirit
would travel far into fiends' keeping.

Then he who had harrowed the hearts of men
with pain and affliction in former times
and had given offence also to God
335 found that his bodily powers failed him.

wail
(wāl) *n.* a long, loud, high-pitched cry expressing grief, sorrow, or fear.

ANALYZE CHARACTERISTICS OF AN EPIC POEM
Annotate: Mark words and phrases in lines 318–331 that tell why Beowulf's companion warriors could not defeat Grendel.

Analyze: What characteristic of an epic poem does this typify?

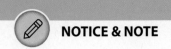

340 Sinews: the tendons that connect muscles to bones.

ANALYZE OLD ENGLISH POETRY

Annotate: Poets often use alliteration to create rhythm, emphasis, and mood. Mark the alliteration in line 340–345.

Infer: How does the poet's use of alliteration enhance the description of Grendel's wounds?

loathsome
(lōth´səm) *adj.* causing loathing; abhorrent.

Hygelac's kinsman kept him helplessly
locked in a handgrip. As long as either lived,
he was hateful to the other. The monster's whole
body was in pain, a tremendous wound
340 appeared on his shoulder. Sinews split
and the bone-lappings burst. Beowulf was granted
the glory of winning; Grendel was driven
under the fen-banks, fatally hurt,
to his desolate lair. His days were numbered,
345 the end of his life was coming over him,
he knew it for certain; and one bloody clash
had fulfilled the dearest wishes of the Danes.
The man who had lately landed among them,
proud and sure, had purged the hall,
350 kept it from harm; he was happy with his nightwork
and the courage he had shown. The Geat captain
had boldly fulfilled his boast to the Danes:
he had healed and relieved a huge distress,
unremitting humiliations,
355 the hard fate they'd been forced to undergo,
no small affliction. Clear proof of this
could be seen in the hand the hero displayed
high up near the roof: the whole of Grendel's
shoulder and arm, his awesome grasp.

360 Then morning came and many a warrior
gathered, as I've heard, around the gift-hall,
clan-chiefs flocking from far and near
down wide-ranging roads, wondering greatly
at the monster's footprints. His fatal departure
365 was regretted by no-one who witnessed his trail,
the ignominious marks of his flight
where he'd skulked away, exhausted in spirit
and beaten in battle, bloodying the path,
hauling his doom to the demons' mere.
370 The bloodshot water wallowed and surged,
there were **loathsome** upthrows and overturnings
of waves and gore and wound-slurry.
With his death upon him, he had dived deep
into his marsh-den, drowned out his life
375 and his heathen soul: hell claimed him there.

Then away they rode, the old retainers
with many a young man following after,
a troop on horseback, in high spirits
on their bay steeds. Beowulf's doings
380 were praised over and over again.

Nowhere, they said, north or south
between the two seas or under the tall sky
on the broad earth was there anyone better
to raise a shield or to rule a kingdom.
385 Yet there was no laying of blame on their lord,
the noble Hrothgar; he was a good king.

At times the war-band broke into a gallop,
letting their chestnut horses race
wherever they found the going good
390 on those well-known tracks. Meanwhile, a thane
of the king's household, a carrier of tales,
a traditional singer deeply schooled
in the lore of the past, linked a new theme
to a strict metre. The man started
395 to recite with skill, rehearsing Beowulf's
triumphs and feats in well-fashioned lines,
entwining his words.

CHECK YOUR UNDERSTANDING

Answer these questions before moving on to the **Analyze the Text** section on
the following page.

1 Why does Grendel hate humanity?

   A He is an outcast member of the nobility.

   B He is cursed and envious of the Danes' celebrations.

   C The Danes had persecuted and exiled him.

   D His home had been destroyed to make way for people.

2 Where does the final battle take place?

   F Hrothgar's mead hall

   G Grendel's cave lair

   H Beowulf's castle

   J Wulfgar's beach

3 Beowulf defeats Grendel by —

   A using a magic sword

   B setting fire to his lair

   C chasing him out to sea

   D fighting without weapons

ANALYZE THE TEXT

Support your responses with evidence from the text. 📓 NOTEBOOK

1. **Analyze** Identify two kennings associated with Grendel. How do these phrases convey the poet's attitude toward the character?

2. **Draw Conclusions** Reread lines 85–103, which describe how Hrothgar's followers prayed for protection from Grendel's attacks. Are these Christian ideas fully integrated into the epic? Explain why or why not.

3. **Evaluate** Reread lines 268–313. The poet uses various techniques— alliteration, caesura, kennings—in the description of the battle between Grendel and Beowulf. How might these techniques have helped Anglo-Saxon poets chant or sing the poem and convey its meaning?

4. **Analyze** Identify and explain a universal theme conveyed by the description of the battle between Beowulf and Grendel.

5. **Notice & Note** Reread Hrothgar's speech in lines 191–225. What values are reflected in his recollection of his relationship with Beowulf's father and of the efforts of his followers to stop Grendel?

RESEARCH

RESEARCH TIP
When you research online, use reliable websites. Often these have .org or .edu web addresses. Be wary of information from publicly sourced sites; information that can be changed, supplemented, and otherwise edited by the general public is not always accurate.

Traditional epic poems reflect the values and beliefs of the prevailing culture, as *Beowulf* reflects values of Anglo-Saxon society. Many cultures have produced epic poetry. Briefly research other epic poems and use a chart like the one below to pose and answer research questions about the epics.

QUESTION	ANSWER
What culture is represented in the *Iliad*, and who is its author?	
In what language was *Emperor Shaka the Great* originally compiled?	
***Paradise Lost*, by John Milton, is based on what famous story?**	

Connect Consider which kinds of stories in today's society might be seen as epics. Make a list of several books, movies, TV shows, songs, or other kinds of stories that feature heroes and reflect the values and beliefs of our culture. Share your list with a partner and discuss what makes a story an epic.

CREATE AND PRESENT

Write a Poem Write a poem about someone whose ideals and values you admire. Review your notes on the Quick Start activity before you begin.

❑ Employ at least one technique that you have learned about in this lesson, such as alliteration or kennings.

❑ Think about the form and tone that will best suit your message.

❑ Use a strong rhythm to help make your poem memorable.

❑ Have a partner read your poem and give you feedback. Make revisions, if necessary.

Present an Epic *Beowulf* is full of action and drama and is best appreciated when read aloud. With a partner, present a passage from the epic poem.

❑ Select a passage that features exciting action, rich poetic language, or dialogue between two characters.

❑ With your partner, decide how you will divide the passage and who will read each part.

❑ Practice reading with expression, gestures, and appropriate volume.

❑ Present your reading of the epic to your classmates.

Go to **Giving a Presentation: Delivering Your Presentation** in the **Speaking and Listening Studio** for more on giving a presentation.

RESPOND TO THE ESSENTIAL QUESTION

? What makes someone a hero?

Gather Information Review your annotations and notes on *Beowulf*. Then, add relevant information to your Response Log. As you determine which information to include, think about:

- the motivation of a hero
- the importance of cultural values
- how the actions of one person can benefit the community

ACADEMIC VOCABULARY
As you write and discuss what you learned from the poem, be sure to use the Academic Vocabulary words. Check off each of the words that you use.

❑ **collapse**

❑ **displace**

❑ **military**

❑ **violate**

❑ **visual**

WORD BANK
aghast
unrelenting
affliction
plight
baleful
wail
loathsome

CRITICAL VOCABULARY

Practice and Apply Choose the letter of the best answer to each question. Explain your answer.

1. Which is an example of a **baleful** action?
   a. throwing a rock intentionally   **b.** dropping a rock accidentally

2. Which is more likely to sound like a **wail**?
   a. a child shouting for joy   **b.** a child having a tantrum

3. Which can be described as an **affliction**?
   a. a case of hiccups   **b.** a case of chickenpox

4. Which is likely to be **unrelenting**?
   a. a persistent suitor   **b.** a casual acquaintance

5. Which is more likely to leave you **aghast**?
   a. finding a scratch on your car   **b.** witnessing a car accident

6. Which is more likely to be considered a **plight**?
   a. finding a wallet at a store   **b.** leaving your wallet at a store

7. Which would make you feel **loathsome**?
   a. doing a mud run   **b.** wading through a sewer

VOCABULARY STRATEGY:
Homophones

Go to **Homonyms, Homographs, and Homophones** in the **Vocabulary Studio** for more on homophones.

When listening to poetry read aloud, the audience has to be able to recognize **homophones.** These are words that have the same pronunciation but different spellings and meanings. Listeners use context clues to figure out which word is intended. For instance, the critical vocabulary word *wail* is a homophone found in line 306: "Then an extraordinary / wail arose . . . " *Wail* is pronounced the same as the word for a large sea mammal, but the context helps the listener understand that this word means "to make a long, loud, high-pitched cry, as in grief, sorrow, or fear."

Practice and Apply Complete each sentence with the correct choice from the homophones in parentheses. Define the word you choose.

1. At one point, Grendel grabbed 30 men from (their, there) resting places and took them to his lair.

2. Grendel's powers of destruction were (plane, plain) to (sea, see).

3. He always struck at nighttime, and his mayhem was complete before (morning, mourning) came.

4. When Beowulf (herd, heard) about Grendel, he was at home in Geatland.

5. His plan was to (sail, sale) the swan's road and offer to defend the king.

LANGUAGE CONVENTIONS:
Mood

Mood is the feeling or atmosphere that a writer creates for the reader. Poets may use imagery, figurative language, alliteration or other sound devices, and word choices to create mood.

In lines 41–52, the Beowulf poet describes the scene at the banquet hall. Read this passage from the poem:

> Then as dawn brightened and the day broke
> Grendel's powers of destruction were plain:
> their wassail was over, they wept to heaven
> and mourned under morning. Their mighty prince,
> the storied leader, sat stricken and helpless,
> humiliated by the loss of his guard,
> bewildered and stunned, staring aghast
> at the demon's trail, in deep distress.
> He was numb with grief, but got no respite
> for one night later merciless Grendel
> struck again with more gruesome murders.
> Malignant by nature, he never showed remorse.

The chart gives examples of literary devices used in these lines:

LITERARY DEVICE	EXAMPLES
Imagery	wept to heaven, numb with grief
Alliteration	and mourned under morning. Their mighty prince
Word Choice	mourned, helpless, humiliated, distress, grief

These devices create a mood of sadness and despair. This mood helps underscore the difficult situation facing King Hrothgar. It also helps to establish Grendel as a vicious, uncaring beast, imbued with supernatural powers. The mood also builds suspense as readers wonder how Beowulf will conquer such an evil, dangerous opponent.

Practice and Apply Complete these activities independently.

1. Choose a passage from the poem that conveys a distinct mood—for example, lines 14–40 or 234–268. Identify the mood of the passage you've chosen and the literary devices that help to create this mood.

2. With the passage from *Beowulf* as a guide, use what you learned about literary devices to write an original passage that creates a similar mood.

3. Read your passage aloud to a partner. Have your partner identify the mood and evaluate your success in conveying it.

THE WIFE OF BATH'S TALE

from THE CANTERBURY TALES

Narrative Poem by **Geoffrey Chaucer**
translated by **Nevill Coghill**

? *ESSENTIAL QUESTION:*

What is true chivalry?

QUICK START

What do you think is most important for a successful romantic relationship? Write a paragraph in response to this question. Then discuss your thoughts with a partner.

ANALYZE STRUCTURE

The Canterbury Tales has a complex structure that features a **frame story**—a story that surrounds and binds together one or more different narratives in a single work. The frame story in *The Canterbury Tales* begins with a General Prologue, in which the characters, setting, and storytelling premise are introduced. It also includes interactions among characters in the breaks between tales, when they often interrupt and argue with one another.

In addition to unifying the tales told by the pilgrims, the frame story provides a vivid portrait of each pilgrim. Through the initial descriptions as well as the later interactions among the pilgrims, readers learn about the positions they occupy in medieval society. These interactions enable Chaucer to present insights about practices and institutions in this time period; for example, his portrayals of clergy and church officials reveal corruption in the church.

Chaucer also uses the frame story to explore relationships between pilgrims. In "The Wife of Bath's Prologue," the Friar interrupts the Wife of Bath's long account of her five husbands, which prefaces her actual story: "Well, Ma'am . . . as God may send me bliss, / This is a long preamble to a tale!" She finds an opportunity to get back at him as she starts to tell her tale.

ANALYZE NARRATOR

The **narrator** of a story is the character or voice that tells the story's events to the reader. Chaucer used multiple narrators for *The Canterbury Tales*. The narrator of the frame story describes the pilgrims and records their exchanges with one another. The pilgrims, in turn, narrate their own tales. You can gain insight into the Wife of Bath by examining the following elements in her narration:

GENRE ELEMENTS: NARRATIVE POETRY

• tells a story using elements of prose fiction such as character, setting, plot, narrator, and theme

• written in verse, with techniques such as rhyme, meter, and figurative language

• includes epic poems and ballads

SUBJECT AND THEME	DIRECT STATEMENTS	TONE
When narrators are also characters in a story, they usually choose subjects and themes relevant to their own experiences. For example, the Wife of Bath, who has been married five times, tells a tale about relationships between men and women.	Narrators sometimes comment directly on characters and events. The Wife of Bath makes statements on several topics, such as the type of husband she values and the ability of women to keep secrets.	A narrator's tone, or attitude toward a subject, provides clues about the narrator's personality. Usually tone is communicated through word choice and details. Notice the words that the Wife of Bath uses to describe the knight's plight. What kind of person comes across through this tone?

CRITICAL VOCABULARY

preamble   virtue   sovereignty   bequeath   rebuke

To see how many Critical Vocabulary words you already know, use them to complete the sentences.

1. The Wife of Bath chose some of her husbands based on what they could _____ to her.

2. Nuns' habits are designed to reflect the _____ and modesty of the wearer.

3. Since the Wife of Bath has _____ over her financial affairs, she can spend her money on whatever she likes.

4. The Friar objected to the lengthy _____ to the Wife of Bath's tale.

5. The Summoner responded to the Friar's comments with a _____.

LANGUAGE CONVENTIONS

Inverted Sentences In this lesson, you will learn about inverted sentences, where the normal order of a subject followed by a verb is reversed. Notice how Chaucer uses inversion in this line:

> But truly poor are they who whine and fret.

Notice that the verb *are* precedes the subject *they*. As you read "The Wife of Bath's Tale," note other examples of inverted sentences.

ANNOTATION MODEL   NOTICE & NOTE

As you read, note clues about the personality of the Wife of Bath and also about the frame story that surrounds her tale. This model shows one reader's notes about the prologue to the tale.

The Friar laughed when he had heard all this.	
"Well, Ma'am," he said, "as God may send me bliss,	This suggests that the Wife of Bath likes to talk for a long time.
This is a long preamble to a tale!"	
But when the Summoner heard the Friar rail,	
"Just look!" he cried, "by the two arms of God!	Seems like the Summoner doesn't like the Friar. Maybe they quarreled earlier.
These meddling friars are always on the prod!	
Don't we all know a friar and a fly	
Go prod and buzz in every dish and pie!"	

BACKGROUND

Geoffrey Chaucer *(1342?–1400) came from a prosperous, though not noble, family. His father was a wine merchant who could afford to give him a good education. Chaucer grew up in London at a time when the city was growing due to expansion of commerce. In 1357 he became an attendant in an aristocrat's court, which put him in contact with influential people such as John of Gaunt, who became his lifelong patron. Two years later he went to France to fight in the Hundred Years' War. When he was captured, his family's connections to King Edward III helped secure his safe return.*

THE WIFE OF BATH'S TALE

Narrative Poem by Geoffrey Chaucer
translated by Nevill Coghill

In 1366 Chaucer married Philippa Roet, whose ties to the court benefitted his career. During the next two decades he held various royal posts and traveled to Italy, Flanders, and France on diplomatic missions. He also served at home as a justice of the peace and as a member of parliament. While fulfilling these public roles, Chaucer began to write the literary works for which he is famous.

Chaucer is widely considered to be the first great English author. He wrote in Middle English, which was starting to replace French and Latin as England's main literary language. Chaucer's best-known work, The Canterbury Tales, *is a collection of mostly verse tales in a variety of genres. The book is distinguished by its realism, earthy humor, and shrewd insights into human nature. Chaucer depicts a group of pilgrims traveling to the shrine of St. Thomas à Becket in Canterbury. At the beginning of their journey, the host of a tavern where they stop to rest proposes a storytelling contest, with the winner to receive a free dinner. Chaucer's pilgrims represent a cross-section of medieval society, allowing him to satirize institutions of his time. Each tale is preceded by a prologue in which the characters exchange commentary.*

In addition to The Canterbury Tales, *Chaucer wrote other notable works including the tragic verse romance* Troilus *and* Criseyde. *Upon his death, he was buried in Westminster Abbey, an honor rarely given to a commoner.*

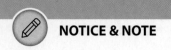

NOTICE & NOTE

Notice & Note

Use the side margins to notice and note signposts in the text.

ANALYZE STRUCTURE

Annotate: Mark phrases in lines 1–28 that show how the frame story provides details about relationships between pilgrims.

Draw Conclusions: What is the relationship between the Friar and the Summoner? The Friar and the Wife of Bath?

preamble
(prē̆ăm´bəl, prē-ăm´-) *n.* a preliminary statement.

33 mead: meadow.

SETTING A PURPOSE

As you read, pay attention to details that reveal the personality of the Wife of Bath and her opinions about men and women.

from The Wife of Bath's Prologue

The Friar laughed when he had heard all this.
"Well, Ma'am," he said, "as God may send me bliss,
This is a long **preamble** to a tale!"
But when the Summoner heard the Friar rail,
5 "Just look!" he cried, "by the two arms of God!
These meddling friars are always on the prod!
Don't we all know a friar and a fly
Go prod and buzz in every dish and pie!
What do you mean with your 'preambulation'?
10 Amble yourself, trot, do a meditation!
You're spoiling all our fun with your commotion."
The Friar smiled and said, "Is that your motion?
I promise on my word before I go
To find occasion for a tale or so
15 About a summoner that will make us laugh."
"Well, damn your eyes, and on my own behalf,"
The Summoner answered, "mine be damned as well
If I can't think of several tales to tell
About the friars that will make you mourn
20 Before we get as far as Sittingbourne.
Have you no patience? Look, he's in a huff!"
  Our Host called out, "Be quiet, that's enough!
Shut up, and let the woman tell her tale.
You must be drunk, you've taken too much ale.
25 Now, Ma'am, you go ahead and no demur."
"All right," she said, "it's just as you prefer,
If I have licence from this worthy friar."
"Nothing," said he, "that I should more desire."

The Wife of Bath's Tale

When good King Arthur ruled in ancient days
30 (A king that every Briton loves to praise)
This was a land brim-full of fairy folk.
The Elf-Queen and her courtiers joined and broke
Their elfin dance on many a green mead,
Or so was the opinion once, I read,
35 Hundreds of years ago, in days of yore.
But no one now sees fairies any more.
For now the saintly charity and prayer

Of holy friars seem to have purged the air;
They search the countryside through field and stream
40 As thick as motes that speckle a sun-beam,
Blessing the halls, the chambers, kitchens, bowers,
Cities and boroughs, castles, courts and towers,
Thorpes, barns and stables, outhouses and dairies,
And that's the reason why there are no fairies.
45 Wherever there was wont to walk an elf
Today there walks the holy friar himself
As evening falls or when the daylight springs,
Saying his matins and his holy things,
Walking his limit round from town to town.
50 Women can now go safely up and down
By every bush or under every tree;
There is no other incubus but he,
So there is really no one else to hurt you
And he will do no more than take your **virtue**.

55   Now it so happened, I began to say,
Long, long ago in good King Arthur's day,
There was a knight who was a lusty liver.
One day as he came riding from the river
He saw a maiden walking all forlorn
60 Ahead of him, alone as she was born.
And of that maiden, spite of all she said,
By very force he took her maidenhead.
        This act of violence made such a stir,
So much petitioning to the king for her,
65 That he condemned the knight to lose his head
By course of law. He was as good as dead
(It seems that then the statutes took that view)
But that the queen, and other ladies too,
Implored the king to exercise his grace
70 So ceaselessly, he gave the queen the case
And granted her his life, and she could choose
Whether to show him mercy or refuse.

        The queen returned him thanks with all her might,
And then she sent a summons to the knight
75 At her convenience, and expressed her will:
"You stand, for such is the position still,
In no way certain of your life," said she,
"Yet you shall live if you can answer me:
What is the thing that women most desire?
80 Beware the axe and say as I require.

40 motes: specks of dust.

41 bowers: bedrooms.

43 thorpes: villages;
outhouses: sheds.

45 wherever . . . elf: wherever
an elf was accustomed to walk.

49 limit: the area to which
a friar was restricted in his
begging for donations.

52 incubus (ĭnˊkyə-bəs): an evil
spirit believed to descend on
women.

virtue
(vûrˊchoo) *n. Archaic* chastity,
especially in a woman.

**61 of that maiden . . .
maidenhead:** in spite of the
maiden's protests, he robbed
her of her virginity.

**CONTRASTS AND
CONTRADICTIONS**

Notice & Note: In lines 66–72,
mark the words or phrases
indicating behavior that
would not be consistent with
the behavior of a traditional
medieval king.

Infer: What does this
contradiction demonstrate
about the Wife of Bath's views
on the relationship between
men and women?

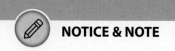

"If you can't answer on the moment, though,
I will concede you this: you are to go
A twelvemonth and a day to seek and learn
Sufficient answer, then you shall return.
85 I shall take gages from you to extort
Surrender of your body to the court."
  Sad was the knight and sorrowfully sighed,
But there! All other choices were denied,
And in the end he chose to go away
90 And to return after a year and day
Armed with such answer as there might be sent
To him by God. He took his leave and went.

  He knocked at every house, searched every place,
Yes, anywhere that offered hope of grace.
95 What could it be that women wanted most?
But all the same he never touched a coast,
Country or town in which there seemed to be
Any two people willing to agree.

  Some said that women wanted wealth and treasure,
100 "Honor," said some, some "Jollity and pleasure,"
Some "Gorgeous clothes" and others "Fun in bed,"
"To be oft widowed and remarried," said
Others again, and some that what most mattered
Was that we should be cosseted and flattered.
105 That's very near the truth, it seems to me;
A man can win us best with flattery.
To dance attendance on us, make a fuss,
Ensnares us all, the best and worst of us.

  Some say the things we most desire are these:
110 Freedom to do exactly as we please,
With no one to reprove our faults and lies,
Rather to have one call us good and wise.
Truly there's not a woman in ten score
Who has a fault, and someone rubs the sore,
115 But she will kick if what he says is true;
You try it out and you will find so too.
However vicious we may be within
We like to be thought wise and void of sin.
Others assert we women find it sweet
120 When we are thought dependable, discreet
And secret, firm of purpose and controlled,
Never betraying things that we are told.
But that's not worth the handle of a rake;

85 gages: pledges.

104 cosseted (kŏs´ĭ-tĭd): pampered.

ANALYZE NARRATOR

Annotate: Mark words or phrases in lines 99–108 that convey the Wife of Bath's tone.

Infer: What is her attitude toward the knight's quest for an answer?

113 ten score: 200.

115 but she will: who will not.

118 void of sin: sinless.

Women conceal a thing? For Heaven's sake!
125 Remember Midas? Will you hear the tale?

Among some other little things, now stale,
Ovid relates that under his long hair
The unhappy Midas grew a splendid pair
Of ass's ears; as subtly as he might,
130 He kept his foul deformity from sight;
Save for his wife, there was not one that knew.
He loved her best, and trusted in her too.
He begged her not to tell a living creature
That he possessed so horrible a feature.
135 And she—she swore, were all the world to win,
She would not do such villainy and sin
As saddle her husband with so foul a name;
Besides to speak would be to share the shame.
Nevertheless she thought she would have died
140 Keeping this secret bottled up inside;
It seemed to swell her heart and she, no doubt,
Thought it was on the point of bursting out.

Fearing to speak of it to woman or man,
Down to a reedy marsh she quickly ran
145 And reached the sedge. Her heart was all on fire
And, as a bittern bumbles in the mire,
She whispered to the water, near the ground,
"Betray me not, O water, with thy sound!
To thee alone I tell it: it appears
150 My husband has a pair of ass's ears!
Ah! My heart's well again, the secret's out!
I could no longer keep it, not a doubt."
And so you see, although we may hold fast
A little while, it must come out at last,
155 We can't keep secrets; as for Midas, well,
Read Ovid for his story; he will tell.

This knight that I am telling you about
Perceived at last he never would find out
What it could be that women loved the best.
160 Faint was the soul within his sorrowful breast,
As home he went, he dared no longer stay;
His year was up and now it was the day.

As he rode home in a dejected mood
Suddenly, at the margin of a wood,
165 He saw a dance upon the leafy floor

125 Midas: a legendary king of Phrygia, in Asia Minor.

127 Ovid (ŏv´ĭd): an ancient Roman poet whose *Metamorphoses* is a storehouse of Greek and Roman legends.

131 save: except.

ANALYZE NARRATOR

Annotate: Reread lines 143–156. Mark the Wife of Bath's hint that Midas's secret will not be safe after his wife whispers it to the water.

Draw Conclusions: Why might Chaucer have chosen to include this long digression in the narrator's story?

145 sedge: marsh grasses.

146 bumbles in the mire: booms in the swamp. (The bittern, a wading bird, is famous for its loud call.)

Of four and twenty ladies, nay, and more.
Eagerly he approached, in hope to learn
Some words of wisdom ere he should return;
But lo! Before he came to where they were,
170 Dancers and dance all vanished into air!
There wasn't a living creature to be seen
Save one old woman crouched upon the green.
A fouler-looking creature I suppose
Could scarcely be imagined. She arose
175 And said, "Sir knight, there's no way on from here.
Tell me what you are looking for, my dear,
For peradventure that were best for you;
We old, old women know a thing or two."

"Dear Mother," said the knight, "alack the day!
180 I am as good as dead if I can't say
What thing it is that women most desire;
If you could tell me I would pay your hire."
"Give me your hand," she said, "and swear to do
Whatever I shall next require of you
185 —If so to do should lie within your might—
And you shall know the answer before night."
"Upon my honor," he answered, "I agree."
"Then," said the crone, "I dare to guarantee
Your life is safe; I shall make good my claim.
190 Upon my life the queen will say the same.
Show me the very proudest of them all
In costly coverchief or jewelled caul
That dare say no to what I have to teach.
Let us go forward without further speech."
195 And then she crooned her gospel in his ear
And told him to be glad and not to fear.

They came to court. This knight, in full array,
Stood forth and said, "O Queen, I've kept my day
And kept my word and have my answer ready."

200   There sat the noble matrons and the heady
Young girls, and widows too, that have the grace
Of wisdom, all assembled in that place,
And there the queen herself was throned to hear
And judge his answer. Then the knight drew near
205 And silence was commanded through the hall.

The queen gave order he should tell them all
What thing it was that women wanted most.

177 peradventure: maybe; possibly.

179 alack the day: an exclamation of sorrow, roughly equivalent to "Woe is me!"

192 coverchief: kerchief; **caul** (kaul): an ornamental hairnet.

195 gospel: message.

197 in full array: in all his finery.

200 heady: giddy; impetuous.

201 grace: gift.

He stood not silent like a beast or post,
But gave his answer with the ringing word
210 Of a man's voice and the assembly heard:

     "My liege and lady, in general," said he,
"A woman wants the self-same **sovereignty**
Over her husband as over her lover,
And master him; he must not be above her.
215 That is your greatest wish, whether you kill
Or spare me; please yourself. I wait your will."

     In all the court not one that shook her head
Or contradicted what the knight had said;
Maid, wife and widow cried, "He's saved his life!"

220   And on the word up started the old wife,
The one the knight saw sitting on the green,
And cried, "Your mercy, sovereign lady queen!
Before the court disperses, do me right!
'Twas I who taught this answer to the knight,
225 For which he swore, and pledged his honor to it,
That the first thing I asked of him he'd do it,

211 liege (lēj): lord.

sovereignty
(sŏv´ər-ĭn-tē, sŏv´rĭn-tē) *n.*
complete independence and
self-government.

LANGUAGE CONVENTIONS
Annotate: Mark the inverted
phrase in lines 217–222.

Analyze: How does this
inversion help maintain the
pattern of the verse?

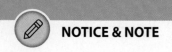

NOTICE & NOTE

So far as it should lie within his might.
Before this court I ask you then, sir knight,
To keep your word and take me for your wife;
230 For well you know that I have saved your life.
If this be false, deny it on your sword!"

"Alas!" he said, "Old lady, by the Lord
I know indeed that such was my behest,
But for God's love think of a new request,
235 Take all my goods, but leave my body free."
"A curse on us," she said, "if I agree!
I may be foul, I may be poor and old,
Yet will not choose to be, for all the gold
That's bedded in the earth or lies above,
240 Less than your wife, nay, than your very love!"

"My love?" said he. "By heaven, my damnation!
Alas that any of my race and station
Should ever make so foul a misalliance!"
Yet in the end his pleading and defiance
245 All went for nothing, he was forced to wed.
He takes his ancient wife and goes to bed.

Now peradventure some may well suspect
A lack of care in me since I neglect
To tell of the rejoicing and display
250 Made at the feast upon their wedding-day.
I have but a short answer to let fall;
I say there was no joy or feast at all,

Nothing but heaviness of heart and sorrow.
He married her in private on the morrow
255 And all day long stayed hidden like an owl,
It was such torture that his wife looked foul.

Great was the anguish churning in his head
When he and she were piloted to bed;
He wallowed back and forth in desperate style.
260 His ancient wife lay smiling all the while;
At last she said, "Bless us! Is this, my dear,
How knights and wives get on together here?
Are these the laws of good King Arthur's house?
Are knights of his all so contemptuous?
265 I am your own beloved and your wife,
And I am she, indeed, that saved your life;

233 behest (bǐ-hĕst´): promise.

242 race and station: family and rank.

243 misalliance (mǐs´ə-lī´əns): an unsuitable marriage.

ANALYZE NARRATOR
Annotate: Mark words and phrases in lines 247–256 that convey the Wife of Bath's tone.

Draw Conclusions: How does her tone influence readers' views of their wedding night?

258 piloted: led. (In the Middle Ages, the wedding party typically escorted the bride and groom to their bedchamber.)

259 wallowed: (wŏl´ōd) rolled around; thrashed about.

And certainly I never did you wrong.
Then why, this first of nights, so sad a song?
You're carrying on as if you were half-witted.
270 Say, for God's love, what sin have I committed?
I'll put things right if you will tell me how."

"Put right?" he cried. "That never can be now!
Nothing can ever be put right again!
You're old, and so abominably plain,
275 So poor to start with, so low-bred to follow;
It's little wonder if I twist and wallow!
God, that my heart would burst within my breast!"

"Is that," said she, "the cause of your unrest?"

"Yes, certainly," he said, "and can you wonder?"

280   "I could set right what you suppose a blunder,
That's if I cared to, in a day or two,
If I were shown more courtesy by you.
Just now," she said, "you spoke of gentle birth,
Such as descends from ancient wealth and worth.
285 If that's the claim you make for gentlemen
Such arrogance is hardly worth a hen.
Whoever loves to work for virtuous ends,
Public and private, and who most intends
To do what deeds of gentleness he can,
290 Take him to be the greatest gentleman.
Christ wills we take our gentleness from Him,
Not from a wealth of ancestry long dim,
Though they **bequeath** their whole establishment
By which we claim to be of high descent.
295 Our fathers cannot make us a bequest
Of all those virtues that became them best
And earned for them the name of gentlemen,
But bade us follow them as best we can.

"Thus the wise poet of the Florentines,
300 Dante by name, has written in these lines,
For such is the opinion Dante launches:
'Seldom arises by these slender branches
Prowess of men, for it is God, no less,
Wills us to claim of Him our gentleness.'
305 For of our parents nothing can we claim
Save temporal things, and these may hurt and maim.

ANALYZE NARRATOR
Annotate: Reread lines 272–286. Mark phrases that suggest the old woman doesn't take the knight's rejection seriously.

Compare: What does the old woman have in common with the Wife of Bath?

bequeath
(bĭ-kwēth´, -kwēth´) tr.v.
to pass (something) on to another; hand down.

299 Florentines: the people of Florence, Italy.

300 Dante (dän´tā): a famous medieval Italian poet. Lines 302–304 refer to a passage in Dante's most famous work, *The Divine Comedy*.

306 temporal: worldly, rather than spiritual.

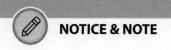

308 gentility (jĕn-tĭl´ĭ-tē): the quality possessed by a gentle, or noble, person.

314 Caucasus (kô´kə-səs): a region of western Asia between the Black and Caspian seas.

321 possessions: beliefs; ideals

325 lording: lord; nobleman.

332 churl (chûrl): low-class person; boor.

339 Valerius (və-lîr´ē-əs): Valerius Maximus, a Roman writer who compiled a collection of historical anecdotes.

340 Tullius (tŭl´ē-əs) **surnamed Hostilius** (hŏ-stĭl´ē-əs): the third king of the Romans.

342 Boethius (bō-ē´thē-əs): a Christian philosopher of the Dark Ages; **Seneca** (sĕn´ĭ-kə): an ancient Roman philosopher, writer, teacher, and politician.

"But everyone knows this as well as I;
For if gentility were implanted by
The natural course of lineage down the line,
310 Public or private, could it cease to shine
In doing the fair work of gentle deed?
No vice or villainy could then bear seed.

"Take fire and carry it to the darkest house
Between this kingdom and the Caucasus,
315 And shut the doors on it and leave it there,
It will burn on, and it will burn as fair
As if ten thousand men were there to see,
For fire will keep its nature and degree,
I can assure you, sir, until it dies.

320 "But gentleness, as you will recognize,
Is not annexed in nature to possessions.
Men fail in living up to their professions;
But fire never ceases to be fire.
God knows you'll often find, if you enquire,
325 Some lording full of villainy and shame.
If you would be esteemed for the mere name
Of having been by birth a gentleman
And stemming from some virtuous, noble clan,
And do not live yourself by gentle deed
330 Or take your father's noble code and creed,
You are no gentleman, though duke or earl.
Vice and bad manners are what make a churl.

"Gentility is only the renown
For bounty that your fathers handed down,
335 Quite foreign to your person, not your own;
Gentility must come from God alone.
That we are gentle comes to us by grace
And by no means is it bequeathed with place.

"Reflect how noble (says Valerius)
340 Was Tullius surnamed Hostilius,
Who rose from poverty to nobleness.
And read Boethius, Seneca no less,
Thus they express themselves and are agreed:
'Gentle is he that does a gentle deed.'
345 And therefore, my dear husband, I conclude
That even if my ancestors were rude,
Yet God on high—and so I hope He will—
Can grant me grace to live in virtue still,

© Houghton Mifflin Harcourt Publishing Company

A gentlewoman only when beginning
350 To live in virtue and to shrink from sinning.

"As for my poverty which you reprove,
Almighty God Himself in whom we move,
Believe and have our being, chose a life
Of poverty, and every man or wife,
355 Nay, every child can see our Heavenly King
Would never stoop to choose a shameful thing.
No shame in poverty if the heart is gay,
As Seneca and all the learned say.
He who accepts his poverty unhurt
360 I'd say is rich although he lacked a shirt.
But truly poor are they who whine and fret
And covet what they cannot hope to get.
And he that, having nothing, covets not,
Is rich, though you may think he is a sot.

365 "True poverty can find a song to sing.
Juvenal says a pleasant little thing:
'The poor can dance and sing in the relief
Of having nothing that will tempt a thief.'
Though it be hateful, poverty is good,
370 A great incentive to a livelihood,
And a great help to our capacity
For wisdom, if accepted patiently.
Poverty is, though wanting in estate,
A kind of wealth that none calumniate.
375 Poverty often, when the heart is lowly,
Brings one to God and teaches what is holy,
Gives knowledge of oneself and even lends
A glass by which to see one's truest friends.
And since it's no offense, let me be plain;
380 Do not **rebuke** my poverty again.

"Lastly you taxed me, sir, with being old.
Yet even if you never had been told
By ancient books, you gentlemen engage,
Yourselves in honor to respect old age.
385 To call an old man 'father' shows good breeding,
And this could be supported from my reading.

"You say I'm old and fouler than a fen.
You need not fear to be a cuckold, then.
Filth and old age, I'm sure you will agree,

364 sot: fool.

366 Juvenal (jo͞o′və-nəl): an ancient Roman satirist.

373 wanting in estate: lacking in grandeur.

374 calumniate (kə-lŭm′nē-āt′): criticize with false statements; slander.

380 rebuke (rĭ-byo͞ok′) *v.* to criticize sharply or reprimand.

387 fen: marsh.

388 cuckold: (kŭk′əld): a husband whose wife is unfaithful.

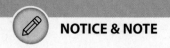
TOUGH QUESTIONS

Notice & Note: Mark the tough question in lines 393–401.

Analyze: What internal conflict must the knight resolve to answer this question?

398 chance your arm: take your chance on.

390 Are powerful wardens over chastity.
Nevertheless, well knowing your delights,
I shall fulfil your worldly appetites.

"You have two choices; which one will you try?
To have me old and ugly till I die,
395 But still a loyal, true, and humble wife
That never will displease you all her life,
Or would you rather I were young and pretty
And chance your arm what happens in a city
Where friends will visit you because of me,
400 Yes, and in other places too, maybe.
Which would you have? The choice is all your own."

The knight thought long, and with a piteous groan
At last he said, with all the care in life,
"My lady and my love, my dearest wife,
405 I leave the matter to your wise decision.
You make the choice yourself, for the provision
Of what may be agreeable and rich
In honor to us both, I don't care which;
Whatever pleases you suffices me."

410 "And have I won the mastery?" said she,
"Since I'm to choose and rule as I think fit?"
"Certainly, wife," he answered her, "that's it."
"Kiss me," she cried. "No quarrels! On my oath
And word of honor, you shall find me both,
415 That is, both fair and faithful as a wife;
May I go howling mad and take my life
Unless I prove to be as good and true
As ever wife was since the world was new!
And if tomorrow when the sun's above
420 I seem less fair than any lady-love,
Than any queen or empress east or west,
Do with my life and death as you think best.
Cast up the curtain, husband. Look at me!"

And when indeed the knight had looked to see,
425 Lo, she was young and lovely, rich in charms.
In ecstasy he caught her in his arms,
His heart went bathing in a bath of blisses
And melted in a hundred thousand kisses,

ANALYZE NARRATOR

Annotate: Reread lines 424–430. Mark words and phrases that describe the knight's feelings.

Draw Conclusions: Do you think the Wife of Bath wants readers to sympathize with the knight at this point in the story? Why or why not?

And she responded in the fullest measure
430 With all that could delight or give him pleasure.

      So they lived ever after to the end
In perfect bliss; and may Christ Jesus send
Us husbands meek and young and fresh in bed,
And grace to overbid them when we wed.
435 And—Jesu hear my prayer!—cut short the lives
Of those who won't be governed by their wives;
And all old, angry niggards of their pence,
God send them soon a very pestilence!

ANALYZE STRUCTURE

Annotate: Mark the phrases in lines 432–438 that express the Wife of Bath's thoughts about husbands.

Analyze: In the frame story we learn that the Wife of Bath had five husbands. How does this conclusion relate to her background?

CHECK YOUR UNDERSTANDING

Answer these questions before moving on to the **Analyze the Text** section on the following page.

1 What action leads to the knight's death sentence?

   A He insults the queen.

   B He assaults a maiden.

   C He is unable to answer the queen's question.

   D He assaults the old woman.

2 How does the old woman get the knight to marry her?

   F She gives him money that she received from her father.

   G She magically becomes a beautiful elf like he wants.

   H She makes him pledge to honor her first request.

   J She tricks the Queen into making him marry her.

3 According to the old woman, why should the knight trust that she will be a faithful wife?

   A She is too poor to attract other men.

   B She has vowed to be faithful.

   C She will always be at his side.

   D She looks old and ugly.

RESPOND

ANALYZE THE TEXT

Support your responses with evidence from the text. 📓 NOTEBOOK

1. **Identify** Chaucer's frame story includes the interaction between the Wife of Bath and the Friar in "The Wife of Bath's Prologue." How is their relationship reflected in the tale itself?

2. **Infer** As a narrator, the Wife of Bath comments extensively about the various answers to the knight's question. What do her comments reveal about her own values and ideas? Use evidence from the poem to support the analysis.

3. **Draw Conclusions** Does the knight gain a better understanding of women over the course of the story, or is he basically the same as he was at the beginning? Explain your response.

4. **Critique** In the "Wife of Bath's Prologue," the Friar complains about the Wife of Bath's long, rambling preamble. How effective is she at narrating her tale about the knight? Explain your response.

5. **Notice & Note** In the last four stanzas, the knight's response to the old woman's question resolves the conflict between them. Do you find this conclusion satisfying? Explain why or why not.

RESEARCH

Chaucer's tale reflects the period in which he lived. During the Middle Ages, England's legal system was not nearly as developed as it is today, and women's roles were limited. Do some research on the following questions to find out more about the background to the story.

QUESTION	ANSWER
What rights did women have in medieval Europe?	
What opportunities did women have outside of marriage?	
What kind of legal system existed in this period?	

RESEARCH TIP

When you conduct online research, use specific search terms. If you just type "women's roles," your search might return some relevant information, but most of it won't relate to your topic. However, if you search "women's roles in the Middle Ages," you're more likely to find useful information.

Extend Find another narrative poem with a female speaker. Discuss with a partner what elements of the poem, including vocabulary and imagery, are similar to or different from "The Wife of Bath's Tale." Then, determine which poem speaks more to your own beliefs and discuss this with your partner.

CREATE AND PRESENT

Write a Short Story Write a short story in which the pilgrims who appear in the "Wife of Bath's Prologue" resume their conversation after she finishes her tale. Reread the prologue before you begin.

❑ Think about how the Friar, the Summoner, and the Host might react to the tale.

❑ Introduce and develop the characters in a way that is consistent with the prologue.

❑ Use dialogue and descriptive details.

❑ Provide a conclusion that resolves the conflict in the story.

Present a Short Story Read your story aloud to a small group.

❑ Practice reading the story so you can present it smoothly.

❑ When reading dialogue, adjust the tone of your voice to reflect how each character would speak.

❑ Use facial expressions and gestures to convey the emotions of the characters.

Go to the **Writing Narratives** in **Writing Studio** for help.

Go to **Giving a Presentation: Delivering Your Presentation** in the **Speaking and Listening Studio** for help.

RESPOND TO THE ESSENTIAL QUESTION

 What is true chivalry?

Gather Information Review your annotations and notes on "The Wife of Bath's Tale." Then, add relevant information to your Response Log. As you determine which information to include, think about:

- the crime that got the knight into trouble
- the knight's reaction when the old woman insists that he marry her
- the lessons that the old woman teaches the knight about true gentility
- the conclusion of the tale

ACADEMIC VOCABULARY

As you write and discuss what you learned from "The Wife of Bath's Tale," be sure to use the Academic Vocabulary words. Check off each of the words that you use.

❑ **collapse**

❑ **displace**

❑ **military**

❑ **violate**

❑ **visual**

WORD BANK
preamble
virtue
sovereignty
bequeath
rebuke

CRITICAL VOCABULARY

Practice and Apply Circle the letter of the best answer to each question. Explain your answer.

1. Which is an example of **sovereignty**?
   a. a monarch's authority   **b.** a subject's loyalty

2. Which is likely to involve **virtue**?
   a. running a fast food restaurant   **b.** running a free food bank

3. Which is likely to prompt a **rebuke**?
   a. doing household chores quickly   **b.** refusing to do household chores

4. Which is used to **bequeath** a gift?
   a. a last will and testament   **b.** an invoice

5. Which is involved in a **preamble**?
   a. an introduction   **b.** a conclusion

VOCABULARY STRATEGY:
Usage

Go to **Words with Multiple Meanings** in the **Vocabulary Studio** for more.

Language is dynamic—new words are continually added, other words are dropped, and still others are used in different ways than they were originally intended. When Geoffrey Chaucer uses the word *virtue* in the line, "And he will do no more than take your virtue," the word *virtue* means "chastity" or "purity." To most readers today, though, *virtue* means "goodness" or "a beneficial quality." Here are other words found in "The Wife of Bath's Tale" that have a different meaning, or usage, today:

WORD IN THE POEM	WHAT IT MEANT IN THE 14TH CENTURY
gentle: "Gentle is he that does a gentle deed."	noble
rude: "even if my ancestors were rude"	of low birth
fair: "And if tomorrow when the sun's above / I seem less fair than any lady-love"	beautiful

Practice and Apply Complete the following steps:

1. Write the current definition of each word in the chart.

2. Use each word in a sentence.

3. Form a small group to identify other words in the poem that have changed their meanings over the years. Share the words and their old and new usages with the class.

LANGUAGE CONVENTIONS:
Inverted Sentences

An inverted sentence is one in which the normal order of a subject followed by a verb is reversed. Notice how Chaucer uses inversion in these lines from the poem:

> This knight that I am telling you about
> Perceived at last he never would find out
> What it could be that women loved the best.
> Faint was the soul within his sorrowful breast,
> As home he went, he dared no longer stay;
> His year was up and now it was the day.

If Chaucer had chosen not to use inversion, his lines might have appeared this way:

> This knight that I am telling you about
> At last perceived he never would find out
> What it could be that women loved the best.
> His soul within his sorrowful breast was faint,
> As he went home, he dared stay no longer;
> His year was up and now it was the day.

By inverting the sentence in the fourth line, Chaucer preserves the rhyming couplet. Just as importantly, he maintains the effective rhythm of the poem. In the second version of the lines with the subject placed before the verb, the rhythm is lost. In addition the rhythm of the line is stilted and awkward and takes away from the effectiveness of the whole stanza.

Prose writers also use inversion. Varying sentence structure enables writers to refocus the readers' attention. In addition, inverted sentences build up suspense with words and phrases before arriving at the verb and subject. Make sure that your subject and verb agree when writing inverted sentences.

REGULAR ORDER	INVERTED ORDER
"A promise is a promise," the old woman declared.	"A promise is a promise," declared the old woman.
The groom stepped mournfully into the bedroom.	Mournfully into the bedroom stepped the groom.

Practice and Apply Write three inverted sentences about events in "The Wife of Bath's Tale."

from

LE MORTE D'ARTHUR

Romance by **Sir Thomas Malory**
retold by **Keith Baines**

? ***ESSENTIAL QUESTION:***

What makes someone a hero?

QUICK START

According to the code of chivalry, knights must always be loyal to their king and country. Write a paragraph about your loyalty to a person or group. Discuss how this sense of loyalty affects your behavior and whether you sometimes struggle to remain loyal.

ANALYZE CONFLICT

Medieval romances typically have exciting plots driven by conflict, a struggle between opposing forces. **External conflict** occurs between a character and an outside force. **Internal conflict** is a struggle within the mind of a character. Both types of conflict can play an important role in the same event. For example, as a knight enters into battle with an enemy, he may struggle internally with doubts about his courage. Often an internal conflict results when a character faces a moral dilemma—a problem in which the character must decide what is morally right. In medieval romances, many characters face moral dilemmas related to their efforts to live up to the code of chivalry. As you read *Le Morte d'Arthur,* look for examples of both external and internal conflict. Analyze how the behavior and underlying motivations of King Arthur, Sir Launcelot, and other knights help create moral dilemmas that influence the plot and theme of the romance.

GENRE ELEMENTS: ROMANCE

- portrays idealized or larger-than-life characters who perform daring deeds
- involves a love relationship
- includes mysterious or supernatural events
- expresses themes related to the code of chivalry

MAKE PREDICTIONS

When you **make predictions,** you use text clues and prior knowledge to guess what will happen in a story. These predictions may be influenced by your knowledge of the story's genre. For example, if you are reading a romance, you can expect the heroes to act bravely and to make great sacrifices for their ideals. As you read *Le Morte d'Arthur,* use a chart like this one to record your predictions. When you finish reading the text, reflect on any incorrect predictions you made and what caused you to guess wrong about the outcome.

PREDICTION	REASON FOR PREDICTION	OUTCOME

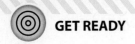

CRITICAL VOCABULARY

dominion	incumbent	redress	usurp	guile

To see how many Critical Vocabulary words you already know, use them to complete the sentences.

1. It is _____ upon each individual to complete his or her assigned section for the group project.

2. Beware of those who might lead you astray with words of _____.

3. His violent attempts to _____ the president's power failed.

4. After the war, the people found themselves under the _____ of a new ruler.

5. The employees demanded _____ for poor working conditions.

LANGUAGE CONVENTIONS

Tone In this lesson you will learn to identify tone, or the writer's or narrator's attitude toward the subject. This is communicated through devices such as word choice, detail, and sentence structure, as well as direct statements. While mood refers to the feelings evoked in the reader, tone refers to the attitude and feelings of the speaker, which may not be the same.

ANNOTATION MODEL   NOTICE & NOTE

As you read the selection, identify internal and external conflicts to find evidence of possible moral dilemmas faced by the characters. Mark supporting details you find in the text. In the model, you can see one reader's notes and evaluations.

> Then Sir Galyhud: "Sir, you command knights of royal blood; you cannot expect them to remain meekly within the city walls. I pray you, <u>let us encounter the enemy on the open field</u>, and they will soon repent of their expedition."
>
> And to <u>this the seven knights of West Britain all muttered their assent.</u> Then Sir Launcelot spoke:
>
> "My lords, <u>I am reluctant to shed Christian blood in a war against my own liege</u>; and yet I do know that these lands have already suffered depredation in the wars between King Claudas and my father and uncle, King Ban and King Bors. Therefore <u>I will next send a messenger to King Arthur and sue for peace</u>, for peace is always preferable to war."

Launcelot wishes to support his knights and protect his lands, but he is conflicted because he doesn't want to fight his lord, King Arthur.

BACKGROUND

As a young man, Sir Thomas Malory fought in the Hundred Years' War and was knighted in about 1442. Between 1451 and 1469, he collected all of the legends of King Arthur and his knights into one work, Le Morte d'Arthur (The Death of Arthur), which was published in 1485. However, the legends themselves date back much earlier, to the sixth century, having been passed down orally through many generations. Some historians believe that the fictional Arthur was modeled on a real Celtic military leader, although the historical Arthur was undoubtedly very different from Malory's Arthur, who ruled an idealized world of romance, chivalry, and magic.

from

LE MORTE D'ARTHUR

Romance by Sir Thomas Malory
retold by Keith Baines

SETTING A PURPOSE

As you read, pay attention to the conflicts that each character experiences. Think about whether these conflicts reveal heroic qualities.

King Arthur's favorite knight, Sir Launcelot, has fallen in love with the king's wife, Queen Gwynevere. The secret love affair is exposed by Sir Modred, Arthur's son by another woman, and Gwynevere is sentenced to burn at the stake. While rescuing the imprisoned Gwynevere, Launcelot slays two knights who, unknown to him at the time, are the brothers of Sir Gawain, a favorite nephew of Arthur's. After a reconciliation, Launcelot returns Gwynevere to Arthur to be reinstated as queen. At the urging of Gawain, who still wants revenge on Launcelot, the king banishes Launcelot to France, where the following excerpt begins.

～ THE SIEGE OF BENWICK ～

1   When Sir Launcelot had established **dominion** over France, he garrisoned the towns and settled with his army in the fortified city of Benwick, where his father King Ban had held court.

2   King Arthur, after appointing Sir Modred ruler in his absence, and instructing Queen Gwynevere to obey him, sailed to

Notice & Note

Use the side margins to notice and note signposts in the text.

dominion
(də-mĭn´yən) *n.* rule or power to rule; mastery.

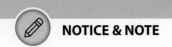
France with an army of sixty thousand men, and, on the advice of Sir Gawain, started laying waste[1] all before him.

3   News of the invasion reached Sir Launcelot, and his counselors advised him. Sir Bors[2] spoke first:

4   "My lord Sir Launcelot, is it wise to allow King Arthur to lay your lands waste when sooner or later he will oblige you to offer him battle?"

5   Sir Lyonel[3] spoke next: "My lord, I would recommend that we remain within the walls of our city until the invaders are weakened by cold and hunger, and then let us sally forth[4] and destroy them."

6   Next, King Bagdemagus: "Sir Launcelot, I understand that it is out of courtesy that you permit the king to ravage your lands, but where will this courtesy end? If you remain within the city, soon everything will be destroyed."

7   Then Sir Galyhud: "Sir, you command knights of royal blood; you cannot expect them to remain meekly within the city walls. I pray you, let us encounter the enemy on the open field, and they will soon repent of their expedition."

8   And to this the seven knights of West Britain all muttered their assent. Then Sir Launcelot spoke:

9   "My lords, I am reluctant to shed Christian blood in a war against my own liege;[5] and yet I do know that these lands have already suffered depredation[6] in the wars between King Claudas and my father and uncle, King Ban and King Bors. Therefore I will next send a messenger to King Arthur and sue[7] for peace, for peace is always preferable to war."

10   Accordingly a young noblewoman accompanied by a dwarf was sent to King Arthur. They were received by the gentle knight Sir Lucas the Butler.

11   "My lady, you bring a message from Sir Launcelot?" he asked.

12   "My lord, I do. It is for the king."

13   "Alas! King Arthur would readily be reconciled to Sir Launcelot, but Sir Gawain forbids it; and it is a shame, because Sir Launcelot is certainly the greatest knight living."

14   The young noblewoman was brought before the king, and when he had heard Sir Launcelot's entreaties for peace he wept, and would readily have accepted them had not Sir Gawain spoken up:

15   "My liege, if we retreat now we will become a laughingstock, in this land and in our own. Surely our honor demands that we pursue this war to its proper conclusion."

16   "Sir Gawain, I will do as you advise, although reluctantly, for Sir Launcelot's terms are generous and he is still dear to me. I beg you make a reply to him on my behalf."

ANALYZE CONFLICT

Annotate: Mark details and statements in paragraphs 14–16 that reveal King Arthur's internal conflict.

Draw Conclusions: Does Arthur reject Launcelot's offer because he is convinced by Gawain's argument? Explain why or why not.

---

[1] **laying waste:** destroying.
[2] **Sir Bors:** Sir Bors de Ganis, Launcelot's cousin and the son of King Bors.
[3] **Sir Lyonel** (līʹən-əl): another of Launcelot's cousins.
[4] **sally forth:** rush out suddenly in an attack.
[5] **liege** (lēj): a lord or ruler to whom one owes loyalty and service.
[6] **depredation** (dĕpʹrĭ-dāʹshən): destruction caused by robbery or looting.
[7] **sue:** appeal; beg.

17   Sir Gawain addressed the young noblewoman:

18   "Tell Sir Launcelot that we will not bandy words with him, and it is too late now to sue for peace. Further that I, Sir Gawain, shall not cease to strive against him until one of us is killed."

19   The young noblewoman was escorted back to Sir Launcelot, and when she had delivered Sir Gawain's message they both wept. Then Sir Bors spoke:

20   "My lord, we beseech you, do not look so dismayed! You have many trustworthy knights behind you; lead us onto the field and we will put an end to this quarrel."

21   "My lords, I do not doubt you, but I pray you, be ruled by me: I will not lead you against our liege until we ourselves are endangered; only then can we honorably sally forth and defeat him."

22   Sir Launcelot's nobles submitted; but the next day it was seen that King Arthur had laid siege to the city of Benwick. Then Sir Gawain rode before the city walls and shouted a challenge:

23   "My lord Sir Launcelot: have you no knight who will dare to ride forth and break spears with me? It is I, Sir Gawain."

24   Sir Bors accepted the challenge. He rode out of the castle gate, they encountered, and he was wounded and flung from his horse. His comrades helped him back to the castle, and then Sir Lyonel offered to joust. He too was overthrown and helped back to the castle.

25   Thereafter, every day for six months Sir Gawain rode before the city and overthrew whoever accepted his challenge. Meanwhile, as a result of skirmishes, numbers on both sides were beginning to dwindle. Then one day Sir Gawain challenged Sir Launcelot:

26   "My lord Sir Launcelot: traitor to the king and to me, come forth if you dare and meet your mortal foe, instead of lurking like a coward in your castle!"

27   Sir Launcelot heard the challenge, and one of his kinsmen spoke to him:

28   "My lord, you must accept the challenge, or be shamed forever."

29   "Alas, that I should have to fight Sir Gawain!" said Sir Launcelot. "But now I am obliged to."

30   Sir Launcelot gave orders for his most powerful courser[8] to be harnessed, and when he had armed, rode to the tower and addressed King Arthur:

31   "My lord King Arthur, it is with a heavy heart that I set forth to do battle with one of your own blood; but now it is **incumbent** upon my honor to do so. For six months I have suffered your majesty to lay my lands waste and to besiege me in my own city. My courtesy is repaid with insults, so deadly and shameful that now I must by force of arms seek **redress**."

32   "Have done, Sir Launcelot, and let us to battle!" shouted Sir Gawain.

---

[8] **courser:** a horse trained for battle.

ANALYZE CONFLICT

Annotate: Reread paragraphs 20–21. Mark the reason Launcelot gives for delaying the battle.

Analyze: How do the rules of chivalry complicate Launcelot's situation?

incumbent
(ĭn-kŭm´bənt) *adj.* required as a duty or an obligation.

redress
(rĭ-drĕs´) *n.* repayment for a wrong or an injury.

33   Sir Launcelot rode from the city at the head of his entire army. King Arthur was astonished at his strength and realized that Sir Launcelot had not been boasting when he claimed to have acted with forbearance.[9] "Alas, that I should ever have come to war with him!" he said to himself.

34   It was agreed that the two combatants should fight to the death, with interference from none. Sir Launcelot and Sir Gawain then drew apart and galloped furiously together, and so great was their strength that their horses crashed to the ground and both riders were overthrown.

35   A terrible sword fight commenced, and each felt the might of the other as fresh wounds were inflicted with every blow. For three hours they fought with scarcely a pause, and the blood seeped out from their armor and trickled to the ground. Sir Launcelot found to his dismay that Sir Gawain, instead of weakening, seemed to increase in strength as they proceeded, and he began to fear that he was battling not with a knight but with a fiend incarnate.[10] He decided to fight defensively and to conserve his strength.

AHA MOMENT

Notice & Note: Mark the sentence in paragraphs 36–38 that indicates when Launcelot discovers Gawain's secret.

Predict: What do you think Launcelot will do with this newly discovered knowledge?

36   It was a secret known only to King Arthur and to Sir Gawain himself that his strength increased for three hours in the morning, reaching its zenith[11] at noon, and waning again. This was due to an enchantment that had been cast over him by a hermit[12] when he was still a youth. Often in the past, as now, he had taken advantage of this.

37   Thus when the hour of noon had passed, Sir Launcelot felt Sir Gawain's strength return to normal, and knew that he could defeat him.

---

[9] **forbearance** (fôr-bâr´əns): self-control; patient restraint.
[10] **fiend incarnate:** devil in human form.
[11] **zenith:** highest point; peak.
[12] **hermit:** a person living in solitude for religious reasons.

38   "Sir Gawain, I have endured many hard blows from you these last three hours, but now beware, for I see that you have weakened, and it is I who am the stronger."

39   Thereupon Sir Launcelot redoubled his blows, and with one, catching Sir Gawain sidelong on the helmet, sent him reeling to the ground. Then he courteously stood back.

40   "Sir Launcelot, I still defy you!" said Sir Gawain from the ground. "Why do you not kill me now? for I warn you that if ever I recover I shall challenge you again."

41   "Sir Gawain, by the grace of God I shall endure you again," Sir Launcelot replied, and then turned to the king:

42   "My liege, your expedition can find no honorable conclusion at these walls, so I pray you withdraw and spare your noble knights. Remember me with kindness and be guided, as ever, by the love of God."

43   "Alas!" said the king, "Sir Launcelot scruples[13] to fight against me or those of my blood, and once more I am beholden to him."

44   Sir Launcelot withdrew to the city and Sir Gawain was taken to his pavilion, where his wounds were dressed. King Arthur was doubly grieved, by his quarrel with Sir Launcelot and by the seriousness of Sir Gawain's wounds.

45   For three weeks, while Sir Gawain was recovering, the siege was relaxed and both sides skirmished only halfheartedly. But once recovered, Sir Gawain rode up to the castle walls and challenged Sir Launcelot again:

46   "Sir Launcelot, traitor! Come forth, it is Sir Gawain who challenges you."

47   "Sir Gawain, why these insults? I have the measure of your strength and you can do me but little harm."

48   "Come forth, traitor, and this time I shall make good my revenge!" Sir Gawain shouted.

49   "Sir Gawain, I have once spared your life; should you not beware of meddling with me again?"

50   Sir Launcelot armed and rode out to meet him. They jousted and Sir Gawain broke his spear and was flung from his horse. He leaped up immediately, and putting his shield before him, called on Sir Launcelot to fight on foot.

51   "The issue[14] of a mare has failed me; but I am the issue of a king and a queen and I shall not fail!" he exclaimed.

52   As before, Sir Launcelot felt Sir Gawain's strength increase until noon, during which period he defended himself, and then weaken again.

53   "Sir Gawain, you are a proved knight, and with the increase of your strength until noon you must have overcome many of your opponents, but now your strength has gone, and once more you are at my mercy."

ANALYZE CONFLICT

Annotate: Mark words and phrases in paragraphs 42–44 that indicate Arthur's feelings toward Launcelot.

Evaluate: What is your opinion of Arthur's handling of this conflict?

---

[13] **scruples:** hesitates for reasons of principle.
[14] **issue:** offspring.

54   Sir Launcelot struck out lustily and by chance reopened the wound he had made before. Sir Gawain fell to the ground in a faint, but when he came to he said weakly:

55   "Sir Launcelot, I still defy you. Make an end of me, or I shall fight you again!"

56   "Sir Gawain, while you stand on your two feet I will not gainsay[15] you; but I will never strike a knight who has fallen. God defend me from such dishonor!"

57   Sir Launcelot walked away and Sir Gawain continued to call after him: "Traitor! Until one of us is dead I shall never give in!"

58   For a month Sir Gawain lay recovering from his wounds, and the siege remained; but then, as Sir Gawain was preparing to fight Sir Launcelot once more, King Arthur received news which caused him to strike camp and lead his army on a forced march to the coast, and thence to embark for Britain.

∽ THE DAY OF DESTINY ∽

59   During the absence of King Arthur from Britain, Sir Modred, already vested with sovereign powers,[16] had decided to **usurp** the throne. Accordingly, he had false letters written—announcing the death of King Arthur in battle—and delivered to himself. Then, calling a parliament, he ordered the letters to be read and persuaded the nobility to elect him king. The coronation took place at Canterbury and was celebrated with a fifteen-day feast.

60   Sir Modred then settled in Camelot and made overtures to Queen Gwynevere to marry him. The queen seemingly acquiesced, but as soon as she had won his confidence, begged leave to make a journey to London in order to prepare her trousseau.[17] Sir Modred consented, and the queen rode straight to the Tower which, with the aid of her loyal nobles, she manned and provisioned for her defense.

61   Sir Modred, outraged, at once marched against her, and laid siege to the Tower, but despite his large army, siege engines, and guns, was unable to effect a breach. He then tried to entice the queen from the Tower, first by **guile** and then by threats, but she would listen to neither. Finally the Archbishop of Canterbury came forward to protest:

62   "Sir Modred, do you not fear God's displeasure? First you have falsely made yourself king; now you, who were begotten by King Arthur on his aunt,[18] try to marry your father's wife! If you do not revoke your evil deeds I shall curse you with bell, book, and candle."[19]

usurp
(yo͞o-sûrp´) *v.* to seize unlawfully by force.

ANALYZE CONFLICT

Annotate: Mark the details of Modred's actions in paragraphs 59–61.

Compare: How does Modred differ from Launcelot as an opponent of King Arthur?

guile
(gīl) *n.* clever trickery; deceit.

---

[15] **gainsay:** deny.

[16] **vested with sovereign powers:** given the authority of a king.

[17] **trousseau** (tro͞o´sō): clothes and linens that a bride brings to her marriage.

[18] **begotten . . . aunt:** Modred is the son of Arthur and Queen Margawse, the sister of Arthur's mother, Queen Igraine.

[19] **I shall curse you with bell, book, and candle:** The archbishop is threatening to excommunicate Modred—that is, to deny him participation in the rites of the church. In the medieval ritual of excommunication, a bell was rung, a book was shut, and a candle was extinguished.

63   "Fie on you! Do your worst!" Sir Modred replied.

64   "Sir Modred, I warn you take heed! or the wrath of the Lord will descend upon you."

65   "Away, false priest, or I shall behead you!"

66   The Archbishop withdrew, and after excommunicating Sir Modred, abandoned his office and fled to Glastonbury. There he took up his abode as a simple hermit, and by fasting and prayer sought divine intercession[20] in the troubled affairs of his country.

67   Sir Modred tried to assassinate the Archbishop, but was too late. He continued to assail the queen with entreaties and threats, both of which failed, and then the news reached him that King Arthur was returning with his army from France in order to seek revenge.

68   Sir Modred now appealed to the barony to support him, and it has to be told that they came forward in large numbers to do so. Why? it will be asked. Was not King Arthur, the noblest sovereign Christendom had seen, now leading his armies in a righteous cause? The answer lies in the people of Britain, who, then as now, were fickle. Those who so readily transferred their allegiance to Sir Modred did so with the excuse that whereas King Arthur's reign had led them into war and strife, Sir Modred promised them peace and festivity.

69   Hence it was with an army of a hundred thousand that Sir Modred marched to Dover to battle against his own father, and to withhold from him his rightful crown.

70   As King Arthur with his fleet drew into the harbor, Sir Modred and his army launched forth in every available craft, and a bloody battle ensued in the ships and on the beach. If King Arthur's army were the smaller, their courage was the higher, confident as they were of the righteousness of their cause. Without stint[21] they battled through the burning ships, the screaming wounded, and the corpses floating on the bloodstained waters. Once ashore they put Sir Modred's entire army to flight.

71   The battle over, King Arthur began a search for his casualties, and on peering into one of the ships found Sir Gawain, mortally wounded. Sir Gawain fainted when King Arthur lifted him in his arms; and when he came to, the king spoke:

72   "Alas! dear nephew, that you lie here thus, mortally wounded! What joy is now left to me on this earth? You must know it was you and Sir Launcelot I loved above all others, and it seems that I have lost you both."

73   "My good uncle, it was my pride and my stubbornness that brought all this about, for had I not urged you to war with Sir Launcelot your subjects would not now be in revolt. Alas, that Sir Launcelot is not here, for he would soon drive them out! And it is at Sir Launcelot's hands that I suffer my own death: the wound which he

MAKE PREDICTIONS
Annotate: Mark the explanation in paragraph 68 for the support Modred receives.

Predict: Do you think Modred will keep this support for long? Why or why not?

---

[20] **divine intercession:** assistance from God.
[21] **stint:** holding back.

dealt me has reopened. I would not wish it otherwise, because is he not the greatest and gentlest of knights?

74   "I know that by noon I shall be dead, and I repent bitterly that I may not be reconciled to Sir Launcelot; therefore I pray you, good uncle, give me pen, paper, and ink so that I may write to him."

75   A priest was summoned and Sir Gawain confessed; then a clerk brought ink, pen, and paper, and Sir Gawain wrote to Sir Launcelot as follows:

76   "Sir Launcelot, flower of the knighthood: I, Sir Gawain, son of King Lot of Orkney and of King Arthur's sister, send you my greetings!

77   "I am about to die; the cause of my death is the wound I received from you outside the city of Benwick; and I would make it known that my death was of my own seeking, that I was moved by the spirit of revenge and spite to provoke you to battle.

78   "Therefore, Sir Launcelot, I beseech you to visit my tomb and offer what prayers you will on my behalf; and for myself, I am content to die at the hands of the noblest knight living.

79   "One more request: that you hasten with your armies across the sea and give succor[22] to our noble king. Sir Modred, his bastard son, has usurped the throne and now holds against him with an army of a hundred thousand. He would have won the queen, too, but she fled to the Tower of London and there charged her loyal supporters with her defense.

80   "Today is the tenth of May, and at noon I shall give up the ghost; this letter is written partly with my blood. This morning we fought our way ashore, against the armies of Sir Modred, and that is how my wound came to be reopened. We won the day, but my lord King Arthur needs you, and I too, that on my tomb you may bestow your blessing."

81   Sir Gawain fainted when he had finished, and the king wept. When he came to he was given extreme unction,[23] and died, as he had anticipated, at the hour of noon. The king buried him in the chapel at Dover Castle, and there many came to see him, and all noticed the wound on his head which he had received from Sir Launcelot.

82   Then the news reached Arthur that Sir Modred offered him battle on the field at Baron Down. Arthur hastened there with his army, they fought, and Sir Modred fled once more, this time to Canterbury.

83   When King Arthur had begun the search for his wounded and dead, many volunteers from all parts of the country came to fight under his flag, convinced now of the rightness of his cause. Arthur marched westward, and Sir Modred once more offered him battle. It was assigned for the Monday following Trinity Sunday, on Salisbury Down.

84   Sir Modred levied fresh troops from East Anglia and the places about London, and fresh volunteers came forward to help Arthur.

---

[22] **succor** (sŭk´ər): *n.* aid in a time of need; relief.

[23] **extreme unction:** a ritual in which a priest anoints and prays for a dying person.

Then, on the night of Trinity Sunday, Arthur was vouchsafed[24] a strange dream:

85   He was appareled in gold cloth and seated in a chair which stood on a pivoted scaffold. Below him, many fathoms deep, was a dark well, and in the water swam serpents, dragons, and wild beasts. Suddenly the scaffold tilted and Arthur was flung into the water, where all the creatures struggled toward him and began tearing him limb from limb.

86   Arthur cried out in his sleep and his squires hastened to waken him. Later, as he lay between waking and sleeping, he thought he saw Sir Gawain, and with him a host of beautiful noblewomen. Arthur spoke:

87   "My sister's son! I thought you had died; but now I see you live, and I thank the lord Jesu! I pray you, tell me, who are these ladies?"

88   "My lord, these are the ladies I championed[25] in righteous quarrels when I was on earth. Our lord God has vouchsafed that we visit you and plead with you not to give battle to Sir Modred tomorrow, for if you do, not only will you yourself be killed, but all your noble followers too. We beg you to be warned, and to make a treaty with Sir Modred, calling a truce for a month, and granting him whatever terms he may demand. In a month Sir Launcelot will be here, and he will defeat Sir Modred."

89   Thereupon Sir Gawain and the ladies vanished, and King Arthur once more summoned his squires and his counselors and told them his vision. Sir Lucas and Sir Bedivere were commissioned to make a treaty with Sir Modred. They were to be accompanied by two bishops and to grant, within reason, whatever terms he demanded.

90   The ambassadors found Sir Modred in command of an army of a hundred thousand and unwilling to listen to overtures of peace.

MAKE PREDICTIONS

Annotate: Reread paragraphs 86–88. Mark Gawain's warning to Arthur.

Predict: Romance plots often involve supernatural events. How do you think Arthur will respond to this vision? What may be the outcome of his response?

---

[24]**vouchsafed:** granted.
[25]**championed:** defended or fought for.

However, the ambassadors eventually prevailed on him, and in return for the truce granted him suzerainty[26] of Cornwall and Kent, and succession to the British throne when King Arthur died. The treaty was to be signed by King Arthur and Sir Modred the next day. They were to meet between the two armies, and each was to be accompanied by no more than fourteen knights.

91   Both King Arthur and Sir Modred suspected the other of treachery, and gave orders for their armies to attack at the sight of a naked sword. When they met at the appointed place the treaty was signed and both drank a glass of wine.

92   Then, by chance, one of the soldiers was bitten in the foot by an adder[27] which had lain concealed in the brush. The soldier unthinkingly drew his sword to kill it, and at once, as the sword flashed in the light, the alarums[28] were given, trumpets sounded, and both armies galloped into the attack.

93   "Alas for this fateful day!" exclaimed King Arthur, as both he and Sir Modred hastily mounted and galloped back to their armies. There followed one of those rare and heartless battles in which both armies fought until they were destroyed. King Arthur, with his customary valor, led squadron after squadron of cavalry into the attack, and Sir Modred encountered him unflinchingly. As the number of dead and wounded mounted on both sides, the active combatants continued dauntless until nightfall, when four men alone survived.

94   King Arthur wept with dismay to see his beloved followers fallen; then, struggling toward him, unhorsed and badly wounded, he saw Sir Lucas the Butler and his brother, Sir Bedivere.[29]

95   "Alas!" said the king, "that the day should come when I see all my noble knights destroyed! I would prefer that I myself had fallen. But what has become of the traitor Sir Modred, whose evil ambition was responsible for this carnage?"

96   Looking about him King Arthur then noticed Sir Modred leaning with his sword on a heap of the dead.

97   "Sir Lucas, I pray you give me my spear, for I have seen Sir Modred."

98   "Sire, I entreat you, remember your vision—how Sir Gawain appeared with a heaven-sent message to dissuade you from fighting Sir Modred. Allow this fateful day to pass; it is ours, for we three hold the field, while the enemy is broken."

99   "My lords, I care nothing for my life now! And while Sir Modred is at large I must kill him: there may not be another chance."

100   "God speed you, then!" said Sir Bedivere.

101   When Sir Modred saw King Arthur advance with his spear, he rushed to meet him with drawn sword. Arthur caught Sir Modred below the shield and drove his spear through his body; Sir Modred, knowing that the wound was mortal, thrust himself up to the handle

ANALYZE CONFLICT

Annotate: Reread paragraphs 96–99. Mark Arthur's explanation for why he must confront Modred now.

Interpret: What theme about chivalry is suggested by Arthur's decision to ignore Gawain's warning?

---

[26] **suzerainty** (sŏŏ′zər-ən-tē): the position of feudal lord.

[27] **adder:** a poisonous snake.

[28] **alarums:** calls to arms.

[29] **Sir Lucas . . . Bedivere:** brothers who are members of King Arthur's court.

of the spear, and then, brandishing his sword in both hands, struck Arthur on the side of the helmet, cutting through it and into the skull beneath; then he crashed to the ground, gruesome and dead.

102   King Arthur fainted many times as Sir Lucas and Sir Bedivere struggled with him to a small chapel nearby, where they managed to ease his wounds a little. When Arthur came to, he thought he heard cries coming from the battlefield.

103   "Sir Lucas, I pray you, find out who cries on the battlefield," he said.

104   Wounded as he was, Sir Lucas hobbled painfully to the field, and there in the moonlight saw the camp followers stealing gold and jewels from the dead, and murdering the wounded. He returned to the king and reported to him what he had seen, and then added:

105   "My lord, it surely would be better to move you to the nearest town?"

106   "My wounds forbid it. But alas for the good Sir Launcelot! How sadly I have missed him today! And now I must die—as Sir Gawain warned me I would—repenting our quarrel with my last breath."

107   Sir Lucas and Sir Bedivere made one further attempt to lift the king. He fainted as they did so. Then Sir Lucas fainted as part of his intestines broke through a wound in the stomach. When the king came to, he saw Sir Lucas lying dead with foam at his mouth.

108   "Sweet Jesu, give him succor!" he said. "This noble knight has died trying to save my life—alas that this was so!"

109   Sir Bedivere wept for his brother.

110   "Sir Bedivere, weep no more," said King Arthur, "for you can save neither your brother nor me; and I would ask you to take my sword Excalibur[30] to the shore of the lake and throw it in the water. Then return to me and tell me what you have seen."

111   "My lord, as you command, it shall be done."

112   Sir Bedivere took the sword, but when he came to the water's edge, it appeared so beautiful that he could not bring himself to throw it in, so instead he hid it by a tree, and then returned to the king.

113   "Sir Bedivere, what did you see?"

114   "My lord, I saw nothing but the wind upon the waves."

115   "Then you did not obey me; I pray you, go swiftly again, and this time fulfill my command."

116   Sir Bedivere went and returned again, but this time too he had failed to fulfill the king's command.

117   "Sir Bedivere, what did you see?"

118   "My lord, nothing but the lapping of the waves."

119   "Sir Bedivere, twice you have betrayed me! And for the sake only of my sword: it is unworthy of you! Now I pray you, do as I command, for I have not long to live."

[30]**Excalibur** (ĕk-skăl´ə-bər): Arthur's remarkable sword, which originally came from the Lady of the Lake.

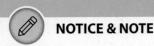

ANALYZE CONFLICT

Annotate: In paragraph 120, mark the description of what happens to Excalibur.

Infer: How does this description help us understand why Arthur was so upset at Bedivere?

120   This time Sir Bedivere wrapped the girdle around the sheath and hurled it as far as he could into the water. A hand appeared from below the surface, took the sword, waved it thrice, and disappeared again. Sir Bedivere returned to the king and told him what he had seen.

121   "Sir Bedivere, I pray you now help me hence, or I fear it will be too late."

122   Sir Bedivere carried the king to the water's edge, and there found a barge in which sat many beautiful ladies with their queen. All were wearing black hoods, and when they saw the king, they raised their voices in a piteous lament.

123   "I pray you, set me in the barge," said the king.

124   Sir Bedivere did so, and one of the ladies laid the king's head in her lap; then the queen spoke to him:

125   "My dear brother, you have stayed too long: I fear that the wound on your head is already cold."

126   Thereupon they rowed away from the land and Sir Bedivere wept to see them go.

127   "My lord King Arthur, you have deserted me! I am alone now, and among enemies."

128   "Sir Bedivere, take what comfort you may, for my time is passed, and now I must be taken to Avalon[31] for my wound to be healed. If you hear of me no more, I beg you pray for my soul."

129   The barge slowly crossed the water and out of sight while the ladies wept. Sir Bedivere walked alone into the forest and there remained for the night.

130   In the morning he saw beyond the trees of a copse[32] a small hermitage. He entered and found a hermit kneeling down by a fresh tomb. The hermit was weeping as he prayed, and then Sir Bedivere recognized him as the Archbishop of Canterbury, who had been banished by Sir Modred.

131   "Father, I pray you, tell me, whose tomb is this?"

132   "My son, I do not know. At midnight the body was brought here by a company of ladies. We buried it, they lit a hundred candles for the service, and rewarded me with a thousand bezants."[33]

133   "Father, King Arthur lies buried in this tomb."

134   Sir Bedivere fainted when he had spoken, and when he came to he begged the Archbishop to allow him to remain at the hermitage and end his days in fasting and prayer.

135   "Father, I wish only to be near to my true liege."

136   "My son, you are welcome; and do I not recognize you as Sir Bedivere the Bold, brother to Sir Lucas the Butler?"

137   Thus the Archbishop and Sir Bedivere remained at the hermitage, wearing the habits of hermits and devoting themselves to the tomb with fasting and prayers of contrition.[34]

---

[31] **Avalon:** an island paradise of Celtic legend, where heroes are taken after death.
[32] **copse** (kŏps): a grove of small trees.
[33] **bezants** (bĕz´ənts): gold coins.
[34] **contrition** (kən-trĭsh´ən): sincere regret for wrongdoing.

138   Such was the death of King Arthur as written down by Sir Bedivere. By some it is told that there were three queens on the barge: Queen Morgan le Fay, the Queen of North Galys, and the Queen of the Waste Lands; and others include the name of Nyneve, the Lady of the Lake who had served King Arthur well in the past, and had married the good knight Sir Pelleas.

139   In many parts of Britain it is believed that King Arthur did not die and that he will return to us and win fresh glory and the Holy Cross of our Lord Jesu Christ; but for myself I do not believe this, and would leave him buried peacefully in his tomb at Glastonbury, where the Archbishop of Canterbury and Sir Bedivere humbled themselves, and with prayers and fasting honored his memory. And inscribed on his tomb, men say, is this legend:

HIC IACET ARTHURUS,
REX QUONDAM REXQUE FUTURUS.[35]

---
[35] *Hic iacet Arthurus, rex quondam rexque futurus* (hĭk yä´kĕt är-tōō´rŏŏs rāks kwôn´däm rāk´skwĕ fŏŏ-tōō´rŏŏs)
Latin: Here lies Arthur, the once and future king.

Annotate: In paragraph 139, mark the direct statement the author makes about Arthur.

Identify: Which word in this statement most directly conveys the narrator's tone in this paragraph?

CHECK YOUR UNDERSTANDING

Answer these questions before moving on to the **Analyze the Text** section.

1 After besieging Sir Launcelot at Benwick, what news compels Arthur to return to Britain?

   A Gwynevere has married Modred.

   B Gwynevere has died.

   C Modred has usurped the throne.

   D Modred has beheaded the Archbishop.

2 How is the conflict between Gawain and Launcelot resolved?

   F Launcelot strikes down Gawain and Gawain surrenders.

   G As Gawain is dying from a wound, he writes a letter to Launcelot asking for his forgiveness.

   H They resolve their problems before Gawain leaves for Britain.

   J After the battle at Dover, Launcelot finds Gawain, and they are able to reconcile their differences.

3 What happens to Arthur at the end of the story?

   A He is killed in a fight with Bedivere after an argument over his sword.

   B He drowns in the lake on his way to Avalon.

   C He is later found living at the hermitage in disguise.

   D Modred mortally wounds him in battle.

© Houghton Mifflin Harcourt Publishing Company

Le Morte d'Arthur   59

ANALYZE THE TEXT

Support your responses with evidence from the text. ▤ NOTEBOOK

1. **Analyze** Reread the headnote that explains what has occurred earlier in the romance. How does Launcelot's past behavior lead to the conflict and the moral dilemma he faces in the siege of Benwick?

2. **Evaluate** Compare the actions and motivation of Gawain and Launcelot. Which knight is a greater model of chivalry? Explain.

3. **Predict** A writer's use of hints or clues to indicate events that will occur later in a story is called **foreshadowing.** Does Malory provide enough clues for you to have predicted that Modred will kill Arthur, or does Arthur's death surprise you? Explain.

4. **Draw Conclusions** Reread paragraph 139. Why might Malory have chosen to mention these rumors about Arthur and to share the legend inscribed on Arthur's tomb?

5. **Notice & Note** Reread paragraphs 71–74. What realization does Gawain have about his role in the conflict with Launcelot? Do you agree with the blame he places on himself? Why or why not?

RESEARCH

RESEARCH TIP
When looking for history-related information, focus on more reliable sites, such as history.com, rather than less credible sources. Also, look for articles written by professors and other scholars found in magazines and journals such as *Archaeology Magazine*, which will offer up-to-date findings.

Was Arthur a real historical figure? Historians disagree. Conduct an Internet search to find evidence for both sides of the argument. Use the chart below to record your findings.

EVIDENCE FOR A REAL ARTHUR	EVIDENCE AGAINST A REAL ARTHUR

Connect In spite of the uncertainty of King Arthur's actual existence, his legend has endured for generations. In small groups, discuss the following: Why do you think Arthur and his knights make such compelling heroes? Do you think their struggles with moral dilemmas make them more appealing? If so, why? Discuss the importance of heroes in literature and in real life.

CREATE AND PRESENT

Create a Hero Write a character sketch of a modern-day hero—real or imaginary. Before you begin, think about the traits of heroes in *Le Morte d'Arthur*. However, keep in mind your hero doesn't need to show physical courage; consider other equally important kinds of heroism.

❑ Describe your hero in terms of both personal traits and behavior. How does he or she exhibit heroic qualities through words and actions?

❑ How do others view him or her?

❑ Relate an incident in which your hero faces a conflict, internal or external, which creates a moral dilemma. How is the conflict resolved?

Direct a Scene Work in small groups to prepare a dramatic scene of a heroic incident. With your group, work out subject matter, mood, and staging of your scene, with one of you serving as the director.

❑ As a group, select one incident to dramatize and choose a director.

❑ Decide how you will present the scene. As a traditional skit? An impromptu presentation? A dramatic reading? Experiment and clarify questions as you work out the most effective way to present it.

❑ Practice and then present to the whole class. Request feedback for how well your group conveyed ideas about the qualities of heroism.

 Go to **Writing Narratives** in the **Writing Studio** to find out more.

 Go to **Giving a Presentation: Delivering Your Presentation** in the **Speaking and Listening Studio** for help.

RESPOND TO THE ESSENTIAL QUESTION

 ? What makes someone a hero?

Gather Information Review your annotations and notes on *Le Morte d'Arthur*. Then, add relevant information to your Response Log. As you determine which information to include, think about:

• the definition of a hero and some qualities a hero might possess
• how a hero might face conflicts and moral dilemmas
• the importance of heroes in real life

ACADEMIC VOCABULARY
As you write and discuss what you learned from *Le Morte d'Arthur*, be sure to use the Academic Vocabulary words. Check off each of the words that you use.

❑ **collapse**
❑ **displace**
❑ **military**
❑ **violate**
❑ **visual**

CRITICAL VOCABULARY

WORD BANK
dominion
incumbent
redress
usurp
guile

Practice and Apply Choose the vocabulary word that best completes each sentence. Use the context clues in the sentence to help you decide.

1. _____ might be observed in the actions of an unscrupulous salesman.

2. A kingdom or nation has _____ over its lands.

3. A wronged person might seek _____.

4. It is _____ upon children to do their chores.

5. The cat tried to _____ control of the dog's bed.

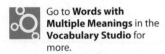 Go to **Words with Multiple Meanings** in the **Vocabulary Studio** for more.

VOCABULARY STRATEGY:
Multiple Meaning Words

Incumbent has more than one possible meaning. To determine which meaning applies in a particular instance, readers must consider the **context,** or clues in the surrounding words, sentences, or paragraphs. For example, in the sentence *It is incumbent on my honor to do so,* the context suggests that *incumbent* means "required as a duty or obligation."

Practice and Apply In the passage below, use context to determine the likely meaning of each boldfaced word. Then explain which context clues in the paragraph helped you determine the word's correct meaning.

> The legend of Arthur has captured the imagination of writers since at least 1136, with the appearance of Geoffrey of Monmouth's *History of the Kings of Britain*. From this text, later writers would **adopt** some of the essential **elements** of Arthurian lore: Merlin, Excalibur, and Arthur's final **repose** at Avalon. A few decades later, the French poet Chrétien de Troyes introduced the character of Launcelot to the growing **body** of Arthurian literature. *Le Morte d'Arthur* (1469), one of the earliest books printed in English, would eventually become the **ultimate** source for writers of Arthurian literature.

LANGUAGE CONVENTIONS:
Tone

The **tone** of a text is the writer's attitude toward the subject. One way to identify the tone in a narrative work is to look for the **connotations** or emotions that are evoked by the words. Think carefully about the writer's **diction,** or word choices, and what deliberate responses such choices are meant to evoke. Such words might be positive, negative, or neutral.

The tone of the narrator in *Le Morte D'Arthur* is moralizing, expressing judgment about the events and the actions of the characters. Read these examples of the narration to detect the tone:

> **A terrible sword fight commenced, and each felt the might of the other as fresh wounds were inflicted with every blow.**

> **Hence it was with an army of a hundred thousand that Sir Modred marched to Dover to battle against his own father, and to withhold from him his rightful crown.**

In the first sentence, the word *terrible* expresses the narrator's negative feelings about the fight that occurred. In the second example, the phrase *withhold from him his rightful crown* shows that the narrator believes Sir Modred's actions are wrong.

Look at the two examples above and think about how the words might change if the narrator had a different attitude toward the subjects and the action. For instance, consider how the second sentence might change if the narrator approved of Sir Modred's action in making himself king and battling his father.

Practice and Apply Write a short narrative using two different tones.

First, write a short narrative of a recent personal experience that you have strong feelings about. For example, you might write about a mistake that you regret or something new that you did that turned out to be really fun. Be sure to use descriptive and precise language.

Now, imagine that you have a completely different attitude about the event and rewrite your narrative to reflect those different feelings. For example, you might imagine that the really fun thing you did was not fun at all and you regret deciding to do it.

Finally, exchange your work with a partner. Describe your partner's tone in each narrative. Talk about how the words your partner used changed when he or she wrote with a different tone.

CHIVALRY

Short Story by **Neil Gaiman**

? **ESSENTIAL QUESTION:**

What is true chivalry?

QUICK START

Imagine that a person from the Middle Ages traveled through time to meet you. What would you ask this person? What do you think this person would want to ask you? Make a list of questions for yourself and the time traveler.

ANALYZE CHARACTERIZATION

A writer's method of revealing characters' personalities is called **characterization**. Writers use four basic methods to develop their characters:

- describing a character's physical appearance

- presenting a character's actions, thoughts, and speech

- revealing other characters' reactions to a character

- directly commenting on a character

Characterization is related to other elements of fiction. For example, a writer may place a character in a setting where he or she stands out in some way, which could affect how others view the character. As you read "Chivalry," notice the methods Neil Gaiman uses to develop the two main characters. In addition, pay attention to how the story's setting influences our perception of the characters.

ANALYZE FANTASY

Fantasy is a type of fiction that intentionally portrays unrealistic events, settings, or characters. For example, a story may be set in a nonexistent world, or the characters might have supernatural powers. Although fantasies are often written mainly for entertainment, they can express serious themes about life or society. Neil Gaiman is known for his highly imaginative fantasy writing. In "Chivalry" he mixes elements of the Arthurian legends into the story of an elderly woman living in a dull English town. Use a chart like the one shown to note down realistic and fantasy details in the story.

REALISTIC DETAILS	FANTASY DETAILS
Mrs. Whitaker stops in at a secondhand shop every week on her way home from the post office.	She finds the Holy Grail for sale in the shop.

As you read "Chivalry," keep an eye out for other elements of fantasy and think about how these elements help to move the plot forward.

GENRE ELEMENTS: SHORT STORY

- includes the basic elements of fiction—setting, characters, plot, conflict, and theme

- centers on a particular moment or event or follows the life of one character

- can be read in one sitting

- may include elements of fantasy, such as supernatural events

CRITICAL VOCABULARY

pension	flotsam	appraise	forge	ignoble	bereft

To see how many Critical Vocabulary words you already know, use them to complete the sentences.

1. After the storm, heaps of _____ washed up on the shore.

2. The metal for the sword was fired in a crude _____.

3. The _____ from her job at the shipbuilding company helped pay her rent and other living expenses.

4. When his grandmother died, he felt _____ for the first time.

5. Some of the crudest, most _____ people have succeeded in politics.

6. I will have an expert _____ the house before I bid on it.

LANGUAGE CONVENTIONS

Appositives and Appositive Phrases In this lesson, you will learn to identify and use appositives and appositive phrases. An appositive is a noun or pronoun that identifies, or renames, another noun or pronoun right beside it. An appositive phrase includes an appositive and its modifiers. Here is an example of an appositive phrase that renames *Arthur:*

> **It was signed by Arthur, King of all Britons.**

As you read "Chivalry," look out for appositives and appositive phrases.

ANNOTATION MODEL

NOTICE & NOTE

As you read, take note of the contrast between the realistic and the fantasy to see how the writer creates humor and surprise by juxtaposing the two. This model shows one reader's notes analyzing fantasy elements in "Chivalry."

It was a sword, its blade almost four feet long. There were words and symbols traced elegantly along the length of the blade. The hilt was worked in silver and gold, and a large jewel was set in the pommel.

"It's very nice," said Mrs. Whitaker, doubtfully.

"This," said Galaad, "is the sword Balmung, forged by Wayland Smith in the dawntimes. Its twin is Flamberge. Who wears it is unconquerable in war, and invincible in battle. Who wears it is incapable of a cowardly act or an ignoble one."

Mrs. Whitaker reacts to the remarkable sword in such an understated way.

It's funny to think of her using the superhuman powers that the sword would provide.

BACKGROUND

Neil Gaiman (b. 1960) is a popular and prolific author who has written novels, comic books, graphic novels, and film and television scripts. He was born and raised in England. As a child, his favorite authors included C. S. Lewis, J. R. R. Tolkien, Ursula K. Le Guin, and other fantasy writers. Gaiman's own writing often features fantasy elements, such as the character Galaad in "Chivalry," who is based on Sir Galahad of the Arthurian legends. The purest of King Arthur's knights, Galahad led the quest to find the Holy Grail, a vessel associated with Christ that was said to have miraculous powers.

CHIVALRY

Short Story by Neil Gaiman

SETTING A PURPOSE

As you read, pay attention to how Mrs. Whitaker reacts to Galaad and the fantastic objects she comes across in the story.

1   Mrs. Whitaker found the Holy Grail; it was under a fur coat.

2   Every Thursday afternoon Mrs. Whitaker walked down to the post office to collect her **pension**, even though her legs were no longer what they were, and on the way back home she would stop in at the Oxfam Shop and buy herself a little something.

3   The Oxfam Shop sold old clothes, knickknacks, oddments, bits and bobs, and large quantities of old paperbacks, all of them donations: secondhand **flotsam**, often the house clearances of the dead. All the profits went to charity.

4   The shop was staffed by volunteers. The volunteer on duty this afternoon was Marie, seventeen, slightly overweight, and dressed in a baggy mauve jumper that looked like she had bought it from the shop.

5   Marie sat by the till with a copy of *Modern Woman* magazine, filling out a "Reveal Your Hidden Personality" questionnaire. Every now and then, she'd flip to the back of the magazine and check the relative points assigned to an A), B), or C) answer before making up her mind how she'd respond to the question.

Notice & Note

Use the side margins to notice and note signposts in the text.

pension
(pĕn´shən) *n.* a sum of money paid regularly as a retirement benefit.

ANALYZE CHARACTERIZATION

Annotate: Mark the details used to characterize Mrs. Whitaker in paragraph 2.

Infer: What can you tell about her from these details?

flotsam
(flŏt´səm) *n.* discarded or unimportant things.

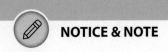

Mrs. Whitaker puttered around the shop.

They still hadn't sold the stuffed cobra, she noted. It had been there for six months now, gathering dust, glass eyes gazing balefully at the clothes racks and the cabinet filled with chipped porcelain and chewed toys.

Mrs. Whitaker patted its head as she went past.

She picked out a couple of Mills & Boon novels from a bookshelf—*Her Thundering Soul* and *Her Turbulent Heart*, a shilling each—and gave careful consideration to the empty bottle of Mateus Rosé with a decorative lampshade on it before deciding she really didn't have anywhere to put it.

ANALYZE FANTASY

Annotate: Mark the element of fantasy in paragraph 10.

Interpret: Why is this detail humorous in the context of the paragraph?

appraise
(ə-prāz´) *tr.v.* to estimate the price or value of.

She moved a rather threadbare fur coat, which smelled badly of mothballs. Underneath it was a walking stick and a water stained copy of *Romance and Legend of Chivalry* by A. R. Hope Moncrieff, priced at five pence. Next to the book, on its side, was the Holy Grail. It had a little round paper sticker on the base, and written on it, in felt pen, was the price: 30p.

Mrs. Whitaker picked up the dusty silver goblet and **appraised** it through her thick spectacles.

"This is nice," she called to Marie.

Marie shrugged.

"It'd look nice on the mantelpiece."

Marie shrugged again.

Mrs. Whitaker gave fifty pence to Marie, who gave her ten pence change and a brown paper bag to put the books and the Holy Grail in. Then she went next door to the butcher's and bought herself a nice piece of liver. Then she went home.

The inside of the goblet was thickly coated with a brownish-red dust. Mrs. Whitaker washed it out with great care, then left it to soak for an hour in warm water with a dash of vinegar added.

Then she polished it with metal polish until it gleamed, and she put it on the mantelpiece in her parlor, where it sat between a small soulful china basset hound and a photograph of her late husband, Henry, on the beach at Frinton in 1953.

She had been right: It did look nice.

For dinner that evening she had the liver fried in breadcrumbs with onions. It was very nice.

The next morning was Friday; on alternate Fridays Mrs. Whitaker and Mrs. Greenberg would visit each other. Today it was Mrs. Greenberg's turn to visit Mrs. Whitaker. They sat in the parlor and ate macaroons and drank tea. Mrs. Whitaker took one sugar in her tea, but Mrs. Greenberg took sweetener, which she always carried in her handbag in a small plastic container.

"That's nice," said Mrs. Greenberg, pointing to the Grail. "What is it?"

"It's the Holy Grail," said Mrs. Whitaker. "It's the cup that Jesus drunk out of at the Last Supper. Later, at the Crucifixion, it caught His precious blood when the centurion's spear pierced His side."

© Houghton Mifflin Harcourt Publishing Company

24   Mrs. Greenberg sniffed. She was small and Jewish and didn't hold with unsanitary things. "I wouldn't know about that," she said, "but it's very nice. Our Myron got one just like that when he won the swimming tournament, only it's got his name on the side."

25   "Is he still with that nice girl? The hairdresser?"

26   "Bernice? Oh yes. They're thinking of getting engaged," said Mrs. Greenberg.

27   "That's nice," said Mrs. Whitaker. She took another macaroon.

28   Mrs. Greenberg baked her own macaroons and brought them over every alternate Friday: small sweet light brown biscuits with almonds on top.

29   They talked about Myron and Bernice, and Mrs. Whitaker's nephew Ronald (she had had no children), and about their friend Mrs. Perkins who was in hospital with her hip, poor dear.

30   At midday Mrs. Greenberg went home, and Mrs. Whitaker made herself cheese on toast for lunch, and after lunch Mrs. Whitaker took her pills; the white and the red and two little orange ones.

31   The doorbell rang.

32   Mrs. Whitaker answered the door. It was a young man with shoulder-length hair so fair it was almost white, wearing gleaming silver armor, with a white surcoat.

33   "Hello," he said.

34   "Hello," said Mrs. Whitaker.

35   "I'm on a quest," he said.

36   "That's nice," said Mrs. Whitaker, noncommittally.

37   "Can I come in?" he asked.

38   Mrs. Whitaker shook her head. "I'm sorry, I don't think so," she said.

39   "I'm on a quest for the Holy Grail," the young man said. "Is it here?"

40   "Have you got any identification?" Mrs. Whitaker asked. She knew that it was unwise to let unidentified strangers into your home when you were elderly and living on your own. Handbags get emptied, and worse than that.

41   The young man went back down the garden path. His horse, a huge gray charger, big as a shire-horse, its head high and its eyes intelligent, was tethered to Mrs. Whitaker's garden gate. The knight fumbled in the saddlebag and returned with a scroll.

42   It was signed by Arthur, King of All Britons, and charged all persons of whatever rank or station to know that here was Galaad, Knight of the Table Round, and that he was on a Right High and Noble Quest. There was a drawing of the young man below that. It wasn't a bad likeness.

43   Mrs. Whitaker nodded. She had been expecting a little card with a photograph on it, but this was far more impressive.

44   "I suppose you had better come in," she said.

45   They went into her kitchen. She made Galaad a cup of tea, then she took him into the parlor.

© Houghton Mifflin Harcourt Publishing Company

LANGUAGE CONVENTIONS

Annotate: Mark all the appositives in paragraph 29.

Analyze: How do they clarify the meaning of the nouns that precede them?

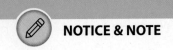

ANALYZE
CHARACTERIZATION

Annotate: Reread paragraphs 47–56. Mark details in Galaad's dialogue that help develop his character.

Analyze: How does Galaad's speech reflect the time period of the Arthurian legends?

46   Galaad saw the Grail on her mantelpiece, and dropped to one knee. He put down the teacup carefully on the russet carpet. A shaft of light came through the net curtains and painted his awed face with golden sunlight and turned his hair into a silver halo.

47   "It is truly the Sangrail,"[1] he said, very quietly. He blinked his pale blue eyes three times, very fast, as if he were blinking back tears.

48   He lowered his head as if in silent prayer.

49   Galaad stood up again and turned to Mrs. Whitaker. "Gracious lady, keeper of the Holy of Holies, let me now depart this place with the Blessed Chalice, that my journeyings may be ended and my geas[2] fulfilled."

50   "Sorry?" said Mrs. Whitaker.

51   Galaad walked over to her and took her old hands in his. "My quest is over," he told her. "The Sangrail is finally within my reach."

52   Mrs. Whitaker pursed her lips. "Can you pick your teacup and saucer up, please?" she said.

53   Galaad picked up his teacup apologetically.

54   "No. I don't think so," said Mrs. Whitaker. "I rather like it there. It's just right, between the dog and the photograph of my Henry."

55   "Is it gold you need? Is that it? Lady, I can bring you gold . . ."

56   "No," said Mrs. Whitaker. "I don't want any gold thank *you*. I'm simply not interested."

57   She ushered Galaad to the front door. "Nice to meet you," she said.

58   His horse was leaning its head over her garden fence, nibbling her gladioli. Several of the neighborhood children were standing on the pavement, watching it.

59   Galaad took some sugar lumps from the saddlebag and showed the braver of the children how to feed the horse, their hands held flat. The children giggled. One of the older girls stroked the horse's nose.

60   Galaad swung himself up onto the horse in one fluid movement. Then the horse and the knight trotted off down Hawthorne Crescent.

61   Mrs. Whitaker watched them until they were out of sight, then sighed and went back inside.

62   The weekend was quiet.

63   On Saturday Mrs. Whitaker took the bus into Maresfield to visit her nephew Ronald, his wife Euphonia, and their daughters, Clarissa and Dillian. She took them a currant cake she had baked herself.

64   On Sunday morning Mrs. Whitaker went to church. Her local church was St. James the Less, which was a little more "Don't think of this as a church, think of it as a place where like-minded friends hang out and are joyful" than Mrs. Whitaker felt entirely comfortable with, but she liked the vicar, the Reverend Bartholomew, when he wasn't actually playing the guitar.

---

[1] **Sangrail:** another name for the Holy Grail.
[2] **geas:** an obligation magically imposed on a person.

65   After the service, she thought about mentioning to him that she had the Holy Grail in her front parlor, but decided against it.

66   On Monday morning Mrs. Whitaker was working in the back garden. She had a small herb garden she was extremely proud of: dill, vervain, mint, rosemary, thyme, and a wild expanse of parsley. She was down on her knees, wearing thick green gardening gloves, weeding, and picking out slugs and putting them in a plastic bag.

67   Mrs. Whitaker was very tenderhearted when it came to slugs. She would take them down to the back of her garden, which bordered on the railway line, and throw them over the fence.

68   She cut some parsley for the salad. There was a cough behind her. Galaad stood there, tall and beautiful, his armor glinting in the morning sun. In his arms he held a long package, wrapped in oiled leather.

69   "I'm back," he said.

70   "Hello," said Mrs. Whitaker. She stood up, rather slowly, and took off her gardening gloves. "Well," she said, "now you're here, you might as well make yourself useful."

71   She gave him the plastic bag full of slugs and told him to tip the slugs out over the back of the fence.

72   He did.

73   Then they went into the kitchen.

74   "Tea? Or lemonade?" she asked.

75   "Whatever you're having," Galaad said.

76   Mrs. Whitaker took a jug of her homemade lemonade from the fridge and sent Galaad outside to pick a sprig of mint. She selected two tall glasses. She washed the mint carefully and put a few leaves in each glass, then poured the lemonade.

77   "Is your horse outside?" she asked.

78   "Oh yes. His name is Grizzel."

79   "And you've come a long way, I suppose."

80   "A very long way."

81   "I see," said Mrs. Whitaker. She took a blue plastic basin from under the sink and half-filled it with water. Galaad took it out to Grizzel. He waited while the horse drank and brought the empty basin back to Mrs. Whitaker.

82   "Now," she said, "I suppose you're still after the Grail."

83   "Aye, still do I seek the Sangrail," he said. He picked up the leather package from the floor, put it down on her tablecloth and unwrapped it. "For it, I offer you this."

84   It was a sword, its blade almost four feet long. There were words and symbols traced elegantly along the length of the blade. The hilt was worked in silver and gold, and a large jewel was set in the pommel.

85   "It's very nice," said Mrs. Whitaker, doubtfully.

86   "This," said Galaad, "is the sword Balmung, **forged** by Wayland Smith in the dawn times. Its twin is Flamberge. Who wears it is unconquerable in war, and invincible in battle. Who wears it is incapable of a cowardly act or an **ignoble** one. Set in its pommel is

© Houghton Mifflin Harcourt Publishing Company

ANALYZE CHARACTERIZATION

Annotate: Reread paragraphs 68–70. Mark details used to describe Galaad.

Analyze: What does Mrs. Whitaker's reaction to Galaad reveal about her character?

forge
(fôrj) *v.* to form (metal, for example) by heating in a forge and beating or hammering into shape.

ignoble
(ĭg-nō′bəl) *adj.* not noble in quality, character, or purpose; base or dishonorable.

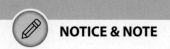

the sardonynx[3] Bircone, which protects its possessor from poison slipped into wine or ale, and from the treachery of friends."

87   Mrs. Whitaker peered at the sword. "It must be very sharp," she said, after a while.

88   "It can slice a falling hair in twain. Nay, it could slice a sunbeam," said Galaad proudly.

89   "Well, then, maybe you ought to put it away," said Mrs. Whitaker.

90   "Don't you want it?" Galaad seemed disappointed.

91   "No, thank you," said Mrs. Whitaker. It occurred to her that her late husband, Henry, would have quite liked it. He would have hung it on the wall in his study next to the stuffed carp he had caught in Scotland, and pointed it out to visitors.

92   Galaad rewrapped the oiled leather around the sword Balmung and tied it up with white cord.

93   He sat there, disconsolate.

94   Mrs. Whitaker made him some cream cheese and cucumber sandwiches for the journey back and wrapped them in greaseproof paper. She gave him an apple for Grizzel. He seemed very pleased with both gifts.

95   She waved them both good-bye.

96   That afternoon she took the bus down to the hospital to see Mrs. Perkins, who was still in with her hip, poor love. Mrs. Whitaker took her some homemade fruitcake, although she had left out the walnuts from the recipe, because Mrs. Perkins's teeth weren't what they used to be.

97   She watched a little television that evening, and had an early night.

98   On Tuesday the postman called. Mrs. Whitaker was up in the boxroom at the top of the house, doing a spot of tidying, and, taking each step slowly and carefully, she didn't make it downstairs in time. The postman had left her a message which said that he'd tried to deliver a packet, but no one was home.

99   Mrs. Whitaker sighed.

100   She put the message into her handbag and went down to the post office.

101   The package was from her niece Shirelle in Sydney, Australia. It contained photographs of her husband, Wallace, and her two daughters, Dixie and Violet, and a conch shell packed in cotton wool.

102   Mrs. Whitaker had a number of ornamental shells in her bedroom. Her favorite had a view of the Bahamas done on it in enamel. It had been a gift from her sister, Ethel, who had died in 1983.

103   She put the shell and the photographs in her shopping bag. Then, seeing that she was in the area, she stopped in at the Oxfam Shop on her way home.

104   "Hullo, Mrs. W.," said Marie.

---

[3] **sardonynx:** a type of stone.

105   Mrs. Whitaker stared at her. Marie was wearing lipstick (possibly not the best shade for her, nor particularly expertly applied, but, thought Mrs. Whitaker, that would come with time) and a rather smart skirt. It was a great improvement.

106   "Oh. Hello, dear," said Mrs. Whitaker.

107   "There was a man in here last week, asking about that thing you bought. The little metal cup thing. I told him where to find you. You don't mind, do you?"

108   "No, dear," said Mrs. Whitaker. "He found me."

109   "He was really dreamy. Really, really dreamy," sighed Marie wistfully. "I could of gone for him.

110   "And he had a big white horse and all," Marie concluded. She was standing up straighter as well, Mrs. Whitaker noted approvingly.

111   On the bookshelf Mrs. Whitaker found a new Mills & Boon novel—*Her Majestic Passion*—although she hadn't yet finished the two she had bought on her last visit.

112   She picked up the copy of *Romance and Legend of Chivalry* and opened it. It smelled musty. *EX LIBRIS FISHER* was neatly handwritten at the top of the first page in red ink.

113   She put it down where she had found it.

114   When she got home, Galaad was waiting for her. He was giving the neighborhood children rides on Grizzel's back, up and down the street.

115   "I'm glad you're here," she said. "I've got some cases that need moving."

116   She showed him up to the boxroom in the top of the house. He moved all the old suitcases for her, so she could get to the cupboard at the back.

117   It was very dusty up there.

118   She kept him up there most of the afternoon, moving things around while she dusted.

119   Galaad had a cut on his cheek, and he held one arm a little stiffly.

120   They talked a little while she dusted and tidied. Mrs. Whitaker told him about her late husband, Henry; and how the life insurance had paid the house off; and how she had all these things, but no one really to leave them to, no one but Ronald really and his wife only liked modern things. She told him how she had met Henry during the war, when he was in the ARP and she hadn't closed the kitchen blackout curtains all the way; and about the sixpenny dances they went to in the town; and how they'd gone to London when the war had ended, and she'd had her first drink of wine.

121   Galaad told Mrs. Whitaker about his mother Elaine, who was flighty and no better than she should have been and something of a witch to boot; and his grandfather, King Pelles, who was well-meaning although at best a little vague; and of his youth in the Castle of Bliant on the Joyous Isle; and his father, whom he knew as "Le Chevalier Mal Fet," who was more or less completely mad, and was in reality Lancelot du Lac, greatest of knights, in disguise and **bereft** of his wits; and of Galaad's days as a young squire in Camelot.

ANALYZE FANTASY

Annotate: Reread paragraphs 120–121. Mark examples of fantasy details.

Analyze: What effect does Gaiman create by offering these parallel descriptions of the two characters sharing stories of their backgrounds?

bereft
(bĭ-rĕft´) *adj.* deprived of something.

ANALYZE FANTASY

Annotate: Reread paragraphs 126–139. Mark the descriptions of the items Galaad offers to Mrs. Whitaker in exchange for the Holy Grail.

Evaluate: Identify the significance of the stone, the egg, and the apple. Does Mrs. Whitaker seem to realize the significance of these items? Explain.

122   At five o'clock Mrs. Whitaker surveyed the boxroom and decided that it met with her approval; then she opened the window so the room could air, and they went downstairs to the kitchen, where she put on the kettle.

123   Galaad sat down at the kitchen table.

124   He opened the leather purse at his waist and took out a round white stone. It was about the size of a cricket ball.

125   "My lady," he said, "This is for you, an you give me the Sangrail."

126   Mrs. Whitaker picked up the stone, which was heavier than it looked, and held it up to the light. It was milkily translucent, and deep inside it flecks of silver glittered and glinted in the late-afternoon sunlight. It was warm to the touch.

127   Then, as she held it, a strange feeling crept over her: Deep inside she felt stillness and a sort of peace. *Serenity*, that was the word for it; she felt serene.

128   Reluctantly she put the stone back on the table.

129   "It's very nice," she said.

130   "That is the Philosopher's Stone, which our forefather Noah hung in the Ark to give light when there was no light; it can transform base metals into gold; and it has certain other properties," Galaad told her proudly. "And that isn't all. There's more. Here." From the leather bag he took an egg and handed it to her.

131   It was the size of a goose egg and was a shiny black color, mottled with scarlet and white. When Mrs. Whitaker touched it, the hairs on the back of her neck prickled. Her immediate impression was one of incredible heat and freedom. She heard the crackling of distant fires, and for a fraction of a second she seemed to feel herself far above the world, swooping and diving on wings of flame.

132   She put the egg down on the table, next to the Philosopher's Stone.

133   "That is the Egg of the Phoenix," said Galaad. "From far Araby it comes. One day it will hatch out into the Phoenix Bird itself; and when its time comes, the bird will build a nest of flame, lay its egg, and die, to be reborn in flame in a later age of the world."

134   "I thought that was what it was," said Mrs. Whitaker.

135   "And, last of all, lady," said Galaad, "I have brought you this."

136   He drew it from his pouch, and gave it to her. It was an apple, apparently carved from a single ruby, on an amber stem.

137   A little nervously, she picked it up. It was soft to the touch—deceptively so: Her fingers bruised it, and ruby-colored juice from the apple ran down Mrs. Whitaker's hand.

138   The kitchen filled—almost imperceptibly, magically—with the smell of summer fruit, of raspberries and peaches and strawberries and red currants. As if from a great way away she heard distant voices raised in song and far music on the air.

139   "It is one of the apples of the Hesperides," said Galaad, quietly. "One bite from it will heal any illness or wound, no matter how deep; a second bite restores youth and beauty; and a third bite is said to grant eternal life."

140   Mrs. Whitaker licked the sticky juice from her hand. It tasted like fine wine.

141   There was a moment, then, when it all came back to her—how it was to be young: to have a firm, slim body that would do whatever she wanted it to do; to run down a country lane for the simple unladylike joy of running; to have men smile at her just because she was herself and happy about it.

142   Mrs. Whitaker looked at Sir Galaad, most comely of all knights, sitting fair and noble in her small kitchen.

143   She caught her breath.

144   "And that's all I have brought for you," said Galaad. "They weren't easy to get, either."

145   Mrs. Whitaker put the ruby fruit down on her kitchen table. She looked at the Philosopher's Stone, and the Egg of the Phoenix, and the Apple of Life.

146   Then she walked into her parlor and looked at the mantelpiece: at the little china basset hound, and the Holy Grail, and the photograph of her late husband Henry, shirtless, smiling and eating an ice cream in black and white, almost forty years away.

147   She went back into the kitchen. The kettle had begun to whistle. She poured a little steaming water into the teapot, swirled it around, and poured it out. Then she added two spoonfuls of tea and one for the pot and poured in the rest of the water. All this she did in silence.

148   She turned to Galaad then, and she looked at him.

149   "Put that apple away," she told Galaad, firmly. "You shouldn't offer things like that to old ladies. It isn't proper."

150   She paused, then. "But I'll take the other two," she continued, after a moment's thought. "They'll look nice on the mantelpiece. And two for one's fair, or I don't know what is."

151   Galaad beamed. He put the ruby apple into his leather pouch. Then he went down on one knee, and kissed Mrs. Whitaker's hand.

152   "Stop that," said Mrs. Whitaker. She poured them both cups of tea, after getting out the very best china, which was only for special occasions.

CONTRASTS AND CONTRADICTIONS

Notice & Note: Mark words and phrases in paragraphs 141–143 that sharply contrast with the portrayal of Mrs. Whitaker elsewhere in the story.

Interpret: What do you make of the way she looks at Galaad in paragraph 143?

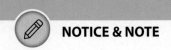
153   They sat in silence, drinking their tea.

154   When they had finished their tea they went into the parlor.

155   Galaad crossed himself, and picked up the Grail.

156   Mrs. Whitaker arranged the Egg and the Stone where the Grail had been. The Egg kept tipping on one side, and she propped it up against the little china dog.

157   "They do look very nice," said Mrs. Whitaker.

158   "Yes," agreed Galaad. "They look very nice."

159   "Can I give you anything to eat before you go back?" she asked.

160   He shook his head.

161   "Some fruitcake," she said. "You may not think you want any now, but you'll be glad of it in a few hours' time. And you should probably use the facilities. Now, give me that, and I'll wrap it up for you."

162   She directed him to the small toilet at the end of the hall, and went into the kitchen, holding the Grail. She had some old Christmas wrapping paper in the pantry, and she wrapped the Grail in it, and tied the package with twine. Then she cut a large slice of fruitcake and put it in a brown paper bag, along with a banana and a slice of processed cheese in silver foil.

163   Galaad came back from the toilet. She gave him the paper bag, and the Holy Grail. Then she went up on tiptoes and kissed him on the cheek.

164   "You're a nice boy," she said. "You take care of yourself."

ANALYZE
CHARACTERIZATION

Annotate: Mark the detail in paragraph 165 that conveys Mrs. Whitaker's emotional reaction after Galaad leaves.

Infer: Why do you think she reacts this way?

165   He hugged her, and she shooed him out of the kitchen, and out of the back door, and she shut the door behind him. She poured herself another cup of tea, and cried quietly into a Kleenex, while the sound of hoof-beats echoed down Hawthorne Crescent.

166   On Wednesday Mrs. Whitaker stayed in all day.

167   On Thursday she went down to the post office to collect her pension. Then she stopped in at the Oxfam Shop.

168   The woman on the till was new to her. "Where's Marie?" asked Mrs. Whitaker.

169   The woman on the till, who had blue-rinsed gray hair and blue spectacles that went up into diamante points, shook her head and shrugged her shoulders. "She went off with a young man," she said. "On a horse. Tch. I ask you. I'm meant to be down in the Heathfield shop this afternoon. I had to get my Johnny to run me up here, while we find someone else."

170   "Oh," said Mrs. Whitaker. "Well, it's nice that she's found herself a young man."

171   "Nice for her, maybe," said the lady on the till, "But some of us were meant to be in Heathfield this afternoon."

172   On a shelf near the back of the shop Mrs. Whitaker found a tarnished old silver container with a long spout. It had been priced at sixty pence, according to the little paper label stuck to the side. It looked a little like a flattened, elongated teapot.

173   She picked out a Mills & Boon novel she hadn't read before. It was called *Her Singular Love*. She took the book and the silver container up to the woman on the till.

174   "Sixty-five pee,[4] dear," said the woman, picking up the silver object, staring at it. "Funny old thing, isn't it? Came in this morning." It had writing carved along the side in blocky old Chinese characters and an elegant arching handle. "Some kind of oil can, I suppose."

175   "No, it's not an oil can," said Mrs. Whitaker, who knew exactly what it was. "It's a lamp."

176   There was a small metal finger ring, unornamented, tied to the handle of the lamp with brown twine.

177   "Actually," said Mrs. Whitaker, "on second thoughts, I think I'll just have the book."

178   She paid her five pence for the novel, and put the lamp back where she had found it, in the back of the shop. After all, Mrs. Whitaker reflected, as she walked home, it wasn't as if she had anywhere to put it.

---

[4] **pee:** slang for pence.

ANALYZE FANTASY

Annotate: Reread paragraph 174–178. Mark the details that describe the lamp.

Draw Conclusions: What might be special about this lamp? Does Mrs. Whitaker really leave it behind because she has no room for it, or might she have some other reason?

CHECK YOUR UNDERSTANDING

Answer these questions before moving on to the **Analyze the Text** section on the following page.

1 Who has sent Galaad to get the Holy Grail from Mrs. Whitaker?

   A Marie

   B Mrs. Greenberg

   C Sir Lancelot

   D King Arthur

2 What does Mrs. Whitaker have Galaad do for her?

   F Play a song on his lute

   G Make a roast mutton and salad

   H Help her in the garden and move some boxes

   J Teach her how to saddle a horse

3 In exchange for the Holy Grail, Mrs. Whitaker accepts —

   A a beautiful sword

   B a stone and an egg

   C the gift of eternal youth

   D a silver lamp

ANALYZE THE TEXT

Support your responses with evidence from the text.   📓 NOTEBOOK

1. **Draw Conclusions** Consider how Mrs. Whitaker is characterized in the story. What conclusions can you make about how she lives her life?

2. **Analyze** How does Gaiman use the setting of a modern English town to help develop the story's fantastic plot?

3. **Infer** Why does Mrs. Whitaker reject Galaad's offer of the apple of the Hesperides while accepting his other two gifts?

4. **Evaluate** Legends and fairy tales are often structured in patterns of three. In "Chivalry," Galaad visits Mrs. Whitaker three times. How effectively does Gaiman use these visits to develop the relationship between these characters? Explain.

5. **Notice & Note** Does Mrs. Whitaker's behavior at the end of the story suggest that she has been changed by her experience with Galaad and the Holy Grail? Why or why not?

RESEARCH

RESEARCH TIP
When researching, focus on reliable sources. Web addresses that end in *.gov, .org,* and *.edu* are mostly reliable and credible websites. Also, try to distinguish between primary and secondary sources and analyze which documents serve as fact-based information versus opinions. Finally, keep an eye out for articles written by historians or literary critics who have studied a subject in depth.

Sir Galahad was considered one of the greatest knights at King Arthur's court. With a partner, conduct an Internet search to discover more about the legend of Sir Galahad. Use the chart below to record your findings.

QUESTION	ANSWER
What were the circumstances of Galahad's birth?	
How did Galahad become one of the Knights of the Round Table?	
What happened on Galahad's quest to find the Holy Grail?	

Extend Find another modern story, novel, or film in which Sir Galahad makes an appearance. Discuss with your partner how the presence of Galahad in this work compares with Gaiman's portrayal of him in "Chivalry."

CREATE AND DRAMATIZE

Write a Fantasy Scene Collaborate with a partner to write a short scene involving the mingling of a legendary or historical character with a present-day character. Review your list of questions from the Quick Start activity. Also, think about any fantasy elements from "Chivalry" that would translate well to your scene.

❏ Decide where your scene will take place, and think about how the characters might react to this setting.

❏ Determine the nature of the interaction between the two characters (for example, it may be humorous or confrontational). Make sure an audience can readily grasp each character's traits and motivations.

❏ Convey a message about the past or about contemporary life.

Present the Scene With your partner, prepare a dramatic presentation based on your fantasy scene.

❏ Discuss elements of presentation needed to act it out for the rest of the class. Is it part of a traditional play or an impromptu skit? Plan how to stage the scene and figure out what simple props you can use.

❏ Determine the emotions you want to stir with the fantasy scene. Are the fantasy elements meant to be humorous, inspiring, or touching? Think of ways to capture and keep your audience's attention.

❏ Practice the scene and present it to the class. Ask for feedback.

 Go to **Writing Narratives** in the **Writing Studio** to develop your scene.

 Go to **Giving a Presentation** in the **Speaking and Listening Studio** to learn more.

RESPOND TO THE ESSENTIAL QUESTION

 What is true chivalry?

Gather Information Review your annotations and notes on "Chivalry." Then add relevant information to your Response Log. As you determine which information to include, think about:

• the definition and key qualities of chivalry
• Galaad's interactions with others throughout the story
• the importance of chivalry in real life

ACADEMIC VOCABULARY
As you write and discuss what you learned from the short story, be sure to use the Academic Vocabulary words. Check off each of the words that you use.

❏ collapse
❏ displace
❏ military
❏ violate
❏ visual

RESPOND

WORD BANK

pension

flotsam

appraise

forge

ignoble

bereft

CRITICAL VOCABULARY

Practice and Apply Read each scenario. Then select the correct vocabulary word from the word bank to match the scenario.

1. Jennifer took her ring to a jeweler to find out how much it's worth.	_____
2. By combining the two metals, the jeweler was able to create an object that was as durable as it was beautiful.	_____
3. The CEO of the company was forced to resign for embezzling from company accounts.	_____
4. Mrs. Donaldson, after retiring from 30 years as a teacher, will receive regular monthly payments.	_____
5. James went hungry at lunchtime because he left his sandwich on the counter.	_____
6. The Harrison family had a yard sale because they had many items they regarded as "junk" in their garage.	_____

VOCABULARY STRATEGY:
Context Clues

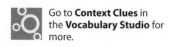 Go to **Context Clues** in the **Vocabulary Studio** for more.

When reading a text, there are times you'll have to use **context clues** in order to determine the meaning of a word or phrase. Context clues include the other words or descriptions surrounding the unknown term. Understanding the context of a sentence or paragraph can help you to better determine the meaning of unknown words or phrases.

Practice and Apply Follow the instructions to complete the activity:

1. Look at the underlined word in each sentence in the chart.

2. Circle, or highlight, the context clues in the sentence that help the reader to understand the underlined term.

3. Based on the context clues, define the meaning of the underlined word or phrase. Explain how the context clues helped you to determine the meaning.

SENTENCE WITH UNKNOWN TERM	MEANING
1. They sat in the parlor and ate <u>macaroons</u> and drank tea.	
2. It was milky and <u>translucent</u>, and deep inside it flecks of silver glittered in the late-afternoon sunlight.	
3. It was the size of a goose egg and was a shiny black color, <u>mottled</u> with scarlet and white.	

© Houghton Mifflin Harcourt Publishing Company

80   Unit 1

LANGUAGE CONVENTIONS:
Appositives and Appositive Phrases

An **appositive** is a noun or pronoun that identifies, or renames, another noun or pronoun. An **appositive phrase** is made up of an appositive plus its modifiers. Writers use appositives and appositive phrases to add important details without being wordy. Appositives can be either restrictive or nonrestrictive. **Restrictive appositives** provide information necessary for identifying the noun or pronoun that precedes it. In the following sentence, the appositive *Balmung* is needed to identify the preceding noun:

> "This," said Galaad, "is the sword Balmung."

Nonrestrictive appositives only provide additional, or nonessential, information about a noun or pronoun whose meaning is already clear. In this sentence, the appositive phrase *the Reverend Bartholomew* adds extra information that is not needed to understand the basic meaning of the sentence.

> . . . she liked the vicar, the Reverend Bartholomew, when he wasn't actually playing the guitar."

Nonrestrictive appositives and appositive phrases are set off with commas.

Practice and Apply   Each sentence below contains an appositive or an appositive phrase. Use a dotted line to mark the appositive or appositive phrase. Then underline the noun or pronoun it identifies or renames.

1. The newspaper *The New York Times* included a famous article about the historical significance of the Holy Grail.

2. Sir Galaad, son of Sir Lancelot, was destined to lead the quest for the Holy Grail.

3. Award-winning author Neil Gaiman enjoys including themes of love in many of his fantasy writings.

Now write a short, detailed paragraph describing a personal possession that is of great importance to you. Use as many appositives and appositive phrases as possible. Exchange paragraphs with a partner, and circle the appositives and appositive phrases in your partner's paragraph.

 Go to **Appositives and Appositive Phrases** in the **Grammar Studio** to learn more.

LETTERS

from
THE PASTON LETTERS

by the **Paston Family**

pages 85–91

COMPARE PRIMARY SOURCES

As you read, identify the intended audience and the clues that indicate the writer's message for each text. Think about how the writer wants the reader to react. As you read about the events described, consider factors that affect the credibility of the account, such as whether the writer witnessed the events firsthand or if the writer has a bias. After you read both selections, you will collaborate with a small group on a final project.

? ***ESSENTIAL QUESTION:***

What happens when a society unravels?

DIARY

from
MY SYRIAN DIARY

by **Marah**

pages 99–103

The Paston Letters

QUICK START

When we have a problem or conflict in our lives, we often reach out to friends or family members for support. Think about a situation in your life for which you would like support from a friend or family member, and write a quick message to the person you choose explaining the situation.

ANALYZE PRIMARY SOURCES

Primary sources such as diaries and letters are materials created by people who took part in or witnessed the events portrayed. These documents can help you learn about the people who wrote them and the period in which they lived. For example, this letter written by a member of the Paston family reveals that the English suffered from terrible plagues in the 1400s.

> **Please send me word if any of our friends or well-wishers are dead, for I fear that there is great mortality in Norwich and in other boroughs and towns in Norfolk: I assure you that it is the most widespread plague I ever knew of in England, for by my faith I cannot hear of pilgrims going through the country nor of any other man who rides or goes anywhere, that any town or borough in England is free from the sickness.**

As you read these letters, analyze them to see if they are credible sources. Consider whether the writer witnessed the events firsthand or is relying on someone else's account. Also, look for bias in the writer's description of events.

© Houghton Mifflin Harcourt Publishing Company

GENRE ELEMENTS: LETTERS

- correspondence exchanged between relatives, friends, or acquaintances
- intended to be private rather than for publication
- sometimes published for a wider audience because of the literary or historical importance

MAKE INFERENCES

When you make **inferences**, you are making logical guesses about a text or character based on your own experiences and the evidences or clues you find in the text. Making inferences is sometimes called "reading between the lines" because you come to understand something in the text that the author has not stated explicitly. For example, when Margaret urges her husband to "take care when you eat or drink in any other men's company, for no one can be trusted," you can infer that she fears his enemies will try to poison him.

As you read the letters from the Paston family, pay close attention to their descriptions of events and people. Record your inferences in a chart like the one shown.

DETAILS FROM THE TEXT	INFERENCES
I am very surprised that you do not send me more news than you have done.	She is afraid that her husband may be in trouble.

CRITICAL VOCABULARY

commend   **quell**   **affairs**   **bailiff**   **writ**   **ransack**

Complete the sentences using the Critical Vocabulary words.

1. After hearing both sides of the case, the judge issued a _____ concerning the lord's ownership of the disputed property.

2. The _____ of the estate informed the tenants of the rent increase.

3. While they are out of the country on business, they will _____ the care of their children to their aunt and uncle.

4. We have asked the king to send soldiers to _____ the riot.

5. The villagers feared that the invaders would _____ their homes.

6. My grandfather is very sick and has asked my father to look after his _____ until he can recover.

LANGUAGE CONVENTIONS

Subject-Verb Agreement The subject and verb in a clause must agree in number. The present simple form of a verb will be either **singular** or **plural**, depending on whether the subject of the clause is singular or plural.

Verbs that have compound subjects with *and* are plural. Compound subjects with *or* and *nor* may take either a plural or singular verb, depending on the implied meaning. For pronouns, agreement with the verb will depend on the pronoun's antecedent.

ANNOTATION MODEL

NOTICE & NOTE

As you read, you can make inferences about the author's purpose. In the model, you can see one reader's notes about Margaret's letter to John I.

Right worshipful husband, I commend myself to you, . . . begging that you will not be angry at my leaving the place where you left me. On my word, such news was brought to me by various people who are sympathetic to you and me that I did not dare stay there any longer. I will tell you who the people were when you come home. They let me know that various of Lord Moleyns' men said that if they could get their hands on me they would carry me off and keep me in the castle.

The writer asks that her husband not be angry with her for leaving.

She was afraid to stay and then explains why she was afraid.

I can infer that the writer is afraid and wants her husband to know she is in danger.

BACKGROUND

The Paston Family *(c. 1421–1500) exchanged many letters that offer valuable insight into a period of war and plague in England. With two noble families battling for the kingdom, landowners often attacked neighbors' estates. The Pastons were prosperous landowners, and their wealth attracted enemies. John I inherited property from his father and acquired more through his marriage to Margaret. Other families challenged the Pastons' claims; John I, who was a lawyer, spent much time in London on these disputes, leaving Margaret to manage their estates alone. The letters you will read are from members of the Paston family to one another.*

from
THE PASTON LETTERS
Letters by the Paston Family

PREPARE TO COMPARE

As you read, use the details given in the text to make inferences about what life was like in 15th-century England and what kinds of challenges people faced. This will help you to compare this primary source with the diary entry from "My Syrian Diary" that follows.

Margaret Paston was able to deal equally well with small housekeeping problems and with family disasters that included attacks against the Paston manors in the absence of her husband, John I. While she was living at the Paston estate of Gresham, it was attacked by a Lord Moleyns, who claimed rights to the property and ejected Margaret from her home. Margaret first escaped to a friend's house about a mile away; but later, fearing that Moleyns's band of men might kidnap her, she fled to the city of Norwich, where she wrote the following letter to her husband.

Margaret to John I
28 February 1449

1 *Right worshipful husband,* I **commend** myself to you, wishing with all my heart to hear that you are well, and begging that you will not be angry at my leaving the place where you left me. On

Notice & Note

Use the side margins to notice and note signposts in the text.

commend
(kə-mĕnd´) *tr. v.* to commit to the care of another; entrust.

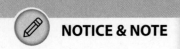

NOTICE & NOTE

my word, such news was brought to me by various people who are sympathetic to you and me that I did not dare stay there any longer. I will tell you who the people were when you come home. They let me know that various of Lord Moleyns' men said that if they could get their hands on me they would carry me off and keep me in the castle. They wanted you to get me out again, and said that it would not cause you much heart-ache. After I heard this news, I could not rest easy until I was here, and I did not dare go out of the place where I was until I was ready to ride away. Nobody in the place knew that I was leaving except the lady of the house, until an hour before I went. And I told her that I would come here to have clothes made for myself and the children, which I wanted made, and said I thought I would be here a fortnight[1] or three weeks. Please keep the reason for my departure a secret until I talk to you, for those who warned me do not on any account want it known.

2   I spoke to your mother as I came this way, and she offered to let me stay in this town, if you agree. She would very much like us to stay at her place, and will send me such things as she can spare so that I can set up house until you can get a place and things of your own to set up a household. Please let me know by the man who brings this what you would like me to do. I would be very unhappy to live so close to Gresham as I was until this matter is completely settled between you and Lord Moleyns.

3   Barow[2] told me that there was no better evidence in England than that Lord Moleyns has for [his title to] the manor of Gresham. I told him that I supposed the evidence was of the kind that William Hasard said yours was, and that the seals were not yet cold.[3] That, I said, was what I expected his lord's evidence to be like. I said I knew that your evidence was such that no one could have better evidence, and the seals on it were two hundred years older than he was. Then Barow said to me that if he came to London while you were there he would have a drink with you, to **quell** any anger there was between you. He said that he only acted as a servant, and as he was ordered to do. Purry[4] will tell you about the conversation between Barow and me when I came from Walsingham.[5] I beg you with all my heart, for reverence of God, beware of Lord Moleyns and his men, however pleasantly they speak to you, and do not eat or drink with them; for they are so false that they cannot be trusted. And please take care when you eat or drink in any other men's company, for no one can be trusted.

4   I beg you with all my heart that you will be kind enough to send me word how you are, and how your **affairs** are going, by the man who brings this. I am very surprised that you do not send me more news than you have done. . . .

ANALYZE PRIMARY SOURCES

Annotate: Reread paragraph 3. Mark Margaret Paston's reply to Barow about Lord Moleyns' claims.

Cite Evidence: Was Margaret a participant in the events described in this paragraph? Cite evidence from the text in your response.

quell
(kwĕl) *tr. v.* to pacify; quiet.

affairs
(ə-fâr´) *n.* personal business.

---
[1] **fortnight:** 14 nights, or two weeks.
[2] **Barow:** one of Lord Moleyns' men.
[3] **the seals . . . cold:** A seal, often made by impressing a family emblem on hot wax, was placed on a document to show its authenticity. Margaret is suggesting that Lord Moleyns' documents are recent forgeries.
[4] **Purry:** perhaps a servant or tenant of the Pastons'.
[5] **Walsingham** (wôl´sĭng-əm): a town near Lynn in the English county of Norfolk.

In 1465, in still another property dispute, the Paston estate of Hellesdon was attacked by the Duke of Suffolk, who had gained the support of several local officials. Although Margaret and John were not living at Hellesdon at the time, many of their servants and tenants suffered from the extensive damage. In the following two letters, Margaret tells her husband about the devastation.

Margaret to John I
17 October 1465

5 . . . On Tuesday morning John Botillere, also John Palmer, Darcy Arnald your cook and William Malthouse of Aylsham were seized at Hellesdon by the **bailiff** of Eye,[6] called Bottisforth, and taken to Costessey,[7] and they are being kept there still without any warrant or authority from a justice of the peace; and they say they will carry them off to Eye prison and as many others of your men and tenants as they can get who are friendly towards you or have supported you, and they threaten to kill or imprison them.

6   The duke came to Norwich at 10 o'clock on Tuesday with five hundred men and he sent for the mayor, aldermen and sheriffs, asking them in the king's name that they should inquire of the constables of every ward within the city which men had been on your side or had helped or supported your men at the time of any of these gatherings and if they could find any they should take them and arrest them and punish them; which the mayor did, and will do anything he can for him and his men. At this the mayor has arrested a man who was with me, called Robert Lovegold, a brazier,[8] and threatened him that he shall be hanged by the neck. So I would be glad if you could get a **writ** sent down for his release, if you think it can be done. He was only with me when Harlesdon and others attacked me at Lammas.[9] He is very true and faithful to you, so I would like him to be helped. I have no one attending me who dares to be known, except Little John. William Naunton is here with me, but he dares not be known because he is much threatened. I am told that the old lady and the duke have been frequently set against us by what Harlesdon, the bailiff of Costessey, Andrews and Doget the bailiff's son and other false villains have told them, who want this affair pursued for their own pleasure; there are evil rumors about it in this part of the world and other places.

7   As for Sir John Heveningham, Sir John Wyndefeld and other respectable men, they have been made into their catspaws,[10] which will not do their reputation any good after this, I think. . . .

---

[6] **bailiff of Eye:** an administrative official of Eye, a town in the English county of Suffolk.

[7] **Costessey:** an estate owned by the duke of Suffolk.

[8] **brazier** (brā′zhər): a person who makes articles of brass.

[9] **when Harlesdon . . . Lammas** (lăm′əs): when Harlesdon and others of the duke of Suffolk's men attacked on Lammas, a religious feast celebrated on August 1.

[10] **catspaws:** people who are deceived and used as tools by others; dupes.

bailiff
(bā′lĭf) *n.* an overseer of an estate; a steward.

LANGUAGE CONVENTIONS
Annotate: In paragraph 5, underline the relative clause *who are friendly towards you or have supported you.* Circle the two verbs.

Subject-Verb Agreement: Are the two verbs singular or plural? Why?

writ
(rĭt) *n.* a written order issued by a court, commanding the party to whom it is addressed to perform or cease performing a specified act.

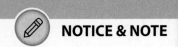
8   The lodge and remainder of your place was demolished on Tuesday and Wednesday, and the duke rode on Wednesday to Drayton and then to Costessey while the lodge at Hellesdon was being demolished. Last night at midnight Thomas Slyford, Green, Porter and John Bottisforth the bailiff of Eye and others got a cart and took away the featherbeds and all the stuff of ours that was left at the parson's and Thomas Water's house for safe-keeping. I will send you lists later, as accurately as I can, of the things we have lost. Please let me know what you want me to do, whether you want me to stay at Caister[11] or come to you in London.

9   I have no time to write any more. God have you in his keeping. Written at Norwich on St. Luke's eve.[12]

M.P.

Margaret to John I
27 October 1465

10   . . . I was at Hellesdon last Thursday and saw the place there, and indeed no one can imagine what a horrible mess it is unless they see it. Many people come out each day, both from Norwich and elsewhere, to look at it, and they talk of it as a great shame. The duke would have done better to lose £1000[13] than to have caused this to be done, and you have all the more goodwill from people because it has been done so foully. And they made your tenants at Hellesdon and Drayton, and others, help them to break down the walls of both the house and the lodge: God knows, it was against their will, but they did not dare do otherwise for fear. I have spoken with your tenants both at Hellesdon and Drayton, and encouraged them as best I can.

11   The duke's men **ransacked** the church, and carried off all the goods that were left there, both ours and the tenants, and left little behind; they stood on the high altar and ransacked the images, and took away everything they could find. They shut the parson out of the church until they had finished, and ransacked everyone's house in the town five or six times. The ringleaders in the thefts were the bailiff of Eye and the bailiff of Stradbroke, Thomas Slyford. And Slyford was the leader in robbing the church and, after the bailiff of Eye, it is he who has most of the proceeds of the robbery. As for the lead, brass, pewter, iron, doors, gates, and other household stuff, men from Costessey and Cawston have got it, and what they could not carry they hacked up in the most spiteful fashion. If possible, I would like some reputable men to be sent for from the king, to see how things are both there and at the lodge, before any snows come, so that they can report the truth, because otherwise it will not be so plain as it is

ransack
(rănˊsăkˊ) *tr. v.* to go through (a place) stealing valuables and causing disarray.

EXTREME OR ABSOLUTE LANGUAGE

Notice & Note: In paragraphs 10 and 11, which strong negative words and phrases does the writer use to describe the situation and actions of Lord Suffolk's men? Mark them.

Infer: How does the writer feel about the events she is recounting? What reaction does the writer of this letter want from the recipient?

---

[11] **Caister:** one of the Paston estates.

[12] **St. Luke's eve:** the eve of St. Luke's Day, October 18. The feasts of major saints were celebrated on specific days throughout the year, and writers often dated letters with the name of a saint's day or eve instead of using days and months.

[13] **£1000:** a thousand pounds (British money).

now. For reverence of God, finish your business now, for the expense and trouble we have each day is horrible, and it will be like this until you have finished; and your men dare not go around collecting your rents, while we keep here every day more than twenty people to save ourselves and the place; for indeed, if the place had not been strongly defended, the duke would have come here. . . .

12   For the reverence of God, if any respectable and profitable method can be used to settle your business, do not neglect it, so that we can get out of these troubles and the great costs and expenses we have and may have in future. It is thought here that if my lord of Norfolk would act on your behalf, and got a commission to inquire into the riots and robberies committed on you and others in this part of the world, then the whole county will wait on him and do as you wish, for people love and respect him more than any other lord, except the king and my lord of Warwick.[14] . . .

13   Please do let me know quickly how you are and how your affairs are going, and let me know how your sons are. I came home late last night, and will be here until I hear from you again. Wykes came home on Saturday, but he did not meet your sons.

14   God have you in his keeping and send us good news from you. Written in haste on the eve of St. Simon and St. Jude.

By yours, M.P.

---

[14] **the king . . . Warwick** (wŏr´ĭk): King Edward IV and the earl of Warwick, a figure so influential that he was known as Warwick the Kingmaker. Warwick put his friend, the Yorkist King Edward IV, on the throne but later turned against him and fought with the Lancastrian faction, who opposed the Yorkists in the War of the Roses.

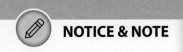

NOTICE & NOTE

Although the Pastons were considered wealthy, they faced continual struggles. They even experienced occasional financial difficulties, particularly after the death of John I in 1466. Margaret's son John II, though frequently in London to deal with family legal matters, seems at times to have paid more attention to his own interests. The Pastons were also affected by the ravages of warfare and disease. The following three letters deal with some of their hardships.

Margaret to her oldest son, John II
28 October 1470

MAKE INFERENCES

Annotate: Mark the warnings that the writer gives to her son in paragraphs 15 and 16.

Infer: What can you assume about the writer's son's behavior from the warnings she gives him? What kind of person is her son?

15 . . . Unless you pay more attention to your expenses, you will bring great shame on yourself and your friends, and impoverish them so that none of us will be able to help each other, to the great encouragement of our enemies.

16   Those who claim to be your friends in this part of the world realize in what great danger and need you stand, both from various of your friends and from your enemies. It is rumored that I have parted with so much to you that I cannot help either you or any of my friends, which is no honor to us and causes people to esteem us less. At the moment it means that I must disperse my household and lodge somewhere, which I would be very loath to do if I were free to choose. It has caused a great deal of talk in this town and I would not have needed to do it if I had held back when I could. So for God's sake pay attention and be careful from now on, for I have handed over to you both my own property and your father's, and have held nothing back, either for myself or for his sake. . . .

John II to Margaret
April 1471

17 *Mother,* I commend myself to you and let you know, blessed be God, my brother John is alive and well, and in no danger of dying. Nevertheless he is badly hurt by an arrow in his right arm below the elbow, and I have sent a surgeon to him, who has dressed the wound; and he tells me that he hopes he will be healed within a very short time. John Mylsent is dead. God have mercy on his soul; William Mylsent is alive and all his other servants seem to have escaped.[15] . . .

John II to John III
15 September 1471

18 . . . Please send me word if any of our friends or well-wishers are dead, for I fear that there is great mortality in Norwich and in

---

[15] **my brother John . . . escaped:** John II is describing the battle of Barnet in the Wars of the Roses. The Pastons fought on the Lancastrian side, which King Edward IV's Yorkist forces defeated.

© Houghton Mifflin Harcourt Publishing Company

other boroughs and towns in Norfolk: I assure you that it is the most widespread plague I ever knew of in England, for by my faith I cannot hear of pilgrims going through the country nor of any other man who rides or goes anywhere, that any town or borough in England is free from the sickness. May God put an end to it, when it please him. So, for God's sake, get my mother to take care of my younger brothers and see that they are not anywhere where the sickness is prevalent, and that they do not amuse themselves with other young people who go where the sickness is. If anyone has died of the sickness, or is infected with it in Norwich, for God's sake let her send them to some friend of hers in the country; I would advise you to do the same. I would rather my mother moved her household into the country. . . .

NOTICE & NOTE

ANALYZE PRIMARY SOURCES

Annotate: John II makes requests of and gives warnings to his brother. Mark them.

Infer: Based on this letter, how well did people in the 15th century understand how the plague spread?

CHECK YOUR UNDERSTANDING

Answer these questions before moving on to the **Analyze the Text** section on the following page.

1 Which event does Margaret experience or see firsthand?

   A The execution of Robert Lovegold

   B The aftermath of the ransacking of Hellesdon

   C The excessive spending of John II

   D The battle of Barnet

2 Which sentence from paragraphs 6 and 7 suggests that the Pastons may be able to appeal for recourse to a higher authority than the mayor?

   F *The duke came to Norwich . . . asking them in the king's name that they should inquire of the constables . . . which men had been on your side . . .*

   G *[T]hey have been made into their catspaws . . .*

   H *So I would be glad if you could get a writ sent down for his release, . . .*

   J *I am told that the old lady and the duke have been frequently set against us by what Harlesdon, . . . and other false villains have told them, . . .*

3 The last line of paragraph 14 starts with the phrase "written in haste." What can the reader infer about Margaret Paston from this phrase?

   A She is an impatient and unsympathetic person.

   B She is in a rush to get her letter to a messenger.

   C She is concerned about getting the plague.

   D She is distressed and feels in constant danger.

ANALYZE THE TEXT

Support your responses with evidence from the text. 📓 NOTEBOOK

1. **Infer** In the first letter from Margaret to her husband, she explains her conversation with Barow, one of Lord Moleyns' men. What do you think is Margaret's opinion of Barow? Why might she have a bias against him?

2. **Interpret** In paragraph 6, Margaret writes, "So I would be glad if you could get a writ sent down for his release, if you think it can be done." Why is Margaret uncertain as to whether her husband can obtain the writ?

3. **Cause/Effect** What made the Paston family vulnerable to attacks?

4. **Draw Conclusions** What can you determine about women's roles in 15th-century English society from reading these primary sources?

5. **Notice & Note** In her letter to her son John II, Margaret uses strong negative language: *great shame*, *great encouragement of our enemies*, *great danger*, *great deal of talk*. Do you think that Margaret's account is credible? Why might she exaggerate?

RESEARCH

RESEARCH TIP
It's always easier to begin a research project by creating a research plan. First, identify exactly what you want to learn. Then make a step-by-step plan to guide your research.

All these letters except for the first one were written during the Wars of the Roses, a period of great political instability in England. With a partner, research the history of this long conflict. Develop research questions, locate answers in the sources you find, and record the results of your research in a chart like the one below.

QUESTIONS	ANSWERS

Extend How did warfare in medieval England differ from the way wars are fought today? Discuss with your partner.

CREATE AND PRESENT

Write a Short Dramatic Scene The letters contain reports of arguments and conflicts. In pairs or in a small group, write a short dramatic scene with at least two characters to recreate one of these scenes through dialogue. You can also imagine that John Paston meets Barow in London, as Barow proposes, and write that scene.

❑ Think about the conflict between the characters and what each character wants or believes they are entitled to.

❑ Make sure that the dialogue goes back and forth with the characters responding to each other, rather than each character presenting their case alone.

❑ Use language to show the emotions of each character. Remember that people often use strong language when they are upset.

❑ People are not always truthful when they are arguing about something. Consider having one or more of your characters lie or exaggerate.

Enact the Scene With your partner or group, present your dramatic scene by acting it out in front of the class.

❑ Use a narrator to set the scene and provide some context before the dialogue begins.

❑ When you read your part, think about how that person feels at that moment; try to convey that feeling in the way you talk and in your movements and facial expressions.

❑ After you present your scene, ask your classmates to summarize what happened.

Go to **Writing Narratives** in the **Writing Studio** for more help with writing a dramatic scene.

RESPOND TO THE ESSENTIAL QUESTION

? What happens when a society unravels?

Gather Information Review your annotations and notes on *The Paston Letters*. Then add relevant details to your Response Log. As you determine which information to include, think about:

• the challenges Margaret Paston faces
• which strategies the Pastons use to survive and defend themselves
• how the usual rules of society change in wartime

ACADEMIC VOCABULARY

As you write and discuss what you learned from *The Paston Letters*, be sure to use the Academic Vocabulary words. Check off each of the words that you use.

❑ **collapse**
❑ **displace**
❑ **military**
❑ **violate**
❑ **visual**

commend
quell
affairs
bailiff
writ
ransack

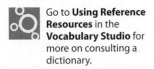

Go to **Using Reference Resources** in the **Vocabulary Studio** for more on consulting a dictionary.

CRITICAL VOCABULARY

Practice and Apply Write the Critical Vocabulary word that has the same or similar meaning as the given word or phrase.

1. Which vocabulary word has a meaning similar to *business*?

2. Which vocabulary word has a meaning similar to *bring to an end*?

3. Which vocabulary word has a meaning similar to *rob and destroy*?

4. Which vocabulary word has a meaning similar to *court order*?

5. Which vocabulary word has a meaning similar to *steward*?

6. Which vocabulary word has a meaning similar to *entrust*?

VOCABULARY STRATEGY:
Consult a Dictionary

At times you may come across a word that looks familiar, but the meaning you know for that word might not make sense in the way it is being used, making it difficult to understand a sentence. Be aware when reading older texts that the meanings and usage of words change over time, so that an author may use a word in a way that was very common in his or her time, but is now uncommon. An example of this can be found in the first letter you read with Margaret's use of the word *commend*.

It is useful to consult a dictionary to see all the meanings and senses of a word. **Senses** are slightly different usages of the same meaning of a word. The dictionary will list meanings and senses of a word in order from most common to least common. The most common meaning of *commend* is "to praise." However, that meaning doesn't make sense in the context of the letter. A different meaning of *commend* best fits its use in the context: "to entrust."

Practice and Apply Look up each Critical Vocabulary word in the dictionary, and write its most common meaning in the chart. When necessary, write a less common meaning to reflect the word's meaning in *The Paston Letters*.

CRITICAL VOCABULARY WORD	MOST COMMON MEANING	MEANING IN THE PASTON LETTERS
commend	to praise	to entrust
quell		
affairs		
bailiff		
writ		
ransack		

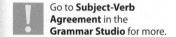

LANGUAGE CONVENTIONS:
Subject-Verb Agreement

Subject–verb agreement means that if the subject is singular, the verb is also singular, and if the subject is plural, the verb is also plural. Verbs in the present simple form, including auxiliary verbs, are plural or singular depending on their subject.

- Nouns in modifying phrases that come between the verb and the subject do not change whether the verb is singular or plural.
- Verbs with compound subjects might be singular or plural depending on the conjunction in the compound subject and the noun closest to the verb.
- Some pronouns always take a singular or plural verb, while for some it will depend on the **antecedent**.

Look at these examples:

> The (people) dying of the plague **are** mostly in the towns.

The verb *are* is plural because the subject is *people*, which is plural. The underlined phrase modifies *people*.

> We still have not heard from your (sisters) who **have** been away for a month.

> We have heard from the (husband) of one of them, who **has** gotten word that (neither) has become ill.

In the underlined clauses, the verb is either singular or plural depending on the antecedent of the pronoun *who*. The pronoun *neither* is always singular.

> People have tried many ways to avoid getting the plague, but *none is certain to work*.

> Half the people in the town are dead from the plague and *none are yet buried*.

In the underlined clauses, *none* is either singular or plural depending on its meaning. In the first sentence, *none* means "not one." In the second sentence, *none* means "not any."

> A few (people) have stayed in the town, but most **have** left for the country to try to avoid the plague.

> There is very little (food) left, as most **has** been eaten or destroyed by invading soldiers.

Some pronouns take a singular or plural verb depending on whether they are referring to a count or noncount noun. *People* is a count noun, so it takes the plural verb *have*. *Food* is a noncount noun, so it takes the singular verb *has*.

Practice and Apply Write four pairs of sentences, two using pronouns that always take a singular verb and two using pronouns that can take a singular or plural verb. The first sentence should contain the pronoun's antecedent.

Go to **Subject-Verb Agreement** in the **Grammar Studio** for more.

© Houghton Mifflin Harcourt Publishing Company

DIARY

from
MY SYRIAN DIARY

by **Marah**

pages 99–103

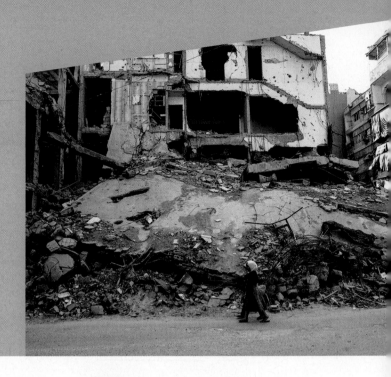

COMPARE PRIMARY SOURCES

Now that you've read selections from *The Paston Letters*, read selections from *My Syrian Diary* and explore how Marah's experiences in 21st-century Syria connect to the experiences of the Paston family in 15th-century England. As you read, think about how *My Syrian Diary* relates to your own experiences, the experiences of other teens, and events that you have seen or heard about in the news. After you are finished, you will complete a final project that involves comparing and contrasting both texts.

? ***ESSENTIAL QUESTION:***

What happens when a society unravels?

LETTERS

from
THE PASTON LETTERS

by the **Paston Family**

pages 85–91

My Syrian Diary

QUICK START

Imagine that your society has completely broken down. Schools are closed, and your parents are afraid to let you go outside to see friends. How would you spend your time? What would you do to make your voice heard? Discuss your responses with a classmate.

EVALUATE AUTHOR'S PURPOSE

Authors write for one or more **purposes**: to inform, to entertain, to persuade, to express opinions and feelings, or to provoke emotions in readers. As you read the excerpt from *My Syrian Diary*, make inferences about Marah's purpose or purposes for writing. Try also to determine her **message,** or the main idea she wants to convey.

Authors often use text structure to help them achieve their purposes. The diary excerpt you're about to read combines organizational patterns of chronological order, compare and contrast, and cause and effect. Consider how these structures contribute to the purpose and message of the text.

Another important aspect to keep in mind with relation to the author's purpose is the intended **audience,** or the people the author hopes will read the piece of writing.

As you read, evaluate how well Marah accomplishes her purposes, as well as how effectively she gets her message across and how well she reaches her intended audience.

GENRE ELEMENTS: DIARY

- personal accounts of day-to-day events
- written from the first-person point of view
- usually kept private
- occasionally published for writing quality or historical significance

CONNECT

When readers **connect** to a text, they relate the content to their own knowledge and experience. Published diaries allow readers to gain direct insight into a person's thoughts and feelings about events. As you read excerpts from *My Syrian Diary*, use these questions to help you make connections to the text:

QUESTIONS	ANSWERS
Does the author remind me of myself or of someone I know?	
What do I know about the time, place, events, or situations described in the text?	
How is the text similar to other works I have read?	

CRITICAL VOCABULARY

extract	sustenance	exorbitant	deprivation
superficial	mandatory		

Complete each sentence using one of the Critical Vocabulary words. Use what you know about word meanings, word parts, and context clues.

1. The _____ prices of the food on display discouraged hungry shoppers from entering the store.

2. After the hurricane, the governor ordered a _____ 9:00 p.m. curfew.

3. Having suffered through the _____ of war, the refugees were overwhelmed by the abundance of _____ they saw in other countries.

4. I could not _____ the splinter from the dog's paw even though the injury appeared to be _____.

LANGUAGE CONVENTIONS

Formal and Informal Language Writing may be divided into two categories: formal language and informal language. **Formal language** follows all rules of grammar and punctuation. It does not include such elements of "everyday" spoken English as slang words and contractions. **Informal language** may not always follow language rules and may include elements taken from spoken language. Pieces written in the first person often use informal language. As you read *My Syrian Diary*, watch for examples of informal language.

ANNOTATION MODEL

NOTICE & NOTE

As you read, mark up details that allow you to make inferences about the author's purpose. Note connections to your own experiences and ideas. In the model, you can see one reader's notes about the selection.

Every day, we open our eyes to our bleak reality: to the mortar shells that bring fear, death, disease and destruction. It has robbed us of our loved ones, destroyed our special places, hurt our close friends. Take my neighbor's daughter. At just seven years old, she has lost the ability to speak after a rocket landed close to our street.

The language of this passage sounds like it is addressed to people outside of Syria.

If my younger sister couldn't speak due to shock, I would be heartbroken and angry.

BACKGROUND

The Syrian civil war began in 2011 with clashes between the government and antigovernment demonstrators, who protested the lack of freedom under Syrian leader Bashar al-Assad. Rebel factions within the country fought Assad's regime and one another for control of the country. Assad's actions sparked worldwide outrage, prompting many countries to provide funding for the rebels, which escalated the conflict. By 2017, over 400,000 Syrians had died and 11 million were either displaced or had fled abroad. The author of this diary, who was 15 years old in 2011, lived in a besieged neighborhood until she fled Syria for Europe in 2016. She used the pen name Marah to protect her identity.

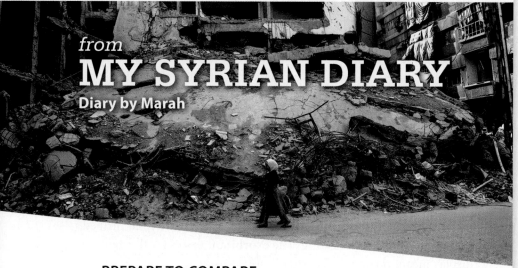

from
MY SYRIAN DIARY
Diary by Marah

PREPARE TO COMPARE

As you read, pay attention to Marah's descriptions of life under siege and how her experiences changed her. Note details that help identify Marah's message and motives for writing.

April 15, 2014

1   My city was once magnificent. In spring, it bloomed. We used to wake up to the sound of birds chirping and to the fragrant scent of flowers. Today, spring is here again. But what kind of spring is this? We now wake up to the sound of falling bombs.

2   Every day, we open our eyes to our bleak reality: to the mortar shells that bring fear, death, disease and destruction. It has robbed us of our loved ones, destroyed our special places, hurt our close friends. Take my neighbor's daughter. At just seven years old, she has lost the ability to speak after a rocket landed close to our street.

3   Today, my city's familiar face has been replaced by the suffering of its residents: the young boy who has been exposed to chemical weapons and is unable to receive treatment. An old man feels powerless after he lost his legs. A young man wears black sunglasses as if to hide a severely scarred face that frightens

Notice & Note

Use the side margins to notice and note signposts in the text.

CONTRASTS AND CONTRADICTIONS

Notice & Note: What contrasts does Marah describe in the opening paragraphs?

Analyze: Why does Marah choose to start her diary by describing such striking contrasts?

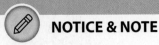

NOTICE & NOTE

extract
(ĭk-străkt´) *v.* to draw or pull out, often with great force or effort.

children. A young woman is now blind after doctors couldn't **extract** the shrapnel from her eyes because they lacked the proper medical equipment and medication.

4 The shelling has turned my city into a ghost town of decrepit buildings and charred trees. Even our animals weren't spared. You often see a limping dog, a dead cat or a bird mourning its destroyed nest.

5 The bombings have not only altered my city's face, but also fundamentally changed its people.

6 During the hardest times, when bombs fell from the sky, we dreamed of bread. We rationed our food intake to one meal a day, depending on whatever greens we could find for **sustenance**.

sustenance
(sŭs´tə-nəns) *n.* something, especially food, that sustains life or health.

7 I remember well the day cattle food, or fodder, was smuggled into the city. We milled the animal feed to make dough. It didn't take us long to get used to the bad taste and weird texture of our new "bread." It brought us a semblance of happiness with the little olives, juice or yogurt—Syrian food staples—that we had. Our only concern was to eat. One can never get used to sleeping on an empty stomach.

8 Our collective will to eat meant we started getting creative with the cattle feed. We cooked it as if we were cooking rice or wheat. We became so accustomed to it that we almost forgot what chicken, meat and fruit looked like.

9 One of the hardest days was when we heard that a car carrying fruit and candy had entered the city. At first, we were beyond thrilled, but our happiness was fleeting. The **exorbitant** prices for the items on display meant no one could actually afford them.

exorbitant
(ĭg-zôr´bĭ-tənt) *adj.* beyond what is reasonable or customary, especially in cost or price.

10 That day, a young boy with holes in his shoes squeezed his mother's hand as they passed by the fruit car. He begged her for an apple. Holding back her tears, she promised to make him "fodder cake" when they got home. Similarly, a father ignored the car carrying the goods and picked up the pace as he dragged his daughter, who was demanding a banana or an orange. Who would believe that the availability of fruit would be worse than the lack of it? Is it not a child's right to have an apple, a banana or a small piece of candy?

EVALUATE AUTHOR'S PURPOSE

Annotate: A rhetorical question is a question that does not require a reply. Authors often use rhetorical questions to emphasize a point. Mark the rhetorical questions in paragraph 10.

Evaluate: How does the author's use of rhetorical questions help evoke a response from the reader?

11 In this world, we have been stripped of our rights, starting with food. We try to entertain ourselves to forget our hunger, but there is no power and it is difficult to be without electricity after our lives once depended on it. I feel as if I'm living in the Stone Age. We wash our laundry by hand and burn wood to keep warm. In this new world, everything we know is gone. We miss the things we took for granted, like TVs and laptops.

12 Nowadays, the children refuse to stay indoors. My younger brother gets bored quickly, so my mother keeps him busy by delegating him the task of breaking firewood. His small hands have become thick and calloused. He executes his chore with anger and an air of rebellion. He now lives with a prevailing sense of **deprivation**. His feelings, along with mine, have altered without our knowledge or will.

deprivation
(dĕp´rə-vā´shən) *n.* the condition of being deprived; lacking the basic necessities or comforts of life.

13   I find myself forming a grudge against people who live outside my city. I wonder, why did this happen to us? What fault have we committed to live this bitter reality? Why were our childhoods stolen?

April 23, 2014

14   I begin my article by asking for help. I feel like I am lost in the middle of a rough sea. I don't know where these crushing waves might take me—to a safe place or to forgetfulness and loss?

15   I am very concerned about my education. It's my greatest priority. I grew up in a family that appreciated education. They enrolled me in a kindergarten that I will never forget. It was expensive, but my parents did not mind because all they cared about was to provide us with the best education from the very beginning.

16   I excelled in that kindergarten and went straight to second grade. My parents and grandparents were proud of me and reinforced my self-confidence. Middle school was fantastic. I drifted with my friends, and thanks to my always-conscious mom, who was my savior during that critical preteen stage, I was able to obtain my middle school diploma.

17   I loved my school immensely and I loved my teachers—especially my Arabic teacher. I adored the subject. School, for me, was like a playground or a picnic that I enjoyed with my friends. My parents never hesitated to provide for my school; their goal was that I obtain the best education, refine my personality and arm myself with a degree that would protect me from misfortune.

18   Then high school took me from childhood to the beginning of maturity and awareness. As the years went by, my fondness for my friends and my teachers had grown. I would see my friends during vacations and share all my secrets with them. My friend Rahaf was the closest to me. After she lost her mother, I watched her way of thinking change. She became like a mother to her little siblings.

19   One year after the beginning of the revolution, the conditions in my city worsened and the missiles intensified. My father decided that we should move out to a safer place. His only concern was to protect his family. We moved to a completely new area and I enrolled in the local school, which was a bad fit. But we had no other option. I formed some **superficial** friendships, and during one semester, I did not even manage to open a book. I thought constantly about my old friends and teachers, but staying in this new area was **mandatory**.

20   Finally, the condition deteriorated in the area where we resettled, which made my dad decide to return to our old city again. My sister and I were very happy that we were going home. But when we returned to our city, we were shocked by the amount of destruction. The schools were all destroyed, and after a while they turned basements into classrooms so we would be protected from the missiles.

21   These new schools were dark with dim lights similar to candles, and were smelly and had very poor ventilation. They were hardly real

CONNECT

Annotate: In paragraphs 15–17, circle details that show how the education system in Syria before the war was different from your own experience. Underline details that show how it was the same.

Infer: Why might the author describe her education as her "greatest priority" despite the violence all around her?

superficial
(sōō′pər-fĭsh′əl) *adj.* apparent rather than actual or substantial; shallow.

mandatory
(măn′də-tôr′ē) *adj.* required or commanded by authority; obligatory.

"schools." They felt more like ponds full of diseases. My father refused to send us to such dungeons, but my mom insisted that we should go. A new phase of concern started for them, right there. Do we invest time in such schools that don't even have accreditation?

22   Now I am trying to prepare for Syria's standardized high school tests, but I don't know whether I will pass or whether my score will be officially recognized. Will I take the tests in my city or somewhere else? Will my mom agree to let me go? So many questions stop me from focusing on my studies. My mom refuses to send me out to any other neighborhood because she fears checkpoints and the risks that a young lady like me might face. I've come to hate the fact that I am a girl.

EVALUATE AUTHOR'S PURPOSE

Annotate: In paragraphs 23–25, mark places where the author directly addresses the reader.

Cause/Effect: What effect does the author hope to have on her readers?

23   Can you imagine that my mom, the one who always believed in the importance of education and planted that belief in me, has suddenly changed? Her excuse comes down to one sentence: "I worry for you." I will never understand that fear or accept what she says. My dream had been to enroll in university, choose a major I like and then start my career. Can I still do that? I don't know.

24   What happened? My mom used to push me forward. I want to study. I desire to live. I desire what's beautiful. I miss my teachers and my friends. They have all left the city. I miss seeing the handsome boys gathering in front of my school. When I was little I liked dreaming big, but now my dreams are fading away. My dreams are limited by the checkpoints. Isn't there someone to help my voice be heard?

25   Everyone is busy with the war, and it seems like no one cares. We don't know how this will end or how it will affect us. I want life, but not this troubled and confusing life that I live now. I want to complete my studies. I don't want to be a neglected period on the margin. I do not want to lose my dreams. Help!

May 1, 2014

26   In my city, guys and girls have undergone a radical change. Everything has changed: their opinions, their aspirations, the way they talk, their expressions and even the way they look.

27   Before, we used to have great conversations. We loved music from the West as well as local music, and we would race to listen to the newest albums. We loved movies of all kinds and in all languages, especially the comedies. We were interested in fashion and design.

28   We were attracted to anything that was new. We lived a wonderful life. We made adolescent mistakes.

29   Now we have turned into old women. Our conversations are all about our daily suffering. Our conversations are now about food, electricity, water and firewood. There is no cell phone coverage and no television. We are deprived of our teenage pastimes.

30   Shopping was one of my favorite activities. We used to go window shopping after school. We used to get excited about a colorful purse

or shiny shoes. Now we get that excited about a rare treat, a dessert—even just fruit. Can you believe it?! We never expected this to happen!

31   Even the boys have changed. We used to see them around school, carrying flowers and wrapped presents, wearing their nicest clothes. Their eyes were filled with love, happiness and hope. But now, the street around the school is empty because all the guys are out fighting on the front lines. When we happen to see them, they usually have shaggy hair and dusty shoes, carrying rifles instead of roses. If you look at their faces, all you see is worry and frustration. Because of our horrible reality, they have lost their hope for the future.

32   We have been deprived of fully living this period of our lives. Everything has turned upside down. Everyone is depressed. Sometimes we laugh and cry at the same moment. How did this damned war do this to us?

33   I feel sorry for myself and for all my fellow Syrian youth. I hope that the current situation changes so that our souls and dreams might awaken. I'm afraid we will regret living this period without our rites of passage, not living youth as it is meant to be lived. Will the war impact us for the rest of our lives? How will we make up for what we've lost? Everything is unknown.

LANGUAGE CONVENTIONS
Annotate: Mark examples of informal writing in paragraphs 30–33.

Interpret: Why do you think Marah uses an informal writing style?

CHECK YOUR UNDERSTANDING

Answer these questions before moving on to the **Analyze the Text** section on the following page.

1 Which of the following is true?

  A Marah's mother loses faith in education as a result of the war.

  B Marah resents the war because it has forced her to grow up quickly.

  C Marah's life improves after her father moves the family back to their old neighborhood.

  D Marah hates being a girl because girls cannot fight in the war.

2 Which question best expresses Marah's uncertainty about the future?

  F *Why were our childhoods stolen?*

  G *Isn't there someone to help my voice be heard?*

  H *How did this damned war do this to us?*

  J *How will we make up for what we've lost?*

3 Why does Marah's mother say, *I worry for you*?

  A She knows that the quality of Marah's education is suffering.

  B She wishes that Marah could have a normal teenage life.

  C She is concerned about Marah's physical safety in the city.

  D She is afraid that Marah will give up her hopes and dreams.

RESPOND

ANALYZE THE TEXT

Support your responses with evidence from the text. 📓 NOTEBOOK

1. **Connect** Review paragraph 11. How was life in Syria before the war similar to or different from your own life? If your own life changed like the author's life did, how do you think you would feel and react?

2. **Infer** How did the priorities of Marah's parents change as a result of the war? How might Marah's relationships with her parents have been affected by these changes?

3. **Evaluate** Review paragraphs 4–8. What organizational pattern or text structure does Marah use in this part of the diary? Is this text structure used effectively to achieve the author's purpose? Why or why not?

4. **Analyze** Marah is living in the middle of a civil war, but she does not discuss politics or take a side in her diary entries. Why might she have chosen to omit political references? What does this decision tell you about her purpose for writing?

5. **Notice & Note** Marah begins her diary by giving contrasting descriptions of her city before and after the start of the war. How is contrast used throughout the rest of the diary? What does Marah achieve through the use of contrast?

RESEARCH

RESEARCH TIP
When you research current or recent events, you are likely to find large quantities of information provided by news media. Evaluate news sources critically and remember to check the publication date. Ask yourself: Is this a well-known and credible news source? Is the information presented obviously biased? Is this the most up-to-date information, or is it possible that other important developments have occurred since it was published?

The Syrian civil war grew out of a wider movement of pro-democracy protests known as the Arab Spring that affected many countries in North Africa and the Middle East. Conduct research to explore the outcomes of the Arab Spring protests in countries other than Syria.

COUNTRY	KEY RESULTS OF ARAB SPRING MOVEMENT

Extend The Arab Spring protests and revolutions were covered heavily in the news and drew significant international attention. Explain why other nations were so interested in the events and outcomes of the Arab Spring. What does their interest tell you about the nature of international politics?

© Houghton Mifflin Harcourt Publishing Company

CREATE AND DISCUSS

Write a Compare-and-Contrast Essay Write a three- or four-paragraph essay in which you compare and contrast *My Syrian Diary* with another diary you have read. If you have not read another diary, select another nonfiction personal narrative. Consider reviewing your notes and annotations in the text before you begin.

❏ Introduce the topic of your essay by giving a brief summary or background of *My Syrian Diary* and the other diary.

❏ Then, explain similarities and differences between the two diaries. Include details about the author's purpose(s) and the diaries' main messages to support your ideas.

❏ In your final paragraph, state your conclusion about the two diaries.

Share and Discuss Connections In a small group, discuss your conclusions about the diaries you analyzed. Consider how writing in the diary form affects the way authors achieve their purposes, convey their messages, and reach their audiences.

❏ Review the author's purpose(s) for writing and the message of *My Syrian Diary*.

❏ Discuss the other diaries that group members chose to compare. Make sure all group members have time to briefly describe the other diaries they chose and the main conclusions they reached in their analyses.

❏ Finally, end your discussion by identifying conclusions that group members had in common and summarizing the group's findings.

 Go to **Writing Informative Texts** in the **Writing Studio** for help with organizing ideas.

 Go to **Participating in Collaborative Discussions** in the **Speaking and Listening Studio** for help with group discussion.

RESPOND TO THE ESSENTIAL QUESTION

? What happens when a society unravels?

Gather Information Review your annotations and notes on *My Syrian Diary*. Then add relevant details to your Response Log. As you decide which information to include, think about:

- how the writer contrasts past and present
- which parts of society the writer chooses to describe
- the way the writer uses small details to provide evidence for a broader message

ACADEMIC VOCABULARY

As you write and discuss what you learned about *My Syrian Diary*, be sure to use the Academic Vocabulary words. Check off each of the words that you use.

❏ **collapse**
❏ **displace**
❏ **military**
❏ **violate**
❏ **visual**

RESPOND

WORD BANK

extract
sustenance
exorbitant
deprivation
superficial
mandatory

CRITICAL VOCABULARY

Practice and Apply Determine which vocabulary word best relates to each group of words. Then write a sentence using each vocabulary word.

1. food, comfort, life

2. surface, shallow, insubstantial

3. unreasonable, expensive, high

4. remove, tug, pry

5. required, important, necessary

6. needy, without, underprivileged

Go to **Latin Roots** in the **Vocabulary Studio** for more.

VOCABULARY STRATEGY:
Latin Roots

While the English language includes words and word parts that come from many different languages, one of the root languages you will encounter most often in English is Latin. Knowing the meanings of common Latin prefixes, roots, and suffixes can help you determine the definitions of unfamiliar words.

For example, consider the word *extract*. The word *extract* can be broken down into two main parts, the prefix *ex-* and the root *tract*. Both come from Latin. *Ex-* means "out of" or "away from." *Tract* means "to draw" or "pull." When they are put together, you get the word *extract*, which means "to draw or pull out."

Practice and Apply Examine the list of Latin word parts provided below. Use the list to fill out the chart. Then discuss with a partner how the combined definition you get from using word parts is related to the dictionary definition.

super-: above or on top of
orbit: path or track
-ant: action or condition

-ation: condition or state
-ial: related to or characterized by
-ory: related to or characterized by

WORD	PREFIXES, ROOTS, AND SUFFIXES	COMBINED DEFINITION	DICTIONARY DEFINITION
exorbitant			
	deprive, -ation		
superficial			
	mandate, -ory		

LANGUAGE CONVENTIONS:
Formal and Informal Language

Writing that uses **formal language,** also known as Standard English, follows all of the accepted rules of grammar and punctuation of the English language. Formal language is usually appropriate for academic or professional writing. Essays, news reports, and textbooks are examples of texts that tend to use formal language. Many—but not all—formal writing pieces are written from a third-person perspective.

Writing that uses **informal language** may not always follow language rules and has a more relaxed and conversational tone. Local expressions, slang words, contractions, and sentence fragments that most people use in everyday speech are common in informal writing. Because informal language includes so many elements of spoken English, it is common for pieces written from the first-person perspective to use informal language. Many types of narratives, such as novels, diaries, and personal narratives, use informal language. Informal language is also commonly used for such written communication between individuals as letters and personal (nonprofessional) emails and text messages.

This sentence from *My Syrian Diary* uses informal language:

> **In my city, guys and girls have undergone a radical change.**

Marah writes the sentence the way she would say it if she were having a conversation. She uses the slang term "guys" to refer to her male peers.

If Marah had used more formal language to write her diary, the sentence might look like this:

> **In my city, the young men and women have undergone a radical change.**

If the information had been included in an official report instead of a personal diary, it might sound even more formal:

> **Young Syrian men and women have undergone radical changes as a result of the ongoing war.**

Practice and Apply Select a paragraph or paragraphs from *My Syrian Diary* in which Marah describes her city or an event that took place in her city using informal language. Rewrite the passage using Standard English in the formal style of a news report.

Go to **Writing Informative Texts: Formal Style** for more help.

Collaborate & Compare

COMPARE PRIMARY SOURCES

from
THE PASTON LETTERS
Letters by the Paston Family

from
MY SYRIAN DIARY
Diary by Marah

Both *The Paston Letters* and *My Syrian Diary* are primary sources that provide firsthand accounts of the authors' experiences. However, they were not written for the same reason. An **author's purpose** is his or her reason for writing. The author may or may not state the purpose directly, depending on the type of document or writing style. If the author does not state his or her purpose, then you must infer it based on details in the text.

As you review the primary sources for hints about the author's purpose, consider the following:

- **Context:** Where, when, and under what circumstances was the text produced?
- **Audience:** Who did the author intend for his or her readers to be?
- **Content:** What main ideas, themes, and messages does the author convey?

In a small group, complete the chart with details from both primary sources.

	THE PASTON LETTERS	MY SYRIAN DIARY
Context		
Audience		
Content		

ANALYZE THE TEXTS

Discuss these questions in your group.

1. **Compare** With your group, review the contexts you cited in your chart. In what ways are the contexts of the sources similar? In what ways are they different?

2. **Analyze** The two sources have very different audiences. Discuss how the audience of each source affects the type of content the author included. Cite textual evidence in your discussion.

3. **Evaluate** The authors of the sources address their audiences using text structures that are related but not identical: letters and diary entries. Discuss the effectiveness of the authors' choices. Is one structure more effective than the other? Explain your reasoning.

4. **Critique** Could either the authors of *The Paston Letters* or the author of *My Syrian Diary* have used a different or more effective writing structure to convey their content and accomplish their purpose? Explain why or why not.

COLLABORATE AND PRESENT

Now your group can continue exploring the ideas in these texts by identifying and comparing the authors' purpose. Follow these steps:

Go to **Participating in Collaborative Discussions** in the **Speaking and Listening Studio** for more help.

1. **Decide on the most important details** With your group, review your chart to identify the details that tell you the most about the authors' purposes.

2. **Determine the authors' purposes** Determine the author's purpose for each primary source. Remember, an author may have multiple reasons for writing. Those reasons may all contribute to one unified purpose, or the author may have multiple purposes. As a group, create at least one statement of purpose for each source.

3. **Compare author's purpose** With your group, discuss whether the authors' purposes are similar or different, and the reasons why these similarities and/or differences might exist or not exist. Use a chart to keep track of the ideas your group generates.

	SIMILAR	DIFFERENT
How?		
Why?		

4. **Present to the class** As a group, prepare a presentation of your ideas. Be sure to include clear statements of the author's purpose for each source and discuss how the context, audience, and content evidence support your conclusions. You may choose to use charts or other visuals to present your ideas to the class.

POEM
THE WANDERER

by **Anonymous**
translated by **Burton Raffel**

pages 113–117

COMPARE THEMES

As you read, notice the key details and memorable images that express each poem's theme or message about loneliness. Then think about how the themes relate to each other. After you read both poems, you will collaborate with a small group on a final project.

ESSENTIAL QUESTION:

Can we control our fate?

POEM
LONELINESS

by **Fanny Howe**

pages 118–121

QUICK START

How do you cope when you feel lonely? On the chart below, write two or three things that you can depend on to get you through an emotional slump. Explain how these things help you.

WHAT HELPS	HOW IT HELPS

ANALYZE TONE

Tone is the attitude that the writer shows toward his subject or audience. You can detect the poet's attitude just as you would interpret the attitude of someone speaking to you. The tone of a poem does not necessarily stay the same throughout the work—the author can change it at any time. You can describe the poet's tone using any adjectives that accurately convey attitude.

Some elements in a poem that help identify tone are:

- imagery
- sound devices
- the poet's word choices
- the speaker's feelings or thoughts

Mark up the selection with notes about tone or use a chart like this one:

	"THE WANDERER"	"LONELINESS"
Imagery	"frost-cold foam" and "frozen waves" help develop a gloomy tone.	
Sound devices		
Word choices		
Speaker's feelings and thoughts		

As you analyze "The Wanderer" and "Loneliness," think about how the authors use the elements of lyric poetry to convey tone in their works.

GENRE ELEMENTS: LYRIC POEM

- expresses strong feelings or thoughts
- has a musical quality
- deals with intense emotions surrounding events like death, love, or loss
- includes such forms as ode, elegy, and sonnet

MONITOR COMPREHENSION

Monitoring comprehension involves determining whether you understand what you are reading. If you have difficulty understanding these poems, you can use different techniques to enhance your comprehension. Here are some helpful strategies:

- **Visualize** Read the text aloud and create pictures in your mind based on images in the text.

- **Generate questions** Ask yourself factual questions that can be answered simply and directly from the text (such as *who, what, when, where, why,* or *how*), as well as questions whose answers require gathering information from different parts of the text to make inferences or evaluations.

- **Reread confusing passages** Slow your pace as you read confusing passages a second time. You might also try reading the passages aloud if you won't disturb those around you. If there are words you don't understand, use a dictionary to find synonyms that may fit.

- **Annotate** Mark sections of the text that are meaningful and make notes in the margins in your own words.

- **Paraphrase** Restate the text in your own words. Simplify the text and be sure to maintain the order and meaning of the original.

ANNOTATION MODEL

NOTICE & NOTE

As you read, identify the author's tone and note whether it changes from passage to passage or stays consistent throughout the work. Use the techniques discussed to monitor your comprehension of the poetry. In the model, you can see one reader's notes about lines 1–11 of "The Wanderer."

> This lonely traveler longs for grace,
> for the mercy of God; grief hangs on
> His heart and follows the frost-cold foam
> He cuts in the sea, sailing endlessly,
> Aimlessly, in exile. Fate has opened
> A single port: memory. He sees
> His kinsmen slaughtered again, and cries:
> "I've drunk too many lonely dawns,
> Grey with mourning. Once there were men
> To whom my heart could hurry, hot
> With open longing. They're long since dead.

The alliteration emphasizes words that express a grim attitude.

I am picturing a ship adrift in a frozen sea: what a sad image!

BACKGROUND

"The Wanderer" is an Old English poem found in The Exeter Book, *the largest manuscript collection of Old English poetry that has survived. Before being transcribed sometime in the tenth century, the poem was probably passed down orally. Nothing is known about the poem's author. Like other poems in* The Exeter Book, *"The Wanderer" reflects the hardship and uncertainty of life in Anglo-Saxon times. Most of the poem is spoken by an Anglo-Saxon warrior who wanders as an exile after losing his lord and companions in battle.*

THE WANDERER

Poem by Anonymous
translated by Burton Raffel

PREPARE TO COMPARE

As you read, think about how the speaker is feeling and how the tone is conveyed by the sound devices used. Try to understand and verbalize the main ideas in the poem.

> This lonely traveler longs for grace,
> For the mercy of God; grief hangs on
> His heart and follows the frost-cold foam
> He cuts in the sea, sailing endlessly,
> 5 Aimlessly, in exile. Fate has opened
> A single port: memory. He sees
> His kinsmen slaughtered again, and cries:
> "I've drunk too many lonely dawns,
> Grey with mourning. Once there were men
> 10 To whom my heart could hurry, hot
> With open longing. They're long since dead.
> My heart has closed on itself, quietly
> Learning that silence is noble and sorrow
> Nothing that speech can cure. Sadness

Notice & Note

Use the side margins to notice and note signposts in the text.

ANALYZE TONE
Annotate: Mark words that give clues about the speaker's feelings in lines 8–14.

Analyze: What do the author's word choices make you think about?

NOTICE & NOTE

15 Has never driven sadness off;
Fate blows hardest on a bleeding heart.
So those who thirst for glory smother
Secret weakness and longing, neither
Weep nor sigh nor listen to the sickness
20 In their souls. So I, lost and homeless,
Forced to flee the darkness that fell
On the earth and my lord.
                                    Leaving everything,
Weary with winter I wandered out
On the frozen waves, hoping to find
25 A place, a people, a lord to replace
My lost ones. No one knew me, now,
No one offered comfort, allowed
Me feasting or joy. How cruel a journey
I've traveled, sharing my bread with sorrow
30 Alone, an exile in every land,
Could only be told by telling my footsteps.
For who can hear: "friendless and poor,"
And know what I've known since the long cheerful nights
When, young and yearning, with my lord I yet feasted
35 Most welcome of all. That warmth is dead.
He only knows who needs his lord
As I do, eager for long-missing aid;
He only knows who never sleeps
Without the deepest dreams of longing.
40 Sometimes it seems I see my lord,
Kiss and embrace him, bend my hands
And head to his knee, kneeling as though
He still sat enthroned, ruling his thanes.
And I open my eyes, embracing the air,
45 And see the brown sea-billows heave,
See the sea-birds bathe, spreading
Their white-feathered wings, watch the frost
And the hail and the snow. And heavy in heart
I long for my lord, alone and unloved.
50 Sometimes it seems I see my kin
And greet them gladly, give them welcome,

MONITOR COMPREHENSION

Annotate: Mark the phrases in lines 22–28 that answer the question: What has the speaker lost?

Infer: What can you infer has happened to the speaker? What questions do you have about him?

31 telling: counting.

43 thanes (thānz): followers of a lord.

The best of friends. They fade away,
Swimming soundlessly out of sight,
Leaving nothing.
                      How loathsome become
55 The frozen waves to a weary heart.
    In this brief world I cannot wonder
That my mind is set on melancholy,
Because I never forget the fate
Of men, robbed of their riches, suddenly
60 Looted by death—the doom of earth,
Sent to us all by every rising
Sun. Wisdom is slow, and comes
But late. He who has it is patient;
He cannot be hasty to hate or speak,
65 He must be bold and yet not blind,
Nor ever too craven, complacent, or covetous,
Nor ready to gloat before he wins glory.
The man's a fool who flings his boasts
Hotly to the heavens, heeding his spleen
70 And not the better boldness of knowledge.
What knowing man knows not the ghostly,
Waste-like end of worldly wealth:
See, already the wreckage is there,
The wind-swept walls stand far and wide,
75 The storm-beaten blocks besmeared with frost,
The mead-halls crumbled, the monarchs thrown down
And stripped of their pleasures. The proudest of warriors
Now lie by the wall: some of them war
Destroyed; some the monstrous sea-bird
80 Bore over the ocean; to some the old wolf
Dealt out death; and for some dejected
Followers fashioned an earth-cave coffin.
Thus the Maker of men lays waste
This earth, crushing our callow mirth.
85 And the work of old giants stands withered and still."

MONITOR COMPREHENSION

Annotate: Mark unfamiliar words in lines 62–67 where the actions of a wise person are described. Look up the words in a dictionary.

Paraphrase: Restate lines 62–67 in your own words.

69 spleen: bad temper. The spleen is a body organ that was formerly thought to be the seat of strong emotions.

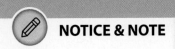

NOTICE & NOTE

He who these ruins rightly sees,
And deeply considers this dark twisted life,
Who sagely remembers the endless slaughters
Of a bloody past, is bound to proclaim:
90   "Where is the war-steed? Where is the warrior?
            Where is his war-lord?
Where now the feasting-places? Where now the mead-hall
      pleasures?
Alas, bright cup! Alas, brave knight!
Alas, you glorious princes! All gone,
Lost in the night, as you never had lived.
95 And all that survives you a serpentine wall,
Wondrously high, worked in strange ways.
Mighty spears have slain these men,
Greedy weapons have framed their fate.
        These rocky slopes are beaten by storms,
100 This earth pinned down by driving snow,
By the horror of winter, smothering warmth
In the shadows of night. And the north angrily
Hurls its hailstorms at our helpless heads.
Everything earthly is evilly born,
105 Firmly clutched by a fickle Fate.
        Fortune vanishes, friendship vanishes,
Man is fleeting, woman is fleeting,
And all this earth rolls into emptiness."

        So says the sage in his heart, sitting alone with His
            thought.
110 It's good to guard your faith, nor let your grief come forth
Until it cannot call for help, nor help but heed
The path you've placed before it. It's good to find your grace
In God, the heavenly rock where rests our every hope.

95 serpentine: (sûr´pən-tēn´) winding or twisting, like a snake.

ANALYZE TONE

Annotate: Mark the alliterative words in lines 110–113.

Analyze: How does this phrasing affect the tone of the poem?

116   Unit 1

CHECK YOUR UNDERSTANDING

Answer these questions about "The Wanderer" before moving on to the next selection.

1 The imagery in the poem suggests the setting is —

   A warm and sandy

   B dry and parched

   C cold and wet

   D hot and lush

2 Which of the following images from the poem sets a hopeful tone?

   F *No one knew me, now, / No one offered comfort*

   G *It's good to find your grace / In God, the heavenly rock*

   H *Weary with winter I wandered out / On the frozen waves*

   J *Alas, you glorious princes! All gone, / Lost in the night*

3 One important theme in this poem is —

   A sea journeys cause grief

   B you can't gain wisdom unless you suffer

   C the wise course is to avoid war

   D grief isolates people emotionally

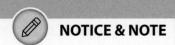
BACKGROUND

Fanny Howe *(1940–) grew up in Cambridge, Massachusetts, part of an artistic and intellectual family. As a girl, she was very close to her father, who taught at Harvard Law School; his influence can be seen in her political and social activism. Howe is an award-winning author of more than 20 books of poetry, fiction, essays, and children's literature. Her poetry is known for its formal experimentation and exploration of religious ideas. Howe has taught literature and fiction writing at various institutions, including Tufts University, Yale University, and the Lannan Center for Poetics and Social Practice at Georgetown University. She now lives back in Cambridge.*

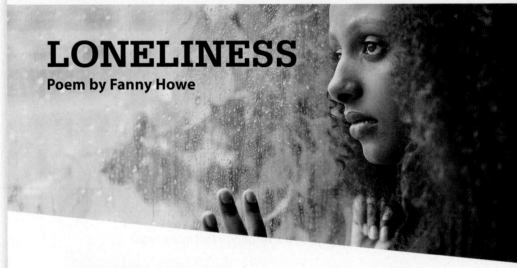

LONELINESS
Poem by Fanny Howe

PREPARE TO COMPARE

As you read, look for details that show the author's tone and how this poem approaches the subject of loneliness.

Loneliness is not an accident or a choice.
It's an uninvited and uncreated companion.
It slips in beside you when you are not aware that a
choice you are making will have consequences.
5 It does you no good even though it's like one of the
elements in the world that you cannot exist without.
It takes your hand and walks with you. It lies down
with you. It sits beside you. It's as dark as a shadow
but it has substance that is familiar.
10 It swims with you and swings around on stools.
It boards the ferry and leans on the motel desk.

Nothing great happens as a result of loneliness.
Your character flaws remain in place. You still stop in
with friends and have wonderful hours among them,
15 but you must run as soon as you hear it calling.

Notice & Note

Use the side margins to notice and note signposts in the text.

MONITOR COMPREHENSION

Annotate: Personification is the attribution of human qualities to an object, animal, or idea. Mark words and phrases in lines 1–11 that exemplify personification.

Analyze: What are some of the comparisons the author makes?

It does call. And you climb the stairs obediently,
pushing aside books and notes to let it know that you
have returned to it, all is well.
If you don't answer its call, you sense that it will sink
20 towards a deep gravity and adopt a limp.

From loneliness you learn very little. It pulls you
back, it pulls you down.

It's the manifestation of a vow never made but kept:
I will go home now and forever in solitude.

25 And after that loneliness will accompany you to
every airport, train station, bus depot, café, cinema,
and onto airplanes and into cars, strange rooms and
offices, classrooms and libraries, and it will hang near
your hand like a habit.
30 But it isn't a habit and no one can see it.

ANALYZE TONE
Annotate: Mark words in lines
21-24 that help set the poem's
tone.

Analyze: Is the speaker hopeful
about ending her loneliness?
Explain.

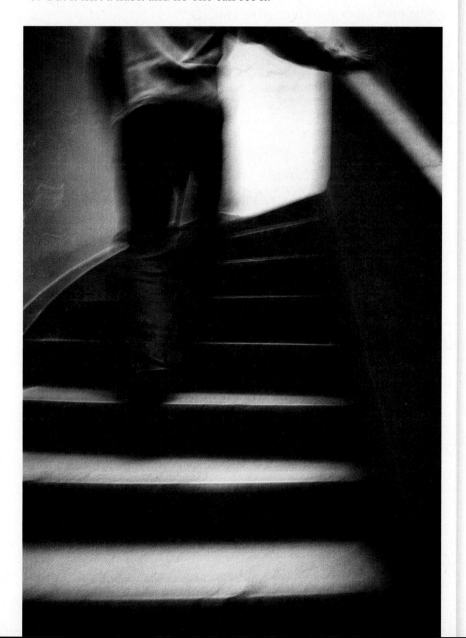

It's your obligation, and your companion warms itself
against you.
You are faithful to it because it was the only vow you
made finally, when it was unnecessary.

35 If you figured out why you chose it, years later, would
you ask it to go?
How would you replace it?

No, saying good-bye would be too embarrassing.
Why?
40 First you might cry.
Because shame and loneliness are almost one.
Shame at existing in the first place. Shame at being
visible, taking up space, breathing some of the sky,
sleeping in a whole bed, asking for a share.

45 Loneliness feels so much like shame, it always seems
to need a little more time on its own.

**MONITOR
COMPREHENSION**

Annotate: Reread lines 38–46.
Mark any ideas or details that
you find confusing.

Draw Conclusions: What
connections do you see
between loneliness and shame?
How do these connections help
you understand this passage?

© Houghton Mifflin Harcourt Publishing Company

CHECK YOUR UNDERSTANDING

Answer these questions about "Loneliness" before moving on to the **Analyze the Texts** section on the following page.

1 The words *You will stop in / with friends and have wonderful hours among them* emphasizes that —

   A you don't have to be alone to be lonely

   B loneliness can be a good friend

   C if you have friends, you won't be lonely

   D you can spend quality time alone

2 In "Loneliness," the feeling named in the title is likened to a —

   F habit

   G choice

   H accident

   J companion

3 The speaker feels like loneliness is —

   A unavoidable in life

   B something to be ashamed of

   C a result of the decisions we make

   D an inherited emotional disability

ANALYZE THE TEXTS

Support your responses with evidence from the text. 　NOTEBOOK

1. **Infer** What can you infer about Anglo-Saxon society from reading lines 22–39 of "The Wanderer"? What questions do you have about the Anglo-Saxons?

2. **Interpret** Reread lines 86–94 of "The Wanderer." How did the speaker incur his loss and become a lonely wanderer?

3. **Analyze** Reread lines 97–103 of "The Wanderer." How does the use of personification help develop the tone in this part of the poem?

4. **Analyze** Reread lines 31–37 of "Loneliness." What is the author's tone in this passage, and how do her word choices convey this tone?

5. **Interpret** Reread lines 19–22 of "Loneliness." How do you visualize and interpret these lines?

RESEARCH

RESEARCH TIP

It is especially important to use verifiable and reliable sources when researching online for help with sensitive issues. For guidance on mental and emotional health issues, sources with the extensions .org and .edu are preferable.

People can feel emotionally isolated for many reasons, including major illness or the loss of a loved one. Do an online search to complete the chart below. Look for details about practical ways to help cope with sadness and maintain a measure of control over one's own fate. Expand the chart if you find other helpful measures in your research.

WHAT CAN YOU DO ABOUT GRIEF?	HOW DOES THIS APPROACH HELP?
Start a grief support group.	
Express your feelings in writing or artwork.	
Seek professional help.	

Extend Your family physician or health-care professional is a good resource for information about dealing with loss and grief. You may be able to visit his or her office and request brochures on this and related subjects.

CREATE AND DISCUSS

Create an Imagery Board With a group, create an imagery board to explore your interpretation of key passages in the poems.

- ❏ With the group, choose three passages from the poems that can be visualized and make a statement about a main idea of the poem.
- ❏ Create a collage from magazine clippings, photos, or your own drawings to represent each passage.
- ❏ Display your collages on a poster board. Under each collage, add the text of the passage it represents.
- ❏ Explain to the class how the images you chose help illustrate the tone of the passages you selected.

Discuss the Poems Have a group discussion on how thoughts and feelings are expressed in medieval literature and in contemporary literature.

- ❏ Think about the differences and similarities in the authors' situations that affect how each presents his or her views.
- ❏ Share your ideas with the group. Support your ideas with details from the poems.
- ❏ As a group, draw a conclusion on how each writer feels about loneliness.

Go to **Participating in a Collaborative Discussion** in the **Speaking and Listening Studio** for help.

RESPOND TO THE ESSENTIAL QUESTION

? Can we control our fate?

Gather Information Review your annotations and notes on "The Wanderer" and "Loneliness." Then add relevant details to your Response Log. As you decide which information to include, think about:

- whether being lonely is an unavoidable part of life
- the effectiveness of literary devices to express the authors' thoughts
- how each speaker responds to his or her loneliness

UNIT 1 RESPONSE LOG

? Essential Question	Details from Texts
What makes someone a hero?	
What is true chivalry?	
Can we control our fate?	
What happens when a society unravels?	

ACADEMIC VOCABULARY

As you write and discuss what you learned from the poems, be sure to use the Academic Vocabulary words. Check off each of the words that you use.

- ❏ **collapse**
- ❏ **displace**
- ❏ **military**
- ❏ **violate**
- ❏ **visual**

THE WANDERER
Poem by Anonymous

LONELINESS
Poem by Fanny Howe

Collaborate & Compare

COMPARE THEMES

Both "The Wanderer" and "Loneliness" express strong thoughts and feelings about loneliness. Even though the poems are about a similar topic, they may express a different theme. A poem's theme is the message about life that it expresses. When you ask yourself, "What significant idea is the poem expressing?" you are asking about the theme.

Often the reader has to infer the theme based on the details presented in the poem. As you review the poems for details that give clues to the theme, consider:

❏ **Key statements** made by the speaker or characters

❏ **Significant events** that occur in the poem

❏ **Memorable images** that describe people or the setting

With your group, complete this chart with details from both poems.

	"THE WANDERER"	"LONELINESS"
Key Statements		
Significant Events		
Memorable Images		

ANALYZE THE TEXTS

Discuss these questions in your group.

1. **Compare** With your group, review the images that you cited in your chart. In what ways are the images similar? In what ways are they different? Explain.

2. **Interpret** Both poems describe the way people have dealt with situations that result in loneliness. Discuss each author's view.

3. **Evaluate** "The Wanderer" is translated from Old English; "Loneliness" is a modern-day poem. What do you find effective about each style of writing? What do you find ineffective?

4. **Interpret** What have you learned about loneliness from these poems?

COLLABORATE AND PRESENT

Your group can continue exploring the ideas in these texts by identifying and comparing their themes. Follow these steps:

 Go to **Giving a Presentation** in the **Speaking and Listening Studio** for more.

1. **Decide on the most important details** With your group, review your chart to identify the most important details from each poem. Identify points you agree on and resolve disagreements through discussion based on evidence from the texts.

2. **Create theme statements** Determine a theme statement for each poem. Remember, it is up to you and your group to infer the theme based on details. You can use a chart like the one below to determine the theme each writer expresses.

"THE WANDERER"

DETAIL	DETAIL	DETAIL

THEME

"LONELINESS"

DETAIL	DETAIL	DETAIL

THEME

3. **Compare themes** With your group, discuss whether the themes of the poems are similar or different. Listen actively to the members of your group and ask them to clarify any points you do not understand.

4. **Present to the class** Now it is time to present your ideas. Be sure to include clear statements on the theme of each poem. Discuss whether the themes are similar or different. You may adapt the charts or other visuals you created to help convey information to the class.

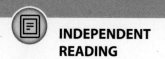

Reader's Choice

? **ESSENTIAL QUESTIONS**

Review the four Essential Questions for this unit on page 1.

Setting a Purpose   Select one or more of these options from your eBook to continue your exploration of the Essential Questions.

- Read the descriptions to see which text grabs your interest.
- Think about which genres you enjoy reading.

Notice & Note

In this unit, you practiced noticing and noting the signposts and asking big questions about nonfiction. As you read independently, these signposts and others will aid your understanding. Below are the key questions to ask when you read literature and nonfiction.

Reading Literature: Stories, Poems, and Plays	
Signpost	**Key Question**
Contrasts and Contradictions	Why did the character act that way?
Aha Moment	How might this change things?
Tough Questions	What does this make me wonder about?
Words of the Wiser	What's the lesson for the character?
Again and Again	Why might the author keep bringing this up?
Memory Moment	Why is this memory important?

Reading Nonfiction: Essays, Articles, and Arguments	
Signpost	**Key Question(s)**
Big Questions	What surprised me? What did the author think I already knew? What challenged, changed, or confirmed what I already knew?
Contrasts and Contradictions	What is the difference, and why does it matter?
Extreme or Absolute Language	Why did the author use this language?
Numbers and Stats	Why did the author use these numbers or amounts?
Quoted Words	Why was this person quoted or cited, and what did this add?
Word Gaps	Do I know this word from someplace else? Does it seem like technical talk for this topic? Do clues in the sentence help me understand the word?

You can preview these texts in Unit 1 of your eBook.

Then, check off the text or texts that you select to read on your own.

EPIC POEM

from **Beowulf**
The Beowulf Poet
translated by Burton Raffel

Beowulf faces one last challenging enemy—a fiery dragon that threatens the safety of his people.

ARTICLE

Beowulf Is Back!
James Parker

Can a medieval poem have value in the modern age? Examine Beowulf's timeless appeal to the imagination.

BALLAD

Barbara Allen
Anonymous

A young man lies dying and calls for the woman he loves. She comes—but cannot forgive him.

ARTICLE

Journeymen Keep the Medieval Past Alive
Melissa Eddy

Young adults continue a medieval tradition of hitting the road to gain valuable on-the-job work experience.

Collaborate and Share   With a partner, discuss what you learned from at least one of your independent readings.

 Go to the **Reading Studio** for more resources on **Notice & Note.**

- Give a brief synopsis or summary of the text.

- Describe any signposts that you noticed in the text and explain what they revealed to you.

- Describe what you most enjoyed or found most challenging about the text. Give specific examples.

- Decide if you would recommend the text to others. Why or why not?

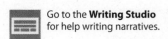

Write a Short Story

Go to the **Writing Studio** for help writing narratives.

This unit focuses on literature from the Anglo-Saxon and medieval periods, when England began to develop as a nation. Many works of these periods portrayed national heroes such as Beowulf and King Arthur. For this writing task, you will write a short story about a hero from the past or from your own world. For an example of well-written fiction, you can review, and use as a mentor text, the short story "Chivalry" by Neil Gaiman.

ORIGIN OF
A NATION
THE ANGLO-SAXON AND MEDIEVAL PERIODS

As you write your short story, you can use the notes from your Response Log, which you filled out after reading texts in this unit.

Writing Prompt

Read the information in the box below.

This is the topic or context for your short story.

> Heroes have appeared in literary works throughout history, though ideas about heroes have changed over time.

Think carefully about the following question.

How might this Essential Question be reflected in a short story?

> What makes someone a hero?

Now mark the word or words that suggest what kind of short story you will write.

Write a short story about a hero from the past or in your own world.

Be sure to—

- ❏ introduce a setting and main character and establish a clear point of view
- ❏ engage readers by presenting a conflict, situation, or observation that sets the short story in motion
- ❏ develop a plot with a clear and logical sequence of events
- ❏ use a variety of narrative techniques to develop characters, plot, theme, and suspense
- ❏ reveal a significant theme related to the Essential Question
- ❏ conclude by resolving the conflict or by conveying your reflection on the experiences described in the short story

Review these points as you write and again when you finish. Make any needed changes.

① Plan

Before you start writing, you need to plan your short story. When you plan a draft, you often start by selecting a genre that is appropriate for a particular topic, purpose, and audience. For this writing task, you already know that the topic is related to heroes, and you know that the genre will be a short story. Next, you should consider your purpose and audience. Also, it can be helpful to use a range of strategies as part of your planning process. These might include discussing the topic with your classmates, reading about heroes from the past, or thinking about people you've met whom you consider to be heroes.

Short Story Planning Table	
Genre	Short Story
Topic	What makes someone a hero?
Purpose	
Audience	
Ideas from discussion with classmates	
Ideas from background reading	
Personal interests related to topic	

Background Reading Review the notes you have taken in your Response Log that relate to the question, "What makes someone a hero?" Texts in this unit provide background reading that will help you formulate the theme and plot of your story.

Go to **Writing as a Process** for help.

Notice & Note
From Reading to Writing

As you plan your short story, apply what you've learned about signposts to your own writing. Remember that writers use common features, called signposts, to help convey their message to readers.

Think about how you can incorporate **Tough Questions** into your short story.

 Go to the **Reading Studio** for more resources on **Notice & Note.**

Use the notes from your Response Log as you plan your short story.

UNIT 1
RESPONSE LOG

WRITING TASK

Go to **Writing Narratives: Narrative Structure** for more help.

Organize Your Ideas After you have gathered ideas from your planning activities, you need to organize them in a way that will help you draft your short story. You can use the chart below to decide on the elements of your story. You can also use the chart to outline the plot of your story.

Story About a Hero	
How does the story begin? What can I do to engage readers and make them want to keep reading?	
What is the central conflict? Are there any other conflicts related to the central one?	
What is the story's plot? Map out the rising action, climax, and falling action.	
How do the setting, characters, conflict, and story events reveal a theme about heroes?	
How does the story end? Is the conflict resolved? How?	

 You might prefer to draft your essay online.

2 Develop a Draft

After planning and organizing, you will be ready to begin drafting your short story. Refer to your planning table and your chart of story elements, as well as any notes you took as you studied the texts in this unit. These will provide a kind of map for you to follow as you write. Using a word processor or online writing application makes it easier to revise your first draft.

Use the Mentor Text

Author's Craft

Your exposition is your first chance to capture the reader's attention. In addition to introducing the main character and the setting, the opening paragraphs should include something that will draw readers into your story. Notice how Neil Gaiman captures the reader's attention in the opening of "Chivalry."

> Mrs. Whitaker found the Holy Grail; it was under a fur coat. Every Thursday afternoon Mrs. Whitaker walked down to the post office to collect her pension, even though her legs were no longer what they were, and on the way back home she would stop in at the Oxfam Shop and buy herself a little something.

The writer starts off with a surprising detail that contrasts with the description of an ordinary setting.

Apply What You've Learned To capture your reader's attention, you might start off with a surprising detail or interesting dialogue.

Genre Characteristics

Sensory details are words, phrases, or sentences that appeal to the reader's senses of sight, hearing, touch, taste, and smell. Notice how the author of "Chivalry" uses sensory details in the following example.

> She moved a rather threadbare fur coat, which smelled badly of mothballs. Underneath it was a walking stick and a water-stained copy of *Romance and Legend of Chivalry* by A. R. Hope Moncrieff, priced at five pence. Next to the book, on its side, was the Holy Grail.

The author provides details that allow you to imagine the smell of the thrift shop and the appearance and position of items that the main character finds there.

Apply What You've Learned The details you include in your own short story should help readers imagine the characters and setting and should draw them into the story. Try to include details that appeal to a variety of senses.

③ Revise

Go to **Writing as a Process: Revising and Editing** for more help.

On Your Own Once you have written your draft, you'll want to go back and look for ways to improve your short story. As you reread and revise, think about whether you have achieved your purpose. The Revision Guide will help you focus on specific elements to make your writing stronger.

Revision Guide		
Ask Yourself	**Tips**	**Revision Techniques**
1. Does the story have an engaging beginning?	**Mark** the exposition.	**Add** interesting or surprising details about the character or situation.
2. Is there anything confusing about the sequence of events?	**Number** each event in the story.	**Reorder** events if necessary so that they have a logical sequence. **Add** appropriate transitions to clarify the sequence of events.
3. Are the characters fully developed?	**Mark** descriptions of the characters' appearance, thoughts, and actions.	**Add** details that provide insight into the characters' feelings and motivation.
4. Does the dialogue sound natural?	**Mark** important dialogue in the story.	**Add** words and phrases to give each character's dialogue a distinctive style. **Include** contractions and incomplete sentences to make dialogue more informal, or natural.
5. Is the conflict resolved in a logical way?	**Mark** the resolution.	**Add** details to make the resolution more satisfying, and tie up loose ends.

ACADEMIC VOCABULARY

As you conduct your **peer review,** be sure to use these words.

❑ **collapse**

❑ **displace**

❑ **military**

❑ **violate**

❑ **visual**

With a Partner Once you and your partner have worked through the Revision Guide on your own, exchange stories and evaluate each other's draft in a **peer review**. Focus on providing revision suggestions for at least three of the items mentioned in the chart. Explain why you think your partner's draft should be revised and what your specific suggestions are.

When receiving feedback from your partner, listen attentively and ask questions to make sure you fully understand the revision suggestions.

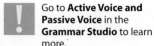

④ Edit

Once you have addressed the plot and other narrative elements in your short story, you can look to improve the finer points of your draft. Edit for proper use of standard English conventions, except in dialogue that you want to be informal. Make sure to correct any misspellings or grammatical errors.

> Go to **Active Voice and Passive Voice** in the **Grammar Studio** to learn more.

Language Conventions

Use Active and Passive Voice Appropriately The voice of a verb tells whether its subject performs or receives the action expressed by the verb.

- A verb is in the **active voice** when the subject performs the action.
- A verb is in the **passive voice** when the subject is the receiver of the action.

Usually you should use the active voice to make your writing more concise and direct. However, sometimes you may want to use the passive voice to emphasize the receiver or because the doer of the action is unknown or unimportant. The chart contains examples of active and passive voice from "Chivalry."

Voice	Example
Active Voice	Mrs. Whitaker picked up the dusty silver goblet and appraised it through her thick spectacles.
Passive Voice	The inside of the goblet was thickly coated with a brownish-red dust.

⑤ Publish

Finalize your short story and choose a way to share it with your audience. Consider these options:

- Read your short story aloud to a small group.
- Publish your story in a zine with other stories by classmates.

Use the scoring guide to evaluate your short story.

Writing Task Scoring Guide: Short Story		
Organization/Plot Development	**Development of Theme**	**Use of Language Conventions and Dialogue**
4 • Exposition captures reader's attention and effectively introduces main character and setting. • Scenes are placed in a logical progression toward a definite climax. • Characters and situations develop clear conflict, which is resolved in the end.	• The story expresses a clear and meaningful theme or message. • Many specific, sensory details are used to add meaning.	• Word choice is appropriate for narration and for character dialogue. • Dialogue helps create strong, vivid characters. • Language elements, such as active and passive voice, are used effectively.
3 • Exposition adequately introduces main character and setting. • Most scenes are placed in a logical progression toward a definite climax. • Characters and situations develop conflict, which is resolved in the end.	• The story expresses a message or theme. • Sufficient, specific sensory details are used to add meaning.	• For the most part, word choice is appropriate for narration and for character dialogue. • Dialogue helps develop characters. • Language elements, such as active and passive voice, are used adequately.
2 • Exposition attempts to introduce main character and setting. • Scenes lack order; weak climax. • Minimal conflict development; no clear resolution.	• Theme is present but poorly developed. • Attempt to use some sensory details is made, but details are general or scarce.	• Basic awareness of proper word choice is clear, but choices often seem awkward or confusing. • Dialogue seems unnatural and not specific to each character. • Weak style and use of language; too many passive voice verbs.
1 • Weak exposition fails to grab reader's attention; main character and setting not adequately introduced. • Scenes are out of order; no definite climax observed. • Little or no obvious conflict.	• Confusing or contradictory themes, or no theme is evident. • Poor use of details.	• Weak word choice. • Minimal dialogue and character development. • Language conventions seem to be ignored.

Create a Podcast

Now that you've written a short story, why not share it with others who enjoy reading tales of heroic adventure? Transform your short story into a podcast—a digital audio file that others can download from the web and listen to.

A strong podcast . . .

- contains sound features such as voice-over narration.
- conveys a distinctive tone and point of view.
- appeals to a specific audience.

Go to the **Speaking and Listening Studio** for help using media in a presentation.

1 Adapt Your Story to Create a Podcast

You will need to first format your story into a script to record your podcast.

Planning the Podcast

You will need to adapt your short story to make it easy for a listening audience to understand. One way is to consider turning your story into a dramatic reading, similar to a radio drama or reader's theater. Follow these suggestions to transform your story into an effective podcast.

❏ **Decide on the Details** Review your story and identify the characters' dialogue and the essential narration. Think about how strategic use of digital media can enhance your ideas.

❏ **Craft Your Script** Your script should indicate the exact words that your story's narrator and characters will say in a recorded audio track. Start by writing your voice-over narration and the dialogue between the characters. Describe which words can be expressed by the characters' manner of speaking rather than with words. For example, the narrator would not need to tell the audience that a character sighed; the audience will hear the sigh in the character's voice. Similarly, omit unnecessary words of attribution, such as *he said* or *she exclaimed*. Then, using the table below, describe the music and sound effects that will match your voice-over narration and dialogue to help convey the tone.

❏ **Choose Your Readers** Gather friends and classmates who will read the various characters in your script, and help create various sound effects.

Voice-over narration and dialogue	Music and sound effects
Harold trudged through the mud, the pouring rain drenching his clothes. He didn't care. All he could think about was getting back to the house where the children were.	Dramatic background music; sounds of pouring rain

② Create and Upload Your Podcast

Use sound, dialogue, and narration to share your short story and to appeal to your specific audience.

As you work to develop and improve your podcast, be sure to work with your classmates respectfully:

❏ listen closely to each other's ideas

❏ don't interrupt

❏ cooperate as you practice reading your scripts

❏ offer helpful suggestions to each other for better dramatic presentation

❏ **Produce the Segment** Using podcasting software, record your short story. (Check with your school's media specialist to make sure you have the equipment you need.) With your script as a guide, record your narration and dialogue. Experiment with sounds to present your story clearly and effectively.

❏ **Respect Copyright** Use only audio elements for which you have permission. To add music to your track, you can search the Internet for royalty-free audio clips, or you can make your own.

❏ **Use Your Voice** The narrator and characters should speak slowly and enunciate words so the audience can understand the events as they unfold. All readers should use intonation in their voices to add emotion and appropriate volume in order to maintain the proper tone.

❏ **Add an Extra Voice** Add depth to your podcast by asking a classmate to introduce your story. Or ask someone to lend a brief commentary at the end of your story.

❏ **Edit Your Work** Did you make a mistake in your recording? Do you need to include more audio elements to appeal to your audience? Add the finishing touches to your track.

❏ **Upload the Final Product** With access to a free podcasting subscription service, you can share your short story with a worldwide audience! Consult available resources for ideas, tips, and additional help, such as knowledgeable peers or a computer or audio/visual teacher. Listen carefully to any instructions you get that will help you produce an engaging podcast and solve potential problems. Then, create and post your podcast for your audience.

Reflect on the Unit

By completing your short story, you have created a writing product that is enriched by your thoughts about the reading selections. Now is a good time to reflect on what you learned.

Reflect on the Essential Questions

- Review the four Essential Questions on page 1. How have your answers to these questions changed in response to the texts you read in this unit?

- How did the heroes you read about in this unit affect other characters?

- Which characters were expected to uphold the code of chivalry? What do you admire or not admire about their behavior?

- Which characters seem to believe that an outside force governs their lives?

- Think about texts in the unit that show a society that is coming apart. How does this social disorder affect people?

Reflect on Your Reading

- Which selections were the most interesting or surprising to you?

- What conclusions can you draw about the period in which most of these texts were written?

Reflect on the Writing Task

- Which parts of the story were the easiest to write? The hardest to write? Why?

- What improvements did you make to your story as you were revising?

© Houghton Mifflin Harcourt Publishing Company

UNIT 1 READING SELECTIONS
- *Beowulf*
- "The Wife of Bath's Tale," from *The Canterbury Tales*
- from *Le Morte d'Arthur*
- "Chivalry"
- from *The Paston Letters*
- from *My Syrian Diary*
- "The Wanderer"
- "Loneliness"

UNIT 2

A CELEBRATION OF HUMAN ACHIEVEMENT

THE ENGLISH RENAISSANCE

" Be not afraid of greatness. "

—William Shakespeare

Discuss the **Essential Questions** with your whole class or in small groups. As you read A Celebration of Human Achievement, consider how the selections explore these questions.

? *ESSENTIAL QUESTION:*
What can drive someone to seek revenge?

Most of us at one time or another have felt the urge to seek retaliation against someone or something that has harmed either us personally or someone we care about. Revenge is also a major plot element of countless books, movies, and television shows. Clearly, the idea of vengeance is one that appeals to many people. But what factors influence some people to take action while others do not act? And why do people feel the need for revenge in the first place?

? *ESSENTIAL QUESTION:*
How does time affect our feelings?

"Time heals all wounds." "Just sleep on it; you'll feel better in the morning." Chances are you have heard these expressions and others like them many times. The central idea is the same: as time passes, human feelings change. But in what ways? Do feelings fade in strength or do they become more powerful? Are there cases in which feelings are unaffected by time? Can a strong feeling a person has at one time be transformed into a completely different feeling?

? *ESSENTIAL QUESTION:*
What's the difference between love and passion?

For millennia, writers, poets, artists, and countless others have struggled to define what constitutes true love. Because love takes so many forms, and is expressed differently by each individual, it often blends into and is sometimes confused with other emotions. To some, romantic love and passion are inseparable concepts. What is love, and what is passion? Why is it so difficult for people to distinguish between the two?

? *ESSENTIAL QUESTION:*
How do you defy expectations?

All of us face them every day: the expectations we have for ourselves and others, and the expectations others and society have for us. High expectations for behavior or achievement can lead to soaring success, if they are met; but can just as easily end in spectacular failure, and crippling blows to self-esteem, if they are unmet or unrealistic. Low expectations, on the other hand, all too often become self-fulfilling prophecies. How are we motivated by the expectations that surround us? What happens when someone chooses to go against the expectations that have been put in place for them?

King Henry VII

THE ENGLISH RENAISSANCE

During the late Middle Ages, Europe suffered from both war and plague. Those who survived wanted to celebrate life and the human spirit. The Renaissance, which literally means "rebirth," was marked by a revival of art and learning, and a rediscovery of classical Greek and Roman ideas. A new emphasis was placed on the individual and human achievement. Artists, writers, and scholars refocused their efforts on exploring the natural world, rather than the spiritual world. Some Europeans even began to question the teachings of the Church, which directed Christians to endure suffering while they awaited their rewards in heaven. After the development of a printing press with movable type in about 1440, Renaissance ideas could be printed in mass and distributed to an increasingly literate population.

The Tudor Dynasty and Religious Reform Although the Renaissance began in the 1300s in Italy and rapidly spread throughout Europe, its influence was delayed in England due to political instability. When King Henry VII assumed the English throne in 1485, the Renaissance finally took hold. King Henry VII was the first in an influential succession of Tudor rulers. A shrewd leader, Henry negotiated favorable treaties, built up the nation's trading fleet, and financed expeditions to the Americas. He also made an alliance with Spain by marrying his son to Princess Catherine of Aragon.

Meanwhile, dissatisfaction with the Roman Catholic Church, and its leader the pope, was spreading in Europe. The great wealth and power of the Church threatened the power of kings, and Church corruption enraged religious reformers. In 1517 Martin Luther, a German monk, responded by writing his 95 Theses and nailing them to a church door. Despite being declared a heretic, Luther's arguments against Church corruption were

© Houghton Mifflin Harcourt Publishing Company • Image Credits: © Peter Horree/Alamy

COLLABORATIVE DISCUSSION
In a small group, review the timeline and discuss which literary or historical events had the greatest impact.

1485
Henry Tudor becomes King Henry VII, the first ruler of the Tudor dynasty.

1534
Henry VIII breaks with the Roman Catholic Church and forms the Church of England.

1485

1517
Martin Luther begins the Protestant Reformation.

1558
Elizabeth I becomes Queen of England.

1564
William Shakespeare is born.

published and spread across Europe. His actions sparked the Reformation, a movement for religious reform, which led to the founding of Christian churches that did not accept the authority of the pope. Christians who belonged to these non-Catholic churches became known as Protestants.

Henry VIII, son of Henry VII, at first remained loyal to the Roman Catholic Church. However, he became obsessed with producing a male heir. When he was only able to produce a female heir, Mary, with his wife, Catherine of Aragon, he asked to annul their marriage. The pope refused, so Henry broke away from the Church, forming the Church of England and declaring himself the head. He divorced Catherine and married Anne Boleyn, who became the mother of his second female heir, Elizabeth.

In all, Henry married six different wives but fathered only one son—the frail and sickly Edward VI, who became king but died when he was just 15. Following Edward, Catherine's daughter Mary succeeded to the throne. To avenge the divorce of her mother, she brought Roman Catholicism back to England and persecuted Protestants, thereby earning the nickname Bloody Mary. When Mary died in 1558, her half-sister Elizabeth became queen.

The Elizabethan Era and the Rise of the Stuarts Elizabeth I was one of the ablest monarchs in English history. During her long reign, England enjoyed a time of unprecedented prosperity and international prestige. The queen kept England out of costly wars, ended the Spanish alliance, and encouraged overseas exploration. In religion, she steered a middle course, reestablishing the Church of England and setting it as a buffer between Catholics and the more radical Protestants known as Puritans. The ideas of the Renaissance flourished, and theater and literature reached new heights. It was during Elizabeth's reign that William Shakespeare began his career, and several of his plays were performed at her court. With Elizabeth's death in 1603, the powerful Tudor dynasty came to an end.

Elizabeth was succeeded by her cousin James Stuart, King of Scotland, who became James I of England. He oversaw a new English translation of the Bible—the King James Bible—but refused to reform the Church of England, angering Puritans, including many in Parliament.

The Defeat of the Monarchy In 1625 James I died and Charles I, his son, became king. In 1629 he dismissed the Puritan-dominated Parliament and

© Houghton Mifflin Harcourt Publishing Company

RESEARCH
What about this historical period interests you? Choose a topic, event, or person to learn more about. Then add your own entry to the timeline.

c. 1590
Shakespeare begins his career as a playwright.

1607
English settlers establish the Jamestown colony in Virginia.

1642
The English Civil War begins; Puritans close England's theaters.

1660

1580
Sir Frances Drake brings great treasures back to England after sailing around the world.

1611
The King James Bible is published.

1660
The monarchy is restored under Charles II.

A Celebration of Human Achievement **141**

did not summon it again for 11 years. During that time, he took strong measures against his opponents, persecuting Puritans and attempting to force the practices of the Church of England on Scotland. When the king finally reconvened Parliament, it stripped him of many of his powers. Charles responded with military force, and civil war resulted.

The English Civil War pitted the Royalists against Parliament. Under Oliver Cromwell, the Puritan army, supporting Parliament, defeated the Royalists, and King Charles I was executed in 1649. Parliament established a commonwealth with Cromwell as head, but the Puritan government was just as autocratic as the Stuart kings, and eventually lost public support. In 1660 a new Parliament invited Charles II, the son of Charles I, to return from exile as king, marking the beginning of a period known as the Restoration.

CHECK YOUR UNDERSTANDING

Choose the best answer to each question.

1 Which event led most directly to the formation of the Church of England?

   A Henry VII made a marriage alliance with Spain.

   B Henry VIII sought to annul his marriage to Catherine of Aragon.

   C Martin Luther protested the corruption of the Catholic Church.

   D The Catholic Church declared Martin Luther a heretic, angering his supporters.

2 Renaissance ideas took hold in England later than in other parts of Europe mainly because —

   F the Catholic Church discouraged people from pursuing the arts and literature

   G the Tudor monarchs stunted England's growth as a nation

   H internal political conflict initially prevented Renaissance ideas from taking root

   J English Puritans disagreed with the Italian Renaissance worldview

3 Which most accurately describes the religious climate in England during this period?

   A England was a predominantly Catholic country.

   B England was a predominantly Puritan country.

   C England became dominated by the Church of England, which promoted the ideas of Martin Luther.

   D England had a few main religious groups that each gained power or popularity under specific rulers.

ACADEMIC VOCABULARY

Academic Vocabulary words are words you use when you discuss and write about texts. In this unit, you will learn the following five words:

☑ ambiguous ☐ anticipate ☐ conceive ☐ drama ☐ integrity

Study the Word Network to learn more about the word **ambiguous**.

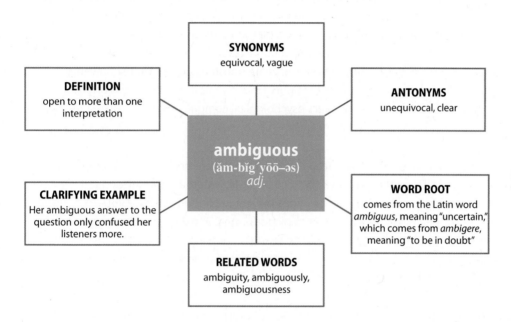

SYNONYMS
equivocal, vague

DEFINITION
open to more than one interpretation

ANTONYMS
unequivocal, clear

ambiguous
(ăm-bĭgʹyōō–əs)
adj.

CLARIFYING EXAMPLE
Her ambiguous answer to the question only confused her listeners more.

WORD ROOT
comes from the Latin word *ambiguus*, meaning "uncertain," which comes from *ambigere*, meaning "to be in doubt"

RELATED WORDS
ambiguity, ambiguously, ambiguousness

Write and Discuss Discuss your completed Word Network with a partner, making sure to talk through all of the boxes until you both understand the word, its synonyms, antonyms, and related forms. Then fill out a Word Network for the remaining four words. Use a dictionary or online resource to help you complete the activity.

Go online to access the Word Networks.

RESPOND TO THE ESSENTIAL QUESTIONS

In this unit, you will explore four different **Essential Questions** related to the literature of the English Renaissance. As you read each selection, you will gather your ideas about one of these questions and write about it in the **Response Log** that appears on page R2. At the end of the unit, you will have the opportunity to write a **literary analysis** related to one of the Essential Questions. Filling out the Response Log after you read each text will help you prepare for this writing task.

You can also go online to access the Response Log.

SHAKESPEAREAN DRAMA

Shakespeare wrote *The Tragedy of Hamlet* around 1600. The story originated in an old folktale that was part of Denmark's legendary history. Shakespeare seems to have based his tragedy mainly on an English play about Hamlet from the 1580s. This earlier play had fallen out of fashion among Elizabethan audiences, but Shakespeare's version was a success. Shakespeare transformed the genre of revenge tragedy by introducing a hero whose insights, doubts, and moral dilemmas often overshadow the play's action. *Hamlet*'s psychological complexity helps explain the play's lasting popularity and influence.

The Globe Theatre In Shakespeare's time, most plays were performed in outdoor public theaters. These theaters resembled courtyards, with the stage surrounded on three sides by galleries. The most famous theater in London was the Globe, where Shakespeare and his acting company performed. The Globe was a three-story wooden structure that could hold up to 3,000 people. Poorer patrons, or "groundlings," stood around the stage to watch the performance. Wealthier patrons sat in the covered galleries.

Elizabethan Staging Plays were performed in the afternoon on a platform stage in the theater's center. The stage was mostly bare, which allowed for quick scene changes. A trapdoor gave the stage added flexibility; in *Hamlet,* it was used for the Ghost's entrances and exits and also in a grave scene. Actors were in close proximity to the groundlings, who were often rowdy. Because the theater was viewed as disreputable, women were not allowed to perform; boys played the female roles.

SHAKESPEAREAN TRAGEDY

Renaissance Drama During the Middle Ages, English drama focused mainly on religious themes, teaching moral lessons or retelling Bible stories to a populace that often couldn't read. In the Renaissance, however, renewed interest in ancient Greek and Roman literature led playwrights to model plays on classical drama. The plays were usually comedies and tragedies. **Comedy** was defined as a dramatic work with a happy ending; many comedies had humor, but it was not required. A **tragedy,** in contrast, was a work in which the main character, or **tragic hero,** came to an unhappy end. The intention of tragedy is to exemplify the idea that human beings are doomed to suffer, fail, or die because of their own flaws, destiny, or fate. Shakespearean tragedy often differs from classical tragedy because Shakespeare's tragic works are not uniformly serious. He often eased the intensity of the action by using comic relief—a light, mildly humorous scene preceding or following a serious one. Shakespeare also wrote plays classified as **histories,** which present stories about England's monarchs.

© Houghton Mifflin Harcourt Publishing Company

SHAKESPEARE'S CONVENTIONS OF DRAMA

Shakespearean plays are divided into **acts** and **scenes. Dialogue** is labeled to show who is speaking. **Stage directions,** written in italics and in parentheses, specify the setting and how the characters should act. Shakespeare also used the following literary devices in his dramas.

Blank Verse Like many plays written before the 19th century, *Hamlet* is a **verse drama,** a play with dialogue consisting mostly of poetry with a fixed pattern of rhythm, or **meter.** Many English verse dramas are written in **blank verse,** or unrhymed **iambic pentameter,** a meter in which the normal line contains five stressed syllables, each preceded by an unstressed syllable.

> A little more than kin and less than kind.

Soliloquy and Aside Shakespeare often used two conventions to express characters' private thoughts and feelings. A **soliloquy** is a speech a character makes while alone to reveal thoughts to the audience. An **aside** is a remark a character quietly makes to the audience or to another character but that others on stage are not supposed to hear. Here is an example from *Hamlet*.

> **Polonius.** Fare you well, my lord.
> **Hamlet** [*aside*]. These tedious old fools.

Dramatic Irony In **dramatic irony,** the audience knows something that one or more characters don't know. For example, the audience knows why Hamlet often behaves strangely in the play, but most characters are confused by this behavior.

SHAKESPEAREAN LANGUAGE

The English language that Shakespeare used was quite different from today's language.

Shakespearean Language	
Grammatical Forms	The pronouns **thou, thee, thy, thine,** and **thyself** *replaced you.* Old verb forms were used, such as **art (are)** and **cometh (comes).**
Unusual Word Order	There is often an unusual word order. For example, Polonius tells Laertes, "Neither a borrower nor a lender be," instead of, "Be neither a borrower nor a lender."
Unfamiliar Vocabulary	The writing used archaic words (**seeling**: "blinding") and words with different modern meanings (**choppy**: "chapped"). He also wrote new words (like **assassination**) commonly used today.

THE TRAGEDY OF HAMLET

Drama by **William Shakespeare**

ESSENTIAL QUESTION:

What can drive someone to seek revenge?

© Houghton Mifflin Harcourt Publishing Company • Image Credits: © Les and Dave Jacobs/cultura/Corbis

QUICK START

Revenge has a central role in the story of *Hamlet*. Is revenge justified in some cases, or is it always misguided? Write a paragraph in response to this question. Then, share your opinion with a partner.

ANALYZE DRAMATIC PLOT

Shakespeare's tragedies have complex plot structures. Critics often refer to distinct stages of a dramatic plot, such as the **exposition,** where the characters and setting are introduced, and the **rising action,** where conflicts arise and suspense builds. The rising action leads to a **climax,** or turning point, where the outcome of the central conflict becomes clear. Events that follow in the **falling action** result in the final outcome, or **resolution.** In Shakespeare's plays, these stages often blend into one another, and a play can have more than one climax.

As the main plot develops, Shakespeare introduces **subplots**—stories that run parallel to the main plot. Subplots may support the main plot by advancing the play's action or by expressing a similar theme. They often involve characters other than the hero and the main opponent. For example, in *Hamlet,* one subplot features a character named Fortinbras, who only makes two brief appearances in the play. However, Fortinbras is important because he serves as a **foil,** a character whose traits contrast with another character, in this case with Hamlet. As you read the play, consider how the subplots connect with the main plot.

ANALYZE CONFLICT

Plots are generally built around **conflict,** a struggle between opposing forces. In tragic drama, conflict often has deadly consequences. The most obvious conflict is external, involving struggles between the main character and opponents.

Hamlet has plenty of violent action, but the play is notable for its exploration of internal conflict, struggles that occur within a character's mind. Prince Hamlet is keenly aware of the potential consequences of his actions. He also understands the consequences of inaction. Shakespeare places him in a situation full of moral dilemmas that are closely tied to the plot and themes of the play. As you read, consider how Hamlet struggles with these questions:

- How can he be certain about what happened to his father?

- How can he live up to his family duties?

- How should he judge his mother's behavior?

- How will his actions affect the fate of his soul as well as his enemy's soul?

- How can he reconcile the corruption and nobility within human nature?

When you finish reading the play, think about whether your views of Hamlet's struggles changed as you learned more about him.

**GENRE ELEMENTS:
TRAGIC DRAMA**

- portrays the downfall of a dignified, courageous character who is generally of importance in society

- hero's downfall occurs because of a character weakness, error in judgment, or circumstances out of his or her control

- events lead to a disastrous or unhappy ending

© Houghton Mifflin Harcourt Publishing Company

ANALYZE SOLILOQUY

A **soliloquy** is a long speech in a play in which a character talks to himself or herself. The character is alone onstage or unaware of the presence of others. Soliloquies help develop characters by revealing their motivations and inner conflicts. They can also express themes and hint at actions to come. Shakespeare uses a variety of techniques in his soliloquies.

Allusions	Act I, Scene 2, 139–140: "So excellent a king, that was to this / Hyperion to a satyr. . . ." Hamlet alludes to the sun god Hyperion to make the point that his father had integrity, unlike his uncle Claudius, whom he compares to a satyr, a mythical figure associated with lechery.
Figures of speech: metaphors, similes, and personification	Act III, Scene I, 59–60: "The slings and arrows of outrageous fortune, / Or to take arms against a sea of troubles. . . ." Shakespeare uses metaphors to express Hamlet's disturbed state of mind.
Powerful imagery; careful word choices	Act III, Scene 2, 393–395: "Now could I drink hot blood / And do such bitter business as the day / Would quake to look on." The imagery and word choices in these lines convey the intensity of Hamlet's feelings.

As you read, think about how Shakespeare uses these literary elements to create memorable and insightful soliloquies.

LANGUAGE CONVENTIONS

A **paradox** is a statement that seems contradictory but actually reveals an element of truth. For example, in Act III, Scene 4, Hamlet says that he "must be cruel only to be kind." Although *cruel* and *kind* have opposite meanings, this paradox suggests that harsh actions are sometimes needed to obtain just outcomes. As you read *Hamlet,* look for other paradoxical statements.

ANNOTATION MODEL　　　　　　　　　　　　　　　**NOTICE & NOTE**

As you read *Hamlet,* note elements of the plot and examine conflicts revealed through dialogue. This model shows one reader's note about a soliloquy in Act I, after Hamlet's mother and uncle suggest he has mourned his father's death for too long.

> **Hamlet.** O, that this too, too sullied flesh would melt,
> Thaw, and resolve itself into a dew,
> Or that the Everlasting had not fixed
> His canon 'gainst self-slaughter! O God, God,
> How weary, stale, flat, and unprofitable
> Seem to me all the uses of this world!
> Fie on 't, ah fie! 'Tis an unweeded garden
> That grows to seed. Things rank and gross in nature
> Possess it merely.

Hamlet feels such despair that he wishes he could disappear.

His choice of words expresses his disgust with everything around him.

BACKGROUND

William Shakespeare *(1564–1616) is considered the finest writer in the English language, admired for his rhetorical power, poetic brilliance, and profound psychological insight. Four centuries after his death, he continues to occupy a central place in literary studies and in our culture. His plays are regularly performed around the world and have been adapted into many films. Ben Jonson, a rival Elizabethan playwright, showed great foresight when he declared that Shakespeare "was not of an age, but for all time."*

THE TRAGEDY OF
HAMLET
Drama by William Shakespeare

Shakespeare was born in Stratford-upon-Avon, a market town in central England. He probably attended Stratford's grammar school, where he would have studied Latin and read classical authors. In 1582, he married Anne Hathaway, who gave birth to their three children within several years. Shakespeare's theatrical career took off in 1594 when he joined the Lord Chamberlain's Men, which became London's most prestigious theater company. Shakespeare, who also acted, soon grew affluent from his share in the company's profits. He bought a large house in Stratford, where his wife and children remained.

Shakespeare mastered all forms of drama. In the 1590s, he focused on comedies and English history plays, such as A Midsummer Night's Dream *and* Henry IV. *Between 1600 and 1607, he wrote his greatest tragedies, including* Hamlet. *The final phase of his career saw the creation of darker comedies, such as* The Tempest. *In addition to his 38 plays, Shakespeare wrote two narrative poems and a highly innovative collection of sonnets.*

Shakespeare died in Stratford when he was 52 years old. At the time, some of his plays existed in cheap, often badly flawed editions; others had never appeared in print. In 1623, two theater colleagues published a collected edition of his plays known as the First Folio, *which ensured the survival of his remarkable work.*

SETTING A PURPOSE

As you read, look for clues to Hamlet's attitude toward his mother and uncle, and notice any changes in his attitude over the course of the act.

CHARACTERS

The Ghost

Hamlet, Prince of Denmark, son of the late King Hamlet and Queen Gertrude

Queen Gertrude, widow of King Hamlet, now married to Claudius

King Claudius, brother to the late King Hamlet

Polonius, councillor to King Claudius

Ophelia, daughter of Polonius

Laertes, son of Polonius

Reynaldo, servant to Polonius

Horatio, Hamlet's friend and confidant

COURTIERS AT THE DANISH COURT

    Voltemand

    Cornelius

    Rosencrantz

    Guildenstern

    Osric

    Gentlemen

    A Lord

DANISH SOLDIERS

    Francisco

    Barnardo

    Marcellus

Fortinbras, Prince of Norway

A Captain in Fortinbras's army

Ambassadors to Denmark from England

Players who take the roles of Prologue, Player King, Player Queen, and Lucianus in *The Murder of Gonzago*

Two Messengers

Sailors

Gravedigger

Gravedigger's companion

Doctor of Divinity

Attendants, Lords, Guards, Musicians, Laertes's Followers, Soldiers, Officers

Place: Denmark

ACT I

Scene 1 *A guard platform at Elsinore Castle.*

[*Enter* Barnardo *and* Francisco, *two sentinels.*]

Barnardo. Who's there?

Francisco. Nay, answer me. Stand and unfold yourself.

Barnardo. Long live the King!

Francisco. Barnardo.

5 **Barnardo.** He.

Francisco. You come most carefully upon your hour.

Barnardo. 'Tis now struck twelve. Get thee to bed, Francisco.

Francisco. For this relief much thanks. 'Tis bitter cold, And I am sick at heart.

10 **Barnardo.** Have you had quiet guard?

Francisco. Not a mouse stirring.

Barnardo. Well, good night.
If you do meet Horatio and Marcellus,
The rivals of my watch, bid them make haste.

[*Enter* Horatio *and* Marcellus.]

15 **Francisco.** I think I hear them.—Stand ho! Who is there?

Horatio. Friends to this ground.

Marcellus. And liegemen to the Dane.

Francisco. Give you good night.

Marcellus. O farewell, honest soldier. Who hath relieved you?

20 **Francisco.** Barnardo hath my place. Give you good night.

[Francisco *exits*.]

Marcellus. Holla, Barnardo.

Barnardo. Say, what, is Horatio there?

Horatio. A piece of him.

Barnardo. Welcome, Horatio.—Welcome, good Marcellus.

25 **Horatio.** What, has this thing appeared again tonight?

Barnardo. I have seen nothing.

2 unfold yourself: show who you are.

14 rivals of my watch: the other soldiers on guard duty with me.

16–17 Horatio and Marcellus identify themselves as friendly to Denmark (**this ground**) and loyal subjects of the Danish king (**the Dane**).

© Houghton Mifflin Harcourt Publishing Company

27–33 Marcellus explains that Horatio doubts their story about having twice seen a ghost (**apparition**), so he has brought Horatio to confirm what they saw (**approve our eyes**).

Marcellus. Horatio says 'tis but our fantasy
And will not let belief take hold of him
Touching this dreaded sight twice seen of us.
30 Therefore I have entreated him along
With us to watch the minutes of this night,
That, if again this apparition come,
He may approve our eyes and speak to it.

Horatio. Tush, tush, 'twill not appear.

Barnardo.   Sit down a while,
35 And let us once again assail your ears,
That are so fortified against our story,
What we have two nights seen.

Horatio.   Well, sit we down,
And let us hear Barnardo speak of this.

Barnardo. Last night of all,

40 star . . . pole: the North Star.
41 his: its.

40 When yond same star that's westward from the pole
Had made his course t' illume that part of heaven
Where now it burns, Marcellus and myself,
The bell then beating one—

[*Enter* Ghost.]

Marcellus. Peace, break thee off! Look where it comes again.

46–50 It was commonly believed that a ghost could only speak after it was spoken to, preferably by someone learned enough (**a scholar**) to ask the proper questions.

48 harrows: torments.

50 usurp'st: unlawfully takes over.

52 majesty of buried Denmark: the buried King of Denmark.

53 sometimes: formerly.

45 **Barnardo.** In the same figure like the King that's dead.

Marcellus [*to* **Horatio**]. Thou art a scholar. Speak to it, Horatio.

Barnardo. Looks he not like the King? Mark it, Horatio.

Horatio. Most like. It harrows me with fear and wonder.

Barnardo. It would be spoke to.

Marcellus.   Speak to it, Horatio.

50 **Horatio.** What art thou that usurp'st this time of night,
Together with that fair and warlike form
In which the majesty of buried Denmark
Did sometimes march? By heaven, I charge thee, speak.

Marcellus. It is offended.

Barnardo.   See, it stalks away.

55 **Horatio.** Stay! speak! speak! I charge thee, speak!

[Ghost *exits*.]

Marcellus. 'Tis gone and will not answer.

Barnardo. How now, Horatio, you tremble and look pale.
Is not this something more than fantasy?
What think you on 't?

60 **Horatio.** Before my God, I might not this believe

Without the sensible and true avouch
Of mine own eyes.

Marcellus. Is it not like the King?

Horatio. As thou art to thyself.
Such was the very armor he had on
65 When he the ambitious Norway combated.
So frowned he once when, in an angry parle,
He smote the sledded Polacks on the ice.
'Tis strange.

Marcellus. Thus twice before, and jump at this dead hour,
70 With martial stalk hath he gone by our watch.

Horatio. In what particular thought to work I know not,
But in the gross and scope of mine opinion
This bodes some strange eruption to our state.

Marcellus. Good now, sit down, and tell me, he that knows,
75 Why this same strict and most observant watch
So nightly toils the subject of the land,
And why such daily cast of brazen cannon
And foreign mart for implements of war,
Why such impress of shipwrights, whose sore task
80 Does not divide the Sunday from the week.
What might be toward that this sweaty haste
Doth make the night joint laborer with the day?
Who is 't that can inform me?

Horatio. That can I.
At least the whisper goes so: our last king,
85 Whose image even but now appeared to us,
Was, as you know, by Fortinbras of Norway,
Thereto pricked on by a most emulate pride,
Dared to the combat; in which our valiant Hamlet
(For so this side of our known world esteemed him)
90 Did slay this Fortinbras, who by a sealed compact,
Well ratified by law and heraldry,
Did forfeit, with his life, all those his lands
Which he stood seized of, to the conqueror.
Against the which a moiety competent
95 Was gagèd by our king, which had returned
To the inheritance of Fortinbras
Had he been vanquisher, as, by the same comart
And carriage of the article designed,
His fell to Hamlet. Now, sir, young Fortinbras,
100 Of unimprovèd mettle hot and full,
Hath in the skirts of Norway here and there
Sharked up a list of lawless resolutes
For food and diet to some enterprise

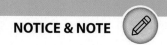

NOTICE & NOTE

61–62 Without . . . eyes: without seeing the proof (**avouch**) with my own eyes.

ANALYZE DRAMATIC PLOT
Annotate: Mark details in lines 63–68 about the former king's actions.

Infer: What does this exposition suggest about his personality?

65 Norway: the King of Norway.

66 parle: parley, meeting with an enemy.

67 smote: defeated; **sledded Polacks:** Polish soldiers riding in sleds.

69 jump: exactly.

72–73 This is a bad omen (**bodes some strange eruption**) for Denmark.

74–78 Can anyone explain why the Danes weary themselves each night with sentry duty and why there is so much casting of armaments (**brazen cannon**) and foreign trade (**mart**) for weapons?

81 toward: approaching, in preparation.

90–104 By prior agreement and according to laws governing combat, Hamlet gained all the land that Fortinbras had possessed (**stood seized of**). Hamlet had pledged an equivalent portion (**moiety competent**) of his land, which would have gone to Fortinbras if he won the battle, as was specified in the same agreement. Young Fortinbras, who has an undisciplined character (**unimprovèd mettle**), has gathered hastily (**Sharked up**) in outlying districts (**skirts**) of Norway a troop of lawless desperadoes to serve in some undertaking that requires courage (**hath a stomach in 't**).

© Houghton Mifflin Harcourt Publishing Company

That hath a stomach in 't; which is no other
105 (As it doth well appear unto our state)
But to recover of us, by strong hand
And terms compulsatory, those foresaid lands
So by his father lost. And this, I take it,
Is the main motive of our preparations,
110 The source of this our watch, and the chief head
Of this posthaste and rummage in the land.

Barnardo. I think it be no other but e'en so.
Well may it sort that this portentous figure
Comes armèd through our watch so like the king
115 That was and is the question of these wars.

Horatio. A mote it is to trouble the mind's eye.
In the most high and palmy state of Rome,
A little ere the mightiest Julius fell,
The graves stood tenantless, and the sheeted dead
120 Did squeak and gibber in the Roman streets;
As stars with trains of fire and dews of blood,
Disasters in the sun; and the moist star,
Upon whose influence Neptune's empire stands,
Was sick almost to doomsday with eclipse.
125 And even the like precurse of feared events,
As harbingers preceding still the fates
And prologue to the omen coming on,
Have heaven and earth together demonstrated
Unto our climatures and countrymen.

[*Enter* Ghost.]

130 But soft, behold! Lo, where it comes again!
I'll cross it though it blast me.—Stay, illusion!

[*It spreads his arms.*]

If thou hast any sound or use of voice,
Speak to me.
If there be any good thing to be done
135 That may to thee do ease and grace to me,
Speak to me.
If thou art privy to thy country's fate,
Which happily foreknowing may avoid,
O, speak!
140 Or if thou hast uphoarded in thy life
Extorted treasure in the womb of earth,
For which, they say, you spirits oft walk in death,
Speak of it.

[*The cock crows.*]

Stay and speak!—Stop it, Marcellus.

110 **head:** source.
111 **rummage:** bustle.

113 **Well . . . sort:** it may be fitting.

116 **mote:** dust speck.

117 **palmy:** thriving.

119 **sheeted:** wrapped in shrouds.

120 **gibber:** chatter.

122 **Disasters:** menacing signs; **moist star:** the moon, which controls the Earth's tides.

123 **Neptune:** Roman god of the sea.

125–129 A similar foreshadowing (**precurse**) has occurred in Denmark, where a terrible event (**omen**) was preceded by signs that were like forerunners (**harbingers**) announcing the approach of someone.

130 **soft:** be quiet, hold off.

131 **cross:** confront.

138 **happily . . . avoid:** perhaps (**happily**) may be avoided if known in advance.

141 **Extorted:** ill-gotten.

Marcellus. Shall I strike it with my partisan?

145 **Horatio.** Do, if it will not stand.

Barnardo. 'Tis here.

Horatio. 'Tis here.

[Ghost *exits.*]

Marcellus. 'Tis gone.
We do it wrong, being so majestical,
150 To offer it the show of violence,
For it is as the air, invulnerable,
And our vain blows malicious mockery.

Barnardo. It was about to speak when the cock crew.

Horatio. And then it started like a guilty thing
155 Upon a fearful summons. I have heard
The cock, that is the trumpet to the morn,
Doth with his lofty and shrill-sounding throat
Awake the god of day, and at his warning,
Whether in sea or fire, in earth or air,
160 Th' extravagant and erring spirit hies
To his confine, and of the truth herein
This present object made probation.

Marcellus. It faded on the crowing of the cock.
Some say that ever 'gainst that season comes
165 Wherein our Savior's birth is celebrated,
This bird of dawning singeth all night long;
And then, they say, no spirit dare stir abroad,
The nights are wholesome; then no planets strike,
No fairy takes, nor witch hath power to charm,
170 So hallowed and so gracious is that time.

Horatio. So have I heard and do in part believe it.
But look, the morn in russet mantle clad
Walks o'er the dew of yon high eastward hill.
Break we our watch up, and by my advice
175 Let us impart what we have seen tonight
Unto young Hamlet; for, upon my life,
This spirit, dumb to us, will speak to him.
Do you consent we shall acquaint him with it
As needful in our loves, fitting our duty?

180 **Marcellus.** Let's do 't, I pray, and I this morning know
Where we shall find him most convenient.

[*They exit.*]

144 partisan: a long-handled weapon.

154 started: made a sudden movement.

160 extravagant and erring: wandering out of bounds.

162 made probation: demonstrated.

164–165 ever . . . celebrated: just before Christmas.

168 strike: put forth an evil influence.

169 takes: bewitches.

© Houghton Mifflin Harcourt Publishing Company

ANALYZE DRAMATIC PLOT

Annotate: Mark phrases that Claudius uses to convey his feelings about his brother's death in lines 1–16.

Draw Conclusions: Do you think that Claudius is speaking sincerely? Why or why not?

8 our sometime sister: my former sister-in-law. (Claudius uses the royal "we.")

9 jointress: a woman who owns property with her husband.

11–12 With . . . eye: with one eye reflecting good fortune and the other eye, sorrow; **dirge:** a song of mourning.

21 Colleaguèd . . . advantage: connected with this false hope of his superior position.

23 Importing: relating to.

29 impotent: helpless.

30–33 Since Fortinbras has obtained all of his troops and supplies from Norway, Claudius has asked the King of Norway to stop him from proceeding further.

37 To business: to negotiate.

38 dilated articles: detailed instructions.

Scene 2 *A state room at the castle.*

[*Flourish. Enter* Claudius, *King of Denmark,* Gertrude the Queen, *the* Council, *as* Polonius, *and his son* Laertes, Hamlet, *with others, among them* Voltemand *and* Cornelius.]

King. Though yet of Hamlet our dear brother's death
The memory be green, and that it us befitted
To bear our hearts in grief, and our whole kingdom
To be contracted in one brow of woe,
5 Yet so far hath discretion fought with nature
That we with wisest sorrow think on him
Together with remembrance of ourselves.
Therefore our sometime sister, now our queen,
Th' imperial jointress to this warlike state,
10 Have we (as 'twere with a defeated joy,
With an auspicious and a dropping eye,
With mirth in funeral and with dirge in marriage,
In equal scale weighing delight and dole)
Taken to wife. Nor have we herein barred
15 Your better wisdoms, which have freely gone
With this affair along. For all, our thanks.
Now follows that you know. Young Fortinbras,
Holding a weak supposal of our worth
Or thinking by our late dear brother's death
20 Our state to be disjoint and out of frame,
Colleaguèd with this dream of his advantage,
He hath not failed to pester us with message
Importing the surrender of those lands
Lost by his father, with all bonds of law,
25 To our most valiant brother—so much for him.
Now for ourself and for this time of meeting.
Thus much the business is: we have here writ
To Norway, uncle of young Fortinbras,
Who, impotent and bedrid, scarcely hears
30 Of this his nephew's purpose, to suppress
His further gait herein, in that the levies,
The lists, and full proportions are all made
Out of his subject; and we here dispatch
You, good Cornelius, and you, Voltemand,
35 For bearers of this greeting to old Norway,
Giving to you no further personal power
To business with the King more than the scope
Of these dilated articles allow.

[*Giving them a paper.*]

Farewell, and let your haste commend your duty.

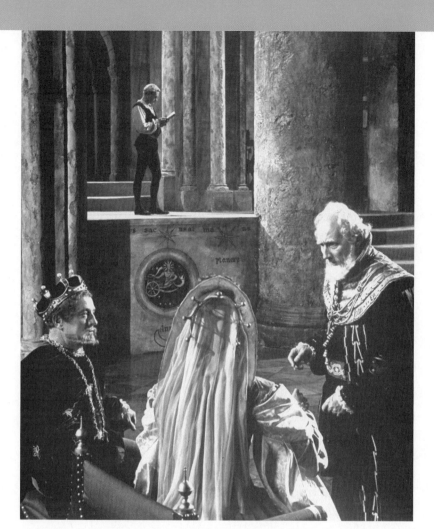

Laurence Olivier's 1948 film *Hamlet*. Background: Hamlet (Laurence Olivier). Foreground, left to right: Claudius (Basil Sidney), Gertrude (Eileen Herlie), Polonius (Felix Aylmer).

40 **Cornelius/Voltemand.** In that and all things will we show our
   duty.

King. We doubt it nothing. Heartily farewell.

[Voltemand *and* Cornelius *exit*.]

And now, Laertes, what's the news with you?
You told us of some suit. What is 't, Laertes?
You cannot speak of reason to the Dane

45 And lose your voice. What wouldst thou beg, Laertes,
That shall not be my offer, not thy asking?
The head is not more native to the heart,
The hand more instrumental to the mouth,
Than is the throne of Denmark to thy father.

50 What wouldst thou have, Laertes?

Laertes.   My dread lord,
Your leave and favor to return to France,
From whence though willingly I came to Denmark
To show my duty in your coronation,

45 lose your voice: waste your breath.

47 native: closely connected.

The Tragedy of Hamlet: Act I, Scene 2   157

Yet now I must confess, that duty done,
55 My thoughts and wishes bend again toward France
And bow them to your gracious leave and pardon.

King. Have you your father's leave? What says Polonius?

Polonius. Hath, my lord, wrung from me my slow leave
By laborsome petition, and at last
60 Upon his will I sealed my hard consent.
I do beseech you give him leave to go.

King. Take thy fair hour, Laertes. Time be thine,
And thy best graces spend it at thy will.—
But now, my cousin Hamlet and my son—

65 **Hamlet** [*aside*]. A little more than kin and less than kind.

King. How is it that the clouds still hang on you?

Hamlet. Not so, my lord; I am too much in the sun.

Queen. Good Hamlet, cast thy nighted color off,
And let thine eye look like a friend on Denmark.
70 Do not forever with thy vailèd lids
Seek for thy noble father in the dust.
Thou know'st 'tis common; all that lives must die,
Passing through nature to eternity.

Hamlet. Ay, madam, it is common.

Queen. If it be,
75 Why seems it so particular with thee?

Hamlet. "Seems," madam? Nay, it is. I know not "seems."
'Tis not alone my inky cloak, good mother,
Nor customary suits of solemn black,
Nor windy suspiration of forced breath,
80 No, nor the fruitful river in the eye,
Nor the dejected havior of the visage,
Together with all forms, moods, shapes of grief,
That can denote me truly. These indeed "seem,"
For they are actions that a man might play;
85 But I have that within which passes show,
These but the trappings and the suits of woe.

King. 'Tis sweet and commendable in your nature, Hamlet,
To give these mourning duties to your father.
But you must know your father lost a father,
90 That father lost, lost his, and the survivor bound
In filial obligation for some term
To do obsequious sorrow. But to persever
In obstinate condolement is a course
Of impious stubbornness. 'Tis unmanly grief.

60 Upon . . . consent: I reluctantly agreed to his wishes.

64 cousin: kinsman.

65 Hamlet plays off two meanings of **kind:** "loving" and "natural." He does not resemble Claudius in nature or feel a son's affection for him.

67 sun: the sunlight of royal favor (also a pun on **son,** suggesting annoyance at Claudius's use of the word).

68 nighted color: dark mood.

70 vailèd lids: lowered eyes.

74 Hamlet plays off two meanings of **common:** "universal" and "vulgar."

75 particular: special, personal.

77–83 'Tis not . . . truly: My feelings are not limited to my black mourning clothes, heavy sighs, tears, downcast expression, and other outward signs of grief.

89–94 Claudius says that a surviving son must dutifully mourn (**do obsequious sorrow**) for a while, but to remain stubbornly in grief (**obstinate condolement**) beyond that appropriate period is perverse.

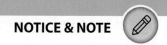

95 It shows a will most incorrect to heaven,
    A heart unfortified, a mind impatient,
    An understanding simple and unschooled.
    For what we know must be and is as common
    As any the most vulgar thing to sense,
100 Why should we in our peevish opposition
    Take it to heart? Fie, 'tis a fault to heaven,
    A fault against the dead, a fault to nature,
    To reason most absurd, whose common theme
    Is death of fathers, and who still hath cried,
105 From the first corse till he that died today,
    "This must be so." We pray you, throw to earth
    This unprevailing woe and think of us
    As of a father; for let the world take note,
    You are the most immediate to our throne,
110 And with no less nobility of love
    Than that which dearest father bears his son
    Do I impart toward you. For your intent
    In going back to school in Wittenberg,
    It is most retrograde to our desire,
115 And we beseech you, bend you to remain
    Here in the cheer and comfort of our eye,
    Our chiefest courtier, cousin, and our son.

    Queen. Let not thy mother lose her prayers, Hamlet.
    I pray thee, stay with us. Go not to Wittenberg.

120 **Hamlet.** I shall in all my best obey you, madam.

    King. Why, 'tis a loving and a fair reply.
    Be as ourself in Denmark.—Madam, come.
    This gentle and unforced accord of Hamlet
    Sits smiling to my heart, in grace where of
125 No jocund health that Denmark drinks today
    But the great cannon to the clouds shall tell,
    And the King's rouse the heaven shall bruit again,
    Respeaking earthly thunder. Come away.

    [*Flourish. All but* Hamlet *exit.*]

    Hamlet. O, that this too, too sullied flesh would melt,
130 Thaw, and resolve itself into a dew,
    Or that the Everlasting had not fixed
    His canon 'gainst self-slaughter! O God, God,
    How weary, stale, flat, and unprofitable
    Seem to me all the uses of this world!
135 Fie on 't, ah fie! 'Tis an unweeded garden
    That grows to seed. Things rank and gross in nature
    Possess it merely. That it should come to this:

96 unfortified: unstrengthened against adversity.

99 As . . . sense: as the most common experience.

104 still: always.

105 corse: corpse.

107 unprevailing: not yielding to persuasion.

108–112 Claudius claims that he offers (**impart toward**) Hamlet, who is next in line (**most immediate**) to succeed to the throne, all the love that the most affectionate father feels for his son.

113 Wittenberg University (founded in 1502) was famous for being the school of German theologian Martin Luther, whose challenge to Roman Catholic doctrine started the Reformation.

114 retrograde: contrary.

125–128 Claudius boasts that he will not merely drink a happy toast (**jocund health**) that day, but a deep drink (**rouse**) accompanied by fanfare, which heaven will echo with thunder.

129 sullied: stained, defiled.

132 canon: law.

ANALYZE SOLILOQUY

Annotate: Mark words in lines 129–159 that convey strong feelings.

Analyze: What is Hamlet most upset about in this soliloquy?

But two months dead—nay, not so much, not two.
So excellent a king, that was to this
140 Hyperion to a satyr; so loving to my mother
That he might not beteem the winds of heaven
Visit her face too roughly. Heaven and earth,
Must I remember? Why, she would hang on him
As if increase of appetite had grown
145 By what it fed on. And yet, within a month
(Let me not think on 't; frailty, thy name is woman!),
A little month, or ere those shoes were old
With which she followed my poor father's body,
Like Niobe, all tears—why she, even she
150 (O God, a beast that wants discourse of reason
Would have mourned longer!), married with my uncle,
My father's brother, but no more like my father
Than I to Hercules. Within a month,
Ere yet the salt of most unrighteous tears
155 Had left the flushing in her gallèd eyes,
She married. O, most wicked speed, to post
With such dexterity to incestuous sheets!
It is not, nor it cannot come to good.
But break, my heart, for I must hold my tongue.

[*Enter* Horatio, Marcellus, *and* Barnardo.]

160 **Horatio.** Hail to your lordship.

Hamlet. I am glad to see you well.
Horatio—or I do forget myself!

Horatio. The same, my lord, and your poor servant ever.

Hamlet. Sir, my good friend. I'll change that name with you.
165 And what make you from Wittenberg, Horatio?—Marcellus?

Marcellus. My good lord.

Hamlet. I am very glad to see you. [*To* Barnardo.] Good
even, sir.—
But what, in faith, make you from Wittenberg?

170 **Horatio.** A truant disposition, good my lord.

Hamlet. I would not hear your enemy say so,
Nor shall you do my ear that violence
To make it truster of your own report
Against yourself. I know you are no truant.
175 But what is your affair in Elsinore?
We'll teach you to drink deep ere you depart.

Horatio. My lord, I came to see your father's funeral.

Hamlet. I prithee, do not mock me, fellow student.

139–140 Hamlet says that comparing his father to Claudius would be like comparing the sun god **Hyperion** to a **satyr** (a mythical creature, half man and half goat, associated with lechery).

141 beteem: allow.

147 or ere: before.

149 Niobe: a Greek mythological figure who continued weeping for her slaughtered children even after she was turned to stone.

155 Had . . . eyes: had stopped reddening her inflamed (**gallèd**) eyes.

157 incestuous: Marriage between a widow and her late husband's brother was often considered incestuous in Shakespeare's time and was prohibited by church law.

163 Horatio refers to himself as a "servant" out of respect for Hamlet.

169 what . . . from: what are you doing away from.

173 truster: believer.

I think it was to see my mother's wedding.

180 **Horatio.** Indeed, my lord, it followed hard upon.

Hamlet. Thrift, thrift, Horatio. The funeral baked meats
Did coldly furnish forth the marriage tables.
Would I had met my dearest foe in heaven
Or ever I had seen that day, Horatio!
185 My father—methinks I see my father.

Horatio. Where, my lord?

Hamlet.   In my mind's eye, Horatio.

Horatio. I saw him once. He was a goodly king.

Hamlet. He was a man. Take him for all in all,
I shall not look upon his like again.

190 **Horatio.** My lord, I think I saw him yesternight.

Hamlet. Saw who?

Horatio. My lord, the King your father.

Hamlet.   The King my father?

Horatio. Season your admiration for a while
With an attent ear, till I may deliver
195 Upon the witness of these gentlemen

This marvel to you.

Hamlet.   For God's love, let me hear!

Horatio. Two nights together had these gentlemen,
Marcellus and Barnardo, on their watch,
In the dead waste and middle of the night,
200 Been thus encountered: a figure like your father,
Armèd at point exactly, cap-à-pie,
Appears before them and with solemn march
Goes slow and stately by them. Thrice he walked
By their oppressed and fear-surprisèd eyes
205 Within his truncheon's length, whilst they, distilled
Almost to jelly with the act of fear,
Stand dumb and speak not to him. This to me
In dreadful secrecy impart they did,
And I with them the third night kept the watch,
210 Where, as they had delivered, both in time,
Form of the thing (each word made true and good),
The apparition comes. I knew your father;
These hands are not more like.

Hamlet.   But where was this?

Marcellus. My lord, upon the platform where we watch.

180 **hard upon:** soon after.

181–182 **The funeral . . . tables:** Leftovers from the funeral were served cold at the marriage feast.

183 **dearest:** most hated.

184 **Or ever:** before.

187 **goodly:** fine, admirable.

193–194 **Season . . . ear:** Control your astonishment for a moment and listen carefully.

201 **Armèd . . . cap-à-pie:** armed properly in every detail, from head to foot.

205 **Within his truncheon's length:** no farther away than the length of his short staff.

205–206 **distilled . . . fear:** reduced almost to jelly by fear.

207–208 **This . . . did:** They told me this in terrified (**dreadful**) secrecy.

210 **delivered:** asserted.

217–218 did . . . speak: began to move as if it were going to speak.

219 even then: just then.

230 beaver: movable front piece of a helmet.

238 While . . . hundred: for as long as one could count (**tell**) to one hundred at a moderate pace.

240 grizzled: gray.

242 A sable silvered: black hair with white hair mixed through it.

215 **Hamlet.** Did you not speak to it?

Horatio.   My lord, I did,
But answer made it none. Yet once methought
It lifted up its head and did address
Itself to motion, like as it would speak;
But even then the morning cock crew loud,
220 And at the sound it shrunk in haste away
And vanished from our sight.

Hamlet.   'Tis very strange.

Horatio. As I do live, my honored lord, 'tis true.
And we did think it writ down in our duty
To let you know of it.

225 **Hamlet.** Indeed, sirs, but this troubles me.
Hold you the watch tonight?

All.   We do, my lord.

Hamlet. Armed, say you?

All.   Armed, my lord.

Hamlet.   From top to toe?

All. My lord, from head to foot.

Hamlet. Then saw you not his face?

230 **Horatio.** O, yes, my lord, he wore his beaver up.

Hamlet. What, looked he frowningly?

Horatio. A countenance more in sorrow than in anger.

Hamlet. Pale or red?

Horatio. Nay, very pale.

Hamlet.   And fixed his eyes upon you?

235 **Horatio.** Most constantly.

Hamlet.   I would I had been there.

Horatio. It would have much amazed you.

Hamlet. Very like. Stayed it long?

Horatio. While one with moderate haste might tell a hundred.

Barnardo/Marcellus. Longer, longer.

240 **Horatio.** Not when I saw 't.

Hamlet.   His beard was grizzled, no?

Horatio. It was as I have seen it in his life,
   A sable silvered.

Hamlet.   I will watch tonight.

Perchance 'twill walk again.

Horatio.   I warrant it will.

Hamlet. If it assume my noble father's person,
245 I'll speak to it, though hell itself should gape
And bid me hold my peace. I pray you all,
If you have hitherto concealed this sight,
Let it be tenable in your silence still;
And whatsomever else shall hap tonight,
250 Give it an understanding but no tongue.
I will requite your loves. So fare you well.
Upon the platform, 'twixt eleven and twelve,
I'll visit you.

All.   Our duty to your Honor.

Hamlet. Your loves, as mine to you. Farewell.

[*All but* Hamlet *exit.*]

255 My father's spirit—in arms! All is not well.
I doubt some foul play. Would the night were come!
Till then, sit still, my soul. Foul deeds will rise,
Though all the earth o'erwhelm them, to men's eyes.

[*He exits.*]

Scene 3 *Polonius's chambers.*

[*Enter* Laertes *and* Ophelia, *his sister.*]

Laertes. My necessaries are embarked. Farewell.
And, sister, as the winds give benefit
And convey is assistant, do not sleep,
But let me hear from you.

Ophelia.   Do you doubt that?

5 **Laertes.** For Hamlet, and the trifling of his favor,
Hold it a fashion and a toy in blood,
A violet in the youth of primy nature,
Forward, not permanent, sweet, not lasting,
The perfume and suppliance of a minute,
10 No more.

Ophelia.   No more but so?

Laertes.   Think it no more.
For nature, crescent, does not grow alone
In thews and bulk, but, as this temple waxes,
The inward service of the mind and soul
Grows wide withal. Perhaps he loves you now,
15 And now no soil nor cautel doth besmirch
The virtue of his will; but you must fear,

248 tenable: held.
249 whatsomever: whatever; **hap:** happen.
251 I . . . loves: I will reward your devotion.
256 doubt: suspect.
6 fashion . . . blood: a temporary enthusiasm and an amorous whim.
7 in . . . nature: at the beginning of its prime.
8 Forward: early blooming.
9–10 The . . . more: a sweet but temporary diversion.
11–14 A growing person does not only increase in strength (**thews**) and size, but as the body grows (**this temple waxes**), the inner life (**inward service**) of mind and soul grows along with it.
15 cautel: deceit.

Ophelia (Jean Simmons)

WORDS OF THE WISER

Notice & Note: Mark Laertes' reasons for his concern in lines 10–35.

Summarize: Why does Laertes think that Ophelia should not trust Hamlet's declaration of his love for her?

17 His . . . weighed: if you consider his high position.

20 Carve: choose.

22–24 And . . . head: His choice must be limited (**circumscribed**) by the opinion and consent (**voice and yielding**) of Denmark.

30 credent: trustful; **list:** listen to.

31–32 your chaste . . . importunity: lose your virginity to his uncontrolled pleading.

34 keep . . . affection: Don't go as far as your emotions would lead.

39 canker galls: cankerworm destroys; **infants:** early flowers.
40 buttons: buds; **disclosed:** opened.

His greatness weighed, his will is not his own,
For he himself is subject to his birth.
He may not, as unvalued persons do,
20 Carve for himself, for on his choice depends
The safety and the health of this whole state.
And therefore must his choice be circumscribed
Unto the voice and yielding of that body
Whereof he is the head. Then, if he says he loves you,
25 It fits your wisdom so far to believe it
As he in his particular act and place
May give his saying deed, which is no further
Than the main voice of Denmark goes withal.
Then weigh what loss your honor may sustain
30 If with too credent ear you list his songs
Or lose your heart or your chaste treasure open
To his unmastered importunity.
Fear it, Ophelia; fear it, my dear sister,
And keep you in the rear of your affection,
35 Out of the shot and danger of desire.
The chariest maid is prodigal enough
If she unmask her beauty to the moon.
Virtue itself 'scapes not calumnious strokes.
The canker galls the infants of the spring
40 Too oft before their buttons be disclosed,

And, in the morn and liquid dew of youth,
Contagious blastments are most imminent.
Be wary, then; best safety lies in fear.
Youth to itself rebels, though none else near.

45 **Ophelia.** I shall the effect of this good lesson keep
As watchman to my heart. But, good my brother,
Do not, as some ungracious pastors do,
Show me the steep and thorny way to heaven,
Whiles, like a puffed and reckless libertine,
50 Himself the primrose path of dalliance treads
And recks not his own rede.

Laertes.   O, fear me not.

[*Enter* Polonius.]

I stay too long. But here my father comes.
A double blessing is a double grace.
Occasion smiles upon a second leave.

55 **Polonius.** Yet here, Laertes? Aboard, aboard, for shame!
The wind sits in the shoulder of your sail,
And you are stayed for. There, my blessing with thee.
And these few precepts in thy memory
Look thou character. Give thy thoughts no tongue,
60 Nor any unproportioned thought his act.
Be thou familiar, but by no means vulgar.
Those friends thou hast, and their adoption tried,
Grapple them unto thy soul with hoops of steel,
But do not dull thy palm with entertainment
65 Of each new-hatched, unfledged courage. Beware
Of entrance to a quarrel, but, being in,
Bear 't that th' opposèd may beware of thee.
Give every man thy ear, but few thy voice.
Take each man's censure, but reserve thy judgment.
70 Costly thy habit as thy purse can buy,
But not expressed in fancy (rich, not gaudy),
For the apparel oft proclaims the man,
And they in France of the best rank and station
Are of a most select and generous chief in that.
75 Neither a borrower nor a lender be,
For loan oft loses both itself and friend,
And borrowing dulls the edge of husbandry.
This above all: to thine own self be true,
And it must follow, as the night the day,
80 Thou canst not then be false to any man.
Farewell. My blessing season this in thee.

Laertes. Most humbly do I take my leave, my lord.

NOTICE & NOTE

42 Contagious blastments: withering blights, harm or injury, catastrophes.

44 Youth . . . near: Youth by nature is prone to rebel.

46–51 Ophelia warns him not to act like a hypocritical pastor, preaching virtue and abstinence, while leading a life of promiscuity and ignoring his own advice.

58–65 Polonius tells Laertes to write down (**character**) these few rules of conduct (**precepts**) in his memory. He should keep his thoughts to himself and not act on any unfit (**unproportioned**) thoughts, be friendly but not vulgar, remain loyal to friends proven (**tried**) worthy of being accepted, but not shake hands with every swaggering youth (**unfledged courage**) who comes along.

73–74 And they . . . that: Upper-class French people especially show their refinement and nobility in their choice of apparel.

77 husbandry: thrift, proper handling of money.

81 Polonius hopes that his advice will ripen (**season**) in Laertes.

83 invests: is pressing.

Polonius. The time invests you. Go, your servants tend.

Laertes. Farewell, Ophelia, and remember well
85 What I have said to you.

Ophelia. 'Tis in my memory locked,
And you yourself shall keep the key of it.

Laertes. Farewell.

[Laertes *exits*.]

Polonius. What is 't, Ophelia, he hath said to you?

90 **Ophelia.** So please you, something touching the Lord Hamlet.

91 Marry: a mild oath, shortened from "by the Virgin Mary."

Polonius. Marry, well bethought.
'Tis told me he hath very oft of late
Given private time to you, and you yourself
Have of your audience been most free and bounteous.

95 put on: told to.

95 If it be so (as so 'tis put on me,
And that in way of caution), I must tell you
You do not understand yourself so clearly
As it behooves my daughter and your honor.
What is between you? Give me up the truth.

100–110 tenders: offers (lines 100 and 107). Polonius uses the word in line 107 to refer to coins that are not legal currency (**sterling**). He then warns Ophelia to offer (**tender**) herself at a higher rate (**more dearly**), or she will tender Polonius a fool—meaning either that she will present herself as a fool, that she will make him look like a fool, or that she will give him a grandchild.

100 **Ophelia.** He hath, my lord, of late made many tenders
Of his affection to me.

Polonius. Affection, puh! You speak like a green girl
Unsifted in such perilous circumstance.
Do you believe his "tenders," as you call them?

105 **Ophelia.** I do not know, my lord, what I should think.

Polonius. Marry, I will teach you. Think yourself a baby
That you have ta'en these tenders for true pay,
Which are not sterling. Tender yourself more dearly,
Or (not to crack the wind of the poor phrase,
110 Running it thus) you'll tender me a fool.

Ophelia. My lord, he hath importuned me with love
In honorable fashion—

Polonius. Ay, "fashion" you may call it. Go to, go to!

Ophelia. And hath given countenance to his speech, my lord,
115 With almost all the holy vows of heaven.

116 springes . . . woodcocks: snares to catch birds that are easily caught.

117 prodigal: lavishly.

118–121 These blazes . . . fire: These blazes, which lose their light and heat almost immediately, should not be mistaken for fire.

Polonius. Ay, springes to catch woodcocks. I do know,
When the blood burns, how prodigal the soul
Lends the tongue vows. These blazes, daughter,
Giving more light than heat, extinct in both
120 Even in their promise as it is a-making,
You must not take for fire. From this time
Be something scanter of your maiden presence.

Set your entreatments at a higher rate
Than a command to parle. For Lord Hamlet,
125 Believe so much in him that he is young,
And with a larger tether may he walk
Than may be given you. In few, Ophelia,
Do not believe his vows, for they are brokers,
Not of that dye which their investments show,
130 But mere implorators of unholy suits,
Breathing like sanctified and pious bawds
The better to beguile. This is for all:
I would not, in plain terms, from this time forth
Have you so slander any moment leisure
135 As to give words or talk with the Lord Hamlet.
Look to 't, I charge you. Come your ways.

Ophelia. I shall obey, my lord.

[*They exit.*]

Scene 4 *A guard platform at the castle.*

[*Enter* Hamlet, Horatio, *and* Marcellus.]

Hamlet. The air bites shrewdly; it is very cold.

Horatio. It is a nipping and an eager air.

Hamlet. What hour now?

Horatio. I think it lacks of twelve.

5 **Marcellus.** No, it is struck.

Horatio. Indeed, I heard it not. It then draws near the season
Wherein the spirit held his wont to walk.

[*A flourish of trumpets and two pieces goes off.*]

What does this mean, my lord?

Hamlet. The King doth wake tonight and takes his rouse,
10 Keeps wassail, and the swagg'ring upspring reels;
And, as he drains his draughts of Rhenish down,
The kettledrum and trumpet thus bray out
The triumph of his pledge.

Horatio. Is it a custom?

15 **Hamlet.** Ay, marry, is 't,
But, to my mind, though I am native here
And to the manner born, it is a custom
More honored in the breach than the observance.
This heavy-headed revel east and west
20 Makes us traduced and taxed of other nations.
They clepe us drunkards and with swinish phrase

ANALYZE DRAMATIC PLOT
Annotate: Reread lines 116–132. Mark phrases that suggest Polonius's attitude toward Hamlet's courtship of Ophelia.

Analyze: Hamlet's relationship with Ophelia is one of the play's subplots. How does Polonius's speech connect with Hamlet's thoughts about his mother and Claudius in lines 129–159 of Act I, Scene 2?

123–135 Polonius, metaphorically referring to Ophelia as a besieged castle, tells her not to enter into negotiations (**entreatments**) for surrender merely because the enemy wants to meet (**parle**) with her. Hamlet's vows are go-betweens (**brokers**) that are not like their outward appearance; these solicitors (**implorators**) of sinful petitions (**unholy suits**) speak in pious terms in order to deceive. Polonius orders her never to disgrace (**slander**) a moment of her time by speaking to Hamlet.

1 shrewdly: keenly.

2 eager: cutting.

9–13 The King stays up tonight drinking and dancing wildly; as he drinks down a glass of wine, kettledrums and trumpets play.

17 to the manner born: familiar since birth with this custom.

19–24 This drunken festivity makes us slandered and blamed by other nations. They call us drunkards and pigs, soiling our good name. Even when we do something outstanding, the essence of our reputation (**pith and marrow of our attribute**) is lost through drunkenness.

© Houghton Mifflin Harcourt Publishing Company

26 mole: defect.

29–32 Hamlet describes reason as a castle whose fortified walls are broken by the excessive growth of a natural trait or by a corrupting habit.

34 nature's . . . star: which they are born with or acquire.

35 His virtues else: their other virtues.

38–40 The dram . . . scandal: A small amount of evil blots out all of a person's good qualities.

45 questionable: capable of responding to questions.

48–50 tell . . . cerements: Tell me why your bones, which were placed in a coffin and received a proper church burial, have escaped from their burial clothes.

57 horridly . . . disposition: disturb us terribly.

61–62 As if . . . alone: as if it has something to tell you on your own.

Soil our addition. And, indeed, it takes
From our achievements, though performed at height,
The pith and marrow of our attribute.
25 So oft it chances in particular men
That for some vicious mole of nature in them,
As in their birth (wherein they are not guilty,
Since nature cannot choose his origin),
By the o'ergrowth of some complexion
30 (Oft breaking down the pales and forts of reason),
Or by some habit that too much o'erleavens
The form of plausive manners—that these men,
Carrying, I say, the stamp of one defect,
Being nature's livery or fortune's star,
35 His virtues else, be they as pure as grace,
As infinite as man may undergo,
Shall in the general censure take corruption
From that particular fault. The dram of evil
Doth all the noble substance of a doubt
40 To his own scandal.

[*Enter* Ghost.]

Horatio.   Look, my lord, it comes.

Hamlet. Angels and ministers of grace, defend us!
Be thou a spirit of health or goblin damned,
Bring with thee airs from heaven or blasts from hell,
Be thy intents wicked or charitable,
45 Thou com'st in such a questionable shape
That I will speak to thee. I'll call thee "Hamlet,"
"King," "Father," "Royal Dane." O, answer me!
Let me not burst in ignorance, but tell
Why thy canonized bones, hearsèd in death,
50 Have burst their cerements; why the sepulcher,
Wherein we saw thee quietly interred,
Hath oped his ponderous and marble jaws
To cast thee up again. What may this mean
That thou, dead corse, again in complete steel,
55 Revisits thus the glimpses of the moon,
Making night hideous, and we fools of nature
So horridly to shake our disposition
With thoughts beyond the reaches of our souls?
Say, why is this? Wherefore? What should we do?

[Ghost *beckons*.]

60 **Horatio.** It beckons you to go away with it
As if it some impartment did desire
To you alone.

Marcellus.   Look with what courteous action
It waves you to a more removèd ground.
But do not go with it.

Horatio.   No, by no means.

65 **Hamlet.** It will not speak. Then I will follow it.

Horatio. Do not, my lord.

Hamlet.   Why, what should be the fear?
I do not set my life at a pin's fee.
And for my soul, what can it do to that,
Being a thing immortal as itself?
70 It waves me forth again. I'll follow it.

Horatio. What if it tempt you toward the flood, my lord?
Or to the dreadful summit of the cliff
That beetles o'er his base into the sea,
And there assume some other horrible form
75 Which might deprive your sovereignty of reason
And draw you into madness? Think of it.
The very place puts toys of desperation,
Without more motive, into every brain
That looks so many fathoms to the sea
80 And hears it roar beneath.

Hamlet. It waves me still.—Go on, I'll follow thee.

Marcellus. You shall not go, my lord.

[*They hold back* Hamlet.]

Hamlet.   Hold off your hands.

Horatio. Be ruled. You shall not go.

Hamlet.   My fate cries out
And makes each petty arture in this body
85 As hardy as the Nemean lion's nerve.
Still am I called. Unhand me, gentlemen.
By heaven, I'll make a ghost of him that lets me!
I say, away!—Go on. I'll follow thee.

[Ghost *and* Hamlet *exit.*]

Horatio. He waxes desperate with imagination.

90 **Marcellus.** Let's follow. 'Tis not fit thus to obey him.

Horatio. Have after. To what issue will this come?

Marcellus. Something is rotten in the state of Denmark.

Horatio. Heaven will direct it.

Marcellus. Nay, let's follow him.

[*They exit.*]

NOTICE & NOTE

67 pin's fee: the value of a pin.

71–76 Horatio is worried that the Ghost might lead Hamlet toward the sea (**flood**) or to the top of the cliff that hangs (**beetles**) over the sea, and then take on some horrible appearance that would drive Hamlet insane.

77 toys of desperation: irrational impulses.

84 arture: artery.

85 Nemean lion's nerve: the sinews of a mythical lion strangled by Hercules.

87 lets: hinders.

91 Have after: Let's go after him.

© Houghton Mifflin Harcourt Publishing Company

Scene 5 *Another part of the fortifications.*

[*Enter* Ghost *and* Hamlet.]

Hamlet. Whither wilt thou lead me? Speak. I'll go no further.

Ghost. Mark me.

Hamlet.   I will.

Ghost.   My hour is almost come
When I to sulf'rous and tormenting flames
Must render up myself.

Hamlet.   Alas, poor ghost!

5   **Ghost.** Pity me not, but lend thy serious hearing
To what I shall unfold.

Hamlet. Speak. I am bound to hear.

Ghost. So art thou to revenge, when thou shalt hear.

Hamlet. What?

10 **Ghost.** I am thy father's spirit.
Doomed for a certain term to walk the night
And for the day confined to fast in fires
Till the foul crimes done in my days of nature
Are burnt and purged away. But that I am forbid
15 To tell the secrets of my prison house,
I could a tale unfold whose lightest word
Would harrow up thy soul, freeze thy young blood,
Make thy two eyes, like stars, start from their spheres,
Thy knotted and combinèd locks to part,
20 And each particular hair to stand an end,
Like quills upon the fearful porpentine.
But this eternal blazon must not be
To ears of flesh and blood. List, list, O list!
If thou didst ever thy dear father love—

7 bound: obligated.

13 crimes: sins.

17 harrow up: tear up, disturb.

18 Make . . . spheres: make your two eyes like stars jump from their assigned places in the universe.

19 knotted . . . locks: carefully arranged hair.

20 an end: on end.

21 fearful porpentine: frightened porcupine.

22–23 The Ghost says he must not describe life beyond death to a living person.

25 **Hamlet.** O God!

Ghost. Revenge his foul and most unnatural murder.

Hamlet. Murder?

Ghost. Murder most foul, as in the best it is,
But this most foul, strange, and unnatural.

30 **Hamlet.** Haste me to know 't, that I, with wings as swift
As meditation or the thoughts of love,
May sweep to my revenge.

Ghost.   I find thee apt;
And duller shouldst thou be than the fat weed
That roots itself in ease on Lethe wharf,
35 Wouldst thou not stir in this. Now, Hamlet, hear.
'Tis given out that, sleeping in my orchard,
A serpent stung me. So the whole ear of Denmark
Is by a forgèd process of my death
Rankly abused. But know, thou noble youth,
40 The serpent that did sting thy father's life
Now wears his crown.

Hamlet. O, my prophetic soul! My uncle!

Ghost. Ay, that incestuous, that adulterate beast,
With witchcraft of his wit, with traitorous gifts—
45 O wicked wit and gifts, that have the power
So to seduce!—won to his shameful lust
The will of my most seeming-virtuous queen.
O Hamlet, what a falling off was there!
From me, whose love was of that dignity
50 That it went hand in hand even with the vow
I made to her in marriage, and to decline
Upon a wretch whose natural gifts were poor
To those of mine.
But virtue, as it never will be moved,
55 Though lewdness court it in a shape of heaven,
So, lust, though to a radiant angel linked,
Will sate itself in a celestial bed
And prey on garbage.
But soft, methinks I scent the morning air.
60 Brief let me be. Sleeping within my orchard,
My custom always of the afternoon,
Upon my secure hour thy uncle stole,
With juice of cursèd hebona in a vial,
And in the porches of my ears did pour
65 The leprous distilment, whose effect
Holds such an enmity with blood of man
That swift as quicksilver it courses through

28 as . . . is: which murder in general (**it**) is at the very least.

32–35 I find . . . this: I think you are willing, and you would have to be duller than the thick weed that grows on the banks of Lethe (the river of forgetfulness in the underworld) to not be roused by this.

36 orchard: garden.

37–39 So . . . abused: Thus all of Denmark is deceived by a false account of my death.

ANALYZE DRAMATIC PLOT
Annotate: Mark the secret the Ghost reveals in lines 32–41.

Infer: Why does Hamlet say in line 42 that his soul was "prophetic"?

43 adulterate: adulterous.

54–58 The Ghost compares virtue, which remains pure even if indecency courts it in a heavenly form, with lust, which grows weary of a virtuous marriage and seeks depravity.

63 hebona: a poisonous plant.

64 porches: entrances.

65 leprous distilment: a distilled liquid that causes disfigurement similar to that caused by leprosy.

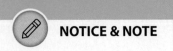
69–71 doth . . . blood: The poison curdles the blood like something sour dropped into milk.

72–74 most instant . . . body: An eruption of sores (**tetter**) instantly covered my smooth body, leper-like (**lazar-like**), with a vile crust like the bark on a tree.

76 dispatched: deprived.

77–80 The Ghost regrets that he had no chance to receive the last rites of the church; he died with all his sins unabsolved.

84 luxury: lust.

86–89 The Ghost tells Hamlet not to think of revenge against his mother.

90 matin: morning.

94 couple: add.

98 globe: head.

99–105 Hamlet vows to erase from the slate (**table**) of his memory all foolish notes (**fond records**), wise sayings (**saws**) he copied from books, and past impressions (**pressures past**) so that the Ghost's command will live in his mind unmixed with ordinary, insignificant thoughts.

The natural gates and alleys of the body,
And with a sudden vigor it doth posset
70 And curd, like eager droppings into milk,
The thin and wholesome blood. So did it mine,
And a most instant tetter barked about,
Most lazar-like, with vile and loathsome crust
All my smooth body.
75 Thus was I, sleeping, by a brother's hand
Of life, of crown, of queen at once dispatched,
Cut off, even in the blossoms of my sin,
Unhouseled, disappointed, unaneled,
No reck'ning made, but sent to my account
80 With all my imperfections on my head.
O horrible, O horrible, most horrible!
If thou hast nature in thee, bear it not.
Let not the royal bed of Denmark be
A couch for luxury and damnèd incest.
85 But, howsomever thou pursues this act,
Taint not thy mind, nor let thy soul contrive
Against thy mother aught. Leave her to heaven
And to those thorns that in her bosom lodge
To prick and sting her. Fare thee well at once.
90 The glowworm shows the matin to be near
And 'gins to pale his uneffectual fire.
Adieu, adieu, adieu. Remember me.

[*He exits.*]

Hamlet. O all you host of heaven! O earth! What else?
And shall I couple hell? O fie! Hold, hold, my heart,
95 And you, my sinews, grow not instant old,
But bear me stiffly up. Remember thee?
Ay, thou poor ghost, whiles memory holds a seat
In this distracted globe. Remember thee?
Yea, from the table of my memory
100 I'll wipe away all trivial, fond records,
All saws of books, all forms, all pressures past,
That youth and observation copied there,
And thy commandment all alone shall live
Within the book and volume of my brain,
105 Unmixed with baser matter. Yes, by heaven!
O most pernicious woman!
O villain, villain, smiling, damnèd villain!
My tables—meet it is I set it down
That one may smile and smile and be a villain.
110 At least I am sure it may be so in Denmark.

[*He writes.*]

So, uncle, there you are. Now to my word.
It is "adieu, adieu, remember me."
I have sworn 't.
[*Enter* Horatio *and* Marcellus.]

Horatio. My lord, my lord!

115 **Marcellus.** Lord Hamlet.

Horatio. Heavens secure him!

Hamlet. So be it.

Marcellus. Illo, ho, ho, my lord!

Hamlet. Hillo, ho, ho, boy! Come, bird, come!

119 Hamlet responds to Marcellus's greeting (**illo, ho, ho**) with the call of a falconer to his hawk.

120 **Marcellus.** How is 't, my noble lord?

Horatio. What news, my lord?

Hamlet. O, wonderful!

Horatio. Good my lord, tell it.

Hamlet. No, you will reveal it.

Horatio. Not I, my lord, by heaven.

Marcellus. Nor I, my lord.

Hamlet. How say you, then? Would heart of man once think it?
125 But you'll be secret?

Horatio/Marcellus. Ay, by heaven, my lord.

Hamlet. There's never a villain dwelling in all Denmark
But he's an arrant knave.

128 arrant knave: thoroughly dishonest person.

Horatio. There needs no ghost, my lord, come from the grave.
130 To tell us this.

Hamlet. Why, right, you are in the right.
And so, without more circumstance at all,
I hold it fit that we shake hands and part,
You, as your business and desire shall point you
(For every man hath business and desire,
135 Such as it is), and for my own poor part,
I will go pray.

131 circumstance: elaboration.

Horatio. These are but wild and whirling words, my lord.

Hamlet. I am sorry they offend you, heartily;
Yes, faith, heartily.

Horatio. There's no offense, my lord.

140 **Hamlet.** Yes, by Saint Patrick, but there is, Horatio,
And much offense, too. Touching this vision here,
It is an honest ghost—that let me tell you.
For your desire to know what is between us,

142 honest: genuine.

O'ermaster 't as you may. And now, good friends,
145 As you are friends, scholars, and soldiers,
Give me one poor request.

Horatio. What is 't, my lord? We will.

Hamlet. Never make known what you have seen tonight.

Horatio/Marcellus. My lord, we will not.

150 **Hamlet.** Nay, but swear 't.

Horatio. In faith, my lord, not I.

Marcellus. Nor I, my lord, in faith.

Hamlet. Upon my sword.

Marcellus. We have sworn, my lord, already.

Hamlet. Indeed, upon my sword, indeed.

155 **Ghost** [*cries under the stage*]. Swear.

Hamlet. Ha, ha, boy, sayst thou so? Art thou there, truepenny?
Come on, you hear this fellow in the cellarage.
Consent to swear.

Horatio. Propose the oath, my lord.

Hamlet. Never to speak of this that you have seen,
160 Swear by my sword.

Ghost [*beneath*]. Swear.

Hamlet. *Hic et ubique*? Then we'll shift our ground.
Come hither, gentlemen,
And lay your hands again upon my sword.
165 Swear by my sword
Never to speak of this that you have heard.

Ghost [*beneath*]. Swear by his sword.

Hamlet. Well said, old mole. Canst work i' th' earth so fast?
A worthy pioner! Once more remove, good friends.

170 **Horatio.** O day and night, but this is wondrous strange.

Hamlet. And therefore as a stranger give it welcome.
There are more things in heaven and earth, Horatio,
Than are dreamt of in your philosophy. But come.
Here, as before, never, so help you mercy,
175 How strange or odd some'er I bear myself
(As I perchance hereafter shall think meet
To put an antic disposition on)
That you, at such times seeing me, never shall,
With arms encumbered thus, or this headshake,
180 Or by pronouncing of some doubtful phrase,
As "Well, well, we know," or "We could an if we would."

153 The hilt of a sword, shaped like a cross, was often used for swearing oaths.

156 truepenny: honest fellow.

162 *Hic et ubique:* here and everywhere (Latin).

169 pioner: digger, miner.

171 Hamlet tells Horatio to welcome, or accept, the night's events as one would welcome a stranger.

173 your philosophy: the general subject of philosophy (not a particular belief of Horatio's).

174–185 Hamlet reveals that he may have to disguise himself with strange behavior (**antic disposition**); he has them swear not to make any gestures or hints that would give him away.

Or "If we list to speak," or "There be an if they might,"
Or such ambiguous giving-out, to note
That you know aught of me—this do swear,
185 So grace and mercy at your most need help you.

Ghost [*beneath*]. Swear.

Hamlet. Rest, rest, perturbèd spirit.—So, gentlemen,
With all my love I do commend me to you,
And what so poor a man as Hamlet is
190 May do t' express his love and friending to you,
God willing, shall not lack. Let us go in together,
And still your fingers on your lips, I pray.
The time is out of joint. O cursèd spite
That ever I was born to set it right!
195 Nay, come, let's go together.

[*They exit.*]

188–191 Hamlet says that he entrusts himself to them and will do his best to reward them.

193 The . . . joint: Everything is in disorder.

CHECK YOUR UNDERSTANDING

Answer these questions before moving on to the **Analyze the Text** section on the following page.

1 At a public gathering in the castle, Claudius criticizes Hamlet for —

   A continuing to mourn his father's death

   B wanting to return to France

   C associating with friends such as Horatio

   D staying up too late at night

2 How does Hamlet react to hearing about his father's Ghost?

   F He is terrified.

   G He does not believe Horatio.

   H He wants to meet the Ghost.

   J He thinks Horatio is insane.

3 How did King Hamlet die?

   A He was killed in battle.

   B He was murdered by Queen Gertrude.

   C He died of illness.

   D He was poisoned by Claudius.

RESPOND

ANALYZE THE TEXT

Support your responses with evidence from the text. ⬛ NOTEBOOK

1. **Infer** In Act I, Scene 2, Claudius urges Hamlet to stay at court instead of returning to Wittenberg. What might he be concerned about?

2. **Draw Conclusions** Reread lines 129–159 of Scene 2. What does this soliloquy suggest about Hamlet's state of mind at this point in the play?

3. **Evaluate** Even before the Ghost reveals Claudius's crime, Hamlet has harsh feelings toward him. What do Claudius's speeches in Scene 2 suggest about his character?

4. **Predict** In Scene 5, lines 173–185, Hamlet asks Horatio and Marcellus not to give him away if he starts to act strangely. What does this remark hint about his plans to deal with Claudius?

5. **Notice & Note** Reread Gertrude's advice to Hamlet in Scene 2, lines 68–73, and Hamlet's reaction to it. What does this exchange reveal about Hamlet's relationship with his mother?

CREATE AND PRESENT

Write a Comparison In Act I, we learn about Hamlet's relationship with his uncle, and we also learn about Ophelia's relations with her father. Write a paragraph in which you compare the two relationships.

❏ First, analyze Hamlet's interaction with Claudius in Scene 2, lines 64–128.

❏ Next, analyze Ophelia's interaction with Polonius in Scene 3, lines 89–137.

❏ Summarize the key similarities and differences in these relationships.

Present a Comparison In a small group, present your paragraph that you wrote comparing the relationships between Hamlet and his uncle, and Ophelia and her father.

❏ Try to focus on the main points; don't read directly from your paragraph.

❏ Practice making eye contact with your group members.

❏ Work to avoid filler words like "uh" and "um." Take a silent pause instead and gather yourself before moving forward.

❏ Practice this until you can comfortably deliver a presentation on your paragraph.

© Houghton Mifflin Harcourt Publishing Company

SETTING A PURPOSE

As you read, pay attention to subplots that develop and consider how they tie into the arc of the larger story.

Notice & Note

Use the side margins to notice and note signposts in the text.

ACT II

Scene 1 *Polonius's chambers.*

[*Enter old* Polonius *with his man* Reynaldo.]

Polonius. Give him this money and these notes, Reynaldo.

Reynaldo. I will, my lord.

Polonius. You shall do marvelous wisely, good Reynaldo,
Before you visit him, to make inquire
5 Of his behavior.

Reynaldo.   My lord, I did intend it.

Polonius. Marry, well said, very well said. Look you, sir,
Inquire me first what Danskers are in Paris;
And how, and who, what means, and where they
  keep,
What company, at what expense; and finding
10 By this encompassment and drift of question
That they do know my son, come you more nearer
Than your particular demands will touch it.
Take you, as 'twere, some distant knowledge of him,
As thus: "I know his father and his friends
15 And, in part, him." Do you mark this, Reynaldo?

Reynaldo. Ay, very well, my lord.

Polonius. "And, in part, him, but," you may say, "not
  well.
But if 't be he I mean, he's very wild,
Addicted so and so." And there put on him
20 What forgeries you please—marry, none so rank
As may dishonor him, take heed of that,
But, sir, such wanton, wild, and usual slips
As are companions noted and most known
To youth and liberty.

6–12 Polonius tells him to start by asking general questions, because he will find out more through this roundabout approach (**encompassment**) than by asking specific questions about Laertes.

13 Take you: assume.

19–20 put on . . . please: accuse him of whatever faults you wish to make up; **rank:** gross.

22 wanton: reckless.

23–24 As are . . . liberty: that are commonly associated with youth and freedom.

24 gaming: gambling.

26 drabbing: going to prostitutes.

28 you . . . charge: You can soften (**season**) the charge by the way you state it.

30 incontinency: habitual sexual misconduct (as opposed to an occasional lapse).

31–35 Polonius tells him to describe Laertes' faults so subtly that they will seem the faults that come with independence (**taints of liberty**), the sudden urges of an excited mind, a wildness in untamed blood that occurs in most men.

37 Wherefore: why.

40 fetch of wit: clever move.

41–46 Polonius wants Reynaldo to put these small stains (**sullies**) on his son's reputation—similar to the way in which cloth might be dirtied when it is handled—and then ask the person whether he has seen Laertes engaged in the offenses Reynaldo has mentioned (**prenominate crimes**).

46 He closes . . . consequence: he agrees with you in the following way.

48 addition: form of address.

59 o'ertook in 's rouse: overcome by drink.

62 *Videlicet:* namely.

Reynaldo.   As gaming, my lord.

25 **Polonius.** Ay, or drinking, fencing, swearing,
Quarreling, drabbing—you may go so far.

Reynaldo. My lord, that would dishonor him.

Polonius. Faith, no, as you may season it in the charge.
You must not put another scandal on him
30 That he is open to incontinency;
That's not my meaning. But breathe his faults so
     quaintly
That they may seem the taints of liberty,
The flash and outbreak of a fiery mind,
A savageness in unreclaimèd blood,
35 Of general assault.

Reynaldo. But, my good lord—

Polonius. Wherefore should you do this?

Reynaldo. Ay, my lord, I would know that.

Polonius. Marry, sir, here's my drift,
40 And I believe it is a fetch of wit.
You, laying these slight sullies on my son,
As 'twere a thing a little soiled i' th' working,
Mark you, your party in converse, him you would
     sound,
Having ever seen in the prenominate crimes
45 The youth you breathe of guilty, be assured
He closes with you in this consequence:
"Good sir," or so, or "friend," or "gentleman,"
According to the phrase or the addition
Of man and country—

Reynaldo.   Very good, my lord.

50 **Polonius.** And then, sir, does he this, he does—what was I
about to say? By the Mass, I was about to say something.
Where did I leave?

Reynaldo. At "closes in the consequence," at "friend, or
so, and gentleman."

55 **Polonius.** At "closes in the consequence"—ay, marry—
He closes thus: "I know the gentleman.
I saw him yesterday," or "th' other day"
(Or then, or then, with such or such), "and as you say,
There was he gaming, there o'ertook in 's rouse,
60 There falling out at tennis"; or perchance
"I saw him enter such a house of sale"—
Videlicet, a brothel—or so forth. See you now

Your bait of falsehood take this carp of truth;
And thus do we of wisdom and of reach,
65 With windlasses and with assays of bias,
By indirections find directions out.
So by my former lecture and advice
Shall you my son. You have me, have you not?

Reynaldo. My lord, I have.

Polonius.   God be wi' you. Fare you well.

70 **Reynaldo.** Good my lord.

Polonius. Observe his inclination in yourself.

Reynaldo. I shall, my lord.

Polonius. And let him ply his music.

Reynaldo. Well, my lord.

75 **Polonius.** Farewell.

[Reynaldo *exits*.]

[*Enter* Ophelia.]

                              How now, Ophelia, what's the matter?

Ophelia. O, my lord, my lord, I have been so affrighted!

Polonius. With what, i' th' name of God?

Ophelia. My lord, as I was sewing in my closet,
Lord Hamlet, with his doublet all unbraced,
80 No hat upon his head, his stockings fouled,
Ungartered, and down-gyvèd to his ankle,
Pale as his shirt, his knees knocking each other,
And with a look so piteous in purport
As if he had been loosèd out of hell
85 To speak of horrors—he comes before me.

Polonius. Mad for thy love?

Ophelia.   My lord, I do not know,
But truly I do fear it.

Polonius.   What said he?

Ophelia. He took me by the wrist and held me hard.
Then goes he to the length of all his arm,
90 And, with his other hand thus o'er his brow,
He falls to such perusal of my face
As he would draw it. Long stayed he so.
At last, a little shaking of mine arm,
And thrice his head thus waving up and down,
95 He raised a sigh so piteous and profound
As it did seem to shatter all his bulk

64–66 **we of . . . out:** we who have wisdom and intelligence (**reach**) find things out indirectly, through roundabout courses (**windlasses**) and indirect tests (**assays of bias**).

ANALYZE DRAMATIC PLOT
Annotate: Underline phrases in lines 55–68 that sum up Polonius's strategy.

Connect: How do his instructions in this subplot relate to Hamlet's thoughts about the Danish court?

71–73 Polonius tells him to observe Laertes' behavior personally and to see that Laertes practices his music.

78 **closet:** private room.

79 **doublet all unbraced:** jacket entirely unfastened.

80 **fouled:** dirty.

81 **down-gyvèd to his ankle:** fallen down to his ankles (like a prisoner's ankle chains, or gyves).

83 **purport:** expression.

96 **bulk:** body.

101 to the last ... me: kept his eyes upon me the whole time.

103–107 Polonius says that the violent nature (**property**) of this love madness (**ecstasy**) often leads people to do something desperate.

113 coted: observed.

114 wrack: ruin, seduce; **beshrew my jealousy:** curse my suspicious nature.

115–118 It is as natural for old people to go too far (**cast beyond ourselves**) with their suspicions as it is for younger people to lack good judgment.

119–120 Polonius decides that although it may anger the King, he must be told about this love because keeping it a secret might create even more grief.

6 Sith ... man: since neither his appearance nor his personality.

10–18 Because Rosencrantz and Guildenstern were childhood friends with Hamlet and are so familiar with his past and his usual manner (**havior**), Claudius asks them to agree to stay (**vouchsafe your rest**) at court awhile to cheer Hamlet up and find out whether he is troubled by something that Claudius is unaware of.

And end his being. That done, he lets me go,
And, with his head over his shoulder turned,
He seemed to find his way without his eyes,
100 For out o' doors he went without their helps
And to the last bended their light on me.

Polonius. Come, go with me. I will go seek the King.
This is the very ecstasy of love,
Whose violent property fordoes itself
105 And leads the will to desperate undertakings
As oft as any passions under heaven
That does afflict our natures. I am sorry.
What, have you given him any hard words of late?

Ophelia. No, my good lord, but as you did command
110 I did repel his letters and denied
His access to me.

Polonius.   That hath made him mad.
I am sorry that with better heed and judgment
I had not coted him. I feared he did but trifle
And meant to wrack thee. But beshrew my jealousy!
115 By heaven, it is as proper to our age
To cast beyond ourselves in our opinions
As it is common for the younger sort
To lack discretion. Come, go we to the King.
This must be known, which, being kept close, might move
120 More grief to hide than hate to utter love.
Come.
[*They exit.*]

Scene 2 *The castle.*

[*Flourish. Enter* King *and* Queen, Rosencrantz *and* Guildenstern *and* Attendants.]

King. Welcome, dear Rosencrantz and Guildenstern.
Moreover that we much did long to see you,
The need we have to use you did provoke
Our hasty sending. Something have you heard
5 Of Hamlet's transformation, so call it,
Sith nor th' exterior nor the inward man
Resembles that it was. What it should be,
More than his father's death, that thus hath put him
So much from th' understanding of himself
10 I cannot dream of. I entreat you both
That, being of so young days brought up with him
And sith so neighbored to his youth and havior,

That you vouchsafe your rest here in our court
Some little time, so by your companies
15 To draw him on to pleasures, and to gather
So much as from occasion you may glean,
Whether aught to us unknown afflicts him thus
That, opened, lies within our remedy.

Queen. Good gentlemen, he hath much talked of you,
20 And sure I am two men there is not living
To whom he more adheres. If it will please you
To show us so much gentry and goodwill
As to expend your time with us awhile
For the supply and profit of our hope,
25 Your visitation shall receive such thanks
As fits a king's remembrance.

Rosencrantz.   Both your Majesties
Might, by the sovereign power you have of us,
Put your dread pleasures more into command
Than to entreaty.

Guildenstern.   But we both obey,
30 And here give up ourselves in the full bent
To lay our service freely at your feet,
To be commanded.

King. Thanks, Rosencrantz and gentle Guildenstern.

Queen. Thanks, Guildenstern and gentle Rosencrantz.
35 And I beseech you instantly to visit
My too much changèd son. Go, some of you,
And bring these gentlemen where Hamlet is.

Guildenstern. Heavens make our presence and our
    practices
Pleasant and helpful to him!

Queen.   Ay, amen!

[Rosencrantz *and* Guildenstern *exit with some* Attendants.]

[*Enter* Polonius.]

40 **Polonius.** Th' ambassadors from Norway, my good lord,
Are joyfully returned.

King. Thou still hast been the father of good news.

Polonius. Have I, my lord? I assure my good liege
I hold my duty as I hold my soul,
45 Both to my God and to my gracious king,
And I do think, or else this brain of mine
Hunts not the trail of policy so sure
As it hath used to do, that I have found
The very cause of Hamlet's lunacy.

18 **opened:** revealed.

22 **gentry:** courtesy.

24 **For . . . hope:** to aid and fulfill our wishes.

29–32 Guildenstern promises that they will devote themselves entirely (**in the full bent**) to the service of the King and Queen.

38 **practices:** doings (sometimes used to mean "trickery").

42 **still:** always.

47–48 **Hunts . . . do:** does not follow the path of political shrewdness as well as it used to.

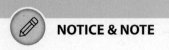

NOTICE & NOTE

52 fruit: dessert.

56 the main: the main matter.

58 sift him: question Polonius carefully.

59 brother: fellow king.

61 Upon our first: as soon as we brought up the matter.

ANALYZE CONFLICT

Annotate: Mark details in lines 60–76 about Fortinbras's plan against Claudius.

Analyze: How was this conflict resolved?

67 borne in hand: deceived; **arrests:** orders to desist.

69 in fine: finally.

71 give . . . against: challenge militarily.

77–80 give . . . down: allow troops to move through Denmark for this expedition, under the conditions set down for Denmark's security and Fortinbras's permission.

80 likes: pleases.

81 our more considered time: a more suitable time for consideration.

50 **King.** O, speak of that! That do I long to hear.

Polonius. Give first admittance to th' ambassadors.
My news shall be the fruit to that great feast.

King. Thyself do grace to them and bring them in.

[Polonius *exits*.]

He tells me, my dear Gertrude, he hath found
55 The head and source of all your son's distemper.

Queen. I doubt it is no other but the main—
His father's death and our o'erhasty marriage.

King. Well, we shall sift him.

[*Enter* Ambassadors Voltemand *and* Cornelius *with* Polonius.]

Welcome, my good friends.
Say, Voltemand, what from our brother Norway?

60 **Voltemand.** Most fair return of greetings and desires.
Upon our first, he sent out to suppress
His nephew's levies, which to him appeared
To be a preparation 'gainst the Polack,
But, better looked into, he truly found
65 It was against your Highness. Whereat, grieved
That so his sickness, age, and impotence
Was falsely borne in hand, sends out arrests
On Fortinbras, which he, in brief, obeys,
Receives rebuke from Norway, and, in fine,
70 Makes vow before his uncle never more
To give th' assay of arms against your Majesty.
Whereon old Norway, overcome with joy,
Gives him three-score thousand crowns in annual
    fee
And his commission to employ those soldiers,
75 So levied as before, against the Polack,
With an entreaty, herein further shown,

[*He gives a paper*.]

That it might please you to give quiet pass
Through your dominions for this enterprise,
On such regards of safety and allowance
80 As therein are set down.

King.   It likes us well,
And, at our more considered time, we'll read,
Answer, and think upon this business.
Meantime, we thank you for your well-took labor.
Go to your rest. At night we'll feast together.
85 Most welcome home!

[Voltemand *and* Cornelius *exit*.]

Polonius.   This business is well ended.
My liege, and madam, to expostulate
What majesty should be, what duty is,
Why day is day, night night, and time is time
Were nothing but to waste night, day, and time.
90 Therefore, since brevity is the soul of wit,
And tediousness the limbs and outward flourishes,
I will be brief. Your noble son is mad.
"Mad" call I it, for, to define true madness,
What is 't but to be nothing else but mad?
95 But let that go.

Queen.   More matter with less art.

Polonius. Madam, I swear I use no art at all.
That he's mad, 'tis true; 'tis true 'tis pity,
And pity 'tis 'tis true—a foolish figure,
But farewell it, for I will use no art.
100 Mad let us grant him then, and now remains
That we find out the cause of this effect,
Or, rather say, the cause of this defect,
For this effect defective comes by cause.
Thus it remains, and the remainder thus.
105 Perpend.
I have a daughter (have while she is mine)
Who, in her duty and obedience, mark,
Hath given me this. Now gather and surmise.

[*He reads*.] *To the celestial, and my soul's idol, the*
110 *most beautified Ophelia*—

That's an ill phrase, a vile phrase; "beautified" is a
vile phrase. But you shall hear. Thus: [*He reads*.]
In her excellent white bosom, these, etc.—

Queen. Came this from Hamlet to her?

115 **Polonius.** Good madam, stay awhile. I will be faithful.

[*He reads the letter*.]
        Doubt thou the stars are fire,
            Doubt that the sun doth move,
        Doubt truth to be a liar,
            But never doubt I love.
120 *O dear Ophelia, I am ill at these numbers. I have not*
art to reckon my groans, but that I love thee
best, O most best, believe it. Adieu.
                Thine evermore, most dear lady, whilst
                    this machine is to him, Hamlet.

86–89 To inquire into (**expostulate**) the nature of one's duty to the crown would be a waste of time, like trying to figure out the reason for day, night, and time.

90 brevity . . . wit: intelligent speech should be concise.

91 flourishes: decorations.

95–99 The Queen asks Polonius to make his point without such a display of rhetoric (**art**). He claims to be speaking plainly about the matter, but then he can't resist making a figure of speech that even he describes as foolish.

105 Perpend: consider.

108 gather and surmise: draw your own conclusions.

114–115 The Queen doubts Hamlet would use such formal and flowery language; Polonius assures her he will read the letter accurately.

116 Doubt: suspect.

120 ill at these numbers: bad at writing in verse.

121 reckon: count, put into metrical verse.

123–124 whilst . . . to him: while I am still in this body (**machine**).

126–128 more above . . . ear: In addition, she has told me all the details of his solicitations as they occurred.

137 played . . . table-book: kept this knowledge hidden within me.

138 given . . . winking: closed the eyes of my heart.

139 with idle sight: saw without really noticing.

142 star: sphere.

143 prescripts: orders.

144 resort: visits.

147–152 Polonius describes the stages of Hamlet's decline: he grew sad, then stopped eating, then suffered from sleeplessness (**a watch**), then turned weak and lightheaded, and finally became mad.

157 The actor playing Polonius might point from his head to his shoulder or make a similar gesture while speaking this line.

160 the center: the Earth's center, the most inaccessible place; **try:** test.

125   This, in obedience, hath my daughter shown me,
And more above, hath his solicitings,
As they fell out by time, by means, and place,
All given to mine ear.

King. But how hath she received his love?

130 **Polonius.** What do you think of me?

King. As of a man faithful and honorable.

Polonius. I would fain prove so. But what might you think,
When I had seen this hot love on the wing
(As I perceived it, I must tell you that,
135 Before my daughter told me), what might you,
Or my dear Majesty your queen here, think,
If I had played the desk or table-book
Or given my heart a winking, mute and dumb,
Or looked upon this love with idle sight?
140 What might you think? No, I went round to work,
And my young mistress thus I did bespeak:
"Lord Hamlet is a prince, out of thy star.
This must not be." And then I prescripts gave her,
That she should lock herself from his resort,
145 Admit no messengers, receive no tokens;
Which done, she took the fruits of my advice,
And he, repelled (a short tale to make),
Fell into a sadness, then into a fast,
Thence to a watch, thence into a weakness,
150 Thence to a lightness, and, by this declension,
Into the madness wherein now he raves
And all we mourn for.

King [*to* Queen].   Do you think 'tis this?

Queen. It may be, very like.

Polonius. Hath there been such a time (I would fain know that)
155 That I have positively said "'Tis so,"
When it proved otherwise?

King.   Not that I know.

Polonius. Take this from this, if this be otherwise.
If circumstances lead me, I will find
Where truth is hid, though it were hid, indeed,
160 Within the center.

King.   How may we try it further?

Polonius. You know sometimes he walks four hours together

© Houghton Mifflin Harcourt Publishing Company

Here in the lobby.

Queen.   So he does indeed.

Polonius. At such a time I'll loose my daughter to him.
[*To the* King.] Be you and I behind an arras then.
165 Mark the encounter. If he love her not,
And be not from his reason fall'n thereon,
Let me be no assistant for a state,
But keep a farm and carters.

King.   We will try it.

[*Enter* Hamlet *reading on a book*.]

Queen. But look where sadly the poor wretch comes
    reading.

170 **Polonius.** Away, I do beseech you both, away.
I'll board him presently. O, give me leave.

[King *and* Queen *exit with* Attendants.]

How does my good Lord Hamlet?

Hamlet. Well, God-a-mercy.

Polonius. Do you know me, my lord?

175 **Hamlet.** Excellent well. You are a fishmonger.

Polonius. Not I, my lord.

163 loose: turn loose (as an animal might be released for mating).

164 arras: a tapestry hung in front of a wall.

171 board him presently: speak to him at once.

ANALYZE CONFLICT
Annotate: As you read lines 172–221, mark insulting comments that Hamlet makes about Polonius.

Infer: Why might he treat Polonius this way?

175 fishmonger: fish seller.

© Houghton Mifflin Harcourt Publishing Company • Image Credits: © Nat Farbman/Time Life Pictures/Getty Images

Hamlet. Then I would you were so honest a man.

Polonius. Honest, my lord?

Hamlet. Ay, sir. To be honest, as this world goes, is to
180 be one man picked out of ten thousand.

Polonius. That's very true, my lord.

Hamlet. For if the sun breed maggots in a dead dog,
being a good kissing carrion—Have you a daughter?

Polonius. I have, my lord.

185 **Hamlet.** Let her not walk i' th' sun. Conception is a
blessing, but, as your daughter may conceive,
friend, look to 't.

Polonius [*aside*]. How say you by that? Still harping on
my daughter. Yet he knew me not at first; he said I
190 was a fishmonger. He is far gone. And truly, in my
youth, I suffered much extremity for love, very
near this. I'll speak to him again.—What do you
read, my lord?

Hamlet. Words, words, words.

195 **Polonius.** What is the matter, my lord?

Hamlet. Between who?

Polonius. I mean the matter that you read, my lord.

Hamlet. Slanders, sir; for the satirical rogue says here
that old men have gray beards, that their faces are
200 wrinkled, their eyes purging thick amber and plum-tree
gum, and that they have a plentiful lack of wit,
together with most weak hams; all which, sir,
though I most powerfully and potently believe, yet
I hold it not honesty to have it thus set down; for
205 yourself, sir, shall grow old as I am, if, like a crab,
you could go backward.

Polonius [*aside*]. Though this be madness, yet there is
method in 't.—Will you walk out of the air, my lord?

Hamlet. Into my grave?

210 **Polonius.** Indeed, that's out of the air. [*Aside.*] How
pregnant sometimes his replies are! A happiness that
often madness hits on, which reason and sanity
could not so prosperously be delivered of. I will
leave him and suddenly contrive the means of
215 meeting between him and my daughter.—My lord,
I will take my leave of you.

183 a good kissing carrion: good flesh for kissing. (Hamlet seems to be reading at least part of this sentence from his book.)

185 Conception: understanding, being pregnant.

188 harping on: sticking to the subject of.

195 matter: subject matter. (Hamlet plays off another meaning, "the basis of a quarrel.")

201 wit: understanding.

204 honesty: good manners.

208 Polonius asks him to come out of the open air.

211 pregnant: full of meaning; **happiness:** talent for expression.

Hamlet. You cannot, sir, take from me anything that I
will more willingly part withal—except my life,
except my life, except my life.

220 **Polonius.** Fare you well, my lord.

Hamlet [*aside*]. These tedious old fools.

[*Enter* Guildenstern *and* Rosencrantz.]

Polonius. You go to seek the Lord Hamlet. There he is.

Rosencrantz [*to* Polonius]. God save you, sir.

[Polonius *exits*.]

Guildenstern. My honored lord.

225 **Rosencrantz.** My most dear lord.

Hamlet. My excellent good friends! How dost thou,
Guildenstern? Ah, Rosencrantz! Good lads, how
do you both?

Rosencrantz. As the indifferent children of the earth.

230 **Guildenstern.** Happy in that we are not overhappy.
On Fortune's cap, we are not the very button.

Hamlet. Nor the soles of her shoe?

Rosencrantz. Neither, my lord.

Hamlet. Then you live about her waist, or in the middle
235 of her favors?

Guildenstern. Faith, her privates we.

Hamlet. In the secret parts of Fortune? O, most true!
She is a strumpet. What news?

Rosencrantz. None, my lord, but that the world's
240 grown honest.

Hamlet. Then is doomsday near. But your news is not
true. Let me question more in particular. What
have you, my good friends, deserved at the hands of
Fortune that she sends you to prison hither?

245 **Guildenstern.** Prison, my lord?

Hamlet. Denmark's a prison.

Rosencrantz. Then is the world one.

Hamlet. A goodly one, in which there are many
confines, wards, and dungeons, Denmark being
250 one o' th' worst.

Rosencrantz. We think not so, my lord.

229 indifferent: ordinary.

234–238 Hamlet exchanges
sexual puns with his childhood
friends. References to Fortune's
sexual favors and private parts
lead up to the traditional saying
that the unfaithful Fortune is a
prostitute (**strumpet**).

249 confines: places of
confinement; **wards:** cells.

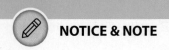

260–262 Guildenstern says that the apparently substantial aims of ambition are even less substantial than dreams.

266–267 Hamlet says that according to their logic, only beggars would have real bodies (since they lack ambition), and monarchs and ambitious (**outstretched**) heroes would be the shadows of beggars.

268 fay: faith.

269 wait upon: escort. (Hamlet takes the word to mean "serve" and replies that he would not categorize them with his servants.)

ANALYZE DRAMATIC PLOT
Annotate: Mark Hamlet's questions in lines 270–280.

Infer: What does he suspect is the real purpose of his friends' visit?

278 too dear a halfpenny: too costly at a halfpenny.

279 free: voluntary.

282 Hamlet sarcastically asks them to give him anything but a straight answer.

285 color: disguise.

288–289 conjure you: ask you earnestly.

289–290 consonancy of our youth: our closeness when we were young.

291–292 by what . . . withal: by whatever you hold more valuable, which someone more skillful than me would use to urge you with.

Hamlet. Why, then, 'tis none to you, for there is nothing either good or bad but thinking makes it so. To me, it is a prison.

255 **Rosencrantz.** Why, then, your ambition makes it one. 'Tis too narrow for your mind.

Hamlet. O God, I could be bounded in a nutshell and count myself a king of infinite space, were it not that I have bad dreams.

260 **Guildenstern.** Which dreams, indeed, are ambition, for the very substance of the ambitious is merely the shadow of a dream.

Hamlet. A dream itself is but a shadow.

Rosencrantz. Truly, and I hold ambition of so airy and
265 light a quality that it is but a shadow's shadow.

Hamlet. Then are our beggars bodies, and our monarchs and outstretched heroes the beggars' shadows. Shall we to th' court? For, by my fay, I cannot reason.

Rosencrantz/Guildenstern. We'll wait upon you.

270 **Hamlet.** No such matter. I will not sort you with the rest of my servants, for, to speak to you like an honest man, I am most dreadfully attended. But, in the beaten way of friendship, what make you at Elsinore?

275 **Rosencrantz.** To visit you, my lord, no other occasion.

Hamlet. Beggar that I am, I am even poor in thanks; but I thank you, and sure, dear friends, my thanks are too dear a halfpenny. Were you not sent for? Is it your own inclining? Is it a free visitation? Come,
280 come, deal justly with me. Come, come; nay, speak.

Guildenstern. What should we say, my lord?

Hamlet. Anything but to th' purpose. You were sent for, and there is a kind of confession in your looks which your modesties have not craft
285 enough to color. I know the good king and queen have sent for you.

Rosencrantz. To what end, my lord?

Hamlet. That you must teach me. But let me conjure you by the rights of our fellowship, by the consonancy
290 of our youth, by the obligation of our everpreserved love, and by what more dear a better proposer can charge you withal: be even and

direct with me whether you were sent for or no.

Rosencrantz [*to* Guildenstern]. What say you?

295 **Hamlet** [*aside*]. Nay, then I have an eye of you.—If you love me, hold not off.

Guildenstern. My lord, we were sent for.

Hamlet. I will tell you why; so shall my anticipation prevent your discovery, and your secrecy to the
300 King and Queen molt no feather. I have of late, but wherefore I know not, lost all my mirth, forgone all custom of exercises, and, indeed, it goes so heavily with my disposition that this goodly frame, the earth, seems to me a sterile promontory; this
305 most excellent canopy, the air, look you, this brave o'er-hanging firmament, this majestical roof, fretted with golden fire—why, it appeareth nothing to me but a foul and pestilent congregation of vapors. What a piece of work is a man, how noble in reason,
310 how infinite in faculties, in form and moving how express and admirable; in action how like an angel, in apprehension how like a god: the beauty of the world, the paragon of animals—and yet, to me, what is this quintessence of dust? Man delights
315 not me, no, nor women neither, though by your smiling you seem to say so.

Rosencrantz. My lord, there was no such stuff in my thoughts.

Hamlet. Why did you laugh, then, when I said "man
320 delights not me"?

Rosencrantz. To think, my lord, if you delight not in man, what Lenten entertainment the players shall receive from you. We coted them on the way, and hither are they coming to offer you service.

325 **Hamlet.** He that plays the king shall be welcome—his Majesty shall have tribute on me. The adventurous knight shall use his foil and target, the lover shall not sigh gratis, the humorous man shall end his part in peace, the clown shall make those laugh
330 whose lungs are tickle o' th' sear, and the lady shall say her mind freely, or the blank verse shall halt for 't. What players are they?

Rosencrantz. Even those you were wont to take such delight in, the tragedians of the city.

335 **Hamlet.** How chances it they travel? Their residence,

295 Hamlet reminds them that he is watching.

298–299 shall my . . . discovery: My saying it first will spare you from revealing your secret.

300 molt no feather: will not be diminished.

304 promontory: a rock jutting out from the sea.

305 brave: splendid.

306 fretted: adorned.

308 congregation: gathering.

309 piece of work: work of art or fine craftsmanship.

311 express: exact, expressive.

312 apprehension: understanding.

314 quintessence of dust: essence, or most refined form, of dust.

322 Lenten entertainment: meager, or spare, reception.

323 coted: passed.

325–332 The king shall receive his praise, the knight shall use his sword and shield, the lover shall not sigh for nothing, the eccentric (**humorous**) character shall play his part in peace, the clown shall make those laugh who do so easily, and the lady shall speak without restraint, or else the blank verse (which has five metrical feet) will limp (**halt**) because of it.

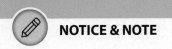

337–349 The players had to leave the city due to competition from a company of boy actors—a nest (**aerie**) of young hawks (**little eyases**) who are loudly applauded for their shrill performances. Many fashionable patrons are afraid to attend the public theaters (**common stages**) where adult actors play, fearing satirical attacks from the pens of those who write for the boy actors.

351 escoted: provided for.

351–352 pursue . . . sing: perform only until their voices change.

353 common: adult.

356 succession: future work as actors.

358 tar: provoke.

359–361 no money . . . question: the only profitable plays were satires about this rivalry.

366–367 Ay . . . load: Yes, they've won over the whole theater world.

368–371 Hamlet says that people who made faces (**mouths**) at his uncle while his father was alive now pay up to 100 gold coins for his miniature portrait.

both in reputation and profit, was better both ways.

Rosencrantz. I think their inhibition comes by the means of the late innovation.

Hamlet. Do they hold the same estimation they did
340 when I was in the city? Are they so followed?

Rosencrantz. No, indeed are they not.

Hamlet. How comes it? Do they grow rusty?

Rosencrantz. Nay, their endeavor keeps in the wonted pace. But there is, sir, an aerie of children, little
345 eyases, that cry out on the top of question and are most tyrannically clapped for 't. These are now the fashion and so berattle the common stages (so they call them) that many wearing rapiers are afraid of goose quills and dare scarce come thither.

350 **Hamlet.** What, are they children? Who maintains 'em? How are they escoted? Will they pursue the quality no longer than they can sing? Will they not say afterwards, if they should grow themselves to common players (as it is most like, if their means are no better),
355 their writers do them wrong to make them exclaim against their own succession?

Rosencrantz. Faith, there has been much to-do on both sides, and the nation holds it no sin to tar them to controversy. There was for a while no
360 money bid for argument unless the poet and the player went to cuffs in the question.

Hamlet. Is 't possible?

Guildenstern. O, there has been much throwing about of brains.

365 **Hamlet.** Do the boys carry it away?

Rosencrantz. Ay, that they do, my lord—Hercules and his load too.

Hamlet. It is not very strange; for my uncle is King of Denmark, and those that would make mouths at
370 him while my father lived give twenty, forty, fifty, a hundred ducats apiece for his picture in little. 'Sblood, there is something in this more than natural, if philosophy could find it out.

[*A flourish for the* Players.]

Guildenstern. There are the players.

375 **Hamlet.** Gentlemen, you are welcome to Elsinore.

Your hands, come then. Th' appurtenance of welcome
is fashion and ceremony. Let me comply with
you in this garb, lest my extent to the players,
which, I tell you, must show fairly outwards,
380 should more appear like entertainment than yours.
You are welcome. But my uncle-father and aunt-
mother are deceived.

Guildenstern. In what, my dear lord?

Hamlet. I am but mad north-north-west. When the
385 wind is southerly, I know a hawk from a handsaw.

[*Enter* Polonius.]

Polonius. Well be with you, gentlemen.

Hamlet. Hark you, Guildenstern, and you too—at
each ear a hearer! That great baby you see there is
not yet out of his swaddling clouts.

390 **Rosencrantz.** Haply he is the second time come to
them, for they say an old man is twice a child.

Hamlet. I will prophesy he comes to tell me of the
players; mark it.—You say right, sir, a Monday
morning, 'twas then indeed.

395 **Polonius.** My lord, I have news to tell you.

Hamlet. My lord, I have news to tell you: when
Roscius was an actor in Rome—

Polonius. The actors are come hither, my lord.

Hamlet. Buzz, buzz.

400 **Polonius.** Upon my honor—

Hamlet. Then came each actor on his ass.

Polonius. The best actors in the world, either for
tragedy, comedy, history, pastoral, pastoral-comical,
historical-pastoral, tragical-historical,
405 tragical-comical-historical-pastoral, scene individable,
or poem unlimited. Seneca cannot be too
heavy, nor Plautus too light. For the law of writ
and the liberty, these are the only men.

Hamlet. O Jephthah, judge of Israel, what a treasure
410 hadst thou!

Polonius. What a treasure had he, my lord?

Hamlet. Why,

> One fair daughter, and no more,
> The which he lovèd passing well.

NOTICE & NOTE

375–381 Hamlet tells Rosencrantz and Guildenstern that since fashion and ceremony should accompany a welcome, he wants to observe these formalities with them so it will not appear that the players get a better reception than they do.

384–385 Hamlet says he is only mad when the wind blows in a certain direction; at other times, he can tell one thing from another.

389 swaddling clouts: cloth used to wrap a newborn baby.

397 Roscius: a famous Roman actor.

399 Hamlet dismisses the announcement as old news.

406 Seneca: a Roman writer of tragedies.

406–407 Plautus: a Roman writer of comedies; **For the . . . liberty:** for plays that follow strict rules of dramatic composition as well as more loosely written plays.

409–426 Jephthah: a biblical figure who sacrifices his beloved daughter after making a thoughtless vow (see Judges 11). Hamlet quotes lines from a ballad based on this story.

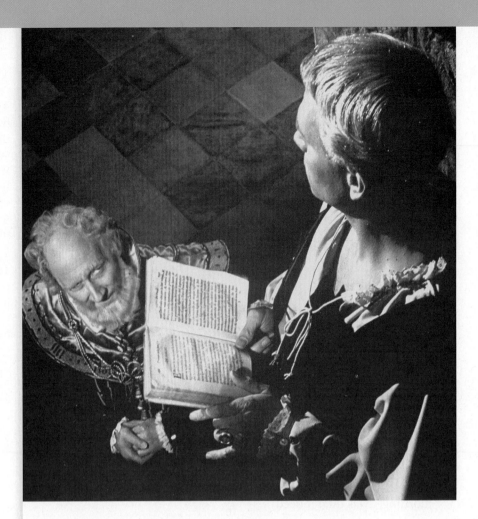

415 **Polonius** [*aside*]. Still on my daughter.

Hamlet. Am I not i' th' right, old Jephthah?

Polonius. If you call me "Jephthah," my lord: I have a daughter that I love passing well.

Hamlet. Nay, that follows not.

420 **Polonius.** What follows then, my lord?

Hamlet. Why,

        As by lot, God wot

and then, you know,

    It came to pass, as most like it was—

425 the first row of the pious chanson will show you more, for look where my abridgment comes.

[*Enter the* Players.]

You are welcome, masters; welcome all.—I am glad to see thee well.—Welcome, good friends.—O my old friend! Why, thy face is valanced since I saw

430 thee last. Com'st thou to beard me in Denmark— What, my young lady and mistress! By'r Lady, your ladyship is nearer to heaven than when I saw you last, by the altitude of a chopine. Pray God your voice, like a piece of uncurrent gold, be not

425 the first ... chanson: the first stanza of the religious song.

429 valanced: fringed (with a beard).

431–435 All female roles were played by boys. Hamlet fears that this boy's voice might crack onstage, since he has grown by the height of a thick-soled shoe.

435 cracked within the ring. Masters, you are all
welcome. We'll e'en to 't like French falconers, fly
at anything we see. We'll have a speech straight.
Come, give us a taste of your quality. Come, a passionate
speech.

440 **First Player.** What speech, my good lord?

Hamlet. I heard thee speak me a speech once, but it
was never acted, or, if it was, not above once; for
the play, I remember, pleased not the million: 'twas
caviary to the general. But it was (as I received it,
445 and others whose judgments in such matters cried
in the top of mine) an excellent play, well digested
in the scenes, set down with as much modesty as
cunning. I remember one said there were no sallets
in the lines to make the matter savory, nor no matter
450 in the phrase that might indict the author of
affectation, but called it an honest method, as
wholesome as sweet and, by very much, more
handsome than fine. One speech in 't I chiefly
loved. 'Twas Aeneas' tale to Dido, and thereabout
455 of it especially when he speaks of Priam's slaughter.
If it live in your memory, begin at this line—let me
see, let me see:
The rugged Pyrrhus, like th' Hyrcanian beast—
'tis not so; it begins with Pyrrhus:
460 *The rugged Pyrrhus, he whose sable arms,*
Black as his purpose, did the night resemble
When he lay couchèd in th' ominous horse,
Hath now this dread and black complexion smeared
With heraldry more dismal. Head to foot,
465 *Now is he total gules, horridly tricked*
With blood of fathers, mothers, daughters, sons,
Baked and impasted with the parching streets,
That lend a tyrannous and a damnèd light
To their lord's murder. Roasted in wrath and fire,
470 *And thus o'ersizèd with coagulate gore,*
With eyes like carbuncles, the hellish Pyrrhus
Old grandsire Priam seeks.
So, proceed you.

Polonius. 'Fore God, my lord, well spoken, with good
475 accent and good discretion.

First Player.   *Anon he finds him*
Striking too short at Greeks. His antique sword,
Rebellious to his arm, lies where it falls,
Repugnant to command. Unequal matched,

© Houghton Mifflin Harcourt Publishing Company

436–437 fly . . . see: take on anything.

437 straight: right away.

444 caviary to the general: like caviar, which is unappreciated by most people.

446 digested: arranged.

447 modesty: restraint.

448 cunning: skill; **sallets:** spicy bits, racey jests.

454–455 Pyrrhus, son of the Greek hero Achilles, killed King Priam to revenge the death of his father during the Trojan War. Aeneas tells the story to Dido, the Queen of Carthage, in Virgil's *Aeneid.*

458 Hyrcanian beast: a tiger.

462 couchèd: concealed; **ominous horse:** wooden horse used by the Greeks to enter Troy.

465 total gules: all red; **tricked:** adorned.

467 The blood is baked and crusted (**impasted**) from the heat of the burning streets.

470 o'ersizèd: smeared over.

471 carbuncles: fiery red stones.

479 Repugnant to: resisting.

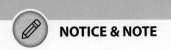

NOTICE & NOTE

482 unnervèd: strengthless; **senseless Ilium:** the inanimate fortress of Troy.

485 Takes . . . ear: captures Pyrrhus' attention.

488–490 So . . . nothing: Pyrrhus stood still like a tyrant in a painting, suspended between his intentions and taking the actions that would fulfill them.

492 rack: mass of high clouds.

497 Cyclops: one-eyed giants who worked for Vulcan, the Roman god of metalworking.

498 Mars: Roman god of war; **for proof eterne:** to last for eternity.

502 synod: assembly.

503 fellies: section of a wheel's rim.

504 nave: hub of a wheel.

508–509 He's for . . . sleeps: Unless he's hearing a comic song and dance (**jig**) or a bawdy tale, he falls asleep.

509 Hecuba: Priam's wife.

510 moblèd: her face was muffled.

514 bisson rheum: blinding tears; **clout:** cloth.

516 o'erteemèd: worn out from childbearing.

519 'Gainst . . . pronounced: would have proclaimed treasonous statements against Fortune's rule.

480 *Pyrrhus at Priam drives, in rage strikes wide;*
But with the whiff and wind of his fell sword
Th' unnervèd father falls. Then senseless Ilium,
Seeming to feel this blow, with flaming top
Stoops to his base, and with a hideous crash
485 *Takes prisoner Pyrrhus' ear. For lo, his sword,*
Which was declining on the milky head
Of reverend Priam, seemed i' th' air to stick.
So as a painted tyrant Pyrrhus stood
And, like a neutral to his will and matter,
490 *Did nothing.*
But as we often see against some storm
A silence in the heavens, the rack stand still,
The bold winds speechless, and the orb below
As hush as death, anon the dreadful thunder
495 *Doth rend the region; so, after Pyrrhus' pause,*
Arousèd vengeance sets him new a-work,
And never did the Cyclops' hammers fall
On Mars's armor, forged for proof eterne,
With less remorse than Pyrrhus' bleeding sword
500 *Now falls on Priam.*
Out, out, thou strumpet Fortune! All you gods
In general synod take away her power,
Break all the spokes and fellies from her wheel,
And bowl the round nave down the hill of heaven
505 *As low as to the fiends!*

Polonius. This is too long.

Hamlet. It shall to the barber's with your beard.—
Prithee say on. He's for a jig or a tale of bawdry, or
he sleeps. Say on; come to Hecuba.

510 **First Player.** *But who, ah woe, had seen the moblèd queen—*

Hamlet. "The moblèd queen"?

Polonius. That's good. "Moblèd queen" is good.

First Player. *Run barefoot up and down, threat'ning the flames*
With bisson rheum, a clout upon that head
515 *Where late the diadem stood, and for a robe,*
About her lank and all o'erteemèd loins
A blanket, in the alarm of fear caught up—
Who this had seen, with tongue in venom steeped,
'Gainst Fortune's state would treason have pronounced.
520 *But if the gods themselves did see her then*
When she saw Pyrrhus make malicious sport

In mincing with his sword her husband's limbs,
The instant burst of clamor that she made
(Unless things mortal move them not at all)
525 *Would have made milch the burning eyes of heaven*
And passion in the gods.

Polonius. Look whe'er he has not turned his color and has tears in 's eyes. Prithee, no more.

Hamlet. 'Tis well. I'll have thee speak out the rest of
530 this soon.—Good my lord, will you see the players well bestowed? Do you hear, let them be well used, for they are the abstract and brief chronicles of the time. After your death you were better have a bad epitaph than their ill report while you live.

535 **Polonius.** My lord, I will use them according to their desert.

Hamlet. God's bodykins, man, much better! Use every man after his desert and who shall 'scape whipping? Use them after your own honor and dignity.
540 The less they deserve, the more merit is in your bounty. Take them in.

Polonius. Come, sirs.

Hamlet. Follow him, friends. We'll hear a play tomorrow. [*As Polonius and* Players *exit,* Hamlet *speaks to*
545 *the* First Player.] Dost thou hear me, old friend? Can you play "The Murder of Gonzago"?

First Player. Ay, my lord.

Hamlet. We'll ha 't tomorrow night. You could, for a need, study a speech of some dozen or sixteen
550 lines, which I would set down and insert in 't, could you not?

First Player. Ay, my lord.

Hamlet. Very well. Follow that lord—and look you mock him not. [First Player *exits*.] My good friends, I'll leave
555 you till night. You are welcome to Elsinore.

Rosencrantz. Good my lord.

Hamlet. Ay, so, good-bye to you.

[Rosencrantz *and* Guildenstern *exit*.]

                     Now I am alone.
O, what a rogue and peasant slave am I!
Is it not monstrous that this player here,
560 But in a fiction, in a dream of passion,

525 milch: milky, moist with tears.

527 whe'er: whether.

532 abstract: summary.

537 God's bodykins: by God's little body.

548 ha 't: have it.

ANALYZE SOLILOQUY
Annotate: As you read lines 558–590, mark phrases Hamlet uses to describe himself.

Interpret: What internal conflict does the speech express?

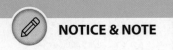

561–562 Could . . . wanned:
could force his soul into such
agreement with his thoughts
that his soul made his face turn
pale.

564–565 his whole . . . conceit:
all of his activity creating
outward appearances that
express his thoughts.

571 cleave . . . speech: pierce
everyone's ears with horrible
words.

572 appall the free: terrify the
innocent.

575 muddy-mettled: weak-
spirited; **peak:** mope.

576 John-a-dreams: a dreamy
idler; **unpregnant of:** not
roused to action by.

579 defeat: destruction.

582–583 gives . . . lungs: calls
me a complete liar.

584 'Swounds: by Christ's
wounds (an oath).

585 pigeon-livered: meek as a
pigeon.

587 kites: birds of prey.

588 offal: entrails.

589 kindless: unnatural.

591 brave: admirable.

595 drab: prostitute.

596 scullion: kitchen servant.

597 About: get to work.

599 cunning of the scene: skill
of the performance.

600 presently: immediately.

601 malefactions: crimes.

606 tent . . . quick: probe him
in his most vulnerable spot;
blench: flinch.

Could force his soul so to his own conceit
That from her working all his visage wanned,
Tears in his eyes, distraction in his aspect,
A broken voice, and his whole function suiting
565 With forms to his conceit—and all for nothing!
For Hecuba!
What's Hecuba to him, or he to Hecuba,
That he should weep for her? What would he do
Had he the motive and the cue for passion
570 That I have? He would drown the stage with tears
And cleave the general ear with horrid speech,
Make mad the guilty and appall the free,
Confound the ignorant and amaze indeed
The very faculties of eyes and ears. Yet I,
575 A dull and muddy-mettled rascal, peak
Like John-a-dreams, unpregnant of my cause,
And can say nothing—no, not for a king
Upon whose property and most dear life
A damned defeat was made. Am I a coward?
580 Who calls me "villain"? breaks my pate across?
Plucks off my beard and blows it in my face?
Tweaks me by the nose? gives me the lie i' th' throat
As deep as to the lungs? Who does me this?
Ha! 'Swounds, I should take it! For it cannot be
585 But I am pigeon-livered and lack gall
To make oppression bitter, or ere this
I should have fatted all the region kites
With this slave's offal. Bloody, bawdy villain!
Remorseless, treacherous, lecherous, kindless villain!
590 O vengeance!
Why, what an ass am I! This is most brave,
That I, the son of a dear father murdered,
Prompted to my revenge by heaven and hell,
Must, like a whore, unpack my heart with words
595 And fall a-cursing like a very drab,
A scullion! Fie upon 't! Foh!
About, my brains!—Hum, I have heard
That guilty creatures sitting at a play
Have, by the very cunning of the scene,
600 Been struck so to the soul that presently
They have proclaimed their malefactions.
For murder, though it have no tongue, will speak
With most miraculous organ. I'll have these players
Play something like the murder of my father
605 Before mine uncle. I'll observe his looks;
I'll tent him to the quick. If he do blench,

I know my course. The spirit that I have seen
May be a devil, and the devil hath power
T' assume a pleasing shape; yea, and perhaps,
610 Out of my weakness and my melancholy,
As he is very potent with such spirits,
Abuses me to damn me. I'll have grounds
More relative than this. The play's the thing
Wherein I'll catch the conscience of the King.

[*He exits.*]

612–613 grounds . . . this: a more solid basis for acting than the Ghost's words.

ANALYZE DRAMATIC PLOT
Annotate: Mark details in lines 597–614 that explain why Hamlet wants to test Claudius's guilt.

Connect: What does this explanation demonstrate about his character?

CHECK YOUR UNDERSTANDING

Answer these questions before moving on to the **Analyze the Text** section on the following page.

1 What does Polonius think is causing Hamlet's moodiness?

  A He suspects Hamlet is plotting revenge against Claudius.

  B He believes Hamlet has a mental illness.

  C He realizes Hamlet is still grieving for his father.

  D He knows Hamlet is lovesick for Ophelia.

2 Why have Claudius and Gertrude invited Rosencrantz and Guildenstern to Elsinore?

  F They want Rosencrantz and Guildenstern to spy on Polonius.

  G They want Rosencrantz and Guildenstern to cheer up Hamlet.

  H Rosencrantz and Guildenstern will manage their land.

  J Rosencrantz and Guildenstern have committed crimes.

3 How does Hamlet plan to test Claudius's guilt?

  A He will ask Claudius to watch a play that depicts a murder similar to that of his father.

  B He hopes to get Claudius to admit to the crime by holding him at knife point.

  C He asks his mother to coax it out of Claudius over dinner.

  D He will confront Claudius as if he already has evidence proving his guilt.

RESPOND

ANALYZE THE TEXT

Support your responses with evidence from the text. 📓 NOTEBOOK

1. **Evaluate** In Act II, Scene 1, lines 78–101, Ophelia describes what happened when Hamlet visited her. Did he just pretend to be mad in that encounter, or could he have been genuinely disturbed because of what he learned about his father's murder? Consider the following:
   • his warning to Horatio and Marcellus at the end of Act I
   • his relationship with Ophelia
   • the details in her description
   • his behavior with other characters in Act II

2. **Interpret** In Scene 2, line 246, Hamlet tells Rosencrantz and Guildenstern that "Denmark's a prison." How does this statement reflect his situation at the Danish court?

3. **Analyze** Reread Hamlet's speech in Scene 2, lines 309–316. What internal conflict does he express here?

4. **Compare** The speech recited by the First Player in Scene 2, lines 475–505, tells the story of Pyrrhus. How does this Greek mythological figure serve as a foil for Hamlet?

5. **Draw Conclusions** At the end of Act II, Hamlet reveals his plan for testing Claudius's guilt. Why might Shakespeare have chosen a theatrical performance for this purpose?

CREATE AND DISCUSS

Discuss with a Small Group Hamlet is not quick to act; instead, he takes time to think through each decision he makes before moving forward. Why is Hamlet so cautious?

   ❏ Gather evidence from the text about Hamlet's pretending to be mad and his plan to test Claudius's guilt.

   ❏ In a small group, discuss why Hamlet takes these measures. Consider what might happen if he tried to immediately take revenge.

   ❏ As group members share ideas and supporting evidence, reflect on and adjust your earlier remarks if their reasons and evidence lead you to change your mind.

   ❏ Respond using appropriate vocabulary and tone.

   ❏ Summarize the group discussion and present your ideas to the class.

SETTING A PURPOSE

As you read, notice how conflicts build to a turning point that leads Hamlet to commit to a course of action.

Notice & Note

Use the side margins to notice and note signposts in the text.

ACT III

Scene 1 *The castle.*

[*Enter* King, Queen, Polonius, Ophelia, Rosencrantz, Guildenstern, *and* Lords.]

King. And can you by no drift of conference
Get from him why he puts on this confusion,
Grating so harshly all his days of quiet
With turbulent and dangerous lunacy?

5 **Rosencrantz.** He does confess he feels himself distracted,
But from what cause he will by no means speak.

Guildenstern. Nor do we find him forward to be sounded,
But with a crafty madness keeps aloof
When we would bring him on to some confession
10 Of his true state.

Queen.   Did he receive you well?

Rosencrantz. Most like a gentleman.

Guildenstern. But with much forcing of his disposition.

Rosencrantz. Niggard of question, but of our demands
    Most free in his reply.

15 **Queen.** Did you assay him to any pastime?

Rosencrantz. Madam, it so fell out that certain players
We o'erraught on the way. Of these we told him,
And there did seem in him a kind of joy
To hear of it. They are here about the court,
20 And, as I think, they have already order
This night to play before him.

Polonius.   'Tis most true,
And he beseeched me to entreat your Majesties
To hear and see the matter.

King. With all my heart, and it doth much content me
25 To hear him so inclined.

1 drift of conference: steering of conversation.

7 forward to be sounded: interested in being questioned.

12 forcing of his disposition: effort.

13–14 Niggard . . . reply: Reluctant to talk, but willing to answer our questions.

15 assay: tempt.

17 o'erraught: overtook.

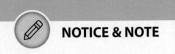

NOTICE & NOTE

26 give . . . edge: sharpen his interest.

29 closely: privately.

31 Affront: meet.

32 espials: spies.

35 as he is behaved: according to his behavior.

43 Gracious: Your Grace (addressing the King).

44–49 Polonius tells Ophelia to read a religious book to provide an excuse for being alone. He remarks that many people are guilty of using worship and a devout appearance to cover their sins.

50–55 Claudius compares the heavy makeup that covers up the flaws on a prostitute's cheek to the beautiful words that cover his crime.

57 To be: to exist, to continue living.

59 slings: something thrown or shot.

ANALYZE SOLILOQUY

Annotate: Mark figurative language in lines 57–89 that expresses how Hamlet feels about life.

Interpret: What reason does he give for continuing to endure life's problems?

Good gentlemen, give him a further edge
And drive his purpose into these delights.

Rosencrantz. We shall, my lord.

[Rosencrantz *and* Guildenstern *and* Lords *exit*.]

King.   Sweet Gertrude, leave us too,
For we have closely sent for Hamlet hither,
30 That he, as 'twere by accident, may here
Affront Ophelia.
Her father and myself (lawful espials)
Will so bestow ourselves that, seeing unseen,
We may of their encounter frankly judge
35 And gather by him, as he is behaved,
If 't be th' affliction of his love or no
That thus he suffers for.

Queen.   I shall obey you.
And for your part, Ophelia, I do wish
That your good beauties be the happy cause
40 Of Hamlet's wildness. So shall I hope your virtues
Will bring him to his wonted way again,
To both your honors.

Ophelia.   Madam, I wish it may.

[Queen *exits*.]

Polonius. Ophelia, walk you here.—Gracious, so please you,
We will bestow ourselves. [*To* Ophelia.] Read on this book,
45 That show of such an exercise may color
Your loneliness.—We are oft to blame in this
('Tis too much proved), that with devotion's visage
And pious action we do sugar o'er
The devil himself.

50 **King** [*aside*]. O, 'tis too true!
How smart a lash that speech doth give my conscience.
The harlot's cheek beautied with plast'ring art
Is not more ugly to the thing that helps it
Than is my deed to my most painted word.
55 O heavy burden!

Polonius. I hear him coming. Let's withdraw, my lord.

[*They withdraw*.]

[*Enter* Hamlet.]

Hamlet. To be or not to be—that is the question:
Whether 'tis nobler in the mind to suffer
The slings and arrows of outrageous fortune,
60 Or to take arms against a sea of troubles
And, by opposing, end them. To die, to sleep—

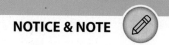

NOTICE & NOTE

No more—and by a sleep to say we end
The heartache and the thousand natural shocks
That flesh is heir to—'tis a consummation
65 Devoutly to be wished. To die, to sleep—
To sleep, perchance to dream. Ay, there's the rub,
For in that sleep of death what dreams may come,
When we have shuffled off this mortal coil,
Must give us pause. There's the respect
70 That makes calamity of so long life.
For who would bear the whips and scorns of time,
Th' oppressor's wrong, the proud man's contumely,
The pangs of despised love, the law's delay,
The insolence of office, and the spurns
75 That patient merit of th' unworthy takes,
When he himself might his quietus make
With a bare bodkin? Who would fardels bear,
To grunt and sweat under a weary life,
But that the dread of something after death,
80 The undiscovered country from whose bourn
No traveler returns, puzzles the will
And makes us rather bear those ills we have
Than fly to others that we know not of?
Thus conscience does make cowards of us all,
85 And thus the native hue of resolution
Is sicklied o'er with the pale cast of thought,
And enterprises of great pitch and moment
With this regard their currents turn awry
And lose the name of action.— Soft you now,
90 The fair Ophelia.— Nymph, in thy orisons
Be all my sins remembered.

Ophelia. Good my lord,
How does your Honor for this many a day?

Hamlet. I humbly thank you, well.

Ophelia. My lord, I have remembrances of yours
95 That I have longèd long to redeliver.
I pray you now receive them.

Hamlet. No, not I. I never gave you aught.

Ophelia. My honored lord, you know right well you did,
And with them words of so sweet breath composed
100 As made the things more rich. Their perfume lost,
Take these again, for to the noble mind
Rich gifts wax poor when givers prove unkind.
There, my lord.

Hamlet. Ha, ha, are you honest?

64 consummation: final ending.

66 rub: obstacle.

68 shuffled . . . coil: cast aside the turmoil of life.

69–70 There's . . . life: That is the consideration that makes us endure misery (**calamity**) for such a long time.

71 time: life in this world.

72 contumely: insults, expressions of contempt.

73 despised: unreturned.

74 office: officials.

74–75 spurns . . . takes: the insults that people of merit receive from the unworthy.

76–77 When . . . bodkin: when he might settle his accounts (**his quietus make**) with merely a dagger (**a bare bodkin**)—that is, end his unhappiness by killing himself.

77 fardels: burdens.

80 bourn: boundary.

81 puzzles: paralyzes.

85 native hue: natural color.

86 cast: shade.

87–89 pitch and moment: height and importance; **With this regard:** for this reason.

89 Soft you: be quiet, enough.

90 orisons: prayers.

104 honest: truthful, chaste.

© Houghton Mifflin Harcourt Publishing Company

108 your honesty . . . beauty: Your chastity should not allow itself to be influenced by your beauty.

110 commerce: dealings.

114 his: its.

115 This . . . paradox: This once went against the common viewpoint.

116 time: the present age.

118–120 Hamlet's metaphor is of grafting a branch onto a fruit tree: If virtue is grafted onto his sinful nature, the fruit of the grafted tree will still taste of his old nature.

122 nunnery: convent (sometimes used as a slang word for "brothel").

123 indifferent honest: reasonably virtuous.

127 beck: command.

105 **Ophelia.** My lord?

Hamlet. Are you fair?

Ophelia. What means your lordship?

Hamlet. That if you be honest and fair, your honesty should admit no discourse to your beauty.

110 **Ophelia.** Could beauty, my lord, have better commerce than with honesty?

Hamlet. Ay, truly, for the power of beauty will sooner transform honesty from what it is to a bawd than the force of honesty can translate beauty into his 115 likeness. This was sometime a paradox, but now the time gives it proof. I did love you once.

Ophelia. Indeed, my lord, you made me believe so.

Hamlet. You should not have believed me, for virtue cannot so inoculate our old stock but we shall relish 120 of it. I loved you not.

Ophelia. I was the more deceived.

Hamlet. Get thee to a nunnery. Why wouldst thou be a breeder of sinners? I am myself indifferent honest, but yet I could accuse me of such things that it 125 were better my mother had not borne me: I am very proud, revengeful, ambitious, with more offenses at my beck than I have thoughts to put

them in, imagination to give them shape, or time to
act them in. What should such fellows as I do
130 crawling between earth and heaven? We are arrant
knaves all; believe none of us. Go thy ways to a
nunnery. Where's your father?

Ophelia. At home, my lord.

Hamlet. Let the doors be shut upon him that he may
135 play the fool nowhere but in 's own house. Farewell.

Ophelia. O, help him, you sweet heavens!

Hamlet. If thou dost marry, I'll give thee this plague
for thy dowry: be thou as chaste as ice, as pure as
snow, thou shalt not escape calumny. Get thee to a
140 nunnery, farewell. Or if thou wilt needs marry,
marry a fool, for wise men know well enough what
monsters you make of them. To a nunnery, go, and
quickly too. Farewell.

Ophelia. Heavenly powers, restore him!

145 **Hamlet.** I have heard of your paintings too, well
enough. God hath given you one face, and you
make yourselves another. You jig and amble, and
you lisp; you nickname God's creatures and make
your wantonness your ignorance. Go to, I'll no
150 more on 't. It hath made me mad. I say we will
have no more marriage. Those that are married
already, all but one, shall live. The rest shall keep
as they are. To a nunnery, go.

[*He exits.*]

Ophelia. O, what a noble mind is here o'erthrown!
155 The courtier's, soldier's, scholar's, eye, tongue, sword,
Th' expectancy and rose of the fair state,
The glass of fashion and the mold of form,
Th' observed of all observers, quite, quite down!
And I, of ladies most deject and wretched,
160 That sucked the honey of his musicked vows,
Now see that noble and most sovereign reason,
Like sweet bells jangled, out of time and harsh;
That unmatched form and stature of blown youth
Blasted with ecstasy. O, woe is me
165 T' have seen what I have seen, see what I see!

King [*advancing with* Polonius]. Love? His affections do
not that way tend;
Nor what he spake, though it lacked form a little,
Was not like madness. There's something in his soul

139 calumny: slander, defamation.

142 monsters: horned cuckolds (men whose wives are unfaithful).

148 nickname: find new names for.
148–149 make . . . ignorance: use ignorance as an excuse for your waywardness.

155–158 Ophelia starts her description of Hamlet's former self by evoking the princely ideal of statesman, soldier, and scholar. He was the hope and ornament (**expectancy and rose**) of Denmark, a model of behavior and appearance for other people, respected (**observed**) by all who looked upon him.

163–164 blown . . . ecstasy: youth in full bloom withered by madness.

166 affections: feelings.

168–171 Claudius says that Hamlet's melancholy broods on something like a bird sits on an egg; he fears that some danger will hatch from it.

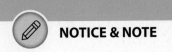

O'er which his melancholy sits on brood,
170 And I do doubt the hatch and the disclose
Will be some danger; which for to prevent,
I have in quick determination
Thus set it down: he shall with speed to England
For the demand of our neglected tribute.
175 Haply the seas, and countries different,
With variable objects, shall expel
This something-settled matter in his heart,
Whereon his brains still beating puts him thus
From fashion of himself. What think you on 't?

180 **Polonius.** It shall do well. But yet do I believe
The origin and commencement of his grief
Sprung from neglected love.— How now, Ophelia?
You need not tell us what Lord Hamlet said;
We heard it all.— My lord, do as you please,
185 But, if you hold it fit, after the play
Let his queen-mother all alone entreat him
To show his grief. Let her be round with him;
And I'll be placed, so please you, in the ear
Of all their conference. If she find him not,
190 To England send him, or confine him where
Your wisdom best shall think.

King.   It shall be so.
Madness in great ones must not unwatched go.

[*They exit.*]

Scene 2 *The castle.*

[*Enter* Hamlet *and three of the* Players.]

Hamlet. Speak the speech, I pray you, as I pronounced
it to you, trippingly on the tongue; but if you mouth
it, as many of our players do, I had as lief the town-crier
spoke my lines. Nor do not saw the air too
5 much with your hand, thus, but use all gently; for in
the very torrent, tempest, and, as I may say, whirlwind
of your passion, you must acquire and beget
a temperance that may give it smoothness. O, it
offends me to the soul to hear a robustious, periwig-
10 pated fellow tear a passion to tatters, to very rags,
to split the ears of the groundlings, who for the
most part are capable of nothing but inexplicable
dumb shows and noise. I would have such a fellow
whipped for o'erdoing Termagant. It out-
15 Herods Herod. Pray you, avoid it.

177 This . . . heart: this unknown thing that has settled in his heart.

187 be round: speak plainly.

189 find him not: does not learn what is disturbing him.

3 I had as lief: I would just as soon.

9 robustious: boisterous.

9–10 periwig-pated: wig-wearing.

11 groundlings: the spectators who paid the cheapest price for admittance to the theater and stood in an open area in front of the stage.

14–15 Termagant, Herod: noisy, violent figures from early drama.

Player. I warrant your Honor.

Hamlet. Be not too tame neither, but let your own discretion
be your tutor. Suit the action to the word,
the word to the action, with this special observance,
20 that you o'erstep not the modesty of nature. For
anything so o'erdone is from the purpose of playing,
whose end, both at the first and now, was and
is to hold, as 'twere, the mirror up to nature, to
show virtue her own feature, scorn her own image,
25 and the very age and body of the time his form and
pressure. Now this overdone or come tardy off,
though it makes the unskillful laugh, cannot but make
the judicious grieve, the censure of the which one
must in your allowance o'erweigh a whole theater
30 of others. O, there be players that I have seen play
and heard others praise (and that highly), not to
speak it profanely, that, neither having th' accent of
Christians nor the gait of Christian, pagan, nor
man, have so strutted and bellowed that I have
35 thought some of nature's journeymen had made
men, and not made them well, they imitated
humanity so abominably.

Player. I hope we have reformed that indifferently
with us, sir.

40 **Hamlet.** O, reform it altogether. And let those that
play your clowns speak no more than is set down
for them, for there be of them that will themselves
laugh, to set on some quantity of barren spectators
to laugh too, though in the meantime some necessary
45 question of the play be then to be considered.
That's villainous and shows a most pitiful ambition
in the fool that uses it. Go make you ready.

[Players *exit*.]

[*Enter* Polonius, Guildenstern, *and* Rosencrantz.]

How now, my lord, will the King hear this piece of
work?

50 **Polonius.** And the Queen too, and that presently.

Hamlet. Bid the players make haste. [Polonius *exits*.]
Will you two help to hasten them?

Rosencrantz. Ay, my lord.

[*They exit*.]

Hamlet. What ho, Horatio!

20 modesty: moderation.

21 is from: strays from.

24 scorn: something scornful.

25–26 the very . . . pressure: a
true impression of the present.

26 come tardy off: done
inadequately.

27 the unskillful: those lacking
in judgment.

28–30 the censure . . . others:
You should value the opinion of
a single judicious theatergoer
over an entire audience that
lacks judgment.

38 indifferently: fairly well.

42 of them: some among
them.

43 barren: dull-witted.

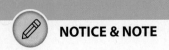

56–57 Hamlet says that Horatio is as honorable as any man he has ever dealt with.

62 candied: flattering.

63 crook . . . knee: bend the ready joint of the knee (kneel down).

64 thrift: profit.

68 one . . . nothing: one who experiences everything but is harmed by nothing.

71 blood: passions; **commeddled:** blended.

72 pipe: small wind instrument.

73 stop: a hole in a wind instrument that controls sound.

81 Even . . . soul: with your most searching observation.

82–86 Hamlet says that if Claudius's hidden (**occulted**) guilt does not reveal (**unkennel**) itself with the speech Hamlet wrote, then the Ghost is in league with the devil and Hamlet's thoughts about Claudius are as foul as the forge of the Roman god of metalworking.

89 censure of his seeming: judgment of how he looks and behaves.

92 be idle: play the fool, be unoccupied.

[*Enter* Horatio.]

55 **Horatio.** Here, sweet lord, at your service.

Hamlet. Horatio, thou art e'en as just a man
As e'er my conversation coped withal.

Horatio. O, my dear lord—

Hamlet.   Nay, do not think I flatter,
For what advancement may I hope from thee
60 That no revenue hast but thy good spirits
To feed and clothe thee? Why should the poor be flattered?
No, let the candied tongue lick absurd pomp
And crook the pregnant hinges of the knee
Where thrift may follow fawning. Dost thou hear?
65 Since my dear soul was mistress of her choice
And could of men distinguish, her election
Hath sealed thee for herself. For thou hast been
As one in suffering all that suffers nothing,
A man that Fortune's buffets and rewards
70 Hast ta'en with equal thanks; and blessed are those
Whose blood and judgment are so well commeddled
That they are not a pipe for Fortune's finger
To sound what stop she please. Give me that man
That is not passion's slave, and I will wear him
75 In my heart's core, ay, in my heart of heart,
As I do thee.—Something too much of this.—
There is a play tonight before the King.
One scene of it comes near the circumstance
Which I have told thee of my father's death.
80 I prithee, when thou seest that act afoot,
Even with the very comment of thy soul
Observe my uncle. If his occulted guilt
Do not itself unkennel in one speech,
It is a damnèd ghost that we have seen,
85 And my imaginations are as foul
As Vulcan's stithy. Give him heedful note,
For I mine eyes will rivet to his face,
And, after, we will both our judgments join
In censure of his seeming.

Horatio.   Well, my lord.
90 If he steal aught the whilst this play is playing
And 'scape detecting, I will pay the theft.

[*Sound a flourish.*]

Hamlet. They are coming to the play. I must be idle.
Get you a place.

[*Enter Trumpets and Kettle Drums. Enter* King, Queen,

Polonius, Ophelia, Rosencrantz, Guildenstern, and other Lords *attendant with the* King's guard *carrying torches*.]

King. How fares our cousin Hamlet?

95 **Hamlet.** Excellent, i' faith, of the chameleon's dish. I eat the air, promise-crammed. You cannot feed capons so.

King. I have nothing with this answer, Hamlet. These words are not mine.

100 **Hamlet.** No, nor mine now. [*To* Polonius.] My lord, you played once i' th' university, you say?

Polonius. That did I, my lord, and was accounted a good actor.

Hamlet. What did you enact?

105 **Polonius.** I did enact Julius Caesar. I was killed i' th' Capitol. Brutus killed me.

Hamlet. It was a brute part of him to kill so capital a calf there.—Be the players ready?

Rosencrantz. Ay, my lord. They stay upon your patience.

110 **Queen.** Come hither, my dear Hamlet, sit by me.

Hamlet. No, good mother. Here's metal more attractive.

[Hamlet *takes a place near* Ophelia.]

Polonius [*to the* King]. Oh, ho! Do you mark that?

Hamlet. Lady, shall I lie in your lap?

Ophelia. No, my lord.

115 **Hamlet.** I mean, my head upon your lap?

Ophelia. Ay, my lord.

Hamlet. Do you think I meant country matters?

Ophelia. I think nothing, my lord.

Hamlet. That's a fair thought to lie between maids' legs.

120 **Ophelia.** What is, my lord?

Hamlet. Nothing.

Ophelia. You are merry, my lord.

Hamlet. Who, I?

Ophelia. Ay, my lord.

125 **Hamlet.** O God, your only jig-maker. What should a man do but be merry? For look you how cheerfully my mother looks, and my father died within 's two hours.

94–97 Hamlet, taking **fares** to mean "feeds," answers that he eats promises. (Chameleons were said to feed on air.)

108 calf: fool.

111 metal more attractive: a substance more magnetic.

117 country matters: something coarse or indecent, which a rustic from the country might propose.

CONTRASTS AND CONTRADICTIONS

Notice & Note: Mark Hamlet's remarks about Ophelia in lines 111–119.

Compare: How does his attitude toward her in this scene compare with his attitude in Scene 1, lines 104–153?

125 Hamlet sarcastically refers to himself as the best jig (comical song and dance) performer.

© Houghton Mifflin Harcourt Publishing Company

129–130 Hamlet sarcastically suggests giving up his mourning clothes for luxurious clothing trimmed with furs.

134 not thinking on: being forgotten; **hobby-horse:** a horse-and-rider figure who once performed in morris and may-day dances. Such traditions had been disappearing.

Dumb show: a scene without dialogue.

138 miching mallecho: sneaking misdeed. (The Spanish word *malhecho* means "misdeed.")

139 Belike: perhaps; **argument:** plot.

148 naught: naughty, indecent.

152 posy of a ring: a motto inscribed in a ring.

Ophelia. Nay, 'tis twice two months, my lord.

Hamlet. So long? Nay, then, let the devil wear black, for
130 I'll have a suit of sables. O heavens, die two months
ago, and not forgotten yet? Then there's hope a great
man's memory may outlive his life half a year. But,
by'r Lady, he must build churches, then, or else shall
he suffer not thinking on, with the hobby-horse, whose
135 epitaph is "For oh, for oh, the hobby-horse is forgot."

[*The trumpets sound. Dumb show follows.*]

[*Enter* a King *and a* Queen, *very lovingly, the* Queen *embracing him and he her. She kneels and makes show of protestation unto him. He takes her up and declines his head upon her neck. He lies him down upon a bank of flowers. She, seeing him asleep, leaves him. Anon comes in another* man, *takes off his crown, kisses it, pours poison in the sleeper's ears, and leaves him. The* Queen *returns, finds the* King *dead, makes passionate action. The* poisoner *with some three or four come in again, seem to condole with her. The dead body is carried away. The* poisoner *woos the* Queen *with gifts. She seems harsh awhile but in the end accepts his love.*]

[Players *exit.*]

Ophelia. What means this, my lord?

Hamlet. Marry, this is miching mallecho. It means mischief.

Ophelia. Belike this show imports the argument of the play.

[*Enter* Prologue.]

140 **Hamlet.** We shall know by this fellow. The players cannot keep counsel; they'll tell all.

Ophelia. Will he tell us what this show meant?

Hamlet. Ay, or any show that you will show him. Be not you ashamed to show, he'll not shame to tell
145 you what it means.

Ophelia. You are naught, you are naught. I'll mark the play.

Prologue.

> For us and for our tragedy,
150 > Here stooping to your clemency,
> We beg your hearing patiently.

[*He exits.*]

Hamlet. Is this a prologue or the posy of a ring?

Ophelia. 'Tis brief, my lord.

Hamlet. As woman's love.

[*Enter the* Player King *and* Queen.]

155　**Player King.** *Full thirty times hath Phoebus' cart gone round*
Neptune's salt wash and Tellus' orbèd ground,
And thirty dozen moons with borrowed sheen
About the world have times twelve thirties been
Since love our hearts and Hymen did our hands
160　*Unite commutual in most sacred bands.*

　　Player Queen. *So many journeys may the sun and moon*
Make us again count o'er ere love be done!
But woe is me! You are so sick of late,
So far from cheer and from your former state,
165　*That I distrust you. Yet, though I distrust,*
Discomfort you, my lord, it nothing must.
For women fear too much, even as they love,
And women's fear and love hold quantity,
In neither aught, or in extremity.
170　*Now what my love is, proof hath made you*
know, And, as my love is sized, my fear is so:
Where love is great, the littlest doubts are fear;
Where little fears grow great, great love grows there.

165　distrust you: am worried about you.

168–169　And women's . . . extremity: Women love and fear in equal measure, loving and fearing either too much or hardly at all.

　　Player King. *Faith, I must leave thee, love, and shortly too.*
175　*My operant powers their functions leave to do.*
And thou shalt live in this fair world behind,
Honored, beloved; and haply one as kind
For husband shalt thou—

175　My . . . do: My vital powers are no longer functioning.

176　behind: after I'm gone.

　　Player Queen. 　　　　　*O, confound the rest!*
Such love must needs be treason in my breast.
180　*In second husband let me be accurst.*
None wed the second but who killed the first.

Hamlet. That's wormwood!

182　wormwood: a bitter herb.

　　Player Queen. *The instances that second marriage move*
Are base respects of thrift, but none of love.
185　*A second time I kill my husband dead*
When second husband kisses me in bed.

183–184　The instances . . . love: People marry a second time for profit, not for love.

　　Player King. *I do believe you think what now you speak,*
But what we do determine oft we break.
Purpose is but the slave to memory,
190　*Of violent birth, but poor validity,*
Which now, the fruit unripe, sticks on the tree
But fall unshaken when they mellow be.
Most necessary 'tis that we forget

189–190 Our intentions are dependent on our memory; they are powerful at first but have little durability (**validity**).

193–194　Most . . . debt: We inevitably forget promises we have made to ourselves.

197–200 When the violence of extreme grief or joy ceases, so too does the willingness to act upon these emotions. People who feel extreme grief also feel extreme joy, and one passion is likely to follow another without much cause (**on slender accident**).

201 for aye: forever.

205 The great . . . flies: When a great man's fortune falls, his closest friend abandons him.

206 advanced: moving up in life.

207 hitherto: to this extent.

210 Directly seasons him: immediately changes him into.

213 devices still: plans always.

218 Sport . . . night: May the day deny (**lock from**) me its pastimes and night its rest.

220 An anchor's cheer: a religious hermit's fare.

221–222 May each obstacle that turns the face of joy pale meet and destroy everything that I wish to see prosper (**what I would have well**).

231 doth protest too much: overstates her case, makes too many assurances.

233 argument: plot.

To pay ourselves what to ourselves is debt.
195 What to ourselves in passion we propose,
The passion ending, doth the purpose lose.
The violence of either grief or joy
Their own enactures with themselves destroy.
Where joy most revels, grief doth most lament;
200 Grief joys, joy grieves, on slender accident.
This world is not for aye, nor 'tis not strange
That even our loves should with our fortunes change;
For 'tis a question left us yet to prove
Whether love lead fortune or else fortune love.
205 The great man down, you mark his favorite flies;
The poor, advanced, makes friends of enemies.
And hitherto doth love on fortune tend,
For who not needs shall never lack a friend,
And who in want a hollow friend doth try
210 Directly seasons him his enemy.
But, orderly to end where I begun:
Our wills and fates do so contrary run
That our devices still are overthrown;
Our thoughts are ours, their ends none of our own.
215 So think thou wilt no second husband wed,
But die thy thoughts when thy first lord is dead.

Player Queen. *Nor earth to me give food, nor heaven light,*
Sport and repose lock from me day and night,
To desperation turn my trust and hope,
220 *An anchor's cheer in prison be my scope.*
Each opposite that blanks the face of joy
Meet what I would have well and it destroy.
Both here and hence pursue me lasting strife,
If, once a widow, ever I be wife.

225 **Hamlet.** If she should break it now!

Player King. *'Tis deeply sworn. Sweet, leave me here awhile.*
My spirits grow dull, and fain I would beguile
The tedious day with sleep.

[*Sleeps.*]

Player Queen.   *Sleep rock thy brain,*
And never come mischance between us twain.

[Player Queen *exits.*]

230 **Hamlet.** Madam, how like you this play?

Queen. The lady doth protest too much, methinks.

Hamlet. O, but she'll keep her word.

King. Have you heard the argument? Is there no offense in 't?

235 **Hamlet.** No, no, they do but jest, poison in jest. No offense i' th' world.

King. What do you call the play?

Hamlet. "The Mousetrap." Marry, how? Tropically. This play is the image of a murder done in Vienna. 240 Gonzago is the duke's name, his wife Baptista. You shall see anon. 'Tis a knavish piece of work, but what of that? Your Majesty and we that have free souls, it touches us not. Let the galled jade wince; our withers are unwrung.

[*Enter* Lucianus.]

245 This is one Lucianus, nephew to the king.

Ophelia. You are as good as a chorus, my lord.

Hamlet. I could interpret between you and your love, if I could see the puppets dallying.

Ophelia. You are keen, my lord, you are keen.

250 **Hamlet.** It would cost you a groaning to take off mine edge.

Ophelia. Still better and worse.

Hamlet. So you mis-take your husbands.—Begin, murderer. Pox, leave thy damnable faces and begin.

238 **Tropically:** metaphorically.

242 **free:** guilt-free.

243–244 **Let . . . unwrung:** a proverbial expression that means, "Let the guilty flinch; our consciences do not bother us."

246 **chorus:** a character who explains what will happen in a play.

247–252 An "interpreter" is a narrator in a puppet show. Hamlet says that he could explain what is going on between Ophelia and her lover if he caught them together. When she comments that he is **keen** (sharp, penetrating), he responds with wordplay (using **keen** to mean "sexually aroused") that she finds even more witty but also more offensive.

253 **mis-take:** take falsely. A reference to the marriage vow to take a husband "for better, for worse."

257 Time is my ally (**Confederate**) and only witness.

259 Hecate's ban: the curse of Hecate, goddess of witchcraft.

261 usurp: steal.

255 Come, the croaking raven doth bellow for revenge.

Lucianus. *Thoughts black, hands apt, drugs fit, and*
  time agreeing,
Confederate season, else no creature seeing,
Thou mixture rank, of midnight weeds collected,
With Hecate's ban thrice blasted, thrice infected,
260 *Thy natural magic and dire property*
On wholesome life usurp immediately.

[*Pours the poison in his ears.*]

Hamlet. He poisons him i' th' garden for his estate.
His name's Gonzago. The story is extant and written
in very choice Italian. You shall see anon how
265 the murderer gets the love of Gonzago's wife.

[Claudius *rises.*]

Ophelia. The King rises.

267 false fire: the discharge of a gun loaded without shot.

Hamlet. What, frighted with false fire?

Queen. How fares my lord?

Polonius. Give o'er the play.

273 ungallèd: uninjured.

270 **King.** Give me some light. Away!

Polonius. Lights, lights, lights!

[*All but* Hamlet *and* Horatio *exit.*]

ANALYZE CONFLICT
Annotate: Reread lines 255–271. Mark Claudius's reaction to Hamlet's comments and the performance.

Predict: How might this incident affect Claudius's plans for Hamlet?

Hamlet. *Why, let the strucken deer go weep,*
    The hart ungallèd play.
  For some must watch, while some must sleep:
275   *Thus runs the world away.*
Would not this, sir, and a forest of feathers (if the
rest of my fortunes turn Turk with me) with two
Provincial roses on my razed shoes, get me a fellowship
in a cry of players?

280 **Horatio.** Half a share.

277–279 turn Turk with me: turn against me. Elizabethan theater costumes often included feathers worn on hats and ribbon rosettes on shoes. A fellowship is a share or partnership in a theater company.

282 Damon: in Roman mythology the friend of Pythias.

285 pajock: either "peacock," which had a reputation for lust and cruelty, or "patchock," a savage person. (Presumably the rhyme Horatio hints at is **ass**.)

Hamlet. A whole one, I.
For thou dost know, O Damon dear,
  This realm dismantled was
Of Jove himself, and now reigns here
285   *A very very—pajock.*

Horatio. You might have rhymed.

Hamlet. O good Horatio, I'll take the ghost's word for
a thousand pound. Didst perceive?

Horatio. Very well, my lord.

290 **Hamlet.** Upon the talk of the poisoning?

Horatio. I did very well note him.

Hamlet. Ah ha! Come, some music! Come, the recorders!
   For if the King like not the comedy,
295   *Why, then, belike he likes it not, perdy.*
Come, some music!

[*Enter* Rosencrantz *and* Guildenstern.]

Guildenstern. Good my lord, vouchsafe me a word with you.

Hamlet. Sir, a whole history.

300 **Guildenstern.** The King, sir—

Hamlet. Ay, sir, what of him?

Guildenstern. Is in his retirement marvelous distempered.

Hamlet. With drink, sir?

Guildenstern. No, my lord, with choler.

305 **Hamlet.** Your wisdom should show itself more richer
to signify this to the doctor, for for me to put him
to his purgation would perhaps plunge him into
more choler.

Guildenstern. Good my lord, put your discourse into
310 some frame and start not so wildly from my affair.

Hamlet. I am tame, sir. Pronounce.

Guildenstern. The Queen your mother, in most great
affliction of spirit, hath sent me to you.

Hamlet. You are welcome.

315 **Guildenstern.** Nay, good my lord, this courtesy is not
of the right breed. If it shall please you to make me
a wholesome answer, I will do your mother's commandment.
If not, your pardon and my return shall
be the end of my business.

320 **Hamlet.** Sir, I cannot.

Rosencrantz. What, my lord?

Hamlet. Make you a wholesome answer. My wit's diseased.
But, sir, such answer as I can make, you
shall command—or, rather, as you say, my mother.
325 Therefore no more but to the matter. My mother,
you say—

Rosencrantz. Then thus she says: your behavior hath
struck her into amazement and admiration.

293 recorders: flute-like wooden wind instruments.

295 perdy: by God (from the French **par dieu**).

302 distempered: upset. (Hamlet takes it in the sense of "drunk.")

304 choler: anger. (Hamlet takes it in the sense of "biliousness.")

307 purgation: cleansing of the body of impurities; spiritual cleansing through confession.

310 frame: order; **start:** shy away like a nervous or wild horse.

318 pardon: permission to leave.

328 admiration: wonder.

© Houghton Mifflin Harcourt Publishing Company

332 closet: private room.

337 pickers and stealers: hands (from the Church catechism, "To keep my hands from picking and stealing").

345–346 The rest of the stale (**musty**) proverb is "the horse starves," suggesting that Hamlet cannot wait so long.

348–350 withdraw: speak privately. Hamlet uses a hunting metaphor: The hunter moves to the windward side of the prey, causing it to flee toward a net (**toil**).

360 ventages: stops, or finger holes, on the recorder.

Hamlet. O wonderful son that can so 'stonish a mother! 330 But is there no sequel at the heels of this mother's admiration? Impart.

Rosencrantz. She desires to speak with you in her closet ere you go to bed.

Hamlet. We shall obey, were she ten times our mother. 335 Have you any further trade with us?

Rosencrantz. My lord, you once did love me.

Hamlet. And do still, by these pickers and stealers.

Rosencrantz. Good my lord, what is your cause of distemper? You do surely bar the door upon your 340 own liberty if you deny your griefs to your friend.

Hamlet. Sir, I lack advancement.

Rosencrantz. How can that be, when you have the voice of the King himself for your succession in Denmark?

345 **Hamlet.** Ay, sir, but "While the grass grows"—the proverb is something musty.

[*Enter the* Players *with recorders.*]

O, the recorders! Let me see one. [*He takes a recorder and turns to* Guildenstern.] To withdraw with you: why do you go about to recover the 350 wind of me, as if you would drive me into a toil?

Guildenstern. O, my lord, if my duty be too bold, my love is too unmannerly.

Hamlet. I do not well understand that. Will you play upon this pipe?

355 **Guildenstern.** My lord, I cannot.

Hamlet. I pray you.

Guildenstern. Believe me, I cannot.

Hamlet. I do beseech you.

Guildenstern. I know no touch of it, my lord.

360 **Hamlet.** It is as easy as lying. Govern these ventages with your fingers and thumb, give it breath with your mouth, and it will discourse most eloquent music. Look you, these are the stops.

Guildenstern. But these cannot I command to any 365 utt'rance of harmony. I have not the skill.

Hamlet. Why, look you now, how unworthy a thing

you make of me! You would play upon me, you
would seem to know my stops, you would pluck
out the heart of my mystery, you would sound me
370 from my lowest note to the top of my compass;
and there is much music, excellent voice, in this little
organ, yet cannot you make it speak. 'Sblood,
do you think I am easier to be played on than a
pipe? Call me what instrument you will, though
375 you can fret me, you cannot play upon me.

[*Enter* Polonius.]

God bless you, sir.

Polonius. My lord, the Queen would speak with you,
and presently.

Hamlet. Do you see yonder cloud that's almost in
380 shape of a camel?

Polonius. By th' Mass, and 'tis like a camel indeed.

Hamlet. Methinks it is like a weasel.

Polonius. It is backed like a weasel.

Hamlet. Or like a whale.

385 **Polonius.** Very like a whale.

Hamlet. Then I will come to my mother by and by.

[*Aside.*] They fool me to the top of my bent.—I will
come by and by.

Polonius. I will say so.

390 **Hamlet.** "By and by" is easily said. Leave me, friends.

[*All but* Hamlet *exit.*]

'Tis now the very witching time of night,
When churchyards yawn and hell itself breathes out
Contagion to this world. Now could I drink hot blood
And do such bitter business as the day
395 Would quake to look on. Soft, now to my mother.
O heart, lose not thy nature; let not ever
The soul of Nero enter this firm bosom.
Let me be cruel, not unnatural.
I will speak daggers to her, but use none.
400 My tongue and soul in this be hypocrites:
How in my words somever she be shent,
To give them seals never, my soul, consent.

[*He exits.*]

369–375 **sound me:** play upon me like an instrument, investigate me; **compass:** an instrument's range; **organ:** musical instrument; **fret me:** annoy me (also punning on **frets,** the raised bars for fingering a stringed instrument).

387 **fool . . . bent:** make me play the fool to the limits of my ability.

388 **by and by:** before long.

397 **Nero:** a Roman emperor who put his mother to death.

401–402 Hamlet tells himself that however much she is rebuked (**shent**) in his words, he must not put those words into action (**give them seals**).

© Houghton Mifflin Harcourt Publishing Company

Scene 3 *The castle.*

[*Enter* King, Rosencrantz, *and* Guildenstern.]

King. I like him not, nor stands it safe with us
To let his madness range. Therefore prepare you.
I your commission will forthwith dispatch,
And he to England shall along with you.
5   The terms of our estate may not endure
Hazard so near 's as doth hourly grow
Out of his brows.

Guildenstern.   We will ourselves provide.
Most holy and religious fear it is
To keep those many many bodies safe
10 That live and feed upon your Majesty.

Rosencrantz. The single and peculiar life is bound
With all the strength and armor of the mind
To keep itself from noyance, but much more
That spirit upon whose weal depends and rests
15 The lives of many. The cess of majesty
Dies not alone, but like a gulf doth draw
What's near it with it; or it is a massy wheel
Fixed on the summit of the highest mount,
To whose huge spokes ten thousand lesser things
20 Are mortised and adjoined, which, when it falls,
Each small annexment, petty consequence,
Attends the boist'rous ruin. Never alone
Did the king sigh, but with a general groan.

King. Arm you, I pray you, to this speedy voyage,
25 For we will fetters put about this fear,
Which now goes too free-footed.

Rosencrantz.   We will haste us.

[Rosencrantz *and* Guildenstern *exit.*]

[*Enter* Polonius.]

Polonius. My lord, he's going to his mother's closet.
Behind the arras I'll convey myself
To hear the process. I'll warrant she'll tax him home;
30 And, as you said (and wisely was it said),
'Tis meet that some more audience than a mother,
Since nature makes them partial, should o'erhear
The speech of vantage. Fare you well, my liege.
I'll call upon you ere you go to bed
35 And tell you what I know.

King.   Thanks, dear my lord.

[Polonius *exits.*]

1 him: his behavior.

3 forthwith dispatch: have prepared at once.

5 The terms of our estate: my position as king.

6 near 's: near us.

11 single and peculiar: individual and private.

13 noyance: harm.

14 weal: well-being.

15 cess: cessation, decease.

16 gulf: whirlpool.

17–22 Rosencrantz alludes to Fortune's massive (**massy**) wheel, with the king traditionally shown on the top; when the king falls, everyone connected with him plunges as well.

24 Arm you: prepare yourself.

29 process: proceedings; **tax him home:** strongly rebuke him.

31 meet: fitting.

33 of vantage: in addition.

O, my offense is rank, it smells to heaven;
It hath the primal eldest curse upon 't,
A brother's murder. Pray can I not,
Though inclination be as sharp as will.
40 My stronger guilt defeats my strong intent,
And, like a man to double business bound,
I stand in pause where I shall first begin
And both neglect. What if this cursèd hand
Were thicker than itself with brother's blood?
45 Is there not rain enough in the sweet heavens
To wash it white as snow? Whereto serves mercy
But to confront the visage of offense?
And what's in prayer but this twofold force,
To be forestallèd ere we come to fall,
50 Or pardoned being down? Then I'll look up.
My fault is past. But, O, what form of prayer
Can serve my turn? "Forgive me my foul murder"?
That cannot be, since I am still possessed
Of those effects for which I did the murder:
55 My crown, mine own ambition, and my queen.
May one be pardoned and retain th' offense?
In the corrupted currents of this world,
Offense's gilded hand may shove by justice,
And oft 'tis seen the wicked prize itself
60 Buys out the law. But 'tis not so above:

37 primal eldest curse: the curse of Cain (the son of Adam and Eve who murdered his brother Abel).

46–47 Whereto . . . offense: What purpose does mercy serve other than to oppose condemnation?

56 th' offense: the benefits of the crime.

57–64 In the corrupt ways (**currents**) of this world, a rich offender can push aside justice, and often the law is bribed with stolen wealth. But that isn't the case in heaven, where there is no evasion (**shuffling**); the true nature of every deed lies exposed, and we must testify against ourselves.

© Houghton Mifflin Harcourt Publishing Company

64 rests: remains.

68 limèd: trapped like a bird caught in quicklime (a sticky substance).

69 engaged: entangled; **Make assay:** make an attempt (addressed to himself).

ANALYZE SOLILOQUY

Annotate: As you read lines 73–96, mark the reason why Hamlet delays killing Claudius.

Analyze: How does this decision relate to what the Ghost told Hamlet about his death in Act I?

73 pat: conveniently.

75 would be scanned: needs to be looked at carefully.

79 hire and salary: something Claudius should pay me to do.

80–84 Hamlet complains that his father was killed without allowing him spiritual preparation (**grossly**). He was immersed in worldly pleasures and his sins were in full bloom. Only heaven knows how his final account stands, but from Hamlet's perspective his father's sins seem a heavy burden.

86 seasoned: prepared.

88 know thou a more horrid hent: wait to be grasped on a more horrible occasion.

95 stays: awaits me.

96 physic: medicine (referring to the postponement of revenge or to Claudius's act of prayer).

There is no shuffling; there the action lies
In his true nature, and we ourselves compelled,
Even to the teeth and forehead of our faults,
To give in evidence. What then? What rests?
65 Try what repentance can. What can it not?
Yet what can it, when one cannot repent?
O wretched state! O bosom black as death!
O limèd soul, that, struggling to be free,
Art more engaged! Help, angels! Make assay.
70 Bow, stubborn knees, and heart with strings of steel
Be soft as sinews of the newborn babe.
All may be well.

[*He kneels.*]

[*Enter* Hamlet.]

Hamlet. Now might I do it pat, now he is a-praying,
And now I'll do 't.

[*He draws his sword.*]

                   And so he goes to heaven,
75 And so am I revenged. That would be scanned:
A villain kills my father, and for that,
I, his sole son, do this same villain send
To heaven.
Why, this is hire and salary, not revenge.
80 He took my father grossly, full of bread,
With all his crimes broad blown, as flush as May;
And how his audit stands who knows save heaven.
But in our circumstance and course of thought
'Tis heavy with him. And am I then revenged
85 To take him in the purging of his soul,
When he is fit and seasoned for his passage?
No.
Up sword, and know thou a more horrid hent.

[*He sheathes his sword.*]

When he is drunk asleep, or in his rage,
90 Or in th' incestuous pleasure of his bed,
At game a-swearing, or about some act
That has no relish of salvation in 't—
Then trip him, that his heels may kick at heaven,
And that his soul may be as damned and black
95 As hell, whereto it goes. My mother stays.
This physic but prolongs thy sickly days.

[Hamlet *exits.*]

King [*rising*]. My words fly up, my thoughts remain
   below;

Words without thoughts never to heaven go.

[*He exits.*]

Scene 4 *The Queen's private chamber.*

[*Enter* Queen *and* Polonius.]

Polonius. He will come straight. Look you lay home to him.
Tell him his pranks have been too broad to bear with
And that your Grace hath screened and stood between
Much heat and him. I'll silence me even here.
5 Pray you, be round with him.

Hamlet [*within*]. Mother, mother, mother!

Queen. I'll warrant you. Fear me not. Withdraw,
I hear him coming.

[Polonius *hides behind the arras.*]

[*Enter* Hamlet.]

Hamlet. Now, mother, what's the matter?

10 **Queen.** Hamlet, thou hast thy father much offended.

Hamlet. Mother, you have my father much offended.

Queen. Come, come, you answer with an idle tongue.

Hamlet. Go, go, you question with a wicked tongue.

Queen. Why, how now, Hamlet?

Hamlet.   What's the matter now?

15 **Queen.** Have you forgot me?

Hamlet.   No, by the rood, not so.
You are the Queen, your husband's brother's wife,
And (would it were not so) you are my mother.

Queen. Nay, then I'll set those to you that can speak.

Hamlet. Come, come, and sit you down; you shall not budge.
20 You go not till I set you up a glass
Where you may see the inmost part of you.

Queen. What wilt thou do? Thou wilt not murder me?
Help, ho!

Polonius [*behind the arras*]. What ho! Help!

25 **Hamlet.** How now, a rat? Dead for a ducat, dead.

[*He kills* Polonius *by thrusting a rapier through the arras.*]

Polonius [*behind the arras*]. O, I am slain!

Queen.   O me, what hast thou done?

Hamlet. Nay, I know not. Is it the King?

1 **straight:** right away; **lay home to:** strongly rebuke.

2 **broad:** unrestrained.

5 **round:** blunt.

12 **idle:** foolish.

15 **forgot me:** forgotten who I am; **rood:** cross.

20 **glass:** mirror.

25 **Dead for a ducat:** I'll wager a ducat that I kill him; I'll kill him for a ducat.

ANALYZE DRAMATIC PLOT
Annotate: Mark Gertrude's reaction to Hamlet's accusations in lines 28–41.

Draw Conclusions: Do you think she knew that Claudius murdered her husband? Why or why not?

34 too busy: too much of a busybody.

38–39 If . . . sense: if habitual wickedness (**damnèd custom**) has not so hardened (**brazed**) your heart that it has become armor (**proof**) and fortification against feeling (**sense**).

47 contraction: the marriage contract.

48 sweet religion: marriage vows.

49 rhapsody: senseless jumble.

Queen. O, what a rash and bloody deed is this!

Hamlet. A bloody deed—almost as bad, good mother,
30 As kill a king and marry with his brother.

Queen. As kill a king?

Hamlet.   Ay, lady, it was my word.

[*He pulls* Polonius' *body from behind the arras.*]

Thou wretched, rash, intruding fool, farewell.
I took thee for thy better. Take thy fortune.
Thou find'st to be too busy is some danger.

[*To* Queen.]

35 Leave wringing of your hands. Peace, sit you down,
And let me wring your heart; for so I shall
If it be made of penetrable stuff,
If damnèd custom have not brazed it so
That it be proof and bulwark against sense.

40 **Queen.** What have I done, that thou dar'st wag thy tongue
In noise so rude against me?

Hamlet.   Such an act
That blurs the grace and blush of modesty,
Calls virtue hypocrite, takes off the rose
From the fair forehead of an innocent love
45 And sets a blister there, makes marriage vows
As false as dicers' oaths—O, such a deed
As from the body of contraction plucks
The very soul, and sweet religion makes
A rhapsody of words! Heaven's face does glow
50 O'er this solidity and compound mass

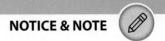

With heated visage, as against the doom,
Is thought-sick at the act.

Queen.   Ay me, what act
That roars so loud and thunders in the index?

Hamlet. Look here upon this picture and on this,
55 The counterfeit presentment of two brothers.
See what a grace was seated on this brow,
Hyperion's curls, the front of Jove himself,
An eye like Mars' to threaten and command,
A station like the herald Mercury
60 New-lighted on a heaven-kissing hill,
A combination and a form indeed
Where every god did seem to set his seal
To give the world assurance of a man.
This was your husband. Look you now what follows.
65 Here is your husband, like a mildewed ear
Blasting his wholesome brother. Have you eyes?
Could you on this fair mountain leave to feed
And batten on this moor? Ha! Have you eyes?
You cannot call it love, for at your age
70 The heyday in the blood is tame, it's humble
And waits upon the judgment; and what judgment
Would step from this to this? Sense sure you have,
Else could you not have motion; but sure that sense
Is apoplexed; for madness would not err,
75 Nor sense to ecstasy was ne'er so thralled,
But it reserved some quantity of choice
To serve in such a difference. What devil was 't
That thus hath cozened you at hoodman-blind?
Eyes without feeling, feeling without sight,
80 Ears without hands or eyes, smelling sans all,
Or but a sickly part of one true sense
Could not so mope. O shame, where is thy blush?
Rebellious hell,
If thou canst mutine in a matron's bones,
85 To flaming youth let virtue be as wax
And melt in her own fire. Proclaim no shame
When the compulsive ardor gives the charge,
Since frost itself as actively doth burn,
And reason panders will.

90 **Queen.** O Hamlet, speak no more!
Thou turn'st my eyes into my very soul,
And there I see such black and grainèd spots
As will not leave their tinct.

Hamlet.   Nay, but to live

49–52 Heaven's face looks down shamefully and is sick with sorrow.

53 index: introduction.

55 counterfeit presentment: portraits.

57 Hyperion: the sun god; **front:** brow.

59–60 A station . . . hill: a stance like that of the winged messenger of the gods.

65–66 Hamlet uses the metaphor of a **mildewed ear** of grain that is blighting (**Blasting**) a nearby healthy plant.

68 batten on: grow fat from feeding on; **moor:** barren land.

70 heyday in the blood: sexual excitement.

72–78 Hamlet says that her senses must be paralyzed, because madness would let her choose correctly between Claudius and Hamlet's father. He wonders what devil tricked her in a game.

80 sans all: without the other senses.

82 so mope: be so dazed.

83–89 If hell can stir up rebellion in an older woman's bones, then in young people virtue should be like a candle melting in its own flame.

92 grainèd: ingrained, indelible.

93 leave their tinct: lose their color, fade.

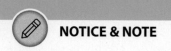

94 enseamèd: greasy, sweaty.

In the rank sweat of an enseamèd bed,
95 Stewed in corruption, honeying and making love
Over the nasty sty!

Queen. O, speak to me no more!
These words like daggers enter in my ears.
No more, sweet Hamlet!

Hamlet.   A murderer and a villain,

100 tithe: tenth part.

101 vice: buffoon. (The Vice was a clownish villain in medieval morality plays.)

102 cutpurse: thief.

103 diadem: crown.

100 A slave that is not twentieth part the tithe
Of your precedent lord; a vice of kings,
A cutpurse of the empire and the rule,
That from a shelf the precious diadem stole
And put it in his pocket—

105 **Queen.** No more!

106 shreds and patches: referring to the patchwork costume of clowns or fools.

Hamlet. A king of shreds and patches—

[*Enter* Ghost.]

Save me and hover o'er me with your wings,
You heavenly guards!— What would your gracious figure?

Queen. Alas, he's mad.

111 lapsed in time and passion: having let time pass and my passion cool.

110 **Hamlet.** Do you not come your tardy son to chide,
That, lapsed in time and passion, lets go by
Th' important acting of your dread command?
O, say!

Ghost. Do not forget. This visitation

116 amazement: bewilderment, shock.

118 Conceit: imagination.

115 Is but to whet thy almost blunted purpose.
But look, amazement on thy mother sits.
O, step between her and her fighting soul.
Conceit in weakest bodies strongest works.
Speak to her, Hamlet.

Hamlet.   How is it with you, lady?

122 incorporal: immaterial.

124–126 Like soldiers awakened by an alarm, your smoothly laid (**bedded**) hair—as if there were life in this outgrowth (**excrements**)—jumps up and stands on end.

130 conjoined: joined together.

131 them capable: the stones responsive.

120 **Queen.** Alas, how is 't with you,
That you do bend your eye on vacancy
And with th' incorporal air do hold discourse?
Forth at your eyes your spirits wildly peep,
And, as the sleeping soldiers in th' alarm,
125 Your bedded hair, like life in excrements,
Start up and stand an end. O gentle son,
Upon the heat and flame of thy distemper
Sprinkle cool patience! Whereon do you look?

Hamlet. On him, on him! Look you how pale he glares.
130 His form and cause conjoined, preaching to stones,
Would make them capable. [*To the* Ghost.] Do not look upon me,

Lest with this piteous action you convert
My stern effects. Then what I have to do
Will want true color—tears perchance for blood.

135 **Queen.** To whom do you speak this?

Hamlet. Do you see nothing there?

Queen. Nothing at all; yet all that is I see.

Hamlet. Nor did you nothing hear?

Queen. No, nothing but ourselves.

140 **Hamlet.** Why, look you there, look how it steals away!
My father, in his habit as he lived!
Look where he goes even now out at the portal!

[Ghost *exits*.]

Queen. This is the very coinage of your brain.
This bodiless creation ecstasy
145 Is very cunning in.

Hamlet.   Ecstasy?
My pulse as yours doth temperately keep time
And makes as healthful music. It is not madness
That I have uttered. Bring me to the test,
And I the matter will reword, which madness
150 Would gambol from. Mother, for love of grace,
Lay not that flattering unction to your soul
That not your trespass but my madness speaks.
It will but skin and film the ulcerous place,
Whiles rank corruption, mining all within,
155 Infects unseen. Confess yourself to heaven,
Repent what's past, avoid what is to come,
And do not spread the compost on the weeds
To make them ranker. Forgive me this my virtue,
For, in the fatness of these pursy times,
160 Virtue itself of vice must pardon beg,
Yea, curb and woo for leave to do him good.

Queen. O Hamlet, thou hast cleft my heart in twain!

Hamlet. O, throw away the worser part of it,
And live the purer with the other half!
165 Good night. But go not to my uncle's bed.
Assume a virtue if you have it not.
That monster, custom, who all sense doth eat,
Of habits devil, is angel yet in this,
That to the use of actions fair and good
170 He likewise gives a frock or livery
That aptly is put on. Refrain tonight,

133–134 convert . . . effects: alter the stern impression I give.

134 want: lack.

LANGUAGE CONVENTIONS
Annotate: Mark the paradox in lines 158–161.

Interpret: What truth does this statement suggest?

142 in his habit as he lived: in the clothes he wore when alive.

145 Madness (**ecstasy**) is very skillful at creating this kind of hallucination (**bodiless creation**).

148–155 Hamlet tells his mother to make him repeat his description word for word, a test that madness would skip (**gambol**) away from. He asks her not to use his madness rather than her misdeeds to explain this visitation; such a soothing ointment (**unction**) would merely cover up the sore on her soul, allowing the infection within to grow unseen.

158 this my virtue: my virtuous talk.

159 fatness: grossness; **pursy:** flabby, bloated.

161 curb: bow; **leave:** permission.

167–171 Custom, which consumes our awareness of the evil we habitually do, can also make us grow used to performing good actions.

174 **stamp of nature:** the traits
we are born with.

175 A word seems to be
missing in this line after *either*.

180 **this:** Polonius.

181 **their scourge and
minister:** heaven's agent of
retribution.

182 **answer well:** explain.

185 **remains behind:** is still to
come.

188 **bloat:** bloated.

189 **mouse:** a term of
endearment.

190 **reechy:** filthy.

191 **paddling in:** fingering on.

194 **in craft:** by clever design
or action.

194–202 Although Hamlet
has asked his mother not to let
Claudius use sexual attentions
to unravel the secret that
Hamlet is only pretending to
be mad, he now sarcastically
urges her to go ahead and tell
Claudius. He refers to a story
about an ape that died trying
to imitate the flight of birds it
released from a cage, hinting
that the Queen will get hurt if
she lets out her secret.

208–211 Rosencrantz and
Guildenstern have been
commanded to escort Hamlet
to some treachery.

212–213 **to have . . . petard:**
to have the maker of military
devices blown up (**hoist**) by his
own bomb (**petard**).

And that shall lend a kind of easiness
To the next abstinence, the next more easy;
For use almost can change the stamp of nature
175 And either . . . the devil or throw him out
With wondrous potency. Once more, good night,
And, when you are desirous to be blest,
I'll blessing beg of you. For this same lord

[*Pointing to* Polonius.]

I do repent; but heaven hath pleased it so
180 To punish me with this and this with me,
That I must be their scourge and minister.
I will bestow him and will answer well
The death I gave him. So, again, good night.
I must be cruel only to be kind.
185 This bad begins, and worse remains behind.
One word more, good lady.

Queen.   What shall I do?

Hamlet. Not this by no means that I bid you do:
Let the bloat king tempt you again to bed,
Pinch wanton on your cheek, call you his mouse,
190 And let him, for a pair of reechy kisses
Or paddling in your neck with his damned fingers,
Make you to ravel all this matter out
That I essentially am not in madness,
But mad in craft. 'Twere good you let him know,
195 For who that's but a queen, fair, sober, wise,
Would from a paddock, from a bat, a gib,
Such dear concernings hide? Who would do so?
No, in despite of sense and secrecy,
Unpeg the basket on the house's top,
200 Let the birds fly, and like the famous ape,
To try conclusions, in the basket creep
And break your own neck down.

Queen. Be thou assured, if words be made of breath
And breath of life, I have no life to breathe
205 What thou hast said to me.

Hamlet. I must to England, you know that.

Queen.   Alack,
I had forgot! 'Tis so concluded on.

Hamlet. There's letters sealed; and my two schoolfellows,
Whom I will trust as I will adders fanged,
210 They bear the mandate; they must sweep my way
And marshal me to knavery. Let it work,
For 'tis the sport to have the enginer

Hoist with his own petard; and 't shall go hard
But I will delve one yard below their mines
215 And blow them at the moon. O, 'tis most sweet
When in one line two crafts directly meet.
This man shall set me packing.
I'll lug the guts into the neighbor room.
Mother, good night indeed. This counselor
220 Is now most still, most secret, and most grave,
Who was in life a foolish prating knave.—
Come, sir, to draw toward an end with you.
Good night, mother.

[*They exit*, Hamlet *tugging in* Polonius.]

213–214 and 't . . . I will: unless I have bad luck I will; **mines:** tunnels.

216 crafts: plots, crafty schemes.

217 Polonius's death will force Hamlet to leave in a hurry.

222 to draw toward an end: to finish up.

CHECK YOUR UNDERSTANDING

Answer these questions before moving on to the **Analyze the Text** section on the following page.

1 Claudius decides to send Hamlet to England because he —

   A feels threatened by Hamlet

   B needs Hamlet to negotiate a treaty

   C hopes the long voyage will cure Hamlet

   D wants to keep Hamlet away from Ophelia

2 Why does Hamlet avoid killing Claudius in this act?

   F Claudius is always surrounded by heavily armed guards.

   G Hamlet is still uncertain about whether Claudius is guilty.

   H He doesn't want to send Claudius to heaven while praying.

   J Someone else must kill Claudius so Hamlet won't be blamed.

3 Why does Hamlet kill Polonius in Gertrude's room?

   A He is angry that Polonius kept Ophelia from him.

   B He thinks the hidden Polonius might be Claudius.

   C Polonius is having an affair with Gertrude.

   D Polonius took part in his father's murder.

ANALYZE THE TEXT

Support your responses with evidence from the text. NOTEBOOK

1. **Evaluate** Review Hamlet's dialogue with Ophelia in Act III, Scene 1, and during the performance by the players in Scene 2. Do these encounters lead you to adjust ideas you formed earlier about his character? Explain why or why not.

2. **Analyze** Reread lines 58–76 in Scene 2. What does Hamlet admire about Horatio? How does Shakespeare use Horatio to help develop the play's plot?

3. **Analyze** In Shakespeare's plays, a climax or turning point usually occurs in the third act when something happens that clarifies the outcome of the central conflict. Where does this climax occur in Act III of *Hamlet*? Explain your response.

4. **Synthesize** Soon after Hamlet decides against killing Claudius while he is praying, he mistakes Polonius for the King and kills him without hesitation. What does this combination of events suggest about revenge?

5. **Notice & Note** Shakespeare reveals Claudius's true thoughts to the audience in his aside in Scene 1, lines 50–55, and his soliloquy in Scene 3, lines 36–72. How does your impression of him in these moments differ from the way he presents himself earlier in the play?

CREATE AND PRESENT

Perform a Scene Act out a brief scene or a section of a longer scene.

❏ In a small group, choose a scene and decide which role will be played by each member.

❏ Read the scene aloud. Discuss the stated and implied motivations of the characters.

❏ Decide where performers will enter or exit and where they will stand while reciting the dialogue. Read the stage directions to determine if any sound or lighting effects are needed.

❏ Practice the performance. There is no need for performers to memorize their parts, but they should read them several times to become familiar with the language. Each performer should use a tone of voice appropriate to his or her character.

❏ Perform the scene in front of the class. You might also videotape the performance and upload it to the Internet.

SETTING A PURPOSE

As you read, notice how new events create conflict and complicate the plot of the play.

ACT IV

Scene 1 *The Castle.*

[*Enter* King and Queen, *with* Rosencrantz *and* Guildenstern.]

King. There's matter in these sighs; these profound heaves
You must translate; 'tis fit we understand them.
Where is your son?

Queen. Bestow this place on us a little while.

[Rosencrantz *and* Guildenstern *exit.*]

5 Ah, mine own lord, what have I seen tonight!

King. What, Gertrude? How does Hamlet?

Queen. Mad as the sea and wind when both contend
Which is the mightier. In his lawless fit,
Behind the arras hearing something stir,
10 Whips out his rapier, cries "A rat, a rat,"
And in this brainish apprehension kills
The unseen good old man.

King. O heavy deed!
It had been so with us, had we been there.
His liberty is full of threats to all—
15 To you yourself, to us, to everyone.
Alas, how shall this bloody deed be answered?
It will be laid to us, whose providence
Should have kept short, restrained, and out of haunt
This mad young man. But so much was our love,
20 We would not understand what was most fit,
But, like the owner of a foul disease,
To keep it from divulging, let it feed
Even on the pith of life. Where is he gone?

Queen. To draw apart the body he hath killed,

Notice & Note

Use the side margins to notice and note signposts in the text.

1 matter: significance.

11 brainish apprehension: frenzied belief.

17–19 Claudius worries that the death will be blamed on him (**laid to us**) because he should have had the foresight (**providence**) to keep Hamlet restrained (**short**) and isolated (**out of haunt**).

22 divulging: being revealed.

25–26 O're . . . mineral: vein of gold in a mine.

25 O'er whom his very madness, like some ore
    Among a mineral of metals base,
    Shows itself pure: he weeps for what is done.

    King. O Gertrude, come away!
    The sun no sooner shall the mountains touch

32 countenance: accept.

30 But we will ship him hence; and this vile deed
    We must with all our majesty and skill
    Both countenance and excuse.—Ho, Guildenstern!

    [*Enter* Rosencrantz *and* Guildenstern.]

33 some further aid: others who can help.

    Friends both, go join you with some further aid.
    Hamlet in madness hath Polonius slain,

35 And from his mother's closet hath he dragged him.
    Go seek him out, speak fair, and bring the body
    Into the chapel. I pray you, haste in this.

    [Rosencrantz *and* Guildenstern *exit.*]

    Come, Gertrude, we'll call up our wisest friends
    And let them know both what we mean to do

40–44 Some words are missing after "untimely done" in line 40. Many editors insert "So haply slander" or a similar phrase. Claudius is hoping that slander, which hits as directly as a cannon fired at point-blank range hits its target, will miss the royal household.

40 And what's untimely done. . . .
    Whose whisper o'er the world's diameter,
    As level as the cannon to his blank
    Transports his poisoned shot, may miss our name
    And hit the woundless air. O, come away!

45 My soul is full of discord and dismay.

    [*They exit.*]

    Scene 2 *The Castle.*

    [*Enter* Hamlet.]

    Hamlet. Safely stowed.

    Gentlemen [*within*]. Hamlet! Lord Hamlet!

    Hamlet. But soft, what noise? Who calls on Hamlet?
    O, here they come.

    [*Enter* Rosencrantz, Guildenstern, *and others.*]

5   **Rosencrantz.** What have you done, my lord, with the
        dead body?

6 Compounded: mixed. Hamlet alludes to Genesis 3.19: "dust thou art, and unto dust shalt thou return."

    Hamlet. Compounded it with dust, whereto 'tis kin.

    Rosencrantz. Tell us where 'tis, that we may take it
        thence

    And bear it to the chapel.

    Hamlet. Do not believe it.

10 **Rosencrantz.** Believe what?

Hamlet. That I can keep your counsel and not mine own. Besides, to be demanded of a sponge, what replication should be made by the son of a king?

Rosencrantz. Take you me for a sponge, my lord?

15 **Hamlet.** Ay, sir, that soaks up the King's countenance, his rewards, his authorities. But such officers do the King best service in the end. He keeps them like an ape an apple in the corner of his jaw, first mouthed, to be last swallowed. When he needs
20 what you have gleaned, it is but squeezing you, and, sponge, you shall be dry again.

Rosencrantz. I understand you not, my lord.

Hamlet. I am glad of it. A knavish speech sleeps in a foolish ear.

25 **Rosencrantz.** My lord, you must tell us where the body is and go with us to the King.

Hamlet. The body is with the King, but the King is not with the body. The King is a thing—

Guildenstern. A "thing," my lord?

30 **Hamlet.** Of nothing. Bring me to him. Hide fox, and all after!

[*They exit.*]

Scene 3 *The castle.*

[*Enter* King *and two or three.*]

King. I have sent to seek him and to find the body. How dangerous is it that this man goes loose! Yet must not we put the strong law on him. He's loved of the distracted multitude,
5 Who like not in their judgment, but their eyes; And, where 'tis so, th' offender's scourge is weighed, But never the offense. To bear all smooth and even, This sudden sending him away must seem Deliberate pause. Diseases desperate grown
10 By desperate appliance are relieved Or not at all.

[*Enter* Rosencrantz.]

　　　　　　　How now, what hath befallen?

Rosencrantz. Where the dead body is bestowed, my lord, We cannot get from him.

King. 　　　　　　　But where is he?

NOTICE & NOTE

12 demanded of: questioned by.

13 replication: response.

15 countenance: favor.

17–18 like an ape . . . jaw: as an ape keeps food in the corner of its mouth.

23 sleeps in: is meaningless to.

27–30 Hamlet may be playing off the idea that the king occupies two "bodies": his own mortal body and the office of kingship. Claudius is a king of no account (**Of nothing**); the office of kingship does not belong to him.

30 Hide fox . . . after: a cry from a children's game such as hide-and-seek.

4–5 He's loved . . . eyes: He's loved by the confused masses, who choose not by judgment but by appearance.

6 scourge: punishment.

7 To bear . . . even: to manage everything smoothly and evenly.

9 Deliberate pause: carefully thought out.

9–11 Diseases . . . all: Desperate diseases require desperate remedies.

Rosencrantz. Without, my lord; guarded, to know
your pleasure.

15 **King.** Bring him before us.

Rosencrantz. Ho! Bring in the lord.

[*They enter with* Hamlet.]

King. Now, Hamlet, where's Polonius?

Hamlet. At supper.

King. At supper where?

Hamlet. Not where he eats, but where he is eaten. A
20 certain convocation of politic worms are e'en at
him. Your worm is your only emperor for diet. We
fat all creatures else to fat us, and we fat ourselves
for maggots. Your fat king and your lean beggar is
but variable service—two dishes but to one table.
25 That's the end.

King. Alas, alas!

Hamlet. A man may fish with the worm that hath eat
of a king and eat of the fish that hath fed of that
worm.

30 **King.** What dost thou mean by this?

Hamlet. Nothing but to show you how a king may go
a progress through the guts of a beggar.

King. Where is Polonius?

Hamlet. In heaven. Send thither to see. If your messenger
35 find him not there, seek him i' th' other place
yourself. But if, indeed, you find him not within
this month, you shall nose him as you go up the
stairs into the lobby.

King [*to* Attendants]. Go, seek him there.

40 **Hamlet.** He will stay till you come.

[Attendants *exit.*]

King. Hamlet, this deed, for thine especial safety
(Which we do tender, as we dearly grieve
For that which thou hast done) must send thee hence
With fiery quickness. Therefore prepare thyself.
45 The bark is ready, and the wind at help,
Th' associates tend, and everything is bent
For England.

Hamlet. For England?

King. Ay, Hamlet.

19–21 Hamlet says that a group of crafty (**politic**) worms are dining on him.

21 Your . . . diet: Worms have the last word when it comes to eating.

24 but variable service: only different courses (of a meal).

32 progress: royal journey.

42 tender: regard, hold dear.

45–47 Claudius says that the sailing vessel (**bark**) is ready, the wind is favorable (**at help**), his fellow travelers wait (**tend**) for him, and everything is ready (**bent**).

50 **Hamlet.** Good.

King. So is it, if thou knew'st our purposes.

Hamlet. I see a cherub that sees them. But come, for
    England.
Farewell, dear mother.

King.   Thy loving father, Hamlet.

Hamlet. My mother. Father and mother is man and wife,
55 Man and wife is one flesh, and so, my mother.—
Come, for England.

[*He exits*.]

King. Follow him at foot; tempt him with speed aboard.
Delay it not. I'll have him hence tonight.
Away, for everything is sealed and done
60 That else leans on th' affair. Pray you, make haste.

[*All but the* King *exit*.]

And England, if my love thou hold'st at aught
(As my great power thereof may give thee sense,
Since yet thy cicatrice looks raw and red
After the Danish sword, and thy free awe
65 Pays homage to us), thou mayst not coldly set
Our sovereign process, which imports at full,
By letters conguring to that effect,
The present death of Hamlet. Do it, England,
For like the hectic in my blood he rages,
70 And thou must cure me. Till I know 'tis done,
Howe'er my haps, my joys were ne'er begun.

[*He exits*.]

Scene 4 *Near the coast of Denmark.*

[*Enter* Fortinbras *with his army over the stage*.]

Fortinbras. Go, Captain, from me greet the Danish king.
Tell him that by his license Fortinbras
Craves the conveyance of a promised march
Over his kingdom. You know the rendezvous.
5 If that his Majesty would aught with us,
We shall express our duty in his eye;
And let him know so.

Captain. I will do 't, my lord.

Fortinbras. Go softly on.

[*All but the* Captain *exit*.]

[*Enter* Hamlet, Rosencrantz, Guildenstern, *and others*.]

52 cherub: angel of knowledge.

ANALYZE DRAMATIC PLOT
Annotate: In lines 61–71, mark what Claudius wants the English king to do.

Draw Conclusions: Why might he want this action done in England instead of Denmark?

57 at foot: closely.

60 leans on: is related to.

61–68 Claudius says that if the King of England values his friendship, he will not ignore Claudius's command to have Hamlet killed immediately.

69 hectic: fever.

71 Howe'er my haps: whatever my fortunes.

2 license: permission.

3 the conveyance of: escort during.

5–7 Fortinbras says that if the King wishes to see him, he will show his respect in person (**in his eye**).

9 softly: slowly, carefully.

© Houghton Mifflin Harcourt Publishing Company

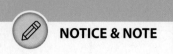

NOTICE & NOTE

10 powers: forces.

16 the main: the main part.

18 Truly . . . addition: to speak plainly.

21 To pay . . . it: I would not pay even five ducats a year to rent it.

23 ranker: higher; **in fee:** outright.

27 Will not . . . straw: are not enough to settle this trifling dispute.

28 impostume: puss-filled swelling.

29 without: on the outside.

ANALYZE SOLILOQUY
Annotate: Mark statements describing Fortinbras in lines 34–68.

Interpret: What does Hamlet admire about Fortinbras?

34 inform against: denounce.

36 market: profit.

38–41 Sure He . . . unused: God would not have given us such a considerable power of reasoning to let it grow moldy from lack of use.

42–43 Bestial . . . event: beast-like forgetfulness or cowardly hesitation from thinking too carefully about the outcome.

48 gross: obvious.

---

10 **Hamlet.** Good sir, whose powers are these?

Captain. They are of Norway, sir.

Hamlet. How purposed, sir, I pray you?

Captain. Against some part of Poland.

Hamlet. Who commands them, sir?

15 **Captain.** The nephew to old Norway, Fortinbras.

Hamlet. Goes it against the main of Poland, sir,
Or for some frontier?

Captain. Truly to speak, and with no addition,
We go to gain a little patch of ground
20 That hath in it no profit but the name.
To pay five ducats, five, I would not farm it;
Nor will it yield to Norway or the Pole
A ranker rate, should it be sold in fee.

Hamlet. Why, then, the Polack never will defend it.

25 **Captain.** Yes, it is already garrisoned.

Hamlet. Two thousand souls and twenty thousand ducats
Will not debate the question of this straw.
This is th' impostume of much wealth and peace,
That inward breaks and shows no cause without
30 Why the man dies.—I humbly thank you, sir.

Captain. God be wi' you, sir.

[*He exits.*]

Rosencrantz. Will 't please you go, my lord?

Hamlet. I'll be with you straight. Go a little before.

[*All but* Hamlet *exit.*]

How all occasions do inform against me
35 And spur my dull revenge. What is a man
If his chief good and market of his time
Be but to sleep and feed? A beast, no more.
Sure He that made us with such large discourse,
Looking before and after, gave us not
40 That capability and godlike reason
To fust in us unused. Now whether it be
Bestial oblivion or some craven scruple
Of thinking too precisely on th' event
(A thought which, quartered, hath but one part wisdom
45 And ever three parts coward), I do not know
Why yet I live to say "This thing's to do,"
Sith I have cause, and will, and strength, and means
To do 't. Examples gross as earth exhort me:

© Houghton Mifflin Harcourt Publishing Company

Witness this army of such mass and charge,
50 Led by a delicate and tender prince,
Whose spirit with divine ambition puffed
Makes mouths at the invisible event,
Exposing what is mortal and unsure
To all that fortune, death, and danger dare,
55 Even for an eggshell. Rightly to be great
Is not to stir without great argument,
But greatly to find quarrel in a straw
When honor's at the stake. How stand I, then,
That have a father killed, a mother stained,
60 Excitements of my reason and my blood,
And let all sleep, while to my shame I see
The imminent death of twenty thousand men
That for a fantasy and trick of fame
Go to their graves like beds, fight for a plot
65 Whereon the numbers cannot try the cause,
Which is not tomb enough and continent
To hide the slain? O, from this time forth
My thoughts be bloody or be nothing worth!

[*He exits.*]

Scene 5 *The castle.*

[*Enter* Horatio, Queen, *and a* Gentleman.]

Queen. I will not speak with her.

Gentleman. She is importunate,
Indeed distract; her mood will needs be pitied.

Queen. What would she have?

5 **Gentleman.** She speaks much of her father, says she hears
There's tricks i' th' world, and hems, and beats her
   heart,
Spurns enviously at straws, speaks things in doubt
That carry but half sense. Her speech is nothing,
Yet the unshaped use of it doth move
10 The hearers to collection. They aim at it
And botch the words up fit to their own thoughts;
Which, as her winks and nods and gestures yield them,
Indeed would make one think there might be thought,
Though nothing sure, yet much unhappily.

15 **Horatio.** 'Twere good she were spoken with, for she
   may strew
Dangerous conjectures in ill-breeding minds.

Queen. Let her come in.

52 Makes mouths . . . event: makes scornful faces at the unforeseeable outcome.

55–58 True greatness does not lie in refraining from action when there is no great cause but in the willingness to fight whenever honor is at stake.

63 fantasy and trick of fame: illusion of honor.

65–67 Whereon . . . slain: The disputed land does not have enough room for so many men to battle on and is too small a burial ground to hold those who will be killed.

3 distract: distracted; **mood . . . pitied:** state of mind must be pitied.

6 tricks: deception.

7 Spurns enviously at straws: takes offense at trifles; **in doubt:** without clear meaning.

8–11 Although Ophelia speaks nonsense, her confused manner of speaking moves her listeners to gather some meaning by patching her words together to fit their conjectures.

16 ill-breeding: intent on making trouble.

19 toy: trifle; **amiss:** misfortune.

20–21 Guilt is so full of clumsy suspicion (**artless jealousy**) that it reveals (**spills**) itself through fear of being revealed.

26 cockle hat: a hat with a scallop shell (worn by pilgrims to show that they had been to an overseas shrine).

27 shoon: shoes.

28 imports: means.

39 Larded: decorated.

41 showers: tears.

43 God dild you: God yield, or reward, you.

43–44 Ophelia refers to a legend about a baker's daughter who was turned into an owl because she refused to give Christ bread.

46 Conceit: brooding.

49–67 This song refers to the ancient custom that the first maiden a man sees on St. Valentine's Day will be his sweetheart.

54 dupped: opened.

[Gentleman *exits.*]

[*Aside*] To my sick soul (as sin's true nature is),
Each toy seems prologue to some great amiss.
20 So full of artless jealousy is guilt,
It spills itself in fearing to be spilt.

[*Enter* Ophelia *distracted.*]

Ophelia. Where is the beauteous Majesty of Denmark?

Queen. How now, Ophelia?

Ophelia [*sings*]. *How should I your true love know*
25 *From another one?*
By his cockle hat and staff
And his sandal shoon.

Queen. Alas, sweet lady, what imports this song?

Ophelia. Say you? Nay, pray you, mark.
30 [*Sings.*] *He is dead and gone, lady,*
He is dead and gone;
At his head a grass-green turf,
At his heels a stone.

Oh, ho!

35 **Queen.** Nay, but Ophelia—

Ophelia. Pray you, mark.

[*Sings.*] *White his shroud as the mountain snow—*
[*Enter* King.]

Queen. Alas, look here, my lord.

Ophelia [*sings*]. *Larded all with sweet flowers;*
40 *Which bewept to the ground did not go*
With true-love showers.

King. How do you, pretty lady?

Ophelia. Well, God dild you. They say the owl was a baker's daughter. Lord, we know what we are but
45 know not what we may be. God be at your table.

King. Conceit upon her father.

Ophelia. Pray let's have no words of this, but when they ask you what it means, say you this:
[*Sings.*] *Tomorrow is Saint Valentine's day,*
50 *All in the morning betime,*
And I a maid at your window,
To be your Valentine.
Then up he rose and donned his clothes
And dupped the chamber door,

59 Gis: Jesus.

62 Cock: a substitution for
"God" in oaths.

63 tumbled: had sexual
intercourse with.

79 spies: soldiers sent ahead
as scouts.

82 muddied: confused.

84–85 Claudius says that
he has only acted foolishly
(**greenly**) by burying Polonius
in haste and secrecy.

89–95 Laertes, who has
secretly returned from France, is
clouded by suspicion and does
not lack gossipers who spread
rumors of his father's death.
And in the absence of facts,
the need for some explanation
means that Claudius will be
accused of the crime.

55 *Let in the maid, that out a maid*
  Never departed more.

King. Pretty Ophelia—

Ophelia. Indeed, without an oath, I'll make an end on 't:
[*Sings.*] *By Gis and by Saint Charity,*
60   *Alack and fie for shame,*
  Young men will do 't, if they come to 't;
    By Cock, they are to blame.
  Quoth she "Before you tumbled me,
    You promised me to wed."
65 *He answers:*
  "So would I 'a done, by yonder sun,
    An thou hadst not come to my bed."

King. How long hath she been thus?

Ophelia. I hope all will be well. We must be patient,
70 but I cannot choose but weep to think they would
lay him i' th' cold ground. My brother shall know
of it. And so I thank you for your good counsel.
Come, my coach! Good night, ladies, good night,
sweet ladies, good night, good night.

[*She exits.*]

75 **King.** Follow her close; give her good watch, I pray you.

[Horatio *exits.*]

O, this is the poison of deep grief. It springs
All from her father's death, and now behold!
O Gertrude, Gertrude,
When sorrows come, they come not single spies,
80 But in battalions: first, her father slain;
Next, your son gone, and he most violent author
Of his own just remove; the people muddied,
Thick, and unwholesome in their thoughts and
   whispers
For good Polonius' death, and we have done but
   greenly
85 In hugger-mugger to inter him; poor Ophelia
Divided from herself and her fair judgment,
Without the which we are pictures or mere beasts;
Last, and as much containing as all these,
Her brother is in secret come from France,
90 Feeds on his wonder, keeps himself in clouds,
And wants not buzzers to infect his ear
With pestilent speeches of his father's death,
Wherein necessity, of matter beggared,
Will nothing stick our person to arraign

95　In ear and ear. O, my dear Gertrude, this,
　　Like to a murd'ring piece, in many places
　　Gives me superfluous death.

　　　[*A noise within.*]

　　Queen. Alack, what noise is this?

　　King. Attend!
100　Where is my Switzers? Let them guard the door.

　　　[*Enter a* Messenger.]

　　What is the matter?

　　Messenger.　　　Save yourself, my lord.
　　The ocean, overpeering of his list,
　　Eats not the flats with more impiteous haste
　　Than young Laertes, in a riotous head,
105　O'erbears your officers. The rabble call him "lord,"
　　And, as the world were now but to begin,
　　Antiquity forgot, custom not known,
　　The ratifiers and props of every word,
　　They cry "Choose we, Laertes shall be king!"
110　Caps, hands, and tongues applaud it to the clouds,
　　"Laertes shall be king! Laertes king!"

　　　[*A noise within.*]

　　Queen. How cheerfully on the false trail they cry.
　　O, this is counter, you false Danish dogs!

　　King. The doors are broke.

　　　[*Enter* Laertes *with others.*]

115　**Laertes.** Where is this king?—Sirs, stand you all without.

　　All. No, let's come in!

　　Laertes. I pray you, give me leave.

　　All. We will, we will.

　　Laertes. I thank you. Keep the door. [Followers *exit.*] O,
　　　thou vile king,
120　Give me my father!

　　Queen.　　　Calmly, good Laertes.

　　Laertes. That drop of blood that's calm proclaims me
　　　bastard,
　　Cries "cuckold" to my father, brands the harlot
　　Even here between the chaste unsmirchèd brow
　　Of my true mother.

　　King.　　　What is the cause, Laertes,
125　That thy rebellion looks so giant-like?—

96 **murd'ring piece:** a cannon that can kill many men simultaneously with its scattered shot.

97 **Gives . . . death:** kills me over and over.

100 **Switzers:** Swiss bodyguards.

102–105 Laertes is overpowering Claudius's officers as quickly as the ocean, rising above its boundary (**list**), floods the level ground.

106–108 **as the world . . . word:** as if the world had just begun, and ancient tradition and custom, which should confirm and support everything one says, were both forgotten.

110 **Caps:** caps thrown into the air.

113 **counter:** a hunting term that means "to follow a trail in the wrong direction."

121–124 Laertes says that no true son could be calm about his father's murder—that being calm would in effect prove that son to be a bastard.

122 **cuckold:** a man whose wife is unfaithful.

124 **true:** faithful.

126–129 Claudius tells Gertrude not to fear for his personal safety; so much divinity protects (**doth hedge**) a king that treason can only peer (**peep**) from afar at what it would like to do.

Let him go, Gertrude. Do not fear our person.
There's such divinity doth hedge a king
That treason can but peep to what it would,
Acts little of his will.—Tell me, Laertes,
130 Why thou art thus incensed.—Let him go,
    Gertrude.—
Speak, man.

Laertes. Where is my father?

King. Dead.

Queen. But not by him.

King.   Let him demand his fill.

135 juggled with: played with, deceived.

135 **Laertes.** How came he dead? I'll not be juggled with.
To hell, allegiance! Vows, to the blackest devil!
Conscience and grace, to the profoundest pit!
I dare damnation. To this point I stand,
That both the worlds I give to negligence,
140 Let come what comes, only I'll be revenged
Most throughly for my father.

ANALYZE CONFLICT
Annotate: Mark emotionally charged language in lines 135–141.

Compare: How does Laertes' speech compare with Hamlet's reaction when he first learned about his father's murder?

King. Who shall stay you?

Laertes. My will, not all the world.
And for my means, I'll husband them so well
145 They shall go far with little.

144 husband: manage, conserve.

King.   Good Laertes,
If you desire to know the certainty
Of your dear father, is 't writ in your revenge
That, swoopstake, you will draw both friend and
    foe,
Winner and loser?

148 swoopstake: a gambling term that means taking all the stakes on the gambling table.

150 **Laertes.** None but his enemies.

King. Will you know them, then?

Laertes. To his good friends thus wide I'll ope my arms
And, like the kind life-rend'ring pelican,
Repast them with my blood.

153 pelican: traditionally thought to feed its young with its own blood.

King.   Why, now you speak
155 Like a good child and a true gentleman.
That I am guiltless of your father's death
And am most sensibly in grief for it,
It shall as level to your judgment 'pear
As day does to your eye.
                [*A noise within*] Let her come in.

157 sensibly: feelingly.

158 level: plain.

160 **Laertes.** How now, what noise is that?

[*Enter* Ophelia.]

O heat, dry up my brains! Tears seven times salt
Burn out the sense and virtue of mine eye!
By heaven, thy madness shall be paid with weight
Till our scale turn the beam! O rose of May,
165 Dear maid, kind sister, sweet Ophelia!
O heavens, is 't possible a young maid's wits
Should be as mortal as an old man's life?
Nature is fine in love, and, where 'tis fine,
It sends some precious instance of itself
170 After the thing it loves.

Ophelia [*sings*]. *They bore him barefaced on the bier,*
   Hey non nonny, nonny, hey nonny,
   And in his grave rained many a tear.
Fare you well, my dove.

175 **Laertes.** Hadst thou thy wits and didst persuade revenge,
It could not move thus.

Ophelia. You must sing "A-down a-down"—and you
"Call him a-down-a."—O, how the wheel becomes
it! It is the false steward that stole his master's
180 daughter.

Laertes. This nothing's more than matter.

Ophelia. There's rosemary, that's for remembrance.
Pray you, love, remember. And there is pansies,
that's for thoughts.

185 **Laertes.** A document in madness: thoughts and
remembrance fitted.

Ophelia. There's fennel for you, and columbines.
There's rue for you, and here's some for me; we
may call it herb of grace o' Sundays. You must
190 wear your rue with a difference. There's a daisy. I
would give you some violets, but they withered all
when my father died. They say he made a good end.
[*Sings.*] *For bonny sweet Robin is all my joy.*

Laertes. Thought and afflictions, passion, hell itself
195 She turns to favor and to prettiness.

Ophelia [*sings*].
And will he not come again?
And will he not come again?
   No, no, he is dead.
   Go to thy deathbed.
200 *He never will come again.*

His beard was as white as snow,

162 virtue: power.

163–164 In his vow to revenge Ophelia's madness, Laertes uses the image of weights being placed on a scale to make it tilt in the opposite direction.

168–169 fine in: refined by; **instance:** token (suggesting that Ophelia has sent her sanity into the grave with her father).

175 persuade: argue rationally for.

176 move thus: have such an effect.

177–178 Ophelia assigns refrains to the others so they can join in the singing.

178 the wheel: perhaps referring to the refrain or a spinning wheel that accompanies the singing.

181 This . . . matter: This nonsense has more meaning than rational speech.

182–192 Rosemary was used to symbolize remembrance at funerals. **Pansies,** a name derived from the French word for thought, **pensée,** was associated with courtship. Ophelia also mentions **fennel** (flattery), **columbines** (adultery or ingratitude), **rue** (repentance, sorrow), the **daisy** (dissembling, false love), and **violets** (faithfulness).

185–186 Laertes finds a lesson (**document**) in Ophelia's linking of thoughts and remembrance.

194 Thought: melancholy; **passion:** suffering.

202 flaxen: pale yellow; **poll:** head.

204 cast away: scatter uselessly.

213 collateral: indirect.

214 find us touched: find me implicated.

221–222 The traditional burial ceremony (**ostentation**) for a knight included hanging his helmet, sword, and a tablet displaying his coat of arms (**hatchment**) over the tomb.

224 That I . . . question: so that I must demand an explanation.

All flaxen was his poll.
  He is gone, he is gone,
    And we cast away moan.
205 *God 'a mercy on his soul.*
And of all Christians' souls, I pray God. God be
wi' you.

[*She exits.*]

Laertes. Do you see this, O God?

King. Laertes, I must commune with your grief,
210 Or you deny me right. Go but apart,
Make choice of whom your wisest friends you will,
And they shall hear and judge 'twixt you and me.
If by direct or by collateral hand
They find us touched, we will our kingdom give,
215 Our crown, our life, and all that we call ours,
To you in satisfaction; but if not,
Be you content to lend your patience to us,
And we shall jointly labor with your soul
To give it due content.

Laertes.   Let this be so.
220 His means of death, his obscure funeral
(No trophy, sword, nor hatchment o'er his bones,
No noble rite nor formal ostentation)
Cry to be heard, as 'twere from heaven to earth,
That I must call 't in question.

King.   So you shall,
225 And where th' offense is, let the great ax fall.
I pray you, go with me.

[*They exit.*]

Scene 6 *The castle.*

[*Enter* Horatio *and others.*]

Horatio. What are they that would speak with me?

Gentleman. Seafaring men, sir. They say they have letters for you.

Horatio. Let them come in. [Gentleman *exits.*] I do not
5 know from what part of the world I should be
greeted, if not from Lord Hamlet.

[*Enter* Sailors.]

Sailor. God bless you, sir.

Horatio. Let Him bless thee too.

Sailor. He shall, sir, an 't please Him. There's a letter
10 for you, sir. It came from th' ambassador that was
bound for England—if your name be Horatio, as I
am let to know it is.

[*He hands* Horatio *a letter.*]

Horatio [*reads the letter*]. *Horatio, when thou shalt
have overlooked this, give these fellows some means*
15 *to the King. They have letters for him. Ere we
were two days old at sea, a pirate of very warlike
appointment gave us chase. Finding ourselves too
slow of sail, we put on a compelled valor, and in the
grapple I boarded them. On the instant, they got*
20 *clear of our ship; so I alone became their prisoner.
They have dealt with me like thieves of mercy, but
they knew what they did: I am to do a good turn
for them. Let the King have the letters I have sent,
and repair thou to me with as much speed as thou*
25 *wouldst fly death. I have words to speak in thine
ear will make thee dumb; yet are they much too
light for the bore of the matter. These good fellows
will bring thee where I am. Rosencrantz and
Guildenstern hold their course for England; of*
30 *them I have much to tell thee. Farewell.
He that thou knowest thine, Hamlet.*

Come, I will give you way for these your letters
And do 't the speedier that you may direct me
To him from whom you brought them.

[*They exit.*]

Scene 7 *The castle.*

[*Enter* King *and* Laertes.]

King. Now must your conscience my acquittance seal,
And you must put me in your heart for friend,
Sith you have heard, and with a knowing ear,
That he which hath your noble father slain
5 Pursued my life.

Laertes.　　　　It well appears. But tell me
Why you proceeded not against these feats,
So criminal and so capital in nature,
As by your safety, greatness, wisdom, all things else,
You mainly were stirred up.

Notes (right column):

9 an 't: if it.

10 th' ambassador: Hamlet.

ANALYZE DRAMATIC PLOT
Annotate: Mark details in lines 13–31 that explain why Hamlet is back in Denmark.

Evaluate: Is Shakespeare's use of the letter an effective way to advance the plot? Why or why not?

14 overlooked: read; means: means of access.

16–17 pirate . . . appointment: pirate ship well equipped for warfare.

21 thieves of mercy: merciful thieves.

22 they knew what they did: their actions were calculated.

24 repair: come.

27 light . . . bore: inadequate for the importance.

32 way: means of access.

1 my acquittance seal: confirm my innocence.

3 Sith: since.

7 capital: punishable by death.

8 safety: concern for your safety.

9 mainly: greatly.

© Houghton Mifflin Harcourt Publishing Company

11 unsinewed: weak.

15 conjunctive: closely joined.

16 star . . . sphere: In Shakespeare's time, it was believed that each planet moves around the Earth in a hollow sphere.

18 count: account, indictment.

19–25 Claudius says that the common people (**general gender**), through their love for Hamlet, act like a spring with such a high concentration of lime that wood placed in it will become petrified; they change his limitations (**gyves**) into attractive qualities, so that the strong wind of their approval would blow back any arrows that Claudius might shoot at Hamlet.

27 terms: condition.

28–30 Whose worth . . . perfections: If praises can recall Ophelia's former self, her worth placed her at the top of the age.

45 naked: destitute, defenseless.

---

10   **King.** O, for two special reasons,
    Which may to you perhaps seem much unsinewed,
    But yet to me they're strong. The Queen his mother
    Lives almost by his looks, and for myself
    (My virtue or my plague, be it either which),
15   She is so conjunctive to my life and soul
    That, as the star moves not but in his sphere,
    I could not but by her. The other motive
    Why to a public count I might not go
    Is the great love the general gender bear him,
20   Who, dipping all his faults in their affection,
    Work like the spring that turneth wood to stone,
    Convert his gyves to graces, so that my arrows,
    Too slightly timbered for so loud a wind,
    Would have reverted to my bow again,
25   But not where I have aimed them.

    Laertes. And so have I a noble father lost,
    A sister driven into desp'rate terms,
    Whose worth, if praises may go back again,
    Stood challenger on mount of all the age
30   For her perfections. But my revenge will come.

    King. Break not your sleeps for that. You must not think
    That we are made of stuff so flat and dull
    That we can let our beard be shook with danger
    And think it pastime. You shortly shall hear more.
35   I loved your father, and we love ourself,
    And that, I hope, will teach you to imagine—

    [*Enter a* Messenger *with letters.*]

    How now? What news?

    Messenger.   Letters, my lord, from Hamlet.
    These to your Majesty, this to the Queen.

    King. From Hamlet? Who brought them?

40   **Messenger.** Sailors, my lord, they say. I saw them not.
    They were given me by Claudio. He received them
    Of him that brought them.

    King.   Laertes, you shall hear them.—
    Leave us.

    [Messenger *exits.*]

    [*Reads.*] *High and mighty, you shall know I am set*
45 *naked on your kingdom. Tomorrow shall I beg*
    leave to see your kingly eyes, when I shall (first

asking your pardon) thereunto recount the occasion
of my sudden and more strange return. Hamlet.
What should this mean? Are all the rest come back?
50 Or is it some abuse and no such thing?

Laertes. Know you the hand?

King. 'Tis Hamlet's character. "Naked"—
And in a postscript here, he says "alone."
Can you advise me?

55 **Laertes.** I am lost in it, my lord. But let him come.
It warms the very sickness in my heart
That I shall live and tell him to his teeth
"Thus didst thou."

King.   If it be so, Laertes
(As how should it be so? how otherwise?),
60 Will you be ruled by me?

Laertes.   Ay, my lord,
So you will not o'errule me to a peace.

King. To thine own peace. If he be now returned,
As checking at his voyage, and that he means
No more to undertake it, I will work him
65 To an exploit, now ripe in my device,
Under the which he shall not choose but fall;
And for his death no wind of blame shall breathe,
But even his mother shall uncharge the practice
And call it accident.

70 **Laertes.** My lord, I will be ruled,
The rather if you could devise it so
That I might be the organ.
King.   It falls right.
You have been talked of since your travel much,
And that in Hamlet's hearing, for a quality
75 Wherein they say you shine. Your sum of parts
Did not together pluck such envy from him
As did that one, and that, in my regard,
Of the unworthiest siege.

Laertes. What part is that, my lord?

80 **King.** A very ribbon in the cap of youth—
Yet needful too, for youth no less becomes
The light and careless livery that it wears
Than settled age his sables and his weeds,
Importing health and graveness. Two months since

© Houghton Mifflin Harcourt Publishing Company

50 Claudius wonders if this is a deception and no such thing has occurred.

52 character: handwriting.

61 So: as long as.

63 checking at: turning away from.

65 device: devising.

68 uncharge the practice: not blame the plot.

72 organ: agent, instrument.

75–84 The rest of Laertes' qualities combined did not inspire as much envy in Hamlet as this one, which ranks lowest in Claudius's regard. Yet this quality is important even if only a mere decoration (**very ribbon**), because light, carefree clothes (**livery**) are as well-suited to youth as more richly trimmed or sober clothes (**his sables and his weeds**) are to old age, suggesting well-being and dignity.

85 Here was a gentleman of Normandy.
I have seen myself, and served against, the French,
And they can well on horseback, but this gallant
Had witchcraft in 't. He grew unto his seat,
And to such wondrous doing brought his horse
90 As had he been encorpsed and demi-natured
With the brave beast. So far he topped my thought
That I in forgery of shapes and tricks
Come short of what he did.

Laertes.   A Norman was 't?

King. A Norman.

95 **Laertes.** Upon my life, Lamord.

King.   The very same.

Laertes. I know him well. He is the brooch indeed
And gem of all the nation.

King. He made confession of you
And gave you such a masterly report
100 For art and exercise in your defense,
And for your rapier most especial,
That he cried out 'twould be a sight indeed
If one could match you. The 'scrimers of their nation
He swore had neither motion, guard, nor eye,
105 If you opposed them. Sir, this report of his
Did Hamlet so envenom with his envy
That he could nothing do but wish and beg
Your sudden coming-o'er, to play with you.
Now out of this—

Laertes.   What out of this, my lord?

110 **King.** Laertes, was your father dear to you?
Or are you like the painting of a sorrow,
A face without a heart?

Laertes.   Why ask you this?

King. Not that I think you did not love your father,
But that I know love is begun by time
115 And that I see, in passages of proof,
Time qualifies the spark and fire of it.
There lives within the very flame of love
A kind of wick or snuff that will abate it,
And nothing is at a like goodness still;
120 For goodness, growing to a pleurisy,
Dies in his own too-much. That we would do

We should do when we would; for this "would"
    changes
And hath abatements and delays as many
As there are tongues, are hands, are accidents;
125 And then this "should" is like a spendthrift sigh,
That hurts by easing. But to the quick of th' ulcer:
Hamlet comes back; what would you undertake
To show yourself indeed your father's son
More than in words?

Laertes.   To cut his throat i' th' church.

130 **King.** No place indeed should murder sanctuarize;
Revenge should have no bounds. But, good Laertes,
Will you do this? Keep close within your chamber.
Hamlet, returned, shall know you are come home.
We'll put on those shall praise your excellence
135 And set a double varnish on the fame
The Frenchman gave you; bring you, in fine, together
And wager on your heads. He, being remiss,
Most generous, and free from all contriving,
Will not peruse the foils, so that with ease,
140 Or with a little shuffling, you may choose
A sword unbated, and in a pass of practice
Requite him for your father.

Laertes.   I will do 't,
And for that purpose I'll anoint my sword.
I bought an unction of a mountebank
145 So mortal that, but dip a knife in it,
Where it draws blood no cataplasm so rare,
Collected from all simples that have virtue
Under the moon, can save the thing from death
That is but scratched withal. I'll touch my point
150 With this contagion, that, if I gall him slightly,
It may be death.

King.   Let's further think of this,
Weigh what convenience both of time and means
May fit us to our shape. If this should fail,
And that our drift look through our bad performance,
155 'Twere better not assayed. Therefore this project
Should have a back or second that might hold
If this did blast in proof. Soft, let me see.
We'll make a solemn wager on your cunnings—
I ha 't!
160 When in your motion you are hot and dry
(As make your bouts more violent to that end)
And that he calls for drink, I'll have prepared him

121–122 That we . . . would: If one wishes to do something, one should act right away.

123 abatements: lessenings.

125–126 spendthrift sigh . . . easing: an allusion to the idea that sighing brings temporary relief but weakens the heart.

130 should murder sanctuarize: should protect a murderer from punishment.

134 put on those shall: arrange for people to.

136 in fine: finally.

137 remiss: carelessly unsuspicious.

138 generous: noble-minded.

141 unbated: not blunted; **pass of practice:** treacherous thrust.

144–149 Laertes bought from a quack doctor an ointment (**unction**) so deadly that no medical dressing (**cataplasm**) can save anyone scratched by it.

150 gall: injure.

153 fit us to our shape: suit our purposes.

153–155 If the plot should fail and our intentions are exposed, it would be better if we never attempted it.

156 back: backup.

157 blast in proof: blow up while tested.

158 cunnings: skills.

159 ha 't: have it.

163 A chalice for the nonce: a cup of wine for the occasion.

164 stuck: thrust.

169 askant: slanting over.

170 his hoar: its gray.

171 Therewith . . . make: she used the willow twigs to make elaborate wreaths.

172 long purples: orchids.

173 liberal: free-spoken.

174 cold: chaste.

175 pendant boughs: overhanging branches; **coronet:** made into a wreath or crown.

176 envious sliver: malicious branch.

180 lauds: hymns.

181 incapable: unaware.

182 native and endued: naturally adapted.

A chalice for the nonce, whereon but sipping,
If he by chance escape your venomed stuck,
165   Our purpose may hold there.—But stay, what noise?

[*Enter* Queen.]

Queen. One woe doth tread upon another's heel,
So fast they follow. Your sister's drowned, Laertes.

Laertes. Drowned? O, where?

Queen. There is a willow grows askant the brook
170   That shows his hoar leaves in the glassy stream.
Therewith fantastic garlands did she make
Of crowflowers, nettles, daisies, and long purples,
That liberal shepherds give a grosser name,
But our cold maids do "dead men's fingers" call them.
175   There on the pendant boughs her coronet weeds
Clamb'ring to hang, an envious sliver broke,
When down her weedy trophies and herself
Fell in the weeping brook. Her clothes spread wide,
And mermaid-like awhile they bore her up,
180   Which time she chanted snatches of old lauds,
As one incapable of her own distress
Or like a creature native and endued
Unto that element. But long it could not be
Till that her garments, heavy with their drink,
185   Pulled the poor wretch from her melodious lay
To muddy death.

Laertes.   Alas, then she is drowned.

Queen. Drowned, drowned.

Laertes. Too much of water hast thou, poor Ophelia,
And therefore I forbid my tears. But yet
190 It is our trick; nature her custom holds,
Let shame say what it will. When these are gone,
The woman will be out.—Adieu, my lord.
I have a speech o' fire that fain would blaze,
But that this folly drowns it.

[*He exits.*]

King.   Let's follow, Gertrude.
195 How much I had to do to calm his rage!
Now fear I this will give it start again.
Therefore, let's follow.

[*They exit.*]

NOTICE & NOTE

189–192 Laertes says that tears are a natural trait (**trick**), which shame cannot prevent. When all his tears are shed, the womanly part of him will be gone.

CHECK YOUR UNDERSTANDING

Answer these questions before moving on to the **Analyze the Text** section on the following page.

1 Why is Fortinbras traveling through Denmark?

  A He wants to overtake the kingdom.

  B He is spying on the king and queen.

  C He is on his way to invade Poland.

  D He wants to open trade routes with Denmark and Poland.

2 Why is Ophelia behaving irrationally?

  F She is sad that Hamlet is traveling to England.

  G She is upset about Fortinbras's visit to Denmark.

  H She misses her brother.

  J She is distraught over her father's death.

3 What happens to Hamlet's ship on the way to England?

  A It capsizes during a storm.

  B It is captured by pirates.

  C It is attacked by a fleet of Fortinbras's ships.

  D It springs a leak and sinks off the coast of England.

RESPOND

ANALYZE THE TEXT

Support your responses with evidence from the text. 📓 NOTEBOOK

1. **Cause/Effect** Which events in Act IV result from Hamlet's killing of Polonius? How does this sequence of events help explain why Hamlet was slow to take action earlier in the play?

2. **Draw Conclusions** Does Gertrude seem sincere in Scene 1 when she tells Claudius that Hamlet killed Polonius in a fit of insanity, or is she trying to protect him? Consider the following:
   • Hamlet's instructions to her at the end of Act III
   • how closely her description matches Hamlet's actual behavior

3. **Evaluate** Reread Hamlet's soliloquy in Scene 4, lines 48–58. This isn't the first time that Hamlet has berated himself for not taking revenge. Is he just repeating himself, or do you sense a change in his attitude? Explain.

4. **Interpret** Ophelia sings fragments of songs when she appears in Scene 5 suffering from mental illness. How do the songs reflect her experiences in the play?

5. **Compare** Shakespeare often highlights the traits of his main characters through the use of foils, characters with contrasting traits. How do Fortinbras and Laertes serve as foils in Act IV?

CREATE AND PRESENT

Write a Journal Entry Write a journal entry by either Rosencrantz or Guildenstern about their mission to take Hamlet to England.

   ❏ Describe Hamlet's behavior toward his old friends and the events that led to Claudius's decision to send him away.

   ❏ Consider the limited knowledge that Rosencrantz and Guildenstern have about these events. Only include information that your character would be aware of.

   ❏ Use an informal, intimate style appropriate for a journal entry.

Present a News Briefing Imagine you are a journalist tracking the rapid development of events in Act IV of Hamlet. Write a news briefing to present.

   ❏ Make sure to cover all the important developments in chronological order.

   ❏ Make sure your news briefing is free from bias and opinion.

   ❏ Practice reading your news briefing until you feel comfortable with the information.

   ❏ Read your news briefing to a small group and respond to questions from your classmates.

© Houghton Mifflin Harcourt Publishing Company

SETTING A PURPOSE

As you read, notice how Shakespeare creates sharp contrasts in the mood of the scenes.

ACT V

Scene 1 *A churchyard.*

[*Enter* Gravedigger *and* Another.]

Gravedigger. Is she to be buried in Christian burial, when she willfully seeks her own salvation?

Other. I tell thee she is. Therefore make her grave straight. The crowner hath sat on her and finds it
5 Christian burial.

Gravedigger. How can that be, unless she drowned herself in her own defense?

Other. Why, 'tis found so.

Gravedigger. It must be se offendendo; it cannot be else.
10 For here lies the point: if I drown myself wittingly, it argues an act, and an act hath three branches—it is to act, to do, to perform. Argal, she drowned herself wittingly.

Other. Nay, but hear you, goodman delver—

15 **Gravedigger.** Give me leave. Here lies the water; good. Here stands the man; good. If the man go to this water and drown himself, it is (will he, nill he) he goes; mark you that. But if the water come to him and drown him, he drowns not himself. Argal, he
20 that is not guilty of his own death shortens not his own life.

Other. But is this law?

Gravedigger. Ay, marry, is 't—crowner's 'quest law.

Other. Will you ha' the truth on 't? If this had not
25 been a gentlewoman, she should have been buried out o' Christian burial.

Gravedigger. Why, there thou sayst. And the more pity that great folk should have count'nance in this

1 Christian burial: Suicides were not allowed Christian funeral rites. The Gravedigger assumes that Ophelia killed herself.

2 salvation: probably a blunder for *damnation.*

4 straight: immediately; **crowner:** coroner; **sat on her:** held an inquest into her death; **finds it:** gave a verdict allowing.

9 se offendendo: a blunder for *se defendendo,* a legal term meaning "in self-defense."

12 Argal: a blunder for Latin *ergo,* "therefore."

13 wittingly: intentionally.

14 goodman: a title used before the name of a profession or craft; **delver:** digger.

17 will he, nill he: willy-nilly, whether he wishes it or not.

23 'quest: inquest.

27 thou sayst: you speak the truth.

28 count'nance: privilege.

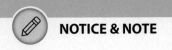
NOTICE & NOTE

30 even-Christian: fellow Christians.

32 hold up: keep up.

34 bore arms: had a coat of arms (the sign of a gentleman).

41 Go to: go on (an expression of impatience).

44 frame: structure.

48–50 Now, thou . . . to thee: Since you blasphemously say that the gallows is stronger than the church, you may be headed for the gallows.

53 unyoke: stop work for the day.

56 Mass: by the Mass.

57–58 The Gravedigger tells him to stop beating his brains to figure it out, because a beating won't make a slow donkey pick up its pace.

62–123 The Gravedigger sings a version of a popular Elizabethan song, with some added grunts (**O** and **a**), as he works.

world to drown or hang themselves more than
30 their even-Christian. Come, my spade. There is no
ancient gentlemen but gard'ners, ditchers, and
grave-makers. They hold up Adam's profession.

Other. Was he a gentleman?

Gravedigger. He was the first that ever bore arms.

35 **Other.** Why, he had none.

Gravedigger. What, art a heathen? How dost thou
understand the scripture? The scripture says Adam
digged. Could he dig without arms? I'll put another
question to thee. If thou answerest me not to the
40 purpose, confess thyself—

Other. Go to!

Gravedigger. What is he that builds stronger than
either the mason, the shipwright, or the carpenter?

Other. The gallows-maker; for that frame outlives a
45 thousand tenants.

Gravedigger. I like thy wit well, in good faith. The gallows
does well. But how does it well? It does well
to those that do ill. Now, thou dost ill to say the
gallows is built stronger than the church. Argal, the
50 gallows may do well to thee. To 't again, come.

Other. "Who builds stronger than a mason, a shipwright,
or a carpenter?"

Gravedigger. Ay, tell me that, and unyoke.

Other. Marry, now I can tell.

55 **Gravedigger.** To 't.

Other. Mass, I cannot tell.

[*Enter* Hamlet *and* Horatio *afar off.*]

Gravedigger. Cudgel thy brains no more about it, for
your dull ass will not mend his pace with beating.
And, when you are asked this question next, say "a
60 grave-maker." The houses he makes lasts till doomsday.
Go, get thee in, and fetch me a stoup of liquor.

[*The* Other Man *exits and the* Gravedigger *digs and sings.*]

In youth when I did love, did love,
  Methought it was very sweet
To contract—O—the time for—a—my behove,
65 *O, methought there—a—was nothing—a—meet.*

© Houghton Mifflin Harcourt Publishing Company

Hamlet. Has this fellow no feeling of his business? He sings in grave-making.

Horatio. Custom hath made it in him a property of easiness.

70 **Hamlet.** 'Tis e'en so. The hand of little employment hath the daintier sense.

Gravedigger [*sings*].
> *But age with his stealing steps*
> *Hath clawed me in his clutch,*
> *And hath shipped me into the land,*
75 > *As if I had never been such.*

[*He digs up a skull.*]

Hamlet. That skull had a tongue in it and could sing once. How the knave jowls it to the ground as if 'twere Cain's jawbone, that did the first murder! This might be the pate of a politician which this
80 ass now o'erreaches, one that would circumvent God, might it not?

Horatio. It might, my lord.

Hamlet. Or of a courtier, which could say "Good morrow, sweet lord! How dost thou, sweet lord?"
85 This might be my Lord Such-a-one that praised my Lord Such-a-one's horse when he went to beg it, might it not?

Horatio. Ay, my lord.

Hamlet. Why, e'en so. And now my Lady Worm's,
90 chapless and knocked about the mazard with a sexton's spade. Here's fine revolution, an we had the trick to see 't. Did these bones cost no more the breeding but to play at loggets with them? Mine ache to think on 't.

Gravedigger [*sings*].
95 > *A pickax and a spade, a spade,*
> *For and a shrouding sheet,*
> *O, a pit of clay for to be made*
> *For such a guest is meet.*

[*He digs up more skulls.*]

Hamlet. There's another. Why may not that be the
100 skull of a lawyer? Where be his quiddities now, his quillities, his cases, his tenures, and his tricks? Why does he suffer this mad knave now to knock him about the sconce with a dirty shovel and will not

68–69 Custom . . . easiness: Habit has made it easy for him.

71 hath the daintier sense: is more sensitive.

77 jowls: dashes.

79–81 The skull, which the Gravedigger gets the better of, might have been the head (**pate**) of a schemer who would have tried to get the better of God.

90 chapless: missing the lower jaw; **mazard:** head.

91 revolution: turn of Fortune's wheel; **an:** if.

92 trick: ability.

92–94 Hamlet asks whether the cost of bringing up these people was so low that one may play a game with their bones.

100 quiddities: subtle arguments, quibbles.

101 quillities: subtle distinctions; **tenures:** terms for the holding of property.

103 sconce: head.

© Houghton Mifflin Harcourt Publishing Company

104–114 Hamlet lists different legal terms related to the buying and holding of property. **Fines** were documents involved in the transfer of estates; Hamlet also uses the word to refer to the "end result" of the lawyer's legal work and his "elegant" head filled with "small particles" of dirt. He plays similarly off the meanings of other terms.

119 assurance in that: safety in legal documents.

120 sirrah: a term used to address inferiors.

125 out on 't: outside of it.

130 quick: living.

139 absolute: strict, precise.

140 by the card: accurately; **equivocation:** use of words that are vague or have more than one meaning.

142–144 The present age has grown so refined (**picked**) that hardly any distinction remains between a peasant and a courtier; the peasant walks so closely that he chafes (**galls**) the courtier's sore heel (**kibe**).

tell him of his action of battery? Hum, this fellow
105 might be in 's time a great buyer of land, with his
statutes, his recognizances, his fines, his double
vouchers, his recoveries. Is this the fine of his fines
and the recovery of his recoveries, to have his fine
pate full of fine dirt? Will his vouchers vouch him
110 no more of his purchases, and double ones too,
than the length and breadth of a pair of indentures?
The very conveyances of his lands will scarcely lie
in this box, and must th' inheritor himself have no
more, ha?

115 **Horatio.** Not a jot more, my lord.

Hamlet. Is not parchment made of sheepskins?

Horatio. Ay, my lord, and of calves' skins too.

Hamlet. They are sheep and calves which seek out
assurance in that. I will speak to this fellow.—
120 Whose grave's this, sirrah?

Gravedigger. Mine, sir.

[*Sings.*] *O, a pit of clay for to be made*
          For such a guest is meet.

Hamlet. I think it be thine indeed, for thou liest in 't.

125 **Gravedigger.** You lie out on 't, sir, and therefore 'tis not
yours. For my part, I do not lie in 't, yet it is mine.

Hamlet. Thou dost lie in 't, to be in 't and say it is
thine. 'Tis for the dead, not for the quick; therefore
thou liest.

130 **Gravedigger.** 'Tis a quick lie, sir; 'twill away again from
me to you.

Hamlet. What man dost thou dig it for?

Gravedigger. For no man, sir.

Hamlet. What woman then?

135 **Gravedigger.** For none, neither.

Hamlet. Who is to be buried in 't?

Gravedigger. One that was a woman, sir, but, rest her
soul, she's dead.

Hamlet. How absolute the knave is! We must speak
140 by the card, or equivocation will undo us. By the
Lord, Horatio, this three years I have took note of
it: the age is grown so picked that the toe of the
peasant comes so near the heel of the courtier, he

galls his kibe.—How long hast thou been grave
145 maker?

Gravedigger. Of all the days i' th' year, I came to 't that
day that our last King Hamlet overcame Fortinbras.

Hamlet. How long is that since?

Gravedigger. Cannot you tell that? Every fool can tell
150 that. It was that very day that young Hamlet was
born—he that is mad, and sent into England?

Hamlet. Ay, marry, why was he sent into England?

Gravedigger. Why, because he was mad. He shall
recover his wits there. Or if he do not, 'tis no great
155 matter there.

Hamlet. Why?

Gravedigger. 'Twill not be seen in him there. There the
men are as mad as he.

Hamlet. How came he mad?

160 **Gravedigger.** Very strangely, they say.

Hamlet. How "strangely"?

Gravedigger. Faith, e'en with losing his wits.

Hamlet. Upon what ground?

Gravedigger. Why, here in Denmark. I have been sexton
165 here, man and boy, thirty years.

Hamlet. How long will a man lie i' th' earth ere he rot?

Gravedigger. Faith, if he be not rotten before he die
(as we have many pocky corses nowadays that will
scarce hold the laying in), he will last you some eight
170 year or nine year. A tanner will last you nine year.

Hamlet. Why he more than another?

Gravedigger. Why, sir, his hide is so tanned with his
trade that he will keep out water a great while; and
your water is a sore decayer of your whoreson
175 dead body. Here's a skull now hath lien you i' th'
earth three-and-twenty years.

Hamlet. Whose was it?

Gravedigger. A whoreson mad fellow's it was. Whose
do you think it was?

180 **Hamlet.** Nay, I know not.

Gravedigger. A pestilence on him for a mad rogue! He
poured a flagon of Rhenish on my head once. This

163 ground: cause. (The Gravedigger takes it in the sense of "land.")

168 pocky: rotten, infected with syphilis.

169 scarce hold the laying in: barely hold together until they are buried.

174–175 your . . . body: Water is a terrible (**sore**) decayer of vile (**whoreson**) corpses.

175 lien you: lain.

NOTICE & NOTE

© Houghton Mifflin Harcourt Publishing Company

The Tragedy of Hamlet: Act V, Scene 1   253

same skull, sir, was, sir, Yorick's skull, the King's
jester.

185 **Hamlet.** This?

Gravedigger. E'en that.

Hamlet [*taking the skull*]. Let me see. Alas, poor Yorick!
I knew him, Horatio—a fellow of infinite jest, of
most excellent fancy. He hath bore me on his back
190 a thousand times, and now how abhorred in my

imagination it is! My gorge rises at it. Here hung
those lips that I have kissed I know not how oft.
Where be your gibes now? your gambols? your
songs? your flashes of merriment that were wont to
195 set the table on a roar? Not one now to mock your
own grinning? Quite chapfallen? Now get you to
my lady's chamber, and tell her, let her paint an
inch thick, to this favor she must come. Make her
laugh at that.—Prithee, Horatio, tell me one thing.

200 **Horatio.** What's that, my lord?

Hamlet. Dost thou think Alexander looked o' this
fashion i' th' earth?

Horatio. E'en so.

Hamlet. And smelt so? Pah!

[*He puts the skull down.*]

205 **Horatio.** E'en so, my lord.

Hamlet. To what base uses we may return, Horatio!
Why may not imagination trace the noble dust of
Alexander till he find it stopping a bunghole?

Horatio. 'Twere to consider too curiously to consider so.

210 **Hamlet.** No, faith, not a jot; but to follow him thither,
with modesty enough and likelihood to lead it, as
thus: Alexander died, Alexander was buried,
Alexander returneth to dust; the dust is earth; of
earth we make loam; and why of that loam whereto
215 he was converted might they not stop a beer barrel?
Imperious Caesar, dead and turned to clay,
Might stop a hole to keep the wind away.
O, that that earth which kept the world in awe
Should patch a wall t' expel the winter's flaw!

[*Enter* King, Queen, Laertes, Lords attendant, *and the corpse of*
Ophelia, *with a* Doctor of Divinity.]

220 But soft, but soft awhile! Here comes the King,
The Queen, the courtiers. Who is this they follow?
And with such maimèd rites? This doth betoken
The corse they follow did with desp'rate hand
Fordo its own life. 'Twas of some estate.
225 Couch we awhile and mark.

[*They step aside.*]

Laertes. What ceremony else?

Hamlet. That is Laertes, a very noble youth. Mark.

193 gibes: taunts; **gambols:** pranks.

196 chapfallen: down in the mouth, missing the lower jaw.

197–198 let her . . . come: Even if she covers her face with an inch of makeup, eventually she will have this appearance (**favor**).

201 Alexander: Alexander the Great.

208 bunghole: a hole in a keg or barrel for pouring liquid.
209 curiously: minutely, closely.

211 modesty: moderation.

214 loam: a mixture of clay, sand, and straw used for plastering.

216 Imperious: imperial.

219 flaw: gust of wind.

222 maimèd: incomplete.

224 Fordo: destroy; **some estate:** high rank.

225 Couch . . . mark: Let us conceal ourselves awhile and observe.

ANALYZE DRAMATIC PLOT
Annotate: Mark details in lines 220–225 that reflect a change in Hamlet's tone.

Predict: Hamlet does not seem to have heard about Ophelia's death. How do you predict he will react to this news?

© Houghton Mifflin Harcourt Publishing Company

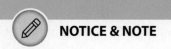
229–233 The priest says he has performed her funeral rites to the extent allowed under church law. The manner of her death was suspicious, and if the King's orders hadn't overruled the procedures, she would have remained buried in unsanctified ground until Judgment Day.

233 For: instead of.

234 Shards: pieces of broken pottery; **should be:** would have been.

235 virgin crants: wreaths placed on the coffin as a sign of virginity.

236 strewments: flowers strewn on a grave.

236–237 bringing . . . burial: being laid to rest in consecrated ground with church bells tolling.

240–241 such rest . . . souls: pray for her to have the same rest as those who died in peace.

245 howling: in hell.

252–253 thy most . . . thee of: deprived you of your excellent mind.

257 Pelion: In Greek mythology, giants placed Mount Pelion on top of Mount Ossa in an attempt to reach the top of Mount Olympus, home of the gods.

260–261 wand'ring stars: planets; **wonder-wounded:** struck with amazement.

Laertes. What ceremony else?

Doctor. Her obsequies have been as far enlarged
230 As we have warranty. Her death was doubtful,
And, but that great command o'ersways the order,
She should in ground unsanctified been lodged
Till the last trumpet. For charitable prayers
Shards, flints, and pebbles should be thrown on her.
235 Yet here she is allowed her virgin crants,
Her maiden strewments, and the bringing home
Of bell and burial.

Laertes. Must there no more be done?

Doctor.   No more be done.
We should profane the service of the dead
240 To sing a requiem and such rest to her
As to peace-parted souls.

Laertes.   Lay her i' th' earth,
And from her fair and unpolluted flesh
May violets spring! I tell thee, churlish priest,
A minist'ring angel shall my sister be
245 When thou liest howling.

Hamlet [*to* Horatio].   What, the fair Ophelia?

Queen. Sweets to the sweet, farewell!

[*She scatters flowers.*]

I hoped thou shouldst have been my Hamlet's wife;
I thought thy bride-bed to have decked, sweet maid,
250 And not have strewed thy grave.

Laertes.   O, treble woe
Fall ten times treble on that cursèd head
Whose wicked deed thy most ingenious sense
Deprived thee of!—Hold off the earth awhile,
Till I have caught her once more in mine arms.

[*Leaps in the grave.*]

255 Now pile your dust upon the quick and dead,
Till of this flat a mountain you have made
T' o'ertop old Pelion or the skyish head
Of blue Olympus.

Hamlet [*advancing*]. What is he whose grief
Bears such an emphasis, whose phrase of sorrow
260 Conjures the wand'ring stars and makes them stand
Like wonder-wounded hearers? This is I,
Hamlet the Dane.

Laertes [*coming out of the grave*].

The devil take thy soul!

Hamlet. Thou pray'st not well.

[*They grapple.*]

I prithee take thy fingers from my throat,
265 For though I am not splenitive and rash,
Yet have I in me something dangerous,
Which let thy wisdom fear. Hold off thy hand.

King. Pluck them asunder.

Queen. Hamlet! Hamlet!

270 **All.** Gentlemen!

Horatio. Good my lord, be quiet.

[Hamlet *and* Laertes *are separated.*]

Hamlet. Why, I will fight with him upon this theme
Until my eyelids will no longer wag!

Queen. O my son, what theme?

275 **Hamlet.** I loved Ophelia. Forty thousand brothers
Could not with all their quantity of love
Make up my sum. What wilt thou do for her?

King. O, he is mad, Laertes!

Queen. For love of God, forbear him.

280 **Hamlet.** 'Swounds, show me what thou't do.
Woo't weep, woo't fight, woo't fast, woo't tear thyself,
Woo't drink up eisel, eat a crocodile?
I'll do 't. Dost thou come here to whine?
To outface me with leaping in her grave?
285 Be buried quick with her, and so will I.
And if thou prate of mountains, let them throw
Millions of acres on us, till our ground,
Singeing his pate against the burning zone,
Make Ossa like a wart. Nay, an thou'lt mouth,
290 I'll rant as well as thou.

Queen.   This is mere madness;
And thus awhile the fit will work on him.
Anon, as patient as the female dove
When that her golden couplets are disclosed,
His silence will sit drooping.

Hamlet.   Hear you, sir,
295 What is the reason that you use me thus?
I loved you ever. But it is no matter.
Let Hercules himself do what he may,
The cat will mew, and dog will have his day.

265 splenitive: quick-tempered.

ANALYZE CONFLICT
Annotate: In lines 272–290, mark statements that explain the cause of Hamlet's anger.

Draw Conclusions: Is Hamlet's response consistent with his earlier treatment of Ophelia? Why or why not?

279 forbear him: leave him alone.

281 Woo't: wilt thou.
282 eisel: vinegar.

285 quick: alive.

288 Singeing his . . . zone: burning its head in the sphere of the sun's orbit.

289 Ossa: See note to line 257, **an thou'lt mouth:** if you rant.

290 mere: utter.

292–294 Soon Hamlet will fall as silent as a dove after its twin baby birds (**couplets**) are hatched.

© Houghton Mifflin Harcourt Publishing Company

[Hamlet *exits.*]

King. I pray thee, good Horatio, wait upon him.

[Horatio *exits.*]

300 [*To* Laertes.] Strengthen your patience in our last
  night's speech.
We'll put the matter to the present push.—
Good Gertrude, set some watch over your son.—
This grave shall have a living monument.
An hour of quiet shortly shall we see;
305 Till then in patience our proceeding be.

[*They exit.*]

Scene 2 *The hall of the castle.*

[*Enter* Hamlet *and* Horatio.]

Hamlet. So much for this, sir. Now shall you see the
  other.
You do remember all the circumstance?

Horatio. Remember it, my lord!

Hamlet. Sir, in my heart there was a kind of fighting
5 That would not let me sleep. Methought I lay
Worse than the mutines in the bilboes. Rashly—
And praised be rashness for it: let us know,
Our indiscretion sometime serves us well
When our deep plots do pall; and that should learn us
10 There's a divinity that shapes our ends,
Rough-hew them how we will—

Horatio.   That is most certain.

Hamlet. Up from my cabin,
My sea-gown scarfed about me, in the dark
Groped I to find out them; had my desire,
15 Fingered their packet, and in fine withdrew
To mine own room again, making so bold
(My fears forgetting manners) to unfold
Their grand commission; where I found, Horatio,
A royal knavery—an exact command,
20 Larded with many several sorts of reasons
Importing Denmark's health and England's too,
With—ho!—such bugs and goblins in my life,
That on the supervise, no leisure bated,
No, not to stay the grinding of the ax,
25 My head should be struck off.

Horatio.   Is 't possible?

299 wait upon: accompany.

301 to the present push: into immediate action.

1 see the other: hear the rest of the story.

6 mutines: mutineers; **bilboes:** shackles, chains.

8 indiscretion: hasty actions.

9 pall: falter; **learn:** teach.

10–11 There's a . . . will: A divine power guides our destinies, despite our clumsy attempts to fashion them ourselves.

13 scarfed: wrapped.

14 them: Rosencrantz and Guildenstern.

15 Fingered: stole; **in fine:** finally.

20 Larded: embellished.

21 Importing: concerning.

22 bugs . . . life: imaginary terrors in my remaining alive.

23 on the supervise: upon reading this; **no leisure bated:** without hesitation.

24 stay: wait for.

Hamlet. Here's the commission. Read it at more leisure.

[*Handing him a paper.*]

But wilt thou hear now how I did proceed?

Horatio. I beseech you.

Hamlet. Being thus benetted round with villainies,
30 Or I could make a prologue to my brains,
They had begun the play. I sat me down,
Devised a new commission, wrote it fair—
I once did hold it, as our statists do,
A baseness to write fair, and labored much
35 How to forget that learning; but, sir, now
It did me yeoman's service. Wilt thou know
Th' effect of what I wrote?

Horatio.   Ay, good my lord.

Hamlet. An earnest conjuration from the King,
As England was his faithful tributary,
40 As love between them like the palm might flourish,
As peace should still her wheaten garland wear
And stand a comma 'tween their amities,
And many suchlike ases of great charge,
That, on the view and knowing of these contents,
45 Without debatement further, more or less,
He should those bearers put to sudden death,
Not shriving time allowed.

Horatio.   How was this sealed?

Hamlet. Why, even in that was heaven ordinant.
I had my father's signet in my purse,
50 Which was the model of that Danish seal;
Folded the writ up in the form of th' other,
Subscribed it, gave 't th' impression, placed it safely,
The changeling never known. Now, the next day
Was our sea-fight; and what to this was sequent
55 Thou knowest already.

Horatio. So Guildenstern and Rosencrantz go to 't.

Hamlet. Why, man, they did make love to this employment.
They are not near my conscience. Their defeat
Does by their own insinuation grow.
60 'Tis dangerous when the baser nature comes
Between the pass and fell incensèd points
Of mighty opposites.

Horatio. Why, what a king is this!

Hamlet. Does it not, think thee, stand me now upon—

30–31 Before Hamlet had time to consider what to do, his brains started working out a plan.

33–36 Like a politician, Hamlet once considered it beneath him to write neatly (as a clerk would), but his handwriting gave him substantial service.

39 tributary: a nation controlled by another.

41 still: always; **wheaten garland:** symbol of peace and prosperity.
42 stand . . . amities: join their friendships.

43 suchlike . . . charge: similar legal phrases of great import beginning with "whereas." (Hamlet is ridiculing official language.)
47 shriving time: time for confession and absolution of sins.

48 ordinant: controlling events.

50 model: likeness.

52 Subscribed . . . impression: signed and sealed it.

53 changeling: substitution.

54 what to this was sequent: what followed.

58 defeat: destruction.

59 insinuation: worming their way in.

60–62 'Tis . . . opposites: It is dangerous for inferior people to come between the fiercely thrusting sword points of mighty antagonists.

© Houghton Mifflin Harcourt Publishing Company

66 The Danish king was elected by a small group of electors.

68 cozenage: deception.

69 quit: pay back.

70–71 come In: grow into.

74–75 Hamlet says that although he only has a short time in which to act, a man's life is also brief, lasting no longer than it takes to count to one.

78 image: likeness.

80 bravery: showiness.

88–89 Let a . . . mess: If a man owns a lot of livestock, no matter how much he resembles them, he may eat at the king's table.

89 chough: chattering bird.

93–106 Men commonly wore their hats indoors but removed them in the presence of superiors. Hamlet mocks not only this show of respect but also Osric's insistence on agreeing with everything Hamlet says.

98 indifferent: somewhat.

100 complexion: temperament.

---

65 He that hath killed my king and whored my mother,
Popped in between th' election and my hopes,
Thrown out his angle for my proper life,
And with such cozenage—is 't not perfect conscience
To quit him with this arm? And is 't not to be damned
70 To let this canker of our nature come
In further evil?

Horatio. It must be shortly known to him from England
What is the issue of the business there.

Hamlet. It will be short. The interim's mine,
75 And a man's life's no more than to say "one."
But I am very sorry, good Horatio,
That to Laertes I forgot myself,
For by the image of my cause I see
The portraiture of his. I'll court his favors.
80 But, sure, the bravery of his grief did put me
Into a tow'ring passion.

Horatio.   Peace, who comes here?

[*Enter* Osric, *a courtier.*]

Osric. Your lordship is right welcome back to Denmark.

Hamlet. I humbly thank you, sir. [*Aside to* Horatio.]
Dost know this waterfly?

85 **Horatio** [*aside to* Hamlet]. No, my good lord.

Hamlet [*aside to* Horatio]. Thy state is the more gracious,
for 'tis a vice to know him. He hath much land,
and fertile. Let a beast be lord of beasts and his
crib shall stand at the king's mess. 'Tis a chough,
90 but, as I say, spacious in the possession of dirt.

Osric. Sweet lord, if your lordship were at leisure, I
should impart a thing to you from his Majesty.

Hamlet. I will receive it, sir, with all diligence of spirit.
Put your bonnet to his right use: 'tis for the head.

95 **Osric.** I thank your lordship; it is very hot.

Hamlet. No, believe me, 'tis very cold; the wind is
northerly.

Osric. It is indifferent cold, my lord, indeed.

Hamlet. But yet methinks it is very sultry and hot for
100 my complexion.

Osric. Exceedingly, my lord; it is very sultry, as
'twere—I cannot tell how. My lord, his Majesty
bade me signify to you that he has laid a great

it himself. There are no tongues else for 's turn.

185 **Horatio.** This lapwing runs away with the shell on his head.

Hamlet. He did comply, sir, with his dug before he sucked it. Thus has he (and many more of the same breed that I know the drossy age dotes on) only
190 got the tune of the time, and, out of an habit of encounter, a kind of yeasty collection, which carries them through and through the most fanned and winnowed opinions; and do but blow them to their trial, the bubbles are out.

[*Enter a* Lord.]

195 **Lord.** My lord, his Majesty commended him to you by young Osric, who brings back to him that you attend him in the hall. He sends to know if your pleasure hold to play with Laertes, or that you will take longer time.

200 **Hamlet.** I am constant to my purposes. They follow the King's pleasure. If his fitness speaks, mine is ready now or whensoever, provided I be so able as now.

Lord. The King and Queen and all are coming down.

205 **Hamlet.** In happy time.

Lord. The Queen desires you to use some gentle entertainment to Laertes before you fall to play.

Hamlet. She well instructs me.

[Lord *exits.*]

Horatio. You will lose, my lord.

210 **Hamlet.** I do not think so. Since he went into France, I have been in continual practice. I shall win at the odds; but thou wouldst not think how ill all's here about my heart. But it is no matter.

Horatio. Nay, good my lord—

215 **Hamlet.** It is but foolery, but it is such a kind of gaingiving as would perhaps trouble a woman.

Horatio. If your mind dislike anything, obey it. I will forestall their repair hither and say you are not fit.

Hamlet. Not a whit. We defy augury. There is a special
220 providence in the fall of a sparrow. If it be now, 'tis not to come; if it be not to come, it will be now; if it be not now, yet it will come. The readiness is all.

185 lapwing: A bird that supposedly left its nest soon after hatching and ran around with its shell on its head—probably a reference to Osric's hat.

187–194 After joking that Osric paid courtesies to his mother's nipple before nursing, Hamlet complains that Osric and his type, popular in this worthless age, have only picked up a fashionable manner of speaking (**the tune of the time**) and a frothy collection of phrases that help them move through refined society (**fanned and winnowed opinions**), but the bubbles burst as soon as they are tested.

201–202 If his . . . whensoever: I am ready at his convenience.

205 In happy time: a polite phrase of welcome.

206 use some gentle entertainment: show some courtesy.

215 gaingiving: misgiving.

218 repair: coming.

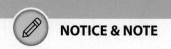

NOTICE & NOTE

219–224 Hamlet rejects **augury** (attempting to foresee the future by interpreting omens) and declares that since the death of even a sparrow is not left to chance, he is ready to accept any circumstances he encounters; his death will come sooner or later. He concludes that since man knows nothing about the life he leaves behind, what does it matter if he leaves early?

227 presence: royal assembly.

229 sore distraction: severe confusion.

230 exception: disapproval.

237 faction: party.

240 purposed evil: intentional harm.

242 That I have: as if I had.

244–250 Laertes is satisfied in regard to his own feelings (**nature**), but in regard to his honor he will wait until men experienced in such matters have given their authoritative judgment (**voice and precedent**) in favor of reconciliation, which would allow him to keep his reputation undamaged (**name ungored**).

253 frankly: without any hard feelings.

255 foil: metallic background used to display a jewel (punning on **foils,** referring to the blunted swords).

Since no man of aught he leaves knows, what is 't
to leave betimes? Let be.

[*A table prepared. Enter Trumpets, Drums, and* Officers *with cushions,*
King, Queen, Osric, *and all the state, foils, daggers, flagons of wine,*
and Laertes.]

225 **King.** Come, Hamlet, come and take this hand from me.

[He *puts* Laertes' *hand into* Hamlet's.]

Hamlet [*to* Laertes]. Give me your pardon, sir. I have
    done you wrong;
But pardon 't as you are a gentleman. This presence
    knows,
And you must needs have heard, how I am punished
With a sore distraction. What I have done
230 That might your nature, honor, and exception
Roughly awake, I here proclaim was madness.
Was 't Hamlet wronged Laertes? Never Hamlet.
If Hamlet from himself be ta'en away.
And when he's not himself does wrong Laertes,
235 Then Hamlet does it not; Hamlet denies it.
Who does it, then? His madness. If 't be so,
Hamlet is of the faction that is wronged;
His madness is poor Hamlet's enemy.
Sir, in this audience
240 Let my disclaiming from a purposed evil
Free me so far in your most generous thoughts
That I have shot my arrow o'er the house
And hurt my brother.

Laertes. I am satisfied in nature,
245 Whose motive in this case should stir me most
To my revenge; but in my terms of honor
I stand aloof and will no reconcilement
Till by some elder masters of known honor
I have a voice and precedent of peace
250 To keep my name ungored. But till that time
I do receive your offered love like love
And will not wrong it.

Hamlet.   I embrace it freely
And will this brothers' wager frankly play.—
Give us the foils. Come on.

Laertes.   Come, one for me.

255 **Hamlet.** I'll be your foil, Laertes; in mine ignorance
Your skill shall, like a star i' th' darkest night,
Stick fiery off indeed.

© Houghton Mifflin Harcourt Publishing Company

Laertes. You mock me, sir.

Hamlet. No, by this hand.

King. Give them the foils, young Osric. Cousin Hamlet,
260 You know the wager?

Hamlet. Very well, my lord.
Your Grace has laid the odds o' th' weaker side.

King. I do not fear it; I have seen you both.
But, since he is better, we have therefore odds.

Laertes. This is too heavy. Let me see another.

265 **Hamlet.** This likes me well. These foils have all a length?

Osric. Ay, my good lord.

[*Prepare to play.*]

King. Set me the stoups of wine upon that table.—
If Hamlet give the first or second hit
Or quit in answer of the third exchange,
270 Let all the battlements their ordnance fire.
The King shall drink to Hamlet's better breath,
And in the cup an union shall he throw,
Richer than that which four successive kings
In Denmark's crown have worn. Give me the cups,
275 And let the kettle to the trumpet speak,
The trumpet to the cannoneer without,
The cannons to the heavens, the heaven to earth,
"Now the King drinks to Hamlet." Come, begin.
And you, the judges, bear a wary eye.

[*Trumpets the while.*]

280 **Hamlet.** Come on, sir.

Laertes. Come, my lord.

[*They play.*]

Hamlet. One.

Laertes. No.

Hamlet. Judgment!

285 **Osric.** A hit, a very palpable hit.

Laertes. Well, again.

King. Stay, give me drink.—Hamlet, this pearl is thine.
Here's to thy health.

[*He drinks and then drops the pearl in the cup. Drum, trumpets, and shot.*]

Give him the cup.

257 **Stick fiery off:** stand out brilliantly.

260–261 Hamlet comments that Claudius has bet on (**laid the odds o'**) the weaker fencer. Claudius expresses confidence in Hamlet, but says he has arranged a handicap (**odds**) for Laertes because he has improved.

265 **likes me:** pleases me; **have all a length:** are all the same length.

269 **quit . . . exchange:** gets back at Laertes by scoring the third hit.

272 **union:** pearl.

275 **kettle:** kettledrum.

Hamlet. I'll play this bout first. Set it by awhile.
290 Come. [*They play.*] Another hit. What say you?

Laertes. A touch, a touch. I do confess 't.

King. Our son shall win.

Queen.   He's fat and scant of breath.
Here, Hamlet, take my napkin; rub thy brows.
The Queen carouses to thy fortune, Hamlet.

[*She lifts the cup.*]

295 **Hamlet.** Good madam.

King. Gertrude, do not drink.

Queen. I will, my lord; I pray you pardon me.

[*She drinks.*]

King [*aside*]. It is the poisoned cup. It is too late.

Hamlet. I dare not drink yet, madam—by and by.

300 **Queen.** Come, let me wipe thy face.

Laertes [*to* Claudius]. My lord, I'll hit him now.

King.   I do not think 't.

Laertes [*aside*]. And yet it is almost against my conscience.

Hamlet. Come, for the third, Laertes. You do but dally.
I pray you pass with your best violence.
305 I am afeard you make a wanton of me.

Laertes. Say you so? Come on. [*Play.*]

Osric. Nothing neither way.

Laertes. Have at you now!

[Laertes *wounds* Hamlet. *Then in scuffling they change rapiers, and* Hamlet *wounds* Laertes.]

King. Part them. They are incensed.

310 **Hamlet.** Nay, come again.

[*The* Queen *falls.*]

Osric. Look to the Queen there, ho!

Horatio. They bleed on both sides.—How is it, my lord?

Osric. How is 't, Laertes?

Laertes. Why as a woodcock to mine own springe,
   Osric.

[*He falls.*]

315 I am justly killed with mine own treachery.

Hamlet. How does the Queen?

---

292 **fat:** sweaty.
293 **napkin:** handkerchief.

304 **pass:** thrust.

305 **make a wanton of me:** indulge me as if I were a spoiled child.

314 Laertes says he's been caught like a **woodcock** (a proverbially stupid bird) in his own trap.

Hamlet dueling with Laertes (Terence Morgan)

King.   She swoons to see them bleed.

Queen. No, no, the drink, the drink! O, my dear
Hamlet!

The drink, the drink! I am poisoned. [*She dies.*]

Hamlet. O villainy! Ho! Let the door be locked.

[Osric *exits.*]

320 Treachery! Seek it out.

Laertes. It is here, Hamlet. Hamlet, thou art slain.
No med'cine in the world can do thee good.
In thee there is not half an hour's life.
The treacherous instrument is in thy hand,

325 unbated: not blunted;
practice: trick.

325 Unbated and envenomed. The foul practice
Hath turned itself on me. Lo, here I lie,
Never to rise again. Thy mother's poisoned.
I can no more. The King, the King's to blame.

Hamlet. The point envenomed too! Then, venom,
to thy work. [*Hurts the* King.]

330 **All.** Treason, treason!

King. O, yet defend me, friends! I am but hurt.

Hamlet. Here, thou incestuous, murd'rous, damnèd Dane,
Drink off this potion. Is thy union here?

333 union: a pun on the
meanings "pearl" and "marriage."
(Claudius is joining his wife in
death.)

[*Forcing him to drink the poison.*]
Follow my mother.

[King *dies.*]

Laertes.   He is justly served.

335 tempered: mixed.

335 It is a poison tempered by himself.
Exchange forgiveness with me, noble Hamlet.
Mine and my father's death come not upon thee,
Nor thine on me.

342 mutes: silent observers
(literally, actors without
speaking parts).

[*Dies.*]

Hamlet. Heaven make thee free of it. I follow thee.—

343 fell sergeant: cruel
arresting officer.

340 I am dead, Horatio.—Wretched queen, adieu.—
You that look pale and tremble at this chance,
That are but mutes or audience to this act,
Had I but time (as this fell sergeant, Death,
Is strict in his arrest), O, I could tell you—

ANALYZE DRAMATIC PLOT
Annotate: Mark Hamlet's
instructions to Horatio in lines
340–356.

345 But let it be.—Horatio, I am dead.
Thou livest; report me and my cause aright
To the unsatisfied.

Analyze: Why is this request so
important to Hamlet?

Horatio.   Never believe it.
I am more an antique Roman than a Dane.
Here's yet some liquor left.

[*He picks up the cup*.]

Hamlet.   As thou'rt a man,
350 Give me the cup. Let go! By heaven, I'll ha 't.
O God, Horatio, what a wounded name,
Things standing thus unknown, shall I leave behind me!
If thou didst ever hold me in thy heart,
Absent thee from felicity awhile
355 And in this harsh world draw thy breath in pain
To tell my story.

[*A march afar off and shot within*.]

                              What warlike noise is this?

[*Enter* Osric.]

Osric. Young Fortinbras, with conquest come from Poland,
To th' ambassadors of England gives
This warlike volley.

Hamlet.   O, I die, Horatio!
360 The potent poison quite o'ercrows my spirit.
I cannot live to hear the news from England.
But I do prophesy th' election lights
On Fortinbras; he has my dying voice.
So tell him, with th' occurrents, more and less,
365 Which have solicited—the rest is silence.
O, O, O, O!

[*Dies*.]

Horatio. Now cracks a noble heart. Good night, sweet
   prince,
And flights of angels sing thee to thy rest.

[*March within*.]

Why does the drum come hither?

[*Enter* Fortinbras *with the* English Ambassadors *with
Drum, Colors, and* Attendants.]

370 **Fortinbras.** Where is this sight?

Horatio. What is it you would see?
If aught of woe or wonder, cease your search.

Fortinbras. This quarry cries on havoc. O proud Death,
What feast is toward in thine eternal cell
375 That thou so many princes at a shot
   So bloodily hast struck?

348 more an antique Roman: a reference to the Roman idea that suicide can be an honorable action following a defeat or the death of a loved one.

354 Absent thee from felicity: deny yourself the pleasure of death.

357–359 Fortinbras, returning triumphant from Poland, has saluted the English ambassadors with a volley of gunfire.

360 o'ercrows: triumphs over (like the winner in a cockfight).

362–363 Hamlet predicts that Fortinbras will be elected the new Danish king and gives him his vote (**voice**).

364 occurrents: occurrences.

365 solicited: prompted, brought about. (Hamlet dies before finishing this thought.)

373 This heap of dead bodies (**quarry**) proclaims a massacre (**cries on havoc**).
374 toward: in preparation.

Ambassador.   The sight is dismal,
And our affairs from England come too late.
The ears are senseless that should give us hearing
To tell him his commandment is fulfilled,
380 That Rosencrantz and Guildenstern are dead.
Where should we have our thanks?

Horatio.   Not from his mouth,
Had it th' ability of life to thank you.
He never gave commandment for their death.
But since, so jump upon this bloody question,
385 You from the Polack wars, and you from England,
Are here arrived, give order that these bodies
High on a stage be placed to the view,
And let me speak to th' yet unknowing world
How these things came about. So shall you hear
390 Of carnal, bloody, and unnatural acts,
Of accidental judgments, casual slaughters,
Of deaths put on by cunning and forced cause,
And, in this upshot, purposes mistook
Fall'n on th' inventors' heads. All this can I
395 Truly deliver.

Fortinbras.   Let us haste to hear it
And call the noblest to the audience.
For me, with sorrow I embrace my fortune.
I have some rights of memory in this kingdom,
Which now to claim my vantage doth invite me.

400 **Horatio.** Of that I shall have also cause to speak,
And from his mouth whose voice will draw on more.
But let this same be presently performed
Even while men's minds are wild, lest more mischance
On plots and errors happen.

Fortinbras.   Let four captains
405 Bear Hamlet like a soldier to the stage,
For he was likely, had he been put on,
To have proved most royal; and for his passage,
The soldier's music and the rite of war
Speak loudly for him.
410 Take up the bodies. Such a sight as this
Becomes the field but here shows much amiss.
Go, bid the soldiers shoot.

[*They exit, marching, after the which a peal of ordnance are shot off.*]

381 his: Claudius's.

384 so jump upon this bloody question: so soon after this bloody quarrel.

387 stage: platform.

390 carnal, bloody, and unnatural acts: Claudius's murder of his brother and marriage to Gertrude.

391 accidental judgments, casual slaughters: punishments that occurred by chance.

392 put on: instigated; **forced:** contrived.

395 deliver: tell the story of.

398–399 Fortinbras says he has some unforgotten claims to Denmark, and this is a favorable time to present them.

401 from his mouth . . . more: the words of Hamlet, whose decision will influence other votes.

402 presently: immediately.

403–404 lest more . . . happen: lest other trouble occur in addition to these plots and accidents.

406 put on: enthroned, and so put to the test.

407 passage: death.

411 field: field of battle.

© Houghton Mifflin Harcourt Publishing Company

ANALYZE THE TEXT

Support your responses with evidence from the text. NOTEBOOK

1. **Analyze** Act V begins with the Gravedigger joking about his profession and Hamlet's witty comments about Yorick's skull. Why might Shakespeare have chosen to include this dark humor in the scene?

2. **Compare** At the start of Scene 2, Hamlet tells Horatio how he handled the plot to have him executed in England. How do his actions on the ship contrast with his earlier behavior? What does this change suggest about the internal conflict he has struggled with for much of the play?

3. **Evaluate** In his closing speech, Fortinbras says that Hamlet was likely to "have proved most royal." Do you agree that Hamlet would probably have made a good king? Why or why not?

4. **Analyze** Briefly analyze one of the play's soliloquies. First, summarize the ideas expressed in the soliloquy and explain how they relate to the plot. Then, discuss how Shakespeare uses literary elements such as figurative language and imagery to make the speech moving and memorable. Choose one of the following:
   • Act I, Scene 2, lines 129–159
   • Act II, Scene 2, lines 558–614
   • Act III, Scene 1, lines 57–89
   • Act IV, Scene 4, lines 34–68

5. **Critique** At the end of *Hamlet*, all of the main characters are dead, and a foreigner is poised to take over Denmark's throne. Is this a satisfying resolution to the revenge plot? Why or why not?

RESEARCH

RESEARCH TIP
Use your sources to find sources. If you have an article that is exactly what you are looking for, use that article's references page to find more relevant sources.

Hamlet pretends to be mad in the play, and Ophelia actually loses her sanity. Do some research on ideas about mental illness in the Renaissance.

QUESTION	ANSWER
What did physicians think caused madness?	
What medical treatments were used on mentally ill people?	
How were the mentally ill viewed by society?	

Extend Research how Shakespeare portrays madness in other plays. Synthesize this information with what you learned from your other sources.

CREATE AND DISCUSS

Write a Eulogy A eulogy is a speech given at a funeral. Typically, a eulogy highlights a person's most important accomplishments and characteristics across their lifespan. Write a eulogy for a character in *Hamlet*.

❏ Many characters die in *Hamlet*. Pick the character you understand the best or feel a personal connection to in some way.

❏ Take note of his or her accomplishments or characteristics. Find a central idea you can focus on in the eulogy.

❏ Use a somber and formal tone and style appropriate for an audience of mourners.

Discuss the Script *Hamlet* is the longest of Shakespeare's plays, and directors often revise the text so their productions won't run too long. In a small group, discuss cuts you would make if you were staging the play.

❏ List all the subplots, and discuss how each one contributes to and advances the action of the play. Critique and evaluate each subplot to determine whether it can be shortened or cut.

❏ Identify long speeches, such as the soliloquies and the speeches of the First Player. Discuss how they reveal conflicts and support the play's themes. Consider what would be lost if they were shortened.

❏ Discuss the comic dialogue involving the Gravedigger and Osric in Act V. Is this dialogue necessary to advance the action, or can it be trimmed or cut out completely?

Go to **Participating in Collaborative Discussions** in the **Speaking and Listening Studio** for help.

RESPOND TO THE ESSENTIAL QUESTION

 What can drive someone to seek revenge?

Gather Information Review your annotations and notes on *Hamlet*. Then, add relevant information to your Response Log. As you determine which information to include, think about:

- how an internal conflict can either spur action or lead to inaction
- how forgiveness can be an antidote to revenge

UNIT 2 RESPONSE LOG	Use this Response Log to record information from the texts that relates to or comments on the *Essential Questions* in Unit 2.
? Essential Question	**Details from Texts**
What can drive someone to seek revenge?	
How does time affect our feelings?	
What's the difference between love and passion?	
How do you defy expectations?	

R2 Student Resources

ACADEMIC VOCABULARY

As you write and discuss what you learned from the play, be sure to use the Academic Vocabulary words. Check off each of the words that you use.

❏ **ambiguous**

❏ **anticipate**

❏ **conceive**

❏ **drama**

❏ **integrity**

VOCABULARY STRATEGY:
Classical Allusion

A **classical allusion** is a reference to a historical or fictional figure, event, or creative work from the ancient world. Shakespeare uses classical allusions several times in *Hamlet*. In Act III, Scene 4, Hamlet compares his father to Hyperion and Jove:

See what a grace was seated on this brow: / Hyperion's curls, the front of Jove himself.

Hyperion is the ancient Greek god of the sun, and Jove is the Roman god of thunder. These classical allusions allow readers and audience members to understand the depth of reverence Hamlet feels for his father.

Practice and Apply Read the classical allusions from *Hamlet* in the chart below. Explain how each allusion relates to its context in the play. Do research if needed.

ALLUSION	EXPLANATION
Act I, Scene 2 . . . A little month, or ere those shoes were old / With which she follow'd my poor father's body, / Like Niobe, all tears . . .	
Act I, Scene 2 . . . My father's brother, but no more like my father / Than I to Hercules . . .	
Act I, Scene 4 My fate cries out / And makes each petty arture in this body / As hardy as the Nemean lion's nerve.	
Act II, Scene 2 What's Hecuba to him, or he to Hecuba, / That he should weep for her?	

LANGUAGE CONVENTIONS:
Paradox

A **paradox** is a statement that seems contradictory but actually reveals an element of truth. Shakespeare uses this literary device frequently in *Hamlet*. By expressing ideas paradoxically, he is able to convey subtle meanings and reinforce the audience's understanding of the duplicitous nature of many of the characters and their actions.

In Act I, Scene 2, Claudius's first speech features examples of paradox and **oxymoron** (a paradox condensed into a brief phrase):

> Have we (as 'twere with a defeated joy,
> With an auspicious and a dropping eye,
> With mirth in funeral and with dirge in marriage,
> In equal scale weighing delight and dole)
> Taken to wife.

He speaks of "defeated joy," "mirth in funeral," "dirge in marriage," and "weighing delight and dole." These paradoxical expressions tell those assembled that he views his marriage and accession to the throne as a mixed blessing, achieved at the expense of his brother's life. The use of paradox also hints at his own contradictory nature: outwardly virtuous, inwardly scheming and self-centered.

Hamlet also uses paradoxical language in the play. For example, in Act II, Scene 2, lines 309–320, he describes humankind in idealistic terms ("how noble in reason, how infinite in faculties . . . in action how like an angel, in apprehension how like a god") but ends the speech with the dismissive remark, "and yet, to me, what is this quintessence of dust? Man delights not me. . . ." This paradox emphasizes Hamlet's obsession with human corruption.

Note these other instances of paradox in the play:

- **Hamlet:** "it is a custom / More honored in the breach than the observance" (Act I, Scene 4, lines 17–18)
- **Polonius:** "Your bait of falsehood takes this carp of truth; / And thus do we of wisdom and of reach, / With windlasses and with assays of bias, / By indirections find directions out." (Act II, Scene 1, lines 63–66)
- **Hamlet:** "I must be cruel only to be kind." (Act III, Scene 4, line 184)

Practice and Apply Review the context of each example of paradox listed above. With a partner, discuss the meaning of each paradox and examine how it deepens the audience's understanding of the character or situation.

MEDIA

from HAMLET

Film Clip by **BBC Shakespeare**

© Houghton Mifflin Harcourt Publishing Company

? ESSENTIAL QUESTION:

What can drive someone to seek revenge?

QUICK START

If you were hired to direct a film adaptation of *Hamlet*, what actors would you cast in the important roles? Would you keep the play's historical setting or chose another time and place? Discuss your choices with a partner.

ANALYZE INTERPRETATIONS OF DRAMA

GENRE ELEMENTS: FILM

- sometimes interprets a literary source such as a play or novel
- uses elements such as visual images, sound, music, and lighting to convey ideas and emotions
- often reflects the director's personal vision

Shakespeare's plays present challenges and opportunities for directors who want to adapt them into films. Shakespeare sometimes included descriptions of characters or setting in the dialogue, but his texts have few stage directions. As a result, directors have a great deal of freedom to imagine a play's details. The director must make decisions that include casting, set design, and lighting.

Casting refers to the selection of actors. Actors may be chosen based on their appearance or age. For example, directors casting Hamlet would most likely choose actors of different ages for the roles of Hamlet and his mother. The choice of actors is crucial to the success of a production; the actors determine how the audience responds to the film as a whole. Directors may stay true to type or cast against type, perhaps choosing a female Hamlet or an actor whose ethnicity differs from what would be expected for a character.

Set design refers to the scenery, props, and physical location that create the setting for the film. The set design may be traditional, modern, futuristic, or primitive, or it may spring from the imagination of the director. The setting in which the action of the film takes place is important to the director's interpretation. It also affects how the audience reacts.

Lighting can have a major influence on the mood and perception of characters and action. Dim lighting conveys an air of mystery or gloominess and obscures actors' features and actions. Bright lighting cheers up the atmosphere and highlights actors' movements and expressions.

BACKGROUND

This BBC adaptation of Hamlet, *produced in 2009, was based on a highly acclaimed stage production by the Royal Shakespeare Company. The film stars David Tennant as Hamlet and Patrick Stewart as both Claudius and the Ghost. Director Gregory Doran came up with interesting ways to bring the film into the present; for example, some of the action is viewed through closed-circuit cameras used for surveillance in the castle. The clip you will view is from Act I, Scene 2 of the play.*

SETTING A PURPOSE

Pay attention to the elements that make the film version unique, and generate a list of questions as you watch. 📝 NOTEBOOK

OBSERVATIONS	QUESTIONS

To view the video, log in online and select **"from HAMLET"** from the unit menu.

As needed, pause the video to make notes about what impresses you or about ideas you might want to talk about later. Replay or rewind so that you can clarify anything you do not understand.

ANALYZE THE MEDIA

Support your responses with evidence from the film clip.

1. **Identify** Describe the setting of the BBC *Hamlet* adaptation. What time and place are indicated by the set and costumes?

2. **Interpret** What mood is evoked by the lighting of this film?

3. **Analyze** What does this adaptation emphasize about Hamlet's personality and his relationships with Gertrude and Claudius? Explain.

4. **Draw Conclusions** Why might the director have chosen to briefly show the action as if we were viewing it through a security camera?

5. **Critique** Reread lines 160–180 in Act I, Scene 2 of the play. What choices did the director make in adapting this passage to the film? How effective are these choices? Explain.

RESEARCH

RESEARCH TIP
To begin researching start by searching the subject, directors, or common setting of the film. Once you locate a possible searchable resource, evaluate the resource, avoid any review based resources or Wikipedia-like platforms to ensure it is credible. Once you find a valid resource take notes and gather only the most usable and factual information.

With a partner, research another film adaptation of *Hamlet* and compare the choices that the directors made in casting, set design, and lighting. If possible, find a clip of the film that shows Act 1, Scene 2. Use a chart such as the one below to record your comparisons.

	BBC *HAMLET* (2009)	OTHER ADAPTATIONS
Casting		
Set Design		
Lighting		

Extend View the entire 2009 BBC adaptation of *Hamlet*. Then write a review of the film. Share your review with the class.

CREATE AND PRESENT

Write a Narrative Imagine why someone might want to seek revenge. Then, write a narrative story about a case of revenge.

- ❏ Establish the story by introducing the event. Where did the story take place? Who is involved?
- ❏ Organize the plot in a logical order.
- ❏ Include dialogue and vivid images to portray the experience.
- ❏ Review your story to edit and add more details if necessary.

Produce a Movie Trailer With a partner, create a trailer for a movie that dramatizes your story.

- ❏ Create a storyboard for a trailer depicting events in your story.
- ❏ Film a video of the trailer storyboard, with voiceover narration.
- ❏ Present your trailer to the class.

Go to **Writing Narratives** in the **Writing Studio** to find out more.

 Go to **Using Media in a Presentation** in the **Speaking and Listening Studio** to find out more.

RESPOND TO THE ESSENTIAL QUESTION

 ? What can drive someone to seek revenge?

Gather Information Review your notes on the film clip as it compares to the play. Then, add relevant information to your Response Log. As you determine which information to include, think about:

- the elements of a film adaptation
- the use of literary devices such as metaphors
- the central theme of revenge established through the play and film clip
- the mental state of the character Hamlet as it pertains to the plot

ACADEMIC VOCABULARY

As you write and discuss what you learned from the film clip, be sure to use the Academic Vocabulary words. Check off each of the words that you use.

- ❏ **ambiguous**
- ❏ **anticipate**
- ❏ **conceive**
- ❏ **drama**
- ❏ **integrity**

HAMLET'S DULL REVENGE

Literary Criticism by **René Girard**

? **ESSENTIAL QUESTION:**

What can drive someone to seek revenge?

QUICK START

The essay you are about to read discusses the genre of revenge tragedy. In your notebook, summarize the plot of a film that centers on revenge. Does the main character face only external obstacles, or does he or she have conflicted feelings about the act of revenge? Share your observations in a small group.

ANALYZE ARGUMENTS

An argument is designed to persuade the reader to agree with the **claim**, or position the author is taking. In order to persuade effectively, the author must back up his or her claim with **reasons** that are supported by **evidence**. In "Hamlet's Dull Revenge," René Girard makes an argument about Shakespeare's motives for writing *Hamlet*. To assess the validity of Girard's argument, you will need to ask questions about the claim he is making, his reasons for the claim, and the evidence he uses to support those reasons. As you read, use a graphic organizer like the one below to analyze Girard's argument.

QUESTION	MY NOTES
What is Girard's claim?	
What reasons does Girard use to support his claim?	
What textual evidence does Girard use to support his reasoning?	
Are there any inconsistencies in the structure of Girard's argument?	

ANALYZE KEY IDEAS

Key ideas are the reasons, or points, that the author wants the reader to understand. In an argument, the claim the author makes is backed up with reasons supported by evidence. Typically, the author divides the argument into sections. In each section, the author provides details that support a specific line of reasoning, or key idea. In turn, each section provides support for the claim the author is making in the argument.

Girard's literary analysis contains several key ideas that he uses to support his claim. By paying attention to how Girard structures his claim and key ideas, the reader can better understand the complex argument Girard is making about Shakespeare's motives for writing *Hamlet*.

CRITICAL VOCABULARY

genre   double entendre   entail   emulation   hierarchy

To see how many Critical Vocabulary words you already know, answer the following questions.

1. Which refers to competitive imitation?
   a. hierarchy   **b.** double entendre   **c.** emulation

2. Which word refers to a category?
   a. hierarchy   **b.** genre   **c.** double entendre

3. Which refers to an expression with two meanings?
   a. double entendre   **b.** emulation   **c.** entail

4. Which refers to a ranking of status?
   a. hierarchy   **b.** emulation   **c.** genre

5. Which word is most closely associated with "involve"?
   a. genre   **b.** entail   **c.** double entendre

LANGUAGE CONVENTIONS

Coordinating Conjunctions Combining sentences can improve the clarity and flow of your writing. Complete sentences can be combined using coordinating conjunctions, such as *and, but,* and *or.* Note this example:

Hamlet is a revenge tragedy, <u>but it is also a criticism of revenge tragedies.</u>

As you read "Hamlet's Dull Revenge," note places where the author chooses to combine or not to combine sentences.

ANNOTATION MODEL   **NOTICE & NOTE**

As you read, note how the author uses a traditional argument structure of claims and evidence to organize his key ideas. You can also mark up evidence that supports your own ideas. In the model, you can see one reader's notes about "Hamlet's Dull Revenge."

Shakespeare can turn this tedious chore into the most brilliant feat of theatrical ***double entendre*** because <u>the tedium of revenge is really what he wants to talk about,</u> and he wants to talk about it in the usual Shakespearean fashion; <u>he will denounce the revenge theater and all its works</u> with the utmost daring without denying his mass audience the *katharsis* it demands, <u>without depriving himself of the dramatic success</u> which is necessary to his own career as a dramatist.

Claim: Shakespeare's motive for writing Hamlet is to criticize revenge theater.

Evidence: He writes a revenge play about the tedium of revenge plays, but includes elements of revenge plays to keep the audience's interest.

BACKGROUND

René Girard *(1923–2015) was born in France and moved to the United States in 1950. He became well known as an influential writer and theorist. Girard's primary theory was that humans are motivated by desire, and their desires are based on imitating the desires of others, a concept he called* mimesis. *His theory of mimesis has influenced other writers, been used to explain economic concepts, and even inspired the founder of a major technology company to invest in social media before it became a major industry. Girard received international recognition for his many achievements in and contributions to the fields of literature, philosophy, and anthropology.*

HAMLET'S DULL REVENGE

Literary Criticism by René Girard

SETTING A PURPOSE

As you read, pay attention to details that show how Girard views Shakespeare as a writer and Hamlet as a character.

1   *Hamlet* belongs to the **genre** of the revenge tragedy, as hackneyed and yet inescapable in Shakespeare's days as the "thriller" in ours to a television writer. In *Hamlet* Shakespeare turned this necessity for a playwright to go on writing the same old revenge tragedies into an opportunity to debate almost openly for the first time the questions I have tried to define. The weariness with revenge and *katharsis*[1] which can be read, I believe, in the margins of the earlier plays must really exist because, in *Hamlet*, it moves to the center of the stage and becomes fully articulated.

2   Some writers who were not necessarily the most unimaginative found it difficult, we are told, to postpone for the whole duration of the lengthy Elizabethan play an action which had never been in doubt in the first place and which is always

© Houghton Mifflin Harcourt Publishing Company • Image Credits: © Louis Monier/Gamma-Rapho/Getty Images; © Moviestore collection Ltd/Alamy

---

[1] **katharsis:** catharsis, the elimination of tension through the release of repressed emotions

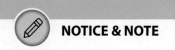

NOTICE & NOTE

double entendre
(dûb´əl än-tän´drə) *n.* an expression having a double meaning.

entail
(ên-tāl´) *v.* involve as a consequence.

ANALYZE ARGUMENTS

Annotate: Mark the specific evidence in paragraph 5 that supports the author's reasoning in paragraph 4.

Summarize: According to Girard, why might Hamlet not "believe" in the justice of his own cause?

the same anyway. Shakespeare can turn this tedious chore into the most brilliant feat of theatrical **double entendre** because the tedium of revenge is really what he wants to talk about, and he wants to talk about it in the usual Shakespearean fashion; he will denounce the revenge theater and all its works with the utmost daring without denying his mass audience the *katharsis* it demands, without depriving himself of the dramatic success which is necessary to his own career as a dramatist.

3   If we assume that Shakespeare really had this double goal in mind, we will find that some unexplained details in the play become intelligible and that the function of many obscure scenes becomes obvious.

4   In order to perform revenge with conviction, you must believe in the justice of your own cause. This is what we noted before, and the revenge seeker will not believe in his own cause unless he believes in the guilt of his intended victim. And the guilt of that intended victim **entails** in turn the innocence of that victim's victim. If the victim's victim is already a killer and if the revenge seeker reflects a little too much on the circularity of revenge, his faith in vengeance must collapse.

5   This is exactly what we have in *Hamlet*. It cannot be without a purpose that Shakespeare suggests the old Hamlet, the murdered king, was a murderer himself. In the various sources of the play there may be indications to that effect, but Shakespeare would have omitted them if he had wanted to strengthen the case for revenge. However nasty Claudius may look, he cannot look nasty enough if he appears in a context of previous revenge; he cannot generate, as a villain, the absolute passion and dedication which is demanded of Hamlet. The problem with Hamlet is that he cannot forget the context. As a result, the crime by Claudius looks to him like one more link in an already long chain, and his own revenge will look like still another link, perfectly identical to all the other links.

6   In a world where every ghost, dead or alive, can only perform the same action, revenge, or clamor for more of the same from beyond the grave, all voices are interchangeable. You can never know with certainty which ghost is addressing whom. It is one and the same thing for Hamlet to question his own identity and to question the ghost's identity, and his authority.

7   To seek singularity in revenge is a vain enterprise but to shrink from revenge, in a world which looks upon it as a "sacred duty" is to exclude oneself from society, to become a nonentity once more. There is no way out for Hamlet and he shifts endlessly from one impasse to the other, unable to make up his mind because neither choice makes sense.

8   If all characters are caught in a cycle of revenge that extends in all directions beyond the limits of its action, *Hamlet* has no beginning

© Houghton Mifflin Harcourt Publishing Company

and no end. The play collapses. The trouble with the hero is that he does not believe in his play half as much as the critics do. He understands revenge and the theater too well to assume willingly a role chosen for him by others. His sentiments are those, in other words, which we have surmised in Shakespeare himself. What the hero feels in regard to the act of revenge, the creator feels in regard to revenge as theater.

9   The public wants vicarious victims and the playwright must oblige. Tragedy is revenge. Shakespeare is tired of revenge, and yet he cannot give it up, or he gives up his audience and his identity as a playwright. Shakespeare turns a typical revenge topic, *Hamlet*, into a meditation on his predicament as a playwright. . . .

10   What Hamlet needs, in order to stir up his vengeful spirit, is a revenge theater more convincing than his own, something less half-hearted than the play Shakespeare is actually writing. Fortunately for the hero and for the spectators who are eagerly awaiting their final bloodbath, Hamlet has many opportunities to watch rousing spectacles during his play and he tries to generate even more, in a conscientious effort to put himself in the right mood for the murder of Claudius. Hamlet must receive from someone else, a mimetic[2] model, the impulse which he does not find in himself. This is what he tried to achieve with his mother, we found, and he did not succeed. He is much more successful with the actor who impersonates for him the role of Hecuba. It becomes obvious, at this point, that the only hope for Hamlet to accomplish what his society—or the spectators—require, is to become as "sincere" a showman as the actor who can shed real tears when he pretends to be the queen of Troy!

> Is it not monstrous that this player here,
> But in a fiction, in a dream of passion,
> Could force his soul so to his own conceit
> That from her working all his visage wanned,
> Tears in his eyes, distraction in's aspect,
> A broken voice, and his whole function suiting
> With forms to his conceit? And all for nothing!
> For Hecuba!
> What's Hecuba to him or he to Hecuba,
> That he should weep for her? What would he do
> Had he the motive and the cue for passion
> That I have?

Another catchy example for Hamlet comes from the army of Fortinbras on its way to Poland. The object of the war is a worthless speck of land. Thousands of people must risk their lives:

---

[2] **mimetic:** relating to imitation

© Houghton Mifflin Harcourt Publishing Company

LANGUAGE CONVENTIONS

Annotate: Underline sentences that have been combined in paragraph 9, and circle the coordinating conjunctions.

Analyze: How does the author's decision to combine these sentences affect the flow of the paragraph?

QUOTED WORDS

Notice & Note: A block quote is often used when quoting several lines of text. Circle the block quote in paragraph 10.

Evaluate: How does the block quote help support the point the author is making?

Even for an eggshell. Rightly to be great
Is not to stir without great argument,
But greatly to find quarrel in a straw
When Honor's at the stake.

11   The scene is as ridiculous as it is sinister. It would not impress Hamlet so much if the hero truly believed in the superiority and urgency of his cause. His words constantly betray him, here as in the scene with his mother. As a cue for passion, his revenge motif is no more compelling, really, than the cue of an actor on the stage. He too must *greatly . . . find quarrel in a straw*, he too must stake everything *even for an eggshell.*

12   The effect of the army scene obviously stems, at least in part, from the large number of people involved, from the almost infinite multiplication of the example which cannot fail to increase its mimetic attraction enormously. Shakespeare is too much a master of mob effects not to remember at this point the cumulative effect of mimetic models. In order to whip up enthusiasm for the war against Claudius, the same irrational contagion is needed as in the war against Poland. The type of mimetic incitement from which Hamlet "benefits" at this point resembles very much the kind of spectacle which governments never fail to organize for their citizenry when they have decided it is time to go to war: a rousing military parade.

13   But it is not the actor, ultimately, or the army of Fortinbras; it is Laertes, I believe, who determines Hamlet to act. Laertes provides the most persuasive spectacle not because he provides the "best" example but because his situation parallels that of Hamlet. Being Hamlet's peer, at least up to a point, his passionate stance constitutes the most powerful challenge imaginable. In such circumstances, even the most apathetic man's sense of **emulation** must rise to such a pitch that the sort of disaster that the fulfillment of the revenge demands can finally be achieved.

14   The simple and unreflective Laertes can shout to Claudius "give me my father" and then leap into his sister's grave in a wild demonstration of grief. Like a well-adjusted gentleman or a consummate actor, he can perform with the utmost sincerity all the actions his social milieu demands, even if they contradict each other. He can mourn the useless death of a human being at one minute and the next he can uselessly kill a dozen more if he is told that his honor is at stake. The death of his father and sister are almost less shocking to him than the lack of pomp and circumstance at their burial. At the rites of Ophelia, Laertes keeps asking the priest for "more ceremony." Laertes is a formalist[3] and he reads the tragedy of which he is a part very much like the formalists of all stripes. He does not question the

© Houghton Mifflin Harcourt Publishing Company

---

[3] **formalist:** one who strictly adheres to accepted rules and conventions

ANALYZE ARGUMENTS

Annotate: Mark the words and phrases in paragraph 13 that show how the author feels about the final piece of evidence he is about to present in support of his claim.

Analyze: Why do you think the author chose to discuss the examples of the actor playing Hecuba, Fortinbras' army, and Laertes in that particular order?

emulation
(ĕm-yə-lā´shən) *n.* competitive imitation.

ANALYZE KEY IDEAS

Annotate: Mark details in paragraph 14 that the author uses to draw comparisons between Laertes and literary critics.

Infer: How does the author seem to feel about his own analysis of *Hamlet* compared to other critics?

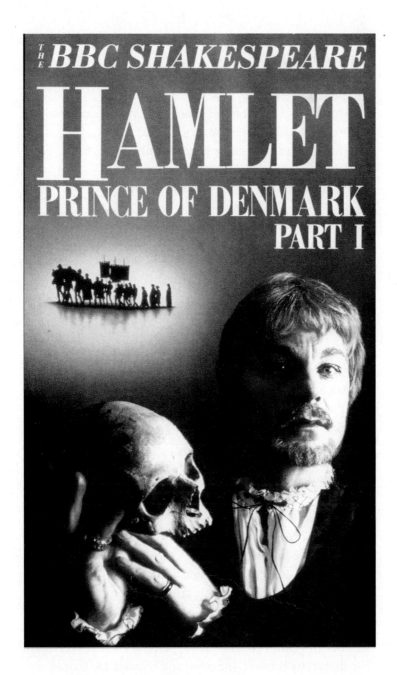

validity of revenge. He does not question the literary *genre*. He does not question the relationship between revenge and mourning. These are not valid critical questions to him; they never enter his mind, just as it never occurs to most critics that Shakespeare himself could question the validity of revenge.

15   Hamlet watches Laertes leap into Ophelia's grave and the effect on him is electrifying. The reflective mood of the conversation with Horatio gives way to a wild imitation of the rival's theatrical mourning. At this point, he has obviously decided that he, too, would act according to the demands of society, that he would become another Laertes in other words. He, too, as a result, must leap into the

ANALYZE ARGUMENTS

Annotate: Mark the details the author cites in paragraph 15 to support the idea that Hamlet's actions are inspired by Hamlet's observations of Laertes.

Analyze: How is the reasoning and evidence presented in paragraph 15 related to the author's overall claim about Shakespeare's double purpose for writing?

Hamlet's Dull Revenge   287

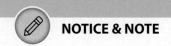

grave of one who has already died, even as he prepares other graves
for those still alive:

> 'Swounds, show me what thou'lt do.
> Woo't weep? Woo't fight? Woo't fast? Woo't tear thyself?
> Woo't drink up eisel? Eat a crocodile?
> I'll do't. Dost thou come here to whine?
> To outface me with leaping in her grave?
> Be buried quick with her, and so will I.
> ....
> I'll rant as well as thou. . . .

ANALYZE KEY IDEAS

Annotate: Mark details in
paragraphs 16 and 17 that
indicate Hamlet undergoes a
change.

Infer: According to Girard, what
is the reason Hamlet changes?

16   Shakespeare can place these incredible lines in the mouth of
Hamlet without undermining the dramatic credibility of what
follows. Following the lead of Gertrude, the spectators will ascribe the
outburst to "madness."

> This is mere madness.
> And thus awhile the fit will work on him.
> Anon, as patient as the female dove
> When that her golden couplets are disclosed,
> His silence will sit drooping.

A little later Hamlet himself, now calmly determined to kill Claudius,
will recall the recent outburst in most significant words:

> I am very sorry, good Horatio,
> That to Laertes I forgot myself,
> For by the image of my cause I see
> The portraiture of his. I'll court his favors.
> But, sure, the bravery of his grief did put me
> Into a towering passion.

hierarchy
(hī'ə-rär'kē) *n.* a ranking of
status within a group.

17   Like all victims of mimetic suggestion, Hamlet reverses the
true **hierarchy** between the other and himself. He should say: "by
the image of *his* cause I see the portraiture of *mine*." This is the
correct formula, obviously, for all the spectacles that have influenced
Hamlet. The actor's tears and the military display of Fortinbras were
already presented as mimetic models. In order to realize that Laertes,
too, functions as a model, the last two lines are essential. The cool
determination of Hamlet, at this point, is the transmutation[4] of the
"towering passion" which he had vainly tried to build up before and
which Laertes has finally communicated to him through the "bravery
of his grief." This transmutation is unwittingly predicted by Gertrude
when she compares Hamlet to the dove who becomes quiet after she

---
[4] **transmutation:** an alteration or conversion into another form

has laid her eggs. Gertrude only thinks of Hamlet's previous changes of mood, as sterile as they were sudden, but her metaphor suggests a more tangible accomplishment, the birth of something portentous:

> Anon, as patient as the female dove
> When that her golden couplets are disclosed,
> His silence will sit drooping.

CHECK YOUR UNDERSTANDING

Answer these questions before moving on to the **Analyze the Text** section.

1   According to Girard, Shakespeare's two goals in writing *Hamlet* were to criticize revenge theater and —

   A to show that revenge is pointless

   B to expose the ways people imitate each other

   C to create a new genre of theater

   D to write the kind of play that his audience wanted

2   According to Girard's analysis, which statement about the character of Hamlet is true?

   F Hamlet struggles with killing Claudius because he does not fully believe in revenge.

   G Hamlet subconsciously imitates the example of Laertes because Laertes is his older brother.

   H Hamlet's mood changes from one of passion to one of calm because he is exhausted by the speech he makes to Laertes.

   J Hamlet finds the sight of Fortinbras' army depressing because he realizes they are dedicated to a worthless cause.

3   Which quotation from the selection shows that Girard believes using mimetic models as a motivating force can be dangerous?

   A *Hamlet must receive from someone else, a mimetic model, the impulse which he does not find in himself.*

   B *Hamlet watches Laertes leap into Ophelia's grave and the effect on him is electrifying.*

   C *Like all victims of mimetic suggestion, Hamlet reverses the true hierarchy between the other and himself.*

   D *The actor's tears and the military display of Fortinbras were already presented as mimetic models.*

RESPOND

ANALYZE THE TEXT

Support your responses with evidence from the text. 📓 NOTEBOOK

1. **Draw Conclusions** What key idea does Girard begin to develop in paragraphs 4–9?

2. **Analyze** What is Girard's tone toward Shakespeare and his play? Explain how his feelings are revealed through his language.

3. **Critique** According to Girard, what is the relationship between the character of Laertes and traditional revenge theater? How well does Girard back up his interpretation of Laertes' role? Explain.

4. **Analyze** *Portend* means to predict that something is likely to occur. What is the "something portentous" that Gertrude's birth metaphor refers to in paragraph 17? In Girard's view, how might the phrase be applied to Shakespeare's play as well?

5. **Notice & Note** Review the lines spoken by Hamlet that are quoted in Girard's essay. Do these lines effectively support his perspective on Hamlet's state of mind? Explain.

RESEARCH

RESEARCH TIP
When conducting research about a scholarly work, be sure to evaluate sources for bias. As you consider the information presented, ask yourself, "Is the information obviously designed to make me agree or disagree with a certain point of view, or is it presented in an objective, or neutral, way? Is the philosophy presented as one possible explanation, or as undeniable fact?"

In his analysis of *Hamlet*, Girard makes frequent references to the idea of mimesis and theories of human motivation. With a partner, research the theories of René Girard. Use what you learn to answer these questions:

QUESTION	ANSWER
In what book did Girard first describe his theory of mimesis?	
How is Girard's concept of mimesis different from imitation?	
Why do some critics and scholars find it difficult to classify Girard's works and ideas?	

Connect In "Hamlet's Dull Revenge," Girard claims that Hamlet's desires and actions are affected by mimetic models. Now that you have learned more about Girard's theory of mimesis, consider what you know about other characters in *Hamlet*. With a partner, discuss whether the actions of any of the other characters in the play can be explained using Girard's theory.

290 Unit 2

© Houghton Mifflin Harcourt Publishing Company

CREATE AND DISCUSS

Write an Argument Write an argumentative essay that answers the following question: Does Girard succeed in presenting a valid interpretation of Shakespeare's play *Hamlet*? Review your annotations and your responses to the analysis questions before you begin.

- ❏ Write a sentence or two summarizing Girard's interpretation.
- ❏ Decide whether or not he convincingly supports this interpretation of the play in his essay.
- ❏ Give reasons for your claim and use details from the essay to provide evidence for your argument.

Discuss an Interpretation Now that you have evaluated Girard's argument, discuss your thoughts about his argument with a partner.

- ❏ Take turns summarizing the findings of your own argumentative essays.
- ❏ Compare and contrast your opinions with those of your partner. Which parts of Girard's argument do you both agree on? Which parts do you disagree on? Cite evidence to support your positions.
- ❏ Ask your partner respectful clarifying questions when you do not understand a point he or she is trying to make.

Go to **Writing Arguments** in the **Writing Studio** to help with the development of your essay.

Go to **Participating in Collaborative Discussions** in the **Speaking and Listening Studio** to find out more.

RESPOND TO THE ESSENTIAL QUESTION

? What can drive someone to seek revenge?

Gather Information Review your annotations and notes on "Hamlet's Dull Revenge." Then, add relevant information to your Response Log. As you determine which information to include, think about:

- how society shapes ideas and expectations about revenge
- when or whether revenge is justified
- how revenge contributes to cycles of violence

UNIT 2 RESPONSE LOG

? Essential Question	Details from Texts
What can drive someone to seek revenge?	
How does time affect our feelings?	
What's the difference between love and passion?	
How do you defy expectations?	

R2   Student Resources

ACADEMIC VOCABULARY

As you write and discuss what you learned from the literary criticism, be sure to use the Academic Vocabulary words. Check off each of the words that you use.

- ❏ **ambiguous**
- ❏ **anticipate**
- ❏ **conceive**
- ❏ **drama**
- ❏ **integrity**

Go to **Specialized Vocabulary** in the **Vocabulary Studio** for more.

CRITICAL VOCABULARY

Practice and Apply Work with a partner to answer the questions below. Discuss which Critical Vocabulary word is most closely associated with the italicized word in each sentence and why.

1. Which word is most closely associated with *requirement*? Why?

2. Which word goes with *drama* or *novel*? Why?

3. Which word is associated with *rivalry*? Why?

4. Which word goes with *rank*? Why?

5. Which word might be associated with *ambiguity*? Why?

VOCABULARY STRATEGY:
Domain-Specific Words and Phrases

To convey his precise meaning, Girard uses **domain-specific words**, terms that are related to the field, or domain, of literary criticism. The Critical Vocabulary words *genre* and *double entendre* are two examples of this specialized vocabulary. Many times domain-specific words are footnoted. If the words are not explained, following these steps will help you define them:

1. Look closely at the context in which the term is used for familiar phrases or words that give clues to its meaning.

2. Identify word parts—roots, prefixes, or suffixes—as well as the word's part of speech, and use them to help define the term.

3. Consult a print or digital dictionary to determine the exact meaning of the term, referring to a specialized dictionary if necessary.

Practice and Apply Work with a partner to define each of the following words that Girard uses in his essay: *tragedy, Elizabethan, vicarious, motif, metaphor*. Make sure that the definition you determine relates to literature or literary criticism. Complete the graphic organizer to show the process that you use.

WORD	STRATEGY: FOOTNOTES, CONTEXT CLUES, WORD PARTS	DICTIONARY DEFINITION
tragedy		
Elizabethan		
vicarious		
motif		
metaphor		

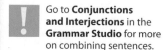

LANGUAGE CONVENTIONS:
Combining Sentences

A series of short sentences can result in a flat, terse style that fails to clearly show the relationship between ideas. One way writers can combine their sentences is by connecting two or more complete sentences with one of these coordinating conjunctions:

> Go to **Conjunctions and Interjections** in the **Grammar Studio** for more on combining sentences.

COORDINATING CONJUNCTION	SAMPLE SENTENCE
and: **builds upon or adds to an idea**	Shakespeare was tired of writing revenge tragedies, *and* his boredom with the genre is demonstrated in *Hamlet*.
but: **shows opposition or contrast**	Shakespeare could have written a play that was not a tragedy, *but* he chose instead to write what his audience wanted.
or: **identifies a choice**	Hamlet had to avenge his father's death, *or* he would risk harsh criticism from society.

In the essay "Hamlet's Dull Revenge," Girard uses coordinating conjunctions to build compound sentences that show how the ideas in each sentence relate to each other. By combining ideas, he creates a smooth, rhythmical prose.

Read this sentence from the essay:

> **Shakespeare is tired of revenge, and yet he cannot give it up, or he gives up his audience and his identity as a playwright.**

This compound sentence could have been written as a series of simple sentences:

> **Shakespeare is tired of revenge. Yet he cannot give it up. He would give up his audience and his identity as a playwright.**

Breaking the sentence into three separate statements takes away from Girard's style and meaning. The first two sentences convey the correct meaning and are grammatically correct, but they have a choppy rhythm. The meaning of the third sentence is completely lost without the conjunction "or," which indicates that Shakespeare has a choice between giving up revenge as a topic or giving up his audience and his identity.

Practice and Apply Return to the argumentative essay you wrote for the Create and Discuss activity for this selection. Find a place where you can improve the clarity of your writing by combining sentences to connect ideas, show opposition, or identify choices with a coordinating conjunction. Record your original sentences and write your new combined sentence. Remember to include a comma before the conjunction. When you have finished, share your changes with a partner.

SONNET 30
SONNET 75

Poems by **Edmund Spenser**

? *ESSENTIAL QUESTION:*

What's the difference between love and passion?

QUICK START

In the two sonnets you will be reading, Spenser deals with both love and passion. What is the difference between love and passion? How would you define each one? What are examples of each? Use the chart to record your initial thoughts. Discuss with your classmates.

LOVE	PASSION

ANALYZE SONNETS

What makes a poem a sonnet? A **sonnet** has fourteen lines and usually follows one of two forms. The Petrarchan, or Italian, sonnet (named after poet Francesco Petrarch) is divided into two parts of eight and six lines. The Shakespearean, or Elizabethan, sonnet consists of three quatrains (four-line units) plus one rhyming couplet at the end. Although the rhyming pattern is the same in each quatrain, the ending rhymes in a Shakespearean sonnet are unique within each grouping—ABAB CDCD EFEF GG. Spenser uses a variation of this rhyme scheme by interlocking the patterns between quatrains—ABAB BCBC CDCD EE.

Sonnets are also written in a particular meter, or rhythm, called **iambic pentameter. Iambic** is a repeating pattern of one unstressed syllable followed by a stressed syllable. **Pentameter** means that the pattern occurs five times in each line. The syllables are marked in the following example:

Mў lóve ĭs líke tŏ íce, ănd Í tŏ fíre;

Most sonnets include a turn (sometimes called the "volta"), or a shift in thought. Since the first two quatrains often present questions or a problem, the poet might turn his thoughts to answering the question or to contradicting an idea previously stated. This turn usually occurs in the third quatrain or the couplet. The turn can resolve the poem or can be followed by a resolution.

As you read each sonnet, notice and mark each quatrain. Indicate the rhyme scheme by placing a letter at the end of each line. Notice the interlocking pattern connecting one quatrain to the next. Find the turn and the resolution in each sonnet. Use the graphic organizer to record your observations.

	TURN	RESOLUTION
Sonnet 30		
Sonnet 75		

GENRE ELEMENTS: SONNET

- consists of 14 lines
- groups the main ideas into three quatrains (four-line units) and one couplet (two rhymed lines) at the end
- written in iambic pentameter
- focuses on one sentiment or emotion
- includes a "turn," or shift in the poet's thoughts, somewhere after the second quatrain
- often includes a revelation or resolution in the couplet

GET READY

SUMMARIZE POETRY

You can often clarify the meaning of a poem by rephrasing it using simpler language. You might **paraphrase** a difficult passage by restating it in your own words. It is important to maintain the passage's meaning and logical order when you paraphrase. Another option would be to **summarize** the entire poem, restating only the key ideas or themes. A summary is much shorter than the original text because it leaves out most details. As you read each sonnet, use a chart like this to help you summarize the idea in each part of the poem.

"Sonnet 75"	
Part of Poem	**Key Idea**
1st Quatrain	Whenever I write my beloved's name in the sand, the waves wash it away.
2nd Quatrain	
3rd Quatrain	
Couplet	

ANNOTATION MODEL

NOTICE & NOTE

As you read, notice how Spenser uses images to express ideas. Paraphrase or summarize the key idea in each quatrain or couplet. This model shows one reader's notes about the first quatrain of "Sonnet 30."

My love is like to (ice,) and I to (fire;)
How comes it then that this her cold so great
Is not dissolved through my so (hot desire,)
But harder grows the more I her entreat?

Why doesn't my flaming desire melt my beloved's coldness?
She only grows icier the more I plead with her.

296   Unit 2

BACKGROUND

Edmund Spenser *(1552?–1599) was a highly innovative poet who rose from humble origins to become one of the most admired Elizabethan writers. He invented a sonnet form based on an intricate pattern of rhymes, called the Spenserian sonnet, and a special stanza form called the Spenserian stanza. Both influenced later poets. Spenser's greatest work is* The Faerie Queene, *an allegorical epic that uses stories of adventurous knights to convey a message about how to lead a virtuous life.*

SONNET 30

SONNET 75

Poems by Edmund Spenser

Spenser was born in London. He attended Cambridge University as a "sizar," or poor scholar. Several years after his graduation, he published his first major work, The Shepheardes Calender. *In 1580, Spenser moved to Ireland to serve as secretary to the lord deputy of Ireland. He became a wealthy landowner in Ireland and wrote most of his remaining works there. Spenser's courtship of his second wife in 1594 inspired him to write a sonnet sequence (a series of related sonnets) called* Amoretti, *which means "little love poems." The sequence includes "Sonnet 30" and "Sonnet 75."*

In 1598, Spenser fled his estate when it was attacked by Irish rebels. He managed to reach London, but he died shortly afterward. In recognition of his literary achievements, he was buried near Geoffrey Chaucer in what is now called the Poets' Corner of Westminster Abbey.

SETTING A PURPOSE

As you read, notice how Spencer uses vivid imagery and figurative language to convey ideas about passion and love in his poems.

Notice & Note

Use the side margins to notice and note signposts in the text.

Sonnet 30

My love is like to ice, and I to fire;
How comes it then that this her cold so great
Is not dissolved through my so hot desire,
But harder grows the more I her entreat?
5 Or how comes it that my exceeding heat
Is not delayed by her heart-frozen cold:
But that I burn much more in boiling sweat,
And feel my flames augmented manifold?
What more miraculous thing may be told
10 That fire which all things melts, should harden ice:
And ice which is congealed with senseless cold,
Should kindle fire by wonderful device.
Such is the pow'r of love in gentle mind,
That it can alter all the course of kind.

8 augmented manifold: greatly increased

11 congealed: solidified.

14 kind: nature.

ANALYZE SONNETS
Annotate: Circle the rhyming pair in the first and third lines. Underline the rhyming pair in the second and fourth lines.

Identify: What conflict does Spencer set up in the first quatrain? What contrasting elements are used to represent each side of the conflict?

CHECK YOUR UNDERSTANDING

Answer these questions about "Sonnet 30" before moving on to the next selection.

1 The speaker wonders why the more he pleads with his beloved —

   A the closer she draws near to him

   B the colder she becomes

   C the more her ice melts

   D the further she runs from him

2 The speaker asks why his beloved's coldness does not —

   F cool his desire

   G dissolve their relationship

   H delay their marriage

   J fade away

3 The speaker concludes that —

   A their love is dying

   B his beloved is preparing to leave him

   C he should give up on his beloved

   D love has supernatural powers

Sonnet 75

One day I wrote her name upon the strand,
But came the waves and washéd it away:
Again I wrote it with a second hand,
But came the tide, and made my pains his prey.
5 "Vain man," said she, "that dost in vain assay,
A mortal thing so to immortalize.
For I myself shall like to this decay,
And eke my name be wipéd out likewise."
"Not so," quod I, "let baser things devise
10 To die in dust, but you shall live by fame:
My verse your virtues rare shall eternize,
And in the heavens write your glorious name,
Where whenas death shall all the world subdue,
Our love shall live, and later life renew."

1 strand: beach.

5 assay: try.

SUMMARIZE POETRY

Annotate: Mark the lines in which the poet's beloved compares herself to the writing in the sand.

Summarize: Write a paraphrase of her comparison.

8 eke: also

9 quod: said.

ANALYZE SONNETS

Annotate: Mark the phrase that expresses the turn.

Interpret: What does the poet state he can do for his beloved?

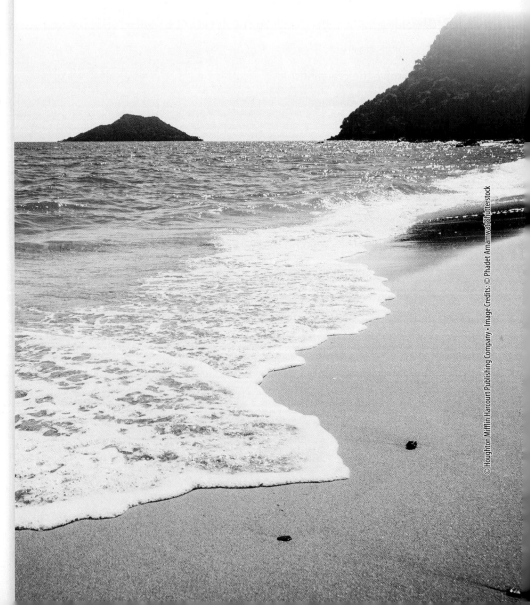

CHECK YOUR UNDERSTANDING

Answer these questions before moving on to the **Analyze the Text** section on the following page.

1 What is the setting of this sonnet?

   A The speaker's beach house

   B On board a ship

   C Along the beach

   D In heaven

2 What does the speaker's beloved say about his efforts to write her name in the sand?

   F She asks him to keep trying so that she can see her name written in the sand.

   G She says it is pointless because, just as she will die someday, her name will be wiped out and forgotten.

   H She scolds him for doing such a ridiculous thing.

   J She praises his efforts for immortalizing her name.

3 Why does the speaker say that his beloved's name, as well as their love, will last forever?

   A Because he has written about them in his poetry

   B Because they have become famous

   C Because songs about her virtues will be sung throughout eternity

   D Because the heavens will declare her glorious name

ANALYZE THE TEXT

Support your responses with evidence from the text. 📓 NOTEBOOK

1. **Summarize** In both sonnets, the first two quatrains introduce a conflict or problem. Summarize the conflict or problem in each poem.

2. **Analyze** How does Spenser's use of an interlocking rhyming pattern in "Sonnet 30" help to connect his ideas across quatrains?

3. **Analyze** Identify the turn in "Sonnet 30." How does this turn resolve the speaker's confusion about the effects of love?

4. **Identify Patterns** In "Sonnet 75," what image is repeated in the first quatrain? How does this underscore the speaker's resolution about the power of poetry?

5. **Compare** Which poem, "Sonnet 30" or "Sonnet 75," seems to focus more on passion? on love? Explain, using details from the poems.

RESEARCH

RESEARCH TIP

Before you begin researching answers to these questions, make a list of key words to use in your search. Rank the search terms on your list from more specific to less specific. If at first you're having difficulty finding answers, broaden your search to include the less-specific key words.

Spenser was one of the greatest poets of the English Renaissance. With a partner, research his literary career. Use what you learn to answer these questions.

QUESTION	ANSWER
Who is represented by the title character of Spenser's epic *The Faerie Queene*?	
Which event inspired Spenser's poem "Epithalamion"?	
What name did Spenser use for a character who represents him in several of his poems?	

Extend "Sonnet 30" and "Sonnet 75" belong to a series of related sonnets called *Amoretti*, which means "little love poems." Read several other sonnets in this series and discuss them with a partner.

CREATE AND PRESENT

Write a Sonnet Write a sonnet that expresses your idea of love or that contrasts your ideas of love and passion. Before you begin, review your notes from the Quick Start activity and reflect on what you have learned from Spenser's sonnets. You may choose to work with a partner.

❏ Decide on the theme. What do you want to say about love or passion?

❏ Start with a question, conflict, or problem that will lead to a resolution.

❏ Decide how your first two quatrains will present your question, problem, or conflict.

❏ Determine a "turn" for the third quatrain of your sonnet and a resolution for the closing couplet. How will you show a new perspective or shift in thought? How will the third quatrain lead into the couplet?

❏ Decide if you will follow the Shakespearean or the Spenserian rhyme scheme. Maintain iambic pentameter and your chosen rhyme scheme.

Present the Sonnets As a class, present the sonnets you have created, using presentational software to project background visuals and transitions.

❏ In teams, plan the design and content of the presentation. Include an introductory screen and select a corresponding image for each sonnet.

❏ Practice reading your sonnets. Work on making eye contact and using your voice to express the appropriate level of emotion. As you practice with others, offer feedback to enhance the presentation.

❏ Pick a date, time, and meeting place for your formal readings. Invite other students to watch the presentation.

 Go to **Writing as a Process** in the **Writing Studio** to help with planning and drafting the sonnet.

 Go to **Using Media in a Presentation** in the **Speaking and Listening Studio** to find out more.

RESPOND TO THE ESSENTIAL QUESTION

 ? What's the difference between love and passion?

Gather Information Review your annotations and notes on "Sonnet 30" and "Sonnet 75." Then, add relevant information to your Response Log. As you determine which information to include, think about:

• the distinctions made between love and passion in Spenser's sonnets
• the relationship between true love and desire
• appropriate expressions of love and passion

ACADEMIC VOCABULARY
As you write and discuss what you learned from the sonnets, be sure to use the Academic Vocabulary words. Check off each of the words that you use.

❏ ambiguous
❏ anticipate
❏ conceive
❏ drama
❏ integrity

© Houghton Mifflin Harcourt Publishing Company

A VALEDICTION: FORBIDDING MOURNING

Poem by **John Donne**

? *ESSENTIAL QUESTION:*

What's the difference between love and passion?

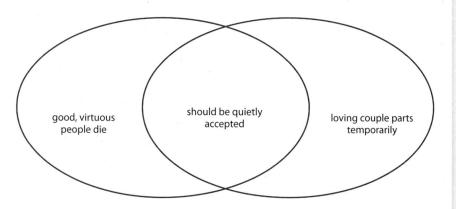
QUICK START

Saying goodbye to someone can be difficult, even if the parting is only temporary. Write a paragraph about a time when you had to be separated from someone you cared about. Use a chart like this one to help you plan your paragraph.

Cause of the separation	
How I felt at the time	
How I feel thinking back on it	

ANALYZE METAPHYSICAL CONCEITS

John Donne was a central figure in a literary group known as the metaphysical poets. In contrast to the ornate, exuberant style of earlier Renaissance poets, they used a more conversational style to explore subjects such as religious devotion, death, physical love, and relationships. Many metaphysical poems are in the form of an argument, giving the poet an opportunity to show off his wit and intellectual subtlety.

The metaphysical poets were admired and sometimes criticized for making unexpected comparisons. A **metaphysical conceit** is an elaborate metaphor or simile in which the comparison is unusually striking and original. It shows likeness in two things that at first seem to have no connection whatsoever. The example below is taken from lines 1–8 of "A Valediction: Forbidding Mourning," where the death of virtuous people is compared to a couple saying goodbye temporarily. The center shows how these two disparate things are made to seem alike in the poem.

GENRE ELEMENTS: LYRIC POETRY

- expresses strong feelings or thoughts
- has a musical quality
- deals with intense emotions surrounding events such as death, love, or loss
- include forms such as ode, elegy, sonnet

good, virtuous people die | should be quietly accepted | loving couple parts temporarily

As you read the poem, look for other examples of metaphysical conceits.

INTERPRET IDEAS IN POETRY

John Donne is known for his highly creative expression of ideas. In many of his poems, the speaker presents an ingenious argument in verse. This complexity of thought makes his poetry rewarding but also sometimes difficult to interpret. To better understand the meaning of "A Valediction: Forbidding Mourning," examine Donne's use of the following literary techniques to express ideas:

Paradox: a statement that seems contradictory or absurd but actually reveals some element of truth

Figurative Language: language that communicates ideas beyond the literal meaning of words, often through comparisons of two unlike things, as in similes and metaphors

Irony: a contrast between expectation and reality

ANNOTATION MODEL

NOTICE & NOTE

As you read, note the author's use of metaphysical conceits as well as other techniques that require interpretation. This model shows how one reader responded to lines 1–8 of "A Valediction: Forbidding Mourning."

As <u>virtuous men pass mildly away,</u>
    And whisper to their souls to go,
Whilst some of their sad friends do say
    The breath goes now, and some say, No;

<u>So let us melt, and make no noise,</u>
    No tear-floods, nor sigh-tempests move,
'Twere <u>profanation</u> of our joys
    To tell the <u>laity</u> our love.

A virtuous person dying quietly is likened to "us" melting, making no noise.

Donne's word choices suggest a comparison between love and religion.

BACKGROUND

John Donne *(1572–1631) was born in London, England. He had planned for a career in government, but his secret marriage to his patron's niece in 1601 got him into trouble. Eventually he became an Anglican priest whose eloquent sermons drew large crowds to St. Paul's Cathedral. "A Valediction: Forbidding Mourning" was written for his wife, Anne, who was upset about his approaching trip to France. (A valediction is a speech or poem that bids farewell.) Anne's death when she was just 33 inspired many of Donne's later spiritual poems.*

A VALEDICTION: FORBIDDING MOURNING

Poem by John Donne

SETTING A PURPOSE

As you read, notice the subtle and often surprising ideas the speaker expresses in the argument he makes to his wife.

> As virtuous men pass mildly away,
>   And whisper to their souls to go,
> Whilst some of their sad friends do say
>   The breath goes now, and some say, No;
>
> 5 So let us melt, and make no noise,
>   No tear-floods, nor sigh-tempests move,
> 'Twere profanation of our joys
>   To tell the laity our love.
>
> Moving of th' earth brings harms and fears,
> 10   Men reckon what it did and meant;
> But trepidation of the spheres,
>   Though greater far, is innocent.

Notice & Note

Use the side margins to notice and note signposts in the text.

5 melt: part; dissolve our togetherness.

7 profanation (prŏf-ə-nā´shən)**:** an act of contempt for what is sacred.

8 laity (lā´ĭ-tē)**:** persons who do not understand the "religion" of love.

9 moving of th' earth: an earthquake.

11 trepidation of the spheres: apparently irregular movements of heavenly bodies.

12 innocent: harmless.

13 sublunary (sŭb-loo'nə-rē) **lovers' love:** the love of earthly lovers, which, like all things beneath the moon, is subject to change and death.

14 soul . . . sense: essence is sensuality.

16 elemented: composed.

19 Inter-assuréd of the mind: confident of each other's love.

22 endure not yet: do not, nevertheless, suffer.

24 like . . . beat: Unlike less valuable metals, gold does not break when beaten thin.

26 twin compasses: the two legs of a compass used for drawing circles.

ANALYZE METAPHYSICAL CONCEITS

Annotate: Mark phrases in lines 25–36 that describe the motion of the two legs of a compass.

Analyze: What does this conceit suggest about the relationship between the speaker and his wife?

32 as that comes home: when the moving foot returns to the center as the compass is closed.

34 obliquely (ō-blēk'lē)**:** not in a straight line.

35 firmness: constancy; **just:** perfect.

Dull sublunary lovers' love
    (Whose soul is sense) cannot admit
15 Absence, because it doth remove
    Those things which elemented it.

But we by a love so much refined
    That our selves know not what it is,
Inter-assuréd of the mind,
20   Care less, eyes, lips, and hands to miss.

Our two souls therefore, which are one,
    Though I must go, endure not yet
A breach, but an expansion,
    Like gold to airy thinness beat.

25 If they be two, they are two so
    As stiff twin compasses are two;
Thy soul, the fixed foot, makes no show
    To move, but doth, if th' other do.

And though it in the center sit,
30   Yet when the other far doth roam,
It leans and hearkens after it,
    And grows erect, as that comes home.

Such wilt thou be to me, who must
    Like th' other foot, obliquely run;
35 Thy firmness makes my circle just,
    And makes me end where I begun.

CHECK YOUR UNDERSTANDING

Answer these questions before moving on to the **Analyze the Text** section on the following page.

1 The speaker in the poem is —

   A terminally ill

   B going on a journey

   C abandoning his family

   D begging his wife to return

2 Which words best describe the speaker's tone?

   F Cold and belittling

   G Sad and regretful

   H Happy and excited

   J Calm and consoling

3 What is an important idea in the poem?

   A Couples need their own personal space.

   B Husbands and wives should not separate.

   C True love is not endangered by physical separation.

   D Women should not travel alone.

ANALYZE THE TEXT

Support your responses with evidence from the text. NOTEBOOK

1. **Analyze** What is ironic about the speaker's comparison in lines 1–8 of the poem?

2. **Analyze** Reread lines 9–20. Explain how Donne compares earthquakes and planetary motion with different kinds of love. What idea does this metaphysical conceit express?

3. **Interpret** Reread lines 21–24. What paradox does Donne express in this stanza? How does the simile comparing their souls to gold help explain the paradox?

4. **Analyze** What hyperbole, or exaggeration for emphasis, does Donne include in lines 5–8? How does this hyperbole affect the speaker's tone?

5. **Connect** John Donne was a very spiritual man who made sacrifices to marry his wife. How is this reflected in his view of his marriage?

RESEARCH

John Donne wrote about subjects such as love and death with great originality and sophistication. With a partner, research other works written by Donne and answer the following questions.

QUESTION	ANSWER
What phrase contained in a John Donne sermon became the title of a novel by Ernest Hemingway?	
Which swashbuckling acquaintance of Donne's was knighted by Queen Elizabeth I and eventually executed in the Tower of London?	
By what other name is John Donne's famous poem "Holy Sonnet 10" known?	

Extend Many professional readings of Donne's poems have been recorded. Listen to a variety of his poems read aloud. Appreciate the rhythm and rhymes of poems such as "The Canonization" and "Holy Sonnet 10." With a partner, discuss the tone and the mood of each poem, and how hearing the poem read aloud affected you.

CREATE AND PRESENT

Write an Essay Write a reflective essay that is inspired by the Donne poem. In the light of your own experience, examine the poet's viewpoints on such ideas as love, family relationships, or coping with separation or loss.

❏ To develop your reflective essay, think about any expectations you may have for significant relationships in the future. As you reflect on your life, include any insights you might have gained from reading "A Valediction: Forbidding Mourning."

❏ Reread the poem more than once as a way to enhance your interpretation. Think about any life lessons it may offer.

❏ Choose a line from the poem that is striking or memorable to you. Consider making the line the theme of your essay.

Present the Essay As a class, read your essays aloud. Use the following suggestions to help prepare.

❏ Practice reading your essay aloud, using an engaging tone to draw listeners into your reflections. Speak at a pace that will hold the interest of your audience.

❏ As you read, make eye contact with your audience and use facial expressions and gestures to help reinforce the essay's points.

Go to **Writing Narratives** in the **Writing Studio** to help develop your essay.

 Go to **Giving a Presentation: Delivering Your Presentation** in the **Speaking and Listening Studio** for help.

RESPOND TO THE ESSENTIAL QUESTION

? What's the difference between love and passion?

Gather Information Review your annotations and notes on "A Valediction: Forbidding Mourning." Then, add relevant information to your Response Log. As you determine which information to include, think about:

• the sacrifices one might make for love
• how well passion can withstand trials, such as separation
• personal characteristics that are needed to make love long-lasting

ACADEMIC VOCABULARY
As you write and discuss what you learned from the poem, be sure to use the Academic Vocabulary words. Check off each of the words that you use.

❏ **ambiguous**
❏ **anticipate**
❏ **conceive**
❏ **drama**
❏ **integrity**

POEM

TO HIS COY MISTRESS

by **Andrew Marvell**

pages 315–317

COMPARE THEMES

As you read each poem, think about the theme, or the central message, and how the author uses figurative language and imagery to convey this theme. Then, think about how the themes of the two poems relate to each other. After you read both poems, you will collaborate on a small group project.

? **ESSENTIAL QUESTION:**

How does time affect our feelings?

POEM

TWENTY-ONE LOVE POEMS (POEM III)

by **Adrienne Rich**

pages 318–319

QUICK START

Sometimes it is better to have patience and take your time with something, while at other times it is better to take advantage of an opportunity while you have it. With a partner, discuss a situation in which it is best to be patient and one in which it is best to act right away. How do the situations differ?

INTERPRET FIGURATIVE LANGUAGE

Figurative language is language that communicates ideas beyond the literal meaning of words. Poets often rely on types of figurative language, including metaphors, similes, personification, and hyperbole, to express ideas in an imaginative yet concrete way. A poet's use of figurative language can transform descriptions, making them more surprising and memorable.

This chart shows examples of figurative language from one of the poems you are about to read.

FIGURATIVE LANGUAGE	EXAMPLE
A **simile** compares two dissimilar things using the word *like* or *as*.	Now therefore, while the youthful hue <u>Sits on thy skin like morning dew</u> —"To His Coy Mistress," lines 33–34
A **metaphor** compares two things directly, without using *like* or *as*.	But at my back I always hear <u>Time's winged chariot</u> hurrying near —"To His Coy Mistress," lines 21–22
Hyperbole is any expression that greatly exaggerates facts or ideas for humorous effect or for emphasis.	<u>An hundred years</u> should go to praise Thine eyes, and on thy forehead gaze —"To His Coy Mistress," lines 13–14

To interpret each poem's use of figurative language, read the poem to grasp its overall meaning. Then, read a second time, focusing your attention on the figurative language:

- Note what is being compared or exaggerated in each instance.
- Consider the effect the poet may be trying to achieve.
- Think about what the comparison reveals, and note your conclusions about the comparison's possible meaning.

GENRE ELEMENTS: LYRIC POETRY

- expresses strong feelings or thoughts
- has a musical quality
- deals with intense emotions surrounding events like death, love, or loss
- includes forms such as ode, elegy, and sonnet

ANALYZE SPEAKER

A poem's **speaker,** like the narrator of a story, is the voice that talks to the reader. The choice of speaker can have a great effect on how a lyric poem develops. Some speakers just offer observations and insights. Other speakers are more like fictional characters who are directly involved in the experience portrayed in the poem. A speaker may express the poet's own thoughts and feelings, but you should not assume that the speaker is the same as the poet, even if he or she uses the pronouns *I* and *me*.

Both poems in this lesson have a speaker who addresses a loved one. As you read each poem, pay attention to the speaker's tone, or attitude, toward this person as well as toward love itself. Notice the word choices and imagery that convey the speaker's tone. You can use a chart like this one to record observations about the speaker.

What do we learn about the speaker?	
What is the speaker's tone?	
What words and images convey this tone?	

ANNOTATION MODEL

NOTICE & NOTE

As you read, mark examples of figurative language. Note each speaker's tone, marking word choices and other elements that help convey the tone. In the model, you can see how one reader annotated the first few lines of "To His Coy Mistress."

> Had we but world enough, and time,
> This (coyness) lady, were no crime.
> We would sit down, and think which way
> To walk, and pass our long love's day.
> Thou by the Indian Ganges' side
> Shouldst rubies find; I by the tide
> Of Humber would complain.

Although he addresses his "mistress," the speaker's tone is pretty formal. "Coyness" suggests he is gently teasing her.

These references to places they would walk to are examples of hyperbole.

BACKGROUND

Andrew Marvell *(1621–1678) was known during his lifetime for his political activities rather than for his poetry. He managed to maintain ties with political figures on both sides of the English Civil War. From 1659 until his death, he served in Parliament. His poetry wasn't published while he was alive, but he did circulate it among friends. "To His Coy Mistress" exemplifies Marvell's graceful use of language and his intellectual depth and wit. The poem develops the ancient theme of carpe diem (Latin for "seize the day"), a call for people to live for the moment. It was only in the 20th century that Marvell gained recognition as a major poet.*

TO HIS COY MISTRESS
Poem by Andrew Marvell

PREPARE TO COMPARE

As you read, note the kind of language used to reveal the character of the speaker, as well as the language used by the speaker to express his emotions and desires. Think about the impression he is trying to make.

     Had we but world enough, and time,
This coyness, lady, were no crime.
We would sit down, and think which way
To walk, and pass our long love's day.
5 Thou by the Indian Ganges' side
Shouldst rubies find; I by the tide
Of Humber would complain. I would
Love you ten years before the flood,
And you should, if you please, refuse
10 Till the conversion of the Jews.
My vegetable love should grow
Vaster than empires and more slow;

© Houghton Mifflin Harcourt Publishing Company • Image Credits: © Peter Horree/Alamy; © Print Collector/Hulton Fine Art Collection/Getty Images

Notice & Note

Use the side margins to notice and note signposts in the text.

5 Ganges (găn´jēz): a great river of northern India.

7 Humber: a river of northern England, flowing through Marvell's hometown; **complain:** sing melancholy love songs.

8 flood: the biblical Flood.

10 till . . . Jews: In Marvell's day, Christians believed that all Jews would convert to Christianity just before the Last Judgment and the end of the world.

3 vegetable love: a love that grows like a plant (an oak tree, for example)—slowly but with the power to become very large.

An hundred years should go to praise
Thine eyes, and on thy forehead gaze;
15 Two hundred to adore each breast,
But thirty thousand to the rest;
An age at least to every part,
And the last age should show your heart.
For, lady, you deserve this state,
20 Nor would I love at lower rate.
      But at my back I always hear
Time's wingèd chariot hurrying near;
And yonder all before us lie
Deserts of vast eternity.
25 Thy beauty shall no more be found,
Nor, in thy marble vault, shall sound
My echoing song; then worms shall try
That long-preserved virginity,
And your quaint honor turn to dust,
30 And into ashes all my lust:
The grave's a fine and private place,
But none, I think, do there embrace.
      Now therefore, while the youthful hue
Sits on thy skin like morning dew,
35 And while thy willing soul transpires
At every pore with instant fires,
Now let us sport us while we may,
And now, like amorous birds of prey,
Rather at once our time devour
40 Than languish in his slow-chapped power.
Let us roll all our strength and all
Our sweetness up into one ball,
And tear our pleasures with rough strife
Thorough the iron gates of life:
45 Thus, though we cannot make our sun
Stand still, yet we will make him run.

19 state: dignity.

INTERPRET FIGURATIVE LANGUAGE

Annotate: Mark the similes in lines 33–40.

Analyze: What comparison is created by each simile? What does each comparison reveal or help express?

35 transpires: breathes.

40 slow-chapped: slow-jawed.

44 thorough: through.

CHECK YOUR UNDERSTANDING

Answer these questions about "To His Coy Mistress" before moving on to the next selection.

1 Which sentence best summarizes the speaker's message in lines 1–20?

    A She is so beautiful that it will take him a very long time to properly love every part of her.

    B If they had all the time in the world, he would be happy for them to take their time in love.

    C He hopes that they will spend a lot of time together and do a lot of traveling.

    D He's in no rush about their relationship because the world is so big and they have so much time.

2 What do the lines *And yonder all before us lie / Deserts of vast eternity* mean?

    F Time stretches on forever.

    G We have to travel across the desert to see each other.

    H If we wait too long, our feelings for each other will dry up.

    J We're both going to be dead one day.

3 Read these lines of the poem: *And while thy willing soul transpires / At every pore with instant fires.* What emotion do these lines evoke?

    A The excitement of youthful love

    B Sorrow for the fate of the soul

    C The discomfort of a high fever

    D Anger at time for going by so fast

BACKGROUND

Adrienne Rich *(1929–2012) was a widely admired poet and one of the leading feminist writers in the United States. She started writing poetry at a young age. In 1951, the same year she graduated from Radcliffe College, she published her first book of poems. She went on to publish over 20 more volumes. Rich's poetry, which combines personal and political content, reflects her passionate interest in social activism and women's rights. She won numerous literary awards for her work.*

TWENTY-ONE LOVE POEMS (POEM III)

Poem by Adrienne Rich

© Houghton Mifflin Harcourt Publishing Company • Image Credits: © Bettmann/Getty Images; © kertu_ee/Getty Images

PREPARE TO COMPARE

Now that you have read "To His Coy Mistress," read this poem and notice how the speaker phrases her sense of urgency and her description of her own experience of love. Later, you will compare the two poems.

Since we're not young, weeks have to do time
for years of missing each other. Yet only this odd warp
in time tells me we're not young.
Did I ever walk the morning streets at twenty,
5 my limbs streaming with a purer joy?
did I lean from any window over the city
listening for the future
as I listen here with nerves tuned for your ring?
And you, you move toward me with the same tempo.
10 Your eyes are everlasting, the green spark
of the blue-eyed grass of early summer,
the green-blue wild cress washed by the spring.
At twenty, yes: we thought we'd live forever.
At forty-five, I want to know even our limits.
15 I touch you knowing we weren't born tomorrow,
and somehow, each of us will help the other live,
and somewhere, each of us must help the other die.

Notice & Note

Use the side margins to notice and note signposts in the text.

ANALYZE SPEAKER

Annotate: Mark references to age and time in lines 1–5.

Infer: What can you infer from these lines about the speaker's relationship with her lover?

CHECK YOUR UNDERSTANDING

Answer these questions before moving on to the **Analyze the Texts** section on the following page.

1 Which of these statements is true?

  A The speaker thinks that her lover is too young for her.

  B The speaker feels the same now as she did when she was young.

  C The speaker's emotions are more intense now than they were when she was young.

  D The speaker regrets that she is too old to love as intensely as she would have when she was young.

2 Which line from "Twenty-One Love Poems (Poem III)" tells us the most about her lover's feelings toward the speaker?

  F *Did I ever walk the morning streets at twenty,*

  G *Your eyes are everlasting, the green spark*

  H *At twenty, yes: we thought we'd live forever.*

  J *And you, you move toward me with the same tempo.*

3 What does the speaker mean when she says, *At forty-five, I want to know even our limits?*

  A They should stay together long enough to face death together.

  B There is always a limit to love, no matter how old you are.

  C Being in love means they can get away with anything.

  D Love is eternal, so there's no reason to worry about death.

ANALYZE THE TEXTS

Support your responses with evidence from the texts. NOTEBOOK

1. **Summarize** In "To His Coy Mistress," the speaker develops his argument in three sections: lines 1–20, 21–32, and 33–46. Summarize the main idea in each section of the poem.

2. **Analyze** In the first stanza of "To His Coy Mistress," how does the speaker use hyperbole to support his argument?

3. **Draw Conclusions** Marvell titled his poem "To His Coy Mistress" instead of "To My Coy Mistress," putting distance between himself and the speaker. Do you think he intended readers to take the speaker's passion seriously? Explain why or why not.

4. **Interpret** In "Twenty-One Love Poems (Poem III)," how does the speaker's use of figurative language reveal her affection for her beloved?

5. **Analyze** What is the overall tone of "Twenty-One Love Poems (Poem III)"? How does the poem's final line contribute to the tone?

RESEARCH

RESEARCH TIP

If you find a source that has a lot of text and you don't have time to read all of it, use the search function [ctrl + f for PC; cmd + f for Apple] to skip to keywords that you are looking for.

At the time that Andrew Marvell wrote "To His Coy Mistress," there were two significant schools of poetry in England: Cavalier and Metaphysical. These two schools, although distinct, shared certain characteristics. Do some research to compare and contrast these two schools of poetry.

SCHOOLS	DIFFERENCES	SIMILARITIES
Cavalier		
Metaphysical		

Extend While Andrew Marvell is usually considered a metaphysical poet, his poetry also has qualities of Cavalier poetry. In what ways might "To His Coy Mistress" be considered Cavalier poetry and in what ways might it be considered Metaphysical poetry?

CREATE AND DISCUSS

Write a Letter Imagine that the speaker of "To His Coy Mistress" finds his old poem to his mistress in a coat pocket 25 years after he had written it. Imagine that he has decided to write her a letter reflecting on the poem. Write that letter.

- ❏ Write in the first person, as if you were the speaker.
- ❏ Consider the perspective of the speaker of "Twenty-One Love Poems (Poem III)."
- ❏ Predict how the speaker's attitude toward love may have changed.
- ❏ Cite specific ideas, images, or lines from his poem.

Discuss the Letter In a group, share the letter you wrote and read or listen to other students' writing. Then, compare letters and critique the tone of each. Evaluate how well your letters portray the speaker's feelings, and provide feedback on qualities you think are most realistic.

 Go to **Writing as a Process** in the **Writing Studio** to find out more.

Go to **Participating in Collaborative Discussions** in the **Speaking and Listening Studio** to find out more.

RESPOND TO THE ESSENTIAL QUESTION

? How does time affect our feelings?

Gather Information Review your annotations and notes on "To His Coy Mistress" and "Twenty-One Love Poems (Poem III)." Then, add relevant details to your Response Log. As you determine which information to include, think about:

- how each author describes the passage of time
- the way that getting older affects the experience of love
- the speakers' emotional responses to time

[Response Log image]

UNIT 2
RESPONSE LOG

Use this Response Log to record information from the texts that relates to or comments on the **Essential Questions** in Unit 2.

| ? Essential Question | Details from Texts |

What can drive someone to seek revenge?

How does time affect our feelings?

What's the difference between love and passion?

How do you defy expectations?

R2 Student Resources

ACADEMIC VOCABULARY

As you write and discuss what you learned from the two lyric poems, be sure to use the Academic Vocabulary words. Check off each of the words that you use.

- ❏ **ambiguous**
- ❏ **anticipate**
- ❏ **conceive**
- ❏ **drama**
- ❏ **integrity**

Collaborate & Compare

COMPARE THEMES

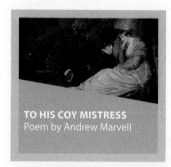

TO HIS COY MISTRESS
Poem by Andrew Marvell

**TWENTY-ONE LOVE POEMS
(POEM III)**
Poem by Adrienne Rich

The poems "To His Coy Mistress" and "Twenty-One Love Poems (Poem III)" express the ancient literary theme of *carpe diem*, Latin for "seize the day." This was one of the most popular themes of Cavalier poetry. *Carpe diem* is often taken to mean that one should enjoy life as much as possible for the present moment. Compare how the poems develop this theme. What reasons do they give for the necessity of enjoying the present moment?

REASONS WE MUST "SEIZE THE DAY"
"To His Coy Mistress"
"Twenty-One Love Poems (Poem III)"

ANALYZE THE TEXTS

Discuss these questions in your group.

1. **Compare** How does the speaker of each poem feel about the passage of time? How are the speakers' feelings similar? How do they differ?

2. **Evaluate** Which speaker is more reasonable in his or her urgency about the relationship? Why do you think this is the case?

3. **Analyze** How does each speaker respond to the inevitability of death?

4. **Synthesize** According to these two texts, how does being in love affect our perception of age and the passing of time?

COLLABORATE AND PRESENT

Now your group can continue exploring the ideas in these texts by discussing the pros and cons of *carpe diem* and living for the moment. Work together to gain an understanding of the arguments pro and con, and then come to an agreement about your position as a group. Follow these steps:

1. **Get some ideas on paper.** Have everyone in the group take some time to think and jot down their answers to the questions, "Is it really best to live for the day? Why or why not?"

2. **Share ideas.** Have everyone in the group explain their thoughts, both pro and con, about living for the moment, and record these thoughts in a chart like the one below.

Go to **Participating in Collaborative Discussions** in the **Speaking and Listening Studio** for more.

LIVING FOR THE MOMENT	
Pros	Cons

3. **Discuss and debate.** Identify the points on which you agree. Then, identify points on which you disagree, and resolve disagreements by presenting and evaluating the evidence. Decide which conclusion (pro or con) is best supported by the evidence.

4. **Present to the class.** Now, present your ideas to the class. Explain why you believe it is or is not better to live for the moment. Remember to provide evidence or examples to support your position.

SPEECH

from
SPEECH BEFORE THE SPANISH ARMADA INVASION

by **Queen Elizabeth I**
pages 327–329

COMPARE ACROSS GENRES

As you read, consider the historical context, time period, and purpose of each text. Next, consider similarities and differences in how each audience is addressed. Finally, make note of the topics and ideas shared by both texts. After you have finished reading, you will collaborate on a small group project.

? ***ESSENTIAL QUESTION:***

How do you defy expectations?

ARTICLE

FOR ARMY INFANTRY'S FIRST WOMEN, HEAVY PACKS AND THE WEIGHT OF HISTORY

by **Dave Philipps**
pages 337–343

© Houghton Mifflin Harcourt Publishing Company • Image Credits: © World History Archive/Alamy; © Scott Olson/Getty Images

---

from Speech Before the Spanish Armada Invasion

QUICK START

Trust is an important factor in motivating people. Think about a time in your life when you tried to motivate someone to take an action you desired. What strategies did you use? Were your efforts successful? Why or why not?

ANALYZE RHETORICAL DEVICES

Elizabeth I was a brilliant speaker who captivated audiences through her command of **rhetorical devices**—techniques that communicate ideas and strengthen arguments. The following devices are often found in persuasive writing:

- **Repetition**—the repeated use of a word or phrase
- **Parallelism**—the use of similar grammatical constructions to express ideas that are related or equal in importance
- **Antithesis**—the use of similar grammatical constructions to express sharply contrasting ideas
- **Rhetorical question**—a question to which no answer is expected
- **Analogy**—a comparison made between two dissimilar things to explain an unfamiliar subject in terms of a familiar one

As you read the speech, pay attention to Elizabeth's use of rhetorical devices.

CONNECT TO HISTORY

Some writing becomes clearer and more meaningful when you make historical connections. A literary work's **historical context** includes the events and social conditions that inspired or influenced its creation. The cultural beliefs and values of a particular period are also part of the historical context.

The background note preceding Queen Elizabeth's speech discusses the event that inspired her address to English soldiers. As you read the text, you should also consider that women's lives in 16th-century England were severely restricted. Most women received a very limited education, suitable for running a household. Women had to be subservient to their fathers and husbands. Elizabeth I was a remarkable exception: Her father, Henry VIII, provided her with an excellent education, and after the deaths of her father, brother, and older sister, she inherited the throne. Because she never married, Elizabeth remained free to make her own decisions.

As you read the speech, pay attention to details that relate to the Spanish Armada invasion. Also notice how in crafting her speech, Elizabeth took into account her audience's views about women and the English monarchy. Consult outside sources such as an encyclopedia if you would like additional information about the historical context of the speech.

GENRE ELEMENTS: SPEECH
- addresses a specific audience
- often explicitly states the speaker's purpose
- uses rhetorical devices and persuasive techniques
- may include a call to action

© Houghton Mifflin Harcourt Publishing Company

CRITICAL VOCABULARY

treachery   feeble   scorn   realm   valor

Replace the boldfaced word in each of the following sentences with a Critical Vocabulary word from the list.

1. **Dishonesty** isn't a concern among the queen's loyal people. _____

2. The queen is a **weak** woman but leads like a fearless king. _____

3. The people's **heroism** gives the queen confidence that her subjects can and will defeat their enemies. _____

4. Outsiders are attempting to invade, but Queen Elizabeth I is willing to fight in order to protect her **kingdom.** _____

5. The act of invading the queen's land is viewed with **disdain.** _____

LANGUAGE CONVENTIONS

Formal Language Writing in emails, texts, and letters to friends often uses informal language. On the other hand, textbooks, reports, and speeches are usually written using formal language. **Formal language** includes sophisticated vocabulary and complex sentence structures. It also follows all writing, grammar, and mechanical rules; it doesn't include slang or contractions. It is less personal and more professional. Queen Elizabeth's speech uses formal language to address her subjects before they went into battle against a formidable enemy. Although the sentiments expressed in the speech are personal and bring her closer to her audience, the language is formal, which fits the situation and her education and rank as queen.

ANNOTATION MODEL

NOTICE & NOTE

As you read, note the queen's tone and the rhetorical devices she uses to appeal to her audience. In the model, you can see one reader's notes about the beginning of the speech.

We have been (persuaded) by some that are careful of our safety, to take heed how we commit our selves to armed multitudes, for fear of treachery; but <u>I assure you</u> I do not desire to live to distrust my faithful and loving people. Let tyrants fear, I have always so behaved myself that, under God, <u>I have placed my chiefest strength and safeguard in the loyal hearts and good-will of my subjects;</u>

She uses "we" to refer to herself. "Persuaded" here means that they tried to persuade her, not that she agreed.

Elizabeth uses a calm, confident tone in addressing her soldiers. This must have reassured them in a time of emergency.

BACKGROUND

Queen Elizabeth I *(1533–1603) enjoyed great popularity, but her life was often in danger. Before becoming queen, she found herself imprisoned by her sister, Mary I, who suspected her of treason. After she took the throne, Elizabeth became the target of assassination plots by Catholics opposed to her Protestant rule. One of the most dangerous events came in 1588, when a fleet of Spanish ships known as the Armada set sail to invade England. Elizabeth delivered the following speech near Tilbury Fort, where her troops were preparing to defend against the invasion. Unknown to her, the Armada had already been defeated at sea.*

SPEECH BEFORE THE SPANISH ARMADA INVASION
Speech by Queen Elizabeth I

PREPARE TO COMPARE

As you read, note the ways Queen Elizabeth I reveals her commitment to her subjects and kingdom. Consider closely the words she chooses to express her loyalty and dedication, as well as her suggestions about women. This analysis will help you compare this speech with the article "For Army Infantry's First Women, Heavy Packs and the Weight of History."

My Loving People,

We have been persuaded by some that are careful of our safety, to take heed how we commit our selves to armed multitudes, for fear of **treachery**; but I assure you I do not desire to live to
5 distrust my faithful and loving people. Let tyrants fear, I have always so behaved myself that, under God, I have placed my chiefest strength and safeguard in the loyal hearts and good-will of my subjects; and therefore I am come amongst you, as you see, at this time, not for my recreation and disport,[1] but
10 being resolved, in the midst and heat of the battle, to live or die amongst you all; to lay down for my God, and for my kingdom,

---
[1] **disport:** entertainment.

© Houghton Mifflin Harcourt Publishing Company • Image Credits: © World History Archive/Alamy

Notice & Note

Use the side margins to notice and note signposts in the text.

treachery
(trĕch´ə-rē) *n.* an act of betrayal.

CONNECT TO HISTORY
Annotate: In lines 1-7, mark Elizabeth's reason for ignoring warnings about her safety.

Connect: Why were some people worried about her giving this speech?

feeble
(fē´bəl) *adj.* lacking strength.

scorn
(skôrn) *n.* contempt or disdain.

realm
(rĕlm) *n.* kingdom.

ANALYZE RHETORICAL DEVICES

Annotate: Mark instances of repetition and parallelism in lines 16–26.

Analyze: What ideas are emphasized by the queen's use of these devices?

valor
(văl´ər) *n.* courage, bravery.

and my people, my honor and my blood, even in the dust. I know I have the body but of a weak and **feeble** woman; but I have the heart and stomach of a king, and of a king of England too, and think foul
15 **scorn** that Parma or Spain, or any prince of Europe,[2] should dare to invade the borders of my **realm**; to which rather than any dishonor shall grow by me, I myself will take up arms, I myself will be your general, judge, and rewarder of every one of your virtues in the field. I know already, for your forwardness you have deserved rewards and
20 crowns; and We do assure you in the word of a prince, they shall be duly paid you. In the mean time, my lieutenant general shall be in my stead,[3] than whom never prince commanded a more noble or worthy subject; not doubting but by your obedience to my general, by your
25 concord[4] in the camp, and your **valor** in the field, we shall shortly have a famous victory over those enemies of my God, of my kingdom, and of my people.

---

[2] **Parma or Spain . . . Europe:** the duke of Parma, the king of Spain, or any other monarch of Europe. Alessandro Farnese, duke of the Italian city of Parma, was a skillful military leader whom Philip II, king of Spain, often relied upon. Philip's plan was to send the Spanish fleet to join the army under Parma's command in the Netherlands and invade England.

[3] **my lieutenant general . . . stead:** Elizabeth refers to Robert Dudley, the Earl of Leicester. He was a courtier who, for a time, was Elizabeth's favorite.

[4] **concord** (kŏn´kôrd): friendly and peaceful relations; harmony; agreement.

CHECK YOUR UNDERSTANDING

Answer these questions before moving on to the **Analyze the Text** section on the following page.

1 How does Queen Elizabeth I address her subjects?

 A Angrily

 B Fearfully

 C Aggressively

 D Passionately

2 The people of England need _____ from their leader.

 F food

 G security

 H clean water

 J warm clothes

3 What is Queen Elizabeth I willing to do in order to defend her kingdom?

 A Give up her position as queen

 B Die for her people

 C Learn from other European monarchs

 D Move to another country

ANALYZE THE TEXT

Support your responses with evidence from the text. ☰ NOTEBOOK

1. **Interpret** What difference does Queen Elizabeth point out between herself and a tyrant in lines 2–8? How does she use this contrast to appeal to her audience's sense of patriotism?

2. **Analyze** What rhetorical device does Elizabeth use to describe herself in lines 12–14? How does this device help her address doubts the soldiers may have had about her ability to lead them?

3. **Connect** In lines 16–18, Elizabeth says that to avoid dishonor, she would take up arms and lead the soldiers into battle. Traditionally, women were not allowed to have professions in this time period, including military roles. Why might she have made this declaration?

4. **Cite Evidence** Which details in lines 19–23 reveal that in addition to being inspirational, Elizabeth was a practical leader?

5. **Evaluate** Given the historical circumstances, do you consider this to be an effective speech? Explain why or why not.

RESEARCH

RESEARCH TIP
Start your Internet research with a few keywords like "Elizabeth I," "Spanish Armada," or even "Spanish Armada loss." As you conduct your research, rely on websites that end in .edu, .org, and .gov. These websites are more likely to have been reviewed for accuracy. Be sure to note website URLs and sources during your research.

The defeat of the Spanish Armada was one of the most important events of the English Renaissance. With a partner, do research on what led up to the attempted invasion and why it failed. Use what you learn to answer these questions.

QUESTION	ANSWER
Why did Spain's king want to invade England?	
What was the plan for the invasion?	
How was the Armada defeated?	

Extend Find another speech by Elizabeth I. With a partner, compare it with her Armada speech, analyzing the ideas she expresses and her use of rhetorical devices.

CREATE AND PRESENT

Write a Speech Write a speech about an issue that is important to you. Your speech should be crafted to appeal to a specific audience—for example, an assembly at your school or a community meeting. Use a variety of rhetorical devices such as repetition and rhetorical questions to help make your speech compelling and persuasive.

Go to **Writing Arguments** in the **Writing Studio** to find out more.

- ❏ Review your Quick Start activity notes.
- ❏ Choose an issue that you are passionate about.
- ❏ Identify and address an audience that faces the same issue.
- ❏ Commit to your purpose and revisit it throughout your speech.

Present a Speech The queen used her words to gain her people's trust and establish herself as a capable leader. Imagine her facial expressions, gestures, and tone as she delivered her speech. Then, use some of those same strategies for delivery in your own presentation.

Go to **Giving a Presentation** in the **Speaking and Listening Studio** to find out more.

- ❏ Practice reading aloud quietly; then try a more assertive tone.
- ❏ Share your speech with a small group. Revise your word choices and approach based on their feedback.
- ❏ Then, present your speech. Pause now and then to give your audience time to think, make eye contact with each member of the audience, and include natural gestures.

RESPOND TO THE ESSENTIAL QUESTION

? How do you defy expectations?

Gather Information Review your notes on "Speech Before the Spanish Armada Invasion." Then, add relevant details to your Response Log. As you decide which information to include, think about:

- how rhetorical devices may be used to motivate people to action
- how connections to historical context help explain and clarify texts
- the relationship between women and power in history

ACADEMIC VOCABULARY

As you write and discuss what you learned from the speech, be sure to use the Academic Vocabulary words. Check off each of the words that you use.

- ❏ **ambiguous**
- ❏ **anticipate**
- ❏ **conceive**
- ❏ **drama**
- ❏ **integrity**

© Houghton Mifflin Harcourt Publishing Company

WORD BANK

treachery
feeble
scorn
realm
valor

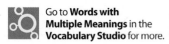

Go to **Words with Multiple Meanings** in the **Vocabulary Studio** for more.

CRITICAL VOCABULARY

Practice and Apply Answer each question by using one of the Critical Vocabulary words in a complete sentence.

1. How might someone describe you if you cannot lift a lightweight object?

2. Which word would be used to describe someone's dishonesty?

3. Which word could you use to describe a kingdom?

4. If you were brave enough to save an entire country what word would be used to describe you?

5. What word would be used to describe a person's feelings towards something contemptible?

VOCABULARY STRATEGY:
Multiple-Meaning Words

Many words have more than one meaning. To make sense of what you read, you need to make sure that you understand which meaning a writer intended. This is particularly true with words used as more than one part of speech or words appearing in older texts. For example, the noun *stomach* usually refers to a digestive organ or to the abdomen, but Elizabeth uses it to mean "courage" or "pride."

As you read texts from earlier periods, be alert to the nuances of meaning in words. If you encounter an unfamiliar word or a familiar word used in a way you find confusing, examine the **context**—the surrounding words, phrases, and sentences—for clues to the writer's meaning.

Practice and Apply Read each word. Then select the correct meaning of the word as it is used in "Speech Before the Spanish Armada Invasion."

1. tyrant _____
   a. an extremely oppressive, harsh, arbitrary person
   b. an absolute ruler who governs without restrictions, especially one who seized power illegally

2. subject _____
   a. prone or disposed
   b. one who is under the rule of another or others

3. general _____
   a. highest or superior in rank
   b. prevalent

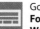

LANGUAGE CONVENTIONS:
Formal Language

Different writing situations call for different levels of formality. For personal communication such as emails and texts, most people tend to use casual or informal language. **Formal language** is often used in academic and professional work; it is also used during formal occasions such as speeches. Queen Elizabeth I uses formal language in her speech marking the occasion when her armed forces went to war with the Spanish Armada. In her speech, the queen uses language that is appropriate for the seriousness of the occasion and the sophistication of her audience. Here is an example from the speech:

> **I know already, for your forwardness you have deserved rewards and crowns; and We do assure you in the word of a prince, they shall be duly paid you.**

Notice that the passage contains key elements of formal language, including complex vocabulary and sentence structure. Note that it does not use slang or contractions.

Practice and Apply   Rewrite the following sentences using formal language. An example sentence has been done for you.

Informal: The battle went back and forth for hours before the guys upstairs decided that we'd just kick back and rest a bit.
Formal: The battle raged on for several hours before the military personnel in charge determined that the soldiers who had been on the frontlines could be relieved for a short rest.

Informal: A battlefield is a really rough place, and I don't think it's any place I want to stick around.

Formal:

Informal: During a battle, people are all over the place with their swords and horses, and everything's just a big, huge mess.

Formal:

© Houghton Mifflin Harcourt Publishing Company

Go to **Writing Arguments: Formal Style** in the **Writing Studio** for more help.

ARTICLE

FOR ARMY INFANTRY'S FIRST WOMEN, HEAVY PACKS AND THE WEIGHT OF HISTORY

by **Dave Philipps**

pages 337–342

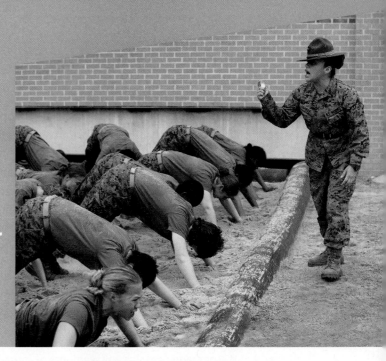

COMPARE ACROSS GENRES

As you read, think about why expectations for women in our culture might make some people question whether they should take combat roles in the military. What motivates some women to overcome these expectations, and what challenges are they willing to face as they do so? After you read this article and the speech, you will collaborate on a small group project.

? **ESSENTIAL QUESTION:**

How do you defy expectations?

SPEECH

from SPEECH BEFORE THE SPANISH ARMADA INVASION

by **Queen Elizabeth I**

pages 327–328

For Army Infantry's First Women, Heavy Packs and the Weight of History

QUICK START

Sometimes we choose to do difficult things—or even things that will make us miserable—because we perceive that they will serve some greater purpose. With a partner or in a small group, think of a time you have challenged yourself by doing something difficult. Why did you do it? Was it worth it?

ANALYZE TEXT FEATURES

Some texts, especially articles in periodicals, include text features that help readers understand the text's organizational structure and readily identify its main ideas. These **text features** include titles, subtitles, subheadings, pull quotes, boldface type, and bulleted and numbered lists.

Before you read, preview the article's text features to make predictions about the text's organization and ideas. Then, as you read, confirm or adjust your predictions. You can use a chart such as the one below to record predictions.

GENRE ELEMENTS: ARTICLE

- provides information about a topic
- uses evidence, including facts and quotations, to support ideas
- may rely on text features to clarify organizational structure

TEXT FEATURES	
TYPE OF FEATURE	PREDICTION
Title	
Subtitle	
Subheadings	

SUMMARIZE AND PARAPHRASE TEXTS

A summary can help clarify how ideas in a text fit together. When you **summarize,** you briefly restate the main ideas and most important details in a text. A summary should follow the order of the original text and be accurate and objective. If you come across passages that are confusing or difficult, you can **paraphrase** the passage, restating ideas and information in your own words. A paraphrase is usually the same length as the original text but contains simpler language.

As you read the article, note ideas and details to include in a summary, and look out for difficult passages that you can simplify by paraphrasing.

CRITICAL VOCABULARY

infantry	smart	esprit de corps	rotation	chow
scrounge	chafe			

Write the Critical Vocabulary word next to its meaning:

1. Food: _____

2. Search: _____

3. Regular variation in a sequence: _____

4. A feeling or spirit shared by a group: _____

5. Soldiers trained to fight on foot: _____

6. To annoy or irritate: _____

7. Feel pain or distress: _____

LANGUAGE CONVENTIONS

Hyphens and dashes look similar but have very different uses. **Hyphens** (-) are used in hyphenated compounds, including some compound modifiers, which are created when two words work together to modify a noun (for example, first-year cadet). An **em dash** (—) is punctuation that can be used instead of a comma, semicolon, or parentheses. An **en dash** (–) has many uses, often to signify the word *to* or *between* in ranges of numbers.

ANNOTATION MODEL

NOTICE & NOTE

As you read, note main ideas and important details, and look for text features that support your understanding.

FORT BENNING, GA. – The first group of women graduated from United States Army infantry training last week, but with soldiers obscured by body armor, camouflage face paint and smoke grenades, it was almost impossible to distinguish the mixed-gender squads in the steamy woods from those of earlier generations.

This feature shows where the article was reported.

The opening detail about it being hard to tell women apart from men may support one of the writer's main ideas.

BACKGROUND

Dave Philipps *(1977–) is a journalist who has written about veterans and the military community for* The New York Times. *He has focused on the unintended consequences of wars in Iraq and Afghanistan, including the presence of women in combat zones. In these wars, women found themselves engaging in combat, although they did not hold official combat positions. They held dangerous frontline roles and often engaged in fierce firefights, even leading battles. Because official combat positions are crucial to career advancement, women felt they were being unfairly held back. Under the Obama administration, these positions were gradually opened to women.*

FOR ARMY INFANTRY'S FIRST WOMEN, HEAVY PACKS AND THE WEIGHT OF HISTORY

Article by Dave Philipps

PREPARE TO COMPARE

As you read, look for details about attitudes toward women serving in combat and how women have overcome them. This analysis will help you compare the article with "Speech Before the Spanish Armada Invasion."

The Army has sought to play down the significance of the mixed-gender milestone. But female grunts see it as monumental and revolutionary.

1   FORT BENNING, Ga. — The first group of women graduated from United States Army **infantry** training in May of 2017 but with soldiers obscured by body armor, camouflage face paint and smoke grenades, it was almost impossible to distinguish the mixed-gender squads in the steamy woods from those of earlier generations.

2   That's just how the Army wants it.

3   After the Obama administration ordered the military in 2013 to open all combat positions to women, the Army developed gender-neutral performance standards to ensure that recruits entering the infantry were all treated the same. Still **smarting** over accusations that it had lowered standards to help the first

Notice & Note

Use the side margins to notice and note signposts in the text.

infantry
(ĭn′fən-trē) *n.* the branch of an army made up of units trained to fight on foot.

smart
(smärt) *v.* to suffer acutely, as from mental distress, wounded feelings, or remorse.

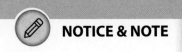
women graduate from its elite Ranger School in 2015, the Army has taken pains to avoid making any exceptions for infantry boot camp. To the pound, men and women lug the same rucksacks, throw the same grenades and shoulder the same machine guns.

4   The Army has also sought to play down the significance of the new female infantrymen — as they are still known — not mentioning, when families gathered . . . for their graduation, that the 18 women who made it through would be the first in more than two centuries for the American infantry.[1]

5   "It's business as usual," the battalion commander overseeing the first class, Lt. Col. Sam Edwards, said as he watched a squad of soldiers run past — including one with French braids and a grenade launcher. "I've tried to not change a thing."

6   Female grunts[2] in the battalion see things differently. In interviews during a series of visits to observe training, many said the fact that they could finally pursue a combat career, and have it treated as no big deal, was for them revolutionary. Now many who dreamed of going into the infantry are no longer barred from the core combat positions that are the clearest career routes to senior leadership.

7   Just before graduation, one female drill sergeant pulled aside a group of female privates, who ranged from high school athletes to a single mother with a culinary[3] degree, and gave them her unofficial assessment out of officers' earshot.

8   "This is a big deal," she said as she looked into one recruit's eyes. She said they were making history.

'Misery is a great equalizer'

9   Rain pounded the roughly 150 troops of Alpha Company, who ranged in age from 17 to 34, as they stood in formation during a tornado warning, waiting to hear if it was too stormy to train.

10   If the downpour let up, they would practice rushing out of armored vehicles. If not, they would tramp back to the foxholes where they had slept the night before and bail out the standing brown water with canteen cups.

11   Either way, by day's end they would be wet, tired, hungry and cold: the four pillars of misery the Army has long relied on to help whip recruits into cohesive fighting teams.

12   "Misery is a great equalizer," one male recruit said with a resigned grin.

13   The rain eventually let up and the sergeants ran the platoons through repeated ambush drills. By the end, while some of the troops

© Houghton Mifflin Harcourt Publishing Company

---

[1] **The Army has also sought .. the American infantry:** Congress authorized the raising of the first infantry battalion units in 1775, shortly after the outbreak of the American Revolution, as part of the Continental Army.

[2] **grunt:** *slang.* infantry soldier.

[3] **culinary** (kŭl´ə-nĕr-ē, kyoō´lə)**:** of or relating to a kitchen or to cookery.

SUMMARIZE AND PARAPHRASE TEXTS

Annotate: Reread paragraphs 3–8. Mark phrases that express the main ideas.

Summarize: Briefly summarize this passage of text.

had buzz cuts and some had their hair in buns, they all shared the drooping weariness that grunts have worn for as long as there's been an infantry.

'She's a hoss'

14 In the woods, after hours of mock raids, Pvt. Kayla Padgett rested her rifle against her rucksack and turned to her platoon, assembling them in three neat rows.

15 It was 90 degrees. A tick crawled along the back of her shirt. The night before, the platoon had slept in the dirt. Everyone was dog tired. Many were covered in ant bites. But as platoon guide, it was her job to make them ready.

16 "All right, hustle it up, let's count off," she said.

17 One by one the platoon of mostly men each shouted until all were accounted for.

18 "O.K., good," Private Padgett said, scanning the group with her blue eyes. "If you haven't done so, keep loading up ammo, all your magazines."

19 Over the years, countless voices have warned that women could never handle the demands of the infantry, and would destroy its all-male **esprit de corps**. None of the recruits or drill sergeants interviewed at Fort Benning shared that fear. They all pointed to women like Private Padgett.

20 The 23-year-old track champion from North Carolina could throw a 20-pound hammer more than 60 meters while on the team at East Carolina University, and showed up at basic training in better shape than many of the men. She is now on her way to Airborne School, and wants to eventually become a Ranger.

21 "She's a hoss," her drill sergeant, Joseph Sapp, said as he watched her. After a tour in Iraq and four in Afghanistan, he has served with his share of soldiers. "Forget male-female; she's one of the best in the company. She's one you're happy to have."

Not 'treated special'

22 In the new integrated infantry companies, women and men train together in mixed-gender squads from before dawn until after dusk: practicing the same raids, kicking in the same doors, doing the same push-ups when their squad messes up. No one gets out of a **rotation** serving **chow**.

23 At night, they sleep in rooms separated by gender, in identical metal bunks with identically scratchy green blankets. To graduate, all must pass tests of the same infantry skills, including hurling a grenade 35 meters, dragging a 268-pound dummy 15 meters, running five miles in less than 45 minutes and completing a 12-mile march carrying 68 pounds.

© Houghton Mifflin Harcourt Publishing Company

ANALYZE TEXT FEATURES
Annotate: Circle the subheading 'She's a hoss.' Then, in paragraph 20, underline details that support the key idea of this section.

Evaluate: How well does the subheading help you predict the details and key idea of this section? Did you need to correct your prediction?

esprit de corps
n. a spirit of devotion and loyalty among group members.

LANGUAGE CONVENTIONS
Annotate: Mark the words *male-female* in paragraph 21.

Analyze: What is the mark between *male* and *female* called and why is it used here? What does the speaker mean by "Forget male-female"?

rotation
n. regular and uniform variation in a sequence or series.

chow
n. food; victuals.

24   Hair is one of the few places where standards still diverge. All men get their heads shaved on arrival. Women don't. Not wanting to be held to a different standard, though, many of the women decided a few weeks into training to shave in solidarity. They would earn back their hair, just like the men.

25   "I loved my hair, but didn't want anyone to look at me and think I was being treated special," said Pvt. Irelynn Donovan.

'I wanted to make history'

26   Private Donovan, 20, grew up outside Philadelphia with five older brothers. She was the only girl on her junior high football team. When assigned to write an essay about an adult she admired, she chose her grandfather, who had served two tours in Vietnam.

27   "She's just always been a badass," said her mother, Cristine Zalewski.

28   She always wanted to join the infantry, despite a ban on women. On her forearm is a tattoo of flowers wrapped around a saying uttered by her single mother, who sometimes had to **scrounge** for change in the house to pay bills: "We'll find a way."

scrounge
(skrounj) *v.intr.* to obtain by salvaging or foraging; round up.

© Houghton Mifflin Harcourt Publishing Company

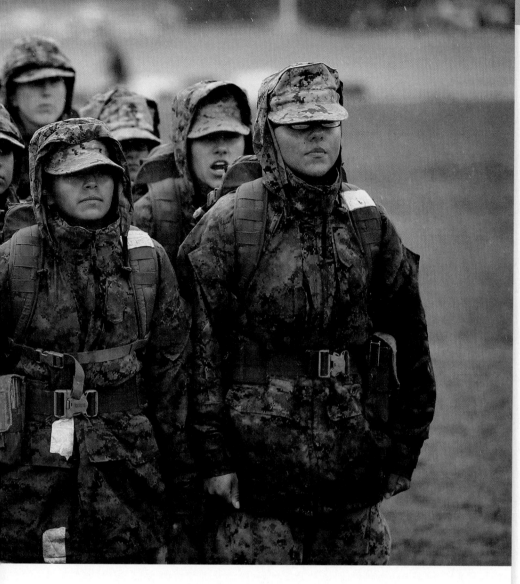

© Houghton Mifflin Harcourt Publishing Company • Image Credits: © Scott Olson/Getty Images

29   As soon as the ban was lifted in 2016, Irelynn Donovan went to a local recruiter.

30   "I wanted to make history," she said. "Pave the way, if not for me, then for others."

31   During training, she wrote home complaining that she was exhausted and tired of being yelled at. "Everything is **chafing**," she wrote. But she became a standout, nailing the physical tests for both men and women when she did 79 push-ups in two minutes.

chafe
(chāf) *v.intr.* to annoy or irritate.

'Hey, the infantry's tough, man'

32   Afghanistan and Iraq were turning points for the Army's thinking on women in combat. The wars forced thousands of women who were not technically combat troops into fire fights. Nearly 14,000 women were awarded the Combat Action Badge for engaging with the enemy. Today most of the men leading the Army have served with women in combat for years.

33   "We saw it can work," said Maj. Gen. Jeffrey Snow, who heads Army Recruiting Command at Fort Knox, Ky. "And now we have a

SUMMARIZE AND PARAPHRASE TEXTS

Annotate: Mark key details in paragraph 32.

Interpret: Write a few sentences paraphrasing this paragraph.

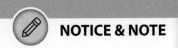

generation that just wants to accomplish the mission and have the most talented people to do it."

34 The Army is determined not to sacrifice performance for the sake of inclusion, and many women have not been able to meet the standard. Of the 32 who showed up at infantry boot camp in February, 44 percent dropped out. For the 148 men in the company, the dropout rate was just 20 percent.

35 Commanders say the higher dropout rate among females is in line with other demanding boot camps for military police and combat engineers, which have been open to women for years. In part, they say, it is a consequence of size. A 5-foot-2 woman has to carry the same weight and perform the same tasks as a man who stands a foot taller, and is more likely to be injured.

36 Why did so many more women fail? One female recruit summed it up by saying simply, "Hey, the infantry's tough, man."

37 "Is it fair?" said the brigade commander overseeing gender-integrated infantry training at Fort Benning, Col. Kelly Kendrick. "I don't care about fair. I care if you can meet the standard."

38 Male soldiers acknowledged in interviews that the women who remain, like Chonell Morgan, 18, are some of the toughest soldiers in the company. During a punishment run the platoons were ordered to undertake on a hot afternoon, Private Morgan, who is from Apple Valley, Calif., was near the front of the pack.

39 The daughter of a NASA engineer, she postponed plans for college when she heard the infantry was opening to women. Her mother is still upset about the decision, but her father, Lorenzo Morgan, who served in the Army in the 1980s, said, "You have to let your children be who they want to be."

An Unspoken Accomplishment

40 After 14 weeks of running and crawling in the dirt, Alpha Company marched onto the parade grounds in crisp dress uniforms and carefully creased berets.

41 The company commander's voice booming over loudspeakers welcomed them to the infantry, but he gave no nod to the women now joining the ranks.

42 The women appeared to take it in stride. Private Donovan, who had won the award for the highest female fitness score in the company, finishing just behind the top man, pushed through the crowd toward her family, then shrank in embarrassment when her mother greeted her with a bouquet of flowers.

43 "Mom," she muttered, looking to see if anyone noticed, "you don't bring flowers to infantry graduation."

CONTRASTS AND CONTRADICTIONS

Notice & Note: Mark details in paragraphs 42–43 that indicate Private Donovan's feelings.

Infer: Why does she respond this way to her mother's gift?

© Houghton Mifflin Harcourt Publishing Company

CHECK YOUR UNDERSTANDING

Answer these questions before moving on to the **Analyze the Text** section on the following page.

1 In paragraph 2, what does the sentence "That's just how the Army wants it" refer to?

 A The soldiers are wearing body armor.

 B Women graduated from U.S. infantry training.

 C Infantry was being trained in the woods of Georgia.

 D It was almost impossible to distinguish the female and male soldiers.

2 In paragraph 5, the speaker is quoted as saying, "It's business as usual." Which sentence from the text contradicts this statement?

 F *"This is a big deal," she said as she looked into one recruit's eyes.*

 G *"I've tried to not change a thing."*

 H *"Misery is a great equalizer," one male recruit said with a resigned grin.*

 J *"I wanted to make history," she said. "Pave the way, if not for me, then for others."*

3 Which detail from the section with the subheading "Not 'treated special'" best supports the main idea of that section?

 A *Hair is one of the few places where standards still diverge.*

 B *To graduate, all must pass tests of the same infantry skills. . . .*

 C *At night, they sleep in rooms separated by gender. . . .*

 D *Not wanting to be held to a different standard, though, many of the women decided a few weeks into training to shave in solidarity.*

ANALYZE THE TEXT

Support your responses with evidence from the text. ⊟ NOTEBOOK

1. **Identify** What are two reasons offered in the text that explain why women want to join the infantry?

2. **Analyze** Why has there been resistance to having women serve in the infantry? What has the U.S. Army done to overcome that resistance?

3. **Summarize** What is the historical significance of the infantry graduation described in the article's final section?

4. **Evaluate** The article's subheadings consist of quotations from people noted by the author. Does this approach communicate organization and key ideas effectively? Explain why or why not.

5. **Notice & Note** How do the women's attitudes about their success in infantry training compare with the Army's official position about them?

RESEARCH

RESEARCH TIP

Don't rely on a single source for your research. Many sources are incomplete or inaccurate. Compare information from multiple sources, and if you find an inaccuracy in a source, consider that source generally unreliable.

Although most women in history have served in domestic roles, such as housekeeping and child rearing, rather than roles suited to the battlefield, history does note some famous female military leaders. Carry out research to discover the facts about some of these women warriors.

MILITARY LEADER	TIME AND PLACE	MILITARY EXPERIENCE
Boudicca		
Joan of Arc		
Zenobia		
Nakano Takeko		
Grace O'Malley		

Extend What motivated these women to become military leaders and what personal qualities might have caused them to do something so unconventional?

CREATE AND DEBATE

Prepare Notes for a Debate In teams of three or four, brainstorm ideas and research supporting information to prepare to debate either for or against allowing women to serve in all roles in the military.

❑ Decide which position your team will defend.

❑ Brainstorm ideas and information to support your argument. You may need to do some research.

❑ Anticipate opposing claims so that you can be prepared to argue against them.

Debate Your team will be matched with another to debate the topic, with each team assigned to be either in favor of allowing women to serve in all roles in the military or against that position. Teams will alternate turns, with each speaker refuting (disagreeing with) the arguments of the previous speaker.

Go to **Writing Arguments** in the **Writing Studio** to find out more about planning an argument.

Go to **Analyzing and Evaluating Presentations** in the **Speaking and Listening Studio** to find out more about tracing a speaker's argument.

DEBATE PLANNING	
In Favor	**Against**

RESPOND TO THE ESSENTIAL QUESTION

 How do you defy expectations?

Gather Information Review your annotations and notes on "For Army Infantry's First Women, Heavy Packs and the Weight of History" and "Speech Before the Spanish Armada Invasion." Then, add relevant details to your Response Log. As you determine which information to include, think about:

• how each author discusses expectations
• the arguments against those expectations
• the motivations of the women to defy expectations

ACADEMIC VOCABULARY

As you write and discuss what you learned from the article, be sure to use the Academic Vocabulary words. Check off each of the words that you use.

❑ **ambiguous**
❑ **anticipate**
❑ **conceive**
❑ **drama**
❑ **integrity**

RESPOND

WORD BANK
infantry
smart
esprit de corps
rotation
chow
scrounge
chafe

Go to **Understanding Word Origins** in the **Vocabulary Studio** for more.

CRITICAL VOCABULARY

Practice and Apply Answer each question by using one of the Critical Vocabulary words in a complete sentence.

1. What might you do if you don't have enough change for the bus?

2. What do you get at the cafeteria?

3. Why do members of a team feel close to each other?

4. What's a fair way to divide up household chores?

5. How might someone feel after getting into trouble?

6. Who might go to fight a battle in the woods?

7. Why might a wet wool suit be uncomfortable?

VOCABULARY STRATEGY:
Foreign Words and Phrases

Sometimes you will come across a word or phrase that is borrowed from another language. The article you just read, for example, includes the phrase *esprit de corps*, a French phrase that translates to "group spirit."

Often, a text provides clues that a word is of non-English origin. Foreign words and phrases frequently use accent marks (à) or unusual letter combinations or pronunciations. Foreign words and phrases may also be set in italic font.

Practice and Apply In each sentence, mark the foreign word or phrase. Then, write it next to the correct origin and translation of the word in the graphic organizer provided. Finally, use your own words to write the meaning of each word, based on how it is used in the sentence.

1. My grandmother believes it is a faux pas to wear white after Labor Day.

2. We've all heard your spiel on that, so there's no sense in repeating it.

3. She's royalty, but she mingles with the hoi polloi with such gracefulness.

4. Well that's it; my car is kaput!

FOREIGN WORD OR PHRASE	ORIGIN AND TRANSLATION	MEANING IN USAGE
	Greek: the many	
	German: broken	
	Yiddish: game	
	French: false step	

© Houghton Mifflin Harcourt Publishing Company

LANGUAGE CONVENTIONS:
Dashes and Hyphenation

Dashes and **hyphenation** can make your writing more interesting, sophisticated, and precise. It is important to understand exactly how these marks function in a text and to know when it is best to use them.

An ***em dash* (—),** also called simply a ***dash*,** can function similarly to a comma, colon, semicolon, or parentheses. Use a dash or pair of dashes to set off text that explains, contrasts, or amplifies.

In this example, dashes set off explanatory text:

> **The Army has also sought to play down the significance of the new female infantrymen—<u>as they are still known</u>—not mentioning, when families gathered last week for their graduation, that the 18 women who made it through would be the first in more than two centuries for the American infantry.**

In the following sentence, the dash sets off an idea that contrasts with the idea before it.

> **"It's business as usual," the battalion commander overseeing the first class, Lt. Col. Sam Edwards, said as he watched a squad of soldiers run past—<u>including one with French braids and a grenade launcher</u>.**

This helps the author convey one of the text's key ideas: having women in infantry training contrasts with our image of women in a way that is still surprising, despite the Army's efforts to normalize the change.

Hyphens are used to create compound nouns and compound modifiers. Hyphens help clarify which word is modifying which. In this example, the compound modifier is made up of an adjective, *mixed*, and a noun, *gender*.

> **It was almost impossible to distinguish the <u>mixed-gender</u> squads in the steamy woods from those of earlier generations.**

Without the hyphen, it would be unclear that there is a squad of mixed gender (male and female), not a "gender squad" that is mixed. It's unlikely that a reader would misunderstand in this instance, but use of hyphens in compound modifiers before a noun is recommended for better readability and to ensure precision.

Practice and Apply Write a short description of an unusual situation or a way that someone you know, or have heard of, has overcome expectations. Use dashes to set off explanations, surprises, or contrasts. Make your writing descriptive and precise by using hyphenated compound modifiers.

© Houghton Mifflin Harcourt Publishing Company

> Go to the **Grammar Studio: Other Marks of Punctuation** for more on dashes and hyphenation.

Collaborate & Compare

COMPARE ACROSS GENRES

Two texts may express similar ideas even though they are written in different genres and address different topics. Sometimes these ideas are explicitly stated. But often the reader must infer the author's general views and values from details in the text.

In a small group, collaborate with classmates to state each author's attitude toward women serving in traditionally male roles. Then, identify ideas and information in each text to support your inferences.

POSITION ABOUT WOMEN IN NONTRADITIONAL ROLES	
"Speech Before the Spanish Armada Invasion"	**"For Army Infantry's First Women, Heavy Packs and the Weight of History"**
SUPPORT	

ANALYZE THE TEXTS

Discuss these questions in your group.

1. **Cite Evidence** How does each author portray the ability of women to demonstrate courage and leadership?

2. **Compare** Which author has the more traditional view of differences between men and women?

3. **Cause and Effect** What motivates the women in these texts to overcome stereotypes about their gender?

4. **Synthesize** How do these texts support the right of women to serve in traditionally male roles?

© Houghton Mifflin Harcourt Publishing Company • Image Credits: © Scott Olson/Getty Images; © World History Archive/Alamy

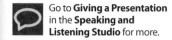

RESEARCH AND SHARE

Now, your group can continue exploring the ideas in these texts by carrying out research and presenting your findings to the class.

Go to **Giving a Presentation** in the **Speaking and Listening Studio** for more.

1. **Choose a Topic** In your group, brainstorm other ways that women have overcome stereotypes concerning their roles in society, either historically or currently. Think about jobs that were not open to women before, rights that women did not always have, and academic subjects or recreational activities for which women were not expected to express an interest. Discuss which examples your group finds most interesting and select one topic to research.

2. **Gather Sources** Look for multiple sources that contain information about your group's topic. Try to find sources that discuss the topic in a variety of ways, rely on different kinds of details, or take different perspectives on the topic.

   ❏ Look for sources that present a position. Remember that authors sometimes imply a position through their use of details and evidence.

   ❏ Watch for extreme or inflammatory language. This is usually an indication that an author is biased and is distorting or altering facts to support a position. Check the provided facts against other sources.

3. **Take Notes** For each source, summarize the author's conclusion and note the details used to support it. Always record source information, such as author, title, publisher, and date of publication.

TOPIC:		
Source	Position	Details

4. **Share Your Findings** Tell the class about the stereotype your group researched, providing details on what your research revealed about how women have overcome that stereotype. Explain and summarize the information you discovered in your sources. If you found examples of authors who altered or distorted facts to support a position, be sure to note this, explaining what led you to this conclusion.

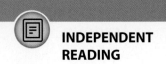

INDEPENDENT READING

Reader's Choice

? *ESSENTIAL QUESTIONS*

Review the four Essential Questions for this Unit on page 139.

Setting a Purpose   Select one or more of these options from your eBook to continue your exploration of the Essential Questions.

- Read the descriptions to see which text is most interesting to you.
- Think about which genres you enjoy reading.

Notice **&** Note

In this unit, you practiced noticing and noting the signposts and asking big questions about nonfiction. As you read independently, these signposts and others will aid your understanding. Below are the key questions to ask when you read literature and nonfiction.

Reading Literature: Stories, Poems, and Plays	
Signpost	**Key Question**
Contrasts and Contradictions	Why did the character act that way?
Aha Moment	How might this action or event change things?
Tough Questions	What does this piece of writing make me wonder about?
Words of the Wiser	What is the lesson for the character?
Again and Again	Why might the author keep bringing up this issue or topic?
Memory Moment	Why is this memory important?

Reading Nonfiction: Essays, Articles, and Arguments	
Signpost	**Key Question(s)**
Big Questions	What surprised me? What did the author think I already knew? What challenged, changed, or confirmed what I already knew?
Contrasts and Contradictions	What is the difference, and why does it matter?
Extreme or Absolute Language	Why did the author use this type of language?
Numbers and Stats	Why did the author use these numbers or amounts?
Quoted Words	Why was this person quoted or cited, and what did this quotation add?
Word Gaps	Do I know this word from some other source? Does the word seem like technical talk for this topic? Do clues in the sentence help me understand the word?

You can preview these texts in Unit 2 of your eBook.

Then check off the text or texts that you select to read on your own.

POEMS

Sonnet 18, Sonnet 29, Sonnet 130

William Shakespeare

Three sonnets reveal Shakespeare's thoughts about true love.

ARTICLE

Elizabeth I: The Reality Behind the Mask

Brenda Ralph Lewis

Discover the real Queen Elizabeth I, who exercised great skill to disguise her true personality.

POEM

The Passionate Shepherd to His Love

Christopher Marlowe

Find out what a shepherd will promise to entice his beloved.

POEM

The Nymph's Reply to the Shepherd

Sir Walter Raleigh

A wise and cautious young woman responds to the shepherd's invitation.

Collaborate and Share   With a partner, discuss what you learned from at least one of your independent readings.

- Give a brief synopsis or summary of the text.
- Describe any signposts that you noticed in the text and explain what they revealed to you.
- Describe what you most enjoyed or found most challenging about the text. Give specific examples.
- Decide if you would recommend the text to others. Why or why not?

Go to the **Reading Studio** for more resources on **Notice & Note.**

Write a Literary Analysis

Go to the **Writing Studio** for help with writing an analysis.

In this unit, you have read just a few great works from the English Renaissance, with a focus on Shakespeare, the dominant literary figure of the period. Your next writing task will focus on what you have learned about the theme of revenge in *Hamlet*. Write a literary analysis of a scene in *Hamlet* that shows the hero struggling to overcome an internal or external conflict. You can use "Hamlet's Dull Revenge" by René Girard as a mentor text.

As you write your literary analysis, you can use the notes from your Response Log to answer the question, "What can drive someone to seek revenge?" which you filled out after reading the texts in this unit.

Writing Prompt

Read the information in the box below.

> Probably more has been written about *Hamlet* than any of Shakespeare's other plays. Despite the fact that it was written more than four hundred years ago, it continues to fascinate readers and stimulate thoughts about revenge.

This is the topic or context for your literary analysis.

Think carefully about the following question.

> What can drive someone to seek revenge?

How might this Essential Question relate to a literary analysis?

Write a literary analysis of a scene in *Hamlet* that shows the hero struggling to overcome an internal or external conflict.

Mark the words that show which type of conflicts you will explore in your analysis.

Be sure to—

Review these points as you write, and again when you finish. Make any needed changes.

- ☐ make a clear thesis statement, or claim
- ☐ present key ideas, or reasons, in a logical order
- ☐ support key ideas with details and evidence from the text
- ☐ quote passages from the text
- ☐ end your analysis with a strong conclusion

① Plan

Plan your analysis carefully before you start to write, using the chart below. First note the genre—literary analysis. Your topic deals with questions about revenge, conflict, and human relationships in *Hamlet*. Think of scenes from the play that contain some sort of conflict or other interaction. Consider the type of interaction involved in each scene. Are there internal or external conflicts? Are these forces struggling against each other? Gather ideas for your analysis of the scene. Perhaps you want to comment on how the scene developed; its significance to the story; what it reveals about Hamlet; how it might lead to another scene in the play; or how the characters are affected by the scene. As you explore the topic for your literary analysis, use any background reading or class discussions to help you generate ideas.

Informative Essay Planning Table	
Genre	Literary analysis
Topic	
Possible scenes	
Ideas about scenes	
Ideas from background reading	
Ideas from class discussion	

Background Reading Review the notes you have taken in your Response Log that relate to the question, "What can drive someone to seek revenge?" Texts in this unit provide background reading that will help you formulate ideas and offer evidence you will use in your literary analysis.

 Go to the **Writing Studio: Using Textual Evidence** for help planning your literary analysis.

Notice & Note
From Reading to Writing

As you plan your literary analysis, apply what you've learned about signposts to your own writing. Remember that writers use common features called signposts to help convey their message to readers.

Think how you can incorporate **Quoted Words** into your essay.

Go to the **Reading Studio** for more resources on **Notice & Note**.

Use the notes from your Response Log as you plan your literary analysis.

WRITING TASK

Go to **Writing Informative Texts: Organizing Ideas** for more help.

Organize Your Ideas After you have gathered ideas from your planning activities, you need to organize them in a way that will help you draft your literary analysis. Choose your scene and identify the type of interaction. Next, decide what the focus of your analysis of the interaction will be. Write a clear thesis statement, or claim, and identify reasons that support it to help develop key ideas. Then find evidence in the text to support your key ideas. You can use the chart below to organize the elements of your analysis.

Topic: Analysis of a Scene in *Hamlet*		
Thesis Statement:		
Key Idea	**Key Idea**	**Key Idea**
Evidence	**Evidence**	**Evidence**

② Develop a Draft

You might prefer to draft your literary analysis online.

Once you have completed your planning, you will be ready to draft your literary analysis. Refer to your Graphic Organizer and your planning chart as well as any notes you took as you studied the texts in this unit. These will provide a map for you to follow as you write. Using a word processor or online writing application makes it easier to make changes or move sentences around later when you are ready to revise your first draft.

Use the Mentor Text

> ### Author's Craft
> State your thesis clearly at the beginning of your literary analysis; tell your reader what you are writing about and the claim you are making. Girard's first paragraph of "Hamlet's Dull Revenge" states his claim about Shakespeare's purpose for writing *Hamlet*.

Hamlet belongs to the **genre** of the revenge tragedy, as hackneyed and yet inescapable in Shakespeare's days as the "thriller" in ours . . . In *Hamlet* Shakespeare turned this necessity for a playwright to go on writing the same old revenge tragedies into an opportunity to debate almost openly for the first time the questions I have tried to define. The weariness with revenge and *katharsis* . . . must really exist because, in *Hamlet*, it moves to the center of the stage and becomes fully articulated.

Girard claims that Shakespeare is trying to make a statement about revenge and revenge theater rather than just producing another clichéd revenge tragedy.

Apply What You've Learned After you've chosen the scene you want to focus on and identified the claim you want to make, begin your analysis with a thesis statement. What interesting insight will you offer your reader?

> ### Genre Characteristics
> You must provide key ideas and evidence from the text to support your thesis. In the text below, Girard makes the point that Hamlet is searching for a model of revenge because he lacks inspiration and passion.

The scene is as ridiculous as it is sinister. . . . [Hamlet's] words constantly betray him, . . . his revenge motif is no more compelling, really, than the cue of an actor on the stage. He too must *greatly . . . find quarrel in a straw,* **he too must stake everything** *even for an eggshell.*

Girard cites a particular instance in the play to support his point. The words in italics are directly quoted from the play.

Apply What You've Learned When you are providing key ideas that support your thesis, be sure to offer evidence from the text to convince your reader. Cite direct evidence from the text, such as quotations, for your major points, and use several pieces of evidence when possible.

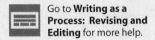

3 Revise

Go to **Writing as a Process: Revising and Editing** for more help.

On Your Own Once you have written your draft, you'll want to go back and look for ways to improve your literary analysis. As you reread and revise, think about whether you have achieved your purpose. The Revision Guide will help you focus on specific elements to strengthen your writing.

Revision Guide		
Ask Yourself	**Tips**	**Revision Techniques**
1. Did I state my thesis clearly and in an interesting way?	**Highlight** your thesis statement, or claim.	If necessary, add a sentence or two to clarify your thesis. Add an interesting example or related quotation to hook your reader.
2. Do I have enough support for my thesis?	**Circle** key ideas and underline details and evidence that provide support.	Read your thesis statement aloud, followed by your key ideas. Are your ideas well-supported? If not, look for more evidence in the text.
3. Are my thoughts logically organized?	**Outline** your key ideas and check for the most logical order.	Reorder ideas if needed so that each idea flows easily to the next.
4. Did I include sufficient evidence from the text?	**Underline** any specific quotations or examples you used.	Add more direct evidence from the text to strengthen your claim.
5. Did I effectively present my claim to the reader by the end of the essay?	**Review** the key points and ideas of your analysis.	Fill in any noticeable gaps or weak points with more relevant details.
6. Is my conclusion strong?	**Highlight** your conclusion.	Add text that summarizes your key ideas to support your conclusion.

ACADEMIC VOCABULARY

As you conduct your **peer review**, be sure to use these words.

❏ **ambiguous**

❏ **anticipate**

❏ **conceive**

❏ **drama**

❏ **integrity**

With a Partner Once you and your partner have worked through the Revision Guide on your own, exchange papers and evaluate each other's draft in a **peer review.** Offer revision suggestions for at least three of the items mentioned in the chart. Explain why you think your partner's draft should be revised and what your specific suggestions include.

When receiving feedback from your partner, listen attentively and ask questions to make sure you fully understand his or her suggestions for revision.

Edit

After you write and revise your literary analysis, it is time to edit some of the finer details. Ensure the proper use of standard English conventions. Look for ways to improve word choice, and be sure to correct all spelling and grammatical errors.

Go to the **Quotation Marks** lesson in the **Grammar Studio** to learn more.

Language Conventions

Indicate Quotations Properly When you are citing words that aren't your own, you must use correct punctuation and format. Even if the words are a short phrase that you want to incorporate, place quotation marks around the phrase. Quotation marks may be appropriate for just one word if that word was used in a particular way or held special significance. Notice that writers use block quotes—setting off the material from the main text in a separate paragraph—when quoting several lines of text. Look at Girard's use of quotation marks, spacing, and indentation in the chart below.

Type of quotation	Example
One word	The only hope for Hamlet to accomplish what his society—or the spectators—require, is to become as "sincere" a showman as the actor who can shed real tears . . . .
Phrase	The cool determination of Hamlet, at this point, is the transmutation of the "towering passion" which he had vainly tried to build up before . . . ;
Block quote	. . . her metaphor suggests a more tangible accomplishment, the birth of something portentous: Anon, as patient as the female dove When that her golden couplets are disclosed, His silence will sit drooping.

Do not use block quotes with fewer than three lines of poetry. Instead, set off the quoted lines within your paragraph with quotation marks, and place a slash mark between each two lines: "Anon, as patient as the female dove/When that her golden couplets are disclosed . . . ."

Publish

Finalize your literary analysis and share it with an audience. Consider these options:

- Save your analysis as a writing sample to include in your college application.
- Research various literary journals and their submission guidelines. Choose at least one and submit your paper.

Use the scoring guide to evaluate your essay.

Writing Task Scoring Guide: Literary Analysis

	Organization/Progression	Development of Ideas	Use of Language and Conventions
4	• Structure is clearly organized and appropriate. • Includes strong thesis statement; all ideas are related to the thesis. • Ideas are in logical order and connected with meaningful transitions.	• Effective development with credible and compelling analysis. • Includes sufficient relevant textual evidence. • Thoughtful and engaging content; demonstrates thorough understanding of the text.	• Precise and appropriate word choice. • Strong and varied sentences. • Consistent command of spelling, punctuation, grammar, and usage conventions.
3	• Structure is for the most part organized and appropriate. • Includes clear thesis statement; most ideas are related to the thesis; minor lapses in unity or focus. • Ideas are generally presented in logical order and connected with sufficient transitions.	• Sufficient development with largely convincing analysis. • Includes sufficient relevant textual evidence; at times could be more complete. • Thoughtful content; demonstrates good understanding of the text.	• For the most part, clear and specific word choice. • Reasonably varied sentences. • Adequate command of spelling, punctuation, grammar, and usage conventions.
2	• Structure is evident but not always appropriate or clear. • Thesis statement is weak or unclear; some irrelevant information affects unity and focus. • Ideas are not always in logical order or connected with sufficient transitions.	• Minimal development with superficial analysis. • Includes textual evidence that is sometimes irrelevant or inaccurate; underdeveloped ideas. • Content reflects little thoughtfulness; demonstrates limited understanding of the text.	• For the most part, general or imprecise word choice. • Some awkward sentences. • Partial command of spelling, punctuation, grammar, and usage conventions.
1	• Structure is inappropriate to the purpose. • Thesis statement is missing, unclear, or illogical; contains irrelevant information. • Weak progression of ideas; includes repetition and wordiness; lacks sufficient transitions.	• Weak development with ineffective analysis. • Includes little if any relevant textual evidence; overall vague development. • Vague or confused response to the text; demonstrates lack of understanding of the text.	• Vague or limited word choice. • Simplistic or awkward sentences. • Little or no command of spelling, punctuation, grammar, and usage conventions.

Reflect on the Unit

By completing your literary analysis, you have a writing product that pulls together and expresses your thoughts about the reading you have done in this unit. Now is a good time to reflect on what you have learned.

Reflect on the Essential Questions

- Review the four Essential Questions on page 139. How have your answers to these questions changed in response to the texts you read in this unit?

- What are some examples from the texts you read that explore individual human nature or celebrate human achievement?

Reflect on Your Reading

- Which selections were the most interesting or surprising to you?

- From which selection did you learn the most about human nature or human achievement?

Reflect on the Writing Task

- What difficulties did you encounter while working on your literary analysis? How might you avoid them next time?

- Which parts of the literary analysis were the easiest to write? The hardest to write? Why?

- What improvements did you make to your literary analysis as you were revising?

© Houghton Mifflin Harcourt Publishing Company

UNIT 2 SELECTIONS
- *The Tragedy of Hamlet*
- *Hamlet* film clip
- "Hamlet's Dull Revenge"
- "Sonnet 30" and "Sonnet 75"
- "A Valediction: Forbidding Mourning"
- "To His Coy Mistress"
- "Twenty-One Love Poems (Poem III)"
- "Speech Before the Spanish Armada Invasion"
- "For Army Infantry's First Women, Heavy Packs and the Weight of History"

UNIT (3)

TRADITION AND REASON

THE RESTORATION AND THE 18TH CENTURY

"Virtue, to deserve the name, must be founded on knowledge."

—Mary Wollstonecraft

Discuss the **Essential Questions** with your whole class or in small groups. As you read Tradition and Reason, consider how the selections explore these questions.

? *ESSENTIAL QUESTION:*

How can satire change people's behavior?

If you have ever read an "Opinion" news column or watched a television show about current events, chances are you have encountered satire. Satire uses exaggeration, irony, and/or humor to make an often serious point about a public figure, event, issue, or situation. Is satire the most effective way for a critic or comic to make a point? Who are the intended audiences of satires? What kinds of reactions do satires evoke from their audiences and, occasionally, their subjects?

? *ESSENTIAL QUESTION:*

What is your most memorable experience?

Memory is extremely personal. After all, there are no two people alive who have the exact same memories. The things we remember about our lives often depend on who we are, what we value, and the emotions we experience during an event. What makes an experience memorable? Does an experience have to be life-changing or have long-term importance to be memorable?

? *ESSENTIAL QUESTION:*

What keeps women from achieving equality with men?

In many parts of the world, women are regarded as second-class citizens and do not have the same access to education, health care, and protection under law as men. Even in lands where gender inequality is supposedly a thing of the past, many women do not receive equal pay for equal work, and women are severely underrepresented in positions of influence. What lies at the root of gender inequality? What must change for gender equality to become a reality?

? *ESSENTIAL QUESTION:*

Why are plagues so horrifying?

Few events strike fear into humans like the threat of disease. Many people take daily precautions to avoid sickness and maintain themselves in the best possible health. When an epidemic or a pandemic occurs, however, avoiding sickness can mean the difference between life and death. How have plagues, both historical and contemporary, shaped the modern world? Have human attitudes toward plagues changed as a result of modern medicine? Why do plague accounts simultaneously fascinate and repel people?

THE RESTORATION AND THE 18TH CENTURY

The year 1660 marked Charles II's ascent to the English throne following more than a decade of exile, during which the country had experienced the Puritan rule of Oliver Cromwell's short-lived Commonwealth. The period that immediately followed this return of the Stuart monarchs became known as the Restoration. At the same time, in England and throughout Europe, other important changes led to the late 1600s and the 1700s being known as the Age of Reason.

The Reign of Charles II Under Charles II, England turned its back on the grim era of Puritan rule and entered a lively period in which upper-class social and political life copied the sophistication and splendor of the French court of Louis XIV. The upper classes attended elegant parties and enjoyed going to the theater, where they were amused by comedies of manners that poked fun at their own glamorous but artificial society. Charles was also an astute politician, and his reign brought relative stability to England. A period of increased growth and prosperity began and led eventually to the growth of the English middle class.

The Restoration brought about the realization that English monarchs would have to share their authority with Parliament, whose influence had increased substantially. Charles at first had widespread support in Parliament, weathering both the Great Plague of 1665 and the Great Fire of London a year later. Soon, though, two factions arose that would become the nation's chief political parties: the Tories, who supported royal authority; and the Whigs, who wanted to limit royal authority.

Royalty and the People Political conflict increased after Charles' death in 1685. Charles had reestablished Anglicanism as the state religion, but his successor James II wanted England to return to Roman Catholicism. When Parliament forced James to abdicate in 1688, the crown passed peacefully to his Protestant daughter Mary and her husband William, demonstrating the power of Parliament over the monarchy. The next year, Parliament passed the English Bill of Rights, which strictly limited royal authority.

The first prime minister, Robert Walpole, was appointed in 1721. The position of prime minister became influential, and although the monarchy remained, people recognized that the time of absolute monarchs was over.

COLLABORATIVE DISCUSSION

In a small group, discuss how historical events influenced writing and literature during the late 1600s and the 1700s.

1660	1687	1707	1719
The Stuart monarchy is restored under Charles II.	Sir Isaac Newton defines the law of gravity.	England, Wales, and Scotland unite as Great Britain.	Daniel Defoe publishes *Robinson Crusoe*.

1660

1665	1666	1690	1718	1721
The Great Plague of London kills thousands.	The Great Fire of London destroys a large section of the city.	John Locke publishes *Two Treatises of Government*.	Smallpox inoculation introduced.	Walpole is prime minister.

The Age of Reason The period including the late 1600s and the 1700s is called the Enlightenment or the Age of Reason because it was during this time that people increasingly made use of scientific thought to understand the world. Sir Isaac Newton formulated the laws of gravity and motion, and developed the scientific method—a process that scientists could use to test hypotheses about how the world works. Newton's findings suggested that the universe operates according to logical principles, an idea that inspired such philosophers as John Locke to apply the rules of logic and reasoning to human nature and society.

During the 1700s, it became common for male writers, artists, politicians, and others to gather in public places and exchange ideas, conduct business, and share gossip. Educated women held private gatherings for the same purpose so that they too could be included in the intellectual life of the day. More women started writing and publishing their work. Some, most notably Mary Wollstonecraft, became advocates for women's rights.

An Era of Change The spirit of the Enlightenment brought about many improvements in living conditions. For example, the practice of inoculation against disease was introduced by Lady Mary Wortley Montagu, and a vaccine for smallpox was developed. The middle class grew and prospered, and ordinary men and women had more money, leisure time, and education than ever before.

For writers, that meant a broad new audience eager to read and willing to pay for literature. The middle classes wanted writing that reflected their

© Houghton Mifflin Harcourt Publishing Company • Image Credits: © National Geographic Creative/Alamy

RESEARCH
What about this historical period interests you? Choose a topic, event, or person to learn more about. Then add your own entry to the timeline.

1755
Samuel Johnson's *A Dictionary of the English Language* is published.

1763
Britain defeats France in the Seven Years' War, acquiring French Canada.

1783
The independence of the United States is recognized in the Treaty of Paris.

1800

1768
The publication of *Encyclopaedia Britannica* begins in Scotland.

1792
Mary Wollstonecraft's *A Vindication of the Rights of Woman* is published.

own concerns and experiences. Thus prose journalism experienced a rise in popularity. Some nonfiction journalists, diarists, and letter writers turned to fictional topics, leading to the birth of the novel. While much poetry was at first still written in a classical style, toward the end of the 1700s some poets began to move toward a simpler and freer poetic style. In the century to come, both prose and poetry would continue to evolve as the new era of Romanticism blossomed.

CHECK YOUR UNDERSTANDING

Choose the best answer to each question.

1 Why was the reign of Charles II known as the Restoration?

    A Parliament passed laws that restored and increased the power of the monarchy.

    B Charles II restored Roman Catholicism as the state religion of England.

    C Peaceful relations between the English and French courts were restored.

    D The Commonwealth ended and the Stuart monarchy was restored.

2 Which factor contributed most to the development of rival political parties in England?

    F Disagreements over how Charles II handled the Great Plague and the Great Fire of London

    G Differing ideas about how much authority the monarchy should have

    H Conflicts between Catholics and Protestants about the appointment of a prime minister

    J Opposing views of the use of reason in society

3 Which best represents how an Enlightenment philosopher would have viewed the Great Plague of 1665?

    A "The Great Plague is a natural event that can be explained through the use of reason."

    B "The Great Plague is a sign that God is displeased with the English people for returning to Anglicanism."

    C "The inability of the king to prevent the Great Plague shows the limits of absolute monarchy."

    D "The devastation caused by the Great Plague indicates a need for the English Bill of Rights."

ACADEMIC VOCABULARY

Academic Vocabulary words are words you use when you discuss and write about texts. In this unit, you will learn the following five words:

☑ encounter   ❑ exploit   ❑ persist   ❑ subordinate   ❑ widespread

Study the Word Network to learn more about the word **encounter.**

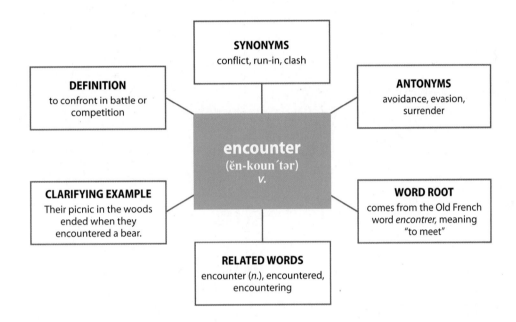

SYNONYMS
conflict, run-in, clash

ANTONYMS
avoidance, evasion, surrender

DEFINITION
to confront in battle or competition

encounter
(ĕn-koun´tər)
v.

WORD ROOT
comes from the Old French word *encontrer,* meaning "to meet"

CLARIFYING EXAMPLE
Their picnic in the woods ended when they encountered a bear.

RELATED WORDS
encounter (*n.*), encountered, encountering

Write and Discuss Discuss your completed Word Network with a partner, making sure to talk through all of the boxes until you both understand the word, its synonyms, antonyms, and related forms. Then fill out a Word Network for the remaining four words. Use a dictionary or online resource to help you complete the activity.

Go online to access the Word Networks.

RESPOND TO THE ESSENTIAL QUESTIONS

In this unit, you will explore four different **Essential Questions** about the Restoration period and the Enlightenment. As you read each selection, you will gather your ideas about one of these questions and write about it in the **Response Log** that appears on page R3. At the end of the unit, you will have the opportunity to write a **personal narrative** related to one of the Essential Questions. Filling out the Response Log after you read each text will help you prepare for this writing task.

You can also go online to access the Response Log.

from

THE RAPE OF THE LOCK

Poem by **Alexander Pope**

? ***ESSENTIAL QUESTION:***

How can satire change people's behavior?

QUICK START

Think of a time when you overreacted to an incident but later realized that what happened was not very important. What made you see that you had overreacted?

ANALYZE SATIRE

Satire is a literary technique in which institutions, practices, or behaviors are ridiculed for the purpose of bringing about reform. Authors write satire to comment on social and political issues and to advocate for improving society. Satirists often use exaggeration and irony to cast a critical eye on human follies and shortcomings. The success of satire depends on readers' ability to distinguish what is stated from what is really meant.

There are two types of satire, named for the Roman satirists Horace and Juvenal. **Juvenalian** satire uses a scathing, scornful tone and dark humor to criticize incompetence or corruption with scorn and outrage. Jonathon Swift's *A Modest Proposal* is an example of Juvenalian satire. *The Rape of the Lock,* on the other hand, is an example of **Horatian** satire, which uses a playful, lighthearted tone to correct foolishness and vice with a combination of gentle mockery and sympathetic understanding.

GENRE ELEMENTS: SATIRE

- ridicules customs, behaviors, or institutions
- purpose is to improve society
- intended to be humorous
- often uses exaggeration
- employs verbal irony

HORATIAN SATIRE	JUVENALIAN SATIRE
Purpose is to improve society	Purpose is to improve society
Lighthearted	Scornful
Gentle humor	Dark humor
Example: Alexander Pope's *The Rape of the Lock*	Example: Jonathan Swift's *A Modest Proposal*

ANALYZE HEROIC COUPLETS

A **heroic couplet** is a pair of rhymed lines in **iambic pentameter,** a metrical pattern of five feet (units). Each foot consists of two syllables, the first unstressed and the second stressed.

> **O thoughtless mortals! ever blind to fate,**
> **Too soon dejected, and too soon elate:**

Pope's adherence to the heroic couplet structure creates some of the unusual syntax in *The Rape of the Lock.* Pope also uses surprising rhymes for a humorous effect.

© Houghton Mifflin Harcourt Publishing Company

GET READY

ANALYZE MOCK EPIC

The Rape of the Lock is a **mock epic,** a form of satire that uses the grandiose style of epic poetry to portray a trivial subject. Mock epics include formal language, supernatural intervention in human affairs, boastful speeches, and elaborate descriptions of weapons and battles to emphasize the subject's insignificance.

In *The Rape of the Lock,* Pope uses elevated language—including **diction** (word choice) and **syntax** (word order)—to shape the reader's perception of how a woman reacts to someone cutting off a lock of her hair. To better understand difficult words and unusual syntax in the poem:

- Use the side notes provided for historical background and unfamiliar words.

- Visualize the action and images.

- Paraphrase sentences with unusual syntax by rearranging words in a more familiar sentence structure.

Here is an example of how you might paraphrase elevated language.

ELEVATED LANGUAGE	PARAPHRASE
"Hither the heroes and the nymphs resort"	The men and young women gather here.

ANNOTATION MODEL

NOTICE & NOTE

As you read, look for juxtapositions, comparisons, and rhymes that Pope makes to achieve a humorous effect. Use paraphrasing to note the meaning of elevated language. This model shows one reader's notes about the excerpt from *The Rape of the Lock.*

Close by those meads, forever crowned with flowers,

Where Thames with pride surveys his rising towers,

There stands a structure of majestic frame,

Which from the neighboring Hampton takes its name.

Here Britain's statesmen oft the fall foredoom

Of foreign tyrants and of nymphs at home;

Here thou, great Anna! whom three realms (obey,)

Dost sometimes counsel take—and sometimes (tea.)

Paraphrase: The majestic Hampton Court stands near the meadows by the Thames River, which are always in bloom.

The elevated diction and the rhyming of "obey" and "tea" create a funny contrast between the serious and the trivial. That dash in the last line is like a pause for comic effect.

© Houghton Mifflin Harcourt Publishing Company

BACKGROUND

Alexander Pope *(1688–1744) is considered one of the best poets and satirists of the early 18th century. He is especially celebrated for his masterful use of the heroic couplet. The Rape of the Lock is based on an actual dispute between two prominent families, the Fermors and the Petres, that resulted when Lord Petre snipped a lock of hair from Arabella Fermor. The feud spiraled out of proportion, and Pope composed the poem in response to a friend's request that he intervene to "laugh them together again."*

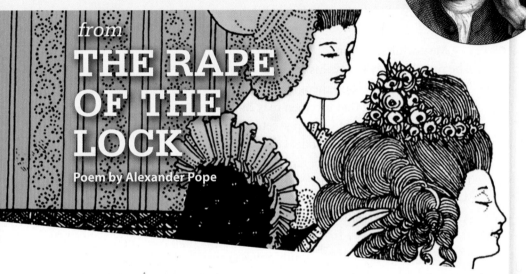

from
THE RAPE OF THE LOCK
Poem by Alexander Pope

SETTING A PURPOSE

As you read, look for ways that Pope makes fun of the aristocracy through his description of this incident, including his use of elevated language and other characteristics of epic poetry.

In the first of the poem's five cantos, a Muse is evoked for inspiration (a tradition in epic poetry) and Belinda is warned of impending danger by Ariel, a spirit sent to protect Belinda. In Canto 2, Belinda rides up the Thames River to a Hampton Court party and is noticed by the scheming Baron, who resolves to possess one of the two curly locks spiraling down Belinda's back.

from CANTO 3

Close by those meads, forever crowned with flowers,
Where Thames with pride surveys his rising towers,
There stands a structure of majestic frame,
Which from the neighboring Hampton takes its name.
5 Here Britain's statesmen oft the fall foredoom
Of foreign tyrants and of nymphs at home;
Here thou, great Anna! whom three realms obey,
Dost sometimes counsel take—and sometimes tea.

Notice & Note

Use the side margins to notice and note signposts in the text.

1 meads: meadows.

2 Thames (tĕmz): a river that flows through southern England.

3–4 structure . . . name: the royal palace of Hampton Court, about 15 miles from London.

6 nymphs (nĭmfs): maidens; young women.

7 Anna . . . obey: Queen Anne, who rules over the three realms of England, Scotland, and Wales.

17 snuff: powdered tobacco that is inhaled.

24 toilet: the process of dressing, fixing one's hair, and otherwise grooming oneself.

27 ombre (ŏm´bər): a popular card game of the day, similar to bridge.

30 King . . . face: the king of diamonds, the only king shown in profile in a deck of cards.

31 refulgent (rĭ-fŏōl´jənt) **Queen:** resplendent or shining queen of diamonds. The Baron is leading his highest diamonds in an effort to win.

34 promiscuous (prə-mĭs´kyōo-əs): confused; **level green:** the green cloth-covered card table.

36 Afric's sable sons: Africa's black soldiers.

41 Knave: jack.

43 the virgin's: Belinda's.

46 Codille (kō-dēl´): a losing hand of cards in ombre.

47 distempered: disordered.

48 nice: delicate; subtle; **trick:** a single round of cards played and won.

Hither the heroes and the nymphs resort,
10 To taste awhile the pleasures of a court;
    In various talk the instructive hours they passed,
    Who gave the ball, or paid the visit last;
    One speaks the glory of the British Queen,
    And one describes a charming Indian screen;
15 A third interprets motions, looks, and eyes;
    At every word a reputation dies.
    Snuff, or the fan, supply each pause of chat,
    With singing, laughing, ogling, and all that.

    Meanwhile declining from the noon of day,
20 The sun obliquely shoots his burning ray;
    The hungry judges soon the sentence sign,
    And wretches hang that jurymen may dine;
    The merchant from the Exchange returns in peace,
    And the long labors of the toilet cease.
25 Belinda now, whom thirst of fame invites,
    Burns to encounter two adventurous knights,
    At ombre singly to decide their doom,
    And swells her breast with conquests yet to come. . . .

    The Baron now his Diamonds pours apace;
30 The embroidered King who shows but half his face,
    And his refulgent Queen, with powers combined,
    Of broken troops an easy conquest find.
    Clubs, Diamonds, Hearts, in wild disorder seen,
    With throngs promiscuous strew the level green.
35 Thus when dispersed a routed army runs,
    Of Asia's troops, and Afric's sable sons,
    With like confusion different nations fly,
    Of various habit, and of various dye,
    The pierced battalions disunited fall
40 In heaps on heaps; one fate o'erwhelms them all.

    The Knave of Diamonds tries his wily arts,
    And wins (oh, shameful chance!) the Queen of Hearts.
    At this, the blood the virgin's cheek forsook,
    A livid paleness spreads o'er all her look;
45 She sees, and trembles at the approaching ill,
    Just in the jaws of ruin, and Codille.
    And now (as oft in some distempered state)
    On one nice trick depends the general fate.
    An Ace of Hearts steps forth: The King unseen
50 Lurked in her hand, and mourned his captive Queen.
    He springs to vengeance with an eager pace,

And falls like thunder on the prostrate Ace.
The nymph exulting fills with shouts the sky,
The walls, the woods, and long canals reply.

55   O thoughtless mortals! ever blind to fate,
Too soon dejected, and too soon elate:
Sudden these honors shall be snatched away,
And cursed forever this victorious day.

     For lo! the board with cups and spoons is crowned,
60 The berries crackle, and the mill turns round;
On shining altars of Japan they raise
The silver lamp; the fiery spirits blaze:
From silver spouts the grateful liquors glide,
While China's earth receives the smoking tide.
65 At once they gratify their scent and taste,
And frequent cups prolong the rich repast.
Straight hover round the fair her airy band;
Some, as she sipped, the fuming liquor fanned,
Some o'er her lap their careful plumes displayed,
70 Trembling, and conscious of the rich brocade.
Coffee (which makes the politician wise,
And see through all things with his half-shut eyes)
Sent up in vapors to the Baron's brain
New stratagems, the radiant Lock to gain.
75 Ah, cease, rash youth! desist ere 'tis too late,
Fear the just Gods, and think of Scylla's fate!
Changed to a bird, and sent to flit in air,
She dearly pays for Nisus' injured hair!

     But when to mischief mortals bend their will,
80 How soon they find fit instruments of ill!
Just then, Clarissa drew with tempting grace
A two-edged weapon from her shining case:
So ladies in romance assist their knight,
Present the spear, and arm him for the fight.
85 He takes the gift with reverence, and extends
The little engine on his fingers' ends;
This just behind Belinda's neck he spread,
As o'er the fragrant steams she bends her head.
Swift to the Lock a thousand sprights repair,
90 A thousand wings, by turns, blow back the hair,
And thrice they twitched the diamond in her ear,
Thrice she looked back, and thrice the foe drew near.
Just in that instant, anxious Ariel sought
The close recesses of the virgin's thought;

© Houghton Mifflin Harcourt Publishing Company

ANALYZE MOCK EPIC

Annotate: In lines 59–70, mark and label two different examples of the characteristics of a mock epic.

Interpret: What actions, real and imaginary, is Pope describing?

61 shining altars of Japan: small lacquered tables. In mock-epic style, Pope elevates the tables to altars.

64 China's earth . . . tide: China cups receive the hot coffee.

66 repast (rĭ-păst´): meal.

67 the fair: Belinda; **her airy band:** the Sylphs (sĭlfs), supernatural creatures attending Belinda. Epic heroes and heroines are generally aided by higher powers.

74 new stratagems (străt´ə-jəmz) **. . . gain:** new schemes for acquiring a lock of Belinda's hair.

76–78 Scylla's (sĭl´əz) **fate . . . Nisus'** (nī´səs) **injured hair:** In ancient Greek legend, Scylla was turned into a bird because she betrayed her father, King Nisus, by giving his enemy the purple lock of his hair on which his safety depended.

89 sprights (sprīts): the Sylphs.

93 Ariel (âr´ē-əl): Belinda's special guardian among the Sylphs.

95 **nosegay:** a small bouquet of flowers.

95 As on the nosegay in her breast reclined,
    He watched the ideas rising in her mind,
    Sudden he viewed, in spite of all her art,
    An earthly lover lurking at her heart.
    Amazed, confused, he found his power expired,
100 Resigned to fate, and with a sigh retired.

101 **the Peer:** the Baron;
forfex: a fancy term for scissors.

        The Peer now spreads the glittering forfex wide,
    To enclose the Lock; now joins it, to divide.
    Even then, before the fatal engine closed,
    A wretched Sylph too fondly interposed;
105 Fate urged the shears, and cut the Sylph in twain
    (But airy substance soon unites again):
    The meeting points the sacred hair dissever
    From the fair head, forever and forever!

ANALYZE SATIRE

Annotate: In lines 109–114, mark phrases that exaggerate Belinda's reaction to having her lock cut.

Analyze: What human folly or flaw is highlighted by this exaggeration?

        Then flashed the living lightning from her eyes,
110 And screams of horror rend the affrighted skies.
    Not louder shrieks to pitying heaven are cast,
    When husbands, or when lapdogs breathe their last;
    Or when rich china vessels fallen from high,
    In glittering dust and painted fragments lie!

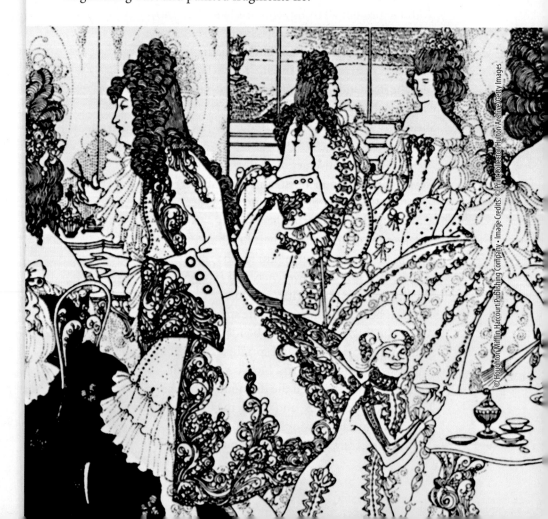

115 "Let wreaths of triumph now my temples twine,"
The victor cried, "the glorious prize is mine!
While fish in streams, or birds delight in air,
Or in a coach and six the British fair,
As long as *Atalantis* shall be read,
120 Or the small pillow grace a lady's bed,
While visits shall be paid on solemn days,
When numerous wax-lights in bright order blaze,
While nymphs take treats, or assignations give,
So long my honor, name, and praise shall live!

125   "What time would spare, from steel receives its date,
And monuments, like men, submit to fate!
Steel could the labor of the Gods destroy,
And strike to dust the imperial towers of Troy;
Steel could the works of mortal pride confound,
130 And hew triumphal arches to the ground.
What wonder then, fair nymph! thy hairs should feel,
The conquering force of unresisted steel?"

In Canto 4, following an epic tradition, a melancholy sprite descends to the Underworld—which Pope calls the "Cave of Spleen"—and returns to the party with a vial of grief and "flowing tears" and a bag of "sobs, sighs, and passions," which are emptied over Belinda's head, fanning her fury even further.

from CANTO 5

"To arms, to arms!" the fierce virago cries,
And swift as lightning to the combat flies.
135 All side in parties, and begin the attack;
Fans clap, silks rustle, and tough whalebones crack;
Heroes' and heroines' shouts confusedly rise,
And bass and treble voices strike the skies.
No common weapons in their hands are found,
140 Like Gods they fight, nor dread a mortal wound. . . .

See, fierce Belinda on the Baron flies,
With more than usual lightning in her eyes;
Nor feared the chief the unequal fight to try,
Who sought no more than on his foe to die.

145   But this bold lord with manly strength endued,
She with one finger and a thumb subdued:
Just where the breath of life his nostrils drew,
A charge of snuff the wily virgin threw;

115 wreaths . . . twine: In epics, victors or champions traditionally wore laurel wreaths as a kind of crown.

118 coach and six: a coach drawn by six horses.

119 *Atalantis*: *The New Atalantis* by Delarivier Manley, a thinly disguised account of scandal among the rich.

ANALYZE SATIRE
Annotate: In lines 117–124, mark the activities of the aristocracy that are mentioned.

Analyze: What do these details suggest about the aristocracy?

125 date: end.

127–128 the labor of the Gods . . . towers of Troy: Troy, an ancient city famous for its towers, whose walls were said to have been built by the Greek gods Apollo and Poseidon.

133 virago (və-rä´gō): a woman who engages in warfare or other fighting. She has come to Belinda's aid at Ariel's request.

136 whalebones: elastic material from whales' mouths, used in corsets or support undergarments.

145 endued (ĕn-dŏŏd´): endowed; provided with.

149 Gnomes (nōmz): supernatural creatures bent on causing mischief.

152 And the high . . . nose: In other words, he sneezes.

154 bodkin (bŏd´kĭn): a long, ornamental hairpin.

157 seal rings: signet rings bearing a person's family crest or initials.

159 Her infant grandame's (grăn´dāmz) **. . . grew:** It was next melted down and turned into a whistle used by Belinda's grandmother as a child. Pope is here making fun of family heirlooms.

168 burn in Cupid's flames: burn with passion.

170 rebound: echo.

171–172 Othello . . . pain: In Shakespeare's *Othello*, the deeply jealous Othello demands the handkerchief that he believes is a sign of his wife's infidelity.

179 mounted to the lunar sphere: climbed up to the moon.

182 beaux' (bōz): the wits of fops.

184 riband (rĭb´ənd): ribbon.

185 Muse (myōōz): the goddess who inspires the writing of the poem. In typical epic fashion, the narrator opens the poem by addressing his Muse and continues to address her throughout the poem.

188 trail of hair: The word *comet* comes from a Greek word that means "long haired."

The Gnomes direct, to every atom just,
150 The pungent grains of titillating dust.
Sudden, with starting tears each eye o'erflows,
And the high dome re-echoes to his nose.

"Now meet thy fate," incensed Belinda cried,
And drew a deadly bodkin from her side.
155 (The same, his ancient personage to deck,
Her great-great-grandsire wore about his neck,
In three seal rings; which after, melted down,
Formed a vast buckle for his widow's gown:
Her infant grandame's whistle next it grew,
160 The bells she jingled, and the whistle blew;
Then in a bodkin graced her mother's hairs,
Which long she wore, and now Belinda wears.)

"Boast not my fall," he cried, "insulting foe!
Thou by some other shalt be laid as low.
165 Nor think to die dejects my lofty mind:
All that I dread is leaving you behind!
Rather than so, ah, let me still survive,
And burn in Cupid's flames—but burn alive."

"Restore the Lock!" she cries; and all around
170 "Restore the Lock!" the vaulted roofs rebound.
Not fierce Othello in so loud a strain
Roared for the handkerchief that caused his pain.
But see how oft ambitious aims are crossed,
And chiefs contend till all the prize is lost!
175 The lock, obtained with guilt, and kept with pain,
In every place is sought, but sought in vain:
With such a prize no mortal must be blessed,
So Heaven decrees! with Heaven who can contest?

Some thought it mounted to the lunar sphere,
180 Since all things lost on earth are treasured there.
There heroes' wits are kept in ponderous vases,
And beaux' in snuffboxes and tweezer cases.
There broken vows and death-bed alms are found,
And lovers' hearts with ends of riband bound. . . .

185 But trust the Muse—she saw it upward rise,
Though marked by none but quick, poetic eyes. . . .
A sudden star, it shot through liquid air,
And drew behind a radiant trail of hair. . . .

Then cease, bright nymph! to mourn thy ravished hair,
190 Which adds new glory to the shining sphere!
 Not all the tresses that fair head can boast
 Shall draw such envy as the Lock you lost.
 For, after all the murders of your eye,
 When, after millions slain, yourself shall die:
195 When those fair suns shall set, as set they must,
 And all those tresses shall be laid in dust,
 This Lock the Muse shall consecrate to fame,
 And 'midst the stars inscribe Belinda's name.

193 murders of your eye: men struck down by your glance.

ANALYZE MOCK EPIC
Annotate: Mark the supernatural intervention in lines 185–198 that resolves the conflict.

Paraphrase: What does this mock epic element suggest about the power of Pope's satire?

CHECK YOUR UNDERSTANDING

Answer these questions before moving on to the **Analyze the Text** section on the following page.

1 In Canto 3, which two common activities of the aristocracy does Pope describe?

A Watching a mock battle and drinking coffee

B Playing cards and drinking coffee

C Dueling and decorating parlors

D Playing cards and reciting epic poetry

2 Reread lines 71–74: *Coffee . . . Sent up in vapors to the Baron's brain / New stratagems, the radiant Lock to gain.* Which sentence best paraphrases this statement?

F Drinking coffee has made the Baron want to steal the lock of hair.

G The coffee gave the Baron new ideas about how to steal the lock of hair.

H The smell of the coffee made the lock of hair seem more attractive.

J The lock of hair looked more radiant because of the steam of the coffee.

3 What happens to the lock of hair at the end of the poem?

A The lock becomes lost and then turns into a star.

B Belinda screams at the Baron until he is forced to return it.

C It becomes lost and goes to the moon with the other lost things.

D When Belinda dies, it turns to dust.

© Houghton Mifflin Harcourt Publishing Company

ANALYZE THE TEXT

Support your responses with evidence from the text. 📓 NOTEBOOK

1. **Interpret** Poets often use heroic couplets to express complete thoughts in a witty and concise way. What flaws or problems in British society does Pope satirize in the following heroic couplets?
   • lines 11–12 ("In various talk . . . the visit last;")
   • lines 15–16 ("A third interprets . . . reputation dies.")
   • lines 21–22 ("The hungry judges . . . jurymen may dine.")

2. **Draw Conclusions** What motivates the Baron to cut Belinda's lock?

3. **Interpret** In lines 115–132, the Baron boasts about his conquest. What flaw does Pope satirize through exaggeration in the speech? Explain.

4. **Analyze** Reread lines 133–152. How does Pope use this mock epic battle to emphasize the foolishness of the quarrel?

5. **Evaluate** Does the poem's ending provide an effective conclusion to Pope's Horatian satire, or is it too scornful of Belinda? Discuss Pope's use of diction and syntax in your response.

RESEARCH

© Houghton Mifflin Harcourt Publishing Company

Pope includes a lot of details about 18th century aristocratic culture in *The Rape of the Lock*. With a partner, do research to learn more about fashions and trends in Britain at the time Pope wrote the poem.

QUESTION	ANSWER
What women's hairstyles were fashionable in the early18th century?	
How did aristocratic men and women dress?	
What types of entertainment were popular?	

Extend With a partner, discuss what 18th century fashions and entertainment suggest about the gender roles of men and women in aristocratic society. Consider how these attitudes about gender are reflected in *The Rape of the Lock*.

RESEARCH TIP

When reading a source on a very unfamiliar subject, use hyperlinks provided in the text for background information that will help you make sense of it. Keep the source you are reading open, and open the new one in a separate tab or window. You can do this by hovering your cursor over the link and right clicking or pressing *ctrl+click* to open a context menu and selecting "Open in new tab" or "Open in new window."

CREATE AND DISCUSS

Write a Rhymed Satirical Poem Think of a behavior common in our culture that you disapprove of. Write a short rhymed poem satirizing that behavior.

❏ Before you start composing, generate ideas through a short free write.

❏ Invent an imaginary incident as an example.

❏ Create humor through the use of elevated language, rhyme, and juxtaposition.

Discuss a Poem Alexander Pope's poem *The Rape of the Lock* makes fun of a young woman for being very upset that a man cut off a lock of her hair as a joke. With your group, talk about whether you think the woman's anger is justified.

❏ Listen as other students explain their ideas, and consider everyone's point of view.

❏ When you disagree with someone, calmly explain why you disagree.

❏ Think of questions you can ask your group to further explore this issue.

Go to **Writing as a Process** in the **Writing Studio** for help.

Go to **Participating in Collaborative Discussions** in the **Speaking and Listening Studio** to find out more about how to respond constructively to other people's ideas.

RESPOND TO THE ESSENTIAL QUESTION

 How can satire change people's behavior?

Gather Information Review your annotations and notes on *The Rape of the Lock*. Then, add relevant information to your Response Log. As you determine which information to include, think about:

• how the use of humor affects the audience
• whether serious matters can be addressed through humor
• how the people being made fun of might respond to satire

ACADEMIC VOCABULARY

As you write and discuss what you learned from *The Rape of the Lock*, be sure to use the Academic Vocabulary words. Check off each of the words that you use.

❏ **encounter**
❏ **exploit**
❏ **persist**
❏ **subordinate**
❏ **widespread**

A MODEST PROPOSAL

Satire by **Jonathan Swift**

? *ESSENTIAL QUESTION:*

How can satire change people's behavior?

QUICK START

Poverty is a problem that affects all societies. What proposals for fighting poverty have you heard about? List a few ideas in your notebook, ranking them in order of their likelihood of success. Discuss your list with a partner.

ANALYZE SATIRICAL DEVICES

Swift's essay is an example of Juvenalian satire, which uses a scornful tone and dark humor to criticize problems such as corruption or incompetence. Swift relies on a variety of rhetorical devices to develop his satire. As you read, use a chart like this one to identify examples of these devices in the essay.

DEVICE	EXAMPLE
Verbal irony occurs when a writer says the opposite of what is meant.	*The title is ironic because the actual proposal is outrageous, not modest.*
Understatement occurs when a writer says less than is expected or appropriate.	
Exaggeration (also called **overstatement** or **hyperbole**) occurs when a writer exaggerates the truth for emphasis or humorous effect.	
Contradiction occurs when a writer expresses two ideas that are in opposition to one another.	
Paradox is a statement that seems contradictory or absurd but actually reveals some element of truth.	

GENRE ELEMENTS: SATIRE

- ridicules customs, behaviors, or institutions
- purpose is to improve society
- can be gently humorous (Horatian) or scornful (Juvenalian)
- uses satirical devices, like irony and exaggeration

UNDERSTAND AUTHOR'S PURPOSE

Swift wrote *A Modest Proposal* in the form of an argument for a public policy. The unnamed narrator who makes this argument bears some resemblance to Swift: both men have previously tried to promote ideas to help Ireland's poor. Despite this ambiguity, Swift's purpose clearly isn't to persuade people to accept the narrator's claim. Instead, he uses the structure of an argument to attack British policies and the callousness of wealthy people in Ireland and England. As you read *A Modest Proposal*, consider whether Swift's satirical argument is an effective way to achieve his intended purpose.

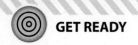

CRITICAL VOCABULARY

sustenance	rudiment	scrupulous	inducement
prodigious	collateral	encumbrance	

To see how many Critical Vocabulary words you already know, use them to complete the sentences.

1. Although some governing rulers are _____ and decent, others are less so.

2. Irony, overstatement, paradox, and other devices are the _____ of satire.

3. During famine, having a large family would be a(n) _____.

4. There were a(n) _____ number of starving children in Ireland.

5. According to Swift, earning good market prices for their children would be a(n) _____ for mothers to have more of them.

6. During a famine, higher food prices are a(n) _____ effect.

7. The narrator of *A Modest Proposal* suggests that one-year-old children would provide the most satisfying _____ for those with enough money to afford the treat.

LANGUAGE CONVENTIONS

In this lesson, you will learn how to differentiate between passive and active voice. In the active voice, the subject performs the action; while in the passive voice, the subject is the receiver of the action.

Active Voice: *Poor families in Ireland starved because of the ruling classes' laws.*
Passive Voice: *Unfair laws were voted on by the ruling classes.*

As you read *A Modest Proposal*, note places where the author chooses to use active or passive voice, and how it affects the meaning of what he's saying.

ANNOTATION MODEL

NOTICE & NOTE

As you read, note how the narrator uses satirical devices like contradiction and overstatement. In the model, you can see one reader's notes for *A Modest Proposal*.

I think it is agreed by all parties that this <u>prodigious number of children</u> in the arms, or on the backs, or at the heels of their mothers, and frequently of their fathers, is in the present deplorable state of the kingdom a <u>very great additional grievance</u>; and therefore whoever could find out a fair, cheap, and easy method of making these children sound, <u>useful members of the commonwealth</u> would deserve so well of the public as to have <u>his statue set up for a preserver of the nation</u>.

The narrator refers to children as a "grievance," contradicting his earlier sympathetic statements.

The sentence about the statue being erected is a humorous exaggeration.

BACKGROUND

In the 1720s Catholics in Ireland suffered from the repressive rule of England, which stripped them of their rights and plunged many into poverty. Their misery increased with a series of crop failures that forced people to beg or face starvation. After his 1713 appointment as dean of St. Patrick's Cathedral in Dublin, Ireland, Jonathan Swift wrote a series of publications attacking England's unjust policies. A Modest Proposal, *his last major work about Ireland, is one of the greatest satires ever written. For Irish Catholics and many Protestants, Swift became a national hero.*

A MODEST PROPOSAL

Satire by Jonathan Swift

Jonathan Swift *(1667–1745) was born of Anglo-Irish parents in Dublin. His father died two months shy of his birth, leaving the family dependent on Swift's uncles for support. After graduating from Trinity College, Swift moved to England. He became ordained as an Anglican priest and started to write satires.*

Swift's first two satires, The Battle of the Books *and* A Tale of the Tub, *quickly established his acerbic style. Whether lampooning modern thinkers and scientists, religious abuses, or humanity in general, Swift raged at the arrogance, phoniness, and shallowness he saw infecting the intellectual and moral life of the time. Though most of his publications were anonymous, people began to recognize his witty and often harsh political writing through his contributions to London periodicals.*

Although, at first, Swift felt exiled when he returned to Ireland to become dean of St. Patrick's Cathedral, he soon regained his interest in politics and in satirical writing. His most famous work is Gulliver's Travels. *This satire is now usually appreciated as a fantasy story, but Swift's main purpose in writing it was to satirize British institutions and human follies. After his death, he was buried in St. Patrick's. Swift wrote his own epitaph for his memorial tablet, saying that he lies "where savage indignation can no longer tear his heart."*

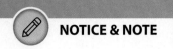

Notice & Note

Use the side margins to notice
and note signposts in the text.

LANGUAGE CONVENTIONS

Annotate: Mark an example
of passive voice in the second
sentence.

Analyze: Why might Swift have
chosen to use passive voice
here?

sustenance
(sŭs´tə-nəns) *n.* something,
especially food, that sustains
life or health.

prodigious
(prə-dĭj´əs) *adj.* enormous.

**UNDERSTAND AUTHOR'S
PURPOSE**

Annotate: In paragraph 4, mark
the sentence where the narrator
compares mothers and their
children to farm animals.

Analyze: How does this
comparison serve the author's
purpose?

SETTING A PURPOSE

*As you read, make note of the elements and devices of satire and think
about how readers might have responded to this essay at the time it was
first published.*

1   It is a melancholy object to those who walk through this great
    town[1] or travel in the country, when they see the streets, the roads,
    and cabin doors, crowded with beggars of the female sex, followed
    by three, four, or six children, all in rags and importuning[2] every
    passenger for an alms. These mothers, instead of being able to work
    for their honest livelihood, are forced to employ all their time in
    strolling to beg **sustenance** for their helpless infants, who, as they
    grow up, either turn thieves for want[3] of work, or leave their dear
    native country to fight for the Pretender[4] in Spain, or sell themselves
    to the Barbadoes.[5]

2   I think it is agreed by all parties that this **prodigious** number
    of children in the arms, or on the backs, or at the heels of their
    mothers, and frequently of their fathers, is in the present deplorable
    state of the kingdom a very great additional grievance; and therefore
    whoever could find out a fair, cheap, and easy method of making
    these children sound, useful members of the commonwealth
    would deserve so well of the public as to have his statue set up for a
    preserver of the nation.

3   But my intention is very far from being confined to provide only
    for the children of professed beggars; it is of a much greater extent,
    and shall take in the whole number of infants at a certain age who are
    born of parents in effect as little able to support them as those who
    demand our charity in the streets.

4   As to my own part, having turned my thoughts for many years
    upon this important subject, and maturely weighed the several
    schemes of other projectors,[6] I have always found them grossly
    mistaken in their computation. It is true, a child just dropped from its

---

[1] **this great town:** Dublin, Ireland.

[2] **importuning** (ĭm-pôr-tōon´ĭng) . . . **alms** (ämz): begging from every passerby for a
charitable handout.

[3] **want:** lack; need.

[4] **Pretender:** James Edward Stuart, who claimed the English throne, from which his
now deceased father, James II, had been removed in 1688. Because James II and his
son were Catholic, the common people of Ireland were loyal to them.

[5] **sell . . . Barbadoes:** To escape poverty, some Irish migrated to the West Indies,
obtaining money for their passage by agreeing to work as slaves on plantations
there for a set period.

[6] **projectors:** persons who propose public projects or plans.

dam[7] may be supported by her milk for a solar year, with little other nourishment; at most not above the value of two shillings, which the mother may certainly get, or the value in scraps, by her lawful occupation of begging; and it is exactly at one year old that I propose to provide for them in such a manner as instead of being a charge upon their parents or the parish, or wanting food and raiment for the rest of their lives, they shall on the contrary contribute to the feeding, and partly to the clothing, of many thousands.

5   There is likewise another great advantage in my scheme, that it will prevent those voluntary abortions, and that horrid practice of women murdering their bastard children, alas, too frequent among us, sacrificing the poor innocent babes, I doubt,[8] more to avoid the expense than the shame, which would move tears and pity in the most savage and inhuman breast.

6   The number of souls in this kingdom being usually reckoned one million and a half, of these I calculate there may be about two hundred thousand couples whose wives are breeders; from which number I subtract thirty thousand couples who are able to maintain their own children, although I apprehend there cannot be so many under the present distresses of the kingdom; but this being granted, there will remain an hundred and seventy thousand breeders. I again subtract fifty thousand for those women who miscarry, or whose children die by accident or disease within the year. There only remain an hundred and twenty thousand children of poor parents annually born. The question therefore is, how this number shall be reared and provided for, which, as I have already said, under the present situation of affairs, is utterly impossible by all the methods hitherto proposed. For we can neither employ them in handicraft or agriculture; we neither build houses (I mean in the country) nor cultivate land. They can very seldom pick up a livelihood by stealing till they arrive at six years old, except where they are of towardly parts;[9] although I confess they learn the **rudiments** much earlier, during which time they can however be looked upon only as probationers, as I have been informed by a principal gentleman in the county of Cavan, who protested to me that he never knew above one or two instances under the age of six, even in a part of the kingdom so renowned for the quickest proficiency in that art.

UNDERSTAND AUTHOR'S PURPOSE

Annotate: In paragraph 6, mark each number from the narrator's calculations.

Infer: Why would Swift include these calculations in his essay?

rudiment:
(rōō′də-mənt) *n.* fundamental element, principle, or skill.

---

[7] **dam** (dăm): female parent. The term is used mostly for farm animals.
[8] **doubt:** suspect.
[9] **are of towardly** (tôrd′lē) **parts:** have a promising talent.

© Houghton Mifflin Harcourt Publishing Company

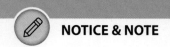

7 I am assured by our merchants that a boy or girl before twelve years old is no salable commodity; and even when they come to this age they will not yield above three pounds, or three pounds and half a crown at most on the Exchange; which cannot turn to account[10] either to the parents or the kingdom, the charge of nutriment and rags having been at least four times that value.

8 I shall now therefore humbly propose my own thoughts, which I hope will not be liable to the least objection.

9 I have been assured by a very knowing American of my acquaintance in London, that a young healthy child well nursed is at a year old a most delicious, nourishing, and wholesome food, whether stewed, roasted, baked, or boiled; and I make no doubt that it will equally serve in a fricassee[11] or a ragout.

UNDERSTAND AUTHOR'S PURPOSE

Annotate: In paragraph 10, mark words and phrases normally used to describe the preparation of meat.

Draw Conclusions: What effects do you think Swift wanted to have on readers by including these details?

10 I do therefore humbly offer it to public consideration that of the hundred and twenty thousand children, already computed, twenty thousand may be reserved for breed,[12] whereof only one fourth part to be males, which is more than we allow to sheep, black cattle, or swine; and my reason is that these children are seldom the fruits of marriage, a circumstance not much regarded by our savages, therefore one male will be sufficient to serve four females. That the remaining hundred thousand may at a year old be offered in sale to the persons of quality and fortune through the kingdom, always advising the mother to let them suck plentifully in the last month, so as to render them plump and fat for a good table. A child will make two dishes at an entertainment for friends; and when the family dines alone, the fore or hind quarter will make a reasonable dish, and seasoned with a little pepper or salt will be very good boiled on the fourth day, especially in winter.

11 I have reckoned upon a medium that a child just born will weigh twelve pounds, and in a solar year if tolerably nursed increaseth to twenty-eight pounds.

12 I grant this food will be somewhat dear, and therefore very proper for landlords, who, as they have already devoured most of the parents, seem to have the best title to the children.

13 Infant's flesh will be in season throughout the year, but more plentiful in March, and a little before and after. For we are told by a grave author, an eminent French physician,[13] that fish being a prolific[14] diet, there are more children born in Roman Catholic countries about nine months after Lent[15] than at any other season;

---

[10]**turn to account:** earn a profit; benefit; prove useful.

[11]**fricassee** (frĭk-ə-sē´) . . . **ragout** (ră-gōō´): types of meat stews.

[12]**reserved for breed:** kept for breeding (instead of being slaughtered).

[13]**grave . . . physician:** François Rabelais (răb´ə-lā) a 16th-century French satirist.

[14]**prolific:** promoting fertility.

[15]**Lent:** Catholics traditionally do not eat meat during Lent, the 40 days leading up to Easter, but instead eat a lot of fish.

therefore, reckoning a year after Lent, the markets will be more glutted than usual, because the number of popish infants is at least three to one in this kingdom; and therefore it will have one other **collateral** advantage, by lessening the number of Papists[16] among us.

14   I have already computed the charge of nursing a beggar's child (in which list I reckon all cottagers, laborers, and four fifths of the farmers), to be about two shillings per annum, rags included; and I believe no gentleman would repine to give ten shillings for the carcass of a good fat child, which, as I have said, will make four dishes of excellent nutritive meat, when he hath only some particular friend or his own family to dine with him. Thus the squire will learn to be a good landlord, and grow popular among the tenants; the mother will have eight shillings net profit, and be fit for work till she produces another child.

15   Those who are more thrifty (as I must confess the times require) may flay the carcass; the skin of which artificially dressed will make admirable gloves for ladies, and summer boots for fine gentlemen.

16   As to our city of Dublin, shambles[17] may be appointed for this purpose in the most convenient parts of it, and butchers we may be assured will not be wanting; although I rather recommend buying the children alive, and dressing them hot from the knife as we do roasting pigs.

17   A very worthy person, a true lover of his country, and whose virtues I highly esteem, was lately pleased in discoursing on this matter to offer a refinement upon my scheme. He said that many gentlemen of this kingdom, having of late destroyed their deer, he conceived that the want of venison might be well supplied by the bodies of young lads and maidens, not exceeding fourteen years of age nor under twelve, so great a number of both sexes in every county being now ready to starve for want of work and service; and these to be disposed of by their parents, if alive, or otherwise by their nearest relations. But with due deference to so excellent a friend and so deserving a patriot, I cannot be altogether in his sentiments; for as to the males, my American acquaintance assured me from frequent experience that their flesh was generally tough and lean, like that of our schoolboys, by continual exercise, and their taste disagreeable; and to fatten them would not answer the charge. Then as to the females, it would, I think with humble submission, be a loss to the public, because they soon would become breeders themselves; and

---

[16] **popish** (pō′pĭsh) . . . **Papists:** hostile or contemptuous terms referring to Roman Catholics.
[17] **shambles:** slaughterhouses.

collateral
(kə-lăt′ər-əl) *adj.* concomitant or accompanying.

ANALYZE SATIRICAL DEVICES
Annotate: In paragraph 17, mark the words and phrases the narrator uses to describe the man who suggested a change to the proposal.

Identify: What satirical device is Swift using in these descriptions?

besides, it is not improbable that some **scrupulous** people might be apt to censure such a practice (although indeed very unjustly) as a little bordering upon cruelty; which, I confess, hath always been with me the strongest objection against any project, how well soever intended.

18   But in order to justify my friend, he confessed that this expedient was put into his head by the famous Psalmanazar, a native of the island Formosa,[18] who came from thence to London above twenty years ago, and in conversation told my friend that in his country when any young person happened to be put to death, the executioner sold the carcass to persons of quality as a prime dainty; and that in his time the body of a plump girl of fifteen, who was crucified for an attempt to poison the emperor, was sold to his Imperial Majesty's prime minister of state, and other great mandarins of the court, in joints from the gibbet,[19] at four hundred crowns. Neither indeed can I deny that if the same use were made of several plump young girls in this town, who without one single groat[20] to their fortunes cannot stir abroad without a chair,[21] and appear at the playhouse and assemblies in foreign fineries which they never will pay for, the kingdom would not be the worse.

19   Some persons of a desponding spirit are in great concern about that vast number of poor people who are aged, diseased, or maimed, and I have been desired to employ my thoughts what course may be taken to ease the nation of so grievous an **encumbrance**. But I am not in the least pain upon that matter, because it is very well known that they are every day dying and rotting by cold and famine, and filth and vermin, as fast as can be reasonably expected. And as to the younger laborers, they are now in almost as hopeful a condition. They cannot get work, and consequently pine away for want of nourishment to a degree that if at any time they are accidentally hired to common labor, they have not strength to perform it; and thus the country and themselves are happily delivered from the evils to come.

20   I have too long digressed, and therefore shall return to my subject. I think the advantages by the proposal which I have made are obvious and many, as well as of the highest importance.

21   For first, as I have already observed, it would greatly lessen the number of Papists, with whom we are yearly overrun, being the principal breeders of the nation as well as our most dangerous enemies; and who stay at home on purpose to deliver the kingdom

© Houghton Mifflin Harcourt Publishing Company

---

[18]**Psalmanazar** (săl′mə-nā′zər) . . . **Formosa** (fôr-mō′sə): a French imposter in London who called himself George Psalmanazar and pretended to be from Formosa (now Taiwan), where, he said, cannibalism was practiced.

[19]**gibbet** (jĭb′ĭt): gallows.

[20]**groat:** an old British coin worth four pennies.

[21]**cannot stir . . . chair:** cannot go outside without using an enclosed chair carried on poles by two men.

scrupulous
(skrōō′pyə-ləs) *adj.* conscientious and exact; having scruples.

encumbrance
(ĕn-kŭm′brəns) *n.* a burden or impediment.

ANALYZE SATIRICAL DEVICES

Annotate: In paragraph 19, mark the example of verbal irony.

Infer: What is ironic about the narrator saying that he is not pained about the fact that so many people are dying?

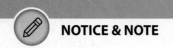
to the Pretender, hoping to take their advantage by the absence of so many good Protestants, who have chosen rather to leave their country than stay at home and pay tithes against their conscience to an Episcopal curate.[22]

22   Secondly, the poorer tenants will have something valuable of their own, which by law may be made liable to distress,[23] and help to pay their landlord's rent, their corn and cattle being already seized and money a thing unknown.

23   Thirdly, whereas the maintenance of an hundred thousand children, from two years old and upwards, cannot be computed at less than ten shillings a piece per annum, the nation's stock will be thereby increased fifty thousand pounds per annum, besides the profit of a new dish introduced to the tables of all gentlemen of fortune in the kingdom who have any refinement in taste. And the money will circulate among ourselves, the goods being entirely of our own growth and manufacture.

24   Fourthly, the constant breeders, besides the gain of eight shillings sterling per annum by the sale of their children, will be rid of the charge of maintaining them after the first year.

25   Fifthly, this food would likewise bring great custom to taverns, where the vintners will certainly be so prudent as to procure the best receipts[24] for dressing it to perfection, and consequently have their houses frequented by all the fine gentlemen, who justly value themselves upon their knowledge in good eating; and a skillful cook, who understands how to oblige his guests, will contrive to make it as expensive as they please.

26   Sixthly, this would be a great **inducement** to marriage, which all wise nations have either encouraged by rewards or enforced by laws and penalties. It would increase the care and tenderness of mothers toward their children, when they were sure of a settlement for life to the poor babes, provided in some sort by the public, to their annual profit instead of expense. We should see an honest emulation among the married women, which of them could bring the fattest child to the market. Men would become as fond of their wives during the time of their pregnancy as they are now of their mares in foal, their cows in calf, or sows when they are ready to farrow; nor offer to beat or kick them (as is too frequent a practice) for fear of a miscarriage.

27   Many other advantages might be enumerated. For instance, the addition of some thousand carcasses in our exportation of barreled beef, the propagation of swine's flesh, and improvement in the art

---

[22]**Protestants . . . curate** (kyŏŏr´ĭt): Swift is criticizing absentee Anglo-Irish landowners who lived—and spent their income from their property—in England.
[23]**distress:** seizure of a person's property for the payment of debts.
[24]**receipts:** recipes.

CONTRASTS AND CONTRADICTIONS

Notice & Note: Mark phrases in paragraph 25 that describe how the narrator expects people to take advantage of his proposal.

Analyze: How do these details contradict your sense of the way any normal person would react to such a practice?

inducement
(ĭn-dōōs´mənt, -dyōōs´-) *n.* an incentive.

of making good bacon, so much wanted among us by the great destruction of pigs, too frequent at our tables, which are no way comparable in taste or magnificence to a well-grown, fat, yearling child, which roasted whole will make a considerable figure at a lord mayor's feast or any other public entertainment. But this and many others I omit, being studious of brevity.

28 Supposing that one thousand families in this city would be constant customers for infants' flesh, besides others who might have it at merry meetings, particularly weddings and christenings, I compute that Dublin would take off annually about twenty thousand carcasses, and the rest of the kingdom (where probably they will be sold somewhat cheaper) the remaining eighty thousand.

29 I can think of no one objection that will possibly be raised against this proposal, unless it should be urged that the number of people will be thereby much lessened in the kingdom. This I freely own, and it was indeed one principal design in offering it to the world. I desire the reader will observe, that I calculate my remedy for this one individual kingdom of Ireland and for no other that ever was, is, or I think ever can be upon earth. Therefore let no man talk to me of other expedients: *of taxing our absentees at five shillings a pound: of using neither clothes nor household furniture except what is of our own growth and manufacture: of utterly rejecting the materials and instruments that promote foreign luxury: of curing the expensiveness of pride, vanity, idleness, and gaming in our women: of introducing a vein of parsimony,[25] prudence, and temperance: of learning to love our country, in the want of which we differ even from Laplanders and the inhabitants of Topinamboo:[26] of quitting our animosities and factions, nor acting any longer like the Jews, who were murdering one another at the very moment their city was taken:[27] of being a little cautious not to sell our country and conscience for nothing: of teaching landlords to have at least one degree of mercy toward their tenants: lastly, of putting a spirit of honesty, industry, and skill into our shopkeepers; who, if a resolution could now be taken to buy only our native goods, would immediately unite to cheat and exact upon us in the price, the measure, and the goodness, nor could ever yet be brought to make one fair proposal of just dealing, though often and earnestly invited to it.*

---

[25] **parsimony** (pär´sə-mō-nē): frugality; thrift.
[26] **Topinamboo** (tŏp´ĭ-năm´boo): an area in Brazil supposedly inhabited by wild savages.
[27] **Jews . . . taken:** In AD 70, during a Jewish revolt against Roman rule, the inhabitants of Jerusalem, by fighting among themselves, made it easier for the Romans to capture the city.

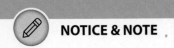
UNDERSTAND AUTHOR'S PURPOSE

Annotate: Underline the statement in paragraph 30 that explains why the narrator dismisses the "expedients" listed in the previous paragraph.

Draw Conclusions: What point does Swift make in describing his own proposals in these paragraphs?

ANALYZE SATIRICAL DEVICES

Annotate: In paragraph 32, mark the question the narrator suggests that people who object to his proposal should ask.

Analyze: What is paradoxical about this question?

30   Therefore I repeat, let no man talk to me of these and the like expedients,[28] till he hath at least some glimpse of hope that there will ever be some hearty and sincere attempt to put them in practice.

31   But as to myself, having been wearied out for many years with offering vain, idle, visionary thoughts, and at length utterly despairing of success, I fortunately fell upon this proposal, which, as it is wholly new, so it hath something solid and real, of no expense and little trouble, full in our own power, and whereby we can incur no danger in disobliging England. For this kind of commodity will not bear exportation, the flesh being of too tender a consistence to admit a long continuance in salt, although perhaps I could name a country which would be glad to eat up our whole nation without it.

32   After all, I am not so violently bent upon my own opinion as to reject any offer proposed by wise men, which shall be found equally innocent, cheap, easy, and effectual. But before something of that kind shall be advanced in contradiction to my scheme, and offering a better, I desire the author or authors will be pleased maturely to consider two points. First, as things now stand, how they will be able to find food and raiment for an hundred thousand useless mouths and backs. And secondly, there being a round million of creatures in human figure throughout this kingdom, whose sole subsistence put into a common stock[29] would leave them in debt two millions of pounds sterling, adding those who are beggars by profession to the bulk of farmers, cottagers, and laborers, with their wives and children who are beggars in effect; I desire those politicians who dislike my overture, and may perhaps be so bold to attempt an answer, that they will first ask the parents of these mortals whether they would not at this day think it a great happiness to have been sold for food at a year old in the manner I prescribe, and thereby have avoided such a perpetual scene of misfortunes as they have since gone through by the oppression of landlords, the impossibility of paying rent without money or trade, the want of common sustenance, with neither house nor clothes to cover them from the inclemencies of the weather, and the most inevitable prospect of entailing the like or greater miseries upon their breed forever.

33   I profess, in the sincerity of my heart, that I have not the least personal interest in endeavoring to promote this necessary work, having no other motive than the public good of my country, by advancing our trade, providing for infants, relieving the poor, and giving some pleasure to the rich. I have no children by which I can propose to get a single penny; the youngest being nine years old, and my wife past childbearing.

---

[28]**let no man ... expedients:** Swift had written pamphlets in support of these proposals, but his efforts were unsuccessful.
[29]**common stock:** ordinary stock in a company or business venture.

CHECK YOUR UNDERSTANDING

Answer these questions before moving on to the **Analyze the Text** section on the following page.

1 The narrator's proposal for easing poverty in Ireland is to —

A eat disadvantaged children

B put disadvantaged children to work

C raise taxes to pay for social services

D ration children's food

2 According to Swift's narrator, the proposal will benefit Irish parents by —

F allowing them to eat their children if necessary

G saving them the difficulties of parenting

H turning mouths to feed into valuable property

J encouraging them to have more children

3 Which idea does the narrator dismiss as impractical?

A Preparing stews from children's flesh

B Making gloves from the skin of children

C Greatly reducing Ireland's population

D Selling adolescents for food

ANALYZE THE TEXT

Support your responses with evidence from the text. 📓 NOTEBOOK

1. **Evaluate** Is Swift's parody of an argument an effective way to achieve his purpose? Explain why or why not.

2. **Analyze** Identify examples of understatement and exaggeration in paragraphs 17 and 19. What effect do these satirical devices have on the reader?

3. **Analyze** Swift's narrator says that he has "digressed" in paragraph 20. Explain how this digression actually serves his purpose of exposing injustice.

4. **Connect** The period from the late 1600s through the 1700s is known as the Enlightenment, a time when many writers promoted scientific reasoning as a means of solving social problems. Swift was often critical of such writers. How is this attitude reflected in *A Modest Proposal*?

5. **Notice & Note** Review the many contrasts and contradictions between accepted behavior and Swift's "modest proposal." Do you think these stark contrasts and contradictions make the satire more powerful? Why or why not?

RESEARCH

RESEARCH TIP
When using the Internet to search for information about a historical event, make sure to use only reliable sources, such as those ending in .edu. Academic institutions are less likely to have an agenda—and more likely to be reliable—than commercial sites.

Swift offers his proposal as a consideration for easing the suffering of those living in Ireland under England's rule. With a partner, research what life was like in Ireland during the 18th century. Use what you learn to answer these questions.

QUESTION	ANSWER
What living conditions did most Irish people experience during English rule in this period?	
How did English policies harm the Irish people?	

Extend Swift presented this proposal in the form of Juvenalian satire to strengthen his message about the suffering in Ireland. With a partner, discuss how this reinforced the points he was trying to make. Then study another work by Swift to determine whether he uses the same type of satire in that text.

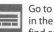

CREATE AND DISCUSS

Write a Satirical Essay Write a short satirical essay that addresses a problem in your school or community. Before you begin drafting, review your notes and analysis of Swift's use of satirical devices such as irony and exaggeration. Then, model your essay on his style.

❑ Identify a problem or behavior that will be the target of your satire.

❑ Think of a solution to the problem or a way to reform the behavior.

❑ Draft your essay using satirical devices to show the problem or behavior in a critical light.

Discuss the Satirical Essay Now that you have written your own satirical essay, discuss the process with a partner.

❑ Take turns sharing your essays.

❑ Evaluate your partner's use of satirical devices and the strength of the argument.

❑ Offer constructive suggestions on ways your partner could polish the essay to make it more effective.

Go to **Writing as a Process** in the **Writing Studio** to find out more.

 Go to **Participating in Collaborative Discussions** in the **Speaking and Listening Studio** to find out more.

RESPOND TO THE ESSENTIAL QUESTION

 ? How can satire change people's behavior?

Gather Information Review your annotations and notes on *A Modest Proposal*. Then, add relevant information to your Response Log. As you determine which information to include, think about:

• current examples of the use of satire to change people's behavior
• satirical devices used in the examples you identified
• whether these satires caused a change in your behavior or in the behavior of others

ACADEMIC VOCABULARY

As you write and discuss what you learned from the satirical essay, be sure to use the Academic Vocabulary words. Check off each of the words that you use.

❑ **encounter**
❑ **exploit**
❑ **persist**
❑ **subordinate**
❑ **widespread**

CRITICAL VOCABULARY

WORD BANK

sustenance   scrupulous

prodigious   encumbrance

rudiment   inducement

collateral

Practice and Apply Choose the situation that fits the meaning of the Critical Vocabulary word. Explain your decision.

1. Which is a rudiment of farming—knowing how to grow plants or knowing how to cook harvested food?

2. Which would a scrupulous landlord be more likely to do for a tenant who is out of work—offer a break on rent or ask for rent earlier than it is due?

3. Which is a collateral effect of heavy rains—a rise in umbrella sales or a decline in raincoat sales?

4. Which is an inducement to exercise more—getting a guitar or getting a skateboard?

5. Which of these provides healthier sustenance—a salad or a cake?

6. Which of these is an encumbrance to maintaining your household—not getting a bigger office at work or not earning a high hourly wage?

7. Which of these is more prodigious—the state of Texas or the state of Rhode Island?

VOCABULARY STRATEGY:
Context Clues

Context clues are often found in the words and sentences around an unknown term. A context clue may consist of a definition or a restatement of the meaning of the unfamiliar word, an example following the word, a comparison or contrast, or a nearby synonym. The unknown word's position or function in a sentence can also be a clue.

For example, the placement and suffix of the Critical Vocabulary word *prodigious* in paragraph 2 tells you that it is an adjective. Knowing this makes the word easier to define.

After using context clues to get a preliminary understanding of a word, you can verify the word's meaning by looking it up in a dictionary.

Go to **Context Clues** in the **Vocabulary Studio** for more.

Practice and Apply Use context clues in each sentence to help you identify the correct words to complete the sentences. Check your answers in a dictionary.

WORD BANK

inclemency

liable

reckoned

1. The farmer was _____ for the loan payment on the farm, even though he was not responsible for the failure of his crops.

2. He _____ the cost of raising a child, computing it to the penny.

3. The _____ of the winter weather, with frequent snow and ice storms, added to the misery of the homeless.

LANGUAGE CONVENTIONS:
Active and Passive Voice

Swift uses both active and passive voice in his essay. When a verb is in the **active voice,** the subject performs the action. When the verb is in the **passive voice,** the subject is the receiver of the action. The passive voice is formed with the verb *to be* and the past participle of a verb. Typically, the active voice is preferred because it conveys more energy and is more direct. To develop a more stilted, formal tone fitting for the narrator of his proposal, however, Swift turns to the passive voice.

Read these sentences from the essay.

> **It is agreed by all parties that this prodigious number of children . . . is . . . a very great additional grievance.**

> **I am assured by our merchants that a boy or girl before twelve years old is no salable commodity.**

Swift could have chosen to use the active voice in both sentences:

> **All parties agree that this prodigious number of children is a very great additional grievance.**

> **Our merchants assure me that a boy or girl before twelve years old is no salable commodity.**

Altering the verb from passive to active makes the writing more vigorous and less like the bureaucratic language that might be used in a real proposal. Sometimes, the passive voice is preferred for other reasons as explained in the chart.

USE OF PASSIVE VOICE	
PURPOSE	EXAMPLE
to emphasize the receiver of the action	The truce was shattered by the accidental firing.
when the doer of the action is not known or not important or when the writer or speaker wants to conceal the identity of the doer	The window was broken.

Practice and Apply Write four sentences about *A Modest Proposal* in the passive voice. Exchange sentences with a partner and rewrite each other's sentences in the active voice. Compare the differences between the two versions.

Go to **Active Voice and Passive Voice** in the **Grammar Studio** for more.

SATIRE IS DYING BECAUSE THE INTERNET IS KILLING IT

Editorial by **Arwa Mahdawi**

? *ESSENTIAL QUESTION:*

How can satire change people's behavior?

QUICK START

What are your favorite sources of satire? Do you generally look for satires in print publications, on the Internet, or on television? With a partner, discuss the kind of satires you enjoy most.

ANALYZE DEVELOPMENT OF IDEAS

In a nonfiction selection, the **main idea** is the most important point the writer wants to make about the topic. This main idea is usually developed through several key points, each of which is supported by details. An author may state a main idea outright; however, more often the reader must infer the main idea from key points and details in the selection.

To develop the main idea stated in its title, "Satire Is Dying Because the Internet Is Killing It," author Arwa Mahdawi presents a series of key points, drawing connections between them. Details and examples support the key points and make the selection meaningful and interesting to readers.

Use a graphic organizer like this one to help analyze how an author develops ideas in a nonfiction selection.

GENRE ELEMENTS: EDITORIAL

• expresses an opinion, often on a controversial subject

• often found on the editorial page of a newspaper

• presents an argument and uses rhetorical techniques to persuade readers

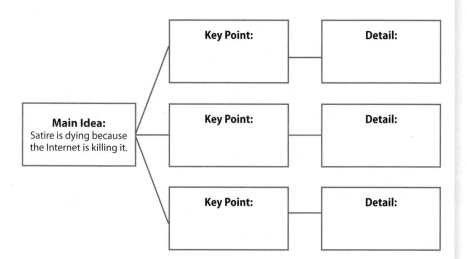

ANALYZE TONE

Tone is the attitude that a writer expresses toward a subject. In nonfiction, tone is often developed through **diction,** or word choice and syntax. The details a writer includes may also contribute to tone. The tone of a text may be intimate or distant, serious or humorous, ironic or earnest, understated or hyperbolic.

To identify the tone in a selection, you might try reading it aloud. What attitude toward the subject and audience do the words, sentence structures, and details convey? An author's tone can powerfully shape readers' perceptions of a selection's topic.

As you read "Satire Is Dying Because the Internet Is Killing It," analyze and evaluate the author's tone. What is the overall tone, and does it help the author to achieve her purpose?

CRITICAL VOCABULARY

algorithm	accolade	curate	eschew	finite
satire	spoof	monetize	meme	

To see how many Critical Vocabulary words you already know, use them to complete the sentences.

1. At this company, the highest _____ is accompanied with a bonus.

2. The _____ they performed poked fun at his self-importance.

3. There are only a(n) _____ number of solutions to the problem.

4. Micha posted a(n) _____ that promised to break the Internet.

5. Darcy was asked to _____ the newest exhibit at the Austen Museum.

6. She tried to _____ her knitting skills selling hats in an online shop.

7. To solve the problem quickly, Joaquin wrote a(n) _____.

8. Since Christian hates chores, he _____ them whenever possible.

9. Although he claimed to enjoy _____, the principal was not happy.

LANGUAGE CONVENTIONS

Effective Words A part of Arwa Mahdawi's style is her use of highly effective words, evocative adjectives, and concrete nouns to critique the digital generation. For example, she uses adjectives like *satire-blindness* and compares the human attention span to that of goldfish. As you read, note how she uses distinctive wording to convey her ideas and perspective.

ANNOTATION MODEL   NOTICE & NOTE

As you read the selection, note how the author develops her argument by overstating certain elements and by using irony to create a humorous tone. This model shows one reader's notes about an excerpt from the editorial.

Forget self-driving cars or virtual reality nano-technology algorithms, <u>the newest innovation</u> to emerge from Silicon Valley is square brackets. Facebook is testing a "satire tag" that will clearly label fake news stories from well-known satire sites like the *Onion* as [satire]. <u>No longer will you need to rely on outdated technology such as common sense</u> to realize that content like Area Facebook User Incredibly Stupid is [satire], the square brackets will do it for you.

The author refers to square brackets as "the newest innovation," even though they aren't as innovative as technology such as self-driving cars, and calls common sense "outdated." This establishes an ironic tone.

BACKGROUND

Arwa Mahdawi *is a Palestinian/British writer based in New York. She writes about pop culture, race, technology, and women's issues. In "Satire Is Dying Because the Internet Is Killing It," she laments the death of satire and points out both reported and underlying reasons for the apparent decline. This editorial was published on August 19, 2014, in the Opinion section of* The Guardian.

SATIRE IS DYING BECAUSE THE INTERNET IS KILLING IT

Editorial by Arwa Mahdawi

SETTING A PURPOSE

As you read, notice the author's diction, or word choice, and how it conveys her viewpoints about the "satire tag."

1   Forget self-driving cars or virtual reality nano-technology[1] **algorithms**, the newest innovation to emerge from Silicon Valley[2] is square brackets. Facebook is testing a "satire tag" that will clearly label fake news stories from well-known **satire** sites like the *Onion* as [satire]. No longer will you need to rely on outdated technology such as common sense to realize that content like Area Facebook User Incredibly Stupid is [satire], the square brackets will do it for you.

2   It should perhaps be noted that Facebook isn't introducing the satire tag because it thinks we're all morons, but rather because it knows we're all morons. In a statement, the social network explained that it had "received feedback that people wanted a clearer way to distinguish satirical articles from others."

---

[1] **nano-technology:** the study of technology and engineering functions at a molecular level.

[2] **Silicon Valley:** located in the Bay Area in California; home to many start-up and global technology companies like Facebook.

© Houghton Mifflin Harcourt Publishing Company • Image Credits: © Ridofranz/Getty Images

---

Notice & Note

Use the side margins to notice and note signposts in the text.

LANGUAGE CONVENTIONS

Annotate: Mark effective words, nouns, and adjectives in paragraphs 1 and 2 that illustrate the author's view of using satire tags in news.

Evaluate: What effect does the author's choice of language create?

algorithm
(ăl´gə-rĭth-əm) *n.* a finite set of unambiguous instructions that, given some set of initial conditions, can be performed in a prescribed sequence to achieve a certain goal and that has a recognizable set of end conditions.

satire
(săt´īr) *n.* a literary work in which human foolishness or vice is attacked through irony, derision, or wit.

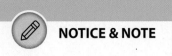

NOTICE & NOTE

accolade
(ăk´ə-lād, -läd) *n.* a special acknowledgment; an award.

spoof
(spoof) *n.* a satirical imitation; a parody or send-up.

ANALYZE DEVELOPMENT OF IDEAS

Annotate: Mark the statements in paragraphs 4 and 5 that explain why it has become so difficult to discern between satire and real news on the Internet.

Draw Conclusions: What might be one solution to this problem?

curate
(kyoor´ ĭt) *tr.vb.* to gather and present to the public.

monetize
(mŏn´ ĭ-tīz, mŭn-) *tr.vb.* to convert into a source of income.

eschew
(ĕ-shoo´, ĕs-choo´) *tr.vb.* to avoid using, accepting, participating in, or partaking of.

meme
(mēm) *n.* a unit of cultural information, such as a cultural practice or idea, that is transmitted verbally or by repeated action from one mind to another.

3   Some of those people may well be journalists who have had embarrassing lapses of satire-blindness in the past. The *Washington Post*, for example, was once fooled into reporting that Sarah Palin[3] was, in a somewhat unlikely career move, taking a job at *Al-Jazeera*.[4] And the English-language arm of China's *People's Daily* fell for an *Onion*[5] article proclaiming the North Korean ruler, Kim Jong-un, the sexiest man alive, even using the **accolade** as an opportunity to run a 55-image slideshow of him, complete with quotes from the *Onion* **spoof**. Although, it's possible this may itself have been satire—I'm unsure.

4   And that's the problem. The Internet has become so weird, so saturated with cats and lists and Buzzfeed[6] quizzes that it's difficult to know what's serious and what's a spoof any more. I challenge you, for example, to identify the *Onion* piece from these headlines:

• U.S. Adults Are Dumber than the Average Human
• Hazelnut Prices Soar, Fueling Fears of Nutella Shortage
• Tips for Being an Unarmed Black Teen
• Serial Chicken Smuggler Caught in Norway
• Definitive Proof Kale Is the Marilyn of Foods

5   The point of this carefully **curated** list[7] is that you often can't tell the difference between satire and real news online. There are several reasons for this. The first is the underlying business model of the Internet. We don't like to pay for stuff online so the Internet is funded by advertising; advertising executives demand eyeballs for their dollars; content providers resort to clickbait headlines and shareable content to secure eyeballs and ad dollars; users get addicted to an endless stream of clickbait.

6   The manner in which we've **monetized** digital media means we often reward reaction over reflection and **eschew** meaning for **meme**-ing. News can't just be news; it has to be entertainment. Indeed, the third law of modern media states that for every moderately important news item published, there will be an obligatory roundup of the funniest Twitter reactions to said news story, generally in slideshow format to maximize clicks.

7   The second big contributor to satire-blindness is our diminishing attention span. The average American attention span in 2000 was

---

³ **Sarah Palin:** American politician who served as governor of Alaska and as the Republican Party nominee for vice-president in 2008 alongside presidential nominee, John McCain.

⁴ *al-Jazeera*: media network that reports on news from the Middle East and worldwide.

⁵ **the *Onion*:** an American digital media company and news satire organization.

⁶ **Buzzfeed:** an American digital media company that reports on social news and entertainment.

⁷ **"Tips for Being an Unarmed Black Teen"** is the only headline from the Onion.

Houghton Mifflin Harcourt Publishing Company

12 seconds; in 2013, it was eight seconds. This is less than the average attention span of a goldfish (nine seconds).

8   As Vladimir Nabokov[8] once said, "Satire is a lesson, parody is a game." But if there's one thing we've learned from the Internet, it's that everyone prefers games to lessons. The problem with satire in an age of **finite** attention and infinite content is that it makes you stop and think. It interrupts the speed and simplicity of the discover-click-share cycle that makes platforms like Facebook lots of money. By introducing satire tagging, Facebook has helpfully gone some way in eliminating the unhelpful friction of thought and, in doing so, made life easier for us all.

_____
[8] **Vladimir Nabokov:** Russian-American novelist, well known for his modern classic, *Lolita*.

© Houghton Mifflin Harcourt Publishing Company

ANALYZE TONE

Annotate: Mark specific evidence in paragraph 7 that supports the author's overall tone.

Summarize: What does the author say about humans' attention span and how it affects their ability to engage with satire?

finite
(fī′nīt) *adj.* having bounds; limited.

CHECK YOUR UNDERSTANDING

Answer these questions before moving on to the **Analyze the Text** section on the following page.

1 What is a "satire tag," as described in this editorial?

   A A trick of social media companies to pass fake stories off as real news

   B A way social media sites help people distinguish satire from parody

   C A label social media sites are considering to alert readers to satire

   D A form of social media advertising

2 Mahdawi cites which of the following as a reason why it is difficult to tell a real news story from a satire?

   F Increasing attention spans

   G Overvaluing of entertainment

   H Innovative technologies across sectors

   J Reduction in social media marketing dollars

3 In paragraph 8, the author explains that the problem with satire is that it makes you stop and think. What is her purpose for this statement?

   A She wants readers to find better ways of sorting their online content.

   B She wants readers to take a stand against satire in the news.

   C She wants readers to recognize the value and importance of satire.

   D She wants readers to know that satire is too difficult to understand.

RESPOND

ANALYZE THE TEXT

Support your responses with evidence from the text. NOTEBOOK

1. **Evaluate** Reread paragraphs 1 and 2. What tone does the author establish at the beginning of the editorial through her word choices and syntax? Do you think this tone is effective? Explain why or why not.

2. **Identify** What details in paragraph 3 support the author's main idea?

3. **Interpret** The author quotes Vladimir Nabokov, who said that "Satire is a lesson, parody is a game." What point does she make with this quotation?

4. **Infer** At the end of the editorial, the author says that social media has "made life easier for us all." Does she intend to praise it with this statement? Explain why or why not.

5. **Draw Conclusions** Throughout the editorial, the author uses elements of satire, such as irony and overstatement. Why do you think she uses these elements of satire?

RESEARCH

RESEARCH TIP

Be sure to use credible and accurate sources when conducting research. Websites with URLs that end in .edu are often good sources of information on academic subjects like Swift's satire.

As you have learned, satire is a form of social commentary that uses ridicule to get people to think about issues in a different way. With a partner, identify three contemporary satires and determine whether they are true satires or parodies. Share your findings with the class.

TITLE OF WORK	AUTHOR	SOCIAL TOPICS THE WORK ADDRESSES	THE AUTHOR'S ATTITUDE TOWARD THE TOPIC

Extend Research another article by Arwa Mahdawi. Then, compare and contrast it with "Satire Is Dying Because the Internet Is Killing It." What are similarities and differences between the two pieces of writing? Share your findings with a partner.

402   Unit 3

© Houghton Mifflin Harcourt Publishing Company

CREATE AND DISCUSS

Write a Satire Write your own brief satirical work about a social issue that interests you. Your satire can be structured as an essay, editorial, poem, play, or song lyric. Make sure you have a clear central, or main, idea that is developed by examples and details. Also, be sure to craft a certain tone and incorporate techniques like overstatement and irony.

❏ Identify a clear central idea. Is your intended purpose clear?

❏ Who is your audience? Will they understand your main idea?

❏ What is the tone you want to convey? Is it clear? Do you want to set different tones at different points? How will you achieve this?

❏ What details will you use to support your main idea?

❏ What elements of satire have you included?

Discuss the Editorial In a small group, discuss whether or not you agree with the author's viewpoint expressed in this editorial.

❏ Take turns sharing your thoughts.

❏ Support your opinions with evidence and examples from the text.

Go to **Writing as a Process** in the **Writing Studio** for help.

 Go to **Participating in Collaborative Discussions** in the **Speaking and Listening Studio** to find out more.

RESPOND TO THE ESSENTIAL QUESTION

 How can satire change people's behavior?

Gather Information Review your annotations and notes on "Satire Is Dying Because the Internet Is Killing It." Then, add relevant details to your Response Log. As you determine which information to include, think about:

- the characteristics of a satire
- how an author of a satire might appeal to readers' emotions
- how language can be used to convey a certain tone

ACADEMIC VOCABULARY

As you write and discuss what you learned from the editorial, be sure to use the Academic Vocabulary words. Check off each of the words that you use.

❏ **encounter**
❏ **exploit**
❏ **persist**
❏ **subordinate**
❏ **widespread**

© Houghton Mifflin Harcourt Publishing Company

CRITICAL VOCABULARY

WORD BANK

algorithm	monetize
satire	eschew
accolade	meme
spoof	finite
curate	

Practice and Apply Complete each sentence in a way that reflects the meaning of the Critical Vocabulary word.

1. An engineer might use an *algorithm* to create . . .

2. A typical response to a *satire* might be . . .

3. The *accolades* she received for her work made it possible to . . .

4. The purpose of a *spoof* is to . . .

5. To *curate* the exhibition, she spent hours . . .

6. The chef *monetized* his skills by . . .

7. The *meme* was passed around by . . .

8. As a vegetarian, she *eschewed* . . .

9. Although money was a *finite* commodity, he . . .

VOCABULARY STRATEGY: Antonyms

Go to **Synonyms and Antonyms** in the **Vocabulary Studio** for more on antonyms.

The **context** of an unfamiliar word—other words, sentences, and paragraphs around the word—often gives clues to its meaning. Sometimes an **antonym,** a word that is opposite of the unfamiliar word, appears in the context. An example of this kind of clue appears in "Satire Is Dying Because the Internet Is Killing It":

> **The problem with satire in an age of finite attention and infinite content is that it makes you stop and think.**

Understanding the word *finite* means "having bounds," you can guess that the word *infinite* means "having no boundaries or limits." Using a print or digital resource can also help you clarify meanings of unfamiliar words.

Practice and Apply In each of the sentences below, underline the antonyms and additional words or phrases that provide clues to the meaning of the italicized words from the selection.

1. As the medicine caused Maxine's fatigue to *diminish*, her energy increased, and she went for a run.

2. The federal organization passed a law indicating that attendance at meetings was *obligatory* for all executive members but voluntary for associate members.

3. Because the director is used to receiving praise and flattery for his work, he was not amused by the witty *parody* of his film.

4. As the rainy season subsided, the once-*saturated* ground dried up and cracked.

LANGUAGE CONVENTIONS:
Effective Words

The use of highly **effective words,** including adjectives and concrete nouns, helps the writer convey ideas clearly and connect with the audience. Whether trying to establish a serious or silly tone, the right choice of words allows a writer to capture the audience's attention and to convey a perspective.

Effective words help writers to infuse their writing with certain meanings. The "weight" of the words a writer might choose can depend on the intensity of the writer's tone and the ideas he or she wants to emphasize. These words might be understood according to their **connotation,** the shade of meaning that might connect to a neutral, positive, or negative feeling.

Neutral: He offered a decent excuse for his actions.
Positive: He offered a valid excuse for his actions.
Negative: He offered a lame excuse for his actions.

An **adjective** modifies nouns and pronouns. Well-chosen adjectives can also convey the "weight" of a writer's ideas.

bad judgment   keen understanding   flagrant injustice

A **concrete noun** names something that can be perceived by the senses. The use of such words might reflect the writer's effort to express ideas plainly and concisely. Concrete writing, which aims to give its audience a clear understanding of what it is about, is most engaging when it includes sensory details.

Vague: I really like satire a lot.
Concrete: I am swept up by fiery satire that seems to singe off my eyelashes.

Practice and Apply Copy paragraph 5 from the selection into your notebook. Then, underline all the effective words, circle the adjectives, and highlight the concrete nouns that you think enable the author to get her point across. Think about how her writing would have been different had she chosen a different set of words, and rewrite the paragraph using your own language.

Go to **Adjectives** in the **Grammar Studio** to learn more.

from

THE JOURNAL AND LETTERS OF FANNY BURNEY: AN ENCOUNTER WITH KING GEORGE III

Diary by **Fanny Burney**

? *ESSENTIAL QUESTION:*

What is your most memorable experience?

QUICK START

What are your most memorable experiences, and why are they memorable? What do you think makes experiences memorable? With a partner, discuss your answers to these questions.

CONNECT TO HISTORY

A diary documents the events in a person's life. To fully appreciate a diary entry from the distant past, readers need some background knowledge of the **historical context** in which the diary was written. Often, this context is not provided in the diary itself but requires some outside research to fully understand.

Footnotes will explain some details. To learn more about a topic mentioned in a diary, you need to do research. As you read this diary entry, you might go online to find information about King George's illness, the king's reign, or Fanny Burney's career.

In Burney's diary, she writes about having a personal encounter with King George III. This would have been an unusual experience for someone like Burney, who was not a member of the royal family or the aristocracy; she had been invited to the court several years earlier to serve Queen Charlotte as second keeper of the robes. As you read the diary, consider how this context helps you understand her reaction to the king.

MAKE INFERENCES

Fanny Burney's diary provides a rare personal account of the illness of King George, including details about his behavior and how it affected life at the royal court. As you read the selection, use text clues and your own knowledge to **make inferences,** or logical guesses, about the king's condition and the reactions of those around him. For example, you can infer from these lines that Burney avoids the king because she is worried about getting into trouble:

> **This morning, when I received my intelligence of the king from Dr. John Willis, I begged to know where I might walk in safety? "In Kew gardens," he said, "as the king would be in Richmond."**

As you read, record your inferences in a chart like the one below.

DETAILS FROM THE TEXT	MY INFERENCES
"…I thought I saw the person of his majesty! Alarmed past all possible expression, I waited not to know more, but turning back, ran off with all my might" (Lines 18–22).	Burney is terrified of the king. She may be afraid because he has displayed erratic or angry behavior in the past.

CRITICAL VOCABULARY

malady	**salutation**	**assent**
undaunted	**expound**	**anecdote**

To see how many Critical Vocabulary words you already know, use them to complete the sentences.

1. Sharice greeted the passengers as they boarded the plane, but they did not return her _____.

2. This particular _____ can be cured with antibiotics.

3. Though she lost her first race, she continued her training _____.

4. Would you care to _____ on that?

5. In her witty _____, Rebecca narrated the story.

6. The vote indicated _____ to the proposed changes.

LANGUAGE CONVENTIONS

Reflexive and Intensive Pronouns A **reflexive pronoun** follows a verb or a preposition and reflects back on an earlier noun or pronoun. Reflexive pronouns end in *-self* or *-selves*. Note the example:

> **I cut my hair myself.**

An **intensive pronoun** also ends in *-self* or *-selves* but has a different use. Intensive pronouns emphasize the antecedent. Note the example:

> **The prince himself sent me the wedding invitation!**

As you read Burney's diary entry, pay attention to how she uses reflexive and intensive pronouns and how this contributes to her tone and style.

ANNOTATION MODEL   **NOTICE & NOTE**

As you read the selection, note how the author, who was not only a diarist but also a novelist, uses many of the techniques of fiction. This model shows one reader's notes about an excerpt from the diary.

> What an adventure had I this morning! one that has occasioned me the severest personal terror I ever experienced in my life.

The author captures readers' attention by introducing the conflict immediately.

BACKGROUND

Frances "Fanny" Burney *(1752–1840) became a successful published novelist at a time when writing for a living was considered unsuitable for a lady. However, Burney's popular novels gained her entrance to the men's world of English literature and paved the way for other women writers. Her success led to her becoming a prominent member of the British social scene. Burney was invited to the royal court of King George III and Queen Charlotte in 1785, where she remained for five years until problems with her health led to her resignation. She documented who and what she observed in a diary that was published several years after her death.*

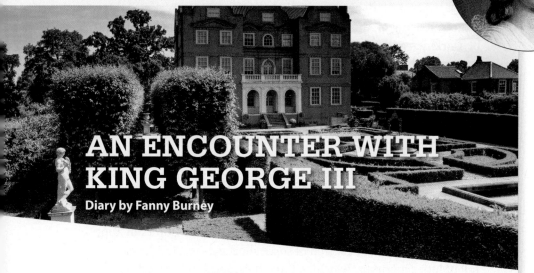

AN ENCOUNTER WITH KING GEORGE III

Diary by Fanny Burney

SETTING A PURPOSE

As you read, pay attention to how King George III and his illness are characterized.

Kew Palace, Monday February 2, 1789

1   What an adventure had I this morning! one that has occasioned me the severest personal terror I ever experienced in my life.

2   Sir Lucas Pepys[1] still persisting that exercise and air were absolutely necessary to save me from illness, I have continued my walks, varying my gardens from Richmond to Kew,[2] according to the accounts I received of the movements of the king. For this I had her majesty's permission, on the representation of Sir Lucas.

3   This morning, when I received my intelligence of the king from Dr. John Willis,[3] I begged to know where I might

---

[1] **Sir Lucas Pepys** (pēps): a physician who was an old friend of the Burney family.

[2] **gardens from Richmond to Kew:** the gardens at Richmond House and Kew House, two adjoining royal residences west of London that were often used by George III and his family.

[3] **Dr. John Willis:** a clergyman and physician who attended George III during his illness. His son, John Willis, also a physician, assisted in treating the king.

© Houghton Mifflin Harcourt Publishing Company • Image Credits: © Mary Evans Picture Library/Alamy; © Mike Kipling Photography/Alamy

Notice & Note

Use the side margins to notice and note signposts in the text.

CONNECT TO HISTORY

Annotate: Mark paragraph 2 where Fanny's diary entry connects to what you just learned about her in the Background feature.

Analyze: How does this part of the diary connect to biographical details from Fanny's life?

walk in safety? "In Kew gardens," he said, "as the king would be in Richmond."

4   "Should any unfortunate circumstance," I cried, "at any time, occasion my being seen by his majesty, do not mention my name, but let me run off without call or notice."

5   This he promised. Everybody, indeed, is ordered to keep out of sight.

6   Taking, therefore, the time I had most at command, I strolled into the gardens. I had proceeded, in my quick way, nearly half the round, when I suddenly perceived, through some trees, two or three figures. Relying on the instructions of Dr. John, I concluded them to be workmen and gardeners; yet tried to look sharp, and in so doing, as they were less shaded, I thought I saw the person of his majesty!

LANGUAGE CONVENTIONS

Annotate: Mark the reflexive pronouns that Burney uses in paragraph 7.

Analyze: What distressful prospect does she face here?

7   Alarmed past all possible expression, I waited not to know more, but turning back, ran off with all my might. But what was my terror to hear myself pursued!—to hear the voice of the king himself loudly and hoarsely calling after me, "Miss Burney! Miss Burney!"

8   I protest I was ready to die. I knew not in what state he might be at the time; I only knew the orders to keep out of his way were universal; that the queen would highly disapprove any unauthorized meeting, and that the very action of my running away might deeply, in his present irritable state, offend him. Nevertheless, on I ran, too terrified to stop, and in search of some short passage, for the garden is full of little labyrinths, by which I might escape.

9   The steps still pursued me, and still the poor hoarse and altered voice rang in my ears:—more and more footsteps resounded frightfully behind me,—the attendants all running, to catch their eager master, and the voices of the two Doctor Willises loudly exhorting him not to heat himself so unmercifully.

10   Heavens, how I ran! I do not think I should have felt the hot lava from Vesuvius—at least not the hot cinders—had I so run during its eruption. My feet were not sensible that they even touched the ground.

11   Soon after, I heard other voices, shriller, though less nervous, call out "Stop! stop! stop!"

12   I could by no means consent; I knew not what was purposed, but I recollected fully my agreement with Dr. John that very morning, that I should decamp if surprised, and not be named.

MAKE INFERENCES

Annotate: Mark the sentence in paragraph 13 that tells you about the king's illness.

Analyze: What can you infer about the king based on this sentence?

malady
(măl´ə-dē) *n.* a disease, disorder, or ailment.

13   My own fears and repugnance, also, after a flight and disobedience like this, were doubled in the thought of not escaping; I knew not to what I might be exposed, should the **malady** be then high,[4] and take the turn of resentment. Still, therefore, on I flew; and

---

[4] **be then high:** then be greater, or worse, than usual.

© Houghton Mifflin Harcourt Publishing Company

such was my speed, so almost incredible to relate or recollect, that I fairly believe no one of the whole party could have overtaken me, if these words, from one of the attendants, had not reached me: "Doctor Willis begs you to stop!"

14   "I cannot! I cannot!" I answered, still flying on, when he called out "You must, ma'am; it hurts the king to run."

15   Then, indeed, I stopped—in a state of fear really amounting to agony. I turned round, I saw the two doctors had got the king between them, and three attendants of Dr. Willis's were hovering about. They all slackened their pace, as they saw me stand still; but such was the excess of my alarm, that I was wholly insensible[5] to the effects of a race which, at any other time, would have required an hour's recruit.[6]

16   As they approached, some little presence of mind happily came to my command; it occurred to me that, to appease the wrath of[7] my flight, I must now show some confidence. I therefore faced them as **undauntedly** as I was able, only charging the nearest of the attendants to stand by my side.

17   When they were within a few yards of me, the king called out, "Why did you run away?"

18   Shocked at a question impossible to answer, yet a little assured by the mild tone of his voice, I instantly forced myself forward, to meet him, though the internal sensation, which satisfied me this was a step the most proper to appease his suspicions and displeasure, was so violently combated by the tremor of my nerves, that I fairly think I may reckon it the greatest effort of personal courage I have ever made.

19   The effort answered:[8] I looked up, and met all his wonted benignity of countenance,[9] though something still of wildness in his eyes. Think, however, of my surprise, to feel him put both his hands round my two shoulders, and then kiss my cheek!

20   I wonder I did not really sink, so exquisite was my affright when I saw him spread out his arms! Involuntarily, I concluded he meant to crush me; but the Willises, who have never seen him till this fatal illness, not knowing how very extraordinary an action this was from him, simply smiled and looked pleased, supposing, perhaps, it was his customary **salutation**!

21   I believe, however, it was but the joy of a heart unbridled, now, by the forms and proprieties of established custom and sober reason. To see any of his household thus by accident, seemed such a near

undaunted
(ŭn-dôn´tĭd, -dän´-) *adj.* not discouraged or disheartened; resolutely courageous.

salutation
(săl-yə-tā´shən) *n.* a polite expression of greeting or goodwill.

---

[5] **wholly insensible:** completely unaware.
[6] **recruit** (rĭ-krōōt´): recovery; renewal of strength.
[7] **appease the wrath of:** make up for the fury of.
[8] **answered:** met the situation; worked.
[9] **his wonted benignity** (wôn´tĭd bĭ-nĭg´nĭ-tē) **of countenance** (koun´tə-nəns): the customary kindness of his facial expression.

approach to liberty and recovery, that who can wonder it should serve rather to elate than lessen what yet remains of his disorder!

22   He now spoke in such terms of his pleasure in seeing me, that I soon lost the whole of my terror; astonishment to find him so nearly well, and gratification to see him so pleased, removed every uneasy feeling, and the joy that succeeded, in my conviction of his recovery, made me ready to throw myself at his feet to express it.

23   What a conversation followed! When he saw me fearless, he grew more and more alive, and made me walk close by his side, away from the attendants, and even the Willises themselves, who, to indulge him, retreated. I own[10] myself not completely composed, but alarm I could entertain no more.

24   Everything that came uppermost in his mind he mentioned; he seemed to have just such remains of his flightiness as heated his imagination without deranging his reason, and robbed him of all control over his speech, though nearly in his perfect state of mind as to his opinions.

25   What did he not say!—He opened his whole heart to me,— **expounded** all his sentiments, and acquainted me with all his intentions.

26   The heads of his discourse[11] I must give you briefly, as I am sure you will be highly curious to hear them, and as no accident can render of much consequence what a man says in such a state of physical intoxication. He assured me he was quite well—as well as he had ever been in his life; and then inquired how I did, and how I went on? and whether I was more comfortable? If these questions, in their implication, surprised me, imagine how that surprise must increase when he proceeded to explain them! He asked after the coadjutrix,[12] laughing, and saying "Never mind her!—don't be oppressed—I am your friend! don't let her cast you down!—I know you have a hard time of it—but don't mind her!"

27   Almost thunderstruck with astonishment, I merely curtsied to his kind "I am your friend," and said nothing.

28   Then presently he added, "Stick to your father—stick to your own family—let them be your objects."

29   How readily I **assented**!

30   Again he repeated all I have just written, nearly in the same words, but ended it more seriously: he suddenly stopped, and held me to stop too, and putting his hand on his breast, in the most solemn manner, he gravely and slowly said, "I will protect you!—I promise you that—and therefore depend upon me!"

---

[10] **own:** admit.

[11] **heads of his discourse:** main points of his conversation.

[12] **coadjutrix** (kō-ə-jü′trĭks): Elizabeth Juliana Schwellenberg, First Keeper of the Robes to Queen Charlotte and Fanny's immediate superior. She was known to be bossy and difficult toward the rest of the royal household staff and gave Fanny a terrible time.

expound
(ĭk-spound′) *v.* to explain in detail; elucidate.

CONNECT TO HISTORY

Annotate: Mark the king's comments in paragraph 26 and then mark in paragraph 27 the author's reaction to his comments.

Analyze: What does Burney's reaction tell you about the king's statement and how kings were expected to behave at the time?

assent
(ə-sĕnt′) *intr.v.* to express agreement or acceptance, as of a proposal.

31   I thanked him; and the Willises, thinking him rather too elevated,[13] came to propose my walking on. "No, no, no!" he cried, a hundred times in a breath; and their good humor prevailed, and they let him again walk on with his new companion.

32   He then gave me a history of his pages,[14] animating almost into a rage, as he related his subjects of displeasure with them, particularly with Mr. Ernst, who he told me had been brought up by himself. I hope his ideas upon these men are the result of the mistakes of his malady.

33   Then he asked me some questions that very greatly distressed me, relating to information given him in his illness, from various motives, but which he suspected to be false, and which I knew he had reason to suspect; yet was it most dangerous to set anything right, as I was not aware what might be the views of their having been stated wrong. I was as discreet as I knew how to be, and I hope I did no mischief; but this was the worst part of the dialogue.

34   He next talked to me a great deal of my dear father, and made a thousand inquiries concerning his "History of Music."[15] This brought him to his favorite theme, Handel;[16] and he told me innumerable **anecdotes** of him, and particularly that celebrated tale of Handel's saying of himself, when a boy, "While that boy lives, my music will never want a protector." And this, he said, I might relate to my father. Then he ran over most of his oratorios, attempting to sing the subjects of several airs and choruses,[17] but so dreadfully hoarse that the sound was terrible.

35   Dr. Willis, quite alarmed at this exertion, feared he would do himself harm, and again proposed a separation. "No! no! no!" he exclaimed, "not yet; I have something I must just mention first."

36   Dr. Willis, delighted to comply, even when uneasy at compliance, again gave way. The good king then greatly affected me. He began upon my revered old friend, Mrs. Delany;[18] and he spoke of her with such warmth—such kindness! "She was my friend!" he cried, "and I loved her as a friend! I have made a memorandum when I lost her—I will show it you."

anecdote
(ăn´ĭk-dōt) *n.* a short account of an interesting or humorous incident.

---

[13] **elevated:** excited.

[14] **pages:** young male servants attending a king or someone else of high rank.

[15] **"History of Music":** Fanny's father, Dr. Charles Burney, was a music historian best known for his *General History of Music,* the third and fourth volumes of which were published in 1789, the same year in which the events in this selection occurred.

[16] **Handel** (hăn´dl): George Frideric Handel (1685–1759), the great composer and a favorite of the king's father, George II.

[17] **oratorios** (ôr-ə-tôr´ē-ōz) **. . . choruses:** long, dramatic musical compositions that contain arias (or "airs"), choruses, and other portions to be sung but that differ from operas in not being performed with stage action, scenery, and costumes.

[18] **Mrs. Delany:** Mary Delany, an elderly friend of Fanny's who had recently died.

37   He pulled out a pocketbook,[19] and rummaged some time, but to no purpose. The tears stood in his eyes—he wiped them, and Dr. Willis again became very anxious. "Come, sir," he cried, "now do you come in and let the lady go on her walk,—come, now you have talked a long while,—so we'll go in,—if your majesty pleases."

38   "No, no!" he cried, "I want to ask her a few questions;—I have lived so long out of the world, I know nothing!"

39   This touched me to the heart. . . . He then told me he was very much dissatisfied with several of his state officers, and meant to form an entire new establishment. He took a paper out of his pocketbook, and showed me his new list.

40   This was the wildest thing that passed; and Dr. John Willis now seriously urged our separating; but he would not consent; he had only three more words to say, he declared, and again he conquered.

41   He now spoke of my father, with still more kindness, and told me he ought to have had the post of master of the band, and not that little poor musician Parsons,[20] who was not fit for it: "But Lord Salisbury,"[21] he cried, "used your father very ill in that business, and so he did me! However, I have dashed out his name, and I shall put your father's in,—as soon as I get loose again!"

42   This again—how affecting was this!

43   "And what," cried he, "has your father got, at last? nothing but that poor thing at Chelsea?[22] O fie! fie! fie! But never mind! I will take care of him! I will do it myself!" Then presently he added, "As to Lord Salisbury, he is out already, as this memorandum will show you, and so are many more. I shall be much better served; and when once I get away, I shall rule with a rod of iron!"

44   This was very unlike himself, and startled the two good doctors, who could not bear to cross him, and were exulting at my seeing his great amendment,[23] but yet grew quite uneasy at his earnestness and volubility.

45   Finding we now must part, he stopped to take leave, and renewed again his charges about the coadjutrix. "Never mind her!" he cried, "depend upon me! I will be your friend as long as I live!—I here

CONTRASTS AND CONTRADICTIONS

Notice & Note: In paragraphs 39–40, mark what the king does that astounds the narrator.

Compare: How does this contrast with the behavior that would be expected from a king?

---

[19] **pocketbook:** a case or folder for carrying money or papers in one's pocket.

[20] **he ought . . . Parsons:** Dr. Burney applied for the position of Master of the King's Band when it became vacant, but the post was instead given to a William Parsons.

[21] **Lord Salisbury** (sôlz´ber-ē): James Cecil, Marquess of Salisbury, who served as the royal household's Lord Chamberlain from 1783 to 1804, would have been involved in deciding who obtained the position of Master of the King's Band.

[22] **that poor thing at Chelsea** (chĕl´sē): Instead of Master of the King's Band, Dr. Burney was made organist in the chapel on the grounds of Chelsea Hospital, a refuge for old and disabled soldiers located in London.

[23] **amendment:** change for the better; improvement.

pledge myself to be your friend!" And then he saluted me again just as at the meeting, and suffered me to go on.

46   What a scene! how variously was I affected by it! but, upon the whole, how inexpressibly thankful to see him so nearly himself—so little removed from recovery!

CHECK YOUR UNDERSTANDING

Answer these questions before moving on to the **Analyze the Text** section on the following page.

1 What does Burney do when she sees King George III in the gardens?

  A She greets him and starts a conversation.

  B She quickly runs away.

  C She joins him for his walk.

  D She does nothing and continues on her walk.

2 Which member of Burney's family does the king speak kindly of?

  F Her father

  G Her mother

  H Her sister-in-law

  J Her brother

3 What did Burney note was the *"wildest thing that had passed"*?

  A The king read a eulogy for a mutual friend who had died.

  B His doctors wanted him to continue with his walk, but the king refused to listen.

  C The king talked about Burney's father's work in music.

  D The king shared with Burney plans for changing his state officers and forming a new establishment.

ANALYZE THE TEXT

Support your responses with evidence from the text. 📓 NOTEBOOK

1. **Infer** In paragraphs 36–38, Dr. Willis is distressed by the king's behavior. What can be inferred from his concern?

2. **Draw Conclusions** Summarize the events in each of the following scenes. To what extent is Burney's initial "terror" of the king justified?
   • her plans for a morning walk (paragraphs 2–4)
   • her flight from the king (paragraphs 7–8)
   • her "disobedience" (paragraphs 10–11)
   • the king's treatment of her (paragraphs 19–20)

3. **Evaluate** Reread paragraph 19. What do the king's appearance and actions toward Burney reveal about him?

4. **Connect** Consider your own familiarity with diaries or journals. Based on reading this account, what insights have you gained into the importance of diaries to life in the 18th century?

5. **Synthesize** Using information from Burney's diary, what is your understanding of George III's condition? Cite specific details in your response.

RESEARCH

RESEARCH TIP
The best search terms are specific. In addition to an author's name, you will want to include a word such as *novels* to help you find the information you need.

It is often said that novelists should write what they know. Do some research on Burney's novels and think about how her life experiences may have contributed to these novels. Use the chart below for your notes.

NOVEL	HOW DOES BURNEY "WRITE WHAT SHE KNOWS" IN THIS NOVEL?

Connect Do some research about the current British royal family. Based on what you have learned from reading this selection, what has changed about the British monarchy and their roles and responsibilities since the time of King George III?

CREATE AND DISCUSS

Write a Diary Entry Imagine that you are a royal court doctor described in Burney's diary entry. You may also choose another person present at the scene. Write your own diary entry depicting the scene from your perspective. Think about how Burney may have misunderstood the motivations of others present in the garden, and try to portray the scene from a new perspective.

❏ Choose one of the king's attendants as your character.

❏ Relate the encounter from his first-person point of view.

❏ Be sure to represent your character's personality in the entry.

Discuss a Diary Entry With a partner, take turns reading your diary entries. Then discuss them. How do your entries compare? In reading aloud, use the enunciation and speaking rate to match your character.

❏ Consider how different perspectives affect the narration of the event.

❏ Think about your character's view of the king and of Burney.

Go to **Writing Narratives** in the **Writing Studio** for help in writing your diary entry.

Go to **Participating in Collaborative Discussions** in the **Speaking and Listening Studio** for more.

RESPOND TO THE ESSENTIAL QUESTION

? What is your most memorable experience?

Gather Information Review your annotations and notes on *The Journal and Letters of Fanny Burney: An Encounter with King George III*. Then, add relevant information to your Response Log. As you determine which information to include, think about:

- how Burney sets up her story by providing background information about herself and the king
- how Burney works in her own thoughts and feelings as she tells the story
- how Burney uses sensory details to make the memory vivid and exciting

UNIT 3 RESPONSE LOG

ACADEMIC VOCABULARY

As you write and discuss what you learned from the diary entry, be sure to use the Academic Vocabulary words. Check off each of the words that you use.

❏ **encounter**

❏ **exploit**

❏ **persist**

❏ **subordinate**

❏ **widespread**

CRITICAL VOCABULARY

Practice and Apply Circle the letter of the best answer to each question. Then explain your answer.

1. Which is an example of a **malady**?

  a. the flu   **b.** a song   **c.** a vehicle

2. Which is an example of an **anecdote**?

  a. a cure for poison   **b.** a story told to illustrate a point in a speech   **c.** a law or regulation

3. Which is an example of **expounding**?

  a. firing someone from their job   **b.** throwing a bad fish overboard   **c.** explaining instructions in further detail

4. Which is an example of a **salutation**?

  a. Hello   **b.** Mrs.   **c.** King

5. Which is an example of someone who is **undaunted**?

  a. a person who flees at danger   **b.** a person who keeps trying no matter what   **c.** a person who speaks to himself or herself

6. Which is an example of giving **assent**?

  a. arguing   **b.** explaining   **c.** agreeing

VOCABULARY STRATEGY: Synonyms

Go to **Synonyms and Antonyms** in the **Vocabulary Studio** for more on synonyms.

Synonyms are words similar in meaning to another word. *Happy* and *content* are synonyms. A synonym is one kind of **context clue** you can use when trying to figure out the meaning of an unfamiliar word. In this example from Burney's diary, notice how the word *anecdotes* has a corresponding synonym:

> This brought him to his favorite theme, Handel; and he told me innumerable <u>anecdotes</u> of him, and particularly that celebrated <u>tale</u> of Handel's saying of himself, when a boy, "While that boy lives, my music will never want a protector."

Practice and Apply Find each of these words in the selection. Define it and identify the synonym used as a context clue that helped you identify its meaning as it is used in the diary entry.

1. astonishment (paragraph 27)

2. oppressed (paragraph 26)

3. compliance (paragraph 36)

LANGUAGE CONVENTIONS:
Reflexive and Intensive Pronouns

There are pronouns that are naturally suited to such personal writing as diary entries, memoirs, and autobiographies. These pronouns are formed by adding *-self* or *-selves* to certain personal pronouns. The forms are the same but differ in how they are used.

REFLEXIVE AND INTENSIVE PRONOUNS	
SINGULAR	**PLURAL**
myself	ourselves
yourself	yourselves
himself, herself, itself	themselves

A **reflexive pronoun** follows a verb or a preposition and reflects back on an earlier noun or pronoun.

> The king threw <u>himself</u> into the chase.

A reflexive pronoun may serve as a direct object, an indirect object, an object of a preposition, or a predicate nominative.

> **DIRECT OBJECT** He might have hurt <u>himself</u> running.

> **INDIRECT OBJECT** All were surprised when she made <u>herself</u> stop.

> **OBJECT OF A PREPOSITION** We are proud of <u>ourselves</u> for showing respect.

> **PREDICATE NOMINATIVE** The king is not <u>himself</u> these days.

An **intensive pronoun** intensifies or emphasizes the nouns and pronouns to which they refer.

> The queen <u>herself</u> stepped in to handle the matter.

> I <u>myself</u> saw no reason to interfere.

Reflexive and intensive pronouns are used throughout Fanny Burney's diary entry. Note the italicized pronouns in this example:

> But what was my terror to hear <u>myself</u> pursued! —to hear the voice of the king <u>himself</u> loudly and hoarsely calling after me, "Miss Burney! Miss Burney!"

Practice and Apply Write a narrative paragraph in which you use both reflexive and intensive pronouns.

ARGUMENT

from

A VINDICATION OF THE RIGHTS OF WOMAN

by **Mary Wollstonecraft**

pages 423–428

COMPARE ACROSS GENRES

As you read, notice how the ideas in both texts relate to the education of women and girls. Then, look for ways that the ideas in the two texts relate to each other. After reading and studying both selections, you will collaborate with a small group on a final project.

 ESSENTIAL QUESTION:

What keeps women from achieving equality with men?

ARTICLE

EDUCATION PROTECTS WOMEN FROM ABUSE

by **Olga Khazan**

pages 437–440

from A Vindication of the Rights of Woman

QUICK START

Think about opportunities for education today. Discuss with a partner of the opposite gender how educational opportunities have improved for women over the years.

EVALUATE ARGUMENTS

Many writers express their opinions on important issues by presenting a formal **argument.** When you read an argument, you should determine whether it is valid by evaluating the argument's main elements.

First, identify the author's **claim.** Is the opinion presented clearly and in detail?

Next, consider the reasons the author gives to support the claim. Are the **reasons** logical? Do they support the claim? As you evaluate the author's reasons, watch out for errors in logic, or **fallacies.** Common fallacies include:

- **Oversimplification** Treating a complex problem as if it were simple
- **Hasty Generalization** Making a generalization that is too broad or is drawn from too little information
- **False Cause-and-Effect** The mistaken assumption that because one event followed another, the first event caused the second one to occur
- **Red Herring** Irrelevant or false reasoning used to divert attention away from an issue

Finally, examine the author's **evidence.** Does the author give relevant facts and sufficient details to support his or her reasons? Is the information verified by reliable sources?

As you read Wollstonecraft's essay, analyze and evaluate the elements of her argument and look out for any logical fallacies.

ANALYZE COUNTERARGUMENTS

Writers often include **counterarguments** in which they anticipate opposing views and refute them. Mary Wollstonecraft provides several counterarguments that acknowledge her opponents' perspectives. This makes readers who might disagree with her more likely to be open to her ideas.

Examine the counterargument in paragraph 3: "In the government of the physical world it is observable that the female in point of strength is, in general, inferior to the male. . . . But not content with this natural preeminence, men endeavor to sink us still lower merely to render us alluring objects for a moment. . . ." Wollstonecraft asserts that men have a physical advantage over women and wrongly use this advantage to treat women as mere ornaments.

As you read, identify other counterarguments the author uses. Try to imagine how these counterarguments might have swayed her audience.

© Houghton Mifflin Harcourt Publishing Company

**GENRE ELEMENTS:
ARGUMENT**

- expresses a position on an issue
- supports the position with reasons and evidence
- considers other points of view, anticipating and answering possible objections raised by opponents
- may be spoken or written

GET READY

CRITICAL VOCABULARY

vindication	prerogative	evanescent	dissimulation
abrogate	inculcate	congenial	Utopian

Answer the questions using a Critical Vocabulary word in a complete sentence.

1. Which word means deceit or pretense?

2. Which word is the opposite of disagreeable?

3. Which word means a right or privilege?

4. Which word means justification?

5. Which word suggests something that is unattainable?

6. Which word suggests something temporary?

7. Which word means to revoke, or take away?

8. Which word suggests instruction?

LANGUAGE CONVENTIONS

Conjunctions help create varied sentences and clarify the relationships between ideas. **Coordinating conjunctions** connect independent clauses (clauses that can stand alone as complete sentences). **Subordinating conjunctions** connect dependent clauses (clauses that can't stand alone as complete sentences).

ANNOTATION MODEL

NOTICE & NOTE

As you read, note how Wollstonecraft develops her argument. This model shows one reader's notes about an excerpt from *A Vindication of the Rights of Woman*.

I have turned over various books written on the subject of education, and patiently observed the conduct of parents and the management of schools; but what has been the result?—a profound conviction that the neglected education of my fellow-creatures is the grand source of the misery I deplore; and that women, in particular, are rendered weak and wretched by a variety of concurring causes, originating from one hasty conclusion. The conduct and manners of women, in fact, evidently prove that their minds are not in a healthy state; for, like the flowers which are planted in too rich a soil, strength and usefulness are sacrificed to beauty; and the flaunting leaves, after having pleased a fastidious eye, fade, disregarded on the stalk, long before the season when they ought to have arrived at maturity.

She seems to be describing the problem first—the misery of women.

She is identifying a cause-effect relationship: Neglected education causes women's misery.

She uses a simile to help readers understand the problem—women are raised to be beautiful rather than productive.

© Houghton Mifflin Harcourt Publishing Company

BACKGROUND

Mary Wollstonecraft *(1759–1797) is considered by many to be the mother of feminism. Inspired by the ideas of liberal reformers, she wrote about the rights of women and others. Her 1790 book,* A Vindication of the Rights of Man, *attacked class and privilege; she followed that with* A Vindication of the Rights of Woman *in 1792.*

In the 18th century, the daughters of English gentlemen were mostly taught reading, languages, playing the piano, singing, drawing, and needlework. This was thought to be adequate preparation for their lives as wives, mothers, governesses, or companions to wealthy ladies.

from

A VINDICATION OF THE RIGHTS OF WOMAN

Argument by Mary Wollstonecraft

PREPARE TO COMPARE

As you read, make note of Wollstonecraft's evaluation of women's education at the time, her suggestion for needed changes, and her conclusions about how these changes would affect the lives of women. This information will help you compare her argument with the article "Education Protects Women from Abuse," which follows it.

1 After considering the historic page, and viewing the living world with anxious solicitude, the most melancholy emotions of sorrowful indignation have depressed my spirits, and I have sighed when obliged to confess, that either nature has made a great difference between man and man, or that the civilization which has hitherto taken place in the world has been very partial. I have turned over various books written on the subject of education, and patiently observed the conduct of parents and the management of schools; but what has been the result?—a profound conviction that the neglected education of my fellow-creatures is the grand source of the misery I deplore; and that women, in particular, are rendered weak and wretched by a variety of concurring causes, originating from one hasty conclusion. The conduct and manners of women, in fact, evidently prove that their minds are not in a healthy state;

Notice & Note

Use the side margins to notice and note signposts in the text.

vindication
(vĭn-dĭ-kā´shən) *n.* justification.

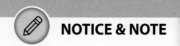
for, like the flowers which are planted in too rich a soil, strength and usefulness are sacrificed to beauty; and the flaunting leaves, after having pleased a fastidious eye, fade, disregarded on the stalk, long before the season when they ought to have arrived at maturity. One cause of this barren blooming I attribute to a false system of education, gathered from the books written on this subject by men who, considering females rather as women than human creatures, have been more anxious to make them alluring mistresses than affectionate wives and rational mothers; and the understanding of the sex has been so bubbled by this specious homage,[1] that the civilized women of the present century, with a few exceptions, are only anxious to inspire love, when they ought to cherish a nobler ambition, and by their abilities and virtues exact respect.

2   In a treatise,[2] therefore, on female rights and manners, the works which have been particularly written for their improvement must not be overlooked; especially when it is asserted, in direct terms, that the minds of women are enfeebled by false refinement; that the books of instruction, written by men of genius, have had the same tendency as more frivolous productions; and that . . . they are treated as a kind of subordinate beings, and not as a part of the human species, when improvable reason is allowed to be the dignified distinction which raises men above the brute creation, and puts a natural scepter in a feeble hand.

3   Yet, because I am a woman, I would not lead my readers to suppose that I mean violently to agitate the contested question respecting the quality or inferiority of the sex; but as the subject lies in my way, and I cannot pass it over without subjecting the main tendency of my reasoning to misconstruction, I shall stop a moment to deliver, in a few words, my opinion. In the government of the physical world it is observable that the female in point of strength is, in general, inferior to the male. This is the law of nature; and it does not appear to be suspended or **abrogated** in favor of woman. A degree of physical superiority cannot, therefore, be denied—and it is a noble **prerogative**! But not content with this natural preeminence, men endeavor to sink us still lower merely to render us alluring objects for a moment; and women, intoxicated by the adoration which men, under the influence of their senses, pay them, do not seek to obtain a durable interest in their hearts, or to become the friends of the fellow creatures who find amusement in their society.

4   I am aware of an obvious inference: from every quarter have I heard exclamations against masculine women; but where are they to be found? If by this appellation men mean to inveigh against their ardor[3] in hunting, shooting, and gaming, I shall most cordially join

abrogate
(ăb´rə-gāt) *v.* to revoke or nullify.

prerogative
(prĭ-rŏg´ə-tĭv) *n.* an exclusive right or privilege held by a person or group, especially a hereditary or official right.

ANALYZE COUNTERARGUMENTS

Annotate: Read paragraphs 4 and 6–8. Mark the sections in which Wollstonecraft addresses counterarguments, or anticipated opposing views.

Interpret: What opposing view is Wollstonecraft acknowledging in these paragraphs? How does she refute it?

---

[1] **bubbled by this specious homage** (spē´shəs hŏm´ĭj): deceived by this false honor.
[2] **treatise:** a formal, detailed article or book on a particular subject.
[3] **If by . . . inveigh** (ĭn-vā´) **against their ardor:** by this term ("masculine women") men mean to condemn some women's enthusiasm.

in the cry; but if it be against the imitation of manly virtues, or, more properly speaking, the attainment of those talents and virtues, the exercise of which ennobles the human character, and which raise females in the scale of animal being, when they are comprehensively termed mankind; all those who view them with a philosophic eye must, I should think, wish with me, that they may every day grow more and more masculine. . . .

5   My own sex, I hope, will excuse me, if I treat them like rational creatures, instead of flattering their *fascinating* graces, and viewing them as if they were in a state of perpetual childhood, unable to stand alone. I earnestly wish to point out in what true dignity and human happiness consists—I wish to persuade women to endeavor to acquire strength, both of mind and body, and to convince them that the soft phrases, susceptibility of heart, delicacy of sentiment, and refinement of taste, are almost synonymous with epithets[4] of weakness, and that those beings who are only the objects of pity and that kind of love, which has been termed its sister, will soon become objects of contempt. . . .

6   The education of women has, of late, been more attended to than formerly; yet they are still reckoned a frivolous sex, and ridiculed or pitied by the writers who endeavor by satire or instruction to improve them. It is acknowledged that they spend many of the first years of their lives in acquiring a smattering of accomplishments;[5] meanwhile strength of body and mind are sacrificed to libertine[6] notions of beauty, to the desire of establishing themselves—the only way women can rise in the world—by marriage. And this desire making mere animals of them, when they marry they act as such children may be expected to act: they dress; they paint, and nickname God's creatures. Surely these weak beings are only fit for a seraglio![7] Can they be expected to govern a family with judgment, or take care of the poor babes whom they bring into the world?

7   If then it can be fairly deduced from the present conduct of the sex, from the prevalent fondness for pleasure which takes place of ambition and those nobler passions that open and enlarge the soul; that the instruction which women have hitherto received has only tended, with the constitution of civil society, to render them insignificant objects of desire—mere propagators of fools!—if it can be proved that in aiming to accomplish them, without cultivating their understandings, they are taken out of their sphere of duties, and made ridiculous and useless when the short-lived bloom of beauty is over, I presume that *rational* men will excuse me for endeavoring to persuade them to become more masculine and respectable.

---

[4] **epithets** (ĕp´ə-thĕts): descriptive terms.

[5] **accomplishments:** This term, when applied to women, designated only those achievements then considered suitable for middle- and upper-class women, such as painting, singing, playing a musical instrument, and embroidery.

[6] **libertine** (lĭb´ər-tēn): indecent or unseemly.

[7] **seraglio** (sə-răl´yō): harem.

EVALUATE ARGUMENTS
Annotate: Mark in paragraph 5 the specific words that indicate the author's claim.

Evaluate: How does the author make her claim clear? How does the placement of her claim affect the strength of her argument?

LANGUAGE CONVENTIONS
Annotate: Circle the coordinating conjunction in the first sentence of paragraph 6. Underline the independent clauses that have been joined together by the conjunction.

Interpret: How does the conjunction clearly show the relationship between the two clauses?

© Houghton Mifflin Harcourt Publishing Company

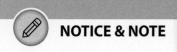
8   Indeed the word masculine is only a bugbear:[8] there is little reason to fear that women will acquire too much courage or fortitude; for their apparent inferiority with respect to bodily strength, must render them, in some degree, dependent on men in the various relations of life; but why should it be increased by prejudices that give a sex to virtue, and confound simple truths with sensual reveries?[9]

❧ From Chapter 2 ❧

9   Youth is the season for love in both sexes; but in those days of thoughtless enjoyment provision should be made for the more important years of life, when reflection takes place of sensation. But Rousseau,[10] and most of the male writers who have followed his steps, have warmly **inculcated** that the whole tendency of female education ought to be directed to one point: to render them[11] pleasing.

10   Let me reason with the supporters of this opinion who have any knowledge of human nature, do they imagine that marriage can eradicate the habitude of life? The woman who has only been taught to please will soon find that her charms are oblique sunbeams, and that they cannot have much effect on her husband's heart when they are seen every day, when the summer is passed and gone. Will she then have sufficient native energy to look into herself for comfort, and cultivate her dormant faculties? or, is it not more rational to expect that she will try to please other men; and, in the emotions raised by the expectation of new conquests, endeavor to forget the mortification her love or pride has received? When the husband ceases to be a lover—and the time will inevitably come, her desire of pleasing will then grow languid, or become a spring of bitterness; and love, perhaps, the most **evanescent** of all passions, gives place to jealousy or vanity.

11   I now speak of women who are restrained by principle or prejudice; such women, though they would shrink from an intrigue with real abhorrence, yet, nevertheless, wish to be convinced by the homage of gallantry that they are cruelly neglected by their husbands; or, days and weeks are spent in dreaming of the happiness enjoyed by **congenial** souls till their health is undermined and their spirits broken by discontent. How then can the great art of pleasing be such a necessary study? it is only useful to a mistress; the chaste wife, and serious mother, should only consider her power to please as the polish of her virtues, and the affection of her husband as one of the comforts that render her talk less difficult and her life happier. But, whether she be loved or neglected, her first wish should be to make

inculcate
(ĭn-kŭl´kāt, ĭn´kŭl-) *v.* to impress (something) upon the mind of another by frequent instruction or repetition; instill.

evanescent
(ĕv-ə-nĕs´ənt) *adj.* vanishing or likely to vanish like vapor.

congenial
(kən-jēn´yəl) *adj.* agreeable, sympathetic.

---

[8] **bugbear:** an object of exaggerated fear.

[9] **confound . . . reveries** (rĕv´ə-rēz): confuse simple truths with men's sexual daydreams.

[10] **Rousseau** (rōō-sō´): The Swiss-born French philosopher Jean-Jacques Rousseau (1712–1778) presented a plan for female education in his famous 1762 novel *Émile*.

[11] **them:** that is, females.

herself respectable, and not to rely for all her happiness on a being subject to like infirmities with herself.

12   The worthy Dr. Gregory fell into a similar error. I respect his heart; but entirely disapprove of his celebrated Legacy to his Daughters.[12] . . .

13   He actually recommends **dissimulation**, and advises an innocent girl to give the lie to her feelings, and not dance with spirit, when gaiety of heart would make her feet eloquent without making her gestures immodest. In the name of truth and common sense, why should not one woman acknowledge that she can take more exercise than another? or, in other words, that she has a sound constitution; and why, to damp innocent vivacity, is she darkly to be told that men will draw conclusions which she little thinks of? Let the libertine draw what inference he pleases; but, I hope, that no sensible mother will restrain the natural frankness of youth by instilling such indecent cautions. Out of the abundance of the heart the mouth speaketh; and a wiser than Solomon[13] hath said, that the heart should be made clean, and not trivial ceremonies observed, which it is not very difficult to fulfil with scrupulous exactness when vice reigns in the heart.

14   Women ought to endeavor to purify their heart; but can they do so when their uncultivated understandings make them entirely dependent on their senses for employment and amusement, when no noble pursuit sets them above the little vanities of the day, or enables them to curb the wild emotions that agitate a reed over which every passing breeze has power? To gain the affections of a virtuous man, is affectation necessary? Nature has given woman a weaker frame than man; but, to ensure her husband's affections, must a wife, who by the exercise of her mind and body whilst she was discharging the duties of a daughter, wife, and mother, has allowed her constitution to retain its natural strength, and her nerves a healthy tone, is she, I say, to condescend to use art and feign a sickly delicacy in order to secure her husband's affection? Weakness may excite tenderness, and gratify the arrogant pride of man; but the lordly caresses of a protector will not gratify a noble mind that pants for, and deserves to be respected. Fondness is a poor substitute for friendship! . . .

15   Besides, the woman who strengthens her body and exercises her mind will, by managing her family and practicing various virtues, become the friend, and not the humble dependent of her husband; and if she, by possessing such substantial qualities, merit his regard, she will not find it necessary to conceal her affection, nor to pretend

dissimulation
(dĭ-sĭm´yə-lā-shən) *n.* deceit or pretense.

---

[12]**Dr. Gregory . . . Daughters:** In his 1774 work *A Father's Legacy for His Daughters*, John Gregory (1724–1773) offered a plan for female education that remained popular for decades.

[13]**a wiser than Solomon:** King David, reputed author of many psalms in the Bible and the father of King Solomon, who was known for his wisdom. The words that follow draw on ideas in Psalm 24, which states that only those with "clean hands and a pure heart" shall ascend into Heaven.

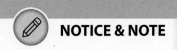

Utopian
(yoo-tō´pē-ən) *adj.* excellent or ideal but impracticable; visionary.

to an unnatural coldness of constitution to excite her husband's passions. . . .

16   If all the faculties of woman's mind are only to be cultivated as they respect her dependence on man; if, when a husband be obtained, she have arrived at her goal, and meanly proud rests satisfied with such a paltry crown, let her grovel contentedly, scarcely raised by her employments above the animal kingdom; but, if, struggling for the prize of her high calling, she look beyond the present scene, let her cultivate her understanding without stopping to consider what character the husband may have whom she is destined to marry. Let her only determine, without being too anxious about present happiness, to acquire the qualities that ennoble a rational being, and a rough inelegant husband may shock her taste without destroying her peace of mind. She will not model her soul to suit the frailties of her companion, but to bear with them: his character may be a trial, but not an impediment to virtue. . . .

17   These may be termed **Utopian** dreams. Thanks to that Being who impressed them on my soul, and gave me sufficient strength of mind to dare to exert my own reason, till, becoming dependent only on him for the support of my virtue, I view, with indignation, the mistaken notions that enslave my sex.

18   I love man as my fellow; but his scepter, real, or usurped, extends not to me, unless the reason of an individual demands my homage; and even then the submission is to reason, and not to man. In fact, the conduct of an accountable being must be regulated by the operations of its own reason; or on what foundation rests the throne of God?

19   It appears to me necessary to dwell on these obvious truths, because females have been insulated, as it were; and, while they have been stripped of the virtues that should clothe humanity, they have been decked with artificial graces that enable them to exercise a short-lived tyranny. Love, in their bosoms, taking place of every nobler passion, their sole ambition is to be fair, to raise emotion instead of inspiring respect; and this ignoble desire, like the servility in absolute monarchies, destroys all strength of character. Liberty is the mother of virtue, and if women be, by their very constitution, slaves, and not allowed to breathe the sharp invigorating air of freedom, they must ever languish like exotics,[14] and be reckoned beautiful flaws in nature.

---

[14]**languish** (lăng´gwĭsh) **like exotics:** wilt like plants grown away from their natural environment.

CHECK YOUR UNDERSTANDING

Answer these questions before moving on to the **Analyze the Text** section on the following page.

1 Wollstonecraft argues that women should be educated to strengthen what two things?

   A Body and soul

   B Beauty and usefulness

   C Mind and body

   D Beauty and emotions

2 Which of the following is an opposing view on which the author builds a counterargument?

   F Education will make women too conceited.

   G The behavior of women proves their lack of intelligence.

   H Women lack the desire for higher education.

   J The point of female education is to make women pleasing to men.

3 According to Wollstonecraft, what is one main cause of women's misery?

   A Their physical weaknesses

   B An obligation to respect their husbands

   C Their suppressed emotions

   D A false system of education

ANALYZE THE TEXT

Support your responses with evidence from the text. 🗒 NOTEBOOK

1. **Interpret** In paragraph 1, the author identifies a logical fallacy, saying that "women, in particular, are rendered weak and wretched by a variety of concurring causes, originating from one hasty conclusion." What is the hasty conclusion to which Wollstonecraft refers?

2. **Critique** How does the author's counterargument to Rousseau's view in paragraphs 9–11 help her to achieve her purpose?

3. **Evaluate** Reread paragraphs 12–13. How does Dr. Gregory's plan for women's education provide evidence to support the author's argument?

4. **Interpret** Wollstonecraft presents her counterargument to Gregory's ideas in paragraphs 14–15. According to Wollstonecraft, how will strengthening her body and mind improve a woman's marriage?

5. **Notice & Note** In paragraph 6, Wollstonecraft makes a claim about the way women gain stature in the world and how this affects them. How might her statements in this paragraph be considered a use of extreme or exaggerated language? What does she most likely wish to accomplish by using this kind of language?

RESEARCH

RESEARCH TIP
Since you'll be searching for specific content included in two texts, be sure to include the titles of the works in the search bar rather than just the authors' names. If you find summaries of their works, use only those from reliable sources.

In support of her argument, Wollstonecraft refers to two writers of her day—Jean-Jacques Rousseau and Dr. John Gregory. She summarizes their general ideas for female education and then presents counterarguments for each one.

But what were some of their other specific ideas on this topic? How did the two men differ in their opinions? Conduct research to find out more about these authors and the works to which Wollstonecraft refers in her essay. Use the chart to record your findings.

ROUSSEAU'S IDEAS ABOUT WOMEN'S EDUCATION—FROM HIS NOVEL *ÉMILE*	GREGORY'S IDEAS ABOUT WOMEN'S EDUCATION—FROM *A FATHER'S LEGACY FOR HIS DAUGHTERS*

Extend In a small group, compare notes from your research and discuss which writers' ideas you believe have more merit.

CREATE AND PRESENT

Write an Argument Use what you have learned from reading and studying Wollstonecraft's essay to write your own argument. Choose a topic related to education or to the Essential Question: What keeps women from achieving equality with men?

When you write your argument, remember the basic structure of an argument:

❏ State your claim, or thesis, clearly in your introduction.

❏ Support your claim with logical reasons. Make sure to avoid relying on logical fallacies.

❏ Use quotations and other evidence from the text and your research to support your reasons.

❏ Anticipate any opposing views to your argument and prepare counterarguments.

Give a Persuasive Speech Once you have written your argument, prepare to present it as a persuasive speech to your class. Practice first with a partner. Critique each other using the following criteria:

❏ clear and logical presentation of argument

❏ effective use of logical, ethical, and emotional appeals

❏ appropriate volume and tone of voice

❏ appropriate use of eye contact, facial expressions, and gestures

Go to **Writing Arguments** in the **Writing Studio** for more help.

Go to **Giving a Presentation** in the **Speaking and Listening Studio** to find out more about making a speech.

RESPOND TO THE ESSENTIAL QUESTION

? What keeps women from achieving equality with men?

Gather Information Review your annotations and notes on *A Vindication of the Rights of Woman*. Then, add relevant details to your Response Log. As you determine which information to include, think about:

- The importance of education for all people
- The meaning of true equality
- How education affects relationships between men and women

UNIT 3 RESPONSE LOG

ACADEMIC VOCABULARY

As you write and discuss what you learned from the argument, be sure to use the Academic Vocabulary words. Check off each of the words that you use.

❏ **encounter**

❏ **exploit**

❏ **persist**

❏ **subordinate**

❏ **widespread**

CRITICAL VOCABULARY

WORD BANK

vindication	evanescent
abrogate	congenial
prerogative	dissimulation
inculcate	Utopian

Practice and Apply Fill in each blank with the most appropriate Critical Vocabulary word.

1. Your friends might try to persuade you to stay, but you have the _____ to change your mind.

2. We lingered on the porch as long as possible in order to enjoy the _____ beauty of the setting sun.

3. His attorney assured him that his actions would not _____ the agreement.

4. The business soon dropped its _____ plans for total participation.

5. Parents should _____ their children with moral values and principles.

6. True friends should avoid any sort of _____ in order to maintain an honest relationship.

7. Although I felt quite homesick during my first week at the university, my discomfort began to fade as my roommate became a _____ companion.

8. When the mayor's innocence was proven, the town rejoiced over his _____.

VOCABULARY STRATEGY:
Literary Allusions

Allusions are indirect references to a person, place, event, or literary work. Writers make allusions to things they assume will be familiar to their readers.

Practice and Apply Wollstonecraft makes four references to literary works to support her argument. How does each allusion strengthen her argument? Use the footnotes in the selection and record answers in the chart below. The last entry in the chart is not footnoted. Can you identify the allusion?

ALLUSION/ REFERENCE	EXPLANATION	HOW IT STRENGTHENS HER ARGUMENT
Paragraph 9		
Paragraph 12		
Paragraph 13		
Paragraph 13: "Out of the abundance of the heart the mouth speaketh."		

LANGUAGE CONVENTIONS:
Coordinating and Subordinating Conjunctions

Wollstonecraft expresses her ideas in long, detailed sentences that rely heavily on coordinating and subordinating conjunctions to connect words, phrases, and clauses smoothly in a way that shows the relationships between ideas.

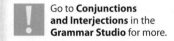

Go to **Conjunctions and Interjections** in the **Grammar Studio** for more.

The charts list the coordinating and subordinating conjunctions and explain how they are used.

COORDINATING CONJUNCTIONS	PURPOSE	SAMPLE SENTENCE
and, but, for, nor, or, so, yet	connect words or groups of words that have the same function in a sentence (examples: two subjects, two phrases, two independent clauses)	She read many books on education, <u>but</u> they did not provide satisfactory answers to her questions.

SUBORDINATING CONJUNCTIONS	PURPOSE	SAMPLE SENTENCE
after, although, as, as if, because, before, if, since, so that, than, though, unless, until, when, whenever, where, wherever, while	introduce subordinate clauses—clauses that cannot stand alone as complete sentences	<u>Although</u> many men read her essay, some were not convinced by the argument she made for the need to enhance the education of women.

Examine the following sentence from Wollstonecraft's essay:

> **I love man as my fellow; but his scepter, real, or usurped, extends not to me, unless the reason of an individual demands my homage; and even then the submission is to reason, and not to man.**

Find the conjunctions between the clauses and identify each one as coordinating or subordinating. What if the author had chosen to write the same ideas in separate sentences, without the use of these conjunctions? Write the resulting sentences below. What effect does removing the conjunctions have on the presentation of ideas?

Practice and Apply Write a brief paragraph providing instructions on how to perform a complex task. Include the correct usage of at least two coordinating conjunctions and two subordinating conjunctions. Remember that the clauses joined by coordinating conjunctions must be able to stand alone as sentences—that is, they must be independent clauses.

ARTICLE

EDUCATION PROTECTS WOMEN FROM ABUSE

by **Olga Khazan**

pages 437–440

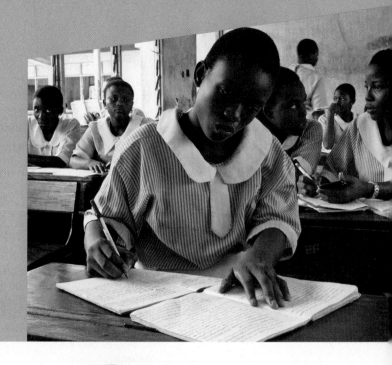

COMPARE ACROSS GENRES

Now that you've read excerpts from *A Vindication of the Rights of Woman*, read "Education Protects Women from Abuse" and explore how the article connects to some of the same ideas. As you read, think about how the author of "Education Protects Women from Abuse" presents and supports her point of view. After you are finished, you will collaborate with a small group on a final project that involves an analysis of both texts.

? **ESSENTIAL QUESTION:**

What keeps women from achieving equality with men?

ARGUMENT

from A VINDICATION OF THE RIGHTS OF WOMAN

by **Mary Wollstonecraft**

pages 423–428

Education Protects Women from Abuse

QUICK START

Imagine you have been invited to promote a United Nations program designed to achieve gender equality and empower all women and girls. In your notebook, list different approaches to empower and educate women to combat inequality. Discuss your ideas with a partner.

MAKE PREDICTIONS

Text features are design elements of a text. They may include titles, subtitles, headings, pull quotes, and boldfaced or italicized text. You will often find a variety of text features in magazine and newspaper articles because they help attract readers' attention. Readers can use text features to make predictions about an article's subject matter, key ideas, and the author's purpose.

In "Education Protects Women from Abuse," Olga Khazan offers strong opinions about the issue she discusses. Use the chart to make predictions about the article based on its text features.

TEXT FEATURE	PREDICTIONS
Title: Education Protects Women from Abuse	
Subtitle: Extremists hate smart girls because smart girls are less likely to be kept down.	
Pull Quote: Girls' schooling . . . has a protective effect against domestic violence, rape, and child marriage.	

ANALYZE GRAPHIC FEATURES

A **multimodal text** combines two or more ways of communicating meaning, such as text, graphic features, and audio. This approach offers the reader a rich learning experience. For example, graphic features can provide at-a-glance information that is difficult to convey in text. Graphic features may include illustrations, photographs, charts, graphs, and maps.

The author of "Education Protects Women from Abuse" integrates two graphic features into her analysis. The first feature is a **thematic map,** a map focused on a specific theme or subject. The second feature is a **scatter plot graph,** which is a type of graph that uses points to show the relationship between two sets of data. As you read the article, note how the information in these features supports the author's ideas about education.

GENRE ELEMENTS: ARTICLE

- provides factual information on a topic or recent event
- includes evidence to support ideas
- often contains text features
- appears in print or online newspapers or magazines

CRITICAL VOCABULARY

extremist	manacle	autonomy	misogyny
mire	condone	inoculate	

To see how many Critical Vocabulary words you already know, use the words to complete the sentences.

1. A person who says disparaging things about women displays _____.

2. A police officer should not _____ the act of speeding.

3. The freed prisoner was thrilled to once again have personal _____.

4. The members of the _____ group used riots to get media attention.

5. Gaining knowledge is a good way to _____ yourself against fear of the unknown.

6. The amount of information available on the Internet can _____ even the most skilled researchers in hours of useless searching.

7. The man would _____ his rival's progress by digging up details about the past.

LANGUAGE CONVENTIONS

Direct and Indirect Quotations In this lesson, you will learn about properly citing others' ideas using direct and indirect quotations. As you read "Education Protects Women from Abuse," look for places where the author uses the exact words of a speaker or writer in a **direct quotation** or uses her own words to paraphrase another writer's work in an **indirect quotation.**

ANNOTATION MODEL
NOTICE & NOTE

As you read, notice how the author uses text features and graphic features. Consider and make note of how these choices add to your experience as a reader and your understanding of the author's purpose for writing. You can mark up evidence that supports your ideas. In the model, you can see one reader's notes about the author's use of the subtitle: "Extremists hate smart girls because smart girls are less likely to be kept down."

The horrifying kidnapping of nearly 300 Nigerian schoolgirls by the extremist group <u>Boko Haram</u> was made even more horrifying by the fact that the group specifically targeted the girls for trying to improve their lives. <u>Boko Haram</u> went after the girls for the same reason the <u>Taliban</u> went after Malala Yousafzai: <u>Extremists fear smart women.</u>

> Boko Haram and the Taliban must be some of the "extremists" referred to in the subtitle.

BACKGROUND

Boko Haram is a militant Islamist group that arose in northeastern Nigeria in 2002. Boko Haram can be roughly translated as "Western education is forbidden." In 2014 Boko Haram sparked international outrage by kidnapping an estimated 276 girls, stating that the girls would be enslaved and married off. In 2015 a coalition of military forces from Nigeria and several other African nations in the region, successfully reclaimed much of the territory the group had gained in its attacks, but Boko Haram remains an influential force in northeastern Nigeria.

EDUCATION PROTECTS WOMEN FROM ABUSE

Extremists hate smart girls because smart girls are less likely to be kept down.

Article by Olga Khazan

PREPARE TO COMPARE

As you read, pay attention to the ideas that the author presents about women's education and rights. Note details and features of the text that help you understand the author's purpose for writing. This will help you compare this text with the excerpt from A Vindication of the Rights of Woman.

1   The horrifying kidnapping of nearly 300 Nigerian schoolgirls by the **extremist** group Boko Haram was made even more horrifying by the fact that the group specifically targeted the girls for trying to improve their lives. Boko Haram went after the girls for the same reason the Taliban went after Malala Yousafzai: Extremists fear smart women.

2   "If you want to **mire** a nation in backwardness, **manacle** your daughters," wrote *New York Times* columnist Nick Kristof. . . .

> **"Girls' schooling . . . has a protective effect against domestic violence, rape, and child marriage."**

© Houghton Mifflin Harcourt Publishing Company • Image Credits: © Picade LLC/Alamy

extremist
(ĭk-strē´mĭst) *adj.* advocating or resorting to measures beyond the norm, especially in politics.

mire
(mīr) *v.* to hinder, entrap, or entangle.

manacle
(măn´ə-kəl) *v.* to restrain the action or progress of something or someone.

MAKE PREDICTIONS
Annotate: Mark the words in the pull quote that provide clues to the author's purpose.

Analyze: Why do you think this quotation was chosen as a pull quote?

3   Kristof listed some of the better-known positive externalities of having an educated female population: Fewer children, and thus less risk of a "youth bulge" and, later, civil war. Not to mention a more skilled labor force and a stronger economy.

4   But a . . . report suggests that the benefit of girls' schooling extends even further—that it has a protective effect against domestic violence, rape, and child marriage.

5   "No place is less safe for a woman than her own home," reads a World Bank report released in 2014. Roughly 30 percent of the world's women have experienced physical or sexual violence at the hands of their partners, and across 33 developing countries surveyed by the organization, nearly one-third of women said they could not refuse sex with their partner.

LANGUAGE CONVENTIONS

Annotate: Mark the direct quotation in paragraph 5.

Analyze: Why does the author most likely include the direct quotation?

ANALYZE GRAPHIC FEATURES

Annotate: Mark the sentence in paragraph 5 that is supported by the thematic map.

Synthesize: How else could the author have chosen to present the information in the map? Would another kind of presentation have been as effective?

Share of Women Who Have Experienced Physical or Sexual Violence by an Intimate Partner

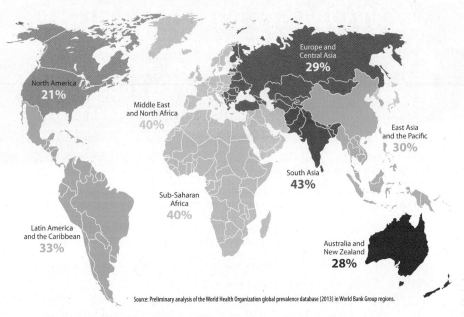

North America **21%**

Europe and Central Asia **29%**

Middle East and North Africa **40%**

East Asia and the Pacific **30%**

South Asia **43%**

Sub-Saharan Africa **40%**

Latin America and the Caribbean **33%**

Australia and New Zealand **28%**

Source: Preliminary analysis of the World Health Organization global prevalence database (2013) in World Bank Group regions.

6   "Yes, it's normal, being beaten, yelled at. If you tell [anyone], your peers will ask you, is this your first time to be beaten? Some of us are used to it, just like the way we are used to eating *ugali*,"[1] one Tanzanian woman said in a World Bank focus group.

7   To make matters worse, one in three women said they thought wife-beating was justifiable, and women who **condoned** domestic violence were more likely to experience it.

condone

(kən-dōnʹ) *v.* to overlook, forgive, or disregard (an offense) without protest or censure.

---

[1] **ugali:** (uːˈgaːli) *n.* a type of maize porridge eaten in eastern and central Africa.

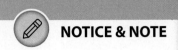
Change in the Percent of Women Who Believe a Husband Is Justified in Beating His Wife if She . . .

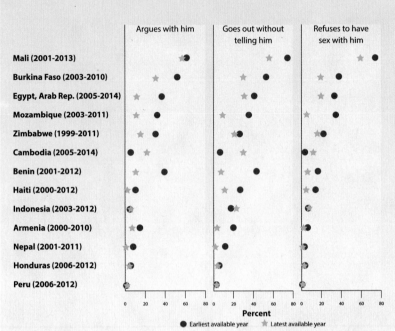

Source: Voice and Agency 2014 team estimates based on Demographic and Heath Surveys for 13 countries for which data over time are available.

ANALYZE GRAPHIC FEATURES

Annotate: Mark details in paragraphs 8 and 9 that demonstrate the effect of education on abuse.

Draw Conclusions: Based on the data presented in the graph and the information in the text, what conclusions can you draw about the education of women in the countries listed?

autonomy
(ô-tŏn´ə-mē) *n.* the condition or quality of being autonomous; independence.

MAKE PREDICTIONS

Annotate: Mark the direct quotation in paragraph 10.

Evaluate: Now that you have nearly finished reading the selection, look back at the predictions you made in the table on page 435. Were your predictions correct? Why or why not?

inoculate
(ĭ-nŏk´yə-lāt) *v.* to safeguard as if by inoculation; to protect.

misogyny
(mĭ-sŏj´ə-nē) *n.* hatred or mistrust of women.

8   But the Bank also found that better-educated women were more likely to not be sexually or physically abused. Each additional year of schooling was associated with a 1-percent increase in their ability to refuse sex with their partner.

9   "The strongest correlate of women's sexual **autonomy** in a relationship is her level of education," the report notes. "Overall, 87 percent of women with a higher education say they can refuse sex. Women with some or completed secondary education have an 11 and 36 percent lower risk of violence, respectively, compared with women with no education."

10   One of the most lasting, damaging impacts of the Boko Haram kidnapping could be making Nigerian girls nervous about attending class. According to recent interviews with some of the escaped girls, when the group arrived at the school in northern Nigeria, they were shouting, "We are Boko Haram. We will burn your school. You shall not do school again. You shall do Islamic school."

11   Of course, it's also crucial to change social norms and laws in countries with high levels of domestic violence, and working with men's groups can go a long way as well. But since female education seems to **inoculate** societies against **misogyny**, it's both unsurprising and heartbreaking that Boko Haram would target classrooms.

CHECK YOUR UNDERSTANDING

Answer these questions before moving on to the **Analyze the Text** section on the following page.

1 Why did the author most likely include the thematic map?

A To emphasize the geopolitical cause of abuse

B To make a point about the importance of maps

C To present complex information in an effective way

D To show that extremist groups are an international threat

2 Which quotation from the selection best supports the claim made by the title of the article?

F *But a . . . report suggests that the benefit of girls' schooling extends even further—that it has a protective effect against domestic violence, rape, and child marriage.*

G *To make matters worse, one in three women said they thought wife-beating was justifiable, and women who condoned domestic violence were more likely to experience it.*

H *Of course, it's also crucial to change social norms and laws in countries with high levels of domestic violence, and working with men's groups can go a long way as well.*

J *One of the most lasting, damaging impacts of the Boko Haram kidnapping could be making Nigerian girls nervous about attending class.*

3 According to the graph, in which country have women's beliefs about justification for domestic violence changed the least?

A Mozambique

B Zimbabwe

C Haiti

D Peru

ANALYZE THE TEXT

Support your responses with evidence from the text.   NOTEBOOK

1. **Summarize** Review paragraphs 4–9. In your own words, summarize the findings of the World Bank report. Explain how the findings relate to the author's purpose.

2. **Analyze** Examine the scatter plot graph. What is the overall trend or pattern in women's opinions regarding domestic violence? Do any countries listed go against the trend?

3. **Compare** Compare the information presented in the map with the information presented in the scatter plot graph. Both present data about domestic violence in different parts of the world. What is an important kind of information presented in the scatter plot graph that the map does not show?

4. **Critique** Review the subtitle and the pull quote. Is the author's use of these text features effective? Why or why not?

5. **Analyze** What are the main ideas of the two graphic features? How does each graphic feature relate to the main idea of the article?

RESEARCH

RESEARCH TIP

When using a search engine to conduct research, choose search terms carefully to obtain relevant results. To research statistical information on education inequality, consider including the term "statistics" in your search phrase.

Inequalities in levels of education for women and men have been extensively researched and reported on by many global organizations. Research some statistics on the education of women and girls worldwide. Use the chart to record your findings.

STATISTIC	SOURCE

Extend Share the statistics you found with a small group. Discuss whether the statistics support the author's claim about the effect of education on the abuse of women.

CREATE AND ADAPT

Write an Analysis Write a three- or four-paragraph essay in which you analyze and evaluate the author's use of graphic features in "Education Protects Women from Abuse." Consider reviewing your notes and annotations of the text before you begin.

- ❏ Introduce your essay by identifying the author's purpose for writing the article.

- ❏ Then, describe the graphic features the author chose to use and explain how they relate to and/or support the author's purpose for writing. Support your ideas with evidence from the text.

- ❏ In your final paragraph, state your conclusion about the effectiveness of the graphic features.

Adapt and Present With a small group, discuss your opinions about what makes a graphic feature effective. Then, adapt information from the article into an effective graphic.

- ❏ Review the article with your group to identify statistics that are presented in a text format but could be adapted to a visual format.

- ❏ Create a graphic that could be used to replace one of the statistics in the article.

- ❏ Present your graphic to the class. Explain possible pros and cons of using your graphic to replace the text.

Go to **Writing Informative Texts** in the **Writing Studio** for more help.

Go to **Giving a Presentation** in the **Speaking and Listening Studio** for more help.

RESPOND TO THE ESSENTIAL QUESTION

? What keeps women from achieving equality with men?

Gather Information Review your annotations and notes on "Education Protects Women from Abuse." Then, add relevant information to your Response Log. As you determine which information to include, think about:

- how abuse is related to inequality
- how education is related to inequality
- how views of the role of women vary from one society to another

ACADEMIC VOCABULARY

As you write and discuss what you learned from "Education Protects Women from Abuse," be sure to use the Academic Vocabulary words. Check off each of the words that you use.

- ❏ **encounter**
- ❏ **exploit**
- ❏ **persist**
- ❏ **subordinate**
- ❏ **widespread**

RESPOND

WORD BANK

extremist	autonomy
mire	inoculate
manacle	misogyny
condone	

Go to **Analyzing Word Structure** in the **Vocabulary Studio** for more on Greek roots and prefixes.

CRITICAL VOCABULARY

Practice and Apply With a partner, discuss and then write down an answer to each of the following questions. Then, work together to write a sentence for each Critical Vocabulary word.

1. Which vocabulary word goes with the idea of excusing behavior?

2. Which vocabulary word is associated with personal freedom?

3. Which vocabulary word could be used to describe outrageous actions?

4. Which vocabulary word goes with the word *safeguard*?

5. Which vocabulary word goes with the idea of holding back or restricting something?

6. Which vocabulary word is associated with gender relations?

7. Which vocabulary word is associated with becoming stuck?

VOCABULARY STRATEGY:
Greek Roots and Prefixes

One of the languages that had a significant impact on the development of the English language was Greek. Knowing the meanings of Greek prefixes and roots can help you determine the meanings of unfamiliar words.

For example, the word *physical* contains the Greek root *phys,* meaning "body." The word *physical* means "relating to the body." When the author of the selection refers to *physical* abuse, she is specifying abuse that involves violence against the human body, as opposed to other forms of abuse.

Practice and Apply Examine the Greek word parts listed below. Use the word parts and the Critical Vocabulary words from this selection to complete the chart. Then, with a partner, brainstorm a list of other English words that use these word parts.

auto: self, same, one   *mis:* bad, wrong, to hate

gyn: woman, female   *nomos:* law

WORD	PREFIXES AND ROOTS	DEFINITION
misogyny		

© Houghton Mifflin Harcourt Publishing Company

LANGUAGE CONVENTIONS:
Direct and Indirect Quotations

Direct quotations are a writer's or speaker's exact words. When included in texts, they are set off by quotation marks. **Indirect quotations** are a writer's restatement of another writer's or speaker's words. They are not punctuated with quotation marks. For detailed instruction on punctuating direct quotations, you can consult a style guide such as the Modern Language Association (MLA) Handbook or the Publication Manual of the American Psychological Association (APA).

Khazan includes a direct quotation from a Tanzanian woman in her article:

> "Yes, it's normal, being beaten, yelled at. If you tell [anyone], your peers will ask you, is this your first time to be beaten? Some of us are used to it, just like the way we are used to eating *ugali*," one Tanzanian woman said in a World Bank focus group.

The author could have instead chosen to present the woman's comments as an indirect quotation:

> A Tanzanian woman told a World Bank focus group that being beaten and yelled at was normal, and that some Tanzanian women are so accustomed to domestic abuse that it seems as normal to them as the food they eat.

Notice the difference between the two versions. In the first, the reader hears the woman's own voice as she matter-of-factly describes being beaten as part of everyday life. The second version conveys the idea that some women view domestic abuse as normal, but it does not have the same impact as the woman's own words.

The chart below shows ways to integrate and punctuate direct quotations, using tags or phrases such as "she said" that indicate the speaker or writer:

PUNCTUATION OF DIRECT QUOTATIONS	
with tag at beginning	The woman said, "In my country, very few girls finish school."
with tag interrupting the quotation	"In my country," the woman said, "very few girls finish school."
with tag after the quotation	"In my country, very few girls finish school," the woman said.
to introduce a long quotation	One woman spoke about her personal experience in the education system: "I entered school at the age of 6. . . ."

Practice and Apply Return to the article. Find a paragraph that includes at least one direct quotation. Rewrite the paragraph using an indirect quotation. When you have finished, share your new paragraph with a partner and work together to analyze how the changes you made affect that part of the article.

Go to **Using Textual Evidence** in the **Writing Studio** for more on using direct and indirect quotations.

Collaborate & Compare

from
A VINDICATION OF THE RIGHTS OF WOMAN
Argument by
Mary Wollstonecraft

EDUCATION PROTECTS WOMEN FROM ABUSE
Article by Olga Khazan

COMPARE ACROSS GENRES

A Vindication of the Rights of Woman and "Education Protects Women from Abuse" reflect two different genres, or types of writing. Wollstonecraft presents her *Vindication* as an argument, while Khazan presents her ideas in an informational article. Despite the difference in genre, both authors address similar themes related to the education of women.

When you compare the ideas in two or more texts, you also synthesize those ideas, making connections, expanding on key concepts, and even developing new questions. In a small group, complete the Venn diagram with similarities and differences in the ideas presented by Wollstonecraft and Khazan.

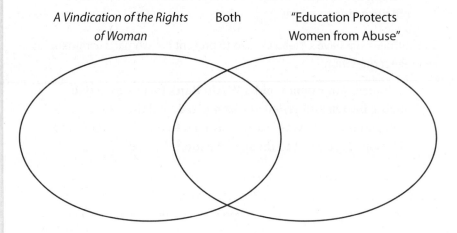

A Vindication of the Rights of Woman   Both   "Education Protects Women from Abuse"

ANALYZE THE TEXTS

Discuss these questions in your group.

1. **Infer** How did Wollstonecraft and Khazan most likely expect their works to be received? How might their expectations have influenced their writing styles? Explain your response.

2. **Contrast** How do Wollstonecraft's and Khazan's interpretations of how lack of education harms women differ?

3. **Interpret** Both Wollstonecraft and Khazan are concerned about the education of women. However, they are writing in very different times and cultures. When Khazan refers to "women" as a group, who is she describing? Does the word *women* used by Wollstonecraft define the same group?

4. **Synthesize** How do you think Mary Wollstonecraft would respond to the information and statistics Khazan presents in her article? Cite evidence to support your response.

COLLABORATE AND PRESENT

Now your group can continue exploring the ideas in these texts by collaborating to compare the texts and present your analyses. Follow these steps:

1. **Determine Central Ideas** In your group, discuss the main ideas of each text, making sure that everyone contributes. Narrow down the ideas presented and try to reach an agreement on one central or controlling idea for each selection.

2. **Identify Supporting Details** Next, identify at least two lines of reasoning each author uses to develop her central idea and at least two specific details she uses to support each line of reasoning. You can use a table to organize your ideas.

SELECTION AND CONTROLLING IDEA	LINES OF REASONING	SUPPORTING DETAILS

3. **Compare and Analyze** With your group, discuss the similarities and differences between the central ideas of the selections and the ways in which each author develops and supports those ideas. Then analyze how the central idea and techniques used by each author reflect her purposes for writing.

4. **Present to the Class** Present your group's findings to the class. Be sure to include your group's conclusions about both the central idea and the author's purpose of each selection, highlighting the primary similarities and differences that you identified. You may adapt the charts you created or use other visuals to convey your ideas to the class.

Go to **Giving a Presentation** in the **Speaking and Listening Studio** for more on presenting.

NOVEL

from

A JOURNAL OF THE PLAGUE YEAR

by **Daniel Defoe**

pages 451–456

COMPARE ACROSS GENRES

As you read, carefully note details about the setting, the narrator, and the plague being described. How does the author use setting to develop the plot and theme? How does the text's point of view affect your impression of events? Later, your answers will help guide you and your group as you compare this text to *Inferno: A Doctor's Ebola Story*.

ESSENTIAL QUESTION:

Why are plagues so horrifying?

MEMOIR

from

INFERNO: A DOCTOR'S EBOLA STORY

by **Steven Hatch, M.D.**

pages 465–470

from **A Journal of the Plague Year**

QUICK START

How do you think you would behave during a major epidemic? Would you flee to a safer place or stay to help others? With a partner, discuss how fear of a dangerous illness can affect people's behavior.

ANALYZE HISTORICAL SETTING

Daniel Defoe's *A Journal of the Plague Year* is a work of fiction. However, the novel realistically portrays historical events in London in the summer of 1665, during the darkest days of the city's outbreak of bubonic plague. In the novel, Defoe incorporates details from mortality records, city maps, and other historical documents to help him achieve **verisimilitude,** or the appearance of truth and actuality. Presented as an eyewitness account, the novel purposefully blurs the line between fact and fiction.

As you read, notice details—such as dates and times, geographical names and information, and numbers and statistics—that establish the novel's historical setting. Note how these details help drive the plot and shape the text's theme.

ANALYZE NARRATOR

Novelists relate the events of their stories through the voices of their narrators. In *A Journal of the Plague Year,* Daniel Defoe uses a first-person **narrator**, a character in the novel who relates events in his own words, using the pronouns *I, me*, and *my*. The perspective of Defoe's narrator affects a reader's impression of what is happening.

As you read, identify details that reveal the character of the narrator, as well as his perspective. Use a chart like the one below to help you analyze Defoe's narrator and to note how that narrator affects your impression of events.

DETAIL ABOUT NARRATOR	CHARACTERISTIC REVEALED	EFFECT ON MY IMPRESSIONS

GENRE ELEMENTS: NOVEL

- includes the basic elements of fiction—plot, characters, conflict, setting, and theme
- often includes more characters and a more complex plot than a short story
- story may be told by one or more narrators
- setting may be real, as in a historical novel, or imagined

CRITICAL VOCABULARY

visitation	discourse	huddle
summon	promiscuously	abate

To preview the Critical Vocabulary words, fill in the blanks with the correct vocabulary word.

1. During their heated _____, Mike and Mary were able to solve their disagreements and continue with plans for the project.

2. There are rules limiting _____ at the college dorm.

3. Joline leaves her laundry strewn _____ across the floor of her room.

4. When it rains, we _____ under the awning to stay warm and dry.

5. Don't worry about the time; a bell will _____ us for our next class.

6. Although you are miserable today, your cold symptoms will _____ soon and you will feel much better.

LANGUAGE CONVENTIONS

A **participle** is a verb form that functions as an adjective, modifying nouns and pronouns. Most participles are present participle forms that end in *-ing* or past participle forms that end in *-ed* or *-en*.

> The <u>wailing</u> man threw himself into the river.
> <u>Confused</u>, he swam in circles.

As you read the excerpt from *A Journal of the Plague Year*, watch for participles.

ANNOTATION MODEL

NOTICE & NOTE

In the model, you can see how one reader marked the text to analyze the historical setting by noting the narrator's language and use of details.

The face of <u>London</u> was now indeed strangely altered, I mean the whole mass of buildings, city, liberties, <u>suburbs, Westminster, Southwark,</u> and altogether; for as to the particular part called the city, or within the walls, that was not yet much infected. <u>But in the whole the face of things, I say, was much altered;</u> <u>sorrow and sadness sat upon every face;</u> and though some parts were not yet overwhelmed, yet all <u>looked deeply concerned;</u> and, as we saw it apparently coming on, so everyone looked on himself and his family as in the <u>utmost danger.</u>

The story takes place in London and surrounding areas. The disaster is widespread.

Emotions are seen on faces, so the author uses the words "the whole face of things, I say, was much altered" to describe the generally sad atmosphere.

All are extremely concerned, so the danger must be great.

BACKGROUND

Daniel Defoe *(c. 1660–1731) is considered a pioneer of modern journalism and the father of the English novel. He was five years old when the bubonic plague broke out in London in 1665, and he and his family survived the epidemic and the Great Fire of London the following year. In* A Journal of the Plague Year, *Defoe chronicles the epidemic through the eyes of his narrator, a saddle maker known as H. F. After agonizing over whether to leave the city, H. F. reads a passage in the Bible and decides to stay to do what he can for those in need.*

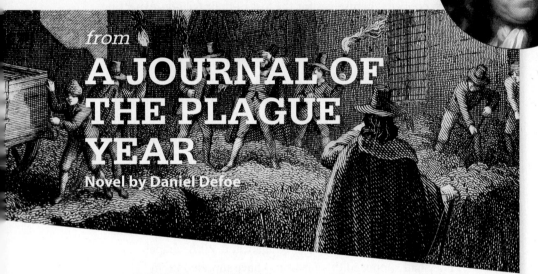

from
A JOURNAL OF THE PLAGUE YEAR
Novel by Daniel Defoe

PREPARE TO COMPARE

As you read, look for details in the text that help describe and develop the historical setting. Also, take time to analyze the narrator so that you can determine the effect his perspective has on the development of the plot and theme. Your analysis will help you compare this narrator's perspective with the perspective of the author of the memoir that follows this selection.

1   The face of London was now indeed strangely altered, I mean the whole mass of buildings, city[1], liberties[2], suburbs, Westminster, Southwark, and altogether; for as to the particular part called the city, or within the walls, that was not yet much infected. But in the whole the face of things, I say, was much altered; sorrow and sadness sat upon every face; and though some parts were not yet overwhelmed, yet all looked deeply concerned; and, as we saw it apparently coming on, so every one looked on himself and his family as in the utmost danger. Were it possible to represent those times exactly to those that did not see them, and give the reader due ideas of the horror that everywhere presented itself, it must make just impressions upon their minds and fill

---

[1] **city:** the portion of London once within the old city walls with Westminster to the west and Southwark to the south.
[2] **liberties:** densely populated area just outside the city walls.

© Houghton Mifflin Harcourt Publishing Company • Image Credits: © GL Archive/Alamy; © Hulton Fine Art Collection/Getty Images

ANALYZE HISTORICAL SETTING
Annotate: In paragraph 1, mark the words or phrases that evoke emotions about the plague.

Analyze: How does the use of this evocative language help readers understand the setting?

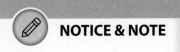
them with surprise. London might well be said to be all in tears; the mourners did not go about the streets indeed, for nobody put on black or made a formal dress of mourning for their nearest friends; but the voice of mourning was truly heard in the streets. The shrieks of women and children at the windows and doors of their houses, where their dearest relations were perhaps dying, or just dead, were so frequent to be heard as we passed the streets, that it was enough to pierce the stoutest heart in the world to hear them. Tears and lamentations were seen almost in every house, especially in the first part of the **visitation**; for towards the latter end men's hearts were hardened, and death was so always before their eyes, that they did not so much concern themselves for the loss of their friends, expecting that themselves should be **summoned** the next hour. . . .

visitation

(vĭz-ĭ-tā´shən) *n.* an instance of being visited.

summon

(sŭm´ən) *v.* to bring into existence or readiness.

2   I went all the first part of the time freely about the streets, though not so freely as to run myself into apparent danger, except when they dug the great pit in the churchyard of our parish of Aldgate.[3] A terrible pit it was, and I could not resist my curiosity to go and see it. As near as I may judge, it was about forty feet in length, and about fifteen or sixteen feet broad, and, at the time I first looked at it, about nine feet deep; but it was said they dug it near twenty feet deep afterwards in one part of it, till they could go no deeper for the water; for they had, it seems, dug several large pits before this. For though the plague was long a-coming to our parish, yet, when it did come, there was no parish in or about London where it raged with such violence as in the two parishes of Aldgate and Whitechapel. . . .[4]

3   They had supposed this pit would have supplied them for a month or more when they dug it, and some blamed the churchwardens for suffering such a frightful thing, telling them they were making preparations to bury the whole parish, and the like; but time made it appear the churchwardens knew the condition of the parish better than they did, for the pit being finished the 4th of September, I think, they began to bury in it the 6th, and by the 20th, which was just two weeks, they had thrown into it 1,114 bodies when they were obliged to fill it up, the bodies being then come to lie within six feet of the surface. . . .

ANALYZE NARRATOR

Annotate: In paragraph 4, mark details that help you understand more about the narrator.

Infer: What can you infer about the narrator's motivations and character?

4   It was about the 10th of September that my curiosity led, or rather drove, me to go and see this pit again, when there had been near 400 people buried in it; and I was not content to see it in the daytime, as I had done before, for then there would have been nothing to have been seen but the loose earth; for all the bodies that were thrown in were immediately covered with earth by those they called the buriers, which at other times were called bearers; but I resolved to go in the night and see some of them thrown in.

5   There was a strict order to prevent people coming to those pits, and that was only to prevent infection. But after some time that order

---

[3] **parish of Aldgate:** the street and area known as Aldgate take their name from the nearby old gate, or Aldgate.

[4] **Whitechapel:** an area just east of Aldgate and the old city walls.

© Houghton Mifflin Harcourt Publishing Company · © Print Collector/Getty Images

was more necessary, for people that were infected and near their end, and delirious also, would run to those pits, wrapt in blankets or rugs, and throw themselves in, and, as they said, bury themselves. I cannot say that the officers suffered any willingly to lie there; but I have heard that in a great pit in Finsbury, in the parish of Cripplegate, it lying open then to the fields, for it was not then walled about, [some] came and threw themselves in, and expired there, before they threw any earth upon them; and that when they came to bury others and found them there, they were quite dead, though not cold.

6   This may serve a little to describe the dreadful condition of that day, though it is impossible to say anything that is able to give a

ANALYZE HISTORICAL SETTING

Annotate: In paragraph 5, mark the phrases that indicate why people were not allowed to go to the burial pit.

Analyze: How does this information add to your understanding of the setting?

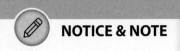
ANALYZE HISTORICAL SETTING

Annotate: Mark phrases in paragraph 7 that highlight the purpose of the conversation between the narrator and the sexton.

Analyze: What does this conversation reveal about the time period and cultural setting?

discourse

(dĭs´kôrs) *n.* verbal exchange or conversation.

AGAIN & AGAIN

Notice & Note: Recurring or similar use of imagery often emphasizes an important point. In paragraph 8, mark imagery used to describe death and suffering.

Analyze: What idea is being emphasized through this use of imagery?

LANGUAGE CONVENTIONS

Annotate: Mark the participles in the first sentence of paragraph 9.

Analyze: What details do these participles add to the description of the grieving man?

true idea of it to those who did not see it, other than this, that it was indeed very, very, very dreadful, and such as no tongue can express.

7   I got admittance into the churchyard by being acquainted with the sexton[5] who attended, who, though he did not refuse me at all, yet earnestly persuaded me not to go, telling me very seriously, for he was a good, religious, and sensible man, that it was indeed their business and duty to venture, and to run all hazards, and that in it they might hope to be preserved; but that I had no apparent call to it but my own curiosity, which, he said, he believed I would not pretend was sufficient to justify my running that hazard. I told him I had been pressed in my mind to go, and that perhaps it might be an instructing sight, that might not be without its uses. "Nay," says the good man, "if you will venture upon that score, name of God go in; for, depend upon it, 't will be a sermon to you, it may be, the best that ever you heard in your life. 'T is a speaking sight," says he, "and has a voice with it, and a loud one, to call us all to repentance;" and with that he opened the door and said, "Go, if you will."

8   His **discourse** had shocked my resolution a little, and I stood wavering for a good while, but just at that interval I saw two links[6] come over from the end of the Minories,[7] and heard the bellman, and then appeared a dead-cart, as they called it, coming over the streets; so I could no longer resist my desire of seeing it, and went in. There was nobody, as I could perceive at first, in the churchyard, or going into it, but the buriers and the fellow that drove the cart, or rather led the horse and cart; but when they came up to the pit they saw a man go to and again, muffled up in a brown cloak, and making motions with his hands under his cloak, as if he was in a great agony, and the buriers immediately gathered about him, supposing he was one of those poor delirious or desperate creatures that used to pretend, as I have said, to bury themselves. He said nothing as he walked about, but two or three times groaned very deeply and loud, and sighed as he would break his heart.

9   When the buriers came up to him they soon found he was neither a person infected and desperate, as I have observed above, or a person distempered[8] in mind, but one oppressed with a dreadful weight of grief indeed, having his wife and several of his children all in the cart that was just come in with him, and he followed in an agony and excess of sorrow. He mourned heartily, as it was easy to see, but with a kind of masculine grief that could not give itself vent by tears; and calmly defying the buriers to let him alone, said he would only see the bodies thrown in and go away, so they left importuning him. But no sooner was the cart turned round and the bodies shot into

---

[5] **sexton:** a church officer or employee responsible for the care and upkeep of church property, sometimes charged with ringing bells and digging graves.

[6] **links:** torches.

[7] **Minories:** a street running from Aldgate to the Tower of London.

[8] **distempered:** afflicted with distemper, or disorder, of the mind; deranged; mentally disturbed.

the pit **promiscuously**, which was a surprise to him, for he at least expected they would have been decently laid in, though indeed he was afterwards convinced that was impracticable; I say, no sooner did he see the sight but he cried out aloud, unable to contain himself. I could not hear what he said, but he went backward two or three steps and fell down in a swoon. The buriers ran to him and took him up, and in a little while he came to himself, and they led him away to the Pie Tavern over against the end of Houndsditch,⁹ where, it seems, the man was known, and where they took care of him. He looked into the pit again as he went away, but the buriers had covered the bodies so immediately with throwing in earth, that though there was light enough, for there were lanterns, and candles in them, placed all night round the sides of the pit, upon heaps of earth, seven or eight, or perhaps more, yet nothing could be seen.

10   This was a mournful scene indeed, and affected me almost as much as the rest; but the other was awful and full of terror. The cart had in it sixteen or seventeen bodies; some were wrapt up in linen sheets, some in rags, some little other than naked, or so loose that what covering they had fell from them in the shooting out of the cart, and they fell quite naked among the rest; but the matter was not much to them, or the indecency much to any one else, seeing they were all dead, and were to be **huddled** together into the common grave of mankind, as we may call it, for here was no difference made, but poor and rich went together; there was no other way of burials, neither was it possible there should, for coffins were not to be had for the prodigious numbers that fell in such a calamity as this. . . .

11   I had some little obligations, indeed, upon me to go to my brother's house, which was in Coleman Street parish,¹⁰ and which he had left to my care, and I went at first every day, but afterwards only once or twice a week.

12   In these walks I had many dismal scenes before my eyes, as particularly of persons falling dead in the streets, terrible shrieks and screechings of women, who, in their agonies, would throw open their chamber windows and cry out in a dismal, surprising manner. It is impossible to describe the variety of postures in which the passions of the poor people would express themselves. . . . People in the rage of the distemper, or in the torment of their swellings,¹¹ which was indeed intolerable, running out of their own government,¹² raving and distracted, and oftentimes laying violent hands upon themselves, throwing themselves out at their windows, shooting themselves, etc.; mothers murdering their own children in their lunacy, some dying of mere grief as a passion, some of mere fright and surprise without any

---

⁹ **Houndsditch:** a street on the site of an old ditch running northwest along the city wall between Aldgate and Bishopgate.

¹⁰ **Coleman Street parish:** an area about half a mile west of the narrator's parish.

¹¹ **swellings:** Bubonic plague is characterized by the painful swelling of inflamed lymph glands, or buboes.

¹² **running out of their own government:** losing the ability to govern, or control, themselves.

promiscuously
(prə-mǐsʹkyo͞o-əs-lə) *adv.*
lacking standards of selection; acting without careful judgment; indiscriminate.

ANALYZE HISTORICAL SETTING
Annotate: Mark details in paragraph 9 that describe the setting.

Analyze: What do these details add to your understanding of the setting's time and location?

huddle
(hŭdʹl) *v.* to crowd together, as from cold or fear (in this case, death).

ANALYZE NARRATOR
Annotate: In paragraph 12, mark details that reveal the narrator's perspective on events.

Compare: How does the narrator's perspective affect your impression of the events he describes?

ANALYZE HISTORICAL SETTING

Annotate: Mark each aspect of the setting used in the narrator's description of events surrounding the infected man.

Evaluate: Do the details of the setting create a sense of verisimilitude in the description? Explain why or why not.

infection at all, others frighted into idiotism and foolish distractions, some into despair and lunacy, others into melancholy madness. . . .

13   I heard of one infected creature who, running out of his bed in his shirt in the anguish and agony of his swellings, of which he had three upon him, got his shoes on and went to put on his coat; but the nurse resisting, and snatching the coat from him, he threw her down, ran over her, ran downstairs and into the street, directly to the Thames in his shirt, the nurse running after him, and calling to the watch to stop him; but the watchman, frighted at the man, and afraid to touch him, let him go on; upon which he ran down to the Stillyard stairs, threw away his shirt, and plunged into the Thames, and, being a good swimmer, swam quite over the river; and the tide being coming in, as they call it, that is, running westward, he reached the land not till he came about the Falcon stairs, where landing, and finding no people there, it being in the night, he ran about the streets there, naked as he was, for a good while, when, it being by that time high water, he takes the river again, and swam back to the Stillyard, landed, ran up the streets again to his own house, knocking at the door, went up the stairs and into his bed again; and that this terrible experiment cured him of the plague, that is to say, that the violent motion of his arms and legs stretched the parts where the swellings he had upon him were, that is to say, under his arms and his groin, and caused them to ripen and break, and that the cold of the water **abated** the fever in his blood.

abate

(ə-bāt´) *v.* to reduce in amount, degree, or intensity; lessen.

CHECK YOUR UNDERSTANDING

Answer these questions before moving on to the **Analyze the Text** section on the following page.

1 Why was there an order to keep people away from the burial pit?

   A To stop mourners from crowding the site

   B To protect citizens from wild animals

   C To keep people from discovering the mass grave

   D To prevent the spread of infection

2 How is the narrator able to get in to see the pit?

   F He bribes the sexton.

   G He knows the sexton.

   H He sneaks past an officer.

   J He goes at night.

3 How does the man at the end of the story supposedly cure himself of the plague?

   A He goes to the doctor.

   B He drinks a lot of fluids.

   C He swims in the river.

   D He takes herbal remedies.

ANALYZE THE TEXT

Support your responses with evidence from the text. ☰ NOTEBOOK

1. **Draw Conclusions** Reread paragraph 1. Which details suggest that the plague affects family relationships and friendships? What conclusions can you draw about the plague's impact on relationships?

2. **Infer** Review the narrator's description of the mass grave in paragraphs 3 and 4. What do details about the historical setting reveal about a possible theme, or message about life or human nature, in the text?

3. **Evaluate** What qualities and characteristics of the narrator help make the historical novel seem realistic? What qualities and characteristics make it seem less than realistic? Explain.

4. **Analyze** List details of the narrator's conversation with the church sexton in paragraph 7. How does the narrator's description of this conversation affect your impression of events?

5. **Notice & Note** Describe images that the narrator repeats again and again in the novel excerpt. What effect does this repetition have on your understanding of events?

RESEARCH

RESEARCH TIP
Once you have chosen a topic, formulate a specific question about that topic to guide your research.

As you studied this fictional journal, did you have any questions about the plague that you would like to have answered? Were you curious about England's history before the event or how London recovered? Generate at least three questions that you have about the plague. Use the categories below to guide you, writing your questions in the row of the chart next to the corresponding category.

Burial and mourning customs	
Beliefs about caring for the sick/poor	
Medicine and treatments	
Economic consequences	
My own category	

Extend Research one of the following topics that are related to the bubonic plague: Pied Piper, positive outcomes of bubonic plague, literature about bubonic plague, CDC (Centers for Disease Control and Prevention). Once you complete your research, share what you learned with a small group.

CREATE AND DISCUSS

Write Notes for a Problem-Solution Essay As Daniel Defoe emphasizes in his novel, epidemics can strike indiscriminately and unpredictably. Even today, despite advances in medicine, diseases capable of triggering epidemics remain threats to public health.

Imagine that you are a public health official. You have just discovered several cases of a highly infectious disease that you fear may develop into an epidemic. Write notes for a problem-solution essay that proposes ways that you might work with different sectors of society—such as the media, politicians, and the elderly—to limit the spread of the disease.

Discuss Share your notes with others in a small group of classmates and discuss which ideas might work best to fight the epidemic. Then, organize your group's final ideas into a structure you could use for a presentation.

- ❏ As a group, set an agenda and establish clear goals for your discussion.
- ❏ Set a time limit for each group member to present his or her ideas.
- ❏ Listen closely and respectfully to all speakers.
- ❏ Take notes to record everyone's ideas and suggestions.
- ❏ Take a vote on the best way(s) your group has come up with to limit the spread of an infectious disease.
- ❏ Work together to organize a presentation of your group's ideas.

Go to the **Writing Studio: Writing Informative Texts** for help with writing notes for a problem-solution essay.

Go to **Participating in Collaborative Discussions** in the **Speaking and Listening Studio** to find out more.

RESPOND TO THE ESSENTIAL QUESTION

 Why are plagues so horrifying?

Gather Information Review your annotations and notes on *A Journal of the Plague Year*. Then, add relevant details to your Response Log. As you determine which information to include, think about:

- how people cope with the fear of getting sick and dying
- how social, religious, and economic structures can be affected
- how people take desperate measures to protect themselves and their families

ACADEMIC VOCABULARY

As you write and discuss what you learned from *A Journal of the Plague Year*, be sure to use the Academic Vocabulary words. Check off each of the words that you use.

- ❏ **encounter**
- ❏ **exploit**
- ❏ **persist**
- ❏ **subordinate**
- ❏ **widespread**

WORD BANK

visitation	promiscuously
summon	huddle
discourse	abate

CRITICAL VOCABULARY

Practice and Apply Write the Critical Vocabulary word that has the same or nearly the same meaning as the given word or phrase.

1. the act of going to a place _____

2. order, call to act upon _____

3. conversation _____

4. indiscriminately _____

5. crowd together _____

6. reduce _____

VOCABULARY STRATEGY:
Denotation and Connotation

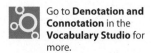

Go to **Denotation and Connotation** in the **Vocabulary Studio** for more.

Dictionary definitions provide the meaning of words, or their **denotations.** However, words also have emotional associations, or connotations. **Connotations** can be positive or negative. The denotation of the word *huddle*, for example, is "to group together." However, *huddle* generally has a negative connotation, an association with crouching together in fear or misery.

Practice and Apply Complete the table below. Under the *Denotation* heading, write a short definition for the vocabulary word. Then, add synonyms that have positive and negative connotations to the chart. Use a thesaurus to help identify synonyms, if needed.

VOCABULARY WORD	DENOTATION (MEANING)	SYNONYMS WITH POSITIVE CONNOTATIONS	SYNONYMS WITH NEGATIVE CONNOTATIONS
huddle	crowd together	nestle, snuggle	crouch, bunch
visitation			
summon			
discourse			
promiscuously			
abate			

LANGUAGE CONVENTIONS:
Participles and Participial Phrases

A **participle** is a verb form that can be used as an adjective. A present participle ends in *-ing*, and a past participle usually ends in *-ed* or *-d*, although some past participles are formed irregularly and end in *-t* or *-n*.

A **participial phrase** consists of a participle together with its modifiers and complements. The entire phrase is used as an adjective.

Writers often use participial phrases to add detail that will make their meaning more precise. They also use participial phrases to vary their sentence structure and keep the attention of their readers.

Defoe's use of participles helps to create a clear picture of what happened in London during the plague.

Here, Defoe uses the past participle *altered* to describe London's appearance:

> **The face of London was now indeed strangely <u>altered</u>.**

Here, he uses the participial phrase *muffled up in a brown coat* to describe a plague victim:

> **. . . they saw a man go to and again, <u>muffled up in a brown coat</u>, and making motions with his hands. . . .**

Practice and Apply

1. Write a sentence about the plague that uses a participle to describe something.

2. Rewrite this sentence from the excerpt so that at least one of the verbs is used as a participle.

> **He said nothing as he walked about, but two or three times groaned very deeply and loud, and sighed as he would break his heart.**

 Go to **Participles and Participial Phrases** in the **Grammar Studio** for more.

MEMOIR

from
INFERNO: A DOCTOR'S EBOLA STORY

by **Steven Hatch, M.D.**
pages 465–470

? ESSENTIAL QUESTION:

Why are plagues so horrifying?

COMPARE ACROSS GENRES

As you read, note the details Hatch uses to portray the experience of witnessing a plague. This will help you later when you compare this text to the excerpt from Defoe's *A Journal of the Plague Year*.

NOVEL

from
A JOURNAL OF THE PLAGUE YEAR

by **Daniel Defoe**
pages 451–456

from **Inferno: A Doctor's Ebola Story**

QUICK START

Think of an important decision you have made. Were you guided by logic and facts or by gut feelings? With a partner, discuss how you made the decision and what happened.

ANALYZE AUTHOR'S PERSPECTIVE

An **author's perspective** is a unique combination of ideas, values, feelings, and beliefs that influence the way the writer looks at a topic. In *Inferno*, Steven Hatch sometimes directly addresses the significance of his perspective as a doctor and as an American in an African country:

> **Say what you will about the potential for cross-cultural misunderstandings . . . but there is simply no mistaking the absolute, unadulterated joyous state of George Beyan in Daniel's portrait.**

In the above statement, Hatch acknowledges the potential for cultural misinterpretation of George Beyan's emotions.

As you read a nonfiction narrative, pause to ask questions about how the author's background, beliefs, and experiences shape his or her perception of people and events. Ask yourself about how the author assesses

- the motives governing the actions and behaviors of people
- the emotional condition and responses of others
- the moral or ethical value of decisions
- the significance and meaning of words and actions

As you read the following excerpt, note comments and clues that provide insight into the author's perspective.

CONNECT TO MEMOIRS

Memoir is a form of autobiographical writing in which the author describes significant personal experiences in a first-person narrative. In addition to recording details of events, memoirs express the author's thoughts and feelings at the time of the events and also upon later reflection.

In their memoirs, authors often address issues of wide social, philosophical, or historical significance. Readers, therefore, can deepen their understanding by connecting the text to their own experiences, to the experiences of people they know, and to their own social and historical contexts.

In *Inferno*, Hatch describes an Ebola outbreak in Liberia through his experience as a doctor in an Ebola treatment unit. His narrative, based on firsthand historical experience, provides valuable insight into how local, extraordinary events can still reflect the universal experience of people across cultures and across the globe.

GENRE ELEMENTS: MEMOIR

- is a narrative of actual events
- recounts author's personal experience in the first-person point of view
- describes author's thoughts and feelings
- author often reflects on events with an understanding gained over time
- may portray and discuss issues of wide social and historical significance

CRITICAL VOCABULARY

abyss	**veracity**	**vexation**	**plateau**
ersatz	**pyrrhic victory**	**vigilance**	**prognosis**

To see how many Critical Vocabulary words you already know, choose the best word to complete each sentence.

1. We can't help but doubt the _____ of the claims.

2. The doctor gave me a worrisome _____.

3. Your running times may _____ after months of improvement.

4. We won, but it was a(n) _____.

5. A(n) _____ medical clinic sprang up at the site of the disaster.

6. His _____ at her rudeness was obvious.

7. Facing the difficulty of the situation was like staring into the _____.

8. We value her constant _____ against many potential threats.

LANGUAGE CONVENTIONS

Writers use subordinate clauses to add descriptive details to their texts. A **subordinate clause** has a subject and verb but does not express a complete idea, so it cannot stand alone as a sentence. Subordinate clauses must be connected to at least one **independent clause.**

Some subordinate clauses, **relative clauses,** function as adjectives. Relative clauses use **relative pronouns,** such as *that, which, who, whom,* or *whose,* as their subjects.

ANNOTATION MODEL

NOTICE & NOTE

As you read, ask questions about how the author's background and experience influence his perception of people and events. This model shows one reader's notes about the beginning of *Inferno.*

Death was part of the daily routine, but some deaths affected us more than others. Each of us grew attached to certain patients as we would have done in any hospital, but one loss hit us all with equal force. We had cared for George Beyan, a quiet man in his mid-thirties who had acquired the virus by tending to a sick friend. George had made the slow recovery after emerging from the abyss in mid-October and waited around for the virus to clear, hardly making a noise as he sat outside listening to Radio Gbarnga in the hot sun.

Hatch is a doctor. He works in hospitals and is used to dealing with patients and growing attached to them at times.

What is it about this case that made it significant enough for the author to write about it? What effect did the case have on him?

BACKGROUND

Dr. Steven Hatch *is an infectious disease and immunology specialist from the United States who spent six weeks as a volunteer at the Ebola Treatment Unit in Liberia during the outbreak of 2013–2014. Fear that the outbreak would spread to the United States was high, and controversy erupted when an American nurse and doctor contracted the virus in Liberia and were flown back to the United States for treatment. Hatch's memoir details his experience, including the extreme measures he had to take to avoid infection, the suffering he witnessed, and the bureaucratic struggles he and the rest of the medical staff faced.*

from
INFERNO: A DOCTOR'S EBOLA STORY
Memoir by Steven Hatch, M.D.

PREPARE TO COMPARE

As you read, make note of the kinds of details Hatch uses to describe his experience as a witness to a devastating plague. Your notes will help you later when you compare this text to A Journal of the Plague Year.

1   Death was part of the daily routine, but some deaths affected us more than others. Each of us grew attached to certain patients as we would have done in any hospital, but one loss hit us all with equal force. We had cared for George Beyan, a quiet man in his mid-thirties who had acquired the virus by tending to a sick friend. George had made the slow recovery after emerging from the **abyss** in mid-October and waited around for the virus to clear, hardly making a noise as he sat outside listening to Radio Gbarnga in the hot sun.

2   Daniel Berehulak had featured George in a photo essay in the *Times* that ran at the end of October. He had created an **ersatz** studio in the lone unused office of the compound taking portraits of the patients and the staff. He used sheets as a white background and the portraits shared a highly formal quality; they reminded me of the work of Robert Mapplethorpe. Say what you will about the potential for cross-cultural misunderstandings, as well as the risks of projecting oneself onto another's inner mental

© Houghton Mifflin Harcourt Publishing Company • Image Credits: © Pascal Guyot/Getty Images

abyss
(ə-bĭs´) *n.* an immeasurably deep chasm, depth, or void.

ersatz
(ĕr´zäts, ĕr-zäts´) *adj.* being an usually inferior imitation or substitute; artificial.

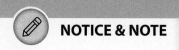
state by looking at their facial expressions, but there is simply no mistaking the absolute, unadulterated joyous state of George Beyan in Daniel's portrait. "I got up in the morning, I prayed. In the evening, I prayed. At dinner, I prayed. Prayed to get well," the caption quotes him as saying. "Yesterday, they said, 'You, you're free.' I danced, I jumped." The picture attests to the **veracity** of his statement.

3   George got the news of his impending freedom from the Navy lab one late afternoon. As much as patients understandably wanted to get the hell out of such confinement upon hearing the news, almost nobody left the day they received it. Coordinating the discharge paperwork and setting up a plan for them to return by alerting family of their departure all took time. Moreover, this was the same time that some of the staff were busying themselves with the patients in the suspect ward whose tests returned as negative, as they were prioritized to leave the high-risk area as soon as possible to avoid further risk of exposure. Others were working on taking the patients whose tests returned positive to the confirmed ward. Patients like George, who had lingered for weeks, were not going to suffer any ill effects from hanging out in the ETU[1] another night. For all their understandable jubilation, in terms of the tasks to be performed at that hour, they were not the top priority.

4   George savored his triumph over death, dancing and jumping, but bad news was about to arrive in the form of his wife and two sons, one aged five, the other a toddler. They all had some form of symptoms. That night he stood at the boundary talking to his wife across the one-meter divide that separated the suspect from the confirmed ward, the boys in tow. The following day would be a waiting game for the blood tests.

5   That next morning we sent George through the decontamination shower as he returned to freedom after nearly three weeks in isolation. I assumed he would have regarded this as a **pyrrhic victory** since his entire family now awaited word as to whether they would have to endure a similar experience, but I was surprised by the serenity of his appearance as he sat outside the main staff quarters. There is always the chance that given the cultural barriers I was misinterpreting his reaction, but I had seen anxiety, dread, and fear on enough Liberian faces to sense that this was different. Having lived through what he had just lived through, however, it was certainly not for me to judge him. Daniel took him into his studio, and his reaction was captured for posterity.

---

[1] **ETU:** Ebola Treatment Unit.

veracity

(və-răs´ĭ-tē) *n.* conformity to fact or truth; accuracy.

pyrrhic victory

n. a victory that is offset by staggering losses.

ANALYZE AUTHOR'S PERSPECTIVE

Annotate: In paragraph 5, underline the author's assessment of George's mental state. Then, circle one reason the author may have misjudged George's emotional state and one reason he may not have misjudged it.

Evaluate: How accurate do you think Hatch's assessment of George's mental state is? Why?

6   The question arose as to whether he should return home in the morning or spend the afternoon waiting for his family's test results. George chose to wait. He was going home with his family, you could almost hear him think. Only fate had a crueler plan in store for him. We again got the call from the Navy guys in the late afternoon. His wife and younger son tested negative, but his elder son, Williams, was positive, and shortly we would need to escort him over to the confirmed side. He was obviously ill and was too young to fend for himself. He was going to need help or he would surely die. The women on the confirmed side could not be expected to provide essentially twenty-four-hour nursing support to this child, busy as they were with other children, to say nothing of their own illnesses. And we would not allow his mother to take him to the confirmed side, even if she wanted to.

7   That left only one obvious choice: We would have to ask George to return to the confirmed ward to nurse Williams. We knew that this was asking an enormous amount of him. Yet we also knew that this would not endanger him and that it was Williams's best chance for survival. After a brief team conference where we all agreed this was the best course to pursue, I walked over to hand George the news and our singular and extremely unpleasant request.

8   Although he did not explicitly say so when I first explained the situation, I had the distinct impression that he thought I was utterly out of my mind. He gave a little shake of his head at first and said quietly that he wasn't going back *in there*. I told him his wife couldn't care for Williams and that I couldn't ask anyone in the confirmed ward—people whom he knew well by this point—to take on such a responsibility. And Williams needed help. After a brief exchange I realized that he was more than simply dreading returning inside, as if the posttraumatic stress of moving back into the nightmarish prison from which he was so recently set free was only the beginning of his **vexations**. I saw that same fear in his eyes that I saw every day with patients in the suspect ward.

9   But what was he concerned about? He was, after all, cured, possessing Ebola-specific antibodies and lymphocytes, which now made him immune to a repeat infection. But . . . did he know that? As I spoke with him, I sat there puzzling this over. Surely he knew at some intuitive level that he was not at risk of getting sick again while he spent day after day convalescing, although maybe he had thought a reset button had been pressed when he emerged from the decontamination shower. But how to explain a concept like acquired immunity to someone who probably had no formal education beyond grade school?

© Houghton Mifflin Harcourt Publishing Company

LANGUAGE CONVENTIONS
Annotate: Mark the sentence in paragraph 6 that includes a subordinate clause.

Infer: What is implied by this subordinate clause?

CONTRASTS AND CONTRADICTIONS

Notice & Note: In paragraph 8, mark details about George's reaction to Hatch's request.

Compare: How does George's reaction compare with your expectations?

vexation
(vĕk-sā´shən) *n.* a source of irritation or annoyance.

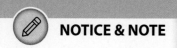

vigilance
(vĭj´ə-ləns) *n.* alert
watchfulness.

plateau
(plă-tō´) *intr.v.* to reach a stable
level; level off.

CONNECT TO MEMOIRS
Annotate: In paragraph 14,
mark the explanation of why
Hatch tries to restrain his
emotions when evaluating a
patient.

Connect: How does his
conflicted view of Williams's
prognosis reflect a common
human struggle?.

prognosis
(prŏg-nō´sĭs) *n.* a prediction
of the probable course and
outcome of a disease.

10   "Look, George," I said. "You're like Superman." It crossed my
mind that he might not be familiar with Superman, but I plowed
ahead. "You have . . . *special blood* now. The virus cannot hurt you.
You can go back in there and you won't be sick. And your son needs
you right now." Some more give-and-take took place, and along with
heaping spoonfuls of reassurance, we convinced him to perform the
nearly unthinkable act of walking back into the high-risk area and
receiving his sick son from his uninfected wife.

11   In the coming days everyone on the staff, Liberian and expat,
followed Williams's progress carefully. Nobody said anything, but
it was easy to see when we discussed everyone's status as we ran the
boards that we were monitoring Williams with heightened **vigilance**
and had attached special emotional importance to his prospects for
survival. We also carefully observed Williams because he had taken
a less typical clinical course. Most patients were on a clear trajectory:
either up, or down. We could usually tell within about a twenty-four-
hour window whether they were getting worse and would likely die,
or had weathered the storm and would likely survive.

12   However, Williams behaved differently: He **plateaued**, then
bounced around. His wet symptoms were not as profound as they
were in so many other patients. We would see him on morning
rounds inside the ward, lying in bed listless, unable even to sit up and
take fluids while his fever raged out of control, the heat draining his
small body of the water and electrolytes that would be critical to his
survival. Then only hours later George would be seen escorting him
by the hand outside to sit on the plastic chairs while he idly munched
on some cookies, and the afternoon rounds would include chattering
among the staff about how he had turned the corner.

13   But over this time his clinical picture had become a canvas onto
which everyone painted different impressions: The more sanguine
among us would view every stirring as an indicator of impending
improvement, while those more naturally predisposed to pessimism
noted that he wasn't looking like the true survivors, who often had
made such progress within twenty-four hours of their worst moments
that one didn't need to be a medical professional to see they would
leave the unit intact.

14   I am much more naturally predisposed to pessimism. When
I try to think scientifically, I do my best to check this pessimism,
along with any other emotions, at the door, lest they interfere
with good clinical judgment. For me, in order to understand his
prognosis, those emotions had to be corralled, which meant

ignoring the small blips of improvement that would get reported and celebrated. Instead, a simple mental equation needed to be performed, and the equation went like this: Fever equaled fluid loss, fluid loss equaled dehydration, and dehydration equaled circulatory collapse. Which, no matter how many ways I turned it over in my head, equaled death. I couldn't explain why he was able to hold on and have moments where he seemed to look, if not well, then definitely better. But unless we could figure out a way to get a lot of fluid into him, I just couldn't see how this would lead to a happy outcome. I didn't say so during rounds, but I wasn't in the mind of putting forth a huzzah just because he was able to hold down a little orange juice. Still, with each passing night, I felt the longer he survived, the more likely it was that he was going home.

15   Then one morning I came in, and I knew something terrible had happened. Everyone was silent. Steve Whiteley, the most unflappable person in the ETU, hardly made eye contact with anyone. The national staff moved about their tasks quietly, and the expat office space felt oppressive. Sheri Fink had been working through the night on a story, and I searched her bloodshot eyes for an explanation, but none came.

16   "Sheri, *what happened*?" I asked.

17   "Williams died last night," she replied in a monotone voice. I blinked, surprised to hear this news, a part of me thinking, No, *that can't be right, he looked good yesterday*, and then was surprised at my surprise, as if the hemispheres of my brain were unhappily squabbling about what to do with this information. I should have surmised instantly why such a pall[2] had been cast over the ETU, and yet it made no sense to me in the moment. I shook my head once as if to rid my ears of what I had just heard, even though I knew not only that it was true but that I had sized it up pretty accurately in the previous days.

18   What she didn't tell me right away, and I would learn only a few days later, was that after Williams had died, George had stayed up the entire night, wailing for his lost son, speaking to him, entreating him to come back, wishing for him to be alive. His lamentations rang throughout the compound for hours. We all knew that the ETU was a place of hellish misery, for by the time that Williams died, about thirty souls that had come to the Bong ETU had been committed to the earth. And we knew there were more to follow, as we fed one new body each day into the maw of the beast. Despite that knowledge, we were able to keep on with our jobs and not let our spirits flag. Our cheer and hope were among our only weapons in the darkness.

---

[2] **pall:** (pôl) a gloomy effect or atmosphere.

ANALYZE AUTHOR'S PERSPECTIVE

Annotate: Mark descriptive details in paragraph 18 that describe George's behavior the night that Williams dies. Then, mark details that explain why the author and others are able to keep working under the circumstances.

Analyze: What do these details illustrate about the differences in perspective among the plague's victims and the author?

19   Yet what made the passing of Williams Beyan harder than the others was not only that we had all become deeply emotionally invested in his survival, but that we had asked George to cross back over in order to help achieve this. If there was a literal place that could be called hell on earth, for George Beyan, the confirmed ward was it, and we had willingly cajoled him into returning to that place of his nightmares only to provide him with one even worse. We asked him to make such sacrifices knowing that this might happen. Indeed, *I* was the one who had asked it of him.

20   Rounds that morning were unlike any other, with the raucous banter that usually accompanied the handoff absent, and the morning meeting a quiet recitation of pertinent items. Everyone silently went about their tasks. I asked Godfrey, who was in charge of burials, when they would inter Williams. He told me it would happen around eleven. I turned to Sambhavi Cheemalapati, who was running the ETU while Sean was on his R & R, and told her that we needed to go. She reluctantly agreed.

AUTHOR'S PERSPECTIVE

Annotate: Mark two reasons that Hatch gives in paragraph 21 for preventing himself from crying at Williams's funeral.

Analyze: What do Hatch's reasons reveal about his personal and cultural perspective?

21   George came back out a second time through the decontamination chamber, glistening from the light bleach shower, and Sambhavi, Godfrey, and I formed the back of a small processional led by two members of the burial team, an empty cart, a sprayer, and George. We moved around the peripheral road of the ETU, stopping at the back fence abutting the morgue, and the staff retrieved Williams's body, covered in two shiny white body bags. George began to wail again, and I struggled like mad to stop the tears from flowing down my face, for this was not my loss, and I didn't dare guess whether such a show of emotion would be considered appropriate. Eventually I had to bite the tip of my tongue so hard to prevent my tears that it bled. We put Williams in the ground in a ceremony that lasted no more than two or three minutes. Godfrey, I believe, spoke some official words.

22   It was the only funeral I attended in the outbreak. Sambhavi, Godfrey, and I had to return to work.

CHECK YOUR UNDERSTANDING

Answer these questions before moving on to the **Analyze the Text** section on the following page.

1 What reason does the author give that George is not immediately released when his results come back as negative?

   A He has to stay because his son has just been admitted.

   B The staff is too busy with other tasks to process his release.

   C The staff believes he might get sick again in a few days.

   D He is afraid to be released because he thinks he might infect his family.

2 Which quotation from the selection shows the author using his experience as a doctor to assess someone's mental state?

   F *He was obviously ill and was too young to fend for himself.*

   G *He was going home with his family, you could almost hear him think.*

   H *His wet symptoms were not as profound as they were in so many other patients.*

   J *I saw that same fear in his eyes that I saw every day with patients in the suspect ward.*

3 Which paragraph explains the statement in paragraph 1 that "one loss hit us all with equal force"?

   A Paragraph 11

   B Paragraph 13

   C Paragraph 14

   D Paragraph 19

ANALYZE THE TEXT

Support your responses with evidence from the text. ⊟ NOTEBOOK

1. **Compare** Review paragraphs 2 and 5, which provide details about George's photo and caption in the *Times*. How is George's portrayal in the *Times* similar to Hatch's portrayal of him in the memoir? How do the two portrayals differ?

2. **Draw Conclusions** Why did the medical staff at the ETU take particular interest in the case of Williams Beyan? What does their interest reveal about them?

3. **Analyze** In paragraphs 13 and 14, how does your understanding of the author's perspective provide insight into his reaction to the course of Williams's illness?

4. **Interpret** In paragraph 20, how does the author use details to convey the emotional effect of Williams's death on the staff?

5. **Notice & Note** What were your thoughts when you first learned of George's reluctance to return to the confirmed ward? Did your thoughts change by the end of the excerpt? Explain why or why not.

RESEARCH

RESEARCH TIP

When you carry out a search, scroll to the bottom of the results page and look for a list of suggested additional search topics. Often, these suggested topics are highly specific and relevant to your inquiry. They also may guide you to interesting, unexpected aspects of the topic.

In paragraph 17, Hatch describes his mental response to the news of Williams's death by saying it was "as if the hemispheres of my brain were unhappily squabbling about what to do with this information." Research popular theories of how the right and left hemispheres of the brain process information. Then, record what you discover in the chart below.

LEFT HEMISPHERE	RIGHT HEMISPHERE

Extend Use what you have discovered to explain why Hatch would describe his response in this way. Base your explanation only on research from reliable sources of information on the brain.

CREATE AND RESEARCH

Take Informal Notes Carry out research to gather information about the steps that are taken to control Ebola outbreaks.

- ❏ Make sure you are using trusted websites, such as those with .org and .gov addresses, with reputable and reliable authors and hosts.
- ❏ Scan for headings to locate the specific information you are interested in.
- ❏ Take informal notes by writing down key words and phrases.

Create an Informational Poster With a group, combine and organize the notes you have gathered through research, and create a poster that tells people what they should do if there is an Ebola outbreak in their community.

- ❏ Make instructions clear and accurate.
- ❏ Use short, imperative sentences.
- ❏ Use visual aids.

Go to **Conducting Research: Taking Notes** in the **Writing Studio** to find out more.

Go to **Giving a Presentation** and **Participating in Collaborative Discussions** in the **Speaking and Listening Studio** for more.

RESPOND TO THE ESSENTIAL QUESTION

 Why are plagues so horrifying?

Gather Information Review your annotations and notes on *Inferno: A Doctor's Ebola Story*. Then, add relevant information to your Response Log. As you determine which information to include, think about:

- how emotions such as fear and hope affect our judgments
- how our understanding of a particular moment changes with time and experience
- how our perception of others' emotions and reactions are influenced by our own perspectives

ACADEMIC VOCABULARY

As you write and discuss what you learned from *Inferno: A Doctor's Ebola Story*, be sure to use the Academic Vocabulary words. Check off each of the words that you use.

- ❏ **encounter**
- ❏ **exploit**
- ❏ **persist**
- ❏ **subordinate**
- ❏ **widespread**

WORD BANK

abyss	vexation
ersatz	vigilance
veracity	plateau
pyrrhic victory	prognosis

Go to the **Vocabulary Studio: Understanding Word Origins** for more on words from classical mythology.

CRITICAL VOCABULARY

Practice and Apply Respond to each question or prompt by using the Critical Vocabulary word in a complete sentence.

1. What does it mean to be "on the edge of an **abyss**"?

2. Give an example of a **pyrrhic victory.**

3. Name a job that requires **vigilance.**

4. How do you determine the **veracity** of a source?

5. What's the most common cause of **vexation** for you?

6. At what time of day does your energy **plateau**?

7. Name something that could be used as an **ersatz** chair.

8. What would you do if your doctor gave you a scary **prognosis**?

VOCABULARY STRATEGY:
Classical Allusions

The title of Steven Hatch's memoir contains an allusion to Dante's epic poem *The Divine Comedy*, in which the first part, *Inferno*, is a detailed description of punishments in an underworld. The English language uses many such **classical allusions,** or indirect references to classical works of literature.

For example, this excerpt from *Inferno: A Doctor's Ebola Story* contains other classical allusions:

> George had made the slow recovery after emerging from the *abyss* in mid-October and waited around for the virus to clear, hardly making a noise as he sat outside listening to Radio Gbarnga in the hot sun.

The word *abyss* is derived from both ancient Greek and Latin and means "an extremely deep or bottomless hole." It is used in classical literature and translations of the New Testament to refer to hell.

> I assumed he would have regarded this as a *pyrrhic victory* since his entire family now awaited word as to whether they would have to endure a similar experience. . . .

The phrase *pyrrhic victory* refers to the victory of King Pyrrhus over the Romans, in which Pyrrhus lost a large portion of his army, including many of his closest friends, as described in Plutarch's classical poem *Pyrrhus*.

Practice and Apply Answer the following questions in complete sentences, citing evidence from the text to support your answers.

Why does Hatch say that George emerged from the abyss?

In what ways might George's recovery be considered a pyrrhic victory?

LANGUAGE CONVENTIONS:
Subordinate Clauses

Subordinate clauses add detail to a text by answering questions such as *where, when, how, what kind*, and *which one*. They cannot stand on their own and must be connected to at least one independent clause, sometimes through the use of a **subordinating conjunction.** Here are some examples of subordinating conjunctions and what they indicate.

Go to **Kinds of Clauses** in the **Grammar Studio** for more.

SUBORDINATING CONJUNCTIONS	WHAT THEY INDICATE
until, when, after, before, as, as soon as, while, whenever	Time relationship
because, as, if, since, unless	Cause/effect or conditional relationship
even though, although, while, whereas	Contrast
where, wherever	Place

Some subordinate clauses function as adjectives, with relative pronouns such as *who, that,* or *which* as their subjects. In this case, the clause is also called a **relative clause,** and it provides information about a noun.

Practice and Apply Summarize some of the specific events in *Inferno* in your own words, incorporating subordinate clauses. Write at least four sentences that use a subordinating conjunction with a clause or that use a relative pronoun as the subject of a clause. For example:

> Williams's father, <u>*who* had survived Ebola infection</u>, stayed with him in the confirmed ward.

> <u>*Although* the staff members were used to seeing people die</u>, they were especially upset about Williams's death.

Collaborate & Compare

COMPARE ACROSS GENRES

Compare and Contrast Details Both Daniel Defoe and Steven Hatch use a variety of details to convey the experience of witnessing a plague to readers. With your group, use a chart like the one below to gather information with which to compare and contrast the types of details used by the two authors.

from
A JOURNAL OF THE PLAGUE YEAR
Novel by Daniel Defoe

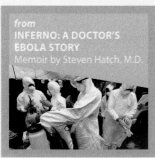

from
INFERNO: A DOCTOR'S EBOLA STORY
Memoir by Steven Hatch, M.D.

	A JOURNAL OF THE PLAGUE YEAR	INFERNO: A DOCTOR'S EBOLA STORY
Images		
Sounds		
Statistics		
Dialogue		
Emotional Language		
Metaphors/ Comparisons		
Examples and Anecdotes		

What similarities and differences do you notice in how the two authors use details in their texts? Which use of details did you find more effective? Why?

ANALYZE THE TEXTS

Discuss these questions in your group.

1. **Contrast** How do the motivations of Defoe's narrator differ from those of the author of *Inferno*? How do these differences affect their perspectives on the events they describe?

2. **Analyze** How do Defoe and Hatch appeal to the sense of hearing to convey the impact and effects of each plague on those who witness it?

3. **Infer** What do the burial scenes in each text reveal about how humans respond to the high number of deaths during a lethal epidemic? What message about human nature is suggested by how humans respond?

4. **Synthesize** Identify examples of both fear and hope in the two texts. What do the texts suggest about the significance of these emotions during an epidemic?

RESEARCH AND SHARE

Now your group can continue exploring the ideas in these texts by researching other examples of how epidemics and plagues are portrayed in literature and the media.

1. **Brainstorm as a group.** Share ideas about how plagues and epidemics have been portrayed through literature and media. The representations can be fictional or nonfictional and can include books, movies, or television shows. Make a list of all the examples you discuss.

2. **Assign a topic to each group member to research.** Assign or have each member of the group choose one book, show, or movie to explore.

3. **Gather information.** Use summaries, reviews, and other sources, including excerpts and clips, to learn about the book, show, or movie you are to research. Note who the narrator or central character is, what details are used to portray the epidemic (such as statistics, visual descriptions, or individual stories), and identify the historical and/or scientific background.

RESEARCH TIP
When looking for works of literature about a particular topic, use the "advanced search" feature of an online library catalogue or a city library's website to search by subject.

Title of book, movie, or show:	
Brief description of epidemic:	
Scientific or historical background:	
Details about narrator or central character:	**Details used to portray epidemic:**

4. **Share with your group.** Have individual members of your group explain the books, shows, or movies they have researched. Then, discuss the various ways that epidemics are portrayed in literature and media, as well as the kinds of reactions these portrayals create in readers and viewers.

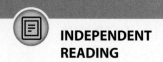

? *ESSENTIAL QUESTIONS:*

Review the four Essential Questions for this unit on page 361.

Reader's Choice

Setting a Purpose   Select one or more of these options from your eBook to continue your exploration of the Essential Questions.

- Read the descriptions to see which text seizes your interest.
- Think about which genres you enjoy reading.

Notice **&** Note

In this unit, you practiced noticing and noting the signposts and asking big questions about nonfiction. As you read independently, these signposts and others will aid your understanding. Below are the key questions to ask when you read literature and nonfiction.

Reading Literature: Stories, Poems, and Plays	
Signpost	**Key Question**
Contrasts and Contradictions	Why did the character act that way?
Aha Moment	How might this moment change things?
Tough Questions	What does this make me wonder about?
Words of the Wiser	What's the lesson for the character?
Again and Again	Why might the author keep bringing this up?
Memory Moment	Why is this memory important?

Reading Nonfiction: Essays, Articles, and Arguments	
Signpost	**Key Question(s)**
Big Questions	What surprised me? What did the author think I already knew? What challenged, changed, or confirmed what I already knew?
Contrasts and Contradictions	What is the difference, and why does it matter?
Extreme or Absolute Language	Why did the author use this language?
Numbers and Stats	Why did the author use these numbers or amounts?
Quoted Words	Why was this person quoted or cited, and what did their words add?
Word Gaps	Do I know this word from someplace else? Does it seem like technical talk for this topic? Do clues in the sentence help me understand the word?

You can preview these texts in Unit 3 of your eBook.

Then check off the text or texts that you select to read on your own.

POEM

Elegy Written in a Country Churchyard

Thomas Gray

A young poet contemplates his own mortality, asking why people are remembered after death.

ARTICLE

Once Below Gas Station, Virginia Cemetery Restored

Wyatt Andrews

Who is buried beneath our feet? And why do people feel a need to identify those strangers from the past?

POEM

On Her Loving Two Equally

Aphra Behn

She loves two very different men. How can she resolve her equally strong affections for them both?

ARTICLE

King George's Letters Betray Madness, Computer Finds

Mindy Weisberger

Historians use a computer to detect signs of mental illness in the letters of America's last king.

Collaborate and Share   With a partner, discuss what you learned from at least one of your independent readings.

- Give a brief synopsis or summary of the text.

- Describe any signposts that you noticed in the text and explain what they showed you.

- Describe what you most enjoyed or found most challenging about the text. Give specific examples.

- Decide if you would recommend the text to others. Why or why not?

Go to the **Reading Studio** for more resources on **Notice & Note**.

Write a Personal Narrative

Go to the **Writing Studio** for help writing narratives.

This unit focuses on literature from the Restoration and 18th century. Although writers in these periods often addressed social issues and historical events, there were also important portrayals of personal experiences, especially in memoirs and journals. For this writing task, you will write about an important personal experience and connect that experience to a topic of wider significance that may be important to a reader. You can use the excerpt from Steven Hatch's memoir *Inferno: A Doctor's Ebola Story* as a mentor text.

As you write your personal narrative, you can use the notes from your Response Log that you filled out after reading the texts in this unit.

Writing Prompt

Read the information in the box below.

> We often gain a better understanding of the significance and meaning of an event after we've had some time to reflect, especially if that event is of historical significance.

This is the context for your personal narrative.

Think carefully about the following question.

> What is your most memorable experience?

How might the Essential Question relate to a personal narrative?

Write a personal narrative about a significant experience you have had.

How might this significant experience relate to a personal narrative?

Be sure to—

- ❏ tell a story that has a beginning, middle, and end
- ❏ use conventions of storytelling, including characterization, scene, and dialogue
- ❏ include concrete sensory details to bring the reader into the experience
- ❏ describe your thoughts and feelings both at the time you had the experience and now as you remember it
- ❏ use the story to relate a "big idea," something of wider social, philosophical, or historical significance that will interest the reader

Review these points as you write and again when you finish. Make any needed changes.

1 Plan

Before you begin your writing, take some time to plan your draft. You should already know which story you want to tell. It's also important to make choices about which details to include, as you don't want to try to include every single detail or clutter your writing with unimportant information. Choose details that best convey something important about the experience, such as an emotion or a mood. You should also think about the significance of this experience that you want to convey. You should always know how your story is going to end *before* you start writing, as your text should be designed to lead your reader to that point.

Personal Narrative Planning Chart	
Genre	Personal narrative
Memorable experience	
Something I learned or understood better because of the experience	
Details I recall	

Background Reading Review the notes you have taken in your Response Log that relate to the question "What is your most memorable experience?" Texts in this unit provide background reading that will help you understand the wider significance of personal experiences.

Go to the **Writing Narratives: Narrative Context** for help planning your personal narrative.

Notice & Note
From Reading to Writing

As you plan your personal narrative, apply what you've learned about signposts to your own writing. Remember that writers use common features called signposts to help convey their message to readers.

Think how you can incorporate **Contrasts and Contradictions** into your essay.

 Go to the **Reading Studio** for more resources on **Notice & Note.**

Use the notes from your Response Log as you plan your personal narrative.

UNIT 3
RESPONSE LOG

Use this Response Log to record information from the texts that relates to or comments on the **Essential Questions** in Unit 3.

? Essential Question	Details from Texts
How can satire change people's behavior?	
What is your most memorable experience?	
What keeps women from achieving equality with men?	
Why are plagues so horrifying?	

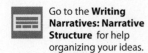

Go to the **Writing Narratives: Narrative Structure** for help organizing your ideas.

Organize Your Ideas After you have gathered ideas from your planning activities, you need to organize them in a way that will help you draft your personal narrative. You can use the chart below to decide on the elements of your story.

Introduction: How can you grab your reader's attention? What is your story about? Where does it take place? Who is involved?	
Second Paragraph: What happens at the beginning of your story?	
Third Paragraph: How does your story develop? Are there any twists or turns?	
Fourth Paragraph What is the climax, or ending, of your story?	
Conclusion: Why does your story matter? What has changed, and what does it mean for the future?	

② Develop a Draft

Once you have completed your planning activities, you will be ready to begin drafting your personal narrative. Refer to your graphic organizers and any notes you took as you studied the texts in the collection. These will provide a kind of map for you to follow as you write. Using a word processor or online writing application makes it easier to make changes or move sentences around later when you are ready to revise your first draft.

You might prefer to draft your personal narrative online.

Use the Mentor Text

Author's Craft

The first few sentences of your opening paragraph should "hook" readers and grab their attention, making them curious about the story to come. In a personal narrative, the introduction may include a description of the place where the story took place, a quote, a thought, or even an interesting fact.

> Death was part of the daily routine, but some deaths affected us more than others. Each of us grew attached to certain patients as we would have done in any hospital, but one loss hit us all with equal force. We had cared for George Beyan, a quiet man in his mid-thirties who had acquired the virus by attending a sick friend.

This is the hook. It seizes the reader's attention because it is shocking. The reader wants to continue reading to find out what was significant about this particular death.

Apply What You've Learned Brainstorm a few ideas for how you might open your personal narrative and try writing a sentence for each one. Think of a surprising or unusual detail you could use to open the story, and make the reader curious to keep reading.

Genre Characteristics

Your personal narrative should have a "big idea," something that you learned from or understood differently after the experience. Help the reader understand this "big idea" by reflecting on events.

> If there was a literal place that could be called hell on earth, for George Beyan, the confirmed ward was it, and we had willingly cajoled him into returning to that place of his nightmares only to provide him with one even worse. We asked him to make sacrifices knowing that this might happen. Indeed, I was the one who had asked it of him.

The author is reflecting on his decision to convince George to go back to the confirmed ward and the terrible experience the man had as a result.

Apply What You've Learned As you tell your story, alternate narration of events with reflection, and give the reader insight into your inner thoughts and feelings, especially at moments when your understanding of the experience changed.

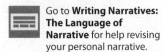

③ Revise

Go to **Writing Narratives: The Language of Narrative** for help revising your personal narrative.

On Your Own Once you have written your draft, you'll want to go back and look for ways to improve your personal narrative. As you reread and revise, think about whether you have conveyed the significance of your experience. The Revision Guide will help you focus on specific elements to make your writing stronger.

Revision Guide		
Ask Yourself	**Tips**	**Revision Techniques**
1. Does my opening paragraph grab the reader's attention?	**Think** about whether you as a reader would want to keep going after the first sentence.	**Add** an interesting detail to your opening to engage your reader's curiosity.
2. Do I include enough sensory details?	**Highlight** the sensory details you used.	**Add** such sensory details as images, sounds, smells, and physical sensations.
3. Does the reader understand my emotions?	**Look** for the moments where you describe your emotions.	**Elaborate** on emotional moments with details that "show" emotion rather than just telling.
4. Is my story organized and logical?	Go through your draft and make a short note to **summarize** each of your paragraphs.	**Break up** and **reorder** paragraphs so the story flows logically.
5. Is my "big idea" clearly conveyed to the reader?	**Write** a sentence or two that summarizes your "big idea."	**Add** reflection, emotions, and details to bring out the "big idea" throughout the story.

ACADEMIC VOCABULARY

As you conduct your **peer review,** be sure to use these words.

❑ encounter

❑ exploit

❑ persist

❑ subordinate

❑ widespread

With a Partner Once you and your partner have worked through the Revision Guide on your own, exchange personal narratives and evaluate each other's draft in a **peer review.** Focus on providing revision suggestions for at least three of the items mentioned in the chart. Explain why you think your partner's draft should be revised and what your specific suggestions are.

When receiving feedback from your partner, listen attentively and ask questions to make sure you fully understand the revision suggestions.

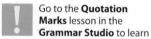

④ Edit

Once you have addressed the narrative flow, development of the "big idea," and other elements of your personal narrative, you can look to improve the finer points of your draft. Edit for proper use of standard English conventions, including syntax, sentence structure, grammar, and spelling.

Language Conventions

One way to really give life to your personal narrative is to include **direct quotations.** Look at your writing to see whether there are places you could add direct quotations or revise to change **indirect quotations** to direct ones.

 Go to the **Quotation Marks** lesson in the **Grammar Studio** to learn more.

Indirect Quotation	Direct Quotation
After half an hour of walking around the island, I asked him whether he was sure there was a beach this way.	"Are you sure there's a beach this way?" I asked after half an hour of walking around the island.

When you write direct quotations, make sure you punctuate them correctly. If you are quoting a conversation, use a paragraph break when the speaker changes.

> We'd been hiking around the rocky edge of the island for half an hour, with no sign of a beach. "Are you sure there's a beach this way?" I asked.
>
> "That's what the locals told me," he retorted. "Why would they lie?"
>
> "Maybe that's a joke for them around here," I said, slightly out of breath from jumping between the rocks. "They send tourists walking around the whole island looking for a beach that isn't there."

⑤ Publish

Finalize your personal narrative and choose a way to share it with your audience. Consider these options:

- Upload it as an article to an open web platform.
- Submit it to a school or local publication.

Use the scoring guide to evaluate your essay.

	Writing Task Scoring Guide: Narrative Essay		
	Organization/Progression	**Development of Ideas**	**Use of Language and Conventions**
4	• The introduction and conclusion are engaging and appropriate, and every part of the narrative is on topic. • Sentences and paragraphs flow smoothly, with every detail adding to the quality of the narrative.	• The writer's imaginative and creative use of details and elaboration effectively supports the important ideas in the narrative.	• The writer's voice and personality are evident, and the writer's word choice and language are vivid and expressive. • The writer shows consistent command of grammar with only minor errors in punctuation or spelling.
3	• The introduction and conclusion add to the narrative, and most of the narrative is on topic. • Most sentences and paragraphs include effective transitions, and most of the details support the focus of the narrative.	• Some details and elaboration help to support important ideas in the narrative.	• The writer's style is mostly effective and appropriate, and parts of the narrative are expressive and engaging. • The writer shows moderate command of grammar with occasional errors in spelling and grammar.
2	• The introduction and conclusion are weak, and sometimes the narrative wanders from the topic. • Few transitions are included; some points are irrelevant and don't contribute to the focus of the narrative.	• Details are present but don't really support the important ideas. Details are often disconnected.	• The writing is formulaic and simple, with no varied sentence structure or expressive language. • The writer's grammar and spelling are often incorrect, but the writer's ideas are still clear.
1	• The introduction or conclusion is missing, and the narrative is often off topic. • Sentences are choppy and paragraphs are disjointed. There is repetition and unnecessary wordiness.	• Very few details are present, and no information is given to support the important ideas.	• The writing is confusing, with simple and awkward sentences. • The writer makes many errors in grammar and spelling that cause ideas to be unclear.

Present a Narrative

You will now adapt your narrative essay for presentation to your classmates. You will also listen to their presentations, will ask questions to better understand their ideas, and will help them improve their work.

Go to **Giving a Presentation** in the **Speaking and Listening Studio** to learn more.

1 Adapt Your Essay for Presentation

Review your personal narrative, and use the chart below to guide you as you adapt your essay and create a script and presentation materials.

Presentation Planning Chart		
Title and Introduction	Is there a clever title or creative way you can introduce your presentation that will draw your audience's attention?	
Audience	What might you need to explain to the audience? What details in your essay might be of particular interest to the audience? What is the best way to present these details to convey your "big idea" to the audience?	
Effective Language and Organization	Which parts of your essay should be condensed for a presentation format? Which parts could you elaborate on? Could any of the language in your narrative be revised to make it more vivid or engaging?	
Visuals and Audio	Which kinds of visuals or props can you include to enrich your presentation? Would sound-effects or music help to enhance your presentation?	

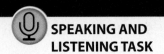

2 Practice with a Partner or Group

Once you've completed the draft of your presentation, practice with a partner or group to improve both the presentation and your delivery.

Practice Effective Verbal Techniques

❑ **Enunciation** Replace words that you stumble over, and rearrange sentences so your delivery is smooth.

❑ **Voice Modulation and Pitch** Use your voice to display enthusiasm and emphasis.

❑ **Speaking Rate** Speak slowly enough that listeners understand you. Pause now and then to let them consider important points.

❑ **Volume** Remember that listeners at the back of the room need to hear you.

Practice Effective Nonverbal Techniques

❑ **Eye Contact** Try to let your eyes rest on each member of the audience at least once.

❑ **Facial Expression** Smile, frown, or raise an eyebrow to show your feelings or to emphasize points.

❑ **Gestures** Stand tall and relaxed, and use natural gestures—shrugs, nods, or shakes of your head—to add meaning and interest to your presentation.

Provide and Consider Advice for Improvement

As a listener, pay close attention. Take notes about ways that presenters can improve their presentations and use verbal and nonverbal techniques more effectively. Summarize each presenter's personal narrative to confirm your understanding, and ask questions to clarify any confusing details.

As a presenter, listen closely to questions and consider ways to revise your presentation to make sure your narrative is clear and logical. Remember to ask for suggestions about how you might change elements of your presentation to make it more clear and more interesting.

3 Deliver Your Presentation

Use the advice you received during practice to make final changes to your presentation. Then, using effective verbal and nonverbal techniques, present your personal narrative to your classmates.

As you work to improve your presentations, be sure to follow discussion rules:

❑ listen closely to each other

❑ don't interrupt

❑ stay on topic

❑ ask only helpful and relevant questions

❑ provide only clear, thoughtful, and direct answers

Reflect on the Unit

By completing your personal narrative, you have created a writing product that pulls together and expresses your thoughts about the reading you have done in this unit. Now is a good time to reflect on what you have learned.

Reflect on the Essential Questions

- Review the four Essential Questions on page 361. How have your answers to these questions changed in response to the texts you've read in this unit?

- What are some examples from the texts you've read that show how personal experiences can have social and historical significance?

Reflect on Your Reading

- Which selections were the most interesting or surprising to you?

- From which selection did you learn the most about the importance of personal experiences?

Reflect on the Writing Task

- What difficulties did you encounter while working on your personal narrative? How might you avoid them next time?

- Which part of the personal narrative was the easiest to write? The hardest to write? Why?

- What improvements did you make to your personal narrative as you were revising?

EMOTION AND EXPERIMENTATION

THE FLOWERING OF ROMANTICISM

" **I will not Reason and Compare; my business is to Create.** "

—William Blake

Discuss the **Essential Questions** with your whole class or in small groups. As you read Emotion and Experimentation, consider how the selections explore these questions.

? *ESSENTIAL QUESTION:*
What can nature offer us?

As the 19th century dawned, England's cities underwent tremendous growth. Urban life had advantages, but some observers worried about the negative consequences of so many people leaving the countryside and losing contact with the natural world. Today, the idea of going outside and "back to nature" holds great appeal for many. Why are people drawn to nature? What does nature offer that we cannot find anywhere else?

? *ESSENTIAL QUESTION:*
How do you define beauty?

Beauty was a topic of great interest during the Romantic period. Writers, artists, and others sought to discover beauty not only in such conventional places as nature, the arts, and the human form, but also in such abstract concepts as emotions, ideals, and the human spirit. Some writers even explored the idea of beauty in failure and tragedy. What does it mean for something to be described as beautiful? How do definitions of beauty vary from person to person and from culture to culture?

? *ESSENTIAL QUESTION:*
How can science go wrong?

The Enlightenment ushered in a new era of scientific progress and confidence in the power of humanity over the natural world. With advances, however, came new responsibilities and new dilemmas, many of which still concern scientists and society today. What happens when scientific discoveries or experiments result in harm or get out of control? When do the risks of pursuing scientific advancement outweigh the benefits to society? Who gets to define ethical scientific practices?

? *ESSENTIAL QUESTION:*
What shapes your outlook on life?

One hallmark of Romanticism was its focus on individual feelings and personal experiences. As humans, we are often shaped by our most emotionally intense experiences. Still, it is not experience alone that molds perspective. Two people can live through the same event and come away from it with completely different perspectives, based on their outlooks on life or how they view and interact with the world. If experience cannot account for all of the differences in perspective, what can?

THE FLOWERING OF ROMANTICISM

The literary movement known as Romanticism developed in reaction to many social influences: the unrest of the French Revolution, the economic excesses of the Industrial Revolution, and the widespread poverty and oppression of workers.

A Time of Revolution During the American Revolution and, later, the French Revolution, George III ruled Britain. He was not a very capable king, and many blamed the loss of the American colonies chiefly on his inflexible attitude toward the colonists. In 1788, the year before the French Revolution began, George III suffered a major attack of mental illness; in 1811 he was declared permanently insane. His son George ruled as prince regent until the king's death in 1820.

Initially, many British citizens, including most of the early Romantic writers and poets, felt sympathy for the French Revolution and its ideals of liberty, equality, and brotherhood. The Romantics saw the revolution as a turning point in human history, a move toward an ideal civilized society in which those who had previously struggled under oppression would find relief. When the revolution turned radical and violent, however, British sympathy dissipated, and the Romantics turned elsewhere for inspiration.

During the Reign of Terror, radical revolutionaries persecuted and massacred thousands of French aristocrats and middle-class citizens. The British upper and middle classes were all too aware that England's lower classes faced many of the same social ills as the French lower classes. The British ruling classes were afraid that any efforts at reform could lead to anarchy as it had in France. As a result, British leaders grew more conservative, suppressing reform and outlawing writing or speech that was critical of the government.

War with France In 1793 Britain entered into a war with France that would last for more than 25 years. It was during this conflict that General Napoleon Bonaparte took control of France's government, made himself emperor, and then proceeded to conquer much of continental Europe. Britain was continually threatened with invasion until the British fleet destroyed the French navy in 1805. After that, Britain was able to loosen Napoleon's hold on Europe, and Napoleon was finally defeated at Waterloo in 1815.

COLLABORATIVE DISCUSSION
In a small group, discuss how the events on the timeline influenced British society. Was this influence mainly direct or indirect?

1780

1789
The French Revolution begins.

1793
The French Revolution gives way to the Reign of Terror; war begins between Britain and France.

1794
William Blake publishes *Songs of Innocence and of Experience.*

© Houghton Mifflin Harcourt Publishing Company

The Downside of Industry During this period, England was an industrial as well as an agricultural country. The Industrial Revolution and improvements in farming brought increased prosperity to the middle and upper classes, but brought degrading poverty to the families employed in the factories and mills. Living and working conditions were appalling. There were no laws to regulate work safety, hours, wages, or child labor. At the time, Britain operated under the doctrine of *laissez-faire* economics, which means that an economy works best without government intervention.

Shortly after George III's son took control as regent, an economic depression resulted in the loss of many factory jobs. Advances in technology caused even more job losses, as fewer workers were needed to run textile mills. In the ensuing Luddite Riots, unemployed mill workers rioted, smashing the machines they blamed for taking their jobs. Frightened by the violence, Parliament, instead of working to solve the root causes of the violence, passed laws that made the rioters' actions punishable by death. Labor unions were illegal, and workers had little power in Parliament. Some workers organized anyway, but were quickly put down by the government.

The Romantics Romantic writers often sympathized with the oppressed lower classes and wrote about their plight. Lord Byron, a Romantic poet

RESEARCH

What about this historical period interests you? Choose a topic, event, or person to learn more about. Then add your own entry to the timeline.

1805
The British fleet defeats the French navy at the Battle of Trafalgar.

1815
Napoleon is defeated at Waterloo.

1820
The Regency ends when George III dies and his son becomes king.

1820

1804
Napoleon crowns himself Emperor of France.

1811
George III is declared insane; his son is named regent.

1818
Mary Shelley anonymously publishes *Frankenstein*.

and a member of Parliament, openly expressed his sympathy for the poor to other members of the British government. In fact, he was one of only three members of Parliament to vote against the law punishing the Luddite rioters with death.

Such political efforts, however, yielded few results. Many of the Romantic writers reacted to the harsh realities of industrialization by turning to nature for truth and beauty. They revolted against the order, propriety, and traditionalism of the Age of Reason and rejected the classical tradition that venerated the achievements of ancient Greece and Rome. The Romantics were influenced by the same forces that gave rise to the American and French revolutions and by the agitation for political, social, and economic change taking place in their own country. For the Romantics, emotion became more important than reason. Thus, they preferred styles of writing that allowed self-expression, like lyric poetry, which came to dominate English literature during this time.

CHECK YOUR UNDERSTANDING

Choose the best answer to each question.

1 Which event caused many British citizens to lose sympathy for the French Revolution?

   A Britain's loss of the American colonies in an earlier revolution

   B The takeover of the French government by Napoleon Bonaparte

   C The execution of French aristocrats during the Reign of Terror

   D The defeat of the French navy by the British fleet

2 Which factor contributed most directly to the Luddite Riots?

   F Instigation by Romantic writers like Lord Byron

   G Appointment of George III's son as regent in his father's place

   H Discontent over the outlawed status of labor unions

   J Loss of factory jobs due to advances in technology

3 Romantic writers valued —

   A traditionalism over revolution

   B emotion over reason

   C industry over nature

   D order over agitation

ACADEMIC VOCABULARY

Academic Vocabulary words are words you use when you discuss and write about texts. In this unit, you will learn the following five words:

☑ **appreciate**　　❑ **insight**　　❑ **intensity**　　❑ **invoke**　　❑ **radical**

Study the Word Network to learn more about the word **appreciate.**

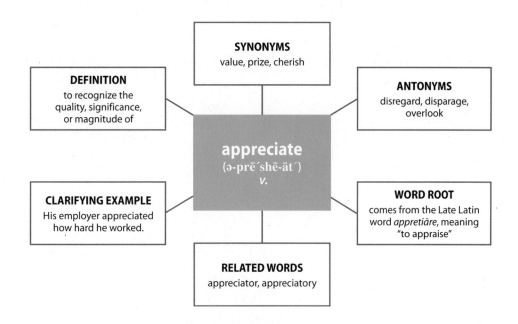

Write and Discuss Discuss your completed Word Network with a partner, making sure to talk through all of the boxes until you both understand the word, its synonyms, antonyms, and related forms. Then fill out a Word Network for the remaining four words. Use a dictionary or online resource to help you complete the activity.

Go online to access the Word Networks.

RESPOND TO THE ESSENTIAL QUESTIONS

In this unit, you will explore four different **Essential Questions** about Emotion and Experimentation. As you read each selection, you will gather your ideas about one of these questions and write about it in the **Response Log** that appears on page R4. At the end of the unit, you will have the opportunity to write an **explanatory essay** related to one of the Essential Questions. Filling out the Response Log after you read each text will help you prepare for this writing task.

You can also go online to access the Response Log.

POEMS BY

WILLIAM WORDSWORTH

? ***ESSENTIAL QUESTION:***

What can
nature offer us?

QUICK START

Think about a time you were in nature and were fully absorbed in the present moment. What do you remember seeing, hearing, and smelling? How did it make you feel?

ANALYZE ROMANTIC POETRY

Romanticism was a literary movement that flourished in Britain and Europe in the 19th century. Unlike the neoclassical poets who preceded them, the Romantics emphasized the importance of the individual's subjective experiences rather than issues that concerned society as a whole. Their philosophy valued emotion, spontaneity, and imagination over reason, analysis, and orderliness.

Romantic poets wrote about personal experiences, often using simple, unadorned language. Many Romantic poems celebrate the beauty and grandeur of the natural world. The Romantics rejected the forces of industrialization that were beginning to transform Europe and tended to idealize the distant past. They looked to nature for inspiration and also for insight into their creative processes.

You are about to read three poems by William Wordsworth, one of the key figures of the Romantic movement. As you read, use a chart such as this one to note details that display the characteristics of Romantic poetry.

GENRE ELEMENTS: LYRIC POETRY

- usually written in the first person
- expresses the feelings and thoughts of the speaker
- uses sound devices such as rhythm and repetition to create a musical quality
- often deals with intense emotions surrounding events like death, love, or loss

DETAILS FROM THE POEMS	CHARACTERISTICS OF ROMANTIC POETRY

ANALYZE IMAGERY

Imagery is language that creates vivid sensory experiences for the reader. Visual imagery, which appeals to the sense of sight, is the most common form of imagery used in literature, but writers also use words and phrases to appeal to the senses of hearing, touch, smell, and taste to deepen their readers' understanding of and connection to their works. For example, in "Lines Composed a Few Miles Above Tintern Abbey," Wordsworth refers to the "soft inland murmur" of the Wye River. This auditory image describes the sound of the moving water and also suggests its calming effect.

As you read Wordsworth's poems, look for sensory language and create mental images of the sights and sounds of the landscapes and experiences the poet describes. Also notice how Wordsworth develops the subject, mood, and theme of each poem through imagery. Consider the following lines from "Lines Composed a Few Miles Above Tintern Abbey":

> **Therefore let the moon**
> **Shine on thee in thy solitary walk;**
> **And let the misty mountain winds be free**
> **To blow against thee:**

The visual image of the moon shining and the tactile image of the misty winds blowing against his sister as she walks alone help develop the solemn, reverent mood of the poem. This imagery also reflects the poet's ideas related to the spiritual nourishment that the natural world can provide and the importance of the individual's unique experience.

ANNOTATION MODEL

NOTICE & NOTE

As you read, note passages in the poems that reflect characteristics of Romanticism, and examine how Wordsworth uses imagery to develop ideas about nature and the experiences of individuals. This model shows one reader's notes about "Lines Composed a Few Miles Above Tintern Abbey."

Five years have passed; five summers, with the length

Of five long winters! and again I hear

These <u>waters, rolling from their mountain-springs</u>

With a soft inland murmur. Once again

Do I behold these steep and lofty cliffs,

That on a <u>wild secluded scene impress</u>

<u>Thoughts of more deep seclusion; and connect</u>

The landscape with the quiet of the sky.

These images suggest the grandeur of the wilderness near Tintern Abbey.

The speaker draws a connection between the landscape and the turning inward of his thoughts.

BACKGROUND

William Wordsworth *(1770–1850) helped launch the Romantic movement in England. Rebelling against the formal diction and lofty writings of many poets of the time, Wordsworth used simple language to celebrate subjects drawn mostly from nature and everyday life.*

As a child, Wordsworth happily explored the countryside near his home. When he was seven, his mother died, and he was sent to boarding school. Fortunately, he was able to continue spending time outdoors there, developing his deep love for the natural world and writing poetry. He went to Cambridge University, graduating in 1791.

POEMS BY
WILLIAM WORDSWORTH

A walking tour of France in 1790 interested Wordsworth in the political changes happening as a result of the French Revolution. In 1791 Wordsworth returned to France and fell in love with a French woman, Annette Vallon. Lacking money, he returned to England in 1792, but when war broke out between France and England he was prevented from reuniting with Annette and their newborn baby.

In 1795 Wordsworth and his sister set up a home together in a rural area in Dorset. There they befriended the poet Samuel Taylor Coleridge. Wordsworth and Coleridge collaborated on a book of poetry, Lyrical Ballads (1798), that ushered in the Romantic movement.

In many of his poems, Wordsworth describes specific natural settings and often shares his thoughts and feelings about them. In "Lines Composed a Few Miles Above Tintern Abbey," Wordsworth reflects on his memories of the beauty of the Wye River Valley in Wales, an area he hiked through extensively. Near this valley are the ruins of Tintern Abbey, a medieval monastery that captivated public imagination with its picturesque decay.

In 1802 Wordsworth married childhood friend Mary Hutchinson. Over the next two decades, he struggled to find readers and critical acceptance for his work. In the 1820s his reputation gradually improved, and by the 1830s he was hugely popular. In 1843 his immense achievement as a poet was recognized when he was named England's poet laureate.

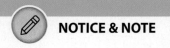
Notice & Note

Use the side margins to notice and note signposts in the text.

---

9 repose: lie at rest.

14 copses (kŏpˈsĭz): thickets of small trees.

16 pastoral (păsˈtər-əl): rural and serene.

20 vagrant: wandering.

ANALYZE ROMANTIC POETRY

Annotate: Mark words and phrases in lines 27–49 that describe the speaker's feelings about the landscape.

Analyze: Why are these feelings important for the speaker?

SETTING A PURPOSE

As you read, pay attention to the ideas expressed in the poems about how people are affected by nature and by city life. Also notice how Wordsworth uses imagery to appeal to the reader's senses.

Lines Composed a Few Miles Above Tintern Abbey

Five years have passed; five summers, with the length
Of five long winters! and again I hear
These waters, rolling from their mountain-springs
With a soft inland murmur. Once again
5 Do I behold these steep and lofty cliffs,
That on a wild secluded scene impress
Thoughts of more deep seclusion; and connect
The landscape with the quiet of the sky.
The day is come when I again repose
10 Here, under this dark sycamore, and view
These plots of cottage ground, these orchard tufts,
Which at this season, with their unripe fruits,
Are clad in one green hue, and lose themselves
'Mid groves and copses. Once again I see
15 These hedgerows, hardly hedgerows, little lines
Of sportive wood run wild; these pastoral farms,
Green to the very door; and wreaths of smoke
Sent up, in silence, from among the trees!
With some uncertain notice, as might seem
20 Of vagrant dwellers in the houseless woods,
Or of some Hermit's cave, where by his fire
The Hermit sits alone.

         These beauteous forms,
Through a long absence, have not been to me
As is a landscape to a blind man's eye;
25 But oft, in lonely rooms, and 'mid the din
Of towns and cities, I have owed to them,
In hours of weariness, sensations sweet,
Felt in the blood, and felt along the heart;
And passing even into my purer mind,
30 With tranquil restoration—feelings too
Of unremembered pleasure; such, perhaps,
As have no slight or trivial influence
On that best portion of a good man's life,
His little, nameless, unremembered, acts
35 Of kindness and of love. Nor less, I trust,
To them I may have owed another gift,

Of aspect more sublime; that blessed mood,
In which the burthen of the mystery,
In which the heavy and the weary weight
40 Of all this unintelligible world,
Is lightened—that serene and blessed mood,
In which the affections gently lead us on—
Until, the breath of this corporeal frame
And even the motion of our human blood
45 Almost suspended, we are laid asleep
In body, and become a living soul;
While with an eye made quiet by the power
Of harmony, and the deep power of joy,
We see into the life of things.

                    If this
50 Be but a vain belief, yet, oh! how oft—
In darkness and amid the many shapes
Of joyless daylight; when the fretful stir
Unprofitable, and the fever of the world,
Have hung upon the beatings of my heart—
55 How oft, in spirit, have I turned to thee,
O sylvan Wye! thou wanderer through the woods,
How often has my spirit turned to thee!

    And now, with gleams of half-extinguished thought
With many recognitions dim and faint,
60 And somewhat of a sad perplexity,
The picture of the mind revives again;
While here I stand, not only with the sense
Of present pleasure, but with pleasing thoughts
That in this moment there is life and food
65 For future years. And so I dare to hope,
Though changed, no doubt, from what I was when first
I came among these hills; when like a roe
I bounded o'er the mountains, by the sides
Of the deep rivers, and the lonely streams,
70 Wherever nature led—more like a man
Flying from something that he dreads than one
Who sought the thing he loved. For nature then
(The coarser pleasures of my boyish days,
And their glad animal movements all gone by)
75 To me was all in all.—I cannot paint
What then I was. The sounding cataract
Haunted me like a passion; the tall rock,
The mountain, and the deep and gloomy wood,
Their colors and their forms, were then to me

© Houghton Mifflin Harcourt Publishing Company

NOTICE & NOTE

38 burthen: burden.

43 corporeal (kôr-pôr´ē-əl):
bodily.

56 sylvan: located in a wood or
forest; **Wye:** a river near Tintern
Abbey.

67 roe: deer.

76 cataract (kăt´ə-răkt):
waterfall.

ANALYZE IMAGERY
Annotate: Mark the auditory
and visual imagery in lines
76–78.

Analyze: How does this
imagery affect the reader's
understanding of the speaker's
experience?

86 Faint I: I lose heart.

88 recompense (rĕkʹəm-pĕns): compensation.

93 chasten (chāʹsən): scold; make modest.

80 An appetite; a feeling and a love,
    That had no need of a remoter charm,
    By thought supplied, nor any interest
    Unborrowed from the eye.—That time is past,
    And all its aching joys are now no more,
85 And all its dizzy raptures. Not for this
    Faint I, nor mourn nor murmur; other gifts
    Have followed; for such loss, I would believe,
    Abundant recompense. For I have learned
    To look on nature, not as in the hour
90 Of thoughtless youth; but hearing oftentimes
    The still, sad music of humanity,
    Nor harsh nor grating, though of ample power
    To chasten and subdue. And I have felt
    A presence that disturbs me with the joy
95 Of elevated thoughts; a sense sublime
    Of something far more deeply interfused,
    Whose dwelling is the light of setting suns,
    And the round ocean and the living air,

© Houghton Mifflin Harcourt Publishing Company

And the blue sky, and in the mind of man:
100 A motion and a spirit, that impels
All thinking things, all objects of all thought,
And rolls through all things. Therefore am I still
A lover of the meadows and the woods,
And mountains; and of all that we behold
105 From this green earth; of all the mighty world
Of eye, and ear—both what they half create,
And what perceive; well pleased to recognize
In nature and the language of the sense
The anchor of my purest thoughts, the nurse,
110 The guide, the guardian of my heart, and soul
Of all my moral being.

            Nor perchance,
If I were not thus taught, should I the more
Suffer my genial spirits to decay:
For thou art with me here upon the banks
115 Of this fair river; thou my dearest Friend,

ANALYZE IMAGERY
Annotate: Mark images of nature in lines 93–102.

Analyze: How do these images support the speaker's idea about a force that affects all things?

111 perchance: by chance; perhaps.
113 genial (jēn´yəl): relating to genius; creative.
115 thou my dearest Friend: Wordsworth´s sister, Dorothy.

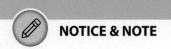

ANALYZE ROMANTIC POETRY

Annotate: Mark the verbs used in lines 123–134 to describe nature's actions.

Analyze: What romantic idea does Wordsworth express in this passage?

My dear, dear Friend; and in thy voice I catch
The language of my former heart, and read
My former pleasures in the shooting lights
Of thy wild eyes. Oh! yet a little while
120 May I behold in thee what I was once,
My dear, dear Sister! and this prayer I make,
Knowing that Nature never did betray
The heart that loved her; 'tis her privilege,
Through all the years of this our life, to lead
125 From joy to joy: for she can so inform
The mind that is within us, so impress
With quietness and beauty, and so feed
With lofty thoughts, that neither evil tongues,
Rash judgments, nor the sneers of selfish men,
130 Nor greetings where no kindness is, nor all
The dreary intercourse of daily life,
Shall e'er prevail against us, or disturb
Our cheerful faith, that all which we behold
Is full of blessings. Therefore let the moon
135 Shine on thee in thy solitary walk;
And let the misty mountain winds be free
To blow against thee: and, in after years,
When these wild ecstasies shall be matured
Into a sober pleasure; when thy mind
140 Shall be a mansion for all lovely forms,
Thy memory be as a dwelling place
For all sweet sounds and harmonies; oh! then,
If solitude, or fear, or pain, or grief
Should be thy portion, with what healing thoughts
145 Of tender joy wilt thou remember me,
And these my exhortations! Nor, perchance—
If I should be where I no more can hear
Thy voice, nor catch from thy wild eyes these gleams
Of past existence—wilt thou then forget
150 That on the banks of this delightful stream
We stood together; and that I, so long
A worshiper of Nature, hither came
Unwearied in that service; rather say
With warmer love—oh! with far deeper zeal
155 Of holier love. Nor wilt thou then forget,
That after many wanderings, many years
Of absence, these steep woods and lofty cliffs,
And this green pastoral landscape, were to me
More dear, both for themselves and for thy sake!

146 exhortations: words of encouraging advice.

149 past existence: the speaker's own past experience five years before (see lines 116–119).

CHECK YOUR UNDERSTANDING

Answer these questions about "Lines Composed a Few Miles Above Tintern Abbey" before moving on to the next selection.

1 How did the speaker's memories of the valley affect him during the past five years?

    A They tormented him.

    B They restored his spirit.

    C They made him resent city life.

    D They caused him to avoid nature.

2 What has the speaker lost since he last visited the valley?

    F His ability to run up the mountains

    G His memory of where the ruined abbey stood

    H His career in the city

    J His passionate reaction to nature

3 What does the speaker observe in his sister?

    A She responds to nature the same way he used to.

    B She fears hurting herself in the valley.

    C She shares his memories of the valley.

    D She behaves recklessly on their hike.

ANALYZE ROMANTIC POETRY

Annotate: Mark language in lines 9–14 that conveys the emotions of the speaker.

Analyze: What emotions does this language convey?

9 steep: soak; saturate.

12 The river: Westminster Bridge spans the Thames (tĕmz)—the principal river in London.

13 houses: possibly a pun on the Houses of Parliament, near Westminster Bridge.

Composed upon Westminster Bridge, September 3, 1802

Earth has not anything to show more fair:
Dull would he be of soul who could pass by
A sight so touching in its majesty;
This City now doth, like a garment, wear
5 The beauty of the morning; silent, bare,
Ships, towers, domes, theaters, and temples lie
Open unto the fields, and to the sky;
All bright and glittering in the smokeless air.
Never did sun more beautifully steep
10 In his first splendor, valley, rock, or hill;
Ne'er saw I, never felt, a calm so deep!
The river glideth at his own sweet will:
Dear God! the very houses seem asleep;
And all that mighty heart is lying still!

CHECK YOUR UNDERSTANDING

Answer these questions about "Composed upon Westminster Bridge, September 3, 1802" before moving on to the next selection.

1 What time of day does "Composed upon Westminster Bridge, September 3, 1802" describe?

A Dawn

B Dusk

C Midnight

D Midday

2 Which of the following best describes the speaker's meaning in lines 2 and 3?

F He prefers being in the city to being in nature.

G He believes people should stop to appreciate the world around them.

H He thinks his soul is better than the souls of other people.

J He feels saddened by the majestic view.

3 How does the scene he describes in the poem make the speaker feel?

A Excited

B Melancholy

C Peaceful

D Disappointed

2 vales: valleys.

I Wandered Lonely As a Cloud

I wandered lonely as a cloud
That floats on high o'er vales and hills,
When all at once I saw a crowd,
A host, of golden daffodils;
5 Beside the lake, beneath the trees,
Fluttering and dancing in the breeze.

Continuous as the stars that shine
And twinkle on the milky way,
They stretched in never-ending line
10 Along the margin of a bay:
Ten thousand saw I at a glance,
Tossing their heads in sprightly dance.

The waves beside them danced; but they
Outdid the sparkling waves in glee;
15 A poet could not but be gay,
In such a jocund company;
I gazed—and gazed—but little thought
What wealth the show to me had brought:

ANALYZE IMAGERY

Annotate: Mark the imagery that describes nature in lines 1–12.

Analyze: How do these images help the reader understand the speaker's experience?

16 jocund (jŏk´ənd): merry.

For oft, when on my couch I lie
20 In vacant or in pensive mood,
They flash upon that inward eye
Which is the bliss of solitude;
And then my heart with pleasure fills,
And dances with the daffodils.

CHECK YOUR UNDERSTANDING

Answer these questions before moving on to the **Analyze the Texts** section on the following page.

1 What sight captures the speaker's attention in "I Wandered Lonely As a Cloud"?

A Clouds

B Daffodils

C Dancers

D Waves

2 The tone of the poem is best described as —

F lonely

G joyful

H solemn

J humorous

3 What does Wordsworth mean in line 21 when he says that the daffodils "flash upon that inward eye"?

A They remind him that he is alone.

B They keep him awake at night.

C They make him feel pensive.

D They appear in his imagination.

ANALYZE THE TEXTS

Support your responses with evidence from the texts. ⊟ NOTEBOOK

1. **Analyze** What details in lines 1–22 of "Lines Composed a Few Miles Above Tintern Abbey" suggest that Wordsworth preferred to celebrate the individual in his work rather than society?

2. **Draw Conclusions** In "Lines Composed a Few Miles Above Tintern Abbey," how has the speaker's relationship with nature changed over time?

3. **Analyze** How does Wordsworth use imagery in "Composed upon Westminster Bridge, September 3, 1802" to support the mood and theme of the poem?

4. **Interpret** Reread lines 17–24 of "I Wandered Lonely As a Cloud." What is the "wealth" that the speaker doesn't initially appreciate when he sees the daffodils?

5. **Synthesize** Which characteristics of Romanticism do all three of these poems share?

RESEARCH

RESEARCH TIP
Before you begin researching, identify key words from the research prompt to help start your online search.

Tintern Abbey and Westminster Bridge are real places in England. With a partner, research these places to find out more about them.

• Read some background information about the history of these places.
• Search for images so you can see what each place looks like.
• Do a map search so you can see where the locations are in reference to the rest of England.

Use a chart like the one below to record the results of your research.

PLACE	HISTORY	APPEARANCE	LOCATION
Tintern Abbey			
Westminster Bridge			

Extend The poem "I Wandered Lonely As a Cloud" describes the scenery of the Lake District, another real place in England. Research the Lake District, add a row to your chart, and record information about its history, appearance, and location.

CREATE AND DISCUSS

Write a Summary Write a summary of "Lines Composed a Few Miles Above Tintern Abbey." To do this, you will briefly retell the events and experiences described in the poem in your own words.

- ❏ Introduce the speaker and the other people mentioned in the poem.
- ❏ Describe the setting of the poem, and explain the effect it has on the speaker.
- ❏ Explain how the imagery in the poem engages the reader's senses and conveys meaning.
- ❏ Include a statement of the poem's theme, or central message.

Discuss Consider the ideas Wordsworth expresses in his poetry about nature and the comfort it can provide. With a partner, discuss any of your own experiences in nature that you've found meaningful or helpful in your life.

- ❏ Listen thoughtfully as your partner tells you about his or her experiences.
- ❏ Ask questions about any ideas or details that are unclear or need elaboration.
- ❏ Brainstorm to come up with ideas as to how you and your partner might seek out additional meaningful experiences in nature.

Go to **Participating in Collaborative Discussions** in the **Speaking and Listening Studio** for more help.

RESPOND TO THE ESSENTIAL QUESTION

 ? What can nature offer us?

Gather Information Review your annotations and notes on the poems by William Wordsworth. Then, add relevant information to your Response Log. As you determine which information to include, think about:

- the mental and emotional solace Wordsworth finds in nature
- the role of memory in Wordsworth's poems
- what you value about your own memories of experiences with nature

ACADEMIC VOCABULARY

As you write and discuss what you learned from the poems, be sure to use the Academic Vocabulary words. Check off each of the words that you use.

- ❏ **appreciate**
- ❏ **insight**
- ❏ **intensity**
- ❏ **invoke**
- ❏ **radical**

ODE ON A GRECIAN URN

Poem by **John Keats**

ESSENTIAL QUESTION:

How do you define beauty?

QUICK START

Write a description of your favorite artwork or a prized possession. Discuss the feelings you associate with this object and why you find it so appealing. Include at least four sensory details in your description.

ANALYZE STANZA STRUCTURE

A **stanza** is a group of lines that form a unit in a poem. In traditional poetic forms, stanzas often contain the same number of lines and have the same rhyme scheme and meter. Stanzas often function like paragraphs in prose, each presenting a discrete idea.

Although odes can vary in structure, the five stanzas of "Ode on a Grecian Urn" have a regular structure of ten lines of **iambic pentameter,** a metrical pattern of five feet, or units. Each iambic foot consists of two syllables, the first unstressed and the second stressed.

> **Thou still unravish'd bride of quietness,**
>
> **Thou foster-child of silence and slow time,**

Keats sometimes varies the meter to emphasize certain words and to keep the poem from sounding monotonous. You can gain insight into the meaning of the poem by reading it aloud and noticing which words are stressed. As you read, also notice the main idea expressed in each stanza.

ANALYZE RHYME SCHEME

The **rhyme scheme** of a poem is the pattern of **end rhyme** that helps establish the structure and unity of a stanza and adds to the poem's musicality. A rhyme scheme is described using letters, such as *abab* or *aabb*, where lines that rhyme are given the same letter. Certain poetic forms, such as the various types of sonnets, follow a set rhyme scheme.

Keats's "Ode on a Grecian Urn" has a complex rhyme scheme. The first four lines of each stanza rhyme *abab*. The next six lines follow one of these patterns: *cdedce, cdeced,* or *cdecde*. Because of these variations, the rhyming becomes subtler and more unexpected as you move farther along in a stanza. While reading the poem, notice how the rhyme scheme appeals to your sense of hearing.

GENRE ELEMENTS: ODE

- lyric poem that develops a single theme
- has a serious tone
- appeals to both the imagination and the intellect
- may commemorate an event or praise people or nature's beauty

ANALYZE APOSTROPHE

Apostrophe is a figure of speech in which the speaker addresses an object, abstract concept, or absent or imaginary person as if present and able to understand. Poets often use apostrophe to express strong emotions. This device was especially popular among the Romantic poets. In "Ode on a Grecian Urn," Keats uses apostrophe to address both the urn itself and the figures portrayed on it.

> **O Attic shape! Fair attitude! with brede**
> **Of marble men and maidens overwrought,**

Here the speaker addresses the urn as one might speak to an admired person, heightening the reader's sense of his emotional response to seeing the urn. As you read the poem, pay attention to the shifting focus of the apostrophe.

ANNOTATION MODEL   **NOTICE & NOTE**

As you read, note words and phrases that convey ideas about the artwork discussed in the poem. Also notice how the rhyme scheme and meter emphasize important words. In the model, you can see one reader's notes about the opening lines of "Ode on a Grecian Urn."

Thou still <u>unravish'd bride</u> of quietness,

Thou <u>foster-child</u> of silence and slow time,

<u>Sylvan historian</u>, who canst thus express

A flowery tale more sweetly than our rhyme:

What leaf-fring'd legend haunts about thy shape

Of deities or mortals, or of both,

In Tempe or the dales of Arcady?

What men or gods are these? What maidens loath?

What mad pursuit? What struggle to escape?

What pipes and timbrels? What wild ecstasy?

The speaker uses phrases that compare the urn to specific types of people. This helps give the impression that he is addressing something that can understand him.

BACKGROUND

John Keats *(1795–1821) only lived to age 25, yet he produced some of the most famous poems in the English language. Keats's life was marred by illness and tragedy. His father died in a riding accident when he was young. Later, both his mother and brother died of tuberculosis, and Keats himself became ill with the disease at 22. His poor health prevented him from marrying his sweetheart, Fanny Brawne. It was during his illness, however, that he produced some of his greatest work. "Ode on a Grecian Urn" was probably inspired by ancient Greek urns that Keats saw at the British Museum. Such urns were often painted with mythological scenes, as described in this poem.*

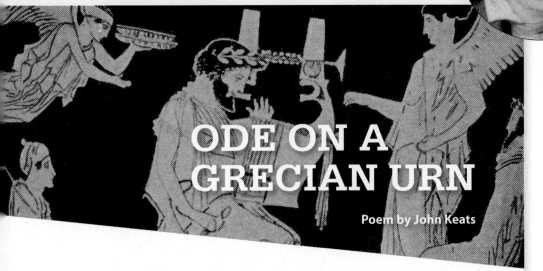

ODE ON A GRECIAN URN

Poem by John Keats

SETTING A PURPOSE

As you read, notice the ideas that the speaker associates with images on the urn.

Thou still unravish'd bride of quietness,
　　Thou foster-child of silence and slow time,
Sylvan historian, who canst thus express
　　A flowery tale more sweetly than our rhyme:
5　What leaf-fring'd legend haunts about thy shape
　　　Of deities or mortals, or of both,
　　　　In Tempe or the dales of Arcady?
　　What men or gods are these? What maidens loath?
What mad pursuit? What struggle to escape?
10　　　What pipes and timbrels? What wild ecstasy?

Heard melodies are sweet, but those unheard
　　Are sweeter; therefore, ye soft pipes, play on;
Not to the sensual ear, but, more endear'd,
　　Pipe to the spirit ditties of no tone:
15　Fair youth, beneath the trees, thou canst not leave
　　Thy song, nor ever can those trees be bare;

© Houghton Mifflin Harcourt Publishing Company • Image Credits: © Time Life Pictures/Mansell/The LIFE Picture Collection/Getty Images; © Hulton Archive/Getty Images

Notice & Note

Use the side margins to notice and note signposts in the text.

3 Sylvan: pertaining to trees or woods.

5 haunts about: surrounds.

7 Tempe (tĕm´pē) **. . . Arcady** (är´kə-dē): two places in Greece that became traditional literary settings for an idealized rustic life. Tempe is a beautiful valley; Arcady (Arcadia) is a mountainous region.

8 loath: unwilling; reluctant.

10 timbrels: tambourines.

ANALYZE RHYME SCHEME

Annotate: Mark the end rhymes in lines 11–20.

Analyze: What is the rhyme scheme in this stanza?

29 cloy'd: having had too much of something; oversatisfied.

ANALYZE APOSTROPHE

Annotate: In lines 32–40, mark the two images that the author addresses.

Interpret: What emotions does the author express about each of these images?

41 Attic: pure and classical; in the style of Attica, the part of Greece where Athens is located; **brede** (brēd): interwoven design.

45 Pastoral (păs′tər-əl): an artistic work that portrays rural life in an idealized way.

ANALYZE STANZA STRUCTURE

Annotate: In lines 41–45, mark the syllables that are stressed.

Identify: Where in the passage does Keats vary the metrical pattern to emphasize certain words?

> Bold lover, never, never canst thou kiss,
> Though winning near the goal—yet, do not grieve;
> She cannot fade, though thou hast not thy bliss,
> 20 For ever wilt thou love, and she be fair!
>
> Ah, happy, happy boughs! that cannot shed
> Your leaves, nor ever bid the spring adieu;
> And, happy melodist, unweariéd,
> For ever piping songs for ever new;
> 25 More happy love! more happy, happy love!
> For ever warm and still to be enjoyed,
> For ever panting, and for ever young;
> All breathing human passion far above,
> That leaves a heart high-sorrowful and cloy'd,
> 30 A burning forehead, and a parching tongue.
>
> Who are these coming to the sacrifice?
> To what green altar, O mysterious priest,
> Lead'st thou that heifer lowing at the skies,
> And all her silken flanks with garlands drest?
> 35 What little town by river or sea shore,
> Or mountain-built with peaceful citadel,
> Is emptied of this folk, this pious morn?
> And, little town, thy streets for evermore
> Will silent be; and not a soul to tell
> 40 Why thou art desolate, can e'er return.
>
> O Attic shape! Fair attitude! with brede
> Of marble men and maidens overwrought,
> With forest branches and the trodden weed;
> Thou, silent form, dost tease us out of thought
> 45 As doth eternity: Cold Pastoral!
> When old age shall this generation waste,
> Thou shalt remain, in midst of other woe
> Than ours, a friend to man, to whom thou say'st,
> "Beauty is truth, truth beauty,"—that is all
> 50 Ye know on earth, and all ye need to know.

© Houghton Mifflin Harcourt Publishing Company

CHECK YOUR UNDERSTANDING

Answer these questions before moving on to the **Analyze the Text** section on the following page.

1 In line 3, the phrase "Sylvan historian" refers to —

   A a Greek writer

   B a man pictured on the urn

   C the reader of the poem

   D the Grecian urn

2 In line 20, why does the author say, "For ever wilt thou love, and she be fair"?

   F True love is everlasting.

   G Their images are frozen in time.

   H They exist only in each other's memories.

   J Their love is immortalized in song.

3 What is the urn's message, delivered in its last two lines?

   A Beauty and truth are unable to stand the test of time.

   B Beauty and truth are equivalent and eternal.

   C Beauty and truth both are important.

   D Beauty and truth are often confused.

ANALYZE THE TEXT

Support your responses with evidence from the text. ☰ NOTEBOOK

1. **Analyze** In lines 1–4, Keats addresses the urn as an "unravish'd bride" and a "Sylvan historian." What characteristics of the urn do these phrases in the apostrophe convey?

2. **Interpret** Reread lines 11–14. How do you interpret the statement, "Heard melodies are sweet, but those unheard / Are sweeter"?

3. **Identify Patterns** What words are repeated in stanza 3? What idea does this repetition help develop in the stanza?

4. **Draw Conclusions** Why might Keats have chosen to vary the rhyme scheme in the last six lines of the stanzas?

5. **Connect** How might Keats's personal circumstances have contributed to the sentiments expressed in the poem?

RESEARCH

RESEARCH TIP
When looking for information in an online source or digital document, use Ctrl + F to do a search of the page. Put phrases in quotation marks to search only for that exact phrase.

Like most educated people of his era, Keats studied classical literature. He was also inspired by Greek art and philosophy. With a partner, research Keats's connections to ancient Greece. Use what you learn to answer these questions.

QUESTION	ANSWER
What artworks in the British Museum probably inspired "Ode on a Grecian Urn"?	
What characteristics of the Greek goddess Psyche does Keats emphasize in his poem "Ode to Psyche"?	
In the poem "On First Looking into Chapman's Homer," what does Keats admire about the translation of the Greek epics referred to in the title?	

Extend Read "Ode to Psyche." With a partner, discuss the poem's ideas and also its formal qualities, such as stanza structure and rhyme scheme. Compare the poem with "Ode on a Grecian Urn."

CREATE AND PRESENT

Write a Poem Using Apostrophe Is there an inanimate object or abstract idea that you have strong feelings about? Perhaps you love winter or are upset about the closing of a local restaurant. Write a poem addressing that inanimate object or abstract idea to express your feelings.

❏ Address the object or idea directly. Use apostrophe to express strong emotion.

❏ Include several stanzas. Decide whether you will use regular patterns of rhyme and meter or if you'll write in free verse, with no regular patterns.

❏ Use sensory details to create a vivid experience for your reader.

Present Your Poem Give a dramatic reading of your poem for a group or the whole class.

❏ Practice your dramatic reading and revise the text as necessary for dramatic effectiveness and ease of speech.

❏ Make notations to remind yourself to emphasize certain words or phrases.

❏ When giving your presentation, use voice inflection, facial expressions, gestures, and eye contact.

Go to **Giving a Presentation** in the **Speaking and Listening Studio** to find out more.

RESPOND TO THE ESSENTIAL QUESTION

? How do you define beauty?

Gather Information Review your annotations and notes on "Ode on a Grecian Urn." Then, add relevant information to your Response Log. As you determine which information to include, think about:

• whether beauty is subjective or objective
• what emotions beauty inspires
• whether your experiences change how you perceive beauty

UNIT 4
RESPONSE LOG

Use this Response Log to record information from the texts that relates to or comments on the **Essential Questions** in Unit 4.

? Essential Question	Details from Texts
What can nature offer us?	
How do you define beauty?	
How can science go wrong?	
What shapes your outlook on life?	

R4 Student Resources

ACADEMIC VOCABULARY

As you write and discuss what you learned from the poem, be sure to use the Academic Vocabulary words. Check off each of the words that you use.

❏ **appreciate**

❏ **insight**

❏ **intensity**

❏ **invoke**

❏ **radical**

Ode on a Grecian Urn 519

from FRANKENSTEIN

Novel by **Mary Shelley**

? *ESSENTIAL QUESTION:*

How can science go wrong?

QUICK START

The name *Frankenstein* is often used to describe scientific research that has gotten out of control. To what extent should scientists be held accountable for the results of their discoveries? Discuss this question with a partner.

ANALYZE SCIENCE FICTION

Frankenstein is a work of gothic horror that is also considered one of the first science fiction novels. **Science fiction** is a literary genre based on imagined scientific or technological developments, such as time travel or encounters with extraterrestrial life. Mary Shelley said that the idea for the book came to her in a dream after spending several stormy nights discussing ghost stories and medical experiments with a group of friends. She wrote a story about a scientist who creates a man from human remains, which she later expanded into the novel *Frankenstein*.

As you read, use a chart like the one below to note how imaginary advances in science or medicine influence important elements of the novel.

Elements of Science Fiction in *Frankenstein*	
Plot	
Characters	
Theme	

© Houghton Mifflin Harcourt Publishing Company

GENRE ELEMENTS: NOVEL
- a long fictional prose narrative
- includes the same fictional elements as a short story
- usually has a more complex plot and a wider range of characters than a short story
- may be written in subgenres such as science fiction, historical fiction, or mystery

ANALYZE MOTIVATION

Motivation is the stated or implied reason behind a fictional character's behavior. Sometimes motivation is directly expressed in a story, but usually readers must infer a character's motivation from dialogue, thoughts, and actions. Characters' motivations often influence the plot and theme of a work, so careful readers look closely for relationships among these elements.

In Shelley's novel, Victor Frankenstein struggles with the moral dilemma of whether to accept or abandon the creature he has created. As you read, analyze the motivations that contribute toward this dilemma. Also, analyze the motivations underlying the creature's behavior toward Frankenstein.

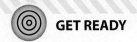

CRITICAL VOCABULARY

infuse	ardor	inarticulate	precipice
inanimate	tumult	misdeed	odious

To see how many Critical Vocabulary words you already know, use them to complete the sentences.

1. Because of his _____ for his experiment, he would stop at nothing to discover how to make the _____ creature come to life.

2. Frankenstein's mind was in a _____ about what he had created, and he felt that he was standing at the edge of a terrifying _____ in the history of science.

3. Though at first the creature was _____, he later learned to speak and even to _____ his speech with the tones and cadences used in real human conversation.

4. The _____ creature, cast out from human society, was determined to find his creator and deny that he had committed any _____.

LANGUAGE CONVENTIONS

Sensory Language In this lesson, you will examine how sensory language is used to help re-create sensory experiences for the reader. Sensory language includes descriptive words or phrases that appeal to one or more of the five senses: sight, hearing, smell, taste, and touch.

In this sentence from *Frankenstein*, Mary Shelley uses sensory language that helps the reader feel the cold wind that the narrator experiences in the novel:

> **I was troubled: a mist came over my eyes, and I felt a faintness seize me; but I was quickly restored by the cold gale of the mountains.**

As you read the excerpt from *Frankenstein*, note places where the author uses sensory language.

ANNOTATION MODEL   **NOTICE & NOTE**

As you read, make note of any elements of horror and science fiction.
In the model, you can see one reader's notes on a passage from *Frankenstein*.

It was <u>on a dreary night</u> of November that I beheld the accomplishment of my toils. With an anxiety that almost amounted to agony, I collected <u>the instruments of life</u> around me, that I <u>might infuse a spark of being</u> into the lifeless thing that lay at my feet.

Shelley opens with a classic horror story phrase to describe the setting.

The details about bringing something dead to life ("the instruments of life" and "might infuse a spark of being") tell me this is a science fiction story.

BACKGROUND

Mary Shelley *(1797–1851) was the daughter of two famous writers, the early feminist Mary Wollstonecraft and the philosopher William Godwin. Shelley's education benefited from access to her father's vast library and the many scientific and literary people she encountered during her upbringing. When she was 19, she married the poet Percy Bysshe Shelley. Although her literary reputation was long overshadowed by those of her parents and husband, in recent decades Shelley has gained increased recognition as an important writer. Written in 1818,* Frankenstein *was first published anonymously, then later under Shelley's name.*

FRANKENSTEIN

Novel by Mary Shelley

SETTING A PURPOSE

As you read, pay attention to Victor Frankenstein's reactions to the creature he created, and consider whether his reactions are out of proportion based on the creature's words and behavior.

A young Swiss scientist named Victor Frankenstein sets out to learn the secret of creating life. For two years he devotes himself to studying chemistry and human anatomy. Finally, after assembling a creature from human remains, he prepares to use an electrical charge to bring it to life.

1   It was on a dreary night of November that I beheld the accomplishment of my toils. With an anxiety that almost amounted to agony, I collected the instruments of life around me, that I might **infuse** a spark of being into the lifeless thing that lay at my feet. It was already one in the morning; the rain pattered dismally against the panes, and my candle was nearly burnt out, when, by the glimmer of the half-extinguished light, I saw the dull yellow eye of the creature open; it breathed hard, and a convulsive motion agitated its limbs.

© Houghton Mifflin Harcourt Publishing Company • Image Credits: © Fine Art Images/Heritage Image Partnership Ltd./Alamy; © Photography by Mangiwau/Getty Images

Notice & Note

Use the side margins to notice and note signposts in the text.

ANALYZE SCIENCE FICTION
Annotate: In paragraph 1, mark the words and phrases that suggest scientific endeavors.

Explain: How do these details support the categorization of *Frankenstein* as one of the first works of science fiction?

infuse
(ĭn-fyōōz´) *v.* to fill or cause to be filled with something.

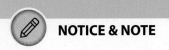
ANALYZE MOTIVATION

Annotate: In paragraph 2, mark the words or phrases that demonstrate the great care Frankenstein took in building his creation.

Analyze: Why would Frankenstein have taken such pains to make his creation?

inanimate
(ĭn-ăn´ə-mĭt) *adj.* not having the qualities associated with active, living organisms.

ardor
(är´dər) *n.* intensity of emotion, especially strong desire, enthusiasm, or devotion.

tumult
(tōō´mŭlt) *n.* a state of agitation of the mind or emotions.

inarticulate
(ĭn-är-tĭk´yə-lĭt) *adj.* uttered without the use of normal words or syllables; incomprehensible as speech or language.

2 How can I describe my emotions at this catastrophe, or how delineate the wretch whom, with such infinite pains and care, I had endeavored to form? His limbs were in proportion, and I had selected his features as beautiful. Beautiful! Great God! His yellow skin scarcely covered the work of muscles and arteries beneath; his hair was of a lustrous black, and flowing; his teeth of a pearly whiteness; but these luxuriances only formed a more horrid contrast with his watery eyes, that seemed almost of the same color as the dun white sockets in which they were set, his shriveled complexion, and straight black lips.

3 The different accidents of life are not so changeable as the feelings of human nature. I had worked hard for nearly two years, for the sole purpose of infusing life into an **inanimate** body. For this I had deprived myself of rest and health. I had desired it with an **ardor** that far exceeded moderation; but now that I had finished, the beauty of the dream vanished, and breathless horror and disgust filled my heart. Unable to endure the aspect of the being I had created, I rushed out of the room, and continued a long time traversing my bed-chamber, unable to compose my mind to sleep. At length lassitude succeeded to the **tumult** I had before endured; and I threw myself on the bed in my clothes, endeavoring to seek a few moments of forgetfulness. But it was in vain: I slept indeed, but I was disturbed by the wildest dreams. I thought I saw Elizabeth, in the bloom of health, walking in the streets of Ingolstadt. Delighted and surprised, I embraced her; but as I imprinted the first kiss on her lips, they became livid with the hue of death; her features appeared to change, and I thought that I held the corpse of my dead mother in my arms; a shroud enveloped her form, and I saw the grave-worms crawling in the folds of the flannel. I started from my sleep with horror; a cold dew covered my forehead, my teeth chattered, and every limb became convulsed; when, by the dim and yellow light of the moon, as it forced its way through the window-shutters, I beheld the wretch, the miserable monster whom I had created. He held up the curtain of the bed; and his eyes, if eyes they may be called, were fixed on me. His jaws opened, and he muttered some **inarticulate** sounds, while a grin wrinkled his cheeks.

4 He might have spoken, but I did not hear; one hand was stretched out, seemingly to detain me, but I escaped, and rushed downstairs. I took refuge in the courtyard belonging to the house which I inhabited; where I remained during the rest of the night, walking up and down in the greatest agitation, listening attentively, catching and fearing each sound as if it were to announce the approach of the demoniacal corpse to which I had so miserably given life. . . .

After fleeing from his creation, Victor Frankenstein falls seriously ill and is cared for by a friend. He learns that the creature has killed his younger brother, William, and framed a family servant for the murder. Frankenstein returns home, but he is unable to save the servant from execution for William's murder. Tormented by guilt, he sets out for a hike in the Swiss Alps, hoping to relieve his despair.

5   It was nearly noon when I arrived at the top of the ascent. For some time I sat upon the rock that overlooks the sea of ice. A mist covered both that and the surrounding mountains. Presently a breeze dissipated the cloud, and I descended upon the glacier. The surface is very uneven, rising like the waves of a troubled sea, descending low, and interspersed by rifts that sink deep. The field of ice is almost a league in width, but I spent nearly two hours in crossing it. The opposite mountain is a bare perpendicular rock. From the side where I now stood Montanvert was exactly opposite, at the distance of a league; and above it rose Mont Blanc, in awful majesty. I remained in a recess of the rock, gazing on this wonderful and stupendous scene. The sea, or rather the vast river of ice, wound among its dependent mountains, whose aerial summits hung over its recesses. Their icy and glittering peaks shone in the sunlight over the clouds. My heart, which was before sorrowful, now swelled with something like joy; I exclaimed — "Wandering spirits, if ye indeed wander, and do not rest in your narrow beds, allow me this faint happiness, or take me as your companion, away from the joys of life."

6   As I said this, I suddenly beheld the figure of a man, at some distance, advancing towards me with superhuman speed. He bounded over the crevices of the ice, among which I had walked with caution; his stature also, as he approached, seemed to exceed that of man.

7   I was troubled: a mist came over my eyes, and I felt a faintness seize me; but I was quickly restored by the cold gale of the mountains. I perceived, as the shape came nearer (sight tremendous and abhorred!), that it was the wretch whom I had created. I trembled with rage and horror, resolving to wait his approach, and then close with him in mortal combat. He approached; his countenance bespoke bitter anguish, combined with disdain and malignity, while its unearthly ugliness rendered it almost too horrible for human eyes. But I scarcely observed this; anger and hatred had at first deprived me of utterance, and I recovered only to overwhelm him with words expressive of furious detestation and contempt.

LANGUAGE CONVENTIONS

Annotate: Mark the language that evokes the senses in paragraph 5.

Infer: What impression of the setting does the sensory language help convey?

ANALYZE MOTIVATION

Annotate: Mark words in paragraph 7 that show how Frankenstein feels about his creation and what he plans to do to it.

Infer: Why might Frankenstein feel this way and resolve to take this action?

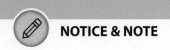

ANALYZE MOTIVATION

Annotate: Mark the words or phrases in paragraph 9 that show what the creature asks of Frankenstein.

Draw Conclusions: What does the creature ask for, and what motivates his request?

misdeed

(mĭs-dēd´) *n.* a wrong or illegal deed; a wrongdoing.

8   "Devil!" I exclaimed, "do you dare approach me? and do you not fear the fierce vengeance of my arm wreaked on your miserable head? Begone, vile insect! or rather stay, that I may trample you to dust! and, oh, that I could, with the extinction of your miserable existence, restore those victims whom you have so diabolically murdered!"

9   "I expected this reception," said the demon. "All men hate the wretched; how then must I be hated, who am miserable beyond all living things! Yet you, my creator, detest and spurn me, thy creature, to whom thou art bound by ties only dissoluble by the annihilation of one of us. You purpose to kill me. How dare you sport thus with life? Do your duty towards me, and I will do mine towards you and the rest of mankind. If you will comply with my conditions, I will leave them and you at peace; but if you refuse, I will glut the maw of death, until it be satisfied with the blood of your remaining friends."

10   "Abhorred monster! fiend that thou art! the tortures of hell are too mild a vengeance for thy crimes. Wretched devil! you reproach me with your creation; come on then, that I may extinguish the spark which I so negligently bestowed."

11   My rage was without bounds; I sprang on him, impelled by all the feelings which can arm one being against the existence of another.
    He easily eluded me, and said, —

12   "Be calm! I entreat you to hear me, before you give vent to your hatred on my devoted head. Have I not suffered enough, that you seek to increase my misery? Life, although it may only be an accumulation of anguish, is dear to me, and I will defend it. Remember, thou hast made me more powerful than thyself; my height is superior to thine; my joints more supple. But I will not be tempted to set myself in opposition to thee. I am thy creature, and I will be even mild and docile to my natural lord and king, if thou wilt also perform thy part, the which thou owest me. Oh, Frankenstein, be not equitable to every other, and trample upon me alone, to whom thy justice, and even thy clemency and affection, is most due. Remember, that I am thy creature: I ought to be thy Adam; but I am rather the fallen angel, whom thou drivest from joy for no **misdeed**. Everywhere I see bliss, from which I alone am irrevocably excluded. I was benevolent and good; misery made me a fiend. Make me happy, and I shall again be virtuous."

13   "Begone! I will not hear you. There can be no community between you and me; we are enemies. Begone, or let us try our strength in a fight, in which one must fall."

14   "How can I move thee? Will no entreaties cause thee to turn a favorable eye upon thy creature, who implores thy goodness and compassion? Believe me, Frankenstein: I was benevolent; my soul glowed with love and humanity: but am I not alone, miserably alone?

You, my creator, abhor me; what hope can I gather from your fellow-creatures, who owe me nothing? They spurn and hate me. The desert mountains and dreary glaciers are my refuge. I have wandered here many days; the caves of ice, which I only do not fear, are a dwelling to me, and the only one which man does not grudge. These bleak skies I hail, for they are kinder to me than your fellow-beings. If the multitude of mankind knew of my existence, they would do as you do, and arm themselves for my destruction. Shall I not then hate them who abhor me? I will keep no terms with my enemies. I am miserable, and they shall share my wretchedness. Yet it is in your power to recompense me, and deliver them from an evil which it only remains for you to make so great, that not only you and your family, but thousands of others, shall be swallowed up in the whirlwinds of its rage. Let your compassion be moved, and do not disdain me. Listen to my tale: when you have heard that, abandon or commiserate me, as you shall judge that I deserve. But hear me. The guilty are allowed, by human laws, bloody as they may be, to speak in their own defense, before they are condemned. Listen to me, Frankenstein. You accuse me of murder; and yet you would, with a satisfied conscience, destroy your own creature. Oh, praise the eternal justice of man! Yet I ask you not to spare me: listen to me; and then, if you can, and if you will, destroy the work of your hands."

15   "Why do you call to my remembrance circumstances of which I shudder to reflect that I have been the miserable origin and author? Cursed be the day, abhorred devil, in which you first saw light! Cursed (although I curse myself) be the hands that formed you! You have made me wretched beyond expression. You have left me no power to consider whether I am just to you or not. Begone! relieve me from the sight of your detested form."

16   "Thus I relieve thee, my creator," he said, and placed his hated hand before my eyes, which I flung from me with violence; "thus I take from thee a sight which you abhor. Still thou canst listen to me, and grant me thy compassion. By the virtues that I once possessed, I demand this from you. Hear my tale; it is long and strange, and the temperature of this place is not fitting to your fine sensations; come to the hut upon the mountain. The sun is yet high in the heavens; before it descends to hide itself behind yon snowy **precipices**, and illuminate another world, you will have heard my story, and can decide. On you it rests, whether I quit forever the neighborhood of man, and lead a harmless life, or become a scourge to your fellow-creatures, and the author of your own speedy ruin."

ANALYZE SCIENCE FICTION

Annotate: In paragraph 14, mark the words or phrases that show that the creature believes he should be treated the same as all humans.

Evaluate: Do you find the creature's argument convincing? Why or why not?

precipice
(prĕs´ə-pĭs) *n.* an overhanging or extremely steep mass of rock; the brink of a dangerous or disastrous situation.

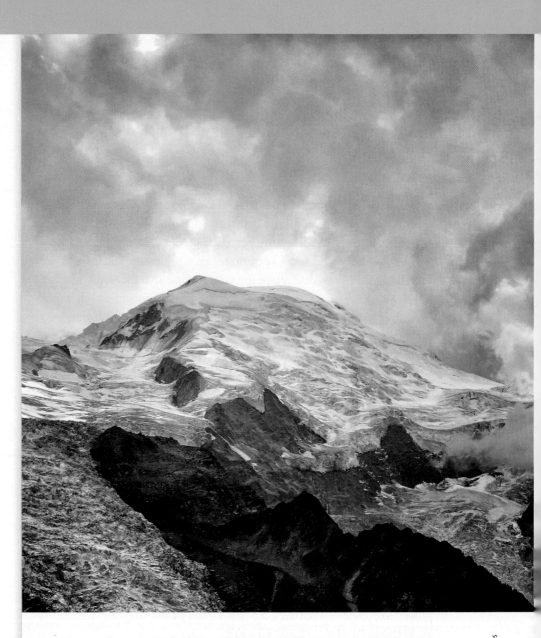

AHA MOMENT

Notice & Note: What does Frankenstein realize for the first time in paragraph 17? Mark the sentence where he expresses this thought.

Evaluate: Is Frankenstein partly responsible for the creature's behavior? Why or why not?

odious
(ō´dē-əs) *adj.* extremely unpleasant; repulsive.

17   As he said this, he led the way across the ice: I followed. My heart was full, and I did not answer him; but, as I proceeded, I weighed the various arguments that he had used, and determined at least to listen to his tale. I was partly urged by curiosity, and compassion confirmed my resolution. I had hitherto supposed him to be the murderer of my brother, and I eagerly sought a confirmation or denial of this opinion. For the first time, also, I felt what the duties of a creator towards his creature were, and that I ought to render him happy before I complained of his wickedness. These motives urged me to comply with his demand. We crossed the ice, therefore, and ascended the opposite rock. The air was cold, and the rain again began to descend: we entered the hut, the fiend with an air of exultation, I with a heavy heart and depressed spirits. But I consented to listen; and, seating myself by the fire which my **odious** companion had lighted, he thus began his tale.

CHECK YOUR UNDERSTANDING

Answer these questions before moving on to the **Analyze the Text** section on the following page.

1 Why does Frankenstein feel disgusted by the creature soon after bringing him to life?

   A The creature acts violently.

   B The creature chases him.

   C The creature has an ugly appearance.

   D The creature is physically weak.

2 How does Frankenstein react when the creature finds him in the Swiss Alps?

   F He is afraid of the creature.

   G He tries to run away.

   H He feels guilty for creating the creature.

   J He wants to kill the creature.

3 The creature demands that Frankenstein —

   A listen to his story

   B protect him from his enemies

   C be his companion

   D improve his appearance

ANALYZE THE TEXT

Support your responses with evidence from the text. ▤ NOTEBOOK

1. **Interpret** In paragraph 3, Frankenstein dreams that Elizabeth, a woman he loves, turns into a corpse after he kisses her. How does this dream reflect his experience in the previous paragraph?

2. **Draw Conclusions** Why does the creature think that he should be forgiven for his crimes? Cite evidence for your conclusion.

3. **Analyze** What moral dilemma does Frankenstein experience in the Swiss Alps? What actions and motivations have contributed to this dilemma?

4. **Critique** Did Shelley choose an effective setting for the confrontation between Frankenstein and the creature? Explain why or why not.

5. **Notice & Note** In paragraph 17, Frankenstein says, "For the first time, also, I felt what the duties of a creator towards his creature were." How does this realization relate to scientific and technological developments today?

RESEARCH

RESEARCH TIP
When researching a subject at a specific time period, use specific search terms like "science early 19th century" or "science and *Frankenstein*." Using specific search terms makes it easier to find relevant information quickly.

Scientific understanding was much different during Mary Shelley's time than it is today. With a partner, research scientific and medical knowledge in the early 19th century. Use the following questions to guide your research.

QUESTION	ANSWER
What did scientists know about electricity by the early 19th century?	
What methods did scientists use to generate electricity?	
What ideas did scientists have about the relationship between electricity and life?	

Extend With a small group, discuss how the information you learned about early 19th-century science relates to *Frankenstein*.

CREATE AND DISCUSS

Write a Science Fiction Story Write a short science fiction story that addresses a moral or ethical issue. The story can be set in the present and involve an imagined scientific or technological development, or it can be set in the future.

- ❏ Identify an imagined scientific or technological advance or invention and evaluate the moral and ethical dilemmas involved with this innovation.
- ❏ Consider the motivations of your characters as you develop the story.
- ❏ Use details to develop the characters and the setting of your story.
- ❏ Think about ways you can use sensory language to give your readers a vivid experience.

Discuss Have a discussion about the possible negative effects and dangers of the rapid advancement of science, medicine, and technology.

- ❏ Discuss possible ways in which people might respond to and address the issues brought on by major advancements in science, medicine, and technology.
- ❏ Listen carefully to your classmates, ask questions, and comment respectfully on others' ideas.
- ❏ As a group, summarize the key points of the discussion and identify points of agreement.

Go to **Writing Narratives** in the **Writing Studio** for more about writing short stories.

Go to **Participating in Collaborative Discussions** in the **Speaking and Listening Studio** for more help with having a discussion.

RESPOND TO THE ESSENTIAL QUESTION

 How can science go wrong?

Gather Information Review your annotations and notes on the excerpt from *Frankenstein*. Then, add relevant information to your Response Log. As you determine which information to include, think about:

- how scientific and medical technologies require ethical consideration
- how science fiction can reflect human nature
- how science can be used for both good and bad purposes

ACADEMIC VOCABULARY

As you write and discuss what you learned from the novel, be sure to use the Academic Vocabulary words. Check off each of the words that you use.

- ❏ **appreciate**
- ❏ **insight**
- ❏ **intensity**
- ❏ **invoke**
- ❏ **radical**

WORD BANK

infuse	inarticulate
inanimate	misdeed
ardor	precipice
tumult	odious

Practice and Apply Use your understanding of the Critical Vocabulary words to answer each question.

1. If a person is **inarticulate,** would that person make an excellent or a poor public speaker?

2. If someone feels **ardor** toward another person, does that person hate or love the other?

3. Would an **odious** meal be one you look forward to eating or one you refuse to eat?

4. If tea is **infused** with lemons, does that mean it is made of lemons or it contains lemons?

5. Which is an **inanimate** object, a rock or a bird?

6. Would a **misdeed** be more likely to be punished or celebrated?

7. If you were afraid of heights, would you be likely to stand near a **precipice**?

8. Which would be more likely to cause a **tumult,** going on a vacation or moving to a new city?

VOCABULARY STRATEGY:
Antonyms

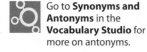

Go to **Synonyms and Antonyms** in the **Vocabulary Studio** for more on antonyms.

An **antonym** is a word with a meaning opposite that of another word. Some antonyms are formed by adding a prefix that means "not" to a word to create one with the opposite meaning. For example, the word *inanimate* is formed by adding the prefix *in-* to the adjective *animate,* which means "living."

Practice and Apply Add the prefix *dis-, il-, im-, in-, ir-, non-,* or *un-* to each word below to create its antonym.

1. violent

2. legitimate

3. responsible

4. mobile

5. conclusive

6. reverent

7. orderly

8. intelligible

LANGUAGE CONVENTIONS:
Sensory Language

Sensory language includes descriptive words and phrases that appeal to one or more of the reader's senses, creating a more vivid experience for the reader. In *Frankenstein*, Mary Shelley often uses sensory words and phrases to provide descriptions that elicit feelings of horror in the reader. For instance, read the following sentence from the novel.

> **It was already one in the morning; the rain pattered dismally against the panes, and my candle was nearly burnt out, when, by the glimmer of the half-extinguished light, I saw the dull yellow eye of the creature open; it breathed hard, and a convulsive motion agitated its limbs.**

Notice that in this sentence, Shelley appeals to the senses of sight ("dull yellow eye") and hearing ("rain pattered dismally"). Now compare that sentence to the following paraphrased version.

> **It was already one in the morning. Rain was falling, and my candle was nearly burnt out. I saw the creature's eye open. It breathed hard and moved its limbs.**

Which version is more effective at establishing a mood and bringing the reader into the story? Why?

Practice and Apply Revisit the science fiction story you wrote. Identify settings, characters, and events in the story that lack vivid description. Look for opportunities to enhance your reader's experience by using sensory language. Revise your story to help bring your reader into the action of the story by adding details that appeal to the senses. Share your revisions with a partner.

Go to the **Writing Studio: Writing Narratives** for more on the language of narratives.

FRANKENSTEIN: GIVING VOICE TO THE MONSTER

Essay by **Langdon Winner**

? ***ESSENTIAL QUESTION:***

How can science go wrong?

QUICK START

Imagine a world in which robots do all of the work. Would such a development make life better? Might there be disadvantages to a fully automated society? Would there be possible dangers to consider? Discuss these questions with a partner.

EVALUATE AN ESSAY

An essay is a brief work of nonfiction that offers an opinion on a subject. A **formal essay** is well organized and has a clear main idea. Formal essays are usually serious and impersonal in tone. Most formal essays are written to inform or persuade or to express ideas. An **informal essay** may be more loosely structured; the tone is conversational, reflecting the personality of the author. The purpose of an informal essay is often to express ideas and feelings or to entertain.

In "Frankenstein: Giving Voice to the Monster," Langdon Winner offers an interesting perspective on the relevance of Mary Shelley's novel today. As you read his essay, notice how he uses his analysis of the novel to support his ideas about science and technology.

MONITOR COMPREHENSION

Some texts are more difficult than others due to their complex ideas, writing style, or unfamiliar content. When you **monitor comprehension,** you check to make sure that you understand what you are reading. One method is to ask questions about a text before, during, and after reading. The following types of questions can help clarify and deepen your understanding:

- **Literal questions** can be answered directly from statements in the text. You might also ask literal questions before you start reading; for example, you might ask yourself what you already know about the topic of an essay or what your purpose is in reading it.

- **Inferential questions** have answers that are not directly stated in the text. Readers make inferences and draw conclusions based on details in a text and their own knowledge and experience.

- **Evaluative questions** are generally asked after reading a text. You might ask whether you agree with ideas in an essay or how effectively you think the author presented them.

As you read this essay, mark up statements that you have trouble understanding, and make note of any questions you have about the content. Review and try to answer your questions after you finish reading.

© Houghton Mifflin Harcourt Publishing Company

GENRE ELEMENTS: ESSAY

- is a short piece of nonfiction
- offers an opinion on a subject
- formal essays have a serious and impersonal tone
- informal essays are loosely structured and have a conversational tone

CRITICAL VOCABULARY

sentient	recoil	ominous	domain
artifice	succinct	calamity	prescient

To see how many Critical Vocabulary words you already know, use them to complete the sentences.

1. The magician used _____ to trick all of the _____ beings in the room.

2. A(n) _____ mood filled the room as the seer used his _____ powers to direct the detectives to the missing child.

3. The nauseated medical student fought the urge to _____ in horror at the sight of the bloody _____.

4. "Welcome to my _____," said the teacher. "Please keep your comments _____ as I dislike long, rambling explanations."

LANGUAGE CONVENTIONS

Parallel Structure In this lesson, you'll learn about parallel structure—the use of similar grammatical constructions to express ideas that are related or equal in importance. Notice the parallel phrases in this example:

> **Mary Shelley's insights on these matters were . . . some of the most ominous hazards and most ghastly calamities. . . .**

The repeated grammatical construction of the adjective *most* plus a second adjective and a noun emphasizes that the two phrases are related and equally important. As you read Winner's essay, notice other uses of parallelism.

ANNOTATION MODEL

NOTICE & NOTE

As you read the essay, practice monitoring your comprehension by taking notes, marking the text, and asking questions. The model below shows one reader's notes in response to the text.

The possibility that artificial creatures, products of human hands, might achieve (sentience) and take on an active role in society is an age-old conception in world cultures, the subject of myths, stories, moral fables, and philosophical speculation.

In Greek mythology one finds the tale of (Pygmalion) who carves a statue named Galatea with whom he falls in love and who eventually comes to life.

What does this word mean?

Why has this been a common theme in literature? What does this say about humans? Does it reflect the need to create?

The writer uses this detail to support his point in the sentence above.

BACKGROUND

Langdon Winner *(1944–present) is a professor and political theorist. He has taught in colleges and universities and lectured on several continents. He currently serves as the humanities and social sciences department chair at Rensselaer Polytechnic Institute in Troy, New York. His essay "Frankenstein: Giving Voice to the Monster" was presented in Geneva in 2016 at the "Frankenstein's Shadow" conference, honoring the 200th anniversary of the writing of Mary Shelley's novel.*

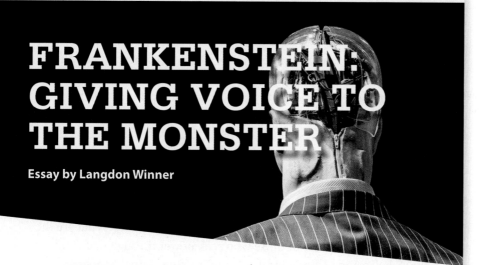

FRANKENSTEIN: GIVING VOICE TO THE MONSTER

Essay by Langdon Winner

SETTING A PURPOSE

As you read, note Winner's ideas about the novel Frankenstein *and how he connects those ideas to society today.*

1   The possibility that artificial creatures, products of human hands, might achieve sentience and take on an active role in society is an age-old conception in world cultures, the subject of myths, stories, moral fables, and philosophical speculation.

2   In Greek mythology one finds the tale of Pygmalion who carves a statue named Galatea with whom he falls in love and who eventually comes to life. In Jewish folklore there are stories of the Golem, an artificial creature animated with surprising results. Norse legends include reports of clay giants able to move on their own accord. An ancient Chinese text describes the work of Yan Shi who in the 10th century B.C. crafted a humanoid figure with lifelike qualities.

3   Both Plato and Aristotle draw upon the myth of the statues of Daedalus[1], mythical creations that could move, perform certain

© Houghton Mifflin Harcourt Publishing Company • Image Credits: © ISAAC LAWRENCE/AFP/Getty Images

---

[1] **Daedalus** (dĕd´l-əs): Greek Mythology; A renowned craftsman, sculptor, and inventor and builder of the Labyrinth. He fashioned the wings with which he and his son Icarus escaped from Crete after their imprisonment by Minos.

Notice & Note

Use the side margins to notice and note signposts in the text.

EVALUATE AN ESSAY

Annotate: Reread paragraph 2. Mark the examples of myths and legends.

Analyze: What is the author's purpose for listing these examples?

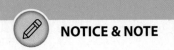
© Houghton Mifflin Harcourt Publishing Company

kinds of work and would wander off on their own unless tied down by a rope. In the *Politics* Aristotle uses the metaphor in his defense of slavery: ". . . if every tool could perform its own work when ordered, or by seeing what to do in advance, like the statues of Daedalus in the story . . . master-craftsmen would have no need of assistants and masters no need of slaves."

4   World literature, not to mention modern science fiction, contains a great many stories of this kind, ones that are often used to shed light upon basic questions about what it means to be alive, what it means to be conscious, what it means to be human, what membership in society entails.

5   Within this tradition of thought Mary Shelley's *Frankenstein* plays a pivotal role. Within popular culture, of course, its story has spawned an astonishing range of novels, stories, movies, television programs, advertisements, toys, and costumes, most of which center upon images of monstrosity, horror and the mad scientist. Beyond these familiar manifestations, however, the novel offers a collection of deeply unsettling reflections upon the human condition, ones brought to focus by modern dreams of creating **sentient**, artificial, humanoid beings.

6   In direct, provocative ways the book asks: What is the relationship between the creator and the thing created? What are the larger responsibilities of those who seek power through scientific knowledge and technological accomplishment? What happens when those responsibilities are not recognized or otherwise left unattended?

7   Questions of this kind concern particular projects that involve attempts to create artificial devices that exhibit features and abilities similar to or even superior to ones associated with human beings. In a larger sense, however, the problems posed by the novel point to situations in which scientific technologies introduced into nature and society seem to run out of control, to achieve a certain autonomy, taking on a life of their own beyond the plans and intentions of the persons involved in their creation.

8   As she addresses issues of this kind, the genius of Mary Shelley is to give voice not only to Victor Frankenstein, his family, friends and acquaintances, but to the creature that sprang from his work and after a time learns to speak, read and form his thoughts, eager to speak his mind about his situation. I do not know whether this is the first time in world literature that one finds a serious dialogue between an artificial creation and its creator. But first instance or not, it is a literary device that Shelley uses with stunning effectiveness.

9   At their climatic meeting high in the Alps, the creature's observations and arguments painfully articulate the perils of unfinished, imperfect, carelessly prepared **artifice**, suddenly released

---

MONITOR COMPREHENSION

Annotate: Mark the reference to technology in the last sentence of paragraph 5.

Infer: What inferential question can you develop in response to this statement? How would you answer it?

sentient
(sĕn´shənt) *adj.* having sense perception; conscious.

artifice
(är´tə-fĭs) *n.* cleverness or ingenuity in making or doing something.

into the world, emphasizing the obligations of the creator as well as the consequences of insensitivity and neglect.

> I am thy creature, and I will be even mild and docile to my natural lord and king if thou wilt also perform thy part, that which thou owest me.

> You propose to kill me. How dare you sport thus with life? Do your duty towards me, and I will do mine toward you and the rest of mankind. If you will comply with my conditions I will leave them and you at peace; but if you refuse, I will glut the maw of death, until it be satiated with the blood of your remaining friends.

10   The creature goes on to explain that his greatest desire is to be made part of the human community, something that has been strongly, even brutally, denied him to that point. His stern admonition to Victor is to recognize that the invention of something powerful, ingenious, even marvelous cannot be the end of the work at hand. Thoughtful care must be given to its place in the sphere of human relationships.

11   At first Victor **recoils** and bitterly denounces the creature's demands that he recognize, affirm and fulfill his obligations. But as the threat of violent revenge becomes clear, Victor finally yields to the validity of the argument. "For the first time," he admits, "I felt what the duties of a creator towards his creature were, and that I ought to render him happy before I complained of his wickedness."

12   Following that flash of recognition the story careens toward a disastrous conclusion. Within the wreckage that envelops both Victor and his creature, the book reveals crucial insight, one before its time and with profound implications for similar projects in the future. It can be stated **succinctly** as follows: The quest for power through scientific technology often tends to override and obscure the recognition of the profound responsibilities that the possession of such power entails.

13   Put even more simply: The impulse to power and control typically comes first, while the recognition of personal and collective moral obligation arrives later, if ever at all. Within that unfortunate gap—between aspirations to power through science and belated recognitions of responsibility—arise generations of monstrosity.

14   Mary Shelley's insights on these matters were well ahead of their time and foreshadow some of the most **ominous** hazards and most ghastly **calamities** found along the path to modernity from the early 19th century up to the present day. . . .

15   One could offer a great many historical and contemporary illustrations of what I would call "Frankenstein's problem." An

---

EVALUATE AN ESSAY

Annotate: Reread the author's analysis of a passage from *Frankenstein* in paragraphs 10–12. Mark words and phrases with strong connotations.

Evaluate: Identify the author's tone. How does his choice of words contribute to the persuasiveness of his essay?

recoil
(rĭ-koil´) *v.* to shrink back, as in fear or repugnance.

succinct
(sək-sĭngkt´) *adj.* characterized by clear, precise expression in few words; concise and terse.

LANGUAGE CONVENTIONS

Annotate: Mark the author's use of parallel structure in the first sentence of paragraph 13.

Evaluate: How does parallelism strengthen the connection between ideas here?

ominous
(ŏm´ə-nəs) *adj.* menacing; threatening.

calamity
(kə-lăm´ĭ-tē) *n.* an event that brings terrible loss, lasting distress, or severe affliction; a disaster.

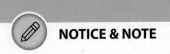
domain
(dō-mān´) *n.* a sphere of activity, influence, or knowledge.

QUOTED WORDS

Notice & Note: Mark the names of notable people the author quotes in paragraphs 16–18.

Critique: Do these quotations provide effective support for the author's opinion about artificial intelligence? Why or why not?

---

appropriate, highly practical, obviously troubling set of developments at present are found within a particular **domain** of scientific inquiry and application, a zone of works not all that dissimilar from the one the fictional Victor Frankenstein explored—today's realm of advanced computerization, smart algorithms, artificial intelligence (AI) and robotics. . . . During the past several years, notable scientists, engineers and luminaries in the technology business sector have stepped forward to express distress at what they see as dire risks that research in AI presents to the human species overall.

16   In a BBC interview last year, Stephen Hawking warned, "The development of full artificial intelligence could spell the end of the human race. . . . Humans, limited by slow biological evolution, couldn't compete and would be superseded by AI. . . . One can imagine such technology outsmarting financial markets, out-inventing human researchers, out-manipulating human leaders, and developing weapons we cannot even understand. Whereas the short-term impact of AI depends on who controls it, the long-term impact depends on whether it can be controlled at all."

17   In a live exchange on the internet, Microsoft cofounder Bill Gates offered similar views. "I am in the camp that is concerned about super intelligence," Gates wrote. "First the machines will do a lot of jobs for us and not be super intelligent. . . . A few decades after that though the intelligence is strong enough to be a concern."

18   In the same vein, British inventor Clive Sinclair recently told the BBC, "Once you start to make machines that are rivaling and surpassing humans with intelligence, it's going to be very difficult for us to survive. It's just an inevitability." . . .

19   Studies of and speculation about issues of this kind has inspired the creation of a collection of new research centers at leading universities. Among them are the Cambridge Center for the Study of Existential Risk and The Future of Life Institute at MIT. Taken together the shelf of books on AI and Robots, the systematic studies of the future of automation and employment, and the excited warnings about artificial devices superseding human beings as the key actors on the stage of world history are, in my view, a contemporary realization of the **prescient** concerns and warnings at the heart of Mary Shelley's book—concerns and warnings about the headlong flight from responsibility.

---

prescient
(prĕsh´ənt) *adj.* of or relating to prescience—which means knowledge of actions or events before they occur.

CHECK YOUR UNDERSTANDING

Answer these questions before moving on to the **Analyze the Text** section on the following page.

1 According to the author, the genius of Shelley is in —

   A setting the climactic meeting place in the Alps

   B giving a voice to Frankenstein's creature

   C anticipating the novel's effect on popular culture

   D introducing the concept of a mad scientist

2 What is one of the deeper questions posed by Shelley's novel?

   F Who should participate in scientific development?

   G What is the relationship between nature and society?

   H What scientific projects should never be attempted?

   J What responsibilities accompany scientific development?

3 The attitude that Gates, Hawking, and Sinclair share about the future of artificial intelligence is one of —

   A concern and caution

   B hope and excitement

   C annoyance and dismay

   D doubt and negativity

ANALYZE THE TEXT

Support your responses with evidence from the text. ≡ NOTEBOOK

1. **Identify** What is the main idea of this essay?

2. **Evaluate** Does the author provide sufficient support for his opinion that Shelley's genius was to "give voice to the monster"? Why or why not?

3. **Critique** How effective is the author's conclusion to the essay? Explain.

4. **Question** Review your markups and notes on "Frankenstein: Giving Voice to the Monster." What questions do you have after reading this essay? What kind of research or investigation might help you answer these questions?

5. **Notice and Note** Reread paragraphs 16–18. Do you think that the author should have included a quotation from someone with a different view of the future of artificial intelligence? Explain why or why not.

RESEARCH

RESEARCH TIP
Look for sources that include up-to-date research and provide evidence in the form of facts, statistics, and logical reasoning.

Winner suggests that some problems resulting from the development of artificial intelligence might be related to the "future of automation and employment." He quotes Bill Gates, who also mentions the issue of machines doing many of our jobs. Research these concerns. What jobs are currently being replaced by machines? What jobs are in danger of being replaced in the future? Use the chart below to record your findings.

JOBS ALREADY REPLACED OR ARE BEING REPLACED	JOBS IN DANGER OF BEING REPLACED IN THE NEAR FUTURE	JOBS PROBABLY NOT IN DANGER OF BEING REPLACED

Extend Use the information you found to think about your own plans for a future career. Write a brief paragraph explaining how the research might influence your planning for the future.

CREATE AND DISCUSS

Write a Reflective Essay Respond to Winner's essay with a **reflective essay** in which you make connections between the text and yourself. Use your own point of view to express your personal reaction to the ideas presented in the essay.

❏ Record your personal reactions to the text. Use the annotations and notes you made while reading. How does the text relate to your life?

❏ Use a topical outline or a chart to organize your thoughts.

❏ Begin your essay with a hook, such as an anecdote or an interesting example.

❏ As you write, stay organized. Maintain a personal tone appropriate to your purpose and audience, using academic vocabulary as applicable.

❏ Conclude by sharing what you discovered about yourself, important insights you gained, or a decision you made as a result of your reflection upon the essay.

Discuss Your Essay Use your reflective essay to generate discussion in a small group.

❏ Read your essay to the members of your group.

❏ Ask each member of the group to give a brief oral response to your essay.

❏ Encourage the group to discuss ideas and questions raised in your essay.

❏ Listen and respond appropriately as other group members read their essays.

Go to the **Writing Studio: Writing as a Process** for help with writing your reflective essay.

Go to **Participating in Collaborative Discussions** in the **Speaking and Listening Studio** to find out more.

RESPOND TO THE ESSENTIAL QUESTION

? How can science go wrong?

Gather Information Review your annotations and notes on "Frankenstein: Giving Voice to the Monster." Then, add relevant information to your Response Log. As you determine which information to include, think about:

• possible dangers and problems related to the development of artificial intelligence
• society's responsibility in controlling scientific developments
• how Shelley's novel relates to Winner's ideas

UNIT 4
RESPONSE LOG

? Essential Question	Details from Texts
What can nature offer us?	
How do you define beauty?	
How can science go wrong?	
What shapes your outlook on life?	

ACADEMIC VOCABULARY
As you write and discuss what you learned from the essay, be sure to use the Academic Vocabulary words. Check off each of the words that you use.

❏ **appreciate**

❏ **insight**

❏ **intensity**

❏ **invoke**

❏ **radical**

RESPOND

CRITICAL VOCABULARY

WORD BANK

sentient	ominous
artifice	calamity
recoil	domain
succinct	prescient

Practice and Apply Choose the word that completes the sentence.

1. The politician used _____ to make it appear as if he wanted to enrich the people when, in fact, he wanted only to enrich himself.

   a. artifice   **b.** sentient

2. Despite the _____ clouds on the near horizon, the skipper pressed onward toward the stricken vessel.

   a. prescient   **b.** ominous

3. When the dam broke above the village, _____ ensued.

   a. calamity   **b.** recoil

4. The professor delivered a _____ lecture that ended well before the class period was over.

   a. succinct   **b.** domain

VOCABULARY STRATEGY:
Latin Roots

Go to the **Vocabulary Studio: Analyzing Word Structure** for more on Latin roots.

Knowing Latin roots can give you clues to the meanings of unfamiliar words. For example, knowing that the Latin root *sent* means "to feel" could help you figure out the meaning of *sentient*, which means "capable of feeling." When the author speaks of sentient beings, you know that he means beings that are aware of their surroundings and capable of emotions. Another word in the essay with the same root is *sentience,* which refers to the state of being sentient.

Practice and Apply The following words are all based on a Latin root. Write the root for each word and then the meaning of the root. Use a dictionary to help you. Notice how the definition of the word is related to its root. Can you think of other words that might be based on each root?

1. artifice

2. domain

3. prescient

4. ominous

LANGUAGE CONVENTIONS:
Parallel Structure

Parallel structure, or parallelism, is the use of similar grammatical constructions to express ideas that are closely related or equal in importance. The grammatical constructions may include phrases, clauses, or sentences. Parallel structure helps writers organize, clarify, and emphasize their thoughts. It can also affect the meaning and tone of a sentence or passage. Read this sentence from Langdon Winner's essay:

> **World literature, . . . contains a great many stories of this kind, ones that are often used to shed light upon basic questions about <u>what it means to be</u> alive, <u>what it means to be</u> conscious, <u>what it means to be</u> human, <u>what membership in society entails.</u>**

Winner uses a series of noun clauses beginning with *what* that are the objects of the preposition *about*. The repetition of this grammatical construction gives equal weight to the "basic questions" he identifies in world literature. The parallelism also gives the sentence a pleasing rhythm that makes it more memorable. Consider that he could have written the sentence like this:

> **World literature, . . . contains a great many stories of this kind, ones that are often used to shed light upon basic questions about what it means to be alive, conscious, and human, and what membership in society entails.**

In this sentence without parallel structure, the relationship between the questions is less clear. The sentence is also less memorable because it lacks a strong rhythm.

Writers can use parallel structure not only within sentences but also in groups of sentences. For example, Winner starts the first two sentences in paragraph 2 with "In Greek mythology" and "In Jewish folklore," using parallelism to tie together examples from different cultural traditions to support his idea.

Practice and Apply Underline the parallel structures in the sentences below. Then, use each sentence as a model to write two sentences of your own with the same parallel structures.

1. "One can imagine such technology outsmarting financial markets, out-inventing human researchers, out-manipulating human leaders, and developing weapons we cannot even understand."

2. "Whereas the short-term impact of AI depends on who controls it, the long-term impact depends on whether it can be controlled at all."

POEM

ODE TO THE WEST WIND

by **Percy Bysshe Shelley**

pages 549–552

COMPARE THEMES

As you read, notice how both poets describe the effects of the wind in autumn. What can you infer about the poems' themes based on their imagery, figurative language, diction, and other elements? Once you have read both poems, you will collaborate with a small group on a research project.

? ESSENTIAL QUESTION:

What shapes your outlook on life?

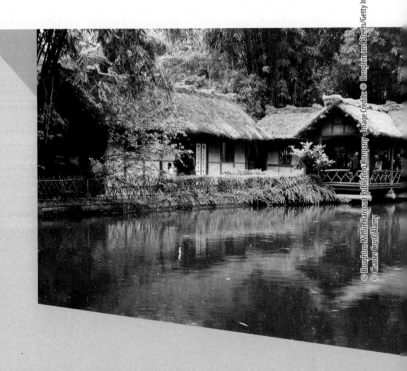

POEM

SONG OF A THATCHED HUT DAMAGED IN AUTUMN WIND

by **Du Fu**

pages 554–555

QUICK START

People constantly learn from nature. Think about a lesson you have learned by observing some aspect of nature, such as a seasonal change. With a partner, discuss the lesson you learned and why it is important.

ANALYZE FORM

In poetry, **form** refers to the arrangement of words into structural patterns, including the length of a poem's lines and their grouping into stanzas. Form can also refer to a poem's rhyme scheme, meter, or its traditional poetic type, such as sonnet or ode. The form of a poem helps support its mood and theme.

Prior to the 20th century, poets usually relied on traditional forms to express their ideas and feelings. One popular form that you have already encountered is the **sonnet,** which has 14 lines and a regular rhyme scheme. Another traditional form is the **ode,** a complex lyric that develops a serious theme. Odes typically have a dignified or reflective tone, and they often commemorate events or praise people, ideas, or elements of nature. Shelley's "Ode to the West Wind," a famous example, employs a complex rhyme scheme and regular meter.

During the 20th century, poets increasingly turned away from traditional forms, often producing **free verse**—poems that do not have regular patterns of rhyme and meter. This form usually gives their poems a rhythm closer to that of everyday speech. Instead of following a fixed structure, lines are organized according to a plan developed by the poet. The poet Du Fu wrote "Song of a Thatched Hut Damaged in Autumn Wind" in a traditional Chinese form; however, the translation you are about to read is composed in free verse.

As you read the two poems, notice these characteristics of their forms:

GENRE ELEMENTS: LYRIC POETRY

- expresses the personal thoughts and feelings of a single speaker
- has a musical quality
- is marked by imagination and evocative language
- creates a strong, unified impression
- can be in a variety of forms covering many subjects

"Ode to the West Wind"	• Follows a regular meter • Written in terza rima, a series of three-line stanzas linked by rhyme • Highly melodic with a dignified tone
"Song of a Thatched Hut Damaged in Autumn Wind"	• Free verse translation • Lines not grouped in stanzas • Rhythms approximate speech • Includes alliteration, figurative language, and other poetic devices

© Houghton Mifflin Harcourt Publishing Company

GET READY

ANALYZE DICTION

Careful control of language is especially important in poetry. To shape the perception of readers, poets must choose appropriate **diction,** a term that refers to both word choice and **syntax,** the order or arrangement of words. Traditionally, poets used a special diction, **inverted syntax,** which reverses the expected order of words. Inverted syntax can help maintain patterns of rhyme and meter. Poets also tended to choose elevated and vivid vocabulary. In contrast, the syntax of modern poetry is usually closer to natural speech, though poets still rely on concrete, vivid words, and distinct poetic elements to appeal to readers' senses.

Use the following questions to help guide your analysis of diction:

- Does the poet use plain or elevated vocabulary?

- Does the poet choose mostly concrete words, which name specific things, or abstract words that identify concepts?

- Does the poet select words with strong connotations, or associated feelings?

- Is the writer's syntax formal or informal? inverted or natural?

ANNOTATION MODEL

NOTICE & NOTE

As you read, note elements of each poem's form and mark distinctive examples of the poet's diction. In the model, you can see one reader's notes about lines 1–6 of "Ode to the West Wind."

O wild West Wind, thou breath of Autumn's being,

Thou, from whose unseen presence the leaves dead

Are driven, like ghosts from an enchanter fleeing,

Yellow, and black, and pale, and hectic red,

Pestilence-stricken multitudes: O thou,

Who chariotest to their dark wintry bed

The poem includes elevated and abstract vocabulary.

The syntax is formal. The phrase "the leaves dead" is an example of inverted syntax.

Words like "dead" and "hectic" and "Pestilence-stricken" have strong, serious connotations.

© Houghton Mifflin Harcourt Publishing Company

BACKGROUND

Percy Bysshe Shelley *(1792–1822) led a turbulent life. As an adolescent, he embraced radical political and social views, which alienated him from his aristocratic relatives. Shelley wrote "Ode to the West Wind" in the autumn of 1819 when he and his family were living in Florence, Italy. Earlier that year, English workers demonstrating for reform were killed by soldiers in the Peterloo Massacre. This event outraged Shelley, who opposed all injustice and dreamed of changing the world through poetry. In 1822, shortly before he would have turned 30, he drowned when his sailboat sank in a storm off the coast of Italy.*

ODE TO THE WEST WIND

Poem by Percy Bysshe Shelley

PREPARE TO COMPARE

As you read, note the ways in which the poet describes and personifies the autumn wind. Think about what this suggests about the poet's view of nature and how these details contribute to the theme of the poem.

I

O wild West Wind, thou breath of Autumn's being,
Thou, from whose unseen presence the leaves dead
Are driven, like ghosts from an enchanter fleeing,

Yellow, and black, and pale, and hectic red,
5 Pestilence-stricken multitudes: O thou,
Who chariotest to their dark wintry bed

The wingéd seeds, where they lie cold and low,
Each like a corpse within its grave, until
Thine azure sister of the Spring shall blow

© Houghton Mifflin Harcourt Publishing Company • Image Credits: © Art Collection 2/Alamy; © Henglein and Steets/Getty Images

---

Notice & Note

Use the side margins to notice and note signposts in the text.

ANALYZE FORM

Annotate: Use letters to mark the patterns of end rhyme in lines 1–14.

Analyze: What is the rhyme scheme? How does rhyme link each stanza to the next?

4 hectic: feverish.

9 sister . . . Spring: the reviving south wind of spring.

---

10 Her clarion o'er the dreaming earth, and fill
(Driving sweet buds like flocks to feed in air)
With living hues and odors plain and hill:

Wild Spirit, which art moving everywhere;
Destroyer and preserver; hear, oh, hear!

II

15 Thou on whose stream, mid the steep sky's commotion,
Loose clouds like earth's decaying leaves are shed,
Shook from the tangled bough of Heaven and Ocean,

Angels of rain and lightning: there are spread
On the blue surface of thine aëry surge,
20 Like the bright hair uplifted from the head

Of some fierce Maenad, even from the dim verge
Of the horizon to the zenith's height,
The locks of the approaching storm. Thou dirge

Of the dying year, to which this closing night
25 Will be the dome of a vast sepulcher,
Vaulted with all thy congregated might

Of vapors, from whose solid atmosphere
Black rain, and fire, and hail will burst: oh, hear!

III

Thou who didst waken from his summer dreams
30 The blue Mediterranean, where he lay,
Lulled by the coil of his crystálline streams,

Beside a pumice isle in Baiae's bay,
And saw in sleep old palaces and towers
Quivering within the wave's intenser day,

35 All overgrown with azure moss and flowers
So sweet, the sense faints picturing them! Thou
For whose path the Atlantic's level powers

Cleave themselves into chasms, while far below
The sea-blooms and the oozy woods which wear
40 The sapless foliage of the ocean, know

Thy voice, and suddenly grow gray with fear,
And tremble and despoil themselves: oh, hear!

---

10 clarion: a trumpet with a clear, ringing tone.

ANALYZE DICTION
Annotate: Mark words and phrases in lines 15–28 that are examples of elevated language.

Analyze: How does Shelley's use of elevated language in this description shape your impression of the wind?

18 Angels: messengers.

19 aëry: airy.

20–22 Like ... height: The clouds lie in streaks from the horizon upward, looking like the streaming hair of a maenad (mē´năd)—a wildly dancing female worshiper of Dionysus, the Greek god of wine.

23 dirge: funeral song.

25 sepulcher (sĕp´əl-kər): tomb.

31 crystálline (krĭs´tə-lĭn) **streams:** the different-colored currents of the Mediterranean Sea.

32 pumice (pŭm´ĭs): a light volcanic rock; **Baiae's** (bī´ēz´) **bay:** the Bay of Naples, site of the ancient Roman resort of Baiae.

37 level powers: surface.

ANALYZE FORM

Annotate: A couplet is two lines of verse that rhyme and form a unit. Mark the words that rhyme at the end of the couplet in section IV.

Analyze: What idea does Shelley emphasize with the rhymed words in this couplet?

50 skyey (skī´ē) **speed:** the swiftness of clouds moving across the sky.

51 vision: something impossible to achieve.

57 lyre: a reference to the Aeolian harp; an instrument whose strings make musical sounds when the wind blows over them.

62 impetuous (ĭm-pĕch´ōō-əs): violently forceful; impulsive.

65 incantation: recitation, as of a magic spell.

IV

If I were a dead leaf thou mightest bear;
If I were a swift cloud to fly with thee;
45 A wave to pant beneath thy power, and share

The impulse of thy strength, only less free
Than thou, O uncontrollable! If even
I were as in my boyhood, and could be

The comrade of thy wanderings over Heaven,
50 As then, when to outstrip thy skyey speed
Scarce seemed a vision; I would ne'er have striven

As thus with thee in prayer in my sore need.
Oh, lift me as a wave, a leaf, a cloud!
I fall upon the thorns of life! I bleed!

55 A heavy weight of hours has chained and bowed
One too like thee: tameless, and swift, and proud.

V

Make me thy lyre, even as the forest is:
What if my leaves are falling like its own!
The tumult of thy mighty harmonies

60 Will take from both a deep, autumnal tone,
Sweet though in sadness. Be thou, Spirit fierce,
My spirit! Be thou me, impetuous one!

Drive my dead thoughts over the universe
Like withered leaves to quicken a new birth!
65 And, by the incantation of this verse,

Scatter, as from an unextinguished hearth
Ashes and sparks, my words among mankind!
Be through my lips to unawakened earth

The trumpet of a prophecy! O Wind,
70 If Winter comes, can Spring be far behind?

CHECK YOUR UNDERSTANDING

Answer these questions about "Ode to the West Wind" before moving on to the next selection.

1 In section I, the speaker refers to the west wind as a "preserver" because it —

  A blows away the dead leaves

  B spreads seeds that will bloom in the spring

  C brings in the warm spring wind

  D protects flocks of sheep from harm

2 In section IV, what does the speaker regret about his adult years?

  F He has lost his appreciation of the seasons.

  G Winter is hard for him to bear.

  H He is all alone in the world.

  J He has become less free and vigorous.

3 Which of the following themes can be inferred from the poem?

  A Life is full of contradictions.

  B Society lacks beauty and grace.

  C The wind is the only constant in life.

  D The world needs to be reawakened.

BACKGROUND

Du Fu *(712–770) is considered by many literary critics to be the greatest figure in Chinese poetry. He was born into a scholarly family and received a traditional Confucian education, but he failed his imperial examinations. As a result, he spent much of his youth traveling and writing poetry. Du Fu is often described as a poet-historian whose body of work addresses a wide range of personal, political, and social issues.*

SONG OF A THATCHED HUT DAMAGED IN AUTUMN WIND

Poem by Du Fu

PREPARE TO COMPARE

As you read the poem, look for images and details that help develop its theme.

Wind howled angrily in high autumn's September
and tore off three layers of reed from my thatched roof.
The reeds flew over the river and scattered on the bank.
Some flew high and hung from the trees.
5 Some flew low and swirled and sank into pools.
The kids from the southern village took advantage of my old age,
played pirate and stole my reeds while I watched them
openly carrying armfuls into the bamboo groves.
My lips cracked, my throat dried, and I couldn't yell out.
10 I returned home and leaned on my stick, sighing.
In a moment the wind stopped and clouds stood ink black,
the autumnal sky stretched into darkness in desert silence.
My cotton quilt is tattered from use and cold as iron.
In an ugly dream, my small son rips the lining with his feet.
15 The roof is leaking by my bed's headboard and nowhere is dry.

Notice & Note

Use the side margins to notice and note signposts in the text.

ANALYZE DICTION

Annotate: Mark the words or phrases in lines 10–14 that suggest how the speaker feels.

Analyze: What tone do these word choices help convey?

The rain like yarn spins down forever.
I've had little sleep since the An Lushan Rebellion.[1]
Such a wet and long night, when will it end!
I wish I had a house with thousands of rooms
20 to shelter all the cold people under the sky and give them happy faces.
We'd be calm as mountains when it stormed and rained.
Oh, let this big house appear before my eyes
and I will die of cold in my damaged hut, happy.

---

[1] **An Lushan Rebellion:** a rebellion lasting almost a decade that began in 755 as a
revolt by a disgruntled general in the Tang Dynasty's army.

ANALYZE FORM

Annotate: Mark the similes in lines 16–23.

Analyze: How does the use of this literary element enrich the poem?

CHECK YOUR UNDERSTANDING

Answer these questions before moving on to the **Analyze the Texts** section on the following page.

1 In "Song of a Thatched Hut Damaged in Autumn Wind," what happens to the speaker's roof?

   A It has been stolen by children.

   B The wind destroys it.

   C It leaks during heavy rains.

   D It was damaged during a rebellion.

2 The speaker wishes for "a house with thousands of rooms" because he wants to —

   F protect his family

   G use the space as a hotel

   H house anyone who needs shelter

   J hide from rebellious soldiers

3 What theme is expressed in the last two lines of the poem?

   A Wealth is just an illusion.

   B Poor people will always struggle.

   C We need comfort to be happy.

   D Imagination can ease our sufferings.

ANALYZE THE TEXTS

Support your responses with evidence from the texts.   NOTEBOOK

1. **Infer** In the last line of "Ode to the West Wind," Shelley poses the question, "If Winter comes, can Spring be far behind?" What theme does this question help convey? How might this theme relate to disturbing political events such as the Peterloo Massacre?

2. **Analyze** How would you describe the diction of "Ode to the West Wind"? What purpose does this use of diction serve? Explain.

3. **Analyze** Which elements of Shelley's poem fit the characteristics of an ode? Why might he have chosen this form to express his ideas?

4. **Evaluate** The translator of "Song of a Thatched Hut Damaged in Autumn Wind" created a free-verse English version of the poem, with plain vocabulary and conversational syntax. Do you think that this was an effective choice? Explain why or why not.

5. **Connect** Du Fu refers to the An Lushan Rebellion in line 17 of his poem. How does this historical reference deepen the poem's meaning?

RESEARCH

RESEARCH TIP
When researching information online, be sure to use various types of reliable sources. For example, you may use a combination of primary sources, which are firsthand accounts of events, and secondary sources, which are secondhand accounts created at a later date.

As you read in their biographies, both Shelley and Du Fu wrote poetry as social or political commentary. Research the times and places in which the poets wrote these two poems. What historical, social, or political events occurred around those times, and how might these events have informed the poets' works? Use the chart below to organize your findings and to explain the connections you discover.

	HISTORICAL CONTEXT	CONNECTIONS
Percy Bysshe Shelley		
Du Fu		

Extend Find another poem by Shelley or Du Fu that addresses a social or political issue. Discuss the poem with a partner, comparing it to the two poems you read in this lesson.

CREATE AND PRESENT

Create a Visual Representation In both selections, the wind is personified in different ways—that is, it is given some human characteristics. Develop a visual representation of the wind in each poem.

- ❏ Think about the similarities and differences in the two poems. How does each poet describe the wind?
- ❏ Identify the human characteristics ascribed to the wind in each selection. Are these descriptions positive or negative?
- ❏ Think about how you can represent these characteristics visually.

Present Your Image Pair up with a partner, and take turns presenting your visual representations.

- ❏ Identify two elements of your visual representation that you would like to present.
- ❏ Present your visual to your partner, and explain two of your choices in creating it. For instance, explain why you chose a certain color or style.
- ❏ Take turns giving each other feedback. If it makes sense, incorporate your partner's feedback into your visual representation.

Go to **Giving a Presentation** in the **Speaking and Listening Studio** to find out more.

RESPOND TO THE ESSENTIAL QUESTION

? What shapes your outlook on life?

Gather Information Review your annotations and notes on "Ode to the West Wind" and "Song of a Thatched Hut Damaged in Autumn Wind." Then, add relevant information to your Response Log. As you determine which information to include, think about:

- how nature affects the way you perceive the world
- the experiences that have shaped the way you relate to people and the world around you
- the relationship between the natural world and human society

UNIT 4
RESPONSE LOG

Use this Response Log to record information from the texts that relate to or comment on the **Essential Questions** in Unit 4.

? Essential Question	Details from Texts
What can nature offer us?	
How do you define beauty?	
How can science go wrong?	
What shapes your outlook on life?	

B4 Student Resources

ACADEMIC VOCABULARY

As you write and discuss what you learned from the poems, be sure to use the Academic Vocabulary words. Check off each of the words that you use.

- ❏ **appreciate**
- ❏ **insight**
- ❏ **intensity**
- ❏ **invoke**
- ❏ **radical**

Collaborate & Compare

COMPARE THEMES

"Ode to the West Wind" and "Song of a Thatched Hut Damaged in Autumn Wind" share a topic—the effects of the wind in autumn. However, the two poems may express different **themes,** or messages about life or human nature.

Poets usually do not state their themes directly. It is up to readers to infer a theme based on a poem's imagery, figurative language, diction, and other elements. Some poems may have multiple themes.

To begin gathering details with which to make inferences about themes, complete the following chart.

ODE TO THE WEST WIND
Poem by Percy Bysshe Shelley

SONG OF A THATCHED HUT DAMAGED IN AUTUMN WIND
Poem by Du Fu

	"ODE TO THE WEST WIND"	**"SONG OF A THATCHED HUT DAMAGED IN AUTUMN WIND"**
Form		
Imagery		
Figurative Language		
Diction		
Other Elements		

ANALYZE THE TEXTS

Discuss these questions in your group.

1. **Compare** With your group, review the imagery that you cited in your chart. How are the images in the two poems similar? How do they differ?

2. **Interpret** Both poems describe some of the ways we relate to nature. Discuss each poem's treatment of nature. Cite evidence in your discussion.

3. **Evaluate** In "Ode to the West Wind," Shelley uses elevated language and formal diction; however, in "Song of a Thatched Hut Damaged in Autumn Wind," Du Fu does the opposite. Which approach do you find most effective, and why?

4. **Draw Conclusions** According to the two poems, what insights about life or human nature can we gain by considering the wind and other elements of the natural world?

COLLABORATE AND PRESENT

With your group, continue exploring the ideas in the poems by identifying and comparing their themes. Follow these steps:

Go to **Giving a Presentation** in the **Speaking and Listening Studio** for more.

1. **Make inferences about themes.** Review your charts as a group, considering details, imagery, figurative language, diction, and other elements from both poems. Then, work together to infer possible themes for each poem.

2. **Agree on a theme.** Determine a theme statement for each poem. You may use a chart like the one below to track the themes and supporting details your group identifies.

	THEME STATEMENT	SUPPORTING DETAILS
"Ode to the West Wind"		
"Song of a Thatched Hut Damaged in Autumn Wind"		

3. **Present to the class.** Organize your ideas, and choose a spokesperson to present them to the class. Include clear statements of the theme for each poem, and explain similarities or differences in the two themes. Be sure to introduce your ideas, to include transitions from idea to idea in the body of your presentation, and to conclude your presentation effectively. You may add visuals or diagrams to help convey information to the class.

PRESENTATION TIPS

When giving a presentation, be sure to pace yourself and enunciate all of your words so your audience can understand you. Also, be sure to make eye contact and address one topic at a time so you don't lose your audience.

POEMS

from
SONGS OF INNOCENCE

by **William Blake**

pages 563–566

COMPARE POEMS

As you read, pay attention to the ways in which William Blake describes the two contrasting states of being—innocence and experience. How are the details in the poems similar or different, and how do they contribute to the themes described?

? **ESSENTIAL QUESTION:**

What shapes your outlook on life?

POEMS

from
SONGS OF EXPERIENCE

by **William Blake**

pages 568–570

QUICK START

What comes to mind when you think of innocence and experience? Write down a list of at least three ideas or images for each state.

INNOCENCE	EXPERIENCE

ANALYZE SYMBOLS

A **symbol** is a person, place, object, or action that has a concrete meaning in itself and also stands for something beyond itself, such as an idea or feeling. For example, a dove is widely known as a symbol of peace. In literature, symbols often take their meaning from the context in which they appear, and the symbolic meaning may be interpreted in different ways.

Symbols play an important role in Blake's poetry. Although at first glance the poems in *Songs of Innocence* and *Songs of Experience* seem simple and straightforward, Blake uses symbols to convey complex spiritual and social themes. As you read these poems, look for clues to help you interpret the symbols. Use this chart to jot down your interpretations.

GENRE ELEMENTS: LYRIC POETRY

- expresses personal thoughts or feelings
- written from a first-person perspective
- has a musical quality
- marked by imagination and evocative language

PERSON, PLACE, OR OBJECT	CONCRETE MEANING	SYMBOLIC IDEA OR FEELING

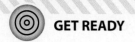

UNDERSTAND HISTORICAL BACKGROUND

Background information on historical, social, cultural, and economic issues may be important for understanding a poem's theme. William Blake sometimes used his poetry to comment on child labor, slavery, science, and other social and cultural issues. In *Songs of Innocence* and *Songs of Experience*, for example, Blake describes the plight of chimney sweepers, boys from poor families who were apprenticed to chimney sweeps and used to clean chimneys in London and other British cities.

During the Romantic period, most fireplaces in England burned coal for fuel, creating sticky soot that had to be brushed or scraped away. Children crawled up narrow chimneys to perform this work. Sometimes their masters would light fires underneath them to make sure they moved quickly. People who worked as sweepers rarely lived past middle age due to respiratory illnesses, cancer, and other diseases.

As early as 1788, legislation was enacted to prohibit children younger than eight from working as sweeps' apprentices. Subsequent legislation raised the minimum age again, but these laws were unenforced and ineffective. In 1834 Parliament passed the Chimney Sweeps Act; however, this too was largely ignored. It was not until 1875 that sweeps were required to be licensed and police were given the power to enforce legislation, bringing an end to the practice of child labor. As you read Blake's poems about chimney sweepers, make connections between this historical information and details of the poems.

ANNOTATION MODEL

NOTICE & NOTE

As you read, note clues to the meaning of symbols in Blake's poems. Also note any details about social conditions in Britain. This model shows one reader's notes about lines 1–6 of "The Lamb."

<u>Little Lamb, who made thee?</u>	*The rhythm and sweet tone remind me of a nursery rhyme.*
Dost thou know who made thee?	
Gave thee life & bid thee feed,	*Details emphasize that the lamb is small and soft. This suggests it is a symbol of gentleness and innocence.*
By the stream & o'er the mead;	
Gave thee clothing of delight,	
<u>Softest clothing wooly bright;</u>	

BACKGROUND

William Blake *(1757–1827) was born into a modest family in London. He learned to read and write at home, while studying the Bible and the works of John Milton. When he was 10, his father sent him to a drawing school. Blake began writing poetry when he was 12. However, the cost of the school was high, so four years later his parents apprenticed him to a master engraver.*

After setting up shop as an engraver, Blake developed a technique that allowed him to print pages of text and illustration from the same plate, which he then hand colored. Blake used this time-consuming process, called illuminated printing, to publish most of his works.

from
SONGS OF INNOCENCE
Poems by William Blake

In 1782 Blake married Catherine Boucher. She was illiterate when they met, but Blake taught her how to read, write, and paint. She was an assistant in his work and became a skilled draftsperson.

In 1789 Blake completed his first illuminated book, Songs of Innocence, *featuring poems written for children that also depicted the innocent nature of childhood. Blake's later works were written on a grand scale, marked by prophetic and mythic visions. Imaginatively illustrated and difficult to understand, these complex works were largely ignored by his contemporaries. More than 100 years passed before people began to recognize Blake's stunning achievements as a poet and artist.*

In this selection, you will read two poems from Blake's first collection. The second collection, Songs of Experience, *which you will read next, includes poems that expand on similar themes, with contrasting perspectives. Two such poems, "The Lamb" and "The Tyger," are an example of companion poems that are in separate volumes.*

PREPARE TO COMPARE

As you read, think about how each poem expresses ideas about innocence or experience.

The Lamb

Little Lamb, who made thee?
Dost thou know who made thee?
Gave thee life & bid thee feed,
By the stream & o'er the mead;
5 Gave thee clothing of delight,
Softest clothing wooly bright;
Gave thee such a tender voice,
Making all the vales rejoice!
Little Lamb who made thee?
10 Dost thou know who made thee?

Little Lamb I'll tell thee,
Little Lamb I'll tell thee!
He is callèd by thy name,
For he calls himself a Lamb:
15 He is meek & he is mild,
He became a little child:
I a child & thou a lamb,
We are callèd by his name.
Little Lamb God bless thee.
20 Little Lamb God bless thee.

4 mead: meadow.

8 vales: valleys.

ANALYZE SYMBOLS

Annotate: Mark references to the lamb's creator in lines 11–18.

Interpret: How does this passage develop the symbolic meaning of the lamb?

13–14 He . . . Lamb: In the New Testament, Jesus is sometimes called the Lamb of God.

CHECK YOUR UNDERSTANDING

Answer these questions about "The Lamb" before moving on to the next selection.

1 In "The Lamb," the speaker begins by asking —

   A whether the lamb is lost

   B how old the lamb is

   C who created the lamb

   D what is the lamb's name

2 Blake reveals that the poem's speaker is —

   F the lamb

   G a child

   H Jesus Christ

   J Blake himself

3 Which of God's characteristics does Blake emphasize in "The Lamb"?

   A Gentleness

   B Power

   C Beauty

   D Creativity

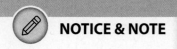
The Chimney Sweeper

When my mother died I was very young,
And my father sold me while yet my tongue
Could scarcely cry "'weep! 'weep! 'weep! 'weep!"
So your chimneys I sweep & in soot I sleep.

5   There's little Tom Dacre, who cried when his head
That curl'd like a lamb's back, was shav'd, so I said,
"Hush, Tom! never mind it, for when your head's bare,
You know that the soot cannot spoil your white hair."

And so he was quiet, & that very night,
10   As Tom was a-sleeping he had such a sight!
That thousands of sweepers, Dick, Joe, Ned, & Jack,
Were all of them lock'd up in coffins of black;

And by came an Angel who had a bright key,
And he open'd the coffins & set them all free;
15   Then down a green plain, leaping, laughing they run,
And wash in a river and shine in the Sun.

Then naked & white, all their bags left behind,
They rise upon clouds, and sport in the wind.
And the Angel told Tom, if he'd be a good boy,
20   He'd have God for his father & never want joy.

And so Tom awoke; and we rose in the dark
And got with our bags & our brushes to work.
Tho' the morning was cold, Tom was happy & warm;
So if all do their duty, they need not fear harm.

3 'weep! 'weep!: the child's attempt to say "Sweep! Sweep!" —a chimney sweeper's street cry.

UNDERSTAND HISTORICAL BACKGROUND

Annotate: Mark details in lines 1–14 that relate to the historical context of the poem.

Infer: What can you infer from these details about social conditions in late 18th century Britain?

18 sport: play or frolic.

20 want: lack.

CHECK YOUR UNDERSTANDING

Answer these questions about "The Chimney Sweeper" before moving on to the next selection.

1 In "The Chimney Sweeper," the speaker knows Tom Dacre because —

   A they go to the same school

   B they are brothers

   C they work together

   D Tom appeared in a dream

2 Why does Tom cry in "The Chimney Sweeper"?

   F His hair is shaved off.

   G His hair becomes dirty.

   H His father sells him.

   J He sees boys in coffins.

3 Tom is "happy & warm" in the morning because he —

   A had a good night's sleep

   B worked over a warm fireplace

   C was allowed to miss work

   D dreamed of an angel comforting him

BACKGROUND

William Blake *(1757–1827) published* Songs of Experience *in 1794 as a companion volume to* Songs of Innocence. *He said his purpose in putting them together was to show "the two contrary states of the human soul." The contrast between the collections lies in the perspectives of the speakers rather than the subjects of the poems. Much darker in mood and tone,* Songs of Experience *includes poems that link to poems in the earlier volume, including some with matching titles.*

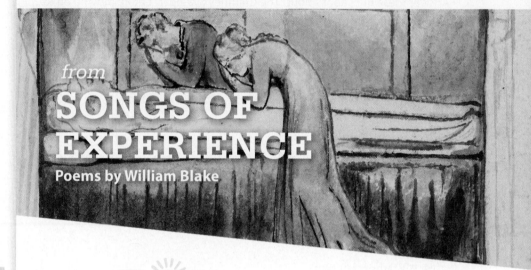

from
SONGS OF EXPERIENCE
Poems by William Blake

Notice & Note

Use the side margins to notice and note signposts in the text.

4 symmetry (sĭm´ĭ-trē): balance or beauty of form.

7 he: the tiger's creator.

ANALYZE SYMBOLS
Annotate: Mark details in lines 1–12 that describe the tiger.

Analyze: What symbolic meaning is suggested by these details?

15 anvil (ăn´vĭl): iron block on which metal objects are hammered into shape.

The Tyger

Tyger! Tyger! burning bright
In the forests of the night,
What immortal hand or eye
Could frame thy fearful symmetry?

5　　In what distant deeps or skies
Burnt the fire of thine eyes?
On what wings dare he aspire?
What the hand dare seize the fire?

And what shoulder, & what art,
10　　Could twist the sinews of thy heart?
And when thy heart began to beat,
What dread hand? & what dread feet?

What the hammer? what the chain?
In what furnace was thy brain?
15　　What the anvil? what dread grasp
Dare its deadly terrors clasp?

When the stars threw down their spears
And watered heaven with their tears,
Did he smile his work to see?
20   Did he who made the Lamb make thee?

Tyger! Tyger! burning bright
In the forests of the night,
What immortal hand or eye
Dare frame thy fearful symmetry?

CHECK YOUR UNDERSTANDING

Answer these questions about "The Tyger" before moving on to the next selection.

1 What does the "immortal hand or eye" in "The Tyger" refer to?

   A God

   B Death

   C Mankind

   D Nature

2 Which aspect of nature does Blake associate with the tiger?

   F Wind

   G Air

   H Water

   J Fire

3 The lines "What the anvil? what dread grasp / Dare its deadly terrors clasp" express —

   A pity for the animals devoured by the tiger

   B fear that the tiger cannot be controlled

   C awe for the creator of such a terrifying creature

   D suspicion that the tiger is not real

The Chimney Sweeper

A little black thing among the snow
Crying "'weep, 'weep," in notes of woe!
"Where are thy father & mother? say?"
"They are both gone up to the church to pray.

5   "Because I was happy upon the heath,
And smil'd among the winter's snow;
They clothed me in the clothes of death,
And taught me to sing the notes of woe.

  "And because I am happy, & dance & sing,
10   They think they have done me no injury,
And are gone to praise God & his Priest & King,
Who make up a heaven of our misery."

2 'weep, 'weep: the child's attempt to say "Sweep, Sweep"—a chimney sweeper's street cry.

5 heath: a tract of open land that cannot be farmed.

UNDERSTAND HISTORICAL BACKGROUND

Annotate: Mark details in lines 5–12 that help create the tone of "The Chimney Sweeper."

Infer: Identify the tone of this poem. What does it suggest about British society?

CHECK YOUR UNDERSTANDING

Answer these questions before moving on to the **Analyze the Texts** section on the following page.

1 What is the "black thing" Blake refers to in "The Chimney Sweeper"?

A A child

B A piece of coal

C A chimney

D Soot-coated snow

2 Why don't the parents of the chimney sweeper see that he is being harmed by his work?

F He lies to them.

G He keeps up a cheerful appearance.

H He has run away from them.

J He praises God for his job.

3 In "The Chimney Sweeper," what does the phrase "make up a heaven of our misery" suggest?

A The church and the king profit from his sweeping.

B The priest and the king also suffer.

C His parents will be rewarded in heaven.

D His parents' religion glorifies suffering.

ANALYZE THE TEXTS

Support your responses with evidence from the texts. NOTEBOOK

1. **Identify** Notice the words, phrases, and lines that Blake repeats in "The Lamb." What mood does this repetition help create?

2. **Interpret** In "The Tyger," the speaker describes the animal as "fearful" and "deadly." Do the negative connotations of this language suggest that the tiger should never have been created? Explain.

3. **Draw Conclusions** In "The Tyger," Blake uses words such as *art, hammer, furnace,* and *anvil* to describe the tiger's creation, as if the animal were a metal sculpture. What does this symbolic meaning of the tiger suggest about Blake's view of art?

4. **Analyze** Describe Blake's use of the colors white and black in "The Chimney Sweeper" poems. What do these colors symbolize?

5. **Notice & Note** In "The Chimney Sweeper" poems, the speakers have two sharply contrasting perspectives on religion. Considered together, what do both poems suggest about Blake's view of the religious establishment of his time? Explain.

RESEARCH

As you've read, poets sometimes draw inspiration from social, historical, and political events. "The Chimney Sweeper" poems, for example, express social commentary on the use and abuse of young boys to clean chimneys before child labor laws were implemented. Research another William Blake poem that addresses a social, historical, or political issue or event. Use the graphic organizer below to explain the poem's social, historical, or political connection.

TITLE OF POEM	SOCIAL, HISTORICAL, OR POLITICAL CONNECTION

RESEARCH TIP

When researching social, historical, or political events, consider referring to an encyclopedia. Encyclopedias are useful because they tend to be organized according to a specific subject or domain. You may, for instance, refer to an encyclopedia of history.

Extend Research another poet who writes about social, historical, or political events. What are some similarities and differences between this poet and William Blake? Consider organizing your findings in a Venn diagram.

© Houghton Mifflin Harcourt Publishing Company

CREATE AND DISCUSS

Write an Essay Choose a social issue that is considered one of the compelling concerns of contemporary times. Write a short problem-solution essay to explore the issue and possible remedies.

- ❏ Focus on a problem that directly affects your community.

- ❏ If you are working actively to confront this social problem, share your firsthand knowledge.

- ❏ Ask yourself questions about the problem as a way to explore ways it might be solved. Your essay might include more than one approach.

- ❏ Identify a symbol that could meaningfully convey your message.

Make a Podcast Form a small group to plan a podcast. Identify the key ideas in your essay and organize them into discussion points. Then record a "talk" on these discussion points to create your podcast.

- ❏ Use your problem-solution essays as well as other research to support your views.

- ❏ Assign a host to keep the conversation flowing. Exchange ideas in a lively manner and try to avoid "talking-down" to your audience.

- ❏ Uphold the basic goal to leave your listeners motivated.

Go to **Writing Informative Texts** in the **Writing Studio** for more help.

Go to **Participating in Collaborative Discussions** in the **Speaking and Listening Studio** for help.

RESPOND TO THE ESSENTIAL QUESTION

 What shapes your outlook on life?

Gather Information Review your annotations and notes on poems from *Songs of Innocence* and *Songs of Experience*. Then, add relevant information to your Response Log. As you determine which information to include, think about:

- the experiences and characteristics of children and of adults—how they are similar and different
- how nature has influenced the way you think about life
- the tension between opposites, like innocence and experience, and how exploring such opposites helps us understand our world

UNIT 4
RESPONSE LOG

Use this Response Log to record information from the texts that relates to or comments on the **Essential Questions** in Unit 4.

? Essential Question	Details from Texts
What can nature offer us?	
How do you define beauty?	
How can science go wrong?	
What shapes your outlook on life?	

R4 Student Resources

ACADEMIC VOCABULARY

As you write and discuss what you learned from the poems, be sure to use the Academic Vocabulary words. Check off each of the words that you use.

- ❏ **appreciate**
- ❏ **insight**
- ❏ **intensity**
- ❏ **invoke**
- ❏ **radical**

Collaborate & Compare

COMPARE POEMS

Compare and contrast the perspectives of the poems from *Songs of Innocence* and *Songs of Experience,* using the following criteria:

- **Word choice:** Look for descriptive words and note how they are used to emphasize characteristics of a subject.
- **Ideas:** Identify common or contrasting ideas expressed in the poems.
- **Tone:** Notice the speaker's attitude toward the subject.

As you read, you may use a chart like this one to record similarities and differences between each linked pair of poems.

	"THE LAMB"	"THE TYGER"
Word Choice		
Ideas		
Tone		

ANALYZE THE TEXTS

Discuss these questions in your group.

1. **Compare** "The Lamb" and "The Tyger" develop around questions posed at the beginning of each poem. How do the speakers' different responses to these questions reflect the contrast between innocence and experience?

2. **Critique** Does Blake use symbols effectively to help convey his themes? Why or why not?

3. **Interpret** Is Blake's view of innocence and experience essentially the same as the idea of good versus evil? Explain your response.

4. **Draw Conclusions** Do these poems suggest that innocence is better than experience? Explain your response.

COLLABORATE AND PRESENT

With your group, continue exploring the ideas in the poems by identifying and comparing word choice, symbols, and themes. Follow these steps:

1. **Decide on the most important details with your group.** Review your chart to identify the most important details from each poem. What words or phrases stood out the most to you? Come to a consensus with your group.

2. **Come up with a message.** Determine a message for each poem based on the details, diction, ideas, and symbols. You may use a chart to keep track of the themes your group members come up with.

	DETAILS	MESSAGE
Songs of Innocence		
Songs of Experience		

3. **Compare ideas.** Compare ideas with your group and discuss whether the messages are similar or different. Listen actively to the members of your group and ask them to clarify any points you do not understand.

4. **Present to the class.** Next, present your ideas to the class. Be sure to include clear statements on the theme for each poem. Discuss whether the messages are similar or different.

© Houghton Mifflin Harcourt Publishing Company

Go to **Participating in a Collaborative Discussion** in the **Speaking and Listening Studio** to support group discussion.

COLLABORATION TIP

When discussing your ideas in a group, be sure to listen attentively. Give your peers an opportunity to share their ideas and respect their views. If you disagree with an idea, present evidence from the selections to support your ideas. Give all group members an opportunity to have a turn.

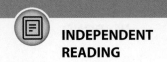

Reader's Choice

? *ESSENTIAL QUESTIONS*

Review the four Essential Questions for this unit on page 491.

Setting a Purpose   Select one or more of these options from your eBook to continue your exploration of the Essential Questions.

- Read the descriptions to see which text attracts your interest.

- Think about which genres you enjoy reading.

Notice **&** Note

In this unit, you practiced noticing and noting the signposts and asking big questions about nonfiction. As you read independently, these signposts and others will aid your understanding. Below are the key questions to ask when you read literature and nonfiction.

Reading Literature: Stories, Poems, and Plays	
Signpost	**Key Question**
Contrasts and Contradictions	Why did the character act that way?
Aha Moment	How might this change things?
Tough Questions	What does this make me wonder about?
Words of the Wiser	What's the lesson for the character?
Again and Again	Why might the author keep bringing this up?
Memory Moment	Why is this memory important?

Reading Nonfiction: Essays, Articles, and Arguments	
Signpost	**Key Question(s)**
Big Questions	What surprised me? What did the author think I already knew? What challenged, changed, or confirmed what I already knew?
Contrasts and Contradictions	What is the difference, and why does it matter?
Extreme or Absolute Language	Why did the author use this language?
Numbers and Stats	Why did the author use these numbers or amounts?
Quoted Words	Why was this person quoted or cited, and what did this citation add?
Word Gaps	Do I know this word from someplace else? Does it seem like technical talk for this topic? Do clues in the sentence help me understand the word?

You can preview these texts in Unit 4 of your eBook.

Then check off the text or texts that you select to read on your own.

**William Blake:
Visions and Verses**
Rachel Galvin

Why was William Blake considered eccentric during his life but is now praised as a creative visionary?

POEM

Frost at Midnight
Samuel Taylor Coleridge

How do the poet's memories of his childhood affect what he wants for his son?

PERSONAL NARRATIVE

Walking with Wordsworth
Bruce Stutz

A naturalist describes continuity as well as change in the landscapes that Wordsworth held dear.

EXPLANATORY ESSAY

from **A Defense of Poetry**
Percy Bysshe Shelley

Why does Shelley believe that poetry is the foundation of society as well as a source of beauty?

POEM

The Skylark
John Clare

Clare contrasts young boys' fanciful view of flight with the skylark's awareness of nature's risks and dangers.

Collaborate and Share   With a partner, discuss what you learned from at least one of your independent readings.

- Give a brief synopsis or summary of the text.
- Describe any signposts that you noticed in the text and explain what they revealed to you.
- Describe what you most enjoyed or found most challenging about the text. Give specific examples.
- Decide if you would recommend the text to others. Why or why not?

Go to the **Reading Studio** for more resources on **Notice & Note.**

Write an Explanatory Essay

In this unit, you have read literature from the Romantic period. Many Romantic writers celebrated nature in their works. Others warned of the dangers of tampering with nature. For your next writing task, you will write an explanatory essay on the relationship between humans and nature, using your readings as sources to support your own ideas. The article "Frankenstein: Giving Voice to the Monster" is an explanatory essay that discusses the concept of the human creation of life using Mary Shelley's *Frankenstein* as a source. You will use this essay as a mentor text as you plan and draft your own essay.

UNIT 4
EMOTION AND EXPERIMENTATION
THE FLOWERING OF ROMANTICISM

As you write your explanatory essay, you can use the notes from your Response Log which you filled out after reading the texts in this unit.

Writing Prompt

Read the information in the box below.

This is the topic or context for your explanatory essay.

> The human relationship with the natural world is a major topic of literature, including fiction, poetry, and literary essays.

Think carefully about the following question.

How might this Essential Question relate to an explanatory essay?

> What can nature offer us?

How might an experience of nature relate to an explanatory essay?

Write an explanatory essay about how experiencing the natural world can alter a person's state of mind.

Be sure to—

❑ have a "big idea" that your essay develops

❑ organize your essay into paragraphs that present a key idea, such as an opinion, an observation, or a claim

Review these points as you write and again when you finish. Make any needed changes.

❑ support your key ideas with such evidence as facts, quotations from texts, expert opinions, or evidence

❑ write an opening that catches your reader's attention while introducing your topic

❑ write a conclusion that wraps up your ideas and leaves the reader with some "food for thought"

1 Plan

Before you begin planning your essay, go through your notes on the texts and look for anything you might use, such as something an author said about nature that you found particularly striking or true, or a thought you had in response. Think about your own experiences with the natural world and how they have affected you.

To generate more ideas for your essay, try these strategies:

- word mapping
- free writing
- group discussion

Review your notes and mark the ones that are most important. Then reflect and come up with your "big idea." You may need to do some more free writing. As E.M. Forster said, "How can I know what I think until I see what I say?"

Use a chart like the one below to plan your essay.

Explanatory Essay Planning Table	
Genre	Explanatory essay
Topic	Human relationship with nature
Details and ideas from texts	
Ideas from word mapping and/or free writing	
Ideas from group discussion	
Ideas from my personal experiences	
My "big idea"	

Background Reading Review the notes you have made in your Response Log that relate to the question "What can nature offer us?" Texts in this unit provide background reading that will help you formulate your "big idea" and your key ideas.

Go to **Writing Informative Texts: Developing a Topic** for help planning your explanatory essay.

Notice & Note

From Reading to Writing

As you plan your explanatory essay, apply what you've learned about signposts to your own writing. Remember that writers use common features called signposts to help convey their message to readers.

Think how you can incorporate **Quoted Words** into your essay.

Go to the **Reading Studio** for more resources on **Notice & Note.**

Use the notes from your Response Log as you plan your explanatory essay.

© Houghton Mifflin Harcourt Publishing Company

Go to **Writing Informative Texts: Organizing Ideas** for help organizing your explanatory essay.

Organize Your Ideas After you have gathered ideas from your planning activities, you need to organize them in a way that will help you draft your explanatory essay. You can use the chart below to help you organize the elements of your essay.

Topic: Human relationship with nature		
Big Idea:		
Key Idea	**Key Idea**	**Key Idea**
Supporting Details	**Supporting Details**	**Supporting Details**
Final Reflection/"Food for Thought"		

② Develop a Draft

You might prefer to draft your explanatory essay online.

Once you have completed your planning activities, you will be ready to begin drafting your explanatory essay. Refer to the elements of an explanatory essay and your organizing chart as well as any notes you took as you studied the texts in this unit. These will provide a kind of map for you to follow as you write. Using a word processor or online writing application makes it easier to make changes or move sentences around later when you are ready to revise your first draft.

Use the Mentor Text

Author's Craft

Your explanatory essay should include several key ideas supported by details. A key idea can be your opinion, an observation, or a claim; supporting details will include facts, quotes from background readings, or short anecdotes from your experiences or those of others. Each key idea and its supporting details should be organized together in a paragraph, but if a paragraph is very long, you should break it into two or more paragraphs.

> The possibility that artificial creatures, products of human hands, might achieve sentience and take on an active role in society is an age-old conception in world cultures. . . .
>
> In Greek mythology one finds the tale of Pygmalion who carves a statue named Galatea with whom he falls in love and who eventually comes to life. In Jewish folklore there are stories of the Golem, an artificial creature animated with surprising results.

The first sentence presents an observation.

These details are facts that support the observation.

Apply What You've Learned To develop a key idea, state an opinion, an observation, or a claim related to your big idea and then provide details that support it. Make sure all of the details you provide are relevant to this key idea.

Genre Characteristics

Bringing in background reading will enrich your essay. When you quote a text, make sure you introduce it by giving the author and the name of the text, as well as some information about the quote's relevance.

> In a live exchange on the internet, Microsoft cofounder Bill Gates offered similar views. "I am in the camp that is concerned about super intelligence," Gates wrote. "First the machines will do a lot of jobs for us and not be super intelligent. . . . A few decades after that though the intelligence is strong enough to be a concern."

Winner identifies where the quote came from, "live exchange on the internet," the author of the quote, Bill Gates, and states that Gates holds "similar views."

Apply What You've Learned Include quotes from your background readings to support your key ideas. For each quote, tell the reader where the quote is from and give some explanation of how it relates to one of your key ideas.

③ Revise

Go to **Writing Informative Texts: Precise Language and Vocabulary** for help revising your explanatory essay.

On Your Own Once you have written your draft, you'll want to go back and look for ways to improve your explanatory essay. As you reread and revise, think about whether you have achieved your purpose. The Revision Guide will help you focus on specific elements to make your writing stronger.

Revision Guide

Ask Yourself	Tips	Revision Techniques
1. Does my first paragraph engage the reader and introduce the topic and my big idea?	**Circle** the part that will grab the reader's interest and **underline** the sentences that introduce the topic and the big idea.	**Add** a surprising detail or vivid image. **Reword** or add a sentence to introduce the topic and big idea more clearly.
2. Do I present a few key ideas that support my big idea?	**Underline** the sentences that state your key ideas.	**Review** your planning notes and **look for** more key ideas to include.
3. Do I provide details that support my key ideas?	**Circle** the first word of each sentence that provides a supporting detail to see if each paragraph has more than one.	**Add** details from your notes or quotes from your background readings.
4. Do I provide smooth transitions between ideas and paragraphs?	**Underline** the transition words and phrases in your essay.	**Add** transition words and phrases to connect ideas.
5. Does my final reflection summarize my big idea?	**Underline** the sentence that summarizes your big idea.	**Look back** at your key ideas to see what conclusions you can draw from all of them.
6. Do I leave my reader with "food for thought"?	**Circle** your "food for thought" statement or question.	**Add** a sentence that invites the reader to consider a question not answered in your essay.

ACADEMIC VOCABULARY
As you conduct your **peer review,** be sure to use these words.

❏ **appreciate**

❏ **insight**

❏ **intensity**

❏ **invoke**

❏ **radical**

With a Partner Once you and your partner have worked through the Revision Guide on your own, exchange explanatory essays and evaluate each other's draft in a **peer review.** Focus on providing revision suggestions for at least three of the items mentioned in the chart. Explain why you think your partner's draft should be revised and what your specific suggestions are.

When receiving feedback from your partner, listen attentively and ask questions to make sure you fully understand the revision suggestions.

4 Edit

Look closely at your essay to make sure you do not have fragments or run-on sentences, that you have used punctuation correctly, and that you have subject-verb agreement. Cut unnecessary words and break up long sentences.

Language Conventions

Sensory Language Sensory language includes descriptive words and phrases that appeal to the reader's senses. This language helps readers imagine they are seeing, hearing, tasting, touching, or smelling what the writer describes in the text.

Here is an example of text revised to make use of sensory language. Note the underlined sensory words and phrases in the revised text.

Original	Revised
The hiking trail near my house is nice in the springtime. There are a lot of wildflowers and pretty insects.	In the springtime, the hiking trail near my house turns <u>balmy</u> in the afternoon, when wildflowers release their <u>sweet scent</u> and the air <u>buzzes</u> with insects whose wings <u>flash with color</u>.

In this example, the writer has revised the text to use words and phrases that appeal to the senses. *Balmy* appeals to the sense of touch, *sweet scent* appeals to the sense of smell, *buzzes* appeals to the sense of hearing, and *flash with color* appeals to the sense of sight. Notice how the use of these words and phrases brings the writing to life for the reader and helps the reader to imagine the hiking trail in detail.

Look back at your writing to find places where you can add detail through sensory language. Try to incorporate all five senses.

5 Publish

Finalize your explanatory essay and choose a way to share it with your audience. Consider these options:

- Record your essay as a podcast.
- Compile the class's essays into an eBook.

Use the scoring guide to evaluate your essay.

Writing Task Scoring Guide: Explanatory Essay

	Organization/Progression	Development of Ideas	Use of Language and Conventions
4	• The introduction engages the reader and establishes the topic. • Every part of the paper supports the big idea. • Key ideas in the essay are organized in a logical manner. • There is a conclusion that summarizes the big idea and leaves the reader with "food for thought."	• Key ideas are presented in a way that clearly supports the big idea. • Details in each paragraph are relevant to the key idea.	• The writer's word choice and language are clear, concise, and appropriate to the expository writing task. • The writer shows consistent command of grammar with only minor errors in punctuation or spelling.
3	• The opening presents the topic but is only somewhat engaging to the reader. • The big idea of the essay is fairly clear but is presented in a formulaic manner. • Key ideas in the essay are mostly logical, although the organizational structure of the paper is weak at some points. • There is a conclusion but it does not fully summarize the big idea.	• Most key ideas are supported by details. • Details presented are mostly relevant to the key ideas, but some seem unnecessary or off topic.	• The writer's word choice and language are mostly clear and unambiguous, and the tone of the paper is appropriate. • The writer shows adequate command of grammar with occasional errors in spelling and punctuation.
2	• The opening does not clearly introduce the topic and does not engage the reader. • The paper contains a big idea, but it is not clearly defined or focused. • The key ideas are not presented in a logical manner, and the organizational structure of the paper is often confused.	• Either the key ideas are not well supported by details, or the details given are irrelevant to the key idea. • Many details are irrelevant or off topic.	• The writing is formulaic and simple, and the tone is not appropriate to expository writing. • The writer shows only moderate command of grammar, spelling, and punctuation, but key ideas are still clear.
1	• The big idea of the paper is not clear at all, and the paper often wanders from the topic. • There is no organizational structure in the presentation of the key ideas.	• Either no details are given, or the details that are provided are irrelevant and do not support key ideas.	• The writing is vague and confusing. Sentences are simple and awkward. • The writer shows little or no command of grammar, spelling, and punctuation, which causes key ideas to be unclear.

Reflect on the Unit

By completing your explanatory essay, you have created a writing product that pulls together and expresses your thoughts about the reading you have done in this unit. Now is a good time to reflect on what you have learned.

Reflect on the Essential Questions

- Review the four Essential Questions on page 491. How have your answers to these questions changed in response to the texts you've read in this unit?

- What are some examples from the texts you've read that show human beings' relationship with the natural world?

Reflect on Your Reading

- Which selections were the most interesting or surprising to you?

- From which selection did you learn the most about human beings' relationship with the natural world?

Reflect on the Writing Task

- What difficulties did you encounter while working on your explanatory essay? How might you avoid them next time?

- Which parts of the essay were the easiest to write? The hardest to write? Why?

- What improvements did you make to your essay as you were revising?

UNIT 4 SELECTIONS

- "Lines Composed a Few Miles Above Tintern Abbey"

- "Composed upon Westminster Bridge, September 3, 1802"

- "I Wandered Lonely As a Cloud"

- "Ode on a Grecian Urn"

- from *Frankenstein*

- "Frankenstein: Giving Voice to the Monster"

- "Ode to the West Wind"

- "Song of a Thatched Hut Damaged in Autumn Wind"

- from *Songs of Innocence*

- from *Songs of Experience*

AN ERA OF RAPID CHANGE

THE VICTORIANS

" The history of England is emphatically the history of progress. "

—Thomas Babington Macaulay

Discuss the **Essential Questions** with your whole class or in small groups. As you read An Era of Rapid Change, consider how the selections explore these questions.

? *ESSENTIAL QUESTION:*

What is a true benefactor?

In 19th-century Great Britain, there was a wide gap between the impoverished many and the wealthy few. Occasionally, well-to-do members of the middle and upper classes would become benefactors, providing financial or other material assistance to those who were less fortunate. How did benefactors determine who would receive their help? What made a person a good benefactor in Victorian Britain? Was the role ever abused? What role do benefactors play in modern society?

? *ESSENTIAL QUESTION:*

How do you view the world?

The 19th century was a time not only of changing technology, but also of changing ideas. As society evolved, so did people's thinking about such topics as religion, science, social structures, and their own place in the world. Some viewed progress with optimism for the future while others noted that progress brought its own set of challenges. When you look at the world around you today, what do you see?

? *ESSENTIAL QUESTION:*

What brings out cruelty in people?

Although the Victorian Era was a time of improvement in the quality of life for many, not all benefited equally. As is the case today, the daily life of some people was marked by needless cruelty. Who are the perpetrators and the victims of cruelty? What might motivate someone to treat another human or an animal cruelly? What roles do society and social structures play in promoting and/or preventing cruelty?

? *ESSENTIAL QUESTION:*

Which invention has had the greatest impact on your life?

The Victorian Era was a time of remarkable technological advancement. Great Britain led the Industrial Revolution, and the strength and influence of the British Empire ensured that British industry and inventions soon spread around the world. Many modern conveniences that we take for granted today were invented, or were in the early stages of development, during that period. Which inventions do you use most in your everyday life? How would your life be different without them?

THE VICTORIANS

"The sun never sets on the British Empire," boasted the Victorians, and it was true: with holdings around the globe, from Africa to India, from New Zealand to Canada, it was always daytime in some part of the vast territory ruled by Great Britain. The phrase also captured the attitude of the era. During the reign of Queen Victoria, Britain was a nation in motion at the height of its power, both politically and economically. Abroad, Britain dominated world politics. At home, the Industrial Revolution was in full swing. For those with wealth and influence, Victoria's reign was a time not only of change but of prosperity. Yet, large segments of the population suffered greatly during this period, leading many writers to criticize the rapid pace and materialism of the age and the injustices that resulted.

The New Monarchy Queen Victoria, for whom the period is named, was just 18 years old when she came to the throne in 1837. She went on to rule for more than 60 years, longer than any English ruler before her. Victoria's devotion to hard work and duty, her insistence on proper behavior, and her support of British imperialism became the hallmarks of the Victorian period.

Victoria knew that previous monarchs had clashed with Parliament, and she realized that the role of royalty had to change. She accepted the concept of a constitutional monarchy in which she gave advice rather than orders, and yielded control of day-to-day governmental affairs to a series of very talented prime ministers. When the queen withdrew from politics and went into mourning in 1861, after the death of her beloved husband Prince Albert, the position of prime minister became even more important.

Progress, Problems, and Reform The Industrial Revolution had already transformed Britain into a modern industrial state by the time Victoria took the throne. By 1850 England boasted 18,000 cotton mills and produced half of the world's iron. Progress also brought new inventions, such as the telephone, light bulb, radio, and automobile, and advances in science and medicine, like the work of British surgeon Joseph Lister. Building on the ideas of Louis Pasteur, Lister developed standards for keeping hospitals clean and germ-free, vastly increasing the survival rates of his patients.

Some writers expressed enthusiasm for the material advantages afforded by the industrial age. Others were appalled by the materialism of the

COLLABORATIVE DISCUSSION
In a small group, review the timeline and discuss which events would have had the greatest effects on everyday life for people in Victorian Britain.

© Houghton Mifflin Harcourt Publishing Company

1837
Victoria becomes Queen of Great Britain.

1842
Britain gains control of Hong Kong.

1847
Charlotte Brontë publishes *Jane Eyre*; Emily Brontë publishes *Wuthering Heights*.

1859
Charles Darwin publishes *On the Origin of Species*.

1835

1844
Samuel Morse sends the first long-distance telegraph message.

1845
The Irish Potato Famine begins.

1860
Charles Dickens publishes the first magazine installment of *Great Expectations*.

1861
Prince Albert dies.

The British Empire, 1880

Victorian upper and middle classes—an attitude they considered tasteless, joyless, and destructive of community.

While the middle class grew more prosperous, conditions for the poor became intolerable. Factory workers, including many children, spent long hours toiling for low wages under harsh and dangerous conditions. In the 1840s, unemployment soared in England and the Great Famine devastated Ireland. Families without income and starving Irish immigrants crowded into England's already squalid slums.

Though Parliament enacted many important reforms during this period, change came slowly. The Great Reform Act of 1832 expanded suffrage, or the right to vote, to wealthy middle-class men. Before this law, only about 5 percent of Britain's population had the right to vote. In 1833 slavery was abolished in the British Empire, and the first laws restricting child labor were enacted. In decades that followed, laws were passed establishing public schools, improving sanitation and housing, legalizing trade unions, easing harsh factory conditions, and giving working-class men the right to vote.

Victorian Poetry Confronted with the harsh realities of the Victorian world, many poets followed the lead of the Romantics, focusing on idealized love and the awe-inspiring beauty of nature. But some poets, especially later in the century, addressed contemporary issues such as spiritual doubt and the loss of old customs, traditions, and values due to the pressures of industrialization and scientific discoveries.

RESEARCH

What about this historical period interests you? Choose a topic, event, or person to learn more about. Then, add your own entry to the timeline.

Houghton Mifflin Harcourt Publishing Company • Image Credits: © Chronicle/Alamy

1874
Alexander Graham Bell develops the telephone.

1883
Robert Louis Stevenson publishes the adventure novel *Treasure Island*.

1893
Henry Ford develops the gasoline-powered automobile.

1905

1867
The Second Reform Act extends voting rights to workingmen.

1876
Queen Victoria gains the title Empress of India.

1884
The Third Reform Act allows nearly all adult males to vote.

1901
Queen Victoria dies after nearly 64 years of rule.

Realism While many poets retreated from modern life, novelists embraced the issues of the age. Victorian novels were weighty affairs, quite literally—so weighty that they typically had to be divided into three volumes. Keen-eyed, sharp-witted writers probed every corner of society—from the drawing room to the slums, exposing problems and pretensions. Victorian readers craved this realism. They wanted to meet characters like themselves and the people they knew; they wanted to learn more about their rapidly changing world. Families often spent evenings reading aloud to each other, laughing at the adventures of Charles Dickens's Mr. Pickwick and his oddball friends or sighing over Heathcliff and Catherine's doomed romance in Emily Brontë's *Wuthering Heights*. In the next century, modernist writers would pick up the torch from their Victorian predecessors and grapple with issues the Victorians could not have imagined.

CHECK YOUR UNDERSTANDING

Choose the best answer to each question.

1 Which **best** describes the British government during the Victorian Era?

A Conflicts between Victoria and Parliament led to the weakening of the monarchy.

B Victoria and Parliament agreed to give primary authority to the prime minister.

C Victoria modified the role of the monarch and strengthened the position of the prime minster.

D Parliament took Victoria's retirement from politics as an opportunity to establish a constitutional monarchy.

2 The reforms enacted by Parliament primarily affected the lower classes by —

F increasing the oppression faced by factory workers

G slowly improving living and working conditions

H addressing the unemployment crisis that arose in the 1840s

J contributing to the development of slums

3 What topic in Victorian novels appealed most to readers?

A Stories about ancient myths and legends

B Celebrations of romantic love

C The awe-inspiring beauty of nature

D Realistic portrayals of everyday people

ACADEMIC VOCABULARY

Academic Vocabulary words are words you use when you discuss and write about texts. In this unit, you will learn the following five words:

☑ abandon ☐ confine ☐ conform ☐ depress ☐ reluctance

Study the Word Network to learn more about the word **abandon**.

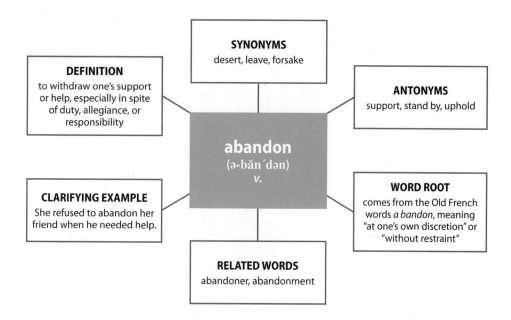

DEFINITION
to withdraw one's support or help, especially in spite of duty, allegiance, or responsibility

SYNONYMS
desert, leave, forsake

ANTONYMS
support, stand by, uphold

abandon
(ə-băn´dən)
v.

WORD ROOT
comes from the Old French words *a bandon*, meaning "at one's own discretion" or "without restraint"

CLARIFYING EXAMPLE
She refused to abandon her friend when he needed help.

RELATED WORDS
abandoner, abandonment

Write and Discuss Discuss your completed Word Network with a partner, making sure to talk through all of the boxes until you both understand the word, its synonyms, antonyms, and related forms. Then, fill out a Word Network for the remaining four words. Use a dictionary or online resource to help you complete the activity.

 Go online to access the Word Networks.

RESPOND TO THE ESSENTIAL QUESTION

In this unit, you will explore four different **Essential Questions** about literature of the Victorian Era. As you read each selection, you will gather your ideas about one of these questions and write about it in the **Response Log** that appears on page R5. At the end of the unit, you will have the opportunity to write a **research report** related to one of the essential questions. Filling out the Response Log after you read each text will help you prepare for this writing task.

 You can also go online to access the Response Log.

from
JANE EYRE

Novel by **Charlotte Brontë**

? ***ESSENTIAL QUESTION:***

What is a true benefactor?

QUICK START

Think about a time of transition in your life, perhaps moving to a new neighborhood or changing schools. What were some of the obstacles you faced? What helped you adjust to your new circumstances? Discuss your experience with a partner.

ANALYZE FIRST-PERSON POINT OF VIEW

Stories are told from a narrative perspective, or **point of view.** In *Jane Eyre*, the story is narrated in the first-person point of view. The narrator is the character Jane, who uses the personal pronouns *I, me,* and *my.* Readers experience everything through her eyes. Jane's thoughts and commentary convey the intensity of her feelings about the Lowood boarding school and its occupants.

As you read, notice how Charlotte Brontë's use of the first-person point of view affects what you learn about the novel's characters, events, setting, and themes.

GENRE ELEMENTS: NOVEL

- is a long work of fiction
- is usually written in the first- or third-person point of view
- can develop characters and conflict more thoroughly than a short story
- often develops complex plot structures, including subplots

ANALYZE SETTING

The **setting** of a novel is the time and place in which the action occurs. This excerpt from *Jane Eyre* is set in a boarding school for girls. During the Victorian period, hundreds of charity schools were established in Britain to provide free education, clothing, lodging, and meals for orphans and poor children. They were funded by contributions from wealthy donors. Some of the people who ran these schools were very idealistic and treated students well. However, many schools were led by harsh disciplinarians and offered only the most basic education. Schools for the poorest children were called "ragged schools," a name inspired by the children's shabby clothing.

As you read, notice how the setting is connected to the novel's plot, characterization, and themes. Use a chart like this one to record details that reveal the historical, economic, and social context of the setting.

SETTING DETAILS	HISTORICAL, ECONOMIC, AND SOCIAL CONTEXT

CRITICAL VOCABULARY

ruddy   dismay   morose   vogue   commence   verandah

To see how many Critical Vocabulary words you already know, identify which underlined word in each sentence is used incorrectly.

1. They <u>commenced</u> the meeting to the <u>verandah</u> after the office air conditioner broke down.

a. commenced   **b.** verandah

2. Her <u>morose</u> face showed how much she appreciated the in-<u>vogue</u> garments presented at the fashion show.

a. morose   **b.** vogue

3. She was quite <u>dismayed</u> at his <u>ruddy</u> complexion, and asked if he ever got outdoors to enjoy the sunshine.

a. dismayed   **b.** ruddy

LANGUAGE CONVENTIONS

Gerunds and Gerund Phrases In this lesson, you will learn about gerunds and gerund phrases. A **gerund** is a verb ending in *-ing* that is used as a noun. You can add modifiers and complements to a gerund to make it a **gerund phrase.** Writers use gerunds and gerund phrases to effectively combine short sentences into one.

As you read the excerpt, notice the author's use of gerunds and gerund phrases.

ANNOTATION MODEL

NOTICE & NOTE

As you read, note the details that Brontë provides about the setting and how the narrator reacts to the treatment she receives from different people at the school. In the model, you can see one reader's notes about the excerpt from *Jane Eyre*.

The refectory was a great, <u>low-ceiled, gloomy room</u>; on two long tables smoked basins of something hot, which, however, to my dismay, sent forth <u>an odor far from inviting</u>. I saw a <u>universal manifestation of discontent</u> when the <u>fumes of the repast met the nostrils of those destined to swallow it</u> . . .

> The room itself seems like it would make you lose your appetite. The narrator uses a formal, restrained tone to describe the food's awful smell, which suggests she's describing it when she's older.

BACKGROUND

Charlotte Brontë *(1816–1855) grew up in a rural area of England, the daughter of a clergyman and a mother who died when she was five. She worked as a governess and teacher before beginning her writing career. Her first book was a collection of poetry that she wrote with two of her sisters, Emily and Anne. Jane Eyre, originally published under a pseudonym, was her first novel. It blended the suspense and moody atmosphere of a Gothic novel with a realistic portrayal of the moral, social, and economic pressures faced by a Victorian woman who lacked family support.*

from

JANE EYRE

Novel by Charlotte Brontë

SETTING A PURPOSE

As you read, pay attention to how Jane reacts to conditions at the school and to the people she meets there.

Orphaned as a young child, Jane Eyre has spent most of her childhood at Gateshead, the home of her wealthy yet heartless aunt, Mrs. Reed. At Gateshead, Jane is tormented by her cousins and repeatedly reminded of her low economic and social status. After a fight with one of her cousins, Jane's aunt decides to send her away to boarding school when she is 10 years old. As this excerpt begins, Jane has left Gateshead and is traveling by coach to the Lowood Institution, a boarding school for orphans and poor girls.

1   The afternoon came on wet and somewhat misty: as it waned into dusk, I began to feel that we were getting very far indeed from Gateshead: we ceased to pass through towns; the country changed; great grey hills heaved up round the horizon: as twilight deepened, we descended a valley, dark with wood, and long after night had overclouded the prospect, I heard a wild wind rushing amongst trees.

© Houghton Mifflin Harcourt Publishing Company • Image Credits: © Pictorial Press Ltd/Alamy; © Lebrecht Music and Arts Photo Library/Alamy

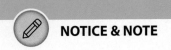

ANALYZE FIRST-PERSON POINT OF VIEW

Annotate: In paragraph 4, mark details about what Jane sees after being lifted from the coach.

Analyze: How does this description give the impression that we see everything through Jane's eyes?

2   Lulled by the sound, I at last dropped asleep: I had not long slumbered when the sudden cessation of motion awoke me; the coach-door was open, and a person like a servant was standing at it: I saw her face and dress by the light of the lamps.

3   "Is there a little girl called Jane Eyre here?" she asked. I answered "Yes," and was then lifted out; my trunk was handed down, and the coach instantly drove away.

4   I was stiff with long sitting, and bewildered with the noise and motion of the coach: gathering my faculties, I looked about me. Rain, wind, and darkness filled the air; nevertheless, I dimly discerned a wall before me and a door open in it. Through this door I passed with my new guide: she shut and locked it behind her. There was now visible a house or houses—for the building spread far—with many windows, and lights burning in some; we went up a broad pebbly path, splashing wet, and were admitted at a door; then the servant led me through a passage into a room with a fire, where she left me alone.

5   I stood and warmed my numbed fingers over the blaze, then looked round; there was no candle, but the uncertain light from the hearth showed, by intervals, papered walls, carpet, curtains, shining mahogany furniture: it was a parlor, not so spacious or splendid as the drawing-room at Gateshead, but comfortable enough. I was puzzling to make out the subject of a picture on the wall, when the door opened, and an individual carrying a light entered; another followed close behind.

6   The first was a tall lady with dark hair, dark eyes, and a pale and large forehead; her figure was partly enveloped in a shawl, her countenance was grave, her bearing erect.

7   "The child is very young to be sent alone," said she, putting her candle down on the table. She considered me attentively for a minute or two, then further added—

8   "She had better be put to bed soon; she looks tired: are you tired?" she asked, placing her hand on my shoulder.

9   "A little, ma'am."

10   "And hungry too, no doubt: let her have some supper before she goes to bed, Miss Miller. Is this the first time you have left your parents to come to school, my little girl?"

11   I explained to her that I had no parents. She inquired how long they had been dead; then how old I was, what was my name, whether I could read, write, and sew a little: then she touched my cheek gently with her forefinger, and saying,

12   "She hoped I should be a good child," dismissed me along with Miss Miller.

13   The lady I had left might be about twenty-nine; the one who went with me appeared some years younger: the first impressed me by her voice, look, and air. Miss Miller was more ordinary; **ruddy** in complexion, though of a careworn countenance; hurried in gait and

ruddy
(rŭd´ē) *adj.* having a healthy, reddish glow.

action, like one who had always a multiplicity of tasks on hand: she looked, indeed, what I afterwards found she really was, an under-teacher. Led by her, I passed from compartment to compartment, from passage to passage, of a large and irregular building; till, emerging from the total and somewhat dreary silence pervading that portion of the house we had traversed, we came upon the hum of many voices, and presently entered a wide, long room, with great deal tables, two at each end, on each of which burnt a pair of candles, and seated all round on benches, a congregation of girls of every age, from nine or ten to twenty. Seen by the dim light of the dips, their number to me appeared countless, though not in reality exceeding eighty; they were uniformly dressed in brown stuff frocks of quaint fashion, and long holland pinafores. It was the hour of study; they were engaged in conning[1] over their tomorrow's task, and the hum I had heard was the combined result of their whispered repetitions.

14   Miss Miller signed to me to sit on a bench near the door, then walking up to the top of the long room, she cried out—

15   "Monitors, collect the lesson-books and put them away!"

16   Four tall girls arose from different tables, and going round, gathered the books and removed them. Miss Miller again gave the word of command—

17   "Monitors, fetch the supper-trays!"

18   The tall girls went out and returned presently, each bearing a tray, with portions of something, I knew not what, arranged thereon, and a pitcher of water and mug in the middle of each tray. The portions were handed round; those who liked took a draught of the water, the mug being common to all. When it came to my turn, I drank, for I was thirsty, but did not touch the food, excitement and fatigue rendering me incapable of eating: I now saw, however, that it was a thin oaten cake, shared into fragments.

19   The meal over, prayers were read by Miss Miller, and the classes filed off, two and two, upstairs. Overpowered by this time with weariness, I scarcely noticed what sort of a place the bedroom was; except that, like the schoolroom, I saw it was very long. Tonight I was to be Miss Miller's bed-fellow; she helped me to undress: when laid down I glanced at the long rows of beds, each of which was quickly filled with two occupants; in ten minutes the single light was extinguished; amid silence and complete darkness, I fell asleep.

20   The night passed rapidly: I was too tired even to dream; I only once awoke to hear the wind rave in furious gusts, and the rain fall in torrents, and to be sensible that Miss Miller had taken her place by my side. When I again unclosed my eyes, a loud bell was ringing: the girls were up and dressing; day had not yet begun to dawn, and a rushlight or two burnt in the room. I too rose reluctantly; it was bitter

ANALYZE SETTING

Annotate: Mark details in paragraph 18 about the girls' supper.

Draw Conclusions: What does this description suggest about living conditions at Lowood?

---

[1] **conning:** examining or studying.

ANALYZE SETTING

Annotate: Mark details about books and reading in paragraphs 22–25.

Analyze: What does this passage reveal about education at Victorian charity schools?

cold, and I dressed as well as I could for shivering, and washed when there was a basin at liberty, which did not occur soon, as there was but one basin to six girls, on the stands down the middle of the room. Again the bell rang: all formed in file, two and two, and in that order descended the stairs and entered the cold and dimly-lit schoolroom: here prayers were read by Miss Miller; afterwards she called out—

21   "Form classes!"

22   A great tumult succeeded for some minutes, during which Miss Miller repeatedly exclaimed, "Silence!" and "Order!" When it subsided, I saw them all drawn up in four semi-circles, before four chairs, placed at the four tables; all held books in their hands, and a great book, like a Bible, lay on each table, before the vacant seat. A pause of some seconds succeeded, filled up by the low, vague hum of numbers; Miss Miller walked from class to class, hushing this indefinite sound.

23   A distant bell tinkled: immediately three ladies entered the room, each walked to a table and took her seat; Miss Miller assumed the fourth vacant chair, which was that nearest the door, and around which the smallest of the children were assembled: to this inferior class I was called, and placed at the bottom of it.

24   Business now began: the day's Collect was repeated, then certain texts of Scripture were said, and to these succeeded a protracted reading of chapters in the Bible, which lasted an hour. By the time that exercise was terminated, day had fully dawned. The indefatigable bell now sounded for the fourth time: the classes were marshalled and marched into another room to breakfast: how glad I was to behold a prospect of getting something to eat! I was now nearly sick from inanition, having taken so little the day before.

25   The refectory[2] was a great, low-ceiled, gloomy room; on two long tables smoked basins of something hot, which, however, to my **dismay**, sent forth an odor far from inviting. I saw a universal manifestation of discontent when the fumes of the repast met the nostrils of those destined to swallow it; from the van of the procession, the tall girls of the first class, rose the whispered words—

26   "Disgusting! The porridge is burnt again!"

27   "Silence!" ejaculated a voice; not that of Miss Miller, but one of the upper teachers, a little and dark personage, smartly dressed, but of somewhat **morose** aspect who installed herself at the top of one table, while a more buxom lady presided at the other. I looked in vain for her I had first seen the night before; she was not visible: Miss Miller occupied the foot of the table where I sat, and a strange, foreign looking, elderly lady, the French teacher, as I afterwards found, took the corresponding seat at the other board. A long grace was said and

dismay
(dĭs-mā´) *v.* to upset or distress.

morose
(mə-rōs´, mô-) *adj.* sullen or gloomy.

---

[2] **refectory:** a room where meals are served in a school or institution.

a hymn sung; then a servant brought in some tea for the teachers, and the meal began.

28   Ravenous, and now very faint, I devoured a spoonful or two of my portion without thinking of its taste; but the first edge of hunger blunted, I perceived I had got in hand a nauseous mess: burnt porridge is almost as bad as rotten potatoes; famine itself soon sickens over it. The spoons were moved slowly: I saw each girl taste her food and try to swallow it; but in most cases the effort was soon relinquished. Breakfast was over, and none had breakfasted. Thanks being returned for what we had not got, and a second hymn chanted, the refectory was evacuated for the schoolroom. I was one of the last to go out, and in passing the tables, I saw one teacher take a basin of the porridge and taste it; she looked at the others; all their countenances expressed displeasure, and one of them, the stout one, whispered—

29   "Abominable stuff! How shameful!"

30   A quarter of an hour passed before lessons again began, during which the schoolroom was in a glorious tumult; for that space of time, it seemed to be permitted to talk loud and more freely, and they used their privilege. The whole conversation ran on the breakfast, which one and all abused roundly. Poor things! it was the sole consolation they had. Miss Miller was now the only teacher in the room: a group of great girls standing about her, spoke with serious and sullen gestures. I heard the name of Mr. Brocklehurst pronounced by some lips; at which Miss Miller shook her head disapprovingly; but she made no great effort to check the general wrath: doubtless she shared in it.

31   A clock in the schoolroom struck nine; Miss Miller left her circle, and standing in the middle of the room, cried—

32   "Silence! To your seats!"

33   Discipline prevailed: in five minutes the confused throng was resolved into order, and comparative silence quelled the Babel clamour of tongues. The upper teachers now punctually resumed their posts: but still, all seemed to wait. Ranged on benches down the sides of the room, the eighty girls sat motionless and erect: a quaint assemblage they appeared, all with plain locks combed from their faces, not a curl visible; in brown dresses, made high and surrounded by a narrow tucker about the throat, with little pockets of holland (shaped something like a Highlander's purse) tied in front of their frocks, and designed to serve the purpose of a work-bag: all too wearing woollen stockings and country-made shoes, fastened with brass buckles. Above twenty of those clad in this costume were full-grown girls, or rather young women; it suited them ill, and gave an air of oddity even to the prettiest.

34   I was still looking at them, and also at intervals examining the teachers—none of whom precisely pleased me; for the stout one was

CONTRASTS AND CONTRADICTIONS

Notice & Note: Mark two statements that express contradictory ideas in paragraph 28.

Infer: What do these statements suggest about how girls are treated at the school?

© Houghton Mifflin Harcourt Publishing Company • Image Credits: © thislife pictures/Alamy

a little coarse, the dark one not a little fierce, the foreigner harsh and grotesque, and Miss Miller, poor thing! looked purple, weather-beaten, and over-worked—when, as my eye wandered from face to face, the whole school rose simultaneously, as if moved by a common spring.

35   What was the matter? I had heard no order given: I was puzzled. Ere I had gathered my wits, the classes were again seated: but as all eyes were now turned to one point, mine followed the general direction, and encountered the personage who had received me last night. She stood at the bottom of the long room, on the hearth; for there was a fire at each end: she surveyed the two rows of girls silently and gravely. Miss Miller approaching, seemed to ask her a question, and having received her answer, went back to her place, and said aloud—

36   "Monitor of the first class, fetch the globes!"

37   While the direction was being executed, the lady consulted moved slowly up the room. I suppose I have a considerable organ of Veneration, for I retain yet the sense of admiring awe with which my eyes traced her steps. Seen now, in broad daylight, she looked tall, fair, and shapely; brown eyes, with a benignant light in their irids,

ANALYZE FIRST-PERSON POINT OF VIEW

Annotate: Mark words and phrases in paragraph 37 that express Jane's admiration for Miss Temple.

Analyze: Which details reveal that Jane has spent time in fashionable society?

and a fine penciling of long lashes round, relieved the whiteness of her large front; on each of her temples her hair, of a very dark brown, was clustered in round curls, according to the fashion of those times, when neither smooth bands nor long ringlets were in **vogue**; her dress, also in the mode of the day, was of purple cloth, relieved by a sort of Spanish trimming of black velvet; a gold watch (watches were not so common then as now) shone at her girdle. Let the reader add, to complete the picture, refined features; a complexion, if pale, clear; and a stately air and carriage, and he will have, at least, as clearly as words can give it, a correct idea of the exterior of Miss Temple— Maria Temple, as I afterwards saw the name written in a prayer-book entrusted to me to carry to church.

vogue
(vōg) *n.* the prevailing fashion, practice, or style.

38   The superintendent of Lowood (for such was this lady) having taken her seat before a pair of globes placed on one of the tables, summoned the first class round her, and **commenced** giving a lesson in geography; the lower classes were called by the teachers: repetitions in history, grammar, etc., went on for an hour; writing and arithmetic succeeded, and music lessons were given by Miss Temple to some of the elder girls. The duration of each lesson was measured by the clock, which at last struck twelve. The superintendent rose—

commence
(kə-mĕns´) *v.* to begin or start.

39   "I have a word to address to the pupils," said she.

40   The tumult of cessation from lessons was already breaking forth, but it sank at her voice. She went on—

41   "You had this morning a breakfast which you could not eat; you must be hungry—I have ordered that a lunch of bread and cheese shall be served to all."

42   The teachers looked at her with a sort of surprise.

43   "It is to be done on my responsibility," she added, in an explanatory tone to them, and immediately afterwards left the room.

44   The bread and cheese was presently brought in and distributed, to the high delight and refreshment of the whole school. The order was now given "To the garden!" Each put on a coarse straw bonnet, with strings of colored calico, and a cloak of grey frieze. I was similarly equipped, and, following the stream, I made my way into the open air.

45   The garden was a wide enclosure, surrounded with walls so high as to exclude every glimpse of prospect: a covered **verandah** ran down one side, and broad walks bordered a middle space divided into scores of little beds: these beds were assigned as gardens for the pupils to cultivate, and each bed had an owner. When full of flowers they would doubtless look pretty; but now, at the latter end of January, all was wintry blight and brown decay. I shuddered as I stood and looked round me: it was an inclement day for outdoor exercise; not positively rainy, but darkened by a drizzling yellow fog; all underfoot was still soaking wet with the floods of yesterday. The stronger among the girls ran about and engaged in active games, but sundry pale and thin

verandah
(və-răn´də) *n.* a porch or balcony.

ANALYZE SETTING

Annotate: Mark details in paragraph 45 showing how the girls feel about their exercise period.

Analyze: What does this description suggest about the school's attitude toward the girls' well-being?

LANGUAGE CONVENTIONS

Annotate: Mark the sentence that contains gerunds in paragraph 46.

Evaluate: What do these gerunds emphasize about Jane's character?

ones herded together for shelter and warmth in the verandah; and amongst these, as the dense mist penetrated to their shivering frames, I heard frequently the sound of a hollow cough.

46   As yet I had spoken to no one, nor did anybody seem to take notice of me; I stood lonely enough: but to that feeling of isolation I was accustomed; it did not oppress me much. I leant against a pillar of the verandah, drew my grey mantle close about me, and, trying to forget the cold which nipped me without, and the unsatisfied hunger which gnawed me within, delivered myself up to the employment of watching and thinking. My reflections were too undefined and fragmentary to merit record: I hardly yet knew where I was; Gateshead and my past life seemed floated away to an immeasurable distance; the present was vague and strange, and of the future I could form no conjecture. I looked round the convent-like garden, and then up at the house; a large building, half of which seemed grey and old, the other half quite new. The new part, containing the schoolroom and dormitory, was lit by mullioned and latticed windows, which gave it a church-like aspect; a stone tablet over the door, bore this inscription—

47   "Lowood Institution.—This portion was rebuilt A.D.—, by Naomi Brocklehurst, of Brocklehurst Hall, in this county."

48   "Let your light so shine before men that they may see your good works, and glorify your Father which is in heaven."— St. Matt. v. 16.

49   I read these words over and over again: I felt that an explanation belonged to them, and was unable fully to penetrate their import. I was still pondering the signification of "Institution," and endeavoring to make out a connection between the first words and the verse of Scripture, when the sound of a cough close behind me, made me turn my head. I saw a girl sitting on a stone bench near; she had bent over a book, on the perusal of which she seemed intent: from where I stood I could see the title—it was "Rasselas;" a name that struck me as strange, and consequently attractive. In turning a leaf she happened to look up, and I said to her directly—

50   "Is your book interesting?" I had already formed the intention of asking her to lend it to me some day.

51   "I like it," she answered, after a pause of a second or two, during which she examined me.

52   "What is it about?" I continued, I hardly know where I found the hardihood thus to open a conversation with a stranger; the step was contrary to my nature and habits: but I think her occupation touched a chord of sympathy somewhere; for I too liked reading, though of a frivolous and childish kind; I could not digest or comprehend the serious or substantial.

53   "You may look at it," replied the girl, offering me the book.

54   I did so; a brief examination convinced me that the contents were less taking than the title: "Rasselas" looked dull to my trifling taste; I saw nothing about fairies, nothing about genii; no bright variety seemed spread over the closely-printed pages. I returned it to her; she received it quietly, and without saying anything she was about to relapse into her former studious mood: again I ventured to disturb her—

55   "Can you tell me what the writing on that stone over the door means? What is Lowood Institution?"

56   "This house where you are come to live."

57   "And why do they call it Institution? Is it in any way different from other schools?"

58   "It is partly a charity-school: you and I, and all the rest of us, are charity-children. I suppose you are an orphan: are not either your father or your mother dead?"

59   "Both died before I can remember."

60   "Well, all the girls here have lost either one or both parents, and this is called an institution for educating orphans."

61   "Do we pay no money? Do they keep us for nothing?"

62   "We pay, or our friends pay, fifteen pounds a year for each."

63   "Then why do they call us charity-children?"

64   "Because fifteen pounds is not enough for board and teaching, and the deficiency is supplied by subscription."

65   "Who subscribes?"

66   "Different benevolent-minded ladies and gentlemen in this neighborhood and in London."

67   "Who was Naomi Brocklehurst?"

68   "The lady who built the new part of this house as that tablet records, and whose son overlooks and directs everything here."

69   "Why?"

70   "Because he is treasurer and manager of the establishment."

71   "Then this house does not belong to that tall lady who wears a watch, and who said we were to have some bread and cheese."

72   "To Miss Temple? Oh, no! I wish it did: she has to answer to Mr. Brocklehurst for all she does. Mr. Brocklehurst buys all our food and all our clothes."

73   "Does he live here?"

74   "No—two miles off, at a large hall."

75   "Is he a good man?"

76   "He is a clergyman, and is said to do a great deal of good."

77   "Did you say that tall lady was called Miss Temple? "

78   "Yes."

79   "And what are the other teachers called?"

80   "The one with red cheeks is called Miss Smith; she attends to the work, and cuts out—for we make our own clothes, our frocks, and pelisses, and every thing; the little one with black hair is Miss

ANALYZE FIRST-PERSON POINT OF VIEW

Annotate: Mark paragraph 57.

Analyze: Why does Jane ask these questions? What do they indicate about the type of person she is?

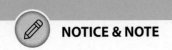
Scatcherd; she teaches history and grammar, and hears the second class repetitions; and the one who wears a shawl, and has a pocket-handkerchief tied to her side with a yellow riband, is Madame Pierrot: she comes from Lisle, in France, and teaches French."

81   "Do you like the teachers?"

82   "Well enough."

83   "Do you like the little black one, and the Madame—?—I cannot pronounce her name as you do."

84   "Miss Scatcherd is hasty—you must take care not to offend her; Madame Pierrot is not a bad sort of person."

85   "But Miss Temple is the best—isn't she?"

86   "Miss Temple is very good, and very clever; she is above the rest, because she knows far more than they do."

87   "Have you been long here?"

88   "Two years."

89   "Are you an orphan?"

90   "My mother is dead."

91   "Are you happy here?"

92   "You ask rather too many questions. I have given you answers enough for the present: now I want to read."

93   But at that moment the summons sounded for dinner: all reentered the house. The odor which now filled the refectory was scarcely more appetizing than that which had regaled our nostrils at breakfast: the dinner was served in two huge tin-plated vessels, whence rose a strong steam redolent of rancid fat. I found the mess to consist of indifferent potatoes and strange shreds of rusty meat, mixed and cooked together. Of this preparation a tolerably abundant plateful was apportioned to each pupil. I ate what I could, and wondered within myself whether every day's fare would be like this.

94   After dinner, we immediately adjourned to the schoolroom: lessons recommenced, and were continued till five o'clock.

95   The only marked event of the afternoon was, that I saw the girl with whom I had conversed in the verandah, dismissed in disgrace, by Miss Scatcherd, from a history class, and sent to stand in the middle of the large schoolroom. The punishment seemed to me in a high degree ignominious, especially for so great a girl—she looked thirteen or upwards. I expected she would show signs of great distress and shame; but to my surprise she neither wept nor blushed: composed, though grave, she stood, the central mark of all eyes. "How can she bear it so quietly—so firmly?" I asked of myself. "Were I in her place, it seems to me I should wish the earth to open and swallow me up. She looks as if she were thinking of something beyond her punishment—beyond her situation: of something not round nor before her. I have heard of daydreams—is she in a daydream now? Her eyes are fixed on the floor, but I am sure they do not see it—her sight seems turned in, gone down into her heart:

ANALYZE FIRST-PERSON POINT OF VIEW

Annotate: Mark the girl's response to Jane's question about Miss Temple.

Compare: How does the girl's response contrast with Jane's reasons for admiring Miss Temple?

she is looking at what she can remember, I believe; not at what is really present. I wonder what sort of a girl she is—whether good or naughty."

96   Soon after five P.M. we had another meal, consisting of a small mug of coffee and half a slice of brown bread. I devoured my bread and drank my coffee with relish; but I should have been glad of as much more—I was still hungry. Half an hour's recreation succeeded, then study; then the glass of water and the piece of oat-cake, prayers, and bed. Such was my first day at Lowood.

CHECK YOUR UNDERSTANDING

Answer these questions before moving on to the **Analyze the Text** section on the following page.

1 What is Miss Temple's reaction when she first meets Jane?

A She is annoyed that Jane has arrived so late.

B She expresses sympathy and concern for Jane.

C She thinks Jane is too young for the school.

D She fears that Jane will misbehave.

2 Why does Miss Temple order bread and cheese to be served on Jane's first day at Lowood?

F She wants to celebrate Jane's arrival.

G Mr. Brocklehurst is coming for a visit.

H The students could not eat their breakfast.

J The school has run out of other food.

3 Who makes the decisions about how Lowood is run?

A Miss Temple

B Miss Miller

C Miss Scatcherd

D Mr. Brocklehurst

© Houghton Mifflin Harcourt Publishing Company

ANALYZE THE TEXT

Support your responses with evidence from the text. 📓 NOTEBOOK

1. **Compare** Reread the introductory note below Setting a Purpose on page 595. How does Jane's experience at Lowood compare with the life she led at Gateshead?

2. **Evaluate** England did not have government-funded schools in the period covered by the novel; because the children at Lowood are poor, they must rely on charity for their education. Based on Jane's descriptions of the setting, how well does this system serve the needs of students? Explain.

3. **Draw Conclusions** What does the excerpt hint about Mr. Brocklehurst's character?

4. **Critique** Is the first-person narration of *Jane Eyre* effective, or should Brontë have used the third-person point of view to tell the story? Give reasons for your opinion.

5. **Notice & Note** Jane is surprised that the older girl shows no emotion when Miss Scatcherd makes her stand in the middle of the room as punishment. What does this incident reveal about Jane's personality?

RESEARCH

RESEARCH TIP
When researching a specific part of a particular time period, it is best to use search strings that include all elements, starting with the most important. For example, for this research, the search string "ragged schools Victorian England" would be most likely to yield useful results.

Research "ragged schools" and other charitable education institutions in England during the Victorian era. Why did these schools exist? Who did they serve? What impact did they have on pupils? Use the following chart to record your findings.

PURPOSE	POPULATION SERVED	IMPACT ON POPULATION

Extend Use the information found in your research to explain how Charlotte Brontë utilized details about education in her writing. Write a brief paragraph analyzing the effectiveness of the author's use of such details.

CREATE AND PRESENT

Write a Comparison Obtain a filmed adaptation of *Jane Eyre* to view the scenes described in the novel excerpt. Focus on how effectively the film version captures the setting and overall atmosphere of the classic.

❏ Isolate a few striking descriptions of setting from the novel excerpt. Find and view similar scenes from film. Pause occasionally to examine shots.

❏ Make a chart, if you wish, to compare details from the novel excerpt and film.

❏ Consider how closely the filmed setting matches the novel excerpt. Think about any deliberate changes the director might have made.

❏ You may include other aspects for comparison, such as character portrayals. Cover how these elements are presented in both versions.

Present Your Comparison Now that you've written a comparison, present it to the group. If possible, play segments of the film version to illustrate your points.

❏ Read your comparison aloud or refer to it as you present your views.

❏ Encourage your listeners to react to your view and offer their own. Ask your listeners how well they followed your points, and if they can add ideas that might strengthen the comparison.

Go to **Writing Informative Texts** in the **Writing Studio** to organize ideas for the comparison.

Go to **Using Media in a Presentation** in the **Speaking and Listening Studio** to learn more.

RESPOND TO THE ESSENTIAL QUESTION

 ? What is a true benefactor?

Gather Information Review your annotations and notes on the excerpt from *Jane Eyre*. Then, add relevant information to your Response Log. As you determine which information to include, think about:

• what a benefactor, or supporter, should provide to someone in need

• how a benefactor would act toward someone he or she was helping

• how a benefactor might try to help, but fail to provide the support a person truly needs

ACADEMIC VOCABULARY

As you write and discuss what you learned from *Jane Eyre*, be sure to use the Academic Vocabulary words. Check off each of the words that you use.

❏ **abandon**

❏ **confine**

❏ **conform**

❏ **depress**

❏ **reluctance**

CRITICAL VOCABULARY

WORD BANK
ruddy
dismay
morose
vogue
commence
verandah

Practice and Apply Choose the situation that best fits with the Critical Vocabulary word.

1. If you're drinking tea on the **verandah,** are you indoors or outside?

2. If your complexion is **ruddy,** have you been exposed to the sun or covered up?

3. If a movie were described as **morose,** would it be sad or funny?

4. If a class is **commencing,** is it beginning or ending?

5. If you are feeling **dismayed,** are you happy or unhappy?

6. If a woman's outfit is said to be in **vogue,** is it in style or out of style?

VOCABULARY STRATEGY:
Foreign Words or Phrases

Go to the **Vocabulary Studio** for more.

Foreign words or phrases are often incorporated into English language usage. Typically, the meaning is similar to the way the word is used in the original language, but not always. Additionally, these words and phrases can be categorized based on use. For example, many German terms used in English refer to philosophy or sociology, while many Latin words deal with the law. French words, like the term *vogue* used in *Jane Eyre*, often refer to food or social class.

In the novel, Jane describes Miss Temple's appearance, including her physical form and how she presents herself through dress and style. The word *vogue* is not only descriptive of the woman's appearance but is also indicative of her social standing, indicating she is above those she is charged with teaching.

Practice and Apply Read each of the clues to identify the foreign word or phrase commonly used in English.

WORD BANK
agenda
genre
café
kindergarten

DESCRIPTION	ORIGIN	WORD OR PHRASE
A restaurant serving coffee or other beverages along with baked goods or light meals	French	
A category or type	French	
A program or class for children aged four to six	German	
A program of things to be done or considered, or an unstated underlying motive	Latin	

LANGUAGE CONVENTIONS:
Gerunds and Gerund Phrases

A **gerund** is a verb form ending in -*ing* that functions as a noun. **Gerund phrases** include the gerund plus its modifiers and complements. Gerunds and gerund phrases may perform any function that a noun performs and can appear in any part of a sentence where a noun could be used. Gerunds can add a sense of motion or action to a sentence.

 Go to **Gerunds and Gerund Phrases** in the **Grammar Studio** to learn more.

PART OF THE SENTENCE	EXAMPLE
subject	**Having little food** was a way of life at Lowood.
direct object	The girls finished **gardening.**
indirect object	They gave **working** their full attention.
subject complement	Her best skill is **coping with hardship.**
object of the preposition	She came home weary from **working all day.**

Practice and Apply Write your own sentences with gerunds or gerund phrases using the sentences above as models.

MEDIA

FACTORY REFORM

Documentary by **Timelines.tv**

? ESSENTIAL QUESTION:

What is a true benefactor?

QUICK START

Write a paragraph about any incident in which an individual took a stand or made efforts on behalf of others. Share your paragraph with a partner.

EVALUATE DOCUMENTARIES

GENRE ELEMENTS: DOCUMENTARY

- informational
- covers a specific person, place, event, or idea
- should rely on facts, but may also express opinions
- uses visual and sound elements
- conveys information through a narrator (or voice-over narration)

Go to the **Speaking and Listening Studio: Using Media in a Presentation** to find out about visual and sound elements.

A **documentary** is a nonfiction film about social, political, or historical subject matter. A historical documentary usually focuses on a particular time period, person, or event and informs viewers by taking a detailed look at the subject. Documentary filmmakers often rely on visual and sound elements to immerse viewers in the subject and to convey certain viewpoints.

VISUAL AND SOUND ELEMENTS	• **Footage** is recorded material used to reveal information about a subject. It can include photos, film clips, even reenactments. • **Illustrations** can be used to help create a storyline by portraying important people and incidents. • **Music** and **sound effects** can be used to set a mood or to capture viewers' attention.
STRATEGIES FOR VIEWING	• Consider the viewpoint of the documentary. Is it **objective,** based strictly on the facts? Or does it make its points in a **subjective** way by sharing only certain views? • Note images used to help you connect ideas. • Think about what the creators emphasize and what impressions they might want to convey.

BACKGROUND

"Factory Reform" is an excerpt from the documentary History of Britain—
Changing Lives *on the website Timelines.tv. It depicts manufacturer Titus Salt's
advocacy for Britain's lower-class factory workers. In the Industrial Revolution,
business owners became quite wealthy, while average citizens lived in poverty.
Workers—men, women, and children—sometimes worked more than 14 hours
per day and made very little money. Many were killed or severely injured; accidents
ranging from falls to explosions were common in Victorian factories.*

SETTING A PURPOSE

*Pay attention to the visual and sound elements in the film. Listen for sounds and
words in the narration that help to connect viewers to the conditions in Victorian
factories. Also, note visual elements that may persuade you to take a certain viewpoint about the subject.* **NOTEBOOK**

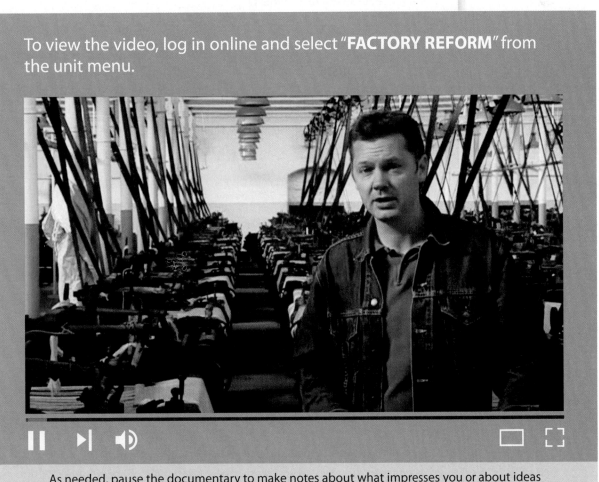

To view the video, log in online and select "**FACTORY REFORM**" from
the unit menu.

As needed, pause the documentary to make notes about what impresses you or about ideas
you might want to talk about later. Replay or rewind so you can clarify anything you do not
understand.

ANALYZE MEDIA

Support your responses with evidence from the documentary. 📋 NOTEBOOK

1. **Identify** At the start of the documentary, what sounds do you hear as the presenter gives background information? What mental images do these sounds conjure up?

2. **Analyze** How does footage of the community of Saltaire help to convey the risk Titus Salt took by moving his factory and investing in living quarters for his workers?

3. **Analyze** What does the appearance of a narrator, as well as the use of his voice-over, contribute to the documentary?

4. **Compare** "Factory Reform" repeatedly shows illustrations in a notebook that depict life in Victorian factories. How are workers depicted compared to images of the wealthy factory owners?

5. **Summarize** According to the documentary, how did Salt's factory influence future factory owners?

RESEARCH

RESEARCH TIP
When choosing sources for your research, look for keywords and synonyms from the class video or text. Use an online dictionary to define unfamiliar words, especially if they make it challenging for you to understand a source.

"Factory Reform" portrays how Titus Salt demonstrated his social concerns, which led to great changes in factories and the lives of working families. The Industrial Revolution in Britain influenced an Industrial Revolution in America. Now that you're familiar with conditions in Victorian factories, research the history of conditions in American factories and the lives of American workers.

	VICTORIAN FACTORIES	AMERICAN FACTORIES
Conditions	Men in Bradford made less than fifty cents per day. Women and children earned half of that. Workers struggled with health and nutrition.	
Child labor	Young children were used because of their low salaries. Boys were even fired once they reached adulthood.	
Risks	Workers were forced to work in dark coal mines and around dangerous machinery. Many lost their eyesight, limbs, and/or their lives while working.	

Connect Recall the visual and sound elements in the documentary. If you were a director, how would you present examples of factory conditions? With a partner, write a description of visual and sound elements you would use to present the subject. You might choose to present your ideas in the form of a storyboard—a pictorial outline that shows a series of scenes.

CREATE AND PRESENT

Write a Short Story Depict a time you received support from someone you might call a benefactor. The short story may be based on a real event or from your imagination.

- ❏ Determine where and when the story takes place.
- ❏ Create events in order to establish the conflict you faced and follow through to a clear resolution. To ensure a solid beginning, middle, and end, use a story map to plan the details of the plot.
- ❏ Use vivid language to paint clear pictures in readers' or listeners' minds.
- ❏ Reread and edit your narrative. Add more details as needed.

Present Your Story Read your short story aloud to a small group. Before you present:

- ❏ Create simple sketches to illustrate your narrative.
- ❏ Change your voice to match the changing events of your story. For example, let your tone convey curiosity, uncertainty, or excitement.

 Go to the **Speaking and Listening Studio: Giving a Presentation** to learn more.

Go to the **Writing Studio: Writing Narratives** for more help.

RESPOND TO THE ESSENTIAL QUESTION

 ? What is a true benefactor?

Gather Information Review your notes on "Factory Reform." Then, add relevant information to your Response Log. As you determine which information to include, think about:

- • the purpose of the documentary
- • the use of visual and sound elements to influence viewers
- • the conditions endured by Victorian factory workers
- • the ways factory workers' lives were altered over time

ACADEMIC VOCABULARY

As you write and discuss what you learned from the documentary, be sure to use the Academic Vocabulary words. Check off each of the words that you use.

- ❏ **abandon**
- ❏ **confine**
- ❏ **conform**
- ❏ **depress**
- ❏ **reluctance**

THE LADY OF SHALOTT

Narrative Poem by **Alfred, Lord Tennyson**

? *ESSENTIAL QUESTION:*

How do you view the world?

QUICK START

Many legends and fairy tales depict a character who is confined to a place and shut off from the world. Imagine what it would be like to experience such isolation. How do you think it would affect you? What risks might you take to gain freedom and live among other people? Write a paragraph in response to these questions. Then, exchange paragraphs with a partner and discuss your thoughts.

ANALYZE ALLEGORY

An **allegory** is a story with two levels of meaning—a literal one and a symbolic one. In allegorical fiction and poetry, characters represent abstract qualities or ideas. Allegory is closely tied to symbolism. These forms of figurative language both use one thing to stand for another, and they allow writers to represent ideas in nontraditional ways. As in a fable or parable, the purpose of an allegory may be to convey truths about life, to teach religious or moral lessons, or to criticize social institutions.

Some critics of *The Lady of Shalott* argue that the poem is an allegory for the life of an artist, while others believe the poem represents the plight of women in Victorian society. As you read *The Lady of Shalott,* use a chart like this one to help you analyze symbolic elements that contribute to the poem's allegorical meaning.

SYMBOLIC ELEMENT	POSSIBLE MEANING	SUPPORTING DETAILS
The island of Shalott		
Camelot		
The loom and the web		
The mirror		
Sir Lancelot		
The boat ride		

GENRE ELEMENTS: NARRATIVE POETRY

- tells a story
- uses elements of fiction, such as character, setting, and plot
- is written in poetic form using lines and stanzas
- may be written with regular patterns of rhyme and meter, or in free verse without a regular structure

ANALYZE MOOD

Mood is the feeling or atmosphere that a writer creates for the reader. Some examples of words describing mood are *mysterious, somber*, and *joyful*. A poem's mood may change as a poem progresses. Elements that help create a poem's mood include diction, imagery, line length, stanza structure, and sound devices, such as repetition and rhyme.

Read these lines from the beginning of *The Lady of Shalott*:

> On either side the river lie
> Long fields of barley and of rye,
> That clothe the wold and meet the sky;
> And through the field the road runs by
>   To many-towered Camelot;

Each line in this passage contains four iambic feet, consisting of an unstressed syllable followed by a stressed syllable. The strong, regular pattern of this meter, the rhyme scheme, and the imagery of King Arthur's mythical realm of Camelot contribute to a tranquil and orderly mood early in the poem. As you read, think about how these elements combine to create that mood or other moods that arise throughout Tennyson's poem.

ANNOTATION MODEL

NOTICE & NOTE

As you read, note the use of vivid imagery and how this contributes to the overall mood of the poem. You can also mark up other places you find symbols or striking images. In the model you can see one reader's notes about *The Lady of Shalott*.

Willows <u>whiten</u>, aspens <u>quiver</u>,

Little breezes <u>dusk</u> and <u>shiver</u>

Through the <u>wave that runs forever</u>

By the island in the river

    Flowing down to Camelot.

Four <u>gray walls</u>, and four <u>gray towers</u>,

Overlook a (space of flowers,)

And the <u>silent isle</u> imbowers

    The Lady of Shalott.

Word choices like <u>whiten</u>, <u>quiver</u>, <u>dusk</u>, and <u>shiver</u> give this stanza a mood of coldness and isolation.

The images of the trees and wind, a wave that runs forever, gray walls and towers, and a silent isle also contribute to the somber mood.

The phrase "space of flowers" adds a tiny element of hope.

BACKGROUND

Alfred, Lord Tennyson *(1809–1892) experienced misfortune early in life, but he became the most celebrated poet of his age. He left Cambridge University without completing his degree due to lack of funds, and soon afterward the death of his closest friend devastated him. Although he struggled financially and professionally for many years, his fortunes turned in 1850 when Queen Victoria named him poet laureate. Decades later, the rank of baron and title of "Lord" were bestowed upon him.* The Lady of Shalott, *an early work, was inspired by the legends of King Arthur.*

THE LADY OF SHALOTT

Narrative Poem by Alfred, Lord Tennyson

SETTING A PURPOSE

As you read, consider the situation in which the Lady of Shalott finds herself, and imagine what it would be like to see the world from her perspective.

Part I

On either side the river lie
Long fields of barley and of rye,
That clothe the wold and meet the sky;
And through the field the road runs by
5   To many-towered Camelot;
And up and down the people go,
Gazing where the lilies blow
Round an island there below,
    The island of Shalott.

Notice & Note

Use the side margins to notice and note signposts in the text.

ANALYZE MOOD

Annotate: Mark the words or phrases that establish the moods of the first and second stanzas.

Analyze: How does the mood change from the first to the second stanza?

3 wold: rolling plain.

7 blow: bloom.

© Houghton Mifflin Harcourt Publishing Company

10 Willows whiten, aspens quiver,
   Little breezes dusk and shiver
   Through the wave that runs forever
   By the island in the river
      Flowing down to Camelot.
15 Four gray walls, and four gray towers,
   Overlook a space of flowers,
   And the silent isle imbowers
      The Lady of Shalott.

   By the margin, willow-veiled,
20 Slide the heavy barges trailed
   By slow horses; and unhailed
   The shallop flitteth silken-sailed
      Skimming down to Camelot:
   But who hath seen her wave her hand?
25 Or at the casement seen her stand?
   Or is she known in all the land,
      The Lady of Shalott?

   Only reapers, reaping early
   In among the bearded barley,
30 Hear a song that echoes cheerly
   From the river winding clearly,
      Down to towered Camelot;
   And by the moon the reaper weary,
   Piling sheaves in uplands airy,
35 Listening, whispers "'Tis the fairy
      Lady of Shalott."

Part II

   There she weaves by night and day
   A magic web with colors gay.
   She has heard a whisper say,
40 A curse is on her if she stay
      To look down to Camelot.
   She knows not what the curse may be,
   And so she weaveth steadily,
   And little other care hath she,
45   The Lady of Shalott.

17 imbowers: encloses; surrounds.

ANALYZE ALLEGORY

Annotate: In lines 19–27, mark details that suggest the Lady of Shalott is invisible or unknown to the citizens of Camelot.

Interpret: How might these details relate to the allegorical meaning of the poem?

22 shallop (shăl´əp): a small open boat.

25 casement: a hinged window that opens outward.

And moving through a mirror clear
That hangs before her all the year,
Shadows of the world appear.
There she sees the highway near
50   Winding down to Camelot;
There the river eddy whirls,
And there the surly village churls,
And the red cloaks of market girls,
        Pass onward from Shalott.

55 Sometimes a troop of damsels glad,
An abbot on an ambling pad,
Sometimes a curly shepherd lad,
Or long-haired page in crimson clad,
        Goes by to towered Camelot;
60 And sometimes through the mirror blue
The knights come riding two and two:
She hath no loyal knight and true,
        The Lady of Shalott.

But in her web she still delights
65 To weave the mirror's magic sights,
For often through the silent nights
A funeral, with plumes and lights
        And music, went to Camelot;
Or when the moon was overhead,
70 Came two young lovers lately wed:
"I am half sick of shadows," said
        The Lady of Shalott.

Part III

A bowshot from her bower eaves,
He rode between the barley sheaves,
75 The sun came dazzling through the leaves,
And flamed upon the brazen greaves
        Of bold Sir Lancelot.
A red-cross knight forever kneeled
To a lady in his shield,
80 That sparkled on the yellow field,
        Beside remote Shalott.

46–48 Weavers often used mirrors while working from the back of a tapestry to view the tapestry's appearance, but this one is used to view the outside world.

52 surly village churls: rude members of the lower class in a village.

55 damsels: young, unmarried women.
56 abbot . . . pad: the head monk in a monastery on a slow-moving horse.
58 page: a boy in training to be a knight.

ANALYZE ALLEGORY
Annotate: In lines 64–72, mark the words or phrases that represent the isolation experienced by the main character.

Infer: What does the Lady's statement in line 71 suggest about her character?

73 bowshot: the distance an arrow can be shot; **bower** (bouʹər) **eaves:** the part of the roof that extends above the Lady's private room.

76 brazen greaves: metal armor for protecting the legs below the knees.

78–79 A red-cross . . . shield: His shield showed a knight wearing a red cross and kneeling to honor a lady. The red cross was a symbol worn by knights who had fought in the Crusades.

82 gemmy: studded with gems.

87 blazoned (blā´zənd) **baldric:** a decorated leather belt worn across the chest to support a sword or, as in this case, a bugle.

The gemmy bridle glittered free,
Like to some branch of stars we see
Hung in the golden Galaxy.
85 The bridle bells rang merrily
    As he rode down to Camelot;
And from his blazoned baldric slung
A mighty silver bugle hung,
And as he rode his armor rung,
90   Beside remote Shalott.

All in the blue unclouded weather
Thick-jeweled shone the saddle leather,
The helmet and the helmet-feather
Burned like one burning flame together,
95   As he rode down to Camelot;
As often through the purple night,
Below the starry clusters bright,
Some bearded meteor, trailing light,
    Moves over still Shalott.

100 His broad clear brow in sunlight glowed;
On burnished hooves his war horse trode;
From underneath his helmet flowed
His coal-black curls as on he rode,
    As he rode down to Camelot.
105 From the bank and from the river
He flashed into the crystal mirror,
"Tirra lirra," by the river
    Sang Sir Lancelot.

AGAIN AND AGAIN

Notice & Note: In lines 109–113, mark the repeated words.

Infer: What effect does this repetition have on the stanza?

She left the web, she left the loom,
110 She made three paces through the room,
She saw the water lily bloom,
She saw the helmet and the plume,
    She looked down to Camelot.
Out flew the web and floated wide;
115 The mirror cracked from side to side;
"The curse is come upon me," cried
    The Lady of Shalott.

Part IV

In the stormy east wind straining,
The pale yellow woods were waning,
120 The broad stream in his banks complaining,
Heavily the low sky raining
    Over towered Camelot;
Down she came and found a boat
Beneath a willow left afloat,
125 And round about the prow she wrote
    The Lady of Shalott.

And down the river's dim expanse
Like some bold seër in a trance,
Seeing all his own mischance—
130 With a glassy countenance
    Did she look to Camelot.

ANALYZE MOOD

Annotate: In lines 118–153, mark instances of imagery and sound devices.

Analyze: How do these images and sound devices help convey a tragic mood?

128 seër (sē´ər): someone who can see into the future; a prophet.

129 mischance: misfortune; bad luck.

The Lady of Shalott **621**

And at the closing of the day
She loosed the chain, and down she lay;
The broad stream bore her far away,
135   The Lady of Shalott.

Lying, robed in snowy white
That loosely flew to left and right—
The leaves upon her falling light—
Through the noises of the night
140   She floated down to Camelot;
And as the boat-head wound along
The willowy hills and fields among,
They heard her singing her last song,
    The Lady of Shalott.

ANALYZE ALLEGORY

Annotate: Mark details about the Lady of Shalott's death in lines 145–153.

Interpret: What idea might be suggested by her death?

150 ere (âr): before.

145 Heard a carol, mournful, holy,
Chanted loudly, chanted lowly,
Till her blood was frozen slowly,
And her eyes were darkened wholly,
    Turned to towered Camelot.
150 For ere she reached upon the tide
The first house by the waterside,
Singing in her song she died,
    The Lady of Shalott.

Under tower and balcony,
155 By garden wall and gallery,
A gleaming shape she floated by,
Dead-pale between the houses high,
    Silent into Camelot.
Out upon the wharfs they came,
160 Knight and burgher, lord and dame,
And round the prow they read her name,
    The Lady of Shalott.

160 burgher: a middle-class citizen of a town.

Who is this? and what is here?
And in the lighted palace near
165 Died the sound of royal cheer;
And they crossed themselves for fear,
    All the knights at Camelot:
But Lancelot mused a little space;
He said, "She has a lovely face;
170 God in his mercy lend her grace,
    The Lady of Shalott."

CHECK YOUR UNDERSTANDING

Answer these questions before moving on to the **Analyze the Text** section on the following page.

1 What will set off the Lady of Shalott's curse?

   A Viewing the world without looking through her mirror

   B Falling in love with a loyal knight

   C Asking forbidden questions

   D Taking a break from weaving her tapestry

2 Before Lancelot appears in her mirror, the Lady of Shalott —

   F feels tormented by her isolation

   G enjoys spending her time weaving

   H tries to undo the curse placed on her

   J yearns to live in Camelot

3 Lines 73–90 show that Lancelot's life is different from the Lady's by —

   A contrasting his boldness with her shyness

   B contrasting the way people react to him with the way they react to her

   C contrasting his freedom with her confinement

   D contrasting the appearance of his armor with the appearance of her gown

ANALYZE THE TEXT

Support your responses with evidence from the text. NOTEBOOK

1. **Infer** Why does the Lady of Shalott decide to look down upon Camelot?

2. **Draw Conclusions** Is it likely that the Lady's actions would be different if she knew more about the curse? Why or why not?

3. **Analyze** Identify the rhyme scheme of the poem. What effect does this rhyme scheme create?

4. **Interpret** Which images, objects, or ideas in *The Lady of Shalott* can be seen as symbols that suggest the poem is an allegory for the experience of women in Victorian society?

5. **Notice & Note** Consider the pattern of repetition of words in the fifth and ninth lines of each stanza. Also note that these lines are indented and usually shorter than the other lines in the stanza. How do these repeating patterns affect the mood of the poem?

RESEARCH

RESEARCH TIP
When researching the laws and rights of a group of people from history, it's best to use reliable sources that focus specifically on that time period. For this research, you should look for a resource that concentrates on the Victorian Era.

The Victorian Era was a difficult one for women. With a partner, research what life was like for women in England during this period (1832–1901).

QUESTION	ANSWER
How were women viewed during the Victorian Era?	
What rights did women have during this time period?	

Extend If, as some critics say, this poem is an allegory for women's life in the Victorian Era, what kinds of allegories could represent what life is like for women in today's society? With a partner, discuss stories, poems, songs, or other forms of media that could be considered allegories for women's lives in today's world.

CREATE AND RECITE

Illustrate a Narrative Poem Create an illustration—such as a painting, drawing, or collage—to depict the characters, setting, and/or events of the story told in *The Lady of Shalott*.

❑ Decide what kind of illustration you will create.

❑ Reread the poem and form mental images of the characters, setting, and events in the poem.

❑ Choose the subject of your illustration by determining which aspect(s) of the story you relate to most strongly.

❑ Present your illustration to the class. Explain what inspired you or why you chose to focus on the subject of your illustration.

Recite a Poem With a group, recite part of *The Lady of Shalott* aloud for the class.

❑ Work with your group to select at least one stanza of the poem.

❑ Discuss how you will recite the section of the poem you've chosen. Will you recite it together as a choral reading? Will each member of your group speak a different part? Will you sing it like a song?

❑ Memorize your lines and rehearse them a few times with your group.

❑ Present the poem to the class, using appropriate volume, enunciation, and gestures.

Go to **Giving a Presentation: Delivering Your Presentation** in the **Speaking and Listening Studio** to find out more.

RESPOND TO THE ESSENTIAL QUESTION

? How do you view the world?

Gather Information Review your annotations and notes on *The Lady of Shalott*. Then, add relevant information to your Response Log. As you determine which information to include, think about:

• how you view your world compared to how others might view your world

• how your mood can affect how you view the world around you

• how something such as an animal or the weather can represent something entirely unrelated

ACADEMIC VOCABULARY

As you write and discuss what you learned from the poem, be sure to use the Academic Vocabulary words. Check off each of the words that you use.

❑ **abandon**

❑ **confine**

❑ **confirm**

❑ **depress**

❑ **reluctance**

from
GREAT EXPECTATIONS

Novel by **Charles Dickens**

? ***ESSENTIAL QUESTION:***

What brings out cruelty in people?

QUICK START

Think about the most unusual or eccentric person you've ever met. What was this person like, and what made him or her unique? Use the chart to note interesting details about the person.

PERSON	CHARACTERISTICS

ANALYZE PLOT

Great Expectations is set in Victorian England following the Industrial Revolution. This social and historical context has an important influence on the **plot**—the series of events that occur in a literary work. During this time, class differences became more pronounced as the middle class grew wealthier while the poor sank deeper into poverty. In the excerpt you are about to read, the main character, Pip, visits the mansion of a wealthy old woman. He feels intimidated in her presence, especially when a girl who lives with her comments negatively about his lower-class background.

A **subplot** is an additional, or secondary, plot in a story. Subplots often concern the backstories of particular characters. The excerpt you will read has a subplot that relates to Miss Havisham, which is revealed in part by the old, yellowing wedding dress she wears. As you read, consider what this detail suggests about Miss Havisham's past and look for other ways the subplot is developed.

ANALYZE CHARACTERIZATION

Characterization is the way a writer creates and develops characters. There are four basic methods of characterization:

- The narrator may comment directly about a character, including discussion of the character's personality, social class, and economic status.

- The writer may describe the character's physical appearance.

- The writer may present the character's own thoughts, speech, and actions.

- The writer may develop the character through the thoughts, speech, and actions of other characters.

Characterization is often affected by the point of view from which a story is told, and it can have important connections to the theme, setting, and plot. As you read the excerpt from *Great Expectations*, pay attention to the way Dickens portrays the characters in the selection. Also consider how these characterizations relate to the theme, setting, and plot of the story.

GENRE ELEMENTS: NOVEL

- is a long work of fiction
- is usually written in the first- or third-person point of view
- can develop characters and conflict more thoroughly than a short story
- often develops complex plot structures, including subplots

CRITICAL VOCABULARY

self-possessed	**trinket**	**aversion**
gilded	**dogged**	**brooding**

To see how many Critical Vocabulary words you already know, use them to complete the sentences.

1. Eva's favorite _____ was the necklace her grandmother gave her.

2. Overcome with _____ determination to complete the race, Andre made it to the finish line in record time.

3. After getting a bad stomach virus, Sarah developed a(n) _____ to strawberries.

4. Although Mary was very upset by the decision made, she was quite _____ at the meeting.

5. The featured exhibit at the museum was a collection of _____ sculptures.

6. When he heard the trip was canceled, he stormed off and sat _____ in the corner of the room.

LANGUAGE CONVENTIONS

Imagery To describe a scene or convey a mood, Dickens uses **imagery**—words and phrases that create vivid sensory experiences for the reader. Dickens frequently creates this imagery through effective use of precise adjectives and other descriptive words. As you read this selection from *Great Expectations*, pay attention to how these descriptions appeal to your senses and help you better understand the characters and setting of the story.

ANNOTATION MODEL

NOTICE & NOTE

As you read, mark adjectives that help to characterize Miss Havisham, Mr. Pumblechook, and others in the novel. The model shows one reader's notes about how Estella is characterized.

> She <u>seemed much older than I</u>, of course, being a girl, and <u>beautiful</u> and <u>self-possessed</u>; and she was as <u>scornful of me</u> as if she had been one-and-twenty, and a queen.

These descriptions characterize Estella as someone who is both self-assured and a bit snobby.

BACKGROUND

Charles Dickens *(1812–1870) was born into a middle-class family in England. After his father went to prison, Dickens had to withdraw from school and work in a factory, an experience that deeply influenced his writing. Great Expectations is considered one of his finest works. The main character, Pip, is an orphan raised by his sister. In this excerpt, a relative named Mr. Pumblechook takes him to play at the house of Miss Havisham, a wealthy and eccentric old woman.*

from

GREAT EXPECTATIONS

Novel by Charles Dickens

SETTING A PURPOSE

As you read, allow yourself to visualize each of the scenes and characters as they are described. Consider how the author's characterization of the people in the story relates to the plot and theme of the selection.

1   Mr. Pumblechook and I breakfasted at eight o'clock in the parlor behind the shop, while the shopman took his mug of tea and hunch of bread-and-butter on a sack of peas in the front premises. I considered Mr. Pumblechook wretched company. Besides being possessed by my sister's idea that a mortifying and penitential character ought to be imparted to my diet—besides giving me as much crumb as possible in combination with as little butter, and putting such a quantity of warm water into my milk that it would have been more candid to have left the milk out altogether—his conversation consisted of nothing but arithmetic. On my politely bidding him Good morning, he said, pompously, "Seven times nine, boy?" And how should *I* be able to answer, dodged in that way, in a strange place, on an empty stomach! I was hungry, but before I had swallowed a morsel, he began a running sum that lasted all through the breakfast.

Notice & Note

Use the side margins to notice and note signposts in the text.

ANALYZE CHARACTERIZATION

Annotate: Mark details in paragraph 1 that reveal aspects of Mr. Pumblechook's character.

Analyze: Which methods of characterization does Dickens use to portray him?

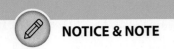
"Seven?" "And four?" "And eight?" "And six?" "And two?" "And ten?" And so on. And after each figure was disposed of, it was as much as I could do to get a bite or a sup, before the next came; while he sat at his ease guessing nothing, and eating bacon and hot roll, in (if I may be allowed the expression) a gorging and gormandising manner.

2   For such reasons I was very glad when ten o'clock came and we started for Miss Havisham's; though I was not at all at my ease regarding the manner in which I should acquit myself under that lady's roof. Within a quarter of an hour we came to Miss Havisham's house, which was of old brick, and dismal, and had a great many iron bars to it. Some of the windows had been walled up; of those that remained, all the lower were rustily barred. There was a courtyard in front, and that was barred; so, we had to wait, after ringing the bell, until some one should come to open it. While we waited at the gate, I peeped in (even then Mr. Pumblechook said, "And fourteen?" but I pretended not to hear him), and saw that at the side of the house there was a large brewery. No brewing was going on in it, and none seemed to have gone on for a long time.

3   A window was raised, and a clear voice demanded "What name?" To which my conductor replied, "Pumblechook." The voice returned, "Quite right," and the window was shut again, and a young lady came across the courtyard, with keys in her hand.

4   "This," said Mr. Pumblechook, "is Pip."

5   "This is Pip, is it?" returned the young lady, who was very pretty and seemed very proud; "come in, Pip."

6   Mr. Pumblechook was coming in also, when she stopped him with the gate.

7   "Oh!" she said. "Did you wish to see Miss Havisham?"

8   "If Miss Havisham wished to see me," returned Mr. Pumblechook, discomfited.

9   "Ah!" said the girl; "but you see she don't."

10   She said it so finally, and in such an undiscussible way, that Mr. Pumblechook, though in a condition of ruffled dignity, could not protest. But he eyed me severely—as if *I* had done anything to him!—and departed with the words reproachfully delivered: "Boy! Let your behavior here be a credit unto them which brought you up by hand!" I was not free from apprehension that he would come back to propound through the gate, "And sixteen?" But he didn't.

11   My young conductress locked the gate, and we went across the courtyard. It was paved and clean, but grass was growing in every crevice. The brewery buildings had a little lane of communication with it; and the wooden gates of that lane stood open, and all the brewery beyond stood open, away to the high enclosing wall; and all was empty and disused. The cold wind seemed to blow colder there, than outside the gate; and it made a shrill noise in howling in and out

LANGUAGE CONVENTIONS

Annotate: Mark Dickens's use of imagery to describe the courtyard and buildings in paragraph 11.

Analyze: What mood does this imagery help create?

© Houghton Mifflin Harcourt Publishing Company

at the open sides of the brewery, like the noise of wind in the rigging of a ship at sea.

12   She saw me looking at it, and she said, "You could drink without hurt all the strong beer that's brewed there now, boy."

13   "I should think I could, miss," said I, in a shy way.

14   "Better not try to brew beer there now, or it would turn out sour, boy, don't you think so?"

15   "It looks like it, miss."

16   "Not that anybody means to try," she added, "for that's all done with, and the place will stand as idle as it is, till it falls. As to strong beer, there's enough of it in the cellars already, to drown the Manor House."

17   "Is that the name of this house, miss?"

18   "One of its names, boy."

19   "It has more than one, then, miss?"

20   "One more. Its other name was Satis; which is Greek, or Latin, or Hebrew, or all three—or all one to me—for enough."

21   "Enough House!" said I: "that's a curious name, miss."

22   "Yes," she replied; "but it meant more than it said. It meant, when it was given, that whoever had this house, could want nothing else. They must have been easily satisfied in those days, I should think. But don't loiter, boy."

23   Though she called me "boy" so often, and with a carelessness that was far from complimentary, she was of about my own age. She seemed much older than I, of course, being a girl, and beautiful and **self-possessed**; and she was as scornful of me as if she had been one-and-twenty, and a queen.

24   We went into the house by a side door—the great front entrance had two chains across it outside—and the first thing I noticed was, that the passages were all dark, and that she had left a candle burning there. She took it up, and we went through more passages and up a staircase, and still it was all dark, and only the candle lighted us.

25   At last we came to the door of a room, and she said, "Go in."

26   I answered, more in shyness than politeness, "After you, miss,"

27   To this, she returned: "Don't be ridiculous, boy; I am not going in." And scornfully walked away, and—what was worse—took the candle with her.

28   This was very uncomfortable, and I was half afraid. However, the only thing to be done being to knock at the door, I knocked, and was told from within to enter. I entered, therefore, and found myself in a pretty large room, well lighted with wax candles. No glimpse of daylight was to be seen in it. It was a dressing-room, as I supposed from the furniture, though much of it was of forms and uses then quite unknown to me. But prominent in it was a draped table with a **gilded** looking-glass, and that I made out at first sight to be a fine lady's dressing-table.

ANALYZE CHARACTERIZATION

Annotate: Mark details in paragraphs 12–23 that characterize the girl.

Draw Conclusions: What does this passage suggest about her personality?

self-possessed
(sĕlf´pə-zĕst´) *adj.* having calm and self-assured command of one's faculties, feelings, and behavior.

gilded
(gĭl´dĭd) *adj.* covered with or having the appearance of being covered with a thin layer of gold.

29   Whether I should have made out this object so soon, if there had been no fine lady sitting at it, I cannot say. In an arm-chair, with an elbow resting on the table and her head leaning on that hand, sat the strangest lady I have ever seen, or shall ever see.

30   She was dressed in rich materials—satins, and lace, and silks—all of white. Her shoes were white. And she had a long white veil dependent from her hair, and she had bridal flowers in her hair, but her hair was white. Some bright jewels sparkled on her neck and on her hands, and some other jewels lay sparkling on the table. Dresses, less splendid than the dress she wore, and half-packed trunks, were scattered about. She had not quite finished dressing, for she had but one shoe on—the other was on the table near her hand—her veil was but half arranged, her watch and chain were not put on, and some lace for her bosom lay with those **trinkets**, and with her handkerchief, and gloves, and some flowers, and a Prayer-book, all confusedly heaped about the looking-glass.

31   It was not in the first few moments that I saw all these things, though I saw more of them in the first moments than might be supposed. But, I saw that everything within my view which ought to be white, had been white long ago, and had lost its luster and was faded and yellow. I saw that the bride within the bridal dress had withered like the dress, and like the flowers, and had no brightness left but the brightness of her sunken eyes. I saw that the dress had been put upon the rounded figure of a young woman, and that the figure upon which it now hung loose, had shrunk to skin and bone. Once, I had been taken to see some ghastly waxwork at the Fair, representing I know not what impossible personage lying in state. Once, I had been taken to one of our old marsh churches to see a skeleton in the ashes of a rich dress, that had been dug out of a vault under the church pavement. Now, waxwork and skeleton seemed to have dark eyes that moved and looked at me. I should have cried out, if I could.

32   "Who is it?" said the lady at the table.

33   "Pip, ma'am."

34   "Pip?"

35   "Mr. Pumblechook's boy, ma'am. Come—to play."

36   "Come nearer; let me look at you. Come close."

37   It was when I stood before her, avoiding her eyes, that I took note of the surrounding objects in detail, and saw that her watch had stopped at twenty minutes to nine, and that a clock in the room had stopped at twenty minutes to nine.

38   "Look at me," said Miss Havisham. " You are not afraid of a woman who has never seen the sun since you were born?"

39   I regret to state that I was not afraid of telling the enormous lie comprehended in the answer "No."

ANALYZE CHARACTERIZATION

Annotate: In paragraphs 30 and 31, mark repeated words used to describe Miss Havisham and her dress.

Analyze: What does Dickens emphasize through the use of repetition in this description?

trinket
(trĭng´kĭt) *n.* a small ornament, such as a piece of jewelry.

dogged
(dô′gĭd, dŏg′ĭd) *adj.* stubbornly persevering; tenacious.

40   "Do you know what I touch here?" she said, laying her hands, one upon the other, on her left side.

41   "Yes, ma'am." (It made me think of the young man.)

42   "What do I touch?"

43   "Your heart."

44   "Broken!"

45   She uttered the word with an eager look, and with strong emphasis, and with a weird smile that had a kind of boast in it. Afterwards, she kept her hands there for a little while, and slowly took them away as if they were heavy.

46   "I am tired," said Miss Havisham. "I want diversion, and I have done with men and women. Play."

47   I think it will be conceded by my most disputatious reader, that she could hardly have directed an unfortunate boy to do anything in the wide world more difficult to be done under the circumstances.

48   "I sometimes have sick fancies," she went on, "and I have a sick fancy that I want to see some play. There, there!" with an impatient movement of the fingers of her right hand; "play, play, play!"

49   For a moment, with the fear of my sister's working me before my eyes, I had a desperate idea of starting round the room in the assumed character of Mr. Pumblechook's chaise-cart. But, I felt myself so unequal to the performance that I gave it up, and stood looking at Miss Havisham in what I suppose she took for a **dogged** manner, inasmuch as she said, when we had taken a good look at each other:

50   "Are you sullen and obstinate?"

51   "No, ma'am, I am very sorry for you, and very sorry I can't play just now. If you complain of me I shall get into trouble with my sister, so I would do it if I could; but it's so new here, and so strange, and so fine—and melancholy—" I stopped, fearing I might say too much, or had already said it, and we took another look at each other.

52   Before she spoke again, she turned her eyes from me, and looked at the dress she wore, and at the dressing-table, and finally at herself in the looking-glass.

53   "So new to him," she muttered, "so old to me; so strange to him, so familiar to me; so melancholy to both of us! Call Estella."

54   As she was still looking at the reflection of herself, I thought she was still talking to herself, and kept quiet.

55   "Call Estella," she repeated, flashing a look at me. "You can do that. Call Estella. At the door."

56   To stand in the dark in a mysterious passage of an unknown house, bawling Estella to a scornful young lady neither visible nor responsive, and feeling it a dreadful liberty so to roar out her name, was almost as bad as playing to order. But, she answered at last, and her light came along the dark passage like a star.

57   Miss Havisham beckoned her to come close, and took up a jewel from the table, and tried its effect upon her fair young bosom and

against her pretty brown hair. "Your own, one day, my dear, and you will use it well. Let me see you play cards with this boy."

58   "With this boy! Why, he is a common laboring-boy!"

59   I thought I overheard Miss Havisham answer—only it seemed so unlikely—"Well? You can break his heart."

60   "What do you play, boy?" asked Estella of myself, with the greatest disdain.

61   "Nothing but beggar my neighbor, Miss."

62   "Beggar him," said Miss Havisham to Estella. So we sat down to cards.

63   It was then I began to understand that everything in the room had stopped, like the watch and the clock, a long time ago. I noticed that Miss Havisham put down the jewel exactly on the spot from which she had taken it up. As Estella dealt the cards, I glanced at the dressing-table again, and saw that the shoe upon it, once white, now yellow, had never been worn. I glanced down at the foot from which the shoe was absent, and saw that the silk stocking on it, once white, now yellow, had been trodden ragged. Without this arrest of everything, this standing still of all the pale decayed objects, not even the withered bridal dress on the collapsed form could have looked so like grave-clothes, or the long veil so like a shroud.

64   So she sat, corpse-like, as we played at cards; the frillings and trimmings on her bridal dress, looking like earthy paper. I knew nothing then of the discoveries that are occasionally made of bodies buried in ancient times, which fall to powder in the moment of being distinctly seen; but, I have often thought since, that she must have looked as if the admission of the natural light of day would have struck her to dust.

65   "He calls the knaves, Jacks, this boy!" said Estella with disdain, before our first game was out. "And what coarse hands he has! And what thick boots!"

66   I had never thought of being ashamed of my hands before; but I began to consider them a very indifferent pair. Her contempt for me was so strong, that it became infectious, and I caught it.

67   She won the game, and I dealt. I misdealt, as was only natural, when I knew she was lying in wait for me to do wrong; and she denounced me for a stupid, clumsy laboring-boy.

68   "You say nothing of her," remarked Miss Havisham to me, as she looked on. "She says many hard things of you, yet you say nothing of her. What do you think of her?"

69   "I don't like to say," I stammered.

70   "Tell me in my ear," said Miss Havisham, bending down.

71   "I think she is very proud," I replied, in a whisper.

72   "Anything else?"

73   "I think she is very pretty."

74   "Anything else?"

AHA MOMENT

Notice & Note: Underline the sentence in paragraph 63 that expresses Pip's realization.

Draw Conclusions: What does this realization help us understand about the subplot involving Miss Havisham?

aversion

(ə-vûr´zhən) *n.* a fixed, intense dislike; repugnance.

ANALYZE PLOT

Annotate: Reread paragraphs 68–80. Mark Miss Havisham's questions to Pip.

Infer: Why do you think Miss Havisham wants to know how Pip feels about Estella?

brooding

(brōō´dĭng) *adj.* thinking about something moodily.

75   "I think she is very insulting." (She was looking at me then with a look of supreme **aversion**.)

76   "Anything else?"

77   "I think I should like to go home."

78   "And never see her again, though she is so pretty?"

79   "I am not sure that I shouldn't like to see her again, but I should like to go home now."

80   "You shall go soon," said Miss Havisham aloud. "Play the game out."

81   Saving for the one weird smile at first, I should have felt almost sure that Miss Havisham's face could not smile. It had dropped into a watchful and **brooding** expression—most likely when all the things about her had become transfixed— and it looked as if nothing could ever lift it up again. Her chest had dropped, so that she stooped; and her voice had dropped, so that she spoke low, and with a dead lull upon her; altogether, she had the appearance of having dropped, body and soul, within and without, under the weight of a crushing blow.

82   I played the game to an end with Estella, and she beggared me. She threw the cards down on the table when she had won them all, as if she despised them for having been won of me.

83   "When shall I have you here again?" said Miss Havisham. "Let me think."

84   I was beginning to remind her that today was Wednesday, when she checked me with her former impatient movement of the fingers of her right hand.

85   "There, there! I know nothing of days of the week; I know nothing of weeks of the year. Come again after six days. You hear?"

86   "Yes, ma'am."

87   "Estella, take him down. Let him have something to eat, and let him roam and look about him while he eats. Go, Pip."

88   I followed the candle down, as I had followed the candle up, and she stood it in the place where we had found it. Until she opened the side entrance, I had fancied, without thinking about it, that it must necessarily be nighttime. The rush of the daylight quite confounded me, and made me feel as if I had been in the candlelight of the strange room many hours.

89   "You are to wait here, you boy," said Estella; and disappeared and closed the door.

CHECK YOUR UNDERSTANDING

Answer these questions before moving on to the **Analyze the Text** section on the following page.

1 What surprises Mr. Pumblechook when he arrives with Pip at Miss Havisham's house?

   A Pip shows poor manners when Estella greets them.

   B Estella doesn't want him to come inside the house.

   C Miss Havisham doesn't come down to say hello.

   D Estella is not how he remembers her.

2 What does Pip find most strange about Miss Havisham when he meets her?

   F She is very thin.

   G She is only wearing one shoe.

   H She is dressed in a wedding gown.

   J She doesn't seem to recognize him.

3 Why is Estella scornful toward Pip?

   A He is unable to play by himself.

   B He stares too much at Miss Havisham.

   C He is very shy and quiet.

   D He comes from a lower-class family.

ANALYZE THE TEXT

Support your responses with evidence from the text. NOTEBOOK

1. **Interpret** In paragraph 10, Mr. Pumblechook says to Pip, "Let your behavior here be a credit unto them which brought you up by hand!" What does this remark suggest about why Pip's family agreed to send him to visit Miss Havisham?

2. **Evaluate** What method of characterization does Dickens rely on most in his characterization of Miss Havisham? Is his use of this method effective? Explain why or why not.

3. **Draw Conclusions** Dickens introduces the subplot involving Miss Havisham's past through clues such as the yellowed wedding dress and her comment about her broken heart. How might this subplot relate to the events of this excerpt? Cite details in your response.

4. **Predict** Miss Havisham tells Pip to return in six days. What do you predict will happen on his future visits to her house?

5. **Notice & Note** In paragraph 66, Pip says that for the first time he feels ashamed of his hands. What has his experience in this wealthy household made him realize about himself?

RESEARCH

RESEARCH TIP
As you research, pay attention whenever you notice that sources disagree on certain points. Try to find out why they disagree and which source, if any, has the most accurate information.

Class differences are an important theme of *Great Expectations*. Conduct research on the class structure of Victorian England and note how this aligns with the excerpt you read from the novel. Use a chart like the one below to make your notes.

CLASS IN VICTORIAN ENGLAND	EXAMPLES FROM THE TEXT

Extend Research some of Charles Dickens's other books, paying special attention to themes that are commonly explored in his writing. How might this information help you better understand the selection from *Great Expectations*?

CREATE AND DISCUSS

Write a Story Write a short story about the most unusual person you've ever met. Use characterization to help your readers understand why this person is unusual.

❏ Describe what he or she looks like.

❏ Describe several of the person's most prominent personality traits.

❏ Use dialogue to bring the characters in your story to life.

❏ Include imagery to help your readers imagine the people, places, and events in the story.

Discuss People are often considered unusual when they behave in ways that fall outside of social norms or expectations. In a small group, discuss what kinds of behavior fall outside of the social norms of today's society. As you discuss, think about how Miss Havisham's behavior would be considered outside of the social norms of her day.

❏ Think about fashions that are accepted as normal in current society.

❏ Discuss what defines "normal" behavior. Make sure each member of your group has a chance to share his or her thoughts.

❏ Consider how the definition of "normal" changes over time, and discuss both the positive and negative results of living a life that others might believe to be strange or unique.

 Go to **Writing Narratives** in the **Writing Studio** for more help writing a short story.

Go to **Participating in Collaborative Discussions** in the **Speaking and Listening Studio** for more help.

RESPOND TO THE ESSENTIAL QUESTION

? What brings out cruelty in people?

Gather Information Review your annotations and notes on *Great Expectations.* Then, add relevant information to your Response Log. As you determine which information to include, think about:

• a person's history and how this affects their decisions

• the times you have been cruel or been tempted to be cruel and what motivated you

• the times when someone has been cruel to you and what might have motivated that person

ACADEMIC VOCABULARY

As you write and discuss what you learned from *Great Expectations,* be sure to use the Academic Vocabulary words. Check off each of the words that you use.

❏ **abandon**

❏ **confine**

❏ **conform**

❏ **depress**

❏ **reluctance**

WORD BANK
self-possessed
gilded
trinket
dogged
aversion
brooding

Go to the **Vocabulary Studio: Using Context Clues** for more on idioms.

CRITICAL VOCABULARY

Practice and Apply Select the word that correctly finishes the sentence.

1. At Laura's church, the ceilings were _____.
   a. gilded   **b.** dogged

2. James found a(n) _____ at the antique store.
   a. aversion   **b.** trinket

3. When Janine met Eric, he was _____ over a book in the library.
   a. self-possessed   **b.** brooding

VOCABULARY STRATEGY:
Idioms

An **idiom** is a common figure of speech whose meaning is different from the literal meaning of its words. For example, the phrase "raining cats and dogs" means that it is raining heavily, not that animals are falling from the sky. A **specialized dictionary** may list common idioms and explain their origins.

Practice and Apply Complete each sentence with the idiom in the diagram that makes the most sense. Use context and your knowledge of dog behavior to help you choose the correct idiom. When you are finished, try to explain the meaning of each idiom you used.

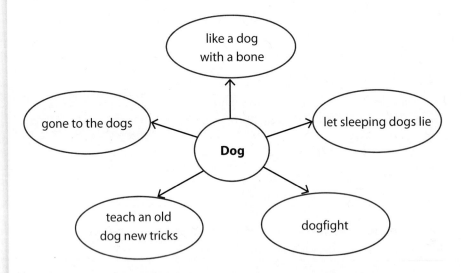

1. The possessive child clutched the toy _____.

2. I tried showing my grandfather a different way to fold his shirts, but you can't _____.

3. The combat flyer had a _____ with an enemy pilot.

4. The service wasn't great here last time, but now it has really _____.

5. Stop raking up the past; it's better to _____.

LANGUAGE CONVENTIONS:
Imagery

Dickens carefully chose precise adjectives and other descriptive words and phrases to create vivid **imagery** in his stories. The majority of imagery in literature is visual, but imagery may also appeal to the readers' senses of smell, hearing, taste, and touch. In addition, images may re-create sensations of heat, movement, or bodily tension. Often the most effective imagery appeals to more than one sense simultaneously. The chart shows several kinds of imagery and provides examples.

Go to **The Language of Narrative** in the **Writing Studio** for more on imagery.

KIND OF IMAGERY	SENSE TO WHICH IT APPEALS	EXAMPLE
Visual	Sight	faded, yellow clothes
Olfactory	Smell	a musty chamber
Auditory	Hearing	a shrill howling of the wind
Gustatory	Taste	sour milk
Tactile	Touch	coarse hands

Practice and Apply Read each of the following lines from *Great Expectations*. Identify the adjectives and verbs in each sentence that create imagery, and then write your own sentence using similar elements to appeal to the senses.

1. **It was paved and clean, but grass was growing in every crevice.** (paragraph 11)

2. **I entered, therefore, and found myself in a pretty large room, well lighted with wax candles.** (paragraph 28)

3. **I glanced down at the foot from which the shoe was absent, and saw that the silk stocking on it, once white, now yellow, had been trodden ragged.** (paragraph 63)

© Houghton Mifflin Harcourt Publishing Company

THE VICTORIANS HAD THE SAME CONCERNS ABOUT TECHNOLOGY AS WE DO

Essay by **Melissa Dickson**

? **ESSENTIAL QUESTION:**

Which invention has had the greatest impact on your life?

QUICK START

Think about and write down the number of times per day that you use technology (e.g., smartphone, social media, Internet, mobile apps, tablets). Imagine a day without these tools. How would you describe that day? List the descriptions in your notebook and share with a partner.

ANALYZE COMPARE AND CONTRAST ESSAY

A **thesis** is an expression of the main idea or purpose of an essay. In this essay, the thesis is articulated in the title. To convince readers to accept this thesis, Melissa Dickson structures her essay as a **point-by-point comparison** of the similarities between Victorian and contemporary concerns about technology. She compares both historical periods one point at a time, instead of discussing the Victorian period first and then the contemporary period. As you read, use a chart like the one below to keep track of the main points presented and Dickson's supporting details related to both the Victorian and current perspectives on this issue.

POINT #1	POINT #2
Victorian:	Victorian:
Current:	Current:

Evaluate the essay's organizational pattern and consider whether this structure effectively serves the author's intended purpose.

EVALUATE MULTIMODAL TEXTS

A **multimodal text** strategically employs two or more modes of communication—words and visuals, for instance—to help the reader construct meaning about the content. Graphic features—such as images, charts, and maps—can play an important role in communicating an author's meaning.

Melissa Dickson reproduces two Victorian Era images in her essay, commenting directly on one of them. As you read, think about how effectively Dickson uses these images to support her ideas.

GENRE ELEMENTS: ESSAY

- has an introduction that includes the broader subject as well as a specific topic, hooks the audience, and briefly describes how the topic will be developed

- contains a thesis statement that offers some original insight on the topic

- contains well-developed body paragraphs, each with a main idea related to the writer's thesis statement or position, and tangible evidence that supports those ideas

- has a conclusion that often neatly summarizes the topic and leaves the audience with something to think about

CRITICAL VOCABULARY

forebear	pervasive	sea change	immersion
underpin	cacophony	posit	Luddite

To see how many Critical Vocabulary words you already know, use them to complete the sentences.

1. Mr. Keller's _____ position on the use of online platforms in the classroom conflicted with the school's plan to engage students by offering complete _____ in new technology.

2. Amid the _____ of fireworks and the cheering crowd, he thought of his _____ who had fought for his country's independence long ago.

3. Some researchers believe a(n) _____ is taking place in the minds of young people because they have allowed social media to have a(n) _____ influence on their ideas and behaviors.

4. Ample moisture and nutrients, the scientists _____, will _____ the bacteria's ability to multiply quickly.

LANGUAGE CONVENTIONS

Sentence Structure Writers use a variety of sentence structures to express ideas clearly. Simple sentences have one main clause, while other structures include more than one clause. These clauses are connected by commas and conjunctions or by semicolons. As you read, take note of the different kinds of sentences the author uses to convey her ideas.

ANNOTATION MODEL   **NOTICE & NOTE**

As you read, notice the parallels between the use of, and attitudes toward, technology in Victorian society and today's culture. Look for details that highlight similarities and differences between the two. In the model, you can see one reader's notes about the text.

Many of us struggle with <u>the bombardment of information</u> we receive and experience anxiety as a result of new media, which we feel <u>threaten our relationships and "usual" modes of human interaction.</u>

Though the technologies may change, these fears actually have a very long history: <u>more than a century ago our forebears had the same concerns.</u>

These details show that people in both Victorian society and today's culture are concerned with how distracting technology can be and the impact it has on relationships.

BACKGROUND

Melissa Dickson *completed her PhD at King's College in London in 2013. In her doctoral thesis, she wrote about the tales of the* Arabian Nights, *exploring how these Middle Eastern folktales influenced British drama, fiction, poetry, travel writing, and children's literature. "The Victorians Had the Same Concerns About Technology as We Do" grew out of her involvement in a project called "Diseases of Modern Life," which investigates 19th-century cultural, literary, and medical understandings of stress, overwork, and other disorders.*

THE VICTORIANS HAD THE SAME CONCERNS ABOUT TECHNOLOGY AS WE DO

Essay by Melissa Dickson

SETTING A PURPOSE

As you read, make note of the author's thesis and the supporting details she uses to develop her main ideas.

1   We live, we are so often told, in an information age. It is an era obsessed with space, time and speed, in which social media inculcates[1] virtual lives that run parallel to our "real" lives and in which communications technologies collapse distances around the globe. Many of us struggle with the bombardment of information we receive and experience anxiety as a result of new media, which we feel threaten our relationships and "usual" modes of human interaction.

2   Though the technologies may change, these fears actually have a very long history: more than a century ago our **forebears** had the same concerns. Literary, medical and cultural responses in the Victorian age to the perceived problems of stress and overwork anticipate many of the preoccupations of our own era to an extent that is perhaps surprising.

---

[1] **inculcate:** to impress (something) upon the mind of another by frequent instruction or repetition; instill.

© Houghton Mifflin Harcourt Publishing Company • Image Credits: © oneinchpunch/Shutterstock

Notice & Note

Use the side margins to notice and note signposts in the text.

ANALYZE COMPARE AND CONTRAST ESSAY

Annotate: Mark details in paragraph 2 about Victorian issues that also concern people today.

Connect: What are some recent complaints about the harmful effects of new technology that you have heard about?

forebear
(fôr´bâr) *n.* a person from whom one is descended; an ancestor.

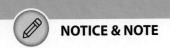

3   This parallel is well illustrated by the following 1906 cartoon from *Punch*, a satirical British weekly magazine:

FORECASTS FOR 1907.

IV.—DEVELOPMENT OF WIRELESS TELEGRAPHY.   SCENE IN HYDE PARK.
[These two figures are not communicating with one another.   The lady is receiving an amatory message, and the gentleman some racing results.]

Worrying trends, 1906.

© Houghton Mifflin Harcourt Publishing Company • Image Credits: © Punch Limited

EVALUATE MULTIMODAL TEXTS

Annotate: Mark details in paragraphs 4 and 5 that support the idea presented in the cartoon.

Analyze: Which details in the cartoon support the author's thesis?

underpin
(ŭn-dər-pĭn´) *tr.v.* to give support or substance to.

4   The caption reads: "These two figures are not communicating with one another. The lady receives an amatory[2] message, and the gentleman some racing results." The development of the "wireless telegraph" is portrayed as an overwhelmingly isolating technology.

5   Replace these strange contraptions with smartphones, and we are reminded of numerous contemporary complaints regarding the stunted social and emotional development of young people, who no longer hang out in person, but in virtual environments, often at great physical distance. Different technology, same statement. And it's **underpinned** by the same anxiety that "real" human interaction is increasingly under threat from technological innovations that we have, consciously or unconsciously, assimilated into daily life. By using such devices, so the popular paranoia would have it, we are somehow damaging ourselves.

Cacophony of voices

6 The 19th century witnessed the rapid expansion of the printing industry. New techniques and mass publishing formats gave rise to a far more **pervasive** periodical press, reaching a wider readership

pervasive
(pər-vā´sĭv,-zĭv) *adj.* having the quality or tendency to pervade or permeate.

---
[2] **amatory:** of, relating to, or expressive of love, especially romantic love.

than ever before. Many celebrated the possibility of instant news and greater communication. But concerns were raised about the overwhelmed middle-class reader who, it was thought, lacked the discernment to judge the new mass of information critically, and so read everything in a superficial, erratic manner.

7   The philosopher and essayist Thomas Carlyle, for example, lamented the new lack of direct contact with society and nature caused by the intervention of machinery in every aspect of life. Print publications were fast becoming the principal medium of public debate and influence, and they were shaping and, in Carlyle's view, distorting human learning and communications.

© Houghton Mifflin Harcourt Publishing Company • Image Credits: © Photo 12/Alamy

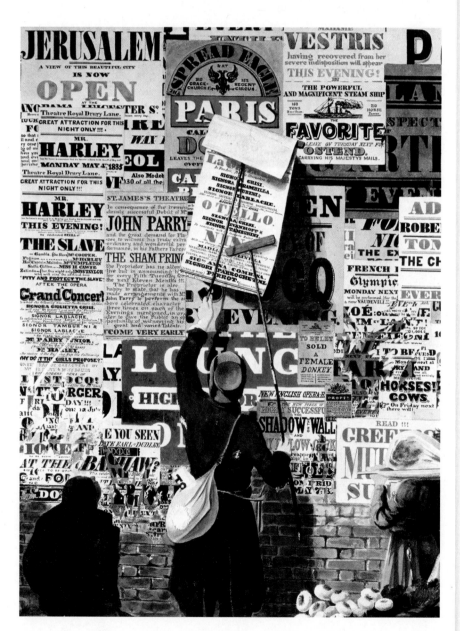

John Orlando Parry, *A London Street Scene*, 1835. © Alfred Dunhill Collection

EVALUATE MULTIMODAL TEXTS

Annotate: Mark details in paragraphs 7 and 8 that are expressed visually in the illustration called *A London Street Scene*.

Analyze: What is the significance of this illustration?

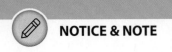
QUOTED WORDS

Notice & Note: Mark the quoted words in paragraph 8.

Evaluate: The author could have paraphrased John Stuart Mill's ideas, or restated the ideas in her own words. What is the effect of including Mill's exact words?

ANALYZE COMPARE AND CONTRAST ESSAY

Annotate: Mark the concern expressed in paragraph 11 about how technology changes the way we read.

Connect: How does this concern relate to a Victorian concern about technology?

8   The philosopher and economist John Stuart Mill heartily agreed, expressing his fears in an essay entitled "Civilisation". He thought that the **cacophony** of voices supposedly overwhelming the general public was creating:

> *A state of society where any voice, not pitched in an exaggerated key, is lost in the hubbub. Success in so crowded a field depends not upon what a person is, but upon what he seems: mere marketable qualities become the object instead of substantial ones, and a man's capital and labor are expended less in doing anything than in persuading other people that he has done it. Our own age has seen this evil brought to its consummation.*

9   Individual authors and writers were becoming disempowered, lost in a glutted marketplace of ideas, opinions, adverts and quacks.

Old complaints

10 The parallels with the concerns of our own society are striking. Arguments along not at all dissimilar lines have been advanced against contemporary means of acquiring information, such as Twitter, Facebook, and our constant access to the internet in general.

11 In his 2008 article, "Is Google Making Us Stupid?", journalist Nicolas Carr speculated that "we may well be in the midst of a **sea change** in the way we read and think". Reading online, he **posits**, discourages long and thoughtful **immersion** in texts in favor of a form of skipping, scanning and digressing via hyperlinks that will ultimately diminish our capacity for concentration and contemplation.

12 Writers, too, have shared Carr's anxieties. Philip Roth and Will Self, for example, have both prophesied these trends as contributing to the death of the novel, arguing that people are increasingly unused to and ill-equipped to engage with its characteristically long, linear form.

13 Of course, all old technologies were once new. People were at one point genuinely concerned about things we take for granted as perfectly harmless now. In the later decades of the 19th century it was thought that the telephone would induce deafness and that sulphurous vapors were asphyxiating passengers on the London Underground. These then-new advancements were replacing older still technologies that had themselves occasioned similar anxieties on their introduction. Plato, as his oral culture began to transition to a literary one, was gravely worried that writing itself would erode the memory.

14　While we cannot draw too strict a line of comparison between 19th-century attitudes to such technologies as the telegraph, train, telephone, and newspaper and our own responses as a culture to the advent of the internet and the mobile phone, there are parallels that almost argue against the **Luddite** position. As dramatically as technology changes, we, at least in the way we regard it, remain surprisingly unchanged.

LANGUAGE CONVENTIONS

Annotate: Mark how the clauses of sentences in paragraph 14 are joined.

Evaluate: How do these complex sentences contribute to the author's style and tone?

Luddite
(lŭd´ĭt) *n.* one who opposes technical or technological change.

CHECK YOUR UNDERSTANDING

Answer these questions before moving on to the **Analyze the Text** section on the following page.

1 The role of the graphic features in the essay is to —

　A Emphasize the ideas expressed by the author

　B Illustrate how distracted people can be

　C Show how pervasive technology is today

　D Suggest that technology has always been in the news

2 Based on the details in the essay, the 21st century is often referred to as the Information Age because people —

　F Always share information

　G Are continually distracted by new information

　H Have access to overwhelming amounts of information

　J Are unsure which information is accurate

3 The author refers to Plato in paragraph 13 to —

　A Suggest that he believed technology should be banned

　B Show that he had concerns about technology

　C Dismiss the opinions of those who fear technology

　D Contrast ancient ideas about technology with current ones

ANALYZE THE TEXT

Support your responses with evidence from the text. ☷ NOTEBOOK

1. **Infer** Reread paragraph 1. Does Dickson agree with the contemporary concerns she summarizes here, or does she seem skeptical of them? Cite details from anywhere in the essay to support your response.

2. **Evaluate** Is point-by-point comparison an effective format for the essay, or should Dickson have discussed the Victorian elements first and then discussed contemporary elements? Explain your response.

3. **Evaluate** Do the images Dickson chose provide good support for her essay? Why or why not?

4. **Critique** Reread paragraph 14. Does Dickson's comparison of Victorian and contemporary fears offer a convincing reason not to worry about current technological changes? Explain your opinion.

5. **Notice & Note** How does the quotation from Nicholas Carr in paragraph 11 support the author's ideas?

RESEARCH

RESEARCH TIP

The four main ways to conduct an online search for an editorial or news article are searching by keywords, subject, title, and author. A keyword search retrieves the most results because it searches for the word(s) throughout the entire catalog or database. A subject search is more focused because it looks for the word in a specific field. If you know the name of an important author or the title of an article in your area of interest, you can search specifically for them.

Go online and find editorials and other arguments on the topic of how teenagers are affected by using smartphones and social media. Analyze how authors reach similar and different conclusions on this topic, and list your findings in the chart below.

AUTHOR'S NAME	TITLE OF WORK	AUTHOR'S POSITION

Connect Think about how social media and other digital tools impact your life. Create a list of pros and cons associated with your access to technology. Share your lists with a partner.

CREATE AND DISCUSS

Write an Op-Ed Analyze the different authors' perspectives and ideas from the research you previously conducted. Then, write a brief opinion editorial that conveys your position on the topic of the impact social media and smartphones have on teenagers.

❏ Identify a clear thesis statement. What is your position on the topic?

❏ Who is your audience? Will your reader understand your argument?

❏ Is your argument organized in a way that effectively engages the reader?

❏ What evidence and details have you included to support your ideas?

Analyze and Discuss Your Ideas Find a partner and take turns reading your opinion editorials to each other. Analyze each other's conclusions and discuss whether or not you agree with each other's positions.

❏ Does your partner have a compelling argument?

❏ What evidence can you point to in your partner's writing that supports his or her thesis?

❏ Are your partner's introduction and conclusion clear and effective?

 Go to **Writing Arguments** in the **Writing Studio** for more help with writing an op-ed.

Go to **Participating in Collaborative Discussions** in the **Speaking and Listening Studio** for more help.

RESPOND TO THE ESSENTIAL QUESTION

 ? Which invention has had the greatest impact on your life?

Gather Information Review your annotations and notes on the essay. Then, add relevant information to your Response Log. As you determine which information to include, think about:

- how technology has impacted your life
- how often you access social media or your smartphone
- how your life would be different if certain technological advances had not been made

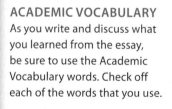

ACADEMIC VOCABULARY

As you write and discuss what you learned from the essay, be sure to use the Academic Vocabulary words. Check off each of the words that you use.

❏ **abandon**

❏ **confine**

❏ **conform**

❏ **depress**

❏ **reluctance**

WORD BANK
forebear
underpin
pervasive
cacophony
sea change
posit
immersion
Luddite

Go to **Synonyms and Antonyms** in the **Vocabulary Studio** for more.

CRITICAL VOCABULARY

Practice and Apply Fill in the blanks with the correct words.

1. Micah's concentration was often interrupted by a(n) _____ of voices and laughter coming from downstairs.

2. Brenda considered her grandfather a(n) _____; her _____ always complained about technology.

3. Your lack of studying is likely to _____ poor scores in math class.

4. The author _____ that the _____ use of social media would ultimately cause people to feel less connected to others.

5. Some people believe video gaming will go through a(n) _____ because we will soon be able to create total _____ in virtual reality environments.

VOCABULARY STRATEGY:
Synonyms and Antonyms

Reference tools help writers understand the precise meaning of words so they can use them correctly. The thesaurus, for example, is used to find **synonyms,** or words with similar meaning, and **antonyms,** words that have opposite meaning. Take a look at this example of a thesaurus entry for the Critical Vocabulary word *pervasive*.

> **pervasive** *adjective*
>   **synonyms:** *prevalent, permeating, extensive, ubiquitous*
>   **antonyms:** *limited, narrow, restricted*

Practice and Apply For each Critical Vocabulary word, follow these steps:

1. Look up each word in a print or digital thesaurus, identify the synonyms appropriate to the meaning of each term as it is used in the selection.

2. Write a sample sentence using each word.

3. In each sentence, replace the vocabulary word with one of your synonyms. Make sure that the sentences make sense by having a partner check your work.

LANGUAGE CONVENTIONS:
Sentence Structure

Good writers use a variety of sentence structures to avoid monotony and to effectively articulate their ideas. The simplest structure has one **clause,** a group of words that contains a subject and a verb. More complex sentence structures include more than one clause. Study the examples in the chart.

> Go to the **Grammar Studio** for more on sentence structure.

SENTENCE STRUCTURE	EXAMPLE
A **simple sentence** has one independent clause and no subordinate clauses.	We live in the Information Age.
A **compound sentence** has two or more independent clauses joined by a comma and a coordinating conjunction, such as *and, or,* or *but.*	People love using social media, but some worry about how it will affect our relationships in the long run.
A **complex sentence** has an independent clause and one or more subordinate clauses. The subordinate clause begins with a subordinating conjunction, such as *when, as, after, because,* or *while.*	After comparing the concerns people had in the 19th century to those of people in the present day, the author concluded that humans will always be fearful of technology.
A **compound-complex sentence** has two or more independent clauses and at least one subordinate clause.	Teenagers are constantly bombarded by information, but they understand the need to think critically when it comes to online sources.

Notice how the conjunctions in the example sentences connect the ideas in the clauses. Without the conjunctions, each sentence would be a **run-on,** or multiple sentences written as if they were one. The writer's meaning would also be less clear without conjunctions.

Run-on example: Teenagers are constantly bombarded by information they understand the need to think critically it comes to online sources.

Practice and Apply Write a paragraph about an invention you believe you cannot live without. Then, go back and review the paragraph, making sure to scan for simple sentences and repeated subjects or verbs in different sentences. Combine these sentences to form complex sentences by compounding verbs and using subordinate clauses to show the relationships among your ideas.

POEM

DOVER BEACH

by **Matthew Arnold**

pages 657–658

COMPARE THEMES

As you read, notice how the speakers in these poems use observations of nature as a springboard to discussing their feelings about the times they live in. Think about how the themes of these poems relate to each other. After you read both poems, you will collaborate with a small group on a final product.

 ESSENTIAL QUESTION:

How do you view the world?

POEM

THE DARKLING THRUSH

by **Thomas Hardy**

pages 660–661

QUICK START

Our personal perspectives have a strong influence on how we react to things. Identify three important issues that affect your community, the country, or the world. Then, work with a partner to describe the different ways an optimist and a pessimist might view these issues. Use this chart to record your ideas.

OPTIMISTIC VIEW	PESSIMISTIC VIEW

ANALYZE EXTENDED METAPHORS

Like any metaphor, an **extended metaphor** is a comparison between two essentially unlike things that nevertheless have something in common. In an extended metaphor, however, the figurative comparison is made at length and in various ways throughout a stanza, a paragraph, or an entire literary work. An extended metaphor is similar to a metaphysical conceit, but the comparison is not as surprising.

Both of the poems you will read in this lesson contain extended metaphors. In "Dover Beach," for example, Matthew Arnold develops a metaphor comparing the sea to traditional religious faith. The poet first offers some specific observations about the sea, then connects these details to his ideas about faith.

As you read each poem, consider how the extended metaphor helps to convey a theme about the period when the poem was written.

GENRE ELEMENTS: LYRIC POETRY

- expresses strong feelings or thoughts
- has a musical quality
- deals with intense emotions surrounding events like death, love, or loss
- includes forms such as ode, elegy, and sonnet

ANALYZE SOUND DEVICES

The earliest poetry was composed to be sung in performance. Poets still use sound devices to create musical effects and to help unify lines and stanzas. The most common sound devices are rhyme and meter. Here are some other types of sound devices.

- **Alliteration**—the repetition of a consonant sound at the beginning of words (*His crypt the cloudy canopy*)

- **Assonance**—the repetition of a vowel sound in two or more stressed syllables that do not end with the same consonant (*The tide is full, the moon lies fair*)

- **Consonance**—the repetition of consonant sounds within and at the end of words (*Like strings of broken lyres*)

- **Onomatopoeia**—the use of words whose sounds echo their meanings (*grating*)

After you read these poems the first time, read them again aloud and notice how the sound devices appeal to your sense of hearing. Also, consider how sound devices support each poem's subject, mood, and theme.

ANNOTATION MODEL

NOTICE & NOTE

As you read, notice how each poet uses nature imagery to appeal to the reader's senses and to develop an extended metaphor. Mark up examples of sound devices. In the model, you can see one reader's notes about the beginning of "Dover Beach."

The sea is <u>calm</u> tonight.

The tide is full, the <u>moon lies fair</u>

Upon the straits – on the French coast the light

Ⓖleams and is Ⓖone; the cliffs of England stand,

Ⓖlimmering and vast, out in the <u>tranquil</u> bay.

Come to the window, sweet is the night air!

The imagery suggests nature's vastness and establishes a peaceful mood at the beginning. Alliteration of the "g" sound contributes to this mood.

The sixth line tells us the speaker is addressing someone in the same room.

© Houghton Mifflin Harcourt Publishing Company • Image Credits: © GL Archive/Alamy; © Norma Cornes/Alamy

BACKGROUND

Matthew Arnold *(1822–1888) was one of the leading poets and essayists of the Victorian era. In his youth, he struggled to live up to the expectations of his father, a famous headmaster of Rugby School. Arnold attended Rugby and then Oxford University; he later held teaching positions at both schools. While at Oxford, he began to gain recognition for his poetry. Arnold's poems are contemplative, often addressing serious themes of isolation and religious doubt.*

DOVER BEACH
Poem by Matthew Arnold

PREPARE TO COMPARE

As you read, note the imagery in the speaker's description of the natural world and the sound devices in his description. Consider the thoughts and feelings the speaker associates with the sea.

The sea is calm tonight.
The tide is full, the moon lies fair
Upon the straits—on the French coast the light
Gleams and is gone; the cliffs of England stand,
5 Glimmering and vast, out in the tranquil bay.
Come to the window, sweet is the night air!
Only, from the long line of spray
Where the sea meets the moon-blanched land,
Listen! you hear the grating roar
10 Of pebbles which the waves draw back, and fling,
At their return, up the high strand,
Begin, and cease, and then again begin,
With tremulous cadence slow, and bring
The eternal note of sadness in.

Notice & Note

Use the side margins to notice and note signposts in the text.

3 straits: the Strait of Dover, a narrow channel separating England and France, located at the northern end of the English Channel.

8 moon-blanched: shining palely in the moonlight.

13 tremulous cadence (trĕmʹyə-ləs kādʹns): trembling rhythm.

15 Sophocles (sŏf´ə-klēz): an ancient Greek writer of tragic plays.

16 Aegean (ĭ-jē´ən): the Aegean Sea, the portion of the Mediterranean Sea between Greece and Turkey.

17 turbid: in a state of turmoil; muddled.

21 Sea of Faith: traditional religious beliefs about God and the world, long viewed as true and unshakable.

23 girdle: a belt or sash worn around the waist.

27 drear: dreary.

28 shingles: pebbly beaches.

ANALYZE SOUND DEVICES
Annotate: Read lines 29–37 aloud. Mark sound devices you notice.

Analyze: What mood do the sound devices help create?

15 Sophocles long ago
Heard it on the Aegean, and it brought
Into his mind the turbid ebb and flow
Of human misery; we
Find also in the sound a thought,
20 Hearing it by this distant northern sea.

The Sea of Faith
Was once, too, at the full, and round earth's shore
Lay like the folds of a bright girdle furled.
But now I only hear
25 Its melancholy, long, withdrawing roar,
Retreating, to the breath
Of the night wind, down the vast edges drear
And naked shingles of the world.

Ah, love, let us be true
30 To one another! for the world, which seems
To lie before us like a land of dreams,
So various, so beautiful, so new,
Hath really neither joy, nor love, nor light,
Nor certitude, nor peace, nor help for pain;
35 And we are here as on a darkling plain
Swept with confused alarms of struggle and flight,
Where ignorant armies clash by night.

CHECK YOUR UNDERSTANDING

Answer these questions about "Dover Beach" before moving on to the next selection.

1 In the poem, the speaker is —

   A looking out to sea from the English coast

   B sailing on a ship in the English Channel

   C swimming in the Aegean Sea

   D fighting in a war in France

2 What does the speaker compare to waves pulling back from the shore?

   F Armed conflict

   G Ships sailing into the channel

   H Loss of religious faith

   J Lovers parting

3 The speaker takes comfort in —

   A his spirituality

   B nature's beauty

   C social progress

   D personal relationships

BACKGROUND

Thomas Hardy *(1840–1928) was born in a small village in southwestern England, the setting of many of his novels and poems. As a young man, he wrote poems and stories in his spare time while working as an architect. Hardy became famous for his novels, although their pessimism and controversial subject matter were often criticized. He published "The Darkling Thrush" just a few days before the end of the 19th century.*

THE DARKLING THRUSH

Poem by Thomas Hardy

PREPARE TO COMPARE

As you read, notice the poet's word choices in describing a landscape.

I leant upon a coppice gate
　　When Frost was specter-gray,
And Winter's dregs made desolate
　　The weakening eye of day.

5　The tangled bine-stems scored the sky
　　Like strings of broken lyres,
And all mankind that haunted nigh
　　Had sought their household fires.

The land's sharp features seemed to be
10　　The Century's corpse outleant,
His crypt the cloudy canopy,
　　The wind his death-lament.
The ancient pulse of germ and birth
　　Was shrunken hard and dry,
15 And every spirit upon earth
　　Seem'd fervorless as I.

At once a voice arose among
　　The bleak twigs overhead
In a full-hearted evensong

Notice & Note

Use the side margins to notice and note signposts in the text.

1 coppice (kŏpˊĭs) **gate:** a gate leading to a coppice, a small wood or thicket.

2 specter-gray: ghost-gray.

5 bine-stems scored: twining stems cut across.

6 lyres: harp-like musical instruments.

7 nigh: near.

10 outleant: outstretched.

13 germ: seed; bud.

19 evensong: evening song.

© Houghton Mifflin Harcourt Publishing Company • Image Credits: © Historica Graphica Collection/Heritage Image Partnership Ltd./Alamy; © Donat Sorokin\TASS via Getty Images

20   Of joy illimited;
   An aged thrush, frail, gaunt, and small,
      In blast-beruffled plume,
   Had chosen thus to fling his soul
      Upon the growing gloom.

25 So little cause for carollings
      Of such ecstatic sound
   Was written on terrestrial things
      Afar or nigh around,
   That I could think there trembled through
30   His happy good-night air
   Some blessed Hope, whereof he knew
      And I was unaware.

NOTICE & NOTE

20 illimited: unlimited.

22 blast-beruffled plume: wind-ruffled feathers.

ANALYZE EXTENDED METAPHORS
Annotate: Underline words that describe natural features in lines 9–16. Circle words that describe the century as it is compared to nature.

Analyze: What idea does this extended metaphor express?

CHECK YOUR UNDERSTANDING

Answer these questions before moving on to the **Analyze the Texts** section on the following page.

1 What is the poem's setting?

  A Sunrise on a mountain slope

  B An open snowy field

  C A lake's frozen shore

  D The edge of the woods in winter

2 The lines "Had chosen thus to fling his soul / Upon the growing gloom" suggest that the thrush —

  F shares the speaker's sense of hopelessness

  G is defying the grimness of its surroundings

  H probably won't live much longer

  J has flown down from the tree branch

3 The speaker says in lines 29–32 that —

  A the thrush may have some unknown reason to be happy

  B he understands why the thrush sings joyfully

  C he mistook the thrush's singing as a sign of hope

  D the singing has plunged him even deeper into despair

ANALYZE THE TEXTS

Support your responses with evidence from the texts. ☷ NOTEBOOK

1. **Analyze** In "Dover Beach," how does Arnold use details about the sea to develop his extended metaphor about faith?

2. **Infer** Arnold refers to Sophocles in lines 15–20 of "Dover Beach." What idea does he suggest through this allusion to the ancient Greek playwright?

3. **Interpret** Reread lines 29–37 of "Dover Beach." How does the speaker's description of the world connect to his plea that he and his love "be true / To one another"?

4. **Analyze** How does Hardy's use of alliteration and assonance in lines 1–4 of "The Darkling Thrush" support the subject and theme of the poem?

5. **Draw Conclusions** In "The Darkling Thrush," why did Hardy choose to describe the bird as an "aged thrush, frail, gaunt, and small"?

RESEARCH

RESEARCH TIP
When researching an aspect of a particular time period, it is easiest to find the answers you're looking for by using specific search strings. In this case, you might use strings like "Victorian + religion" or "how industrialization affected British rural life."

Both of these poems reflect the poets' feelings about changes that occurred during their lifetimes. With a partner, research historical developments during the Victorian era. Use what you learn to answer the following questions.

QUESTION	ANSWER
What challenges to traditional religious beliefs occurred during the Victorian era?	
How did industrialization affect rural life in Britain during this period?	

Extend Although the Victorian era is often characterized as a period of optimism and progress, some of its finest writers expressed a pessimistic outlook. Find other poems by Arnold and Hardy that address subjects such as loss and disillusionment. With a partner, discuss how they compare with the poems you read in this lesson.

CREATE AND DISCUSS

Create a List Select an aspect of nature, such as a season, a type of landscape, or a particular animal. Create a list of words and phrases that describe this aspect of nature, and then list thoughts or feelings that you associate with them. Include at least 20 words or phrases in your list. Review your analysis and interpretation of the two poems to see examples from Arnold and Hardy.

❏ Identify an aspect of nature that is representative of how you view the world.

❏ Review examples of how poets have used nature to represent ideas.

❏ Brainstorm and construct a list of words and phrases.

Discuss Your List People can react to the same sights and experiences in strikingly different ways. Share and discuss your list with a small group.

❏ Review each descriptive word or phrase with your group.

❏ Then, discuss the thoughts and feelings you associated with these details. Ask every group member to explain how their reactions compare with yours.

❏ Make sure to respect everyone's responses. If you are confused by a response, ask the student to clarify it.

RESPOND TO THE ESSENTIAL QUESTION

? How do you view the world?

Gather Information Review your annotations and notes on "Dover Beach" and "The Darkling Thrush." Then, add relevant details to your Response Log. As you determine which information to include, think about:

• how poets describe the natural world in different ways
• how you experience the world around you
• how similar elements can be used to express opposite ideas

ACADEMIC VOCABULARY

As you write and discuss what you learned from the lyric poems, be sure to use the Academic Vocabulary words. Check off each of the words that you use.

❏ **abandon**
❏ **confine**
❏ **conform**
❏ **depress**
❏ **reluctance**

DOVER BEACH
Poem by Matthew Arnold

THE DARKLING THRUSH
Poem by Thomas Hardy

Collaborate & Compare

COMPARE THEMES

A poem's **theme** is the message the author conveys to the reader. Although even a short poem may express several ideas, the theme is the major idea that the poet communicates. Themes are developed through word choice, imagery, figurative language, and other elements.

In both "Dover Beach" and "The Darkling Thrush," the poets use their descriptions of nature to express themes about disillusionment and hopelessness.

Poets seldom directly state their themes, so you must infer them from a close reading of a poem. As you read to understand each poem's message, consider:

- **Key statements**—made by the speaker
- **Imagery**—details that appeal to the reader's senses
- **Figurative language**—language that communicates ideas beyond the literal meaning of the words.

With your group, complete the chart with details from both poems.

	"DOVER BEACH"	"THE DARKLING THRUSH"
Key Statements		
Imagery		
Figurative Language		

ANALYZE THE TEXTS

Discuss these questions in your group:

1. **Analyze** Both poems start out with descriptions of nature. What literary elements does each poet rely on to develop his description?

2. **Compare** How are these two poems similar or different in mood?

3. **Draw Conclusions** Which poem expresses a more hopeful view of the world? Explain.

4. **Analyze** Both poems include extended metaphors comparing something in nature with an abstract idea. How does this technique help the poets develop their poems?

COLLABORATE AND PRESENT

Now, with your group, continue exploring the ideas in the poems by identifying and comparing their themes. Follow these steps:

Go to **Giving a Presentation** in the **Speaking and Listening Studio** for more.

1. **Decide on the most important details** With your group, review your chart to identify the most important details from each poem. Identify points on which you agree, and resolve disagreements by identifying evidence from the poems that support your ideas.

2. **Determine a theme** Based on the word choices, figurative language, sound devices, and feelings evoked from each poem, determine a theme for each. You may use a chart to keep track of the themes your group members suggest.

	DETAILS	THEME
"DOVER BEACH"		
"THE DARKLING THRUSH"		

3. **Compare themes** Compare themes with your group and discuss whether the themes are similar or different. Listen actively to the members of your group and ask them to clarify any points you do not understand.

4. **Present to the class** Next, present your ideas to the class. Be sure to include clear statements on the theme for each poem. Discuss whether the themes are similar or different. You may add other visuals or diagrams to help convey information to the class.

POEM

MY LAST DUCHESS

by **Robert Browning**
pages 669–670

COMPARE THEMES

As you read "My Last Duchess" and "Confession," take note of how each poem addresses the imperfections of human character. After you read both poems, you will collaborate with a small group to create a final presentation comparing their themes.

? **ESSENTIAL QUESTION:**

What brings out cruelty in people?

POEM

CONFESSION

by **Linh Dinh**
page 672

QUICK START

You probably know someone who tends to criticize other people. What is the danger of being overly critical in your interactions with others? Discuss this question with a small group of classmates.

DRAW CONCLUSIONS ABOUT SPEAKERS

The **speaker** of a poem is the voice that talks to the reader. In many poems, the speaker expresses the poet's own thoughts and feelings. However, you should not assume that the speaker is the same as the poet, even if he or she uses the pronouns *I* and *me*.

Some poems have a fictional character, or **persona,** as the speaker. *Persona* is a Latin word meaning "actor's mask." A persona allows the poet to pretend to be someone with a different personality or situation. For example, in "Confession," Linh Dinh uses the persona of a painter to explore an idea about the visual arts.

A **dramatic monologue** is a type of persona poem in which the speaker addresses a silent or absent listener during an intense or emotionally complex moment. Dramatic monologues require readers to make inferences: the speakers reveal themselves by dropping clues that the reader must piece together. Browning's "My Last Duchess," a famous monologue, is set in 16th-century Italy. The speaker is a duke negotiating with an agent to marry a count's daughter. Notice how Browning begins the poem in the middle of their conversation:

> **That's my last Duchess painted on the wall,**
> **Looking as if she were alive.**

As you read, use a chart like the one below to gather evidence and draw conclusions about the character and circumstances of each poem's speaker.

	HOW SPEAKER VIEWS HIMSELF	HOW SPEAKER VIEWS OTHERS
"My Last Duchess"		
"Confession"		

GENRE ELEMENTS: LYRIC POETRY

- usually written in the first person
- expresses the feelings and thoughts of the speaker, who may be a fictional character
- uses sound devices, such as rhythm and repetition, to create a musical quality
- often deals with intense emotions surrounding events like death, love, or loss

ANALYZE IMAGERY

Imagery refers to words and phrases that create vivid sensory experiences for the reader. Most imagery is visual, but imagery can also appeal to the senses of smell, hearing, taste, and touch. Imagery appears in all literary forms, but it is especially important in poetry for establishing a mood, expressing emotions, and conveying ideas.

The two poems in this lesson focus on a painting or the act of painting. Because of this subject, they are both rich in visual imagery. As you read, notice how each poet uses an image or group of images to support the poem's theme. Use a chart like this one to help you analyze ideas and feelings associated with the imagery.

EXAMPLE OF IMAGERY	IDEAS OR FEELINGS LINKED TO IMAGE

ANNOTATION MODEL

NOTICE & NOTE

As you read, draw conclusions about each poem's speaker. Also, note how the imagery in each poem helps create a mood or express a theme. In the model you can see one reader's notes about "My Last Duchess."

That's my last Duchess painted on the wall,

Looking as if she were alive. I call

That piece a wonder, now: Frà Pandolf 's hands

Worked busily a day, and there she stands.

Will't please you sit and look at her?

The Duke uses the term "last Duchess," which is a cold way to refer to his late wife.

He emphasizes how realistic the painting is, like he's describing a real person. The painting seems to have special importance to him.

BACKGROUND

Robert Browning *(1812–1889) showed intellectual brilliance at a young age. When his first book of poetry was harshly criticized for its personal content, he decided to write poems about people and characters other than himself. Browning married the poet Elizabeth Barrett in 1846; they lived happily together in Italy until her death 15 years later. After decades of obscurity, Browning began to gain recognition during the 1860s for his dramatic monologues. He is widely considered one of the most important poets of the Victorian Era.*

MY LAST DUCHESS
Poem by Robert Browning

PREPARE TO COMPARE

As you read, note what the speaker reveals about himself through the course of the poem. Pay close attention to his word choices and the imagery that helps describe his behaviors and feelings for his wife.

That's my last Duchess painted on the wall,
Looking as if she were alive. I call
That piece a wonder, now: Frà Pandolf's hands
Worked busily a day, and there she stands.
5 Will't please you sit and look at her? I said
"Frà Pandolf" by design, for never read
Strangers like you that pictured countenance,
The depth and passion of its earnest glance,
But to myself they turned (since none puts by
10 The curtain I have drawn for you, but I)
And seemed as they would ask me, if they durst,
How such a glance came there; so, not the first
Are you to turn and ask thus. Sir, 'twas not
Her husband's presence only, called that spot
15 Of joy into the Duchess' cheek: perhaps
Frà Pandolf chanced to say "Her mantle laps

© Houghton Mifflin Harcourt Publishing Company • Image Credits: © Lebrecht Music and Arts Photo Library/Alamy; © Heritage Image Partnership Ltd/Alamy

Notice & Note

Use the side margins to notice and note signposts in the text.

3 Frà Pandolf's: of Brother Pandolf, a fictitious friar-painter.

DRAW CONCLUSIONS ABOUT SPEAKERS

Annotate: Mark the phrases in lines 5–13 that hint at the character of the speaker.

Infer: What can you infer about the duke? What details support your inference?

11 durst: dared.

16 mantle: cloak.

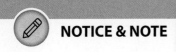
ANALYZE IMAGERY

Annotate: Mark details in lines 22–34 that describe what the duchess was like.

Compare: How does her character differ from that of the duke?

27 officious: offering unwanted services; meddling.

35 trifling: actions of little importance.

41 forsooth: in truth; indeed.

49 munificence (myoo-nĭf´ĭ-səns): generosity.

50 just pretense: legitimate claim.

51 dowry (dou´rə): payment given to a groom by the bride's father.

54 Neptune: in Roman mythology, the god of the sea.

DRAW CONCLUSIONS ABOUT SPEAKERS

Annotate: Mark the words in lines 44–56 that reveal the duke's sense of his own authority and power.

Interpret: What is the duke's motivation for telling the listener the story of his late wife? Has he revealed more than he intended? Explain.

Over my lady's wrist too much," or "Paint
Must never hope to reproduce the faint
Half-flush that dies along her throat": such stuff
20 Was courtesy, she thought, and cause enough
For calling up that spot of joy. She had
A heart—how shall I say?—too soon made glad,
Too easily impressed; she liked whate'er
She looked on, and her looks went everywhere.
25 Sir, 'twas all one! My favor at her breast,
The dropping of the daylight in the West,
The bough of cherries some officious fool
Broke in the orchard for her, the white mule
She rode with round the terrace—all and each
30 Would draw from her alike the approving speech,
Or blush, at least. She thanked men—good! but thanked
Somehow—I know not how—as if she ranked
My gift of a nine-hundred-years-old name
With anybody's gift. Who'd stoop to blame
35 This sort of trifling? Even had you skill
In speech—(which I have not)—to make your will
Quite clear to such an one, and say, "Just this
Or that in you disgusts me; here you miss,
Or there exceed the mark"—and if she let
40 Herself be lessoned so, nor plainly set
Her wits to yours, forsooth, and made excuse
—E'en then would be some stooping; and I choose
Never to stoop. Oh sir, she smiled, no doubt,
Whene'er I passed her; but who passed without
45 Much the same smile? This grew; I gave commands;
Then all smiles stopped together. There she stands
As if alive. Will't please you rise? We'll meet
The company below, then. I repeat,
The Count your master's known munificence
50 Is ample warrant that no just pretense
Of mine for dowry will be disallowed;
Though his fair daughter's self, as I avowed
At starting, is my object. Nay, we'll go
Together down, sir. Notice Neptune, though,
55 Taming a sea horse, thought a rarity,
Which Claus of Innsbruck cast in bronze for me!

CHECK YOUR UNDERSTANDING

Answer these questions about "My Last Duchess" before moving on to the next selection.

1 In the discussion of the duchess's portrait, the duke focuses on the —

    A value of the painting

    B style of the painter

    C duchess's beauty

    D expression on her face

2 The duke thinks that he should be admired because of his —

    F social status

    G intelligence

    H appearance

    J eloquence

3 Why didn't the duke tell his late wife that she was offending him?

    A He was worried she would leave him.

    B He was too proud to complain.

    C He wanted her to figure it out on her own.

    D He knew she would die soon.

BACKGROUND

Linh Dinh *(1963–) is a contemporary poet from Vietnam. He has authored two collections of stories, a novel, and several poetry collections. He is best known for* Postcards from the End of America, *a book of photographs and text documenting life in America. To create that work, he crisscrossed the country by bus, train, and foot, encountering people from all walks of life, including those living on the margins of society. His portrait of the nation underscores the strength it takes to overcome hardship.*

CONFESSION
Poem by Linh Dinh

PREPARE TO COMPARE

As you read this poem, note how the character of its speaker differs from that of the speaker in "My Last Duchess." Consider the ways that both poems express themes about the negative side of human nature.

Perhaps I'm a cruel artist. I always depict
In great details, lovingly, all the defects
On the faces and bodies of my models.
I use my eyes and brushes to thread
5 The jagged gaps of their stiff smiles. I pamper
Each pimple, hump, massage each incrustation.

I cajole my models into poses that are awkward,
Dangerous, unhygienic, sometimes mortifying.
I don't care to paint smooth, poreless skin but collect
10 All manners of rashes and eruptions. Inspired,
I've forced a hundred bodies—impossibly old,
Extremely young—onto appalling heaps,

Democratically naked, viscous with sweat, spit and etc.,
Just so I could render the human condition
15 Most accurately and movingly.

Notice & Note

Use the side margins to notice and note signposts in the text.

ANALYZE IMAGERY

Annotate: Mark contrasting images in lines 9–10.

Interpret: What idea does this contrast help convey?

CHECK YOUR UNDERSTANDING

Answer these questions before moving on to the **Analyze the Texts** section on the following page.

1 What does the poem's use of the phrase *democratically naked* suggest?

   A The speaker's motivations are political.

   B Nakedness creates a natural equality among people.

   C The models never feel embarrassed when they are together.

   D People have voted to take off their clothes before posing.

2 Why does the speaker use such negative imagery to describe the models?

   F The speaker is trying to elicit disgust in a listener or reader.

   G The speaker wants to emphasize the unattractiveness of the models to a listener or reader.

   H The speaker wants a listener or reader to grasp how truly ugly human beings are.

   J The speaker wants a listener or reader to dwell on the flesh-and-bone reality of imperfect human bodies.

3 How would you characterize the artist's purpose in painting people?

   A To see beauty in everyone

   B To express anger by showing humans as ugly

   C To make a statement about society's ideals

   D To idealize human physical imperfections

RESPOND

ANALYZE THE TEXTS

Support your responses with evidence from the texts. 📓 NOTEBOOK

1. **Analyze** Which images does Browning use repeatedly in "My Last Duchess"? What does this repetition reveal about the speaker's personality?

2. **Draw Conclusions** In lines 45–46 of "My Last Duchess," the speaker says, "I gave commands; / Then all smiles stopped together." How do you interpret this statement? Why might Browning have chosen to have the duke describe his actions so ambiguously?

3. **Interpret** Browning devotes most of "My Last Duchess" to discussion of the portrait, and he ends with a description of another artwork. What theme about art and life does he develop in the poem?

4. **Analyze** What mood is created by the images of bodily imperfections and disease in "Confession"? How does this mood support the speaker's ideas about art?

5. **Draw Conclusions** Do you think the speaker of "Confession" really wants us to consider him cruel, or does he have a more idealistic reason for the way he paints? Explain your response.

RESEARCH

RESEARCH TIP

Use websites that give reviews of books, movies, and songs to discover likely titles.

Then, to gather information on years, media types, plots, and themes, search several additional websites.

Feelings of jealousy have been expressed by human beings throughout the ages and across societies. How often does our entertainment industry rely on tales of jealous behavior and its consequences? Research works, such as movies, books, plays, and songs, that address the topic of jealousy. Find several examples from different time periods in a variety of media. Use the graphic organizer below to help you organize and explain your findings.

TITLE	TYPE OF MEDIA	TIME FRAME	SYNOPSIS

Extend Conduct a survey of your classmates to determine their top five favorite movies. Determine if any of the movies address the topic of jealous behavior, and discuss the themes, or messages about life or human nature, those movies express.

CREATE AND PRESENT

Create an Oral Presentation "My Last Duchess" and "Confession" present contrasts in style, tone, and language. The speaker in "My Last Duchess" lived during the Renaissance, so he spoke very differently than the contemporary artist in "Confession." Develop an oral presentation in which you assume the persona of one of the two speakers and recite that poem as a monologue.

❑ Be sure you understand the emotions underlying specific words and phrases, as well as their purposes, and mark the text to indicate style of delivery.

❑ Plan appropriate gestures and movements along with effective intonation to guide emphasis.

❑ Remember to address your audience. Is the speaker talking to a listener or to himself?

Present the Monologue In a small group, present your monologue.

❑ Make sure your presentation helps others understand the poem.

❑ Be clear about the message you impart as the speaker of the poem.

❑ Analyze what you would do differently if you were to recite the second poem.

Go to **Giving a Presentation** in the **Speaking and Listening Studio** for more about presenting to others.

RESPOND TO THE ESSENTIAL QUESTION

? What brings out cruelty in people?

Gather Information Review your annotations and notes on "My Last Duchess" and "Confession." Then, add relevant information to your Response Log. As you determine which information to include, think about:

• human nature and the human condition
• the difference between tolerance and acceptance
• ways that ego and self-obsession motivate behavior

ACADEMIC VOCABULARY
As you write and discuss what you learned from the poems, be sure to use the Academic Vocabulary words. Check off each of the words that you use.

❑ **abandon**

❑ **confine**

❑ **confirm**

❑ **depress**

❑ **reluctance**

MY LAST DUCHESS
Poem by Robert Browning

CONFESSION
Poem by Linh Dinh

Collaborate & Compare

COMPARE THEMES

"My Last Duchess" and "Confession" both focus on art, and they also address cruelty. Still, the two poems express distinct ideas about human nature.

With your group, discuss each area of focus listed in the chart below and record what you notice under the appropriate poem.

	"MY LAST DUCHESS"	"CONFESSION"
Information from the title		
Identity of the speaker		
Primary subject matter		
Use of imagery		
Implied emotions		
The role of art		
View of human nature		

ANALYZE THE TEXTS

Discuss these questions in your group.

1. **Infer** What flaws of human nature are represented by the speakers in the two poems?

2. **Interpret** How does the imagery of the two poems help reveal the identity and character of each speaker? What conclusions about the speakers can you draw based on their word choices?

3. **Compare** What similarities do Frá Pandolf and the painter in "Confession" share? What differences distinguish the two?

4. **Evaluate** How might the duke and the painter in "Confession" pose a threat to their respective societies?

COLLABORATE AND PRESENT

In your group, continue exploring the ideas in the poems by identifying and comparing their themes. Follow these steps:

Go to **Giving a Presentation** in the **Speaking and Listening Studio** for more.

1. **Decide on the most important details.** As a group, review the information you gathered in the previous chart. Determine which points you agree on and resolve disagreements by identifying evidence from the poems that support your ideas.

2. **Determine themes.** Write theme statements, or statements that express each poem's message about life or human nature. Use the chart below to help you track your group's ideas and identify possible themes.

	NOTES	POSSIBLE THEMES
"My Last Duchess"		
"Confession"		

3. **Compare the themes.** Work together as a group to determine similarities and differences between the themes.

4. **Develop your ideas.** Organize your ideas around your points of comparison, and provide evidence and explanations for each.

5. **Present to the class.** Determine how you will present your comparison, who will present it, and if the use of any visuals or diagrams would help clarify your points. Consider using technology as a presentation tool.

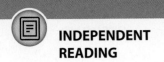
? ESSENTIAL QUESTIONS

Review the four Essential Questions for this unit on page 587.

Reader's Choice

Setting a Purpose   Select one or more of these options from your eBook to continue your exploration of the Essential Questions.

- Read the descriptions to see which text grabs your interest.
- Think about which genres you enjoy reading.

Notice & Note

In this unit, you practiced noticing and noting the signposts and asking big questions about nonfiction. As you read independently, these signposts and others will aid your understanding. Below are the anchor questions to ask when you read literature and nonfiction.

Reading Literature: Stories, Poems, and Plays	
Signpost	**Key Question**
Contrasts and Contradictions	Why did the character act that way?
Aha Moment	How might this change things?
Tough Questions	What does this make me wonder about?
Words of the Wiser	What's the lesson for the character?
Again and Again	Why might the author keep bringing this up?
Memory Moment	Why is this memory important?

Reading Nonfiction: Essays, Articles, and Arguments	
Signpost	**Key Question(s)**
Big Questions	What surprised me? What did the author think I already knew? What challenged, changed, or confirmed what I already knew?
Contrasts and Contradictions	What is the difference, and why does it matter?
Extreme or Absolute Language	Why did the author use this language?
Numbers and Stats	Why did the author use these numbers or amounts?
Quoted Words	Why was this person quoted or cited, and what did this add?
Word Gaps	Do I know this word from someplace else? Does it seem like technical talk for this topic? Do clues in the sentence help me understand the word?

You can preview these texts in Unit 5 of your eBook.

Then check off the text or texts that you select to read on your own.

POEM

Sonnet 43
Elizabeth Barrett Browning

Is love an intense but simple feeling or a complex emotion with many dimensions?

POEM

Remembrance
Emily Brontë

Can love survive a loved one's death, or does it change as the survivor grows older?

ARTICLE

The Great Exhibition
Lara Kriegel

What looked like a giant greenhouse and brought visitors to London from all over the world?

SHORT STORY

Christmas Storms and Sunshine
Elizabeth Cleghorn Gaskell

Can two families divided by politics overcome their differences and discover the benefits of friendship?

ESSAY

Evidence of Progress
Thomas Babington Macaulay

During times of turmoil, how can you tell whether a nation is taking steps toward a better future?

Collaborate and Share Meet with a partner to discuss what you learned from at least one of your independent readings.

- Give a brief synopsis or summary of the text.

- Describe any signposts that you noticed in the text and explain what they revealed to you.

- Describe what you most enjoyed or found most challenging about the text. Give specific examples.

- Decide whether you would recommend the text to others. Why or why not?

Go to the **Reading Studio** for more resources on **Notice & Note.**

Go to the **Writing Studio** for help writing informative texts.

Write a Research Report

This unit focuses on the Victorian period, when rapid technological changes affected nearly every aspect of society, including government, transportation, communication, religious practice, and relations between classes. For this writing task, you will do some research and use outside sources to write about how technology has affected society in our own time. For an example of an essay that uses outside sources well, review the article "The Victorians Had the Same Concerns About Technology As We Do."

As you write your research report, you can use the notes from your Response Log that you filled out after reading the texts in this unit.

Writing Prompt

Read the information in the box below.

This is the topic or context for your research report.

> Both social science research and literature often explore the effects of technological developments on our lives.

Think carefully about the following question.

How might this Essential Question relate to your research report?

> Which invention has had the greatest impact on your life?

How does the research you will do relate to the topic of your report?

Write a research report about one modern invention that has changed the social order or the way people live their daily lives.

Be sure to —

Review these points as you write and again when you finish. Make any needed changes.

- ❏ develop research questions
- ❏ review many possible sources
- ❏ choose the best sources for your essay
- ❏ organize your report logically
- ❏ use evidence from your sources to support your own ideas
- ❏ cite each outside source in the text
- ❏ use quotations, paraphrasing, and summarizing; state most facts and ideas in your own words, using direct quotations when appropriate
- ❏ present a thesis statement
- ❏ include an introduction and conclusion

Plan

Once you have thought about the writing prompt, it's time to plan your research and the writing of your report. First, identify an area of focus related to the topic. It can be helpful to think about background reading you have done or personal interests that you have. As part of your planning, you must also consider your purpose and audience. Follow the steps below to get started planning your research project.

Research Report Planning Table	
Identify research questions	What are some recent inventions? How do they affect my life?
Identify ideas from background reading	
Identify personal interests related to the topic	
Focus on one question/topic	
State your purpose	
Identify your audience	

Background Reading Review the notes you have taken in your Response Log that relate to the question, "Which invention has had the greatest impact on your life?" Texts in this unit provide background reading that will help you formulate and develop the topic for your research report.

 Go to **Writing Informative Texts: Developing a Topic** for help planning your research report.

Notice & Note

From Reading to Writing

As you plan your research report, apply what you've learned about signposts to your own writing. Remember that writers use common features called signposts to help convey their message to readers.

Think how you can incorporate **Quoted Words** into your report.

Go to the **Reading Studio** for more resources on **Notice & Note**.

Use the notes from your Response Log as you plan your research report.

WRITING TASK

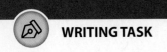 Go to **Writing Informative Texts: Organizing Ideas** for help organizing your research report.

Organize Your Ideas After you have gathered ideas in your planning table, you need to organize them in a way that will help you draft your research report. You can use the chart below to help you organize your draft before you start writing.

Organize Your Research Report	
Write a "hook." *The opening sentence of your report should grab the reader's attention.*	
Write a thesis statement. *Use your planning table to write a thesis statement for your report.*	
Outline the body of your report. *List at least three key ideas that support your thesis statement.*	
Write a conclusion. *Restate your thesis statement, and summarize your key ideas.*	
Keep a list of your sources. *List all of the sources you plan to use along with the relevant publication information. You will use this list later to create your Works Cited page.*	

② Develop a Draft

 You might prefer to draft your research report online.

Once you have completed your planning, you will be ready to begin drafting your research report. Refer to your graphic organizers as well as any notes you took as you studied the texts in this unit. This material will provide ideas for you to develop as you write. Using a word processor or online writing application makes it easier to make changes or move sentences around later when you are ready to revise your first draft.

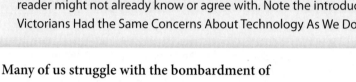

Use the Mentor Text

Author's Craft

Your introduction should start with a "hook" to grab the reader's attention. It should also provide background on the topic. Near the end of your introduction, you should provide a thesis statement that tells the reader the main idea of your report. The thesis statement is a **claim**—something the reader might not already know or agree with. Note the introduction from "The Victorians Had the Same Concerns About Technology As We Do."

Many of us struggle with the bombardment of information we receive and experience anxiety as a result of new media. . . .

> *This is the background that introduces the topic.*

Though the technologies may change, these fears actually have a very long history. . . . <u>Literary, medical, and cultural responses in the Victorian age to the perceived problems of stress and overwork anticipate many of the preoccupations of our own era. . . .</u>

> *This is the thesis statement. The reader should expect the author to present evidence supporting this statement.*

Apply What You've Learned Review the notes from your research and the ideas in your planning table. Then, write a statement supported by your key ideas and evidence from your research. Remember that your thesis statement should present a claim that the reader may not already know or agree with.

Genre Characteristics

When writers use evidence from their sources, they introduce the idea or fact by identifying the source. Then, they present it by paraphrasing, summarizing, or using a direct quotation. Notice how the author of the article uses signal phrases to connect her sources with the ideas the sources support.

<u>Thomas Carlyle</u>, <u>for example</u>, lamented the new lack of direct contact with society and nature. . . . Print publications were fast becoming the principal medium of public debate and influence. . . .

> *The author identifies the source and uses the signal phrase "for example" to show that the source supports the author's key idea.*

Apply What You've Learned Introduce each source you use by giving the name of a person, organization, and/or the publication associated with the source. Use signal phrases to connect the source with the key idea it supports.

③ Revise

Go to **Writing Informative Texts: Precise Language and Vocabulary** for help revising your research report.

On Your Own Once you have written your draft, you'll want to go back and look for ways to improve your research report. As you reread and revise, think about whether you have achieved your purpose. The Revision Guide will help you focus on specific elements to make your writing stronger.

Revision Guide		
Ask Yourself	**Tips**	**Revision Techniques**
1. Does the introduction engage the reader, provide background information, and clearly state the thesis?	**Circle** the engaging introduction, **underline** the background information, and **bracket** the thesis statement.	**Add** a quotation or interesting detail to hook readers. **Add** necessary background information. **Add** a thesis statement.
2. Does the body include only relevant key ideas and supporting evidence?	**Mark** the key ideas. **Number** supporting evidence for each key idea.	**Delete** irrelevant ideas and evidence. **Add** evidence to support ideas.
3. Are sources credited and citations punctuated correctly?	**Place check marks** next to material that requires citation.	**Add** parenthetical citations if necessary, and **correct** punctuation.
4. Does the conclusion restate the thesis?	**Bracket** the restatement of the thesis.	**Add** a sentence or two restating the thesis.
5. Is the Works Cited list complete and correctly formatted?	**Compare** parenthetical citations with the entries in your Works Cited list.	**Add** Works Cited entries if necessary and revise incorrectly formatted entries.

ACADEMIC VOCABULARY

As you conduct your **peer review,** be sure to use these words.

- ❏ **abandon**
- ❏ **confine**
- ❏ **conform**
- ❏ **depress**
- ❏ **reluctance**

With a Partner Once you and your partner have worked through the Revision Guide on your own, exchange research reports and evaluate each other's draft in a **peer review.** Focus on providing revision suggestions for at least three of the items mentioned in the chart. Explain why you think your partner's draft should be revised and what your specific suggestions are.

When receiving feedback from your partner, listen attentively and ask questions to make sure you fully understand the revision suggestions.

4 Edit

Once you have addressed the organization, use of supporting evidence, and logical flow of ideas in your paper, you can look to improve the finer points of your draft. Edit for effective sentence structure, smooth syntax, precise word choice, and Standard English grammar and punctuation.

Language Conventions

Combining Sentences Too many short sentences can result in a stiff style that doesn't clearly show the relationship between ideas. One way that writers connect ideas is by combining sentences using coordinating and subordinating conjunctions. In the examples below, the numbers **[1]** and **[2]** show the two ideas that are combined.

> ! Go to the **Grammar Studio: Conjunctions and Interjections** to learn more about conjunctions.

Coordinating Conjunctions	Example
and, but, or, so, therefore	**[1]** Print publications were fast becoming the principal medium of public debate and influence, **[2] and** they were shaping and, in Carlyle's view, distorting human learning and communications.

Subordinating Conjunctions	Example
Time: *when, as, before, after*	**While [1]** we cannot draw too strict a line of comparison between 19th-century attitudes to such technologies as the telegraph, train, telephone, and newspaper and our own responses as a culture to the advent of the internet and the mobile phone, **[2]** there are parallels that almost argue against the Luddite position.
Contrast: *although, even though, even if, while*	
Cause/effect: *because, if, unless*	

Note that when you use a subordinating conjunction, it can come at the beginning or in the middle of the sentence.

5 Publish

Finalize your research and choose a way to share it with your audience. Consider these options:

- Share it as an article on an open web platform.
- Ask your school librarian to make your work available in the library.

Use the scoring guide to evaluate your essay.

Writing Task Scoring Guide: Research Report

	Organization/Progression	Development of Ideas	Use of Language and Conventions
4	• The organization of the report is clear and appropriate to the purpose. • The writer has a clear thesis with all ideas strongly related to it, and the report is unified and coherent. • The writer's progression of ideas is logical, with meaningful transitions and sentence connections.	• Ideas are effectively developed; examples from outside sources are specific and well chosen. • The report is thoughtful and engaging. The writer uses material from outside sources to support personal thoughts and ideas. • The writer demonstrates a thorough understanding of research and writing.	• Word choice is purposeful and precise, maintains an appropriate tone, and contributes to the quality of the report. • The writer demonstrates a consistent command of spelling, capitalization, punctuation, grammar, and usage. • All sources cited are in correct format.
3	• The organization of the report is generally clear and appropriate to the purpose. • The writer has a clear thesis with most ideas related to it. • The paper is coherent, though it may lack unity in some places. • The writer's progression of ideas is generally logical and controlled, with smooth transitions and sentence connections.	• The development of ideas is sufficient; details and examples from outside sources are generally specific and appropriate. • The report reflects thoughtfulness. The writing is original rather than formulaic; evidence presented supports the writer's ideas. • The writer demonstrates a good understanding of research and writing.	• Word choice is mostly clear and specific, reflecting an awareness of purpose and tone, and contributing to the quality and clarity of the report. • The writer demonstrates adequate command of sentence boundaries, spelling, capitalization, punctuation, grammar, and usage. • Most sources cited are in correct format.
2	• The organizing structure of the report is evident but not always appropriate. • The report lacks clarity because the writer uses unsuitable organizational strategies. • Most ideas are related to the specified topic, but the writer's thesis is weak or unclear. • Transitions and sentence connections do not contribute to the progression of ideas.	• Ideas are only minimally developed. Examples are inappropriate or poorly presented. • The report reflects little thoughtfulness; it presents evidence from outside sources but not personal thoughts and ideas. • The writer demonstrates only a limited understanding of the task. • The writer's progression of ideas is not always logical and controlled.	• Word choice reflects only a basic awareness of the purpose of informative writing. It weakens the quality and clarity of the report. • The writer demonstrates only partial command of sentence boundaries, spelling, capitalization, punctuation, grammar, and usage. • Few sources cited are correctly formatted.
1	• The organizing structure of the report is inappropriate, and its weakness leads to a lack of clarity and direction in the report. • Most ideas are related to the specified topic, but the thesis lacks details or is unclear or illogical. • The writer fails to focus on the topic, includes extraneous information, or shifts abruptly from idea to idea.	• Ideas are poorly developed; the details and examples used are inappropriate, vague, or insufficient. • The writer's response to the prompt is vague or confused. • The report may be only weakly linked to the prompt, or developed in a manner that demonstrates a lack of understanding of the task. • The progression of ideas is weak.	• Word choice is vague or limited, reflecting little or no awareness of the purpose. It fails to establish an appropriate tone and detracts from the quality of the report. • The writer has little or no command of sentence boundaries, spelling, capitalization, punctuation, grammar, and usage. • Sources are not cited.

Give a Multimodal Presentation

You will now adapt your research report for a multimodal presentation to your classmates. You will also listen to their presentations, ask questions to better understand their ideas, and help them improve their work.

Go to the **Speaking and Listening Studio: Using Media in a Presentation** to learn more.

① Adapt Your Report for a Multimodal Presentation

Review your research report. Use the chart below to guide you as you adapt your report to create slides and other presentation materials to convey your thesis, and present your key ideas in a clear and engaging way.

Presentation Planning Chart	
Plan Your Slides How will you present your introduction, thesis statement, key ideas and supporting evidence, and conclusion? What is the best way to convey this information on each slide?	
Use Graphics, Images, and a Consistent Design What design elements will make your slides visually appealing? How will these elements relate to the content of your report?	
Consider Adding Music, Animation, or Sound Effects Would including music, audio clips, or sound effects enhance the content of your presentation?	
Use Verbal Techniques Which sections of your report should be presented slowly? Which sections need emphasis?	
Use Nonverbal Techniques Which slides stand on their own and could be presented with little or no narration?	

2 Practice with a Partner or Group

Once you've completed your draft, practice with a partner or group to improve both your presentation and your delivery.

Practice Effective Verbal Techniques

❏ **Enunciation** Replace words that you stumble over, and rearrange sentences so that your delivery is smooth.

❏ **Voice Modulation and Pitch** Use your voice to display enthusiasm and emphasis.

❏ **Speaking Rate** Speak slowly enough that listeners understand you. Pause now and then to let them consider important points.

❏ **Volume** Remember that listeners at the back of the room must be able to hear you.

Practice Effective Nonverbal Techniques

❏ **Eye Contact** Try to let your eyes rest on each member of the audience at least once.

❏ **Facial Expression** Smile, frown, or raise an eyebrow to show your feelings or to emphasize points.

❏ **Gestures** Stand tall and relaxed, and use natural gestures—shrugs, nods, or shakes of your head—to add meaning and interest to your presentation.

Provide and Consider Advice for Improvement

As a listener, pay close attention. Take notes about ways that presenters can improve their presentations and use verbal and nonverbal techniques more effectively. Paraphrase and summarize each presenter's thesis and key ideas to confirm your understanding, and ask questions to clarify any confusing expressions or ideas.

As a presenter, listen closely to questions and consider ways to revise your presentation to make sure your key ideas are clear and logically sequenced. Remember to ask for suggestions about how you might change onscreen text or images to make your presentation clearer and more interesting.

3 Deliver Your Presentation

Use the advice you received during practice to make final changes to your presentation. Then, using effective verbal and nonverbal techniques, present it to your classmates.

As you work to improve your presentations, be sure to follow discussion rules:

❏ listen closely to each other

❏ don't interrupt

❏ stay on topic

❏ ask only helpful, relevant questions

❏ provide only clear, thoughtful, and direct answers

Reflect on the Unit

By completing your research report, you have created a writing product that pulls together and expresses your thoughts about the reading you have done in this unit. Now is a good time to reflect on what you have learned.

Reflect on the Essential Questions

- Review the four Essential Questions on page 587. How have your answers to these questions changed in response to the texts you've read in this unit?

- What are some examples from the texts you've read that show how technology has altered the social order and the ways in which people live their daily lives?

Reflect on Your Reading

- Which selections were the most interesting or surprising to you?

- From which selection did you learn the most about how technology affects people's lives?

Reflect on the Writing Task

- What difficulties did you encounter while working on your research report? How might you avoid them next time?

- Which parts of the research report were the easiest to write? The hardest to write? Why?

- What improvements did you make to your research report as you were revising?

© Houghton Mifflin Harcourt Publishing Company

UNIT 5 SELECTIONS
- from *Jane Eyre*
- "Factory Reform"
- "The Lady of Shalott"
- from *Great Expectations*
- "The Victorians Had the Same Concerns About Technology As We Do"
- "Dover Beach"
- "The Darkling Thrush"
- "My Last Duchess"
- "Confession"

NEW IDEAS, NEW VOICES

MODERN AND CONTEMPORARY LITERATURE

> **The English language is nobody's special property. It is the property of the imagination; it is the property of the language itself.**
>
> —Derek Walcott

Discuss the Essential Questions with your whole class or in small groups. As you read New Ideas, New Voices, consider how the selections explore these questions.

? *ESSENTIAL QUESTION:*

What makes people feel insecure?

In the modern world, safety and security seem to be emphasized more than ever before in history. Yet people continue to experience insecurity in their daily lives, their relationships, and even their sense of self. How can insecurity affect a person from within? What types of insecurity come from the world around us? How much control do we have over the sources of insecurity in our lives?

? *ESSENTIAL QUESTION:*

Why is it hard to resist social pressure?

You have probably heard many times that the company you keep can influence your thoughts and actions for good or for bad. Peer pressure is certainly a powerful force, whether it is working on individuals or groups. Why do we feel the need to go along with the crowd? What are the benefits and the dangers of conforming to society's expectations? What happens when social pressure gets out of control?

? *ESSENTIAL QUESTION:*

What is the power of symbols?

At the most basic level, a symbol is anything that represents or stands for something else. We are surrounded by symbols every day. Written symbols appear on road signs and electronic devices. Symbols for individuals and concepts appear in books, music, movies, and TV shows. Why do we use symbols? Are symbols usually more or less effective than literal representations? How do differences in interpretation affect the power of symbols?

? *ESSENTIAL QUESTION:*

When should the government interfere in our decisions?

The question of how much influence a government should have over the lives of its citizens is an old one. Over the centuries, it has sparked debates, influenced the development of political parties, and even contributed to wars. Many people agree that some governmental authority is necessary to keep peace and order, but how much interference is too much? Conversely, when does it become necessary for individual rights to yield to government authority?

MODERN AND CONTEMPORARY LITERATURE

At the turn of the 20th century, Great Britain was a nation at its peak. Under the reign of Victoria's successor, Edward VII, England was a land of prosperity, stability, and world dominance. However, vast changes were on the horizon. Over the course of the next hundred years, Britain would become embroiled in wars, experience economic depression, and face the end of its once-massive empire.

World Wars In 1914 a Serbian nationalist assassinated Archduke Franz Ferdinand, heir to the throne of Austria-Hungary. Austria declared war on Serbia, and like a line of dominoes, alliances fell into place: Austria and Germany on one side; Russia, France, and Britain on the other. Both sides became locked in bloody trench warfare. The Great War, as the conflict was then known, dragged on, devastating Europe, killing or wounding virtually an entire generation of young men, and bringing a profound sense of disillusionment to the people. In 1917 the United States entered the war, leading to Germany's capitulation the following year and an uneasy peace.

Britain had lost 750,000 men, and those who returned from World War I alive came home to unemployment and economic depression. France and Germany were hit even harder, while Russia was plunged into revolution and civil war. War-torn European nations turned to the United States for loans, but in 1929 the United States stock market crashed, causing a worldwide depression. In the economic and political chaos of the 1920s and early 1930s, dictators seized power in Italy, Russia, and Germany. In 1939 German dictator Adolf Hitler made the decision to invade Poland, prompting Britain and France to declare war on Germany. Italy and Japan allied themselves with Germany, and World War II began.

Terrible as the Great War had been, for most British citizens it was a distant tragedy on foreign battlefields. World War II was different. After the fall of France in 1940, German planes began to attack Britain. Bombs rained down on London, and the entire population mobilized to defend the home front. Britain held out against Germany until the United States entered the war in 1941, and Hitler was finally defeated in 1945.

COLLABORATIVE DISCUSSION

In a small group, review the timeline and discuss how outside events influenced British politics and literature.

1901
Queen Victoria dies and is succeeded by her son Edward VII.

1918
World War I ends.

1921
Irish Free State is established; Northern Ireland remains part of Great Britain.

1939
Germany invades Poland and World War II begins.

1947
India and Pakistan are given independence from Great Britain.

1900

1914
Assassination of Archduke Franz Ferdinand sparks World War I.

1921
T. S. Eliot writes his groundbreaking poem *The Waste Land*.

1929
United States stock market crash causes global economic depression.

1945
World War II ends; British losses total 360,000.

The End of Empire After World War II, Britain was financially drained, burdened by debt and the need to rebuild its cities. Everything was rationed. Determined to provide at least the basic necessities, the government transformed Britain with a new national health care system and public education. Concerned with domestic issues, leaders had little desire to cling to colonies that were all too eager for self-rule. After World War I, Britain's grasp on its empire had already begun to loosen as the spirit of nationalism swept Europe and the colonial empires. Britain granted ever-greater degrees of self-determination to its colonies, eventually making some of these lands partners in the British Commonwealth of Nations rather than continuing to treat them as possessions. Soon after World War II, Britain gave India its independence. In the decades that followed, Britain yielded to nationalistic and economic pressures and relinquished control of most of its remaining colonies.

Literature in the 20th Century and Beyond After World War I, Europe was a place of uncertainty and upheaval. In England, the previously stable social order based on community and class distinctions was giving way to the anonymity of urban life. In the arts, modernism was a way of trying to make sense of this new, fragmented world. Visual artists, composers, and writers rejected traditional forms and experimented with new styles that better reflected the realities and values of modern life.

RESEARCH
What about this historical period interests you? Choose a topic, event, or person to learn more about. Then, add your own entry to the timeline.

1952
Elizabeth II ascends the throne.

1997
Great Britain returns Hong Kong to China after 155 years of colonial rule.

2007
British Indian author Salman Rushdie is awarded a knighthood from Queen Elizabeth II.

1949
George Orwell publishes *1984*, a nightmarish vision of a totalitarian England.

1979
Margaret Thatcher becomes the first female prime minister.

2005
Bombs explode on the London Underground and a bus, killing 56.

Present

New narrative styles rejected traditional linear plot and character development, and instead placed the reader inside the character's mind. Many writers felt a sense of alienation from their own society after witnessing the horrors of war, and as a result explored themes of isolation, human relationships and vulnerabilities, and disillusionment.

The end of the British Empire also shaped and continues to shape literature. Writers from former colonies explore issues related to their countries' colonial past, while writers who have immigrated to England often address cultural tensions in their works. The multicultural perspective these writers bring has broadened the horizons of contemporary British literature.

CHECK YOUR UNDERSTANDING

Choose the best answer to each question.

1 Which most directly caused the outbreak of World War II?

   A Italy's and Japan's alliance with Germany

   B The crash of the United States stock market

   C Hitler's seizure of power in Germany

   D The invasion of Poland by Germany

2 British politicians after World War II —

   F wanted to hold the British Empire together as long as possible

   G believed that strengthening the colonies would help Britain recover from the war

   H placed less emphasis on empire and focused more on domestic issues

   J immediately granted independence to all former British colonies

3 Which was a primary aspect of modernism?

   A Focus on nationalistic perspectives in the arts and literature

   B Rejection of traditional forms in the arts and literature

   C Focus on war recovery and domestic affairs in politics

   D Rejection of colonialism and empire building in politics

ACADEMIC VOCABULARY

Academic Vocabulary words are words you use when you discuss and write about texts. In this unit, you will learn the following five words:

☑ **arbitrary**   ☐ **controversy**   ☐ **convince**   ☐ **denote**   ☐ **undergo**

Study the Word Network to learn more about the word **arbitrary.**

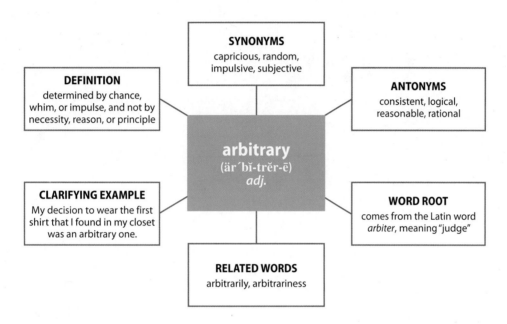

SYNONYMS
capricious, random, impulsive, subjective

DEFINITION
determined by chance, whim, or impulse, and not by necessity, reason, or principle

ANTONYMS
consistent, logical, reasonable, rational

arbitrary
(är´bĭ-trĕr-ē)
adj.

CLARIFYING EXAMPLE
My decision to wear the first shirt that I found in my closet was an arbitrary one.

WORD ROOT
comes from the Latin word *arbiter,* meaning "judge"

RELATED WORDS
arbitrarily, arbitrariness

Write and Discuss Discuss your completed Word Network with a partner, making sure to talk through all of the boxes until you both understand the word, its synonyms, antonyms, and related forms. Then, fill out a Word Network for the remaining four words. Use a dictionary or online resource to help you complete the activity.

   Go online to access the Word Networks.

RESPOND TO THE ESSENTIAL QUESTIONS

In this unit, you will explore four different **Essential Questions** about New Ideas, New Voices. As you read each selection, you will gather your ideas about one of these questions and write about it in the **Response Log** that appears on page R6. At the end of the unit, you will have the opportunity to write an **argument** related to one of the Essential Questions. Filling out the Response Log after you read each text will help you prepare for this writing task.

   You can also go online to access the Response Log.

A CUP OF TEA

Short Story by **Katherine Mansfield**

? *ESSENTIAL QUESTION:*

What makes people feel insecure?

QUICK START

How can social status affect a person's self-image? Discuss this question with a small group of students.

ANALYZE THIRD-PERSON POINT OF VIEW

When a writer uses the **third-person point of view,** the narrator is not a character in the story but an outside observer. Sometimes a third-person narrator is **omniscient** and can describe what all the characters are thinking and feeling. In modern fiction, authors more commonly use a **limited** third-person narrator, describing the thoughts, feelings, and observations of only one character. Readers may feel like they are looking over the shoulder of that character as the story's action unfolds. This technique often helps readers become more emotionally involved with the chosen character, but it can also lead to surprises because the narration is limited by the character's awareness and understanding of events.

In "A Cup of Tea," Katherine Mansfield's use of the third-person limited point of view influences the development of the characters. The narrator starts off describing the protagonist, Rosemary Fell, from a distance, as if discussing her with a friend. But soon the narrator focuses in on Rosemary, using slang and exaggeration to mimic Rosemary's speech and suggest how she perceives the world around her. As you read the story, notice how the narrator's conversational tone subtly reveals Rosemary's inner life.

EVALUATE A CHARACTER

Most complex characters are not entirely good or bad, and readers need to take various factors into account when evaluating them. A character's motivation may influence how you view his or her behavior; for example, a charitable donation may be motivated by compassion, vanity, or a combination of both. When evaluating a character, you should also consider the story's historical, social, and economic context. "A Cup of Tea" is set in London in the early 1900s, a time when rigid class distinctions would have made it seem improper for a wealthy woman to socialize with an impoverished one. This context influences the story's plot and theme, as well as Mansfield's characterization of the protagonist, Rosemary.

As you read "A Cup of Tea," use a chart like this one to help you evaluate Rosemary.

ACTION	MOTIVATION	OUTCOME

GENRE ELEMENTS: SHORT STORY

- includes the basic elements of fiction—setting, characters, plot, conflict, and theme
- centers on a particular moment or event or follows the life of one character
- can be read in one sitting
- may be told by a first-person narrator who is a character in the story or a third-person narrator outside the story

CRITICAL VOCABULARY

presentable	tactfully	listless	vile	engagement

To check your familiarity with the Critical Vocabulary words, answer the following questions.

1. What word would you use to describe something you strongly dislike?

2. Which word might describe someone who has fallen ill?

3. Which word describes how you try to look to meet someone's parents?

4. What's a word for when you have social plans?

5. Which word describes how you should handle a delicate situation?

LANGUAGE CONVENTIONS

Precise Details In both fiction and nonfiction, authors use precise details to shape and inform the perception of readers. Readers evaluate an author's use of details to analyze key ideas.

> For he took a pencil, leaned over the counter, and his <u>pale bloodless fingers</u> crept timidly towards those <u>rosy, flashing ones</u>, as he murmured gently: "If I may venture to point out to madam, the flowers on the little lady's bodice."

In this sentence, the detail of how Rosemary perceives her own fingers in comparison to the shopkeeper's gives us an insight into her character and her habit of comparing herself favorably to others. This is a key idea in the development of the story's theme.

ANNOTATION MODEL

NOTICE & NOTE

As you read, notice how the third-person limited point of view shapes your impression of Rosemary. Pay attention to details and word choices that provide hints about Rosemary's character and motivation. In the model you can see one student's notes about the narrator's description of Rosemary in the opening paragraph.

Rosemary Fell was not exactly beautiful. No, you couldn't have called her beautiful. <u>Pretty? Well, if you took her to pieces</u> . . . But why be so cruel as to take anyone to pieces? <u>She was young, brilliant, extremely modern, exquisitely well dressed, amazingly well read</u> in the newest of the new books, and her parties were the most delicious mixture of the really important people and . . . artists—quaint creatures, <u>discoveries of hers, some of them too terrifying for words</u>, but others quite presentable and amusing.

The narrator describes the protagonist as if she is talking about a friend. The tone is conversational and intimate.

The narrator is sympathetic towards Rosemary but also seems to mock her a little bit.

BACKGROUND

Katherine Mansfield *(1888–1923) was born in New Zealand. She disliked her native country and was eager to leave home at 19 to settle in London, where she had attended school several years earlier. Mansfield struggled to earn a living in England and fell into some troubled romantic relationships. When she was 29 she contracted tuberculosis. In the last year of her life, Mansfield wrote some of her finest stories. By the end of her brief career, she gained recognition as a master of the modern short story, emphasizing psychological realism over dramatic action.*

A CUP OF TEA

Short Story by Katherine Mansfield

SETTING A PURPOSE

As you read, pay attention to the author's use of third-person limited point of view and think about how the story might be different if it were told in omniscient point of view.

1   Rosemary Fell was not exactly beautiful. No, you couldn't have called her beautiful. Pretty? Well, if you took her to pieces . . . But why be so cruel as to take anyone to pieces? She was young, brilliant, extremely modern, exquisitely well dressed, amazingly well read in the newest of the new books, and her parties were the most delicious mixture of the really important people and . . . artists—quaint creatures, discoveries of hers, some of them too terrifying for words, but others quite **presentable** and amusing.

2   Rosemary had been married two years. She had a duck[1] of a boy. No, not Peter—Michael. And her husband absolutely adored her. They were rich, really rich, not just comfortably well off, which is odious and stuffy and sounds like one's grandparents. But if Rosemary wanted to shop she would go to Paris as you and I would go to Bond Street.[2] If she wanted to buy flowers, the car

---

[1] **duck:** a British expression for a darling person or thing.
[2] **Bond Street:** a London street famous for its fashionable shops.

© Houghton Mifflin Publishing Company • Image Credits: © Paul Fearn/Alamy; © Matt Child/Alamy

Notice & Note

Use the side margins to notice and note signposts in the text.

LANGUAGE CONVENTIONS

Annotate: Mark words and phrases used to describe Rosemary in paragraph 1.

Draw Conclusions: What do these details suggest about how society views her?

presentable
(prĭ-zĕn′tə-bəl) *adj.* fit for introduction to others.

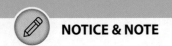
pulled up at that perfect shop in Regent Street, and Rosemary inside the shop just gazed in her dazzled, rather exotic way, and said: "I want those and those and those. Give me four bunches of those. And that jar of roses. Yes, I'll have all the roses in the jar. No, no lilac. I hate lilac. It's got no shape." The attendant bowed and put the lilac out of sight, as though this was only too true; lilac was dreadfully shapeless. "Give me those stumpy little tulips. Those red and white ones." And she was followed to the car by a thin shopgirl staggering under an immense white paper armful that looked like a baby in long clothes. . . .

3   One winter afternoon she had been buying something in a little antique shop in Curzon Street. It was a shop she liked. For one thing, one usually had it to oneself. And then the man who kept it was ridiculously fond of serving her. He beamed whenever she came in. He clasped his hands; he was so gratified he could scarcely speak. Flattery, of course. All the same, there was something . . .

4   "You see, madam," he would explain in his low respectful tones, "I love my things. I would rather not part with them than sell them to someone who does not appreciate them, who has not that fine feeling which is so rare. . . ." And, breathing deeply, he unrolled a tiny square of blue velvet and pressed it on the glass counter with his pale fingertips.

5   Today it was a little box. He had been keeping it for her. He had shown it to nobody as yet. An exquisite little enamel box with a glaze so fine it looked as though it had been baked in cream. On the lid a minute creature stood under a flowery tree, and a more minute creature still had her arms around his neck. Her hat, really no bigger than a geranium petal, hung from a branch; it had green ribbons. And there was a pink cloud like a watchful cherub[3] floating above their heads. Rosemary took her hands out of her long gloves. She always took off her gloves to examine such things. Yes, she liked it very much. She loved it; it was a great duck. She must have it. And, turning the creamy box, opening and shutting it, she couldn't help noticing how charming her hands were against the blue velvet. The shopman, in some dim cavern of his mind, may have dared to think so too. For he took a pencil, leaned over the counter, and his pale bloodless fingers crept timidly towards those rosy, flashing ones, as he murmured gently: "If I may venture to point out to madam, the flowers on the little lady's bodice."[4]

6   "Charming!" Rosemary admired the flowers. But what was the price? For a moment the shopman did not seem to hear. Then a murmur reached her. "Twenty-eight guineas,[5] madam."

---

[3] **cherub** (chĕr´əb): an angel depicted as a chubby child with wings.
[4] **bodice** (bŏd´ĭs): the part of a dress above the waist.
[5] **guineas** (gĭn´ēz): units of British money equal to one pound and one shilling, used mainly for pricing luxury items.

7   "Twenty-eight guineas." Rosemary gave no sign. She laid the little box down; she buttoned her gloves again. Twenty-eight guineas. Even if one is rich . . . She looked vague. She stared at a plump teakettle like a plump hen above the shopman's head, and her voice was dreamy as she answered: "Well, keep it for me—will you? I'll . . ."

8   But the shopman had already bowed as though keeping it for her was all any human being could ask. He would be willing, of course, to keep it for her forever.

9   The discreet door shut with a click. She was outside on the step, gazing at the winter afternoon. Rain was falling, and with the rain it seemed the dark came too, spinning down like ashes. There was a cold bitter taste in the air, and the new-lighted lamps looked sad. Sad were the lights in the houses opposite. Dimly they burned as if regretting something. And people hurried by, hidden under their hateful umbrellas. Rosemary felt a strange pang.[6] She pressed her muff to her breast; she wished she had the little box, too, to cling to. Of course, the car was there. She'd only to cross the pavement. But still she waited. There are moments, horrible moments in life, when one emerges from shelter and looks out, and it's awful. One oughtn't to give way to them. One ought to go home and have an extra-special tea. But at the very instant of thinking that, a young girl, thin, dark, shadowy—where had she come from?—was standing at Rosemary's elbow and a voice like a sigh, almost like a sob, breathed: "Madam, may I speak to you a moment?"

10   "Speak to me?" Rosemary turned. She saw a little battered creature with enormous eyes, someone quite young, no older than herself, who clutched at her coat-collar with reddened hands, and shivered as though she had just come out of the water.

11   "M-madam," stammered the voice. "Would you let me have the price of a cup of tea?"

12   "A cup of tea?" There was something simple, sincere in that voice; it wasn't in the least the voice of a beggar. "Then have you no money at all?" asked Rosemary.

13   "None, madam," came the answer.

14   "How extraordinary!" Rosemary peered through the dusk, and the girl gazed back at her. How more than extraordinary! And suddenly it seemed to Rosemary such an adventure. It was like something out of a novel by Dostoyevsky,[7] this meeting in the dusk. Supposing she took the girl home? Supposing she did do one of those things she was always reading about or seeing on the stage, what would happen? It would be thrilling. And she heard herself saying afterwards to the amazement of her friends: "I simply took her home

EVALUATE A CHARACTER

Annotate: Mark words and phrases in paragraph 14 that reveal Rosemary's thoughts about this encounter.

Evaluate: What is Rosemary's motivation for inviting the girl to her home?

---

[6] **pang** (păng): a sudden sharp pain or feeling.
[7] **Dostoyevsky** (dŏs-tə-yĕf´skē): Feodor Dostoyevsky, a 19th-century Russian author who wrote a number of novels and stories dealing with the lives of the poor.

with me," as she stepped forward and said to that dim person beside her: "Come home to tea with me."

15   The girl drew back startled. She even stopped shivering for a moment. Rosemary put out a hand and touched her arm. "I mean it," she said, smiling. And she felt how simple and kind her smile was. "Why won't you? Do. Come home with me now in my car and have tea."

16   "You—you don't mean it, madam," said the girl, and there was pain in her voice.

17   "But I do," cried Rosemary. "I want you to. To please me. Come along."

18   The girl put her fingers to her lips and her eyes devoured Rosemary. "You're—you're not taking me to the police station?" she stammered.

19   "The police station!" Rosemary laughed out. "Why should I be so cruel? No, I only want to make you warm and to hear—anything you care to tell me."

20   Hungry people are easily led. The footman[8] held the door of the car open, and a moment later they were skimming through the dusk.

21   "There!" said Rosemary. She had a feeling of triumph as she slipped her hand through the velvet strap. She could have said, "Now I've got you," as she gazed at the little captive she had netted. But of course she meant it kindly. Oh, more than kindly. She was going to prove to this girl that—wonderful things did happen in life, that—fairy godmothers were real, that—rich people had hearts, and that women *were* sisters. She turned impulsively, saying: "Don't be frightened. After all, why shouldn't you come back with me? We're both women. If I'm the more fortunate, you ought to expect . . ."

22   But happily at that moment, for she didn't know how the sentence was going to end, the car stopped. The bell was rung, the door opened, and with a charming, protecting, almost embracing movement, Rosemary drew the other into the hall. Warmth, softness, light, a sweet scent, all those things so familiar to her she never even thought about them, she watched that other receive. It was fascinating. She was like the little rich girl in her nursery with all the cupboards to open, all the boxes to unpack.

23   "Come, come upstairs," said Rosemary, longing to begin to be generous. "Come up to my room." And, besides, she wanted to spare this poor little thing from being stared at by the servants; she decided as they mounted the stairs she would not even ring for Jeanne, but take off her things by herself. The great thing was to be natural!

24   And "There!" cried Rosemary again, as they reached her beautiful big bedroom with the curtains drawn, the fire leaping on

© Houghton Mifflin Harcourt Publishing Company

EVALUATE A CHARACTER

Annotate: Mark words and phrases in paragraphs 21–22 that describe how Rosemary views her treatment of the girl.

Evaluate: What do these thoughts suggest about her character?

---

[8] **footman:** a household servant, here functioning as Rosemary's chauffeur.

her wonderful lacquer furniture, her gold cushions and the primrose and blue rugs.

25   The girl stood just inside the door; she seemed dazed. But Rosemary didn't mind that.

26   "Come and sit down," she cried, dragging her big chair up to the fire, "in this comfy chair. Come and get warm. You look so dreadfully cold."

27   "I daren't, madam," said the girl, and she edged backwards.

28   "Oh, please,"—Rosemary ran forward—"you mustn't be frightened, you mustn't, really. Sit down, and when I've taken off my things we shall go into the next room and have tea and be cozy. Why are you afraid?" And gently she half pushed the thin figure into its deep cradle.

29   But there was no answer. The girl stayed just as she had been put, with her hands by her sides and her mouth slightly open. To be quite sincere, she looked rather stupid. But Rosemary wouldn't acknowledge it. She leaned over her, saying: "Won't you take off your hat? Your pretty hair is all wet. And one is so much more comfortable without a hat, isn't one?"

30   There was a whisper that sounded like "Very good, madam," and the crushed hat was taken off.

31   "Let me help you off with your coat, too," said Rosemary.

32   The girl stood up. But she held on to the chair with one hand and let Rosemary pull. It was quite an effort. The other scarcely helped her at all. She seemed to stagger like a child, and the thought came and went through Rosemary's mind, that if people wanted helping they must respond a little, just a little, otherwise it became very difficult indeed. And what was she to do with the coat now? She left it on the floor, and the hat too. She was just going to take a cigarette off the mantelpiece when the girl said quickly, but so lightly and strangely: "I'm very sorry, madam, but I'm going to faint. I shall go off, madam, if I don't have something."

33   "Good heavens, how thoughtless I am!" Rosemary rushed to the bell.

34   "Tea! Tea at once! And some brandy immediately!"

35   The maid was gone again, but the girl almost cried out. "No, I don't want no brandy. I never drink brandy. It's a cup of tea I want, madam." And she burst into tears.

36   It was a terrible and fascinating moment. Rosemary knelt beside her chair.

37   "Don't cry, poor little thing," she said. "Don't cry." And she gave the other her lace handkerchief. She really was touched beyond words. She put her arm round those thin, birdlike shoulders.

38   Now at last the other forgot to be shy, forgot everything except that they were both women, and gasped out: "I can't go on no longer

© Houghton Mifflin Harcourt Publishing Company

ANALYZE THIRD-PERSON POINT OF VIEW

Annotate: In paragraph 32, underline Rosemary's thoughts about the girl's behavior and circle the girl's dialogue.

Analyze: How does the use of third-person limited point of view create irony here?

like this. I can't bear it. I shall *do* away with myself. I can't bear no more."

39   "You shan't have to. I'll look after you. Don't cry anymore. Don't you see what a good thing it was that you met me? We'll have tea and you'll tell me everything. And I shall arrange something. I promise. *Do* stop crying. It's so exhausting. Please!"

40   The other did stop just in time for Rosemary to get up before the tea came. She had the table placed between them. She plied the poor little creature with everything, all the sandwiches, all the bread and butter, and every time her cup was empty she filled it with tea, cream and sugar. People always said sugar was so nourishing. As for herself she didn't eat; she smoked and looked away **tactfully** so that the other should not be shy.

41   And really the effect of that slight meal was marvelous. When the tea table was carried away a new being, a light, frail creature with tangled hair, dark lips, deep, lighted eyes, lay back in the big chair in a kind of sweet languor,[9] looking at the blaze. Rosemary lit a fresh cigarette; it was time to begin.

42   "And when did you have your last meal?" she asked softly.

43   But at that moment the door-handle turned.

44   "Rosemary, may I come in?" It was Philip.

45   "Of course."

46   He came in. "Oh, I'm so sorry," he said, and stopped and stared.

47   "It's quite all right," said Rosemary smiling. "This is my friend, Miss—"

48   "Smith, madam," said the languid figure, who was strangely still and unafraid.

49   "Smith," said Rosemary. "We are going to have a little talk."

50   "Oh, yes," said Philip. "Quite," and his eye caught sight of the coat and hat on the floor. He came over to the fire and turned his back to it. "It's a beastly[10] afternoon," he said curiously, still looking at that **listless** figure, looking at its hands and boots, and then at Rosemary again.

51   "Yes, isn't it?" said Rosemary enthusiastically. "**Vile.**"

52   Philip smiled his charming smile. "As a matter of fact," said he, "I wanted you to come into the library for a moment. Would you? Will Miss Smith excuse us?"

53   The big eyes were raised to him, but Rosemary answered for her. "Of course she will." And they went out of the room together.

54   "I say," said Philip, when they were alone. "Explain. Who is she? What does it all mean?"

---

[9] **languor** (lăng´gər): a dreamy, lazy state.
[10] **beastly:** awful; unpleasant.

tactfully
(tăkt´fəl-lē) *adv.* considerately and discreetly.

EVALUATE A CHARACTER

Annotate: Mark references to the girl's name in paragraphs 47–49.

Evaluate: What does it suggest about Rosemary that she hasn't asked for her name until now?

listless
(lĭst´lĭs) *adj.* lacking energy or disinclined to exert effort; lethargic.

vile
(vīl) *adj.* unpleasant or objectionable.

55   Rosemary, laughing, leaned against the door and said: "I picked her up in Curzon Street. Really. She's a real pick-up. She asked me for the price of a cup of tea, and I brought her home with me."

56   "But what on earth are you going to do with her?" cried Philip.

57   "Be nice to her," said Rosemary quickly. "Be frightfully nice to her. Look after her. I don't know how. We haven't talked yet. But show her—treat her—make her feel—"

58   "My darling girl," said Philip, "you're quite mad, you know. It simply can't be done."

59   "I knew you'd say that," retorted Rosemary. "Why not? I want to. Isn't that a reason? And besides, one's always reading about these things. I decided—"

60   "But," said Philip slowly, and he cut the end of a cigar, "she's so astonishingly pretty."

61   "Pretty?" Rosemary was so surprised that she blushed. "Do you think so? I—I hadn't thought about it."

62   "Good Lord!" Philip struck a match. "She's absolutely lovely. Look again, my child. I was bowled over when I came into your room just now. However . . . I think you're making a ghastly mistake. Sorry, darling, if I'm crude and all that. But let me know if Miss Smith is going to dine with us in time for me to look up *The Milliner's Gazette*."[11]

AHA MOMENT

Notice & Note: Mark the sentence in paragraph 63 that describes how Philip's comments have affected Rosemary.

Infer: Why is Rosemary rushing to give money to Miss Smith?

63   "You absurd creature!" said Rosemary, and she went out of the library, but not back to her bedroom. She went to her writing-room and sat down at her desk. Pretty! Absolutely lovely! Bowled over! Her heart beat like a heavy bell. Pretty! Lovely! She drew her checkbook towards her. But no, checks would be no use, of course. She opened a drawer and took out five pound notes, looked at them, put two back, and holding the three squeezed in her hand, she went back to her bedroom.

64   Half an hour later Philip was still in the library, when Rosemary
65 came in. "I only wanted to tell you," said she, and she leaned against the door again and looked at him with her dazzled exotic gaze, "Miss Smith won't dine with us tonight."

66   Philip put down the paper. "Oh, what's happened? Previous **engagement**?"

67   Rosemary came over and sat down on his knee. "She insisted on going," said she, "so I gave the poor little thing a present of money. I couldn't keep her against her will, could I?" she added softly.

68   Rosemary had just done her hair, darkened her eyes a little, and put on her pearls. She put up her hands and touched Philip's cheeks.

engagement
(ĕn-gāj´mənt) *n.* a promise or agreement to be at a particular place at a particular time.

---

[11] *The Milliner's Gazette*: an imaginary newsletter for working-class women. A milliner is a maker of women's hats.

69   "Do you like me?" said she, and her tone, sweet, husky, troubled him.

70   "I like you awfully," he said, and he held her tighter. "Kiss me."

71   There was a pause.

72   Then Rosemary said dreamily, "I saw a fascinating little box today. It cost twenty-eight guineas. May I have it?"

73   Philip jumped her on his knee. "You may, little wasteful one," said he.

74   But that was not really what Rosemary wanted to say.

75   "Philip," she whispered, and she pressed his head against her bosom, "am I *pretty?*"

CHECK YOUR UNDERSTANDING

Answer these questions before moving on to the **Analyze the Text** section on the following page.

1 In paragraphs 3–5 what can you infer about the shopkeeper?

   A He has a secret crush on Rosemary.

   B He uses flattery to sell expensive things to rich people.

   C He isn't very interested in money.

   D He wishes he didn't have to sell his things.

2 In paragraphs 10–14, which sentence suggests Rosemary's motivation for taking Miss Smith home with her?

   F *"M-madam," stammered the voice. "Would you let me have the price of a cup of tea?"*

   G *There was something simple, sincere in that voice; it wasn't in the least the voice of a beggar.*

   H *It was like something out of a novel by Dostoyevsky, this meeting in the dusk.*

   J *And she heard herself saying afterwards to the amazement of her friends: "I simply took her home with me...."*

3 How does Rosemary's husband convince her to send the girl away?

   A He plays on her insecurity about her looks.

   B He embarrasses her for not reading the paper.

   C He scolds her about money.

   D He flatters her need to feel superior.

ANALYZE THE TEXT

Support your responses with evidence from the text. [≡] NOTEBOOK

1. **Analyze** How does the third-person limited point of view affect your reaction to Rosemary and her plan to help Miss Smith? How might the story have been different if told by an omniscient narrator?

2. **Draw Conclusions** Reread paragraphs 60–62. Why does Philip speak so enthusiastically to his wife about Miss Smith's attractiveness? Explain.

3. **Analyze** What theme about wealthy people does Mansfield convey in "A Cup of Tea"? How do Rosemary's actions and motivation in trying to help Miss Smith relate to this theme?

4. **Connect** "A Cup of Tea" is set in a time when wealthy women did not have professions and were expected to appear fashionable. How does this context influence your evaluation of Rosemary's character?

5. **Notice & Note** Rosemary abandons her plan after Philip makes her aware of Miss Smith's beauty. Has this realization changed Rosemary? Why or why not?

RESEARCH

RESEARCH TIP

When researching many aspects of a broad subject, look for websites run by organizations dedicated to that subject, and look through the website's menu for a "Resources" page. This is a good way to find helpful and credible sources.

"A Cup of Tea" was written in 1922, at a time when British and American women's lives were undergoing radical change. Do some research to find out about some of the social changes of the 1920s, and complete the graphic organizer.

SOCIAL CHANGES FOR WOMEN IN THE 1920s	
Education	
Political Power	
Labor and Employment	
Fashion	

Extend How did these changes affect women's relationships with men on an individual and societal level?

CREATE AND DEBATE

Write a Missing Scene from Another Point of View We know that Rosemary goes back to her bedroom and gives Miss Smith some money before asking her to leave, but the scene is not in the story. Write this scene from Miss Smith's perspective using the third-person limited point of view.

❏ Remember that the third-person narrator is a voice outside of the story.

❏ The narrator should relate only Miss Smith's thoughts and feelings.

Present a Scene Read your scene to the group. Remember your presentational techniques as you convey your meaning.

❏ Practice reading your scene aloud.

❏ Determine the speed at which you will read, including where you will pause for effect.

❏ Select words and phrases you will emphasize.

❏ Determine where you might raise and lower your voice and when you will make eye contact with your audience.

❏ After your presentation, let the group comment or ask questions.

 Go to **Writing Narratives** in the **Writing Studio** to find out more about writing fiction.

Go to **Giving a Presentation** in the **Speaking and Listening Studio** to find out more.

RESPOND TO THE ESSENTIAL QUESTION

 ? What makes people feel insecure?

Gather Information Review your annotations and notes on "A Cup of Tea." Then, add relevant information to your Response Log. As you determine which information to include, think about:

• what we base our opinions of ourselves on
• how people can use our insecurities to manipulate us
• how comparing ourselves to others can affect our self-esteem

ACADEMIC VOCABULARY

As you write and discuss what you learned from the story, be sure to use the Academic Vocabulary words. Check off each of the words that you use.

❏ **arbitrary**
❏ **controversy**
❏ **convince**
❏ **denote**
❏ **undergo**

WORD BANK
presentable
tactfully
listless
vile
engagement

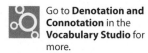

Go to **Denotation and Connotation** in the **Vocabulary Studio** for more.

CRITICAL VOCABULARY

Practice and Apply Complete the sentences with Critical Vocabulary words.

1. The baby is so pale and _____. She must be sick!

2. I'm sorry to cancel our plans, but I have another _____.

3. If I'd known I was having visitors I'd have tried to look _____ instead of wearing sweatpants.

4. I need to _____ remind her that she owes me money.

5. I won't tolerate such _____ language just because you are angry with me.

VOCABULARY STRATEGY:
Denotation and Connotation

Connotation and denotation are ways of describing the meaning of words. **Denotation** is the literal definition of a word found in the dictionary. **Connotation** refers to the emotional associations of a word, which may be positive or negative. The way a word is used may influence its connotation.

> . . . her parties were the most delicious mixture of the really important people and . . . artists—quaint creatures, discoveries of hers, some of them too terrifying for words, but others quite <u>presentable</u> and amusing.

Here, the word *presentable* has a connotation of snobbery and privilege.

Practice and Apply In the sentences below from "A Cup of Tea," look up the underlined word in a dictionary and write its denotation. Then, make some notes about its connotation.

1. Her parties were the most <u>delicious</u> mixture of . . . people.

Denotation:

Connotation:

2. She saw a little battered creature with enormous eyes . . . who <u>clutched</u> at her coat-collar with reddened hands.

Denotation:

Connotation:

3. The girl stayed just as she had been put, with her hands by her sides and her mouth slightly open. To be quite <u>sincere</u>, she looked rather stupid.

Denotation:

Connotation:

LANGUAGE CONVENTIONS:
Precise Details

In order to engage the reader, authors use precise details to illustrate or suggest key ideas. A good writer does not provide details arbitrarily, but rather makes very deliberate choices in using details to develop characters and themes.

> **She had a feeling of triumph as she slipped her hand through the <u>velvet strap</u>.**

In this sentence, the velvet strap reminds the reader that Rosemary lives a life of luxury and comfort.

> **There was a whisper that sounded like "Very good, madam," and the <u>crushed hat</u> was taken off.**

In this sentence, the "crushed hat" gives the reader a sense of the girl's poverty and misfortune.

Practice and Apply In the passages below from "A Cup of Tea," mark the precise details the author uses to develop the characters and theme.

> **"Don't cry, poor little thing," she said. "Don't cry." And she gave the other her lace handkerchief. She really was touched beyond words. She put her arm round those thin, birdlike shoulders.**

> **When the tea table was carried away a new being, a light, frail creature with tangled hair, dark lips, deep, lighted eyes, lay back in the big chair in a kind of sweet languor, looking at the blaze.**

How do these details contribute to the reader's understanding of the characters and the theme of the story?

THE LOVE SONG OF J. ALFRED PRUFROCK

Poem by **T. S. Eliot**

? ***ESSENTIAL QUESTION:***

What makes
people feel
insecure?

QUICK START

Some people appear confident in any situation, while others are filled with doubts about themselves. What circumstances can diminish a person's confidence? Write a paragraph in response to this question. Then, discuss your ideas with a partner.

UNDERSTAND MODERNIST POETRY

Modernist poets such as T. S. Eliot abandoned traditional verse forms and experimented with literary techniques to better reflect the social and technological changes of their times. Eliot's poetry can be difficult to understand because he presents a patchwork of images, symbols, and allusions that readers must connect for themselves. Consider using the following strategies to help you interpret "The Love Song of J. Alfred Prufrock":

- Read the poem aloud, pausing between sections and lingering over striking images.

- Reread the poem more than once.

- Annotate the text by marking difficult lines and passages and paraphrasing or summarizing them.

- Consult the side notes for explanations of literary allusions.

MAKE INFERENCES

In his poetry, Eliot rarely expresses ideas in a straightforward manner. To understand and appreciate these poems, readers must make **inferences,** logical guesses based on clues found in the text. Making inferences is sometimes called "reading between the lines" because you come to an understanding of something that the author has not explicitly stated. For example, we can infer from the following lines that the speaker is going to a social gathering where he thinks he must hide his true personality or feelings from the other guests:

> **There will be time, there will be time**
> **To prepare a face to meet the faces that you meet;**

As you read "The Love Song of J. Alfred Prufrock," look for images that suggest thoughts and feelings. Use a chart like this one to record your inferences.

DETAILS FROM THE TEXT	MY INFERENCES

GENRE ELEMENTS: LYRIC POETRY

- expresses strong feelings or thoughts
- has a musical quality
- often deals with intense emotions surrounding events like death, love, or loss
- includes forms such as ode, elegy, and sonnet

ANALYZE STREAM OF CONSCIOUSNESS

One of the most radical breaks from convention in modernist literature was the development of **stream of consciousness.** This writing technique, used by both poets and fiction writers, presents the random flow of thoughts, emotions, memories, and associations running through the mind of a character or speaker. The goal is to re-create states of mind instead of describing them.

"The Love Song of J. Alfred Prufrock" is a dramatic monologue in which Prufrock addresses a silent listener with a tumble of thoughts, allusions, and figurative language, as in the following stanza:

> **Shall I part my hair behind? Do I dare to eat a peach?**
> **I shall wear white flannel trousers, and walk upon the beach.**
> **I have heard the mermaids singing, each to each.**

As you read the poem, try not to be put off by the seemingly nonsensical nature of the stream-of-consciousness verse, but be alert to any feelings or ideas that the images seem to suggest.

ANNOTATION MODEL   NOTICE & NOTE

As you read, note down associations you can make between thoughts, images, and other elements in the poem. In the model, you can see one reader's notes about the opening lines of "The Love Song of J. Alfred Prufrock."

Let us go then, you and I,

When the evening is spread out against the sky

Like a patient etherised upon a table;

Let us go, through certain half-deserted streets,

The muttering retreats

Of restless nights in one-night cheap hotels

And sawdust restaurants with oyster-shells:

Prufrock addresses the listener—is that us?—with an invitation to walk with him through the city. What a strange simile he uses to describe the night sky!

He seems to be thinking about a tawdry side of town.

BACKGROUND

T. S. Eliot *(1888–1965) was one of the most influential poets and literary critics of the 20th century. He grew up in a cultured household in St. Louis, Missouri. While pursuing his graduate studies, he became involved with a circle of avant-garde writers and settled down in London. He published his first collection of poems,* Prufrock and Other Observations, *in 1917. The book baffled some reviewers but was hailed by modernists. Eliot followed it up in 1922 with* The Waste Land, *which made him internationally famous. The poem expresses the sense of alienation and spiritual loss felt by many in his generation.*

THE LOVE SONG OF J. ALFRED PRUFROCK

Poem by T. S. Eliot

SETTING A PURPOSE

As you read, consider why the speaker asks so many questions and whether or not those questions get answered.

> *S'io credessi che mia risposta fosse*
> *a persona che mai tornasse al mondo,*
> *questa fiamma staria senza più scosse.*
> *Ma per ciò che giammai di questo fondo*
> *non tornò vivo alcun, s'i'odo il vero,*
> *senza tema d'infamia ti rispondo.*

Let us go then, you and I,
When the evening is spread out against the sky
Like a patient etherised upon a table;
Let us go, through certain half-deserted streets,
5 The muttering retreats
Of restless nights in one-night cheap hotels
And sawdust restaurants with oyster-shells:
Streets that follow like a tedious argument
Of insidious intent
10 To lead you to an overwhelming question . . .

© Houghton Mifflin Harcourt Publishing Company • Image Credits: © Mansell/The LIFE Picture Collection/Getty Images; © Piero Cruciatti/Alamy

Notice & Note

Use the side margins to notice and note signposts in the text.

S'io credessi . . . ti rispondo:
These lines are from the *Inferno,* written in the early 14th century by Italian poet Dante Alighieri. As Dante visits hell, one of the damned agrees to speak of his torment only because he believes that Dante cannot return to the living world to repeat the tale.

3 etherised: given ether, a liquid used as an anesthetic.

9 insidious (ĭn-sĭdʹē-əs): more dangerous than it seems.

Oh, do not ask, "What is it?"
Let us go and make our visit.

In the room the women come and go
Talking of Michelangelo.

15 The yellow fog that rubs its back upon the window-panes,
The yellow smoke that rubs its muzzle on the window-panes,
Licked its tongue into the corners of the evening,
Lingered upon the pools that stand in drains,
Let fall upon its back the soot that falls from chimneys,
20 Slipped by the terrace, made a sudden leap,
And seeing that it was a soft October night,
Curled once about the house, and fell asleep.

And indeed there will be time
For the yellow smoke that slides along the street
25 Rubbing its back upon the window-panes;
There will be time, there will be time
To prepare a face to meet the faces that you meet;
There will be time to murder and create,
And time for all the works and days of hands
30 That lift and drop a question on your plate;
Time for you and time for me,
And time yet for a hundred indecisions,
And for a hundred visions and revisions,
Before the taking of a toast and tea.

35 In the room the women come and go
Talking of Michelangelo.

And indeed there will be time
To wonder, "Do I dare?" and, "Do I dare?"
Time to turn back and descend the stair,
40 With a bald spot in the middle of my hair—
(They will say: "How his hair is growing thin!")
My morning coat, my collar mounting firmly to the chin,
My necktie rich and modest, but asserted by a simple pin—
(They will say: "But how his arms and legs are thin!")
45 Do I dare
Disturb the universe?
In a minute there is time
For decisions and revisions which a minute will reverse.

© Houghton Mifflin Harcourt Publishing Company

ANALYZE STREAM OF CONSCIOUSNESS

Annotate: Mark interruptions in Prufrock's train of thought in lines 37–46.

Analyze: What connection can you make between Prufrock's thoughts about his appearance and the question he repeatedly asks in this passage?

For I have known them all already, known them all—
50 Have known the evenings, mornings, afternoons,
I have measured out my life with coffee spoons;
I know the voices dying with a dying fall
Beneath the music from a farther room.
         So how should I presume?

55 And I have known the eyes already, known them all—
The eyes that fix you in a formulated phrase,
And when I am formulated, sprawling on a pin,
When I am pinned and wriggling on the wall,
Then how should I begin
60 To spit out all the butt-ends of my days and ways?
         And how should I presume?

And I have known the arms already, known them all—
Arms that are braceleted and white and bare
(But in the lamplight, downed with light brown hair!)
65 Is it perfume from a dress
That makes me so digress?
Arms that lie along a table, or wrap about a shawl.
         And should I then presume?
         And how should I begin?

                    • • • • •

70 Shall I say, I have gone at dusk through narrow streets
And watched the smoke that rises from the pipes
Of lonely men in shirt-sleeves, leaning out of windows? . . .

I should have been a pair of ragged claws
Scuttling across the floors of silent seas.

                    • • • • •

75 And the afternoon, the evening, sleeps so peacefully!
Smoothed by long fingers,
Asleep . . . tired . . . or it malingers,
Stretched on the floor, here beside you and me.
Should I, after tea and cakes and ices,
80 Have the strength to force the moment to its crisis?
But though I have wept and fasted, wept and prayed,
Though I have seen my head (grown slightly bald) brought in
         upon a platter,
I am no prophet—and here's no great matter;
I have seen the moment of my greatness flicker,
85 And I have seen the eternal Footman hold my coat, and snicker,
And in short, I was afraid.

54 presume: act overconfidently; dare.

55–58 And I have . . . on the wall: Prufrock recalls being scrutinized by women at other parties. He portrays himself as a live insect that has been classified, labeled, and mounted for display.

56 formulated: reduced to a formula.

MAKE INFERENCES
Annotate: Mark the metaphors in lines 55–61.

Infer: What do these metaphors suggest about how Prufrock feels among women at parties?

73–74 I should . . . silent seas: Here Prufrock presents an image of himself as a crayfish.

77 malingers (mə-lĭng´gərz): pretends illness in order to avoid duty or work.

81–83 But though . . . prophet: an allusion to the biblical story of John the Baptist, who is imprisoned by King Herod (Matthew 14; Mark 6). At the request of his wife, Herod had the Baptist's head cut off and brought to him on a platter.

© Houghton Mifflin Harcourt Publishing Company

94 Lazarus: In the biblical story (John 11:17–44), Lazarus lay dead in his tomb for four days before Jesus brought him back to life.

And would it have been worth it, after all,
After the cups, the marmalade, the tea,
Among the porcelain, among some talk of you and me,
90 Would it have been worth while,
To have bitten off the matter with a smile,
To have squeezed the universe into a ball
To roll it towards some overwhelming question,
To say: "I am Lazarus, come from the dead,
95 Come back to tell you all, I shall tell you all"—
If one, settling a pillow by her head,
    Should say: "That is not what I meant at all.
    That is not it, at all."

And would it have been worth it, after all,
100 Would it have been worth while,
After the sunsets and the dooryards and the sprinkled streets,
After the novels, after the teacups, after the skirts that trail along
    the floor—
And this, and so much more?—
It is impossible to say just what I mean!

105 magic lantern: a forerunner of the slide projector.

105 But as if a magic lantern threw the nerves in patterns on a
    screen:
Would it have been worth while
If one, settling a pillow or throwing off a shawl,
And turning toward the window, should say:
    "That is not it at all,
110   That is not what I meant, at all."

• • • • •

UNDERSTAND MODERNIST POETRY

Annotate: Mark the literary allusion in lines 111–119.

Summarize: Write a summary of this stanza.

115 deferential: yielding to someone else's opinion.

116 meticulous: extremely careful and precise about details.

117 obtuse: slow to understand; dull.

No! I am not Prince Hamlet, nor was meant to be;
Am an attendant lord, one that will do
To swell a progress, start a scene or two,
Advise the prince; no doubt, an easy tool,
115 Deferential, glad to be of use,
Politic, cautious, and meticulous;
Full of high sentence, but a bit obtuse;
At times, indeed, almost ridiculous—
Almost, at times, the Fool.

120 I grow old . . . I grow old . . .
I shall wear the bottoms of my trousers rolled.

124–125 mermaids . . . to me: In mythology, mermaids attract mortal men by their beauty and their singing, sometimes allowing men to live with them in the sea.

Shall I part my hair behind? Do I dare to eat a peach?
I shall wear white flannel trousers, and walk upon the beach.
I have heard the mermaids singing, each to each.

125 I do not think that they will sing to me.

I have seen them riding seaward on the waves
Combing the white hair of the waves blown back
When the wind blows the water white and black.

We have lingered in the chambers of the sea
130 By sea-girls wreathed with seaweed red and brown
Till human voices wake us, and we drown.

CHECK YOUR UNDERSTANDING

Answer these questions before moving on to the **Analyze the Text** section on the following page.

1 Which aspect of Prufrock's life is reflected in the simile comparing the evening to *a patient etherised upon a table*?

   A His fear of the evening

   B An illness he is recovering from

   C His profession as a doctor

   D His sense of paralysis

2 How does Prufrock feel about the guests at the party he is going to?

   F He feels alienated from them.

   G He feels hatred toward them.

   H He feels kindness from them.

   J He feels generosity toward them.

3 Lines 87–98 indicate that the woman Prufrock wants to talk to —

   A feels nervous in his presence

   B worries that he has gone insane

   C isn't interested in what he has to say

   D is trying to avoid him

ANALYZE THE TEXT

Support your responses with evidence from the text. **NOTEBOOK**

1. **Analyze** What does Prufrock compare the fog to in lines 15–22? How does this extended metaphor relate to his situation in the poem?

2. **Infer** What thought does Prufrock express in line 51 when he says, "I have measured out my life with coffee spoons"?

3. **Analyze** Read the side margin notes about the quotation from Dante's *Inferno* at the beginning of the poem and the allusion to Lazarus in line 94. What do the quotation and the allusion have in common? How are they connected to Prufrock's experience?

4. **Draw Conclusions** Why might Eliot have chosen not to clarify the nature of Prufrock's "overwhelming question" or what he wants to say to the woman at the party?

5. **Connect** Eliot wrote "The Love Song of J. Alfred Prufrock" at a time when new technology and media were rapidly changing society. How might Eliot's use of stream of consciousness reflect such changes?

RESEARCH

RESEARCH TIP
When researching writers from a specific era or who wrote in a specific style, focus your search on the "top" lists. Use search strings like "top modernist poets" or "best examples of stream-of-consciousness writing."

With a partner, find a work by each author listed in the chart that includes stream-of-consciousness writing. Choose a passage from each work and compare it to Eliot's use of this technique.

WRITER	NOTES ON STREAM OF CONSCIOUSNESS
James Joyce	
Virginia Woolf	
William Faulkner	

Extend For two minutes, write down every thought that goes through your mind. Do not worry about whether your writing is logical or coherent. Once you've finished, review your stream-of-consciousness writing and identify how your thoughts relate to one another.

CREATE AND PRESENT

Write a Poem Modernist poetry often features confusing contradictions or contrasting imagery. Using this style as your base, write a poem that includes seemingly confusing contradictions or contrasting images. Reread examples from Eliot's poem to get ideas. Review your analysis and interpretation of Eliot's creative use of metaphors and analogies to gain a better understanding of how to do this.

❑ Study the examples in Eliot's poem.

❑ Brainstorm contradictions or incongruous images.

❑ Write a poem that includes these contradictions.

❑ Use a free-verse structure, and think about where you will break lines and why.

Present a Poem Now share your poem with the class. When you and your classmates read your poems aloud, provide thoughtful feedback to each other. Discuss your interpretations of the contradictory ideas or images in your poems.

❑ Practice reading your poem. Experiment with stressing different syllables to bring out the musical quality in the text.

❑ Practice making eye contact with your audience, and use facial expressions and natural gestures to convey the meaning of the poem.

❑ Finally, read your poem aloud to the class.

Go to **Giving a Presentation** in the **Speaking and Listening Studio** for more on presenting.

RESPOND TO THE ESSENTIAL QUESTION

? What makes people feel insecure?

Gather Information Review your annotations and notes on "The Love Song of J. Alfred Prufrock." Then, add relevant information to your Response Log. As you determine which information to include, think about:

- how you can feel insecure internally, but look confident externally
- what things might make you feel uncertain about yourself
- how important your self-talk is to how you feel about yourself

ACADEMIC VOCABULARY

As you write and discuss what you learned from the poem, be sure to use the Academic Vocabulary words. Check off each of the words that you use.

❑ **arbitrary**

❑ **controversy**

❑ **convince**

❑ **denote**

❑ **undergo**

SHOOTING AN ELEPHANT

Essay by **George Orwell**

? ***ESSENTIAL QUESTION:***

Why is it hard to resist social pressure?

QUICK START

Think about how you behave with your peers. Then, think about how you behave in the presence of parents or other older adults. Compare and contrast your actions, then discuss with a partner why you may behave differently in these situations.

BEHAVIOR WITH PEERS	BEHAVIOR WITH PARENTS OR ADULTS

ANALYZE REFLECTIVE ESSAY

In a **reflective essay,** the author examines a personal experience and reveals what he or she learned from it. A good reflective essay offers insight into the author's personal growth and also connects a specific observation to some larger idea about life or society. For example, in "Shooting an Elephant," Orwell reflects on an incident he experienced as a young police officer in British-ruled Burma in the 1920s. By exploring this experience, Orwell allows readers to understand what he learned about the true nature of colonialism. As you read, pay attention to the thoughts and feelings that Orwell expresses as he describes the incident.

ANALYZE IRONY

Irony is a contrast between expectation and reality. This contrast often has the effect of surprising the reader or viewer. Irony may be subtle and easily overlooked or misunderstood. There are three main types of irony:

- **Situational irony** occurs when a character or the reader expects one thing to happen but something else actually happens.

- **Verbal irony** occurs when a character or the writer says one thing but means something quite different—often the opposite of what he or she has said.

- **Dramatic irony** occurs when the reader or viewer knows something that a character does not know.

In "Shooting an Elephant," Orwell relies on situational irony to drive home his insight about colonialism. As you read, notice how the young Orwell's expectations are overturned as he tries to carry out his responsibilities. Also pay attention to your own expectations about how he will behave in this situation.

GENRE ELEMENTS: ESSAY

- a short piece of nonfiction
- offers an opinion on a subject
- formal essays have a serious and impersonal tone
- informal essays are loosely structured and have a conversational tone
- a reflective essay examines an experience in the author's life

CRITICAL VOCABULARY

imperialism	supplant	despotic	garish
cowed	prostrate	labyrinth	senility

To see how many Critical Vocabulary words you already know, use them to complete the sentences.

1. _____ in the United States led the president to _____ the rightful queen and annex Hawaii.

2. His words were muffled as he lay _____ on the rug before the _____ ruler.

3. His _____ sometimes made his speech a tangled _____ of half-expressed thoughts.

4. She was _____ by the bright lights and loud sounds of the _____ city.

LANGUAGE CONVENTIONS

In his essay, George Orwell uses **prepositional phrases** to add clarity to his descriptions of the village, the people, and the elephant. Prepositional phrases consist of a preposition, its object, and modifiers of the object.

Common prepositions include *above, at, before, below, by, down, for, from, in, into, near, of, on, out, over, through, to, up, with,* and *without.*

ANNOTATION MODEL   **NOTICE & NOTE**

As you read the essay "Shooting an Elephant," practice taking notes, marking up the text and asking questions, to monitor your comprehension.

In Moulmein, in Lower Burma, <u>I was hated by large numbers of people—the only time in my life that I have been important enough for this to happen to me.</u> I was subdivisional police officer of the town, and in an aimless, petty kind of way anti-European feeling was very bitter. No one had the guts to raise a riot, but if a European woman went through the bazaars alone somebody would probably spit betel juice over her dress. As a police officer <u>I was an obvious target and was baited whenever it seemed safe to do so.</u>

> This statement seems ironic—I expect "important" people to be respected or admired.
>
> Orwell's attitude toward the Burmese people must have been affected by this experience of being targeted.

BACKGROUND

George Orwell *(1903–1950) was born in India. When he was 19, he joined the Indian Imperial police and left to serve in Burma, which at the time was ruled by Britain. Disillusioned with imperialism, he resigned in 1928 and decided to become a writer. In 1936 Orwell went to Spain to fight with antifascist forces in the Spanish Civil War, an experience that greatly influenced his political views. Throughout his life, Orwell spoke out against injustice. His most famous novels, Animal Farm and 1984, reflect his dedication to political freedom.*

SHOOTING AN ELEPHANT

Essay by George Orwell

SETTING A PURPOSE

Read George Orwell's essay to discover his ideas about imperialism and his role as an officer. How can you connect his turmoil with that of 21st-century officers?

1   In Moulmein, in Lower Burma,[1] I was hated by large numbers of people—the only time in my life that I have been important enough for this to happen to me. I was subdivisional police officer of the town, and in an aimless, petty kind of way anti-European feeling was very bitter. No one had the guts to raise a riot, but if a European woman went through the bazaars alone somebody would probably spit betel juice[2] over her dress. As a police officer I was an obvious target and was baited whenever it seemed safe to do so. When a nimble Burman tripped me up on the football[3] field and the referee (another Burman) looked the

---

[1] **Moulmein** (mōōl-mān´), **in Lower Burma:** the main city of British-controlled Burma, now the independent Asian nation of Myanmar. Moulmein is now usually called Mawlamyine.
[2] **betel** (bēt´l) **juice:** the saliva created when chewing a mixture of betel palm nuts, betel palm leaves, and lime.
[3] **football:** soccer.

© Houghton Mifflin Publishing Company • Image Credits: © GL Archive/Alamy; © Santosh Saligram/Alamy

Notice & Note

Use the side margins to notice and note signposts in the text.

LANGUAGE CONVENTIONS
Annotate: Mark the prepositional phrases in the first sentence of paragraph 1.

Evaluate: What do these prepositional phrases suggest about the importance of the experience Orwell is about to describe?

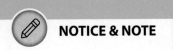
other way, the crowd yelled with hideous laughter. This happened more than once. In the end the sneering yellow faces of young men that met me everywhere, the insults hooted after me when I was at a safe distance, got badly on my nerves. The young Buddhist priests were the worst of all. There were several thousands of them in the town and none of them seemed to have anything to do except stand on street corners and jeer at Europeans.

2   All this was perplexing and upsetting. For at that time I had already made up my mind that **imperialism** was an evil thing and the sooner I chucked up[4] my job and got out of it the better. Theoretically—and secretly, of course—I was all for the Burmese and all against their oppressors, the British. As for the job I was doing, I hated it more bitterly than I can perhaps make clear. In a job like that you see the dirty work of Empire at close quarters. The wretched prisoners huddling in the stinking cages of the lock-ups, the gray, **cowed** faces of the long-term convicts, the scarred buttocks of the men who had been flogged with bamboos—all these oppressed me with an intolerable sense of guilt. But I could get nothing into perspective. I was young and ill-educated and I had had to think out my problems in the utter silence that is imposed on every Englishman in the East. I did not even know that the British Empire is dying, still less did I know that it is a great deal better than the younger empires that are going to **supplant** it. All I knew was that I was stuck between my hatred of the empire I served and my rage against the evil-spirited little beasts who tried to make my job impossible. With one part of my mind I thought of the British Raj[5] as an unbreakable tyranny, as something clamped down, *in saecula saeculorum*,[6] upon the will of **prostrate** peoples; with another part I thought that the greatest joy in the world would be to drive a bayonet into a Buddhist priest's guts. Feelings like these are the normal by-products of imperialism; ask any Anglo-Indian official, if you can catch him off duty.

3   One day something happened which in a roundabout way was enlightening. It was a tiny incident in itself, but it gave me a better glimpse than I had had before of the real nature of imperialism—the real motives for which **despotic** governments act. Early one morning the subinspector at a police station the other end of the town rang me up on the phone and said that an elephant was ravaging the bazaar. Would I please come and do something about it? I did not know what I could do, but I wanted to see what was happening and I got on to a pony and started out. I took my rifle, an old 44 Winchester and much too small to kill an elephant, but I thought the noise might be useful

© Houghton Mifflin Harcourt Publishing Company

---

[4] **chucked up:** threw off; gave up.

[5] **British Raj:** India and adjoining areas (such as Burma) controlled by Britain in the 19th and early 20th centuries. *Raj* is the word for "kingdom" or "rule" in Hindi, a chief language of India.

[6] ***in saecula saeculorum*** (ĭn sĕk´yə-lə sĕk-yə-lôr´əm) *Latin:* forever and ever.

---

imperialism
(ĭm-pîr´ē-ə-lĭz əm): *n.* the extension of a nation's authority by territorial acquisition or by the establishment of economic and political dominance over other nations.

cowed
(koud): *adj.* frightened or subdued with threats or a show of force. **cow** *v.*

ANALYZE IRONY

Annotate: Mark evidence of situational irony in paragraph 2.

Analyze: Explain the situational irony in Orwell's feelings about British colonialism and about the Burmese people.

supplant
(sə-plănt´): *tr.v.* to take the place of or substitute for (another).

prostrate
(prŏs´trāt): *adj.* lying face down, as in submission or adoration.

despotic
(dĭ-spŏt´ĭk): *adj.* of or relating to a person who wields power oppressively, or a tyrant.

in terrorem.[7] Various Burmans stopped me on the way and told me about the elephant's doings. It was not, of course, a wild elephant, but a tame one which had gone "must."[8] It had been chained up as tame elephants always are when their attack of "must" is due, but on the previous night it had broken its chain and escaped. Its mahout,[9] the only person who could manage it when it was in that state, had set out in pursuit, but had taken the wrong direction and was now twelve hours' journey away, and in the morning the elephant had suddenly reappeared in the town. The Burmese population had no weapons and were quite helpless against it. It had already destroyed somebody's bamboo hut, killed a cow and raided some fruit-stalls and devoured the stock; also it had met the municipal rubbish van, and, when the driver jumped out and took to his heels, had turned the van over and inflicted violences upon it.

4   The Burmese subinspector and some Indian constables[10] were waiting for me in the quarter where the elephant had been seen. It was a very poor quarter, a **labyrinth** of squalid bamboo huts, thatched with palm-leaf, winding all over a steep hillside. I remember that it was a cloudy stuffy morning at the beginning of the rains. We began questioning the people as to where the elephant had gone, and, as usual, failed to get any definite information. That is invariably the case in the East; a story always sounds clear enough at a distance, but the nearer you get to the scene of events the vaguer it becomes. Some of the people said that the elephant had gone in one direction, some said that he had gone in another, some professed not even to have heard of any elephant. I had almost made up my mind that the whole story was a pack of lies, when we heard yells a little distance away. There was a loud, scandalized cry of "Go away, child! Go away this instant!" and an old woman with a switch in her hand came round the corner of a hut, violently shooing away a crowd of naked children. Some more women followed, clicking their tongues and exclaiming; evidently there was something there that the children ought not to have seen. I rounded the hut and saw a man's dead body sprawling in the mud. He was an Indian, a black Dravidian coolie,[11] almost naked, and he could not have been dead many minutes. The people said that the elephant had come suddenly upon him round the corner of the hut, caught him with its trunk, put its foot on his back and ground him into the earth. This was the rainy season and the ground was soft, and his face had scored a trench a foot deep and

labyrinth
(lăb´ə-rĭnth): *n.* an intricate structure of interconnecting passages through which it is difficult to find one's way; a maze.

---

[7] *in terrorem* (ĭn tĕ-rôr´əm) *Latin*: for terror.
[8] **gone "must":** had an attack of must, a dangerous frenzy that periodically seizes male elephants.
[9] **mahout** (mə-hout´): an elephant keeper.
[10] **constables:** police officers.
[11] **Dravidian** (drə-vĭd´ē-ən) **coolie:** a dark-skinned menial laborer from the south of India.

British troops patrolling a city in Burma

© Houghton Mifflin Harcourt Publishing Company • Image Credit: ©Bettmann/Getty Images

ANALYZE REFLECTIVE ESSAY

Annotate: Mark details Orwell uses to describe the corpse in paragraph 4.

Analyze: What do these details suggest about how this sight affected him?

a couple of yards long. He was lying on his belly with arms crucified and head sharply twisted to one side. His face was coated with mud, the eyes wide open, the teeth bared and grinning with an expression of unendurable agony. (Never tell me, by the way, that the dead look peaceful. Most of the corpses I have seen looked devilish.) The friction of the great beast's foot had stripped the skin from his back as neatly as one skins a rabbit. As soon as I saw the dead man I sent an orderly[12] to a friend's house nearby to borrow an elephant rifle. I had already sent back the pony, not wanting it to go mad with fright and throw me if it smelled the elephant.

5   The orderly came back in a few minutes with a rifle and five cartridges, and meanwhile some Burmans had arrived and told us that the elephant was in the paddy fields[13] below, only a few hundred yards away. As I started forward practically the whole population of

---

[12] **orderly:** a military aide.
[13] **paddy fields:** rice fields.

the quarter flocked out of the houses and followed me. They had seen the rifle and were all shouting excitedly that I was going to shoot the elephant. They had not shown much interest in the elephant when he was merely ravaging their homes, but it was different now that he was going to be shot. It was a bit of fun to them, as it would be to an English crowd; besides, they wanted the meat. It made me vaguely uneasy. I had no intention of shooting the elephant—I had merely sent for the rifle to defend myself if necessary—and it is always unnerving to have a crowd following you. I marched down the hill, looking and feeling a fool, with the rifle over my shoulder and an ever-growing army of people jostling at my heels. At the bottom, when you got away from the huts, there was a metalled road and beyond that a miry waste of paddy fields a thousand yards across, not yet ploughed but soggy from the first rains and dotted with coarse grass. The elephant was standing eighty yards from the road, his left side towards us. He took not the slightest notice of the crowd's

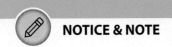
approach. He was tearing up bunches of grass, beating them against his knees to clean them and stuffing them into his mouth.

6   I had halted on the road. As soon as I saw the elephant I knew with perfect certainty that I ought not to shoot him. It is a serious matter to shoot a working elephant—it is comparable to destroying a huge and costly piece of machinery—and obviously one ought not to do it if it can possibly be avoided. And at that distance, peacefully eating, the elephant looked no more dangerous than a cow. I thought then and I think now that his attack of "must" was already passing off; in which case he would merely wander harmlessly about until the mahout came back and caught him. Moreover, I did not in the least want to shoot him. I decided that I would watch him for a little while to make sure that he did not turn savage again, and then go home.

7   But at that moment I glanced round at the crowd that had followed me. It was an immense crowd, two thousand at the least and growing every minute. It blocked the road for a long distance on either side. I looked at the sea of yellow faces above the **garish** clothes—faces all happy and excited over this bit of fun, all certain that the elephant was going to be shot. They were watching me as they would watch a conjurer[14] about to perform a trick. They did not like me, but with the magical rifle in my hands I was momentarily worth watching. And suddenly I realized that I should have to shoot the elephant after all. The people expected it of me and I had got to do it; I could feel their two thousand wills pressing me forward, irresistibly. And it was at this moment, as I stood there with the rifle in my hands, that I first grasped the hollowness, the futility of the white man's dominion in the East. Here was I, the white man with his gun, standing in front of the unarmed native crowd—seemingly the leading actor of the piece; but in reality I was only an absurd puppet pushed to and fro by the will of those yellow faces behind. I perceived in this moment that when the white man turns tyrant it is his own freedom that he destroys. He becomes a sort of hollow, posing dummy, the conventionalized figure of a sahib.[15] For it is the condition of his rule that he shall spend his life in trying to impress the "natives," and so in every crisis he has got to do what the "natives" expect of him. He wears a mask, and his face grows to fit it. I had got to shoot the elephant. I had committed myself to doing it when I sent for the rifle. A sahib has got to act like a sahib; he has got to appear resolute, to know his own mind and do definite things. To come all that way, rifle in hand, with two thousand people marching at my heels, and then to trail feebly away, having done nothing—no, that was impossible. The crowd would laugh at me. And my whole

garish
(gâr´ĭsh, găr´): *adj.* overly bright or ornamented, especially in a vulgar or tasteless way; gaudy.

AHA MOMENT

Notice & Note: In paragraph 7, mark statements expressing Orwell's realization about his role as a colonial officer.

Analyze: How are these statements ironic?

---

[14] **conjurer** (kŏn´jər-ər): magician.
[15] **sahib** (sä´hĭb): a title of respect formerly used by native Indians to address a European gentleman.

life, every white man's life in the East, was one long struggle not to be laughed at.

8   But I did not want to shoot the elephant. I watched him beating his bunch of grass against his knees, with that preoccupied grandmotherly air that elephants have. It seemed to me that it would be murder to shoot him. At that age I was not squeamish about killing animals, but I had never shot an elephant and never wanted to. (Somehow it always seems worse to kill a *large* animal.) Besides, there was the beast's owner to be considered. Alive, the elephant was worth at least a hundred pounds; dead, he would only be worth the value of his tusks—five pounds, possibly. But I had got to act quickly. I turned to some experienced-looking Burmans who had been there when we arrived, and asked them how the elephant had been behaving. They all said the same thing: he took no notice of you if you left him alone, but he might charge if you went too close to him.

9   It was perfectly clear to me what I ought to do. I ought to walk up to within, say, twenty-five yards of the elephant and test his behavior. If he charged I could shoot, if he took no notice of me it would be safe to leave him until the mahout came back. But also I knew that I was going to do no such thing. I was a poor shot with a rifle and the ground was soft mud into which one would sink at every step. If the elephant charged and I missed him, I should have about as much chance as a toad under a steam-roller. But even then I was not thinking particularly of my own skin, only of the watchful yellow faces behind. For at that moment, with the crowd watching me, I was not afraid in the ordinary sense, as I would have been if I had been alone. A white man mustn't be frightened in front of "natives"; and so, in general, he isn't frightened. The sole thought in my mind was that if anything went wrong those two thousand Burmans would see me pursued, caught, trampled on and reduced to a grinning corpse like that Indian up the hill. And if that happened it was quite probable that some of them would laugh. That would never do. There was only one alternative. I shoved the cartridges into the magazine[16] and lay down on the road to get a better aim.

10   The crowd grew very still, and a deep, low, happy sigh, as of people who see the theater curtain go up at last, breathed from innumerable throats. They were going to have their bit of fun after all. The rifle was a beautiful German thing with cross-hair sights. I did not then know that in shooting an elephant one should shoot to cut an imaginary bar running from ear-hole to ear-hole. I ought, therefore, as the elephant was sideways on, to have aimed straight at his ear-hole; actually I aimed several inches in front of this, thinking the brain would be further forward.

ANALYZE REFLECTIVE ESSAY

Annotate: In paragraph 9, mark Orwell's explanation of what he ought to have done in this situation.

Draw Conclusions: What idea does this paragraph convey about how imperialism affects the individuals who serve it?

---

[16]**magazine:** the compartment from which cartridges are fed into the rifle's firing chamber.

senility
(sĭ-nĭl´ ĭ-tē): *n.* relating to or
having diminished cognitive
function, as when memory is
impaired, because of old age.

11   When I pulled the trigger I did not hear the bang or feel the
kick—one never does when a shot goes home—but I heard the
devilish roar of glee that went up from the crowd. In that instant, in
too short a time, one would have thought, even for the bullet to get
there, a mysterious, terrible change had come over the elephant. He
neither stirred nor fell, but every line of his body had altered. He
looked suddenly stricken, shrunken, immensely old, as though the
frightful impact of the bullet had paralyzed him without knocking
him down. At last, after what seemed a long time—it might have
been five seconds, I dare say—he sagged flabbily to his knees. His
mouth slobbered. An enormous **senility** seemed to have settled upon
him. One could have imagined him thousands of years old. I fired
again into the same spot. At the second shot he did not collapse but
climbed with desperate slowness to his feet and stood weakly upright,
with legs sagging and head drooping. I fired a third time. That was
the shot that did for him. You could see the agony of it jolt his whole
body and knock the last remnant of strength from his legs. But in
falling he seemed for a moment to rise, for as his hind legs collapsed
beneath him he seemed to tower upwards like a huge rock toppling,
his trunk reaching skyward like a tree. He trumpeted, for the first
and only time. And then down he came, his belly towards me, with a
crash that seemed to shake the ground even where I lay.

12   I got up. The Burmans were already racing past me across the
mud. It was obvious that the elephant would never rise again, but he
was not dead. He was breathing very rhythmically with long rattling
gasps, his great mound of a side painfully rising and falling. His
mouth was wide open—I could see far down into caverns of pale pink
throat. I waited a long time for him to die, but his breathing did not
weaken. Finally I fired my two remaining shots into the spot where I
thought his heart must be. The thick blood welled out of him like red
velvet, but still he did not die. His body did not even jerk when the
shots hit him, the tortured breathing continued without a pause. He
was dying, very slowly and in great agony, but in some world remote
from me where not even a bullet could damage him further. I felt that
I had got to put an end to that dreadful noise. It seemed dreadful to
see the great beast lying there, powerless to move and yet powerless
to die, and not even to be able to finish him. I sent back for my small
rifle and poured shot after shot into his heart and down his throat.
They seemed to make no impression. The tortured gasps continued
as steadily as the ticking of a clock.

13   In the end I could not stand it any longer and went away. I heard
later that it took him half an hour to die. Burmans were arriving with
dahs[17] and baskets even before I left, and I was told they had stripped
his body almost to the bones by the afternoon.

---

[17] **dahs:** large knives.

14   Afterwards, of course, there were endless discussions about the shooting of the elephant. The owner was furious, but he was only an Indian and could do nothing. Besides, legally I had done the right thing, for a mad elephant has to be killed, like a mad dog, if its owner fails to control it. Among the Europeans opinion was divided. The older men said I was right, the younger men said it was a damn shame to shoot an elephant for killing a coolie, because an elephant was worth more than any damn Coringhee[18] coolie. And afterwards I was very glad that the coolie had been killed; it put me legally in the right and it gave me a sufficient pretext for shooting the elephant. I often wondered whether any of the others grasped that I had done it solely to avoid looking a fool.

_____

[18]**Coringhee:** coming from a port in southeastern India.

© Houghton Mifflin Harcourt Publishing Company

ANALYZE IRONY

Annotate: Mark the opinions of the Europeans in paragraph 14.

Analyze: What is ironic about Orwell's feeling glad that the coolie had been killed?

CHECK YOUR UNDERSTANDING

Answer these questions before moving on to the **Analyze the Text** section on the following page.

1 What annoyed the narrator?

   A The elephant's destruction of trees

   B How the Burmans mocked soldiers

   C The weather in Asia

   D His small gun

2 When Orwell finally sees the elephant, it is —

   F wild

   G ravenous

   H tame

   J gentle

3 The narrator had to shoot the elephant because —

   A so many people were watching

   B the elephant was charging toward him

   C his job was to protect the village people

   D the elephant was already injured

ANALYZE THE TEXT

Support your responses with evidence from the text. 📓 NOTEBOOK

1. **Analyze** Reread paragraphs 5 and 6. What is ironic about Orwell's first sighting of the elephant?

2. **Evaluate** Orwell describes the shooting and slow death of the elephant in excruciating detail. How does this description support his reflections in the essay?

3. **Draw Conclusions** At the end of the essay, Orwell wonders whether other Europeans realized that he shot the elephant "solely to avoid looking a fool." Why was it so important for him to keep up appearances before the Burmans?

4. **Critique** Do you think Orwell provides a reliable account of how the Burmans viewed him? Explain why or why not.

5. **Notice & Note** Orwell says that this experience taught him that "when the white man turns tyrant it is his own freedom that he destroys." In what ways did his role as a colonial policeman end his freedom?

RESEARCH

RESEARCH TIP
Place quotation marks around your search terms to get results that include the exact wording.

Burma (now called Myanmar) was one of many colonies that Britain ruled in the early 20th century. With a partner, research the history of British colonization of Burma. Use what you learn to answer the questions:

QUESTION	ANSWER
How did Britain gain control of Burma?	
What issues fueled Burmese resentment of British rule?	
What role did Buddhist monks play in opposition to colonialism?	
How did Burma gain independence?	

Extend Conduct further research to learn about Burma's history following independence. Did Burmans enjoy greater freedom after the British left? What is life like in Myanmar today?

CREATE AND DISCUSS

Write an Informational Essay Write about a social injustice occurring today. Describe the toll that this injustice takes on individuals. Use evidence from research or what you may have witnessed.

- ❏ Begin your essay with a hook—a stirring incident or anecdote.
- ❏ Create an effective transitional sentence to blend the hook with your informational writing.
- ❏ If you're truly concerned about an injustice, write about that. If a specific social or political wrong moves you, it will come through in the essay.
- ❏ Tease out any ironies you identify in the situation to help provoke deeper thought about the issue.
- ❏ Create a memorable theme or message to share an insight.

Discuss Your Essay Use your essay to generate discussion with your peers. Allow each participant time to share an experience as well as its possible outcomes.

- ❏ Read your essay to the members of your group.
- ❏ Ask each member of the group to give you brief feedback about your essay.
- ❏ Encourage the group to discuss ideas and questions raised in your essay.
- ❏ Listen and respond as other group members read their essays.

 Go to **Writing Informative Texts** in the **Writing Studio** to develop your essay.

Go to **Participating in Collaborative Discussions** in the **Speaking and Listening Studio** for more help.

RESPOND TO THE ESSENTIAL QUESTION

 Why is it hard to resist social pressure?

Gather Information Review your annotations and notes on "Shooting an Elephant." Then, add relevant information to your Response Log. As you determine which information to include, think about:

- the strict roles assigned to men, women, and teens
- the consequences of being different
- social roles and responsibilities

ACADEMIC VOCABULARY

As you write and discuss what you learned from the essay, be sure to use the Academic Vocabulary words. Check off each of the words that you use.

- ❏ **arbitrary**
- ❏ **controversy**
- ❏ **convince**
- ❏ **denote**
- ❏ **undergo**

WORD BANK

imperialism	despotic
cowed	labyrinth
supplant	garish
prostrate	senility

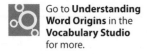

Go to **Understanding Word Origins** in the **Vocabulary Studio** for more.

CRITICAL VOCABULARY

Practice and Apply Choose the word that best completes the sentence.

1. The economic interests of _____ led the British to seize control of local governments and _____ local officials.

2. As the elephant wove through the _____ of the village, the _____ residents sent word to the police of the event.

3. In his _____, he would dress in _____ costumes and relive the scene for any who would stop and listen.

4. As he gazed at the _____ form of the dead man, he felt the _____ expectation of the crowd pushing him toward an action he did not want to take.

VOCABULARY STRATEGY:
Etymology

Etymology is the history of a word. Most dictionary entries include etymologies that identify which language the word came from and what the original word meant. The etymology also traces the route by which a word passed into the English language.

The entry below gives the history of the Critical Vocabulary word *labyrinth*. It shows that *labyrinth* comes from the ancient Greek *laburinthos,* which refers to the Minotaur's maze in the Greek myth of Jason and the Argonauts.

> **lab·y·rinth** (lăb´ə-rĭnth): *n.* an intricate structure of interconnecting passages through which it is difficult to find one's way; a maze. [Middle English *laberinthe,* from Latin *labyrinthus,* from Greek *laburinthos;* possibly akin to *labrus,* double-headed axe used as a ritual weapon and a sign of authority in Minoan civilization, so that Greek *laburinthos* may originally have designated a Minoan palace as "the house of the double-headed axe"]

Practice and Apply Look up the remaining Critical Vocabulary words in a college-level dictionary and trace their etymology. Discuss with a partner how closely the original meaning resembles the usage of the word today.

LANGUAGE CONVENTIONS:
Prepositional Phrases

A **prepositional phrase** begins with the preposition (such as *among* or *with*) and ends with its object. Prepositional phrases tell *where, when, how, what kind,* and other information that makes descriptions clearer and more vivid. Here is an example from the essay, "Shooting an Elephant."

> The orderly came back <u>in a few minutes</u> with a rifle and five cartridges, and meanwhile some Burmans had arrived and told us that the elephant was <u>in the paddy fields below</u>, only a few hundred yards away. As I started forward practically the whole population of the quarter flocked <u>out of the houses</u> and followed me.

Practice and Apply Identify the prepositional phrases in each sentence from "Shooting an Elephant." Then, write your own sentences, using prepositional phrases.

> Finally, I fired my two remaining shots into the spot where I thought his heart must be.

> Burmans were arriving with dahs and baskets even before I left, and I was told they had stripped his body almost to the bones by the afternoon.

> Among the Europeans opinion was divided.

Go to **Prepositional Phrases** in the **Grammar Studio** to learn more.

MY DAUGHTER THE RACIST

Short Story by **Helen Oyeyemi**

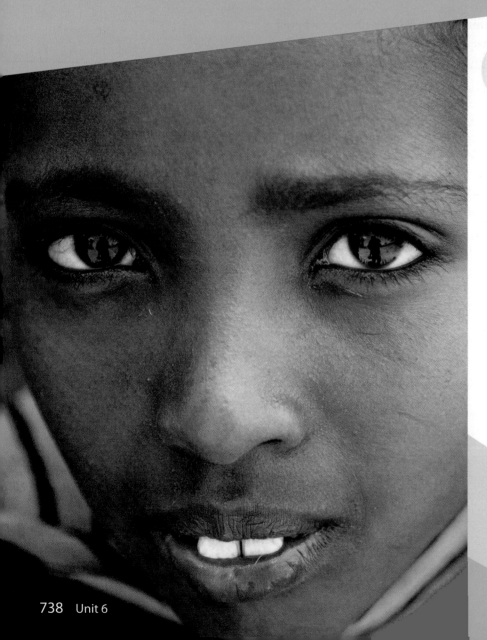

? *ESSENTIAL QUESTION:*

Why is it hard to resist social pressure?

QUICK START

Think of a time when you stood up for something in which you believed. Freewrite about this event, making sure to explain any consequences or outcomes. Share your writing with a partner.

ANALYZE SETTING

Setting is the time and place of the action in a story. Setting also encompasses the culture and customs of the time and place. Religion, historical events, economic conditions, popular beliefs, and political climate are all part of a story's setting. "My Daughter the Racist" takes place in an unnamed country near a desert occupied by foreign troops.

As you read the story, notice how the historical and social context influence the characterization, plot, and theme of the story.

MAKE PREDICTIONS

You can use text clues to make **predictions** about what will happen next in a story. For example, near the beginning of "My Daughter the Racist," the narrator makes the following comment when discussing the tension between people in her village and foreign soldiers:

> **And that girl of mine has really begun to stare at the soldiers, too, . . .**

This remark hints that her daughter will somehow become involved in the tension between villagers and soldiers. As you read this story, try to anticipate what changes will occur in the lives of the main characters. Pay careful attention to the main characters' beliefs about themselves and their way of life, and consider how the events in the story might call these beliefs into question. Use a chart like this one to record your predictions.

© Houghton Mifflin Harcourt Publishing Company

GENRE ELEMENTS: SHORT STORY

- focuses on one incident and has a single plot and setting
- introduces a limited number of characters and covers a short period of time
- told from a first- or third-person point of view
- has one main conflict that the characters must resolve
- includes a theme, or message, about human nature or society

CLUE FROM TEXT	MY PREDICTION	WHAT HAPPENED

CRITICAL VOCABULARY

balmy   **loftily**   **brazen**   **impeccably**

To see how many Critical Vocabulary words you already know, use them to complete the sentences.

1. Loy's _____ disregard of the rules landed him in the principal's office.

2. Cree wished she could trade in this snowy day for a sunny, _____ one.

3. Kaila _____ refused to play with the young boys, claiming she was so much older and more mature.

4. Because Eliot spoke French _____, the locals could not tell he was a foreigner.

LANGUAGE CONVENTIONS

Syntax refers to the way in which words are arranged in a sentence. To keep readers interested and to draw attention to particular ideas, writers vary their syntax. For example, they might use inverted word order, alternate long sentences with short ones, or even include sentence fragments. This selection uses a mixture of short and long sentences, as well as some fragments. As you read, notice how the syntax contributes to the overall mood and tone.

ANNOTATION MODEL   **NOTICE & NOTE**

As you read, notice details about the setting. Underline language that helps you predict what will happen next. In the model, you can see one reader's notes about the setting.

> They <u>fight</u> us and they try to tell us, in our own language, that they're freeing us. Maybe, maybe not. I look through the dusty window (I can never get it clean, <u>the desert is our neighbor</u>) and <u>I see soldiers every day.</u>

These details hint that the story takes place in a setting that is hot, near a desert. There is fighting taking place.

BACKGROUND

Helen Oyeyemi (b. 1984) was born in Nigeria and raised in London. She has published novels, plays, and a collection of short stories. Oyeyemi wrote her first novel while still attending secondary school. Her story "My Daughter the Racist," which is set in an unnamed Middle Eastern or African country, was a finalist for the 2010 BBC National Short Story Award.

MY DAUGHTER THE RACIST

Short Story by Helen Oyeyemi

SETTING A PURPOSE

As you read, notice how the narrator's wish to support her daughter's independent spirit comes into conflict with the need to protect her.

1   One morning my daughter woke up and said all in a rush: "Mother, I swear before you and God that from today onwards I am racist." She's eight years old. She chopped all her hair off two months ago because she wanted to go around with the local boys and they wouldn't have her with her long hair. Now she looks like one of them; eyes dazed from looking directly at the sun, teeth shining white in her sunburnt face. She laughs a lot. She plays. "Look at her playing," my mother says. "Playing in the rubble of what used to be our great country." My mother exaggerates as often as she can. I'm sure she would like nothing more than to be part of a Greek tragedy. She wouldn't even want a large part, she'd be perfectly content with a chorus role, warning that fate is coming to make havoc of all things. My mother is a fine woman, all over wrinkles and she always has a clean handkerchief somewhere about her person, but I don't know what she's talking about with her rubble this, rubble that—we live in a village, and it's not bad here. Not peaceful, but not bad. In

© Houghton Mifflin Harcourt Publishing Company • Image Credits: © Colin McPherson/Corbis via Getty Images
© Eric Lafforgue/Art In All Of Us/Corbis via Getty Images

Notice & Note

Use the side margins to notice and note signposts in the text.

MAKE PREDICTIONS
Annotate: Mark details about the narrator's daughter in paragraph 1.

Predict: What expectations do you have about her personality based on these clues?

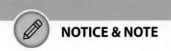
ANALYZE SETTING

Annotate: Mark words and phrases in paragraph 2 that signal the social context. Mark the phrases in paragraph 3 that signal the historical context.

Infer: What do these details help you understand about the characters and plot?

cities it's worse. In the city center, where we used to live, a bomb took my husband and turned his face to blood. I was lucky, another widow told me, that there was something left so that I could know of his passing. But I was ungrateful. I spat at that widow. I spat at her in her sorrow. That's sin. I know that's sin. But half my life was gone, and it wasn't easy to look at what was left.

2 Anyway, the village. I live with my husband's mother, whom I now call my mother, because I can't return to the one who gave birth to me. It isn't done. I belong with my husband's mother until someone else claims me. And that will never happen, because I don't wish it.

3 The village is hushed. People observe the phases of the moon. In the city I felt the moon but hardly ever remembered to look for it. The only thing that disturbs us here in the village is the foreign soldiers. Soldiers, soldiers, soldiers, patrolling. They fight us and they try to tell us, in our own language, that they're freeing us. Maybe, maybe not. I look through the dusty window (I can never get it clean, the desert is our neighbor) and I see soldiers every day. They think someone dangerous is running secret messages through here; that's what I've heard. What worries me more is the young people of the village. They stand and watch the soldiers. And the soldiers don't like it, and the soldiers point their guns, especially at the young men. They won't bother with the women and girls, unless the woman or the girl has an especially wild look in her eyes. I think there are two reasons the soldiers don't like the young men watching them. The first reason is that the soldiers know they are ugly in their boots and fatigues, they are perfectly aware that their presence spoils everything around them. The second reason is the nature of the watching—the boys and the men around here watch with a very great hatred, so great that it feels as if action must follow. I feel that sometimes, just walking past them—when I block their view of the soldiers these boys quiver with impatience.

4 And that girl of mine has really begun to stare at the soldiers, too, even though I slap her hard when I catch her doing that. Who knows what's going to happen? These soldiers are scared. They might shoot someone. Noura next door says: "If they could be so evil as to shoot children then it's in God's hands. Anyway I don't believe that they could do it."

5 But I know that such things can be. My husband was a university professor. He spoke several languages, and he gave me books to read, and he read news from other countries and told me what's possible. He should've been afraid of the world, should've stayed inside with the doors locked and the blinds drawn, but he didn't do that, he went out. Our daughter is just like him. She is part of his immortality. I told him, when I was still carrying her, that that's what I want, that that's how I love him. I had always dreaded and feared pregnancy, for all the usual reasons that girls who daydream more than they live fear

pregnancy. My body, with its pain and mess and hunger—if I could have bribed it to go away, I would have. Then I married my man, and I held fast to him. And my brain, the brain that had told me I would never bear a child for any man, no matter how nice he was, that brain began to tell me something else. Provided the world continues to exist, provided conditions remain favorable, or at least tolerable, our child will have a child and that child will have a child and so on, and with all those children of children come the inevitability that glimpses of my husband will resurface, in their features, in the way they use their bodies, a fearless swinging of the arms as they walk. Centuries from now some quality of a man's gaze, smile, voice, way of standing or sitting will please someone else in a way that they aren't completely aware of, will be loved very hard for just a moment, without inquiry into where it came from. I ignore the women who say that my daughter does things that a girl shouldn't do, and when I want to keep her near me, I let her go. But not too far, I don't let her go too far from me.

6   The soldiers remind me of boys from here sometimes. The way our boys used to be. Especially when you catch them with their helmets off, three or four of them sitting on a wall at lunchtime, trying to enjoy their sandwiches and the sun, but really too restless for both. Then you see the rifles beside their lunchboxes and you remember that they aren't our boys.

7   "Mother... did you hear me? I said that I am now a racist."

8   I was getting my daughter ready for school. She can't tie knots but she loves her shoelaces to make extravagant bows.

9   "Racist against whom, my daughter?"

10   "Racist against soldiers."

11   "Soldiers aren't a race."

12   "Soldiers aren't a race," she mimicked. "Soldiers aren't a race."

13   "What do you want me to say?"

14   She didn't have an answer, so she just went off in a big gang with her schoolfriends. And I worried, because my daughter has always seen soldiers—in her lifetime she hasn't known a time or place when the cedars stood against the blue sky without khaki canvas or crackling radio signals in the way.

15   An hour or so later Bilal came to visit. A great honor, I'm sure, a visit from that troublesome Bilal who had done nothing but pester me since the day I came to this village. He sat down with us and mother served him tea.

16   "Three times I have asked this daughter of yours to be my wife," Bilal said to my mother. He shook a finger at her. As for me, it was as if I wasn't there. "First wife," he continued. "Not even second or third—first wife."

© Houghton Mifflin Harcourt Publishing Company

MAKE PREDICTIONS
Annotate: Mark details in paragraphs 15–23 that describe Bilal's personality.

Predict: At this point in the story, what can you predict about Bilal's involvement in the story?

17   "Don't be angry, son," my mother murmured. "She's not ready. Only a shameless woman could be ready so soon after what happened."

18   "True, true," Bilal agreed. A fly landed just above my top lip and I let it walk.

19   "Rather than ask a fourth time I will kidnap her…"

20   "Ah, don't do that, son. Don't take the light of an old woman's eyes," my mother murmured, and she fed him honey cake. Bilal laughed from his belly, and the fly fled. "I was only joking."

21   The third time Bilal asked my mother for my hand in marriage I thought I was going to have to do it after all. But my daughter said I wasn't allowed. I asked her why. Because his face is fat and his eyes are tiny? Because he chews with his mouth open?

22   "He has a tyrannical mustache," my daughter said. "It would be impossible to live with." I'm proud of her vocabulary. But it's starting to look as if I think I'm too good for Bilal, who owns more cattle than any other man for miles around and could give my mother, daughter and I everything we might reasonably expect from this life.

23   Please, God. You know I don't seek worldly things. If you want me to marry again, so be it. But please—not Bilal. After the love that I have had…you don't believe me, but I would shatter.

LANGUAGE CONVENTIONS

Annotate: Parallel structure is the repetition of a grammatical form within a sentence. Mark an example of parallel structure in paragraph 24.

Analyze: What idea does this use of parallel structure emphasize?

24   My daughter came home for her lunch. After prayers we shared some cold karkedeh,[1] two straws in a drinking glass, and she told me what she was learning, which wasn't much. My mother was there, too, rattling her prayer beads and listening indulgently. She made faces when she thought my daughter talked too much. Then we heard the soldiers coming past as usual, and we went and looked at them through the window. I thought we'd make fun of them a bit, as usual. But my daughter ran out of the front door and into the path of the army truck, yelling: "You! You bloody soldiers!" Luckily the truck's wheels crawled along the road, and the body of the truck itself was slumped on one side, resigned to a myriad of pot holes. Still, it was a very big truck, and my daughter is a very small girl.

25   I was out after her before I knew what I was doing, shouting her name. It's a good name—we chose a name that would grow with her, but she seemed determined not to make it to adulthood. I tried to trip her up, but she was too nimble for me. Everyone around was looking on from windows and the open gates of courtyards. The truck rolled to a stop. Someone inside it yelled: "Move, kid. We've got stuff to do."

26   I tried to pull my daughter out of the way, but she wasn't having any of it. My hands being empty, I wrung them. My daughter began to pelt the soldier's vehicle with stones from her pockets. Her pockets were very deep that afternoon, her arms lashed the air like whips.

---

[1] **karkedeh:** Egyptian drink made from dried hibiscus.

Stone after stone bounced off metal and rattled glass, and I grabbed at her and she screamed: "This is my country! Get out of here!"

27   The people of the village began to applaud her. "Yes," they cried out, from their seats in the audience, and they clapped. I tried again to seize her arm and failed again. The truck's engine revved up and I opened my arms as wide as they would go, inviting everyone to witness. Now I was screaming too: "So you dare? You really dare?"

28   And there we were, mother and daughter, causing problems for the soldiers together.

29   Finally a scrawny soldier came out of the vehicle without his gun. He was the scrawniest fighting man I've ever seen—he was barely there, just a piece of wire, really. He walked towards my daughter, who had run out of stones. He stretched out a long arm, offering her chewing gum, and she swore at him, and I swore at her for swearing. He stopped about thirty centimeters away from us and said to my daughter: "You're brave."

30   My daughter put her hands on her hips and glared up at him.

31   "We're leaving tomorrow," the scrawny soldier told her.

32   Whispers and shouts: *the soldiers are leaving tomorrow!*

33   A soldier inside the truck yelled out: "Yeah, but more are coming to take our place," and everyone piped low. My daughter reached for a stone that hadn't fallen far. Who is this girl? Four feet tall and fighting something she knows nothing about. Even if I explained it to her she wouldn't get it. I don't get it myself.

34   "Can I shake your hand?" the scrawny soldier asked her, before her hand met the stone. I thought my girl would refuse, but she said yes. "You're okay," she told him. "You came out to face me."

35   "Her English is good," the coward from within the truck remarked.

36   "I speak to her in English every day," I called out. "So she can tell people like you what she thinks."

37   We stepped aside then, my daughter and I, and let them continue their patrol.

38   My mother didn't like what had happened. But didn't you see everyone clapping for us, my daughter asked. So what, my mother said. People clap at anything. Some people even clap when they're on an airplane and it lands. That was something my husband had told us from his travels—I hadn't thought she'd remember.

39   My daughter became a celebrity amongst the children, and from what I saw, she used it for good, bringing the shunned ones into the inner circle and laughing at all their jokes.

© Houghton Mifflin Harcourt Publishing Company

MAKE PREDICTIONS

Annotate: Mark details in paragraphs 33–37 that describe the girl's interaction with the soldier.

Predict: What do you think might happen if they meet again?

balmy

(bä´mē) *adj.* mild and pleasant.

ANALYZE SETTING

Annotate: Mark details in paragraphs 40–51 that reveal more about the social context.

Analyze: How does the setting contribute to the plot at this point in the story?

40 The following week a foreigner dressed like one of our men knocked at my mother's door. It was late afternoon, turning to dusk. People sat looking out onto the street, talking about everything as they took their tea. Our people really know how to discuss a matter from head to toe; it is our gift, and such conversation on a **balmy** evening can be sweeter than sugar. Now they were talking about the foreigner who was at our door. I answered it myself. My daughter was at my side and we recognized the man at once; it was the scrawny soldier. He looked itchy and uncomfortable in his djellaba,[2] and he wasn't wearing his keffiyeh[3] at all correctly—his hair was showing.

41 "What a clown," my daughter said, and from her seat on the cushioned floor my mother vowed that clown, or no clown, he couldn't enter her house.

42 "Welcome," I said to him. It was all I could think of to say. See a guest, bid him welcome. It's who we are. Or maybe it's just who I am.

43 "I'm not here to cause trouble," the scrawny soldier said. He was looking to the north, south, east, and west so quickly and repeatedly that for some seconds his head was just a blur. "I'm completely off duty. In fact, I've been on leave since last week. I'm just—I just thought I'd stick around for a little while. I thought I might have met a worthy adversary—this young lady here, I mean." He indicated my

---

2 **djellaba** (jə-lä´bə): a long, loose, hooded garment with full sleeves, worn especially in Muslim countries.
3 **keffiyeh** (kə-fē´ə): a square of cloth, often embroidered, traditionally worn as a headdress by Arab men, either by winding it around the head or by folding it into a triangle, draping it over the head, and securing it with an agal.

daughter, who chewed her lip and couldn't stop herself from looking pleased.

44   "What is he saying?" my mother demanded.

45   "I'll just—go away, then," the soldier said. He seemed to be dying several thousand deaths at once.

46   "He'd like some tea…" my daughter told my mother. "We'll just have a quick cup or two," I added, and we took the tea out onto the verandah, and drank it under the eyes of God and the entire neighborhood. The neighborhood was annoyed. Very annoyed, and it listened closely to everything that was said. The soldier didn't seem to notice. He and my daughter were getting along famously. I didn't catch what exactly they were talking about, I just poured the tea and made sure my hand was steady. *I'm not doing anything wrong*, I told myself. *I'm not doing anything wrong.*

47   The scrawny soldier asked if I would tell him my name. "No," I said. "You have no right to use it." He told me his name, but I pretended he hadn't spoken. To cheer him up, my daughter told him her name, and he said: "That's great. A really, really good name. I might use it myself one day."

48   "You can't—it's a girl's name," my daughter replied, her nostrils flared with scorn.

49   "Ugh," said the soldier. "I meant for my daughter…"

50   He shouldn't have spoken about his unborn daughter out there in front of everyone, with his eyes and his voice full of hope and laughter. I can guarantee that some woman in the shadows was cursing the daughter he wanted to have. Even as he spoke someone was saying, May that girl be born withered for the grief people like you have caused us.

51   "Ugh," said my daughter. "I like that sound. Ugh, ugh, ugh."

52   I began to follow the conversation better. The scrawny soldier told my daughter that he understood why the boys lined the roads with anger. "Inside my head I call them the children of Hamelin."[4]

53   "The what?" my daughter asked.

54   "The who?" I asked.

55   "I guess all I mean is that they're paying the price for something they didn't do."

56   And then he told us the story of the Pied Piper of Hamelin[5] because we hadn't heard it before. We had nightmares that night, all three of us—my mother, my daughter and I. My mother hadn't even heard the story, so I don't know why she joined in. But somehow it was nice that she did.

---

[4] **Hamelin** (hăm´ə-lǐn): a city of northern Germany on the Weser River southwest of Hanover.

[5] **Pied Piper of Hamelin:** a tale of a piper who led children away from their homes using his music.

57 On his second visit the scrawny soldier began to tell my daughter that there were foreign soldiers in his country, too, but that they were much more difficult to spot because they didn't wear uniforms and some of them didn't even seem foreign. They seemed like ordinary citizens, the sons and daughters of shopkeepers and dentists and restaurant owners and big businessmen. "That's the most dangerous kind of soldier. The longer those ones live amongst us, the more they hate us, and everything we do disgusts them…these are people we go to school with, ride the subway with—we watch the same movies and play the same video games. They'll never be with us, though. We've been judged, and they'll always be against us. Always."

58 He'd wasted his breath, because almost as soon as he began with all that I put my hands over my daughter's ears. She protested loudly, but I kept them there. "What you're talking about is a different matter," I said. "It doesn't explain or excuse your being here. Not to this child. And don't say 'always' to her. You have to think harder or just leave it alone and say sorry."

59 He didn't argue, but he didn't apologize. He felt he'd spoken the truth, so he didn't need to argue or apologize.

60 Later in the evening I asked my daughter if she was still racist against soldiers and she said **loftily**: "I'm afraid I don't know what you're referring to." When she's a bit older I'm going to ask her about that little outburst, what made her come out with such words in the first place. And I'm sure she'll make up something that makes her sound cleverer and more sensitive than she really was.

loftily
(lôf′tə·lē) *adv.* arrogantly; haughtily.

MAKE PREDICTIONS

Annotate: Mark details in paragraph 61 that tell how the villagers treated the narrator and her daughter.

Predict: Story plots are driven by conflict. Based on these details about conflict with their neighbors, what might happen to the narrator and her daughter as a result of their friendship with the soldier?

61 We were expecting our scrawny soldier again the following afternoon, my daughter and I. My daughter's friends had dropped her. Even the ones she had helped find favor with the other children forgot that their new position was due to her and urged the others to leave her out of everything. The women I knew snubbed me at market, but I didn't need them. My daughter and I told each other that everyone would come round once they understood that what we were doing was innocent. In fact we were confident that we could convince our soldier of his wrongdoing and send him back to his country to begin life anew as an architect. He'd confessed a love of our minarets.[5] He could take the image of our village home with him and make marvels of it.

---

[5] **minaret** (mĭn′ə-rĕt′): a tall slender tower attached to a mosque, having one or more projecting balconies from which a muezzin or a recording of a muezzin summons the people to prayer.

62   Noura waited until our mothers, mine and hers, were busy gossiping at her house, then she came to tell me that the men were discussing how best to deal with me. I was washing clothes in the bathtub and I almost fell in.

63   My crime was that I had insulted Bilal with my **brazen** pursuit of this soldier…

64   "Noura! This soldier—he's just a boy! He can hardly coax his beard to grow. How could you believe—"

65   "I'm not saying I believe it. I'm just saying you must stop this kind of socializing. And behave **impeccably** from now on. I mean—angelically."

66   Three months before I had come to the village, Noura told me, there had been a young widow who talked back all the time and looked haughtily at the men. A few of them got fed up, and they took her out to the desert and beat her severely. She survived, but once they'd finished with her she couldn't see out of her own eyes or talk out of her own lips. The women didn't like to mention such a matter, but Noura was mentioning it now, because she wanted me to be careful.

67   "I see," I said. "You're saying they can do this to me?"

68   "Don't smile; they can do it. You know they can do it! You know that with those soldiers here our men are twice as fiery. Six or seven of them will even gather to kick a stray dog for stealing food…"

69   "Yes, I saw that yesterday. Fiery, you call it. Did they bring this woman out of her home at night or in the morning, Noura? Did they drag her by her hair?"

70   Noura averted her eyes because I was asking her why she had let it happen and she didn't want to answer.

71   "You're not thinking clearly. Not only can they do this to you but they can take your daughter from you first, and put her somewhere she would never again see the light of day. Better that than have her grow up like her mother. Can't you see that that's how it would go? I'm telling you this as a friend, a true friend…my husband doesn't want me to talk to you anymore. He says your ideas are wicked and bizarre."

72   I didn't ask Noura what her husband could possibly know about my ideas. Instead I said: "You know me a little. Do you find my ideas wicked and bizarre?"

73   Noura hurried to the door. "Yes. I do. I think your husband spoilt you. He gave you illusions…you feel too free. We are not free."

74   I drew my nails down my palm, down then back up the other way, deep and hard. I thought about what Noura had told me. I didn't think for very long. I had no choice—I couldn't afford another visit

© Houghton Mifflin Harcourt Publishing Company

brazen
(brā´zən) *adj.* unrestrained by a sense of shame; rudely bold.

impeccably
(ĭm·pĕk´kə·blē) *adv.* in accordance with having no flaws; perfectly.

WORDS OF THE WISER

Notice & Note: Reread paragraphs 62–71. Mark the advice Noura gives to the narrator.

Draw Conclusions: Based on the information she tells the narrator, do you agree with Noura's advice? Explain why or why not.

MAKE PREDICTIONS

Annotate: Mark the sentences in paragraph 74 that explain how the narrator made sure the villagers no longer believed that she was friendly with the soldier.

Draw Conclusions: Were you expecting this outcome or did her actions surprise you? Explain.

from him. I wrote him a letter. I wonder if I'll ever get a chance to take back all that I wrote in that letter; it was hideous from beginning to end. Human beings shouldn't say such things to each other. I put the letter into an unsealed envelope and found a local boy who knew where the scrawny soldier lived. Doubtless Bilal read the letter before the soldier did, because by evening everyone but my daughter knew what I had done. My daughter waited for the soldier until it was fully dark, and I waited with her, pretending that I was still expecting our friend. There was a song she wanted to sing to him. I asked her to sing it to me instead, but she said I wouldn't appreciate it. When we went inside at last, my daughter asked me if the soldier could have gone home without telling us. He probably hated goodbyes.

75   "He said he would come...I hope he's alright..." my daughter fretted.

76   "He's gone home to build minarets."

77   "With matchsticks, probably."

78   And we were both very sad.

79 My daughter didn't smile for six days. On the seventh she said she couldn't go to school.

80   "You have to go to school," I told her. "How else will you get your friends back again?"

81   "What if I can't," she wailed. "What if I can't get them back again?"

82   "Do you really think you won't get them back again?"

83   "Oh, you don't even care that our friend is gone. Mothers have no feelings and are enemies of progress."

84   (I really wonder who my daughter has been talking to lately. Someone with a sense of humor very like her father's...)

85   I tickled the sole of her foot until she shouted.

86   "Let this enemy of progress tell you something," I said. "I'm never sad when a friend goes far away, because whichever city or country that friend goes to, they turn the place friendly. They turn a suspicious-looking name on the map into a place where a welcome can be found. Maybe the friend will talk about you sometimes, to other friends that live around him, and then that's almost as good as being there yourself. You're in several places at once! In fact, my daughter, I would even go so far as to say that the further away your friends are, and the more spread out they are, the better your chances of going safely through the world..."

87   "Ugh," my daughter said.

CHECK YOUR UNDERSTANDING

Answer these questions before moving on to the **Analyze the Text** section on the following page.

1 Why does the narrator's daughter cut her hair?

  A She wants to look pretty.

  B She wants the boys to notice her.

  C She wants to be able to play with the boys.

  D She wants to blend in with the soldiers.

2 Why is the narrator currently unmarried?

  F She is a widow.

  G She hasn't found a suitor.

  H She has to take care of her mother.

  J She isn't allowed to marry.

3 What can be inferred about the role of women in the society in which the story is set?

  A Women only work in the home.

  B Women are leaders in the community.

  C Women have a limited role in society.

  D Women are not allowed in public spaces.

ANALYZE THE TEXT

Support your responses with evidence from the text. 📓 NOTEBOOK

1. **Infer** Why does the soldier come to visit the narrator and her daughter? Consider:
   • his initial encounter with the daughter
   • what he says about his home country

2. **Compare** In what ways is the narrator different from Noura? What do they have in common?

3. **Analyze** What is the theme of the story? How does this theme relate to the cultural and historical setting?

4. **Predict** How might relations between the villagers and the narrator change after the conclusion of the story? Explain the reasons for your prediction.

5. **Notice & Note** At the end of the story, the narrator tries to console her daughter with wise words about how absent friends enrich our lives, which the daughter undercuts with the comical exclamation "ugh." How has the daughter's life been enriched by her brief friendship with the foreign soldier?

RESEARCH

Although Helen Oyeyemi chose not to name a specific country as the setting for her story, "My Daughter the Racist" seems to have been inspired by Western military operations in countries in the Middle East and Africa. Leaders of those operations say they want to help the people of those countries. However, the narrator reflects a common response to these claims when she says, "They fight us and they try to tell us, in our own language, that they're freeing us. Maybe, maybe not." With a partner, research involvement by Western nations in other countries and answer the following questions.

QUESTION	ANSWER
What set off the conflict?	
Why were Western troops sent to the country?	
How were ordinary citizens of the country affected by the fighting?	

Connect Think about how you would feel living in a country that has been occupied by foreign troops. How would you react? What would you do from day to day? Briefly describe what you think your experience would be like, and share your writing with a partner.

CREATE AND DISCUSS

Write a Fictional Scene In their last scene together, Noura and the narrator exchange harsh words after Noura warns the narrator to cut ties with the soldier. Write a new scene in which the two women get together after the narrator has followed Noura's advice. Will the women resume their former friendship, or does the conflict between them linger?

❏ Reread the scene between the narrator and Noura to refresh your memory of the disagreement between them.

❏ Freewrite some new dialogue between the women.

❏ Use the dialogue as the basis for your scene. Before you begin to write, decide whether you will stick with Oyeyemi's first-person narrator, write the scene with Noura as the narrator, or use a third-person narrator.

Critique and Discuss In a small group, share your impressions of "My Daughter the Racist," informally critiquing the short story.

❏ Focus on the literary devices of setting and first-person point of view. Consider what the narrator relates about the political and social context, and how the setting drives the plot and affects characters.

❏ Evaluate the story in terms of originality. For example, why do you think writer Helen Oyeyemi never clearly identifies the setting? What aspects of the story seem provocative or thought provoking? How are genders represented? What might the writer be expressing through these representations?

❏ Find evidence to support your views.

 Go to **Participating in Collaborative Discussions** in the **Speaking and Listening Studio** to learn more.

 Go to **Writing Narratives** in the **Writing Studio** to learn more.

RESPOND TO THE ESSENTIAL QUESTION

 Why is it hard to resist social pressure?

Gather Information Review your annotations and notes on "My Daughter the Racist." Then, add relevant information to your Response Log. As you determine which information to include, think about:

• the ways in which society impacts your own views and behavior

• a time you had to resist the influence of others

• the repercussions for standing up for what you believe in

ACADEMIC VOCABULARY

As you write and discuss what you learned from the short story, be sure to use the Academic Vocabulary words. Check off each of the words that you use.

❏ **arbitrary**

❏ **controversy**

❏ **convince**

❏ **denote**

❏ **undergo**

WORD BANK
balmy
loftily
brazen
impeccably

CRITICAL VOCABULARY

Practice and Apply Explain whether or not the Critical Vocabulary words are used correctly in the following sentences.

1. When the weather turned **balmy,** Hillary began to shiver on the park bench.

2. Darryl spoke passionately and **loftily** when he told us about his time volunteering at the animal shelter.

3. Alice's **brazen** speech earned praise from teachers.

4. Whenever Sid's parents walk into a room, he behaves **impeccably** so he can get a reward.

VOCABULARY STRATEGY:
Idioms

Go to the **Vocabulary Studio: Using Context Clues** for more on idioms.

An **idiom** is a common figure of speech whose meaning is different from the literal meaning of its words. Idioms are used in everyday speech and are often specific to a dialect. An example of an idiom in "My Daughter the Racist" appears in paragraph 24: "She made faces when she thought my daughter talked too much." *Made faces* does not mean she literally drew or crafted a face. This idiom means she tried to communicate with her granddaughter through facial expressions to prevent her from talking.

Practice and Apply Review the short story once again, this time identifying at least one additional idiom. Jot down each idiom you find and its possible meaning. Then, write a few idioms you know or use. Share your findings with a partner.

LANGUAGE CONVENTIONS:
Syntax

Syntax refers to the order of words or phrases in a sentence. The author of "My Daughter the Racist" varies the syntax throughout the story to create variety, to add emphasis, and to establish a conversational tone.

For example, in paragraph 4, the narrator uses a combination of short and long sentences to call attention to the soldiers:

> **And that girl of mine has really begun to stare at the soldiers, too, even though I slap her hard when I catch her doing that. Who knows what's going to happen? These soldiers are scared. They might shoot someone. Noura next door says: "If they could be so evil as to shoot children then it's in God's hands. Anyway I don't believe that they could do it."**

The varied structure of the sentences places emphasis on the girl's boldness and suggests that something could happen between the daughter and the soldiers. By posing the question, "Who knows what's going to happen?" readers are drawn in and begin to anticipate how the plot will unfold.

In paragraph 58, the narrator uses a sentence fragment in saying:

> **"It doesn't explain or excuse your being here. Not to this child. And don't say 'always' to her. . . ."**

The sentence fragment—following a longer, complete sentence—emphasizes the narrator's protectiveness toward her child and stresses how she wants the soldier to behave. The fragment in this dialogue also mirrors the way people naturally speak. The effect is realistic-sounding dialogue.

Practice and Apply Write a brief paragraph in which you react to the plot in "My Daughter the Racist." Be sure to vary the syntax of your sentences to keep readers engaged and to emphasize certain ideas.

Go to **Sentence Structure** in the **Grammar Studio** to learn more.

© Houghton Mifflin Harcourt Publishing Company • Image Credits: © Sylvie Corriveau/Shutterstock; © everst/Shutterstock

POEM

THE SECOND COMING

by **William Butler Yeats**

pages 759–760

COMPARE THEME

The poems you are about to read make use of symbols—a type of figurative language. As you read, look for people, places, or objects that seem likely to have a symbolic meaning, and consider how these might be related to the themes of the poems. Also make note of the similarities and differences between the two poems. After reading, you will collaborate with a small group on a final project.

? **ESSENTIAL QUESTION:**

What is the power of symbols?

POEM

SYMBOLS? I'M SICK OF SYMBOLS

by **Fernando Pessoa**

pages 762–763

QUICK START

Think about the last time you were expecting something big to happen—something you might be dreading or something you were looking forward to. What was it like to wait, anticipating a big change? How did you feel? Discuss with a partner or a small group.

UNDERSTAND SYMBOLISM

A **symbol** is a person, place, or object that has a concrete meaning in itself and also represents something beyond itself, such as an idea or feeling. This chart provides some examples of common symbols.

SYMBOL	WHAT IT REPRESENTS
dove	peace
fox	cleverness
rose	romantic love
water	purification or cleansing
winter	death

Symbolism is the practice of using symbols, and it is also the name of a literary movement that began in France in the late 19th century. The Symbolists emphasized the use of symbols to suggest states of mind and ideas that cannot be expressed directly. Like many modernist writers, Yeats was strongly influenced by this literary movement. His poems often feature complex symbols drawn from a wide variety of sources, including the Bible, Irish folklore, and occult practices.

Fernando Pessoa was also influenced by symbolism, but nothing about this Portuguese poet's work is easy to pin down. Pessoa wrote his poems through multiple personas, which he called "heteronyms." Each heteronym is a well-defined character who has his own approach to the art of poetry. The poem "Symbols? I'm Sick of Symbols" was written under the heteronym Álvaro de Campos, a naval engineer who lives in London. While some of Pessoa's heteronyms fully embrace symbolism, in this poem Campos playfully criticizes the movement.

As you read, consider which people, places, and objects could be symbolic of ideas or feelings. Also, think about how the poets develop the moods and themes of their poems through the use of symbols.

**GENRE ELEMENTS:
LYRIC POETRY**

- expresses the thoughts and feelings of the speaker
- uses sound devices such as rhyme and rhythm to create a musical quality
- often deals with intense emotions surrounding events such as love, death, or loss

ANALYZE RHYTHMIC PATTERNS

In poetry, **meter** is a pattern of stressed and unstressed syllables. Each unit of meter, known as a **foot,** consists of a combination of stressed and unstressed syllables. These patterns create rhythm, which brings out the musical quality of language and often serves to unify a work of literature.

An **iamb** is a foot that contains one unstressed syllable (˘) followed by one stressed syllable (´). For example, the word *apart* is an iamb. A **trochee** is a foot that contains one stressed syllable followed by one unstressed syllable, as in the word *falcon.* The chart shows the most common types of feet. It also shows terms that describe the number of feet in a line.

RHYTHMIC PATTERNS	
TYPE OF FOOT	iamb (˘ ´) trochee (´ ˘) anapest (˘ ˘ ´) dactyl (´ ˘ ˘)
NUMBER OF FEET	monometer—one dimeter—two trimeter—three tetrameter—four pentameter—five hexameter—six

Many forms of poetry are written in **iambic pentameter,** with five iambic feet in each line. In "The Second Coming," Yeats primarily uses irregular rhythms, but several of the lines are written in perfect iambic pentameter. When he uses regular metrical lines among lines with irregular meter, he creates a dramatic rhythm that helps support his theme.

Pessoa's poem, on the other hand, is written in **free verse,** which is poetry that does not follow any regular patterns of rhyme or meter. Pessoa creates a unique, irregular rhythm by using conversational language and alternating between long and short lines.

ANNOTATION MODEL

NOTICE & NOTE

As you read, mark any people, places, or objects that could be symbolic and make note of what you think they could symbolize. In the model, you can see one reader's notes about "The Second Coming."

Turning and turning in the widening gyre

The falcon cannot hear the falconer;

Things fall apart; the center cannot hold;

The poem starts off dramatically with two dactyl feet. The falcon that cannot hear the falconer may symbolize loss of control.

BACKGROUND

William Butler Yeats *(1865–1939) is widely considered the finest English language poet of the 20th century. He was born in a suburb of Dublin, Ireland, but he spent much of his childhood with his grandparents in the countryside, where he learned about Irish history and mythology—subjects that would heavily influence his writing. In addition to his poetry, Yeats was a dramatist who helped found Dublin's prestigious Abbey Theatre. In 1923 he was awarded the Nobel Prize for Literature. Yeats wrote "The Second Coming" in 1919, shortly after the Russian Revolution and the end of World War I—events that traumatized Europe.*

THE SECOND COMING

Poem by William Butler Yeats

PREPARE TO COMPARE

As you read, look for places and objects in the poem that could be symbols and consider what they might represent.

Turning and turning in the widening gyre
The falcon cannot hear the falconer;
Things fall apart; the center cannot hold;
Mere anarchy is loosed upon the world,
5 The blood-dimmed tide is loosed, and everywhere
The ceremony of innocence is drowned;
The best lack all conviction, while the worst
Are full of passionate intensity.

Surely some revelation is at hand;
10 Surely the Second Coming is at hand.
The Second Coming! Hardly are those words out

Notice & Note

Use the side margins to notice and note signposts in the text.

1 gyre (jīr): spiral.

6 ceremony of innocence: the rituals (such as the rites of baptism and marriage) that give order to life.

10 Second Coming: Christ's return to Earth predicted in the New Testament to be an event preceded by a time of terror and chaos.

ANALYZE RHYTHMIC PATTERNS

Annotate: Mark the meter in lines 7–10.

Analyze: Where does Yeats vary the rhythm from iambic pentameter? What effect does this have?

12 *Spiritus Mundi* (spîr ĭ-
tŏŏs mŏŏn´dē) *Latin:* Spirit
of the World. Yeats used this
term to refer to the collective
unconscious, a supposed
source of images and memories
that all human beings share.

14 This image suggests the
Great Sphinx in Egypt, built
more than 40 centuries ago.

UNDERSTAND SYMBOLISM
Annotate: Mark the symbol in
line 20.

Analyze: What might this object
symbolize?

When a vast image out of *Spiritus Mundi*
Troubles my sight: somewhere in sands of the desert
A shape with lion body and the head of a man,
15 A gaze blank and pitiless as the sun,
Is moving its slow thighs, while all about it
Reel shadows of the indignant desert birds.
The darkness drops again; but now I know
That twenty centuries of stony sleep
20 Were vexed to nightmare by a rocking cradle,
And what rough beast, its hour come round at last,
Slouches towards Bethlehem to be born?

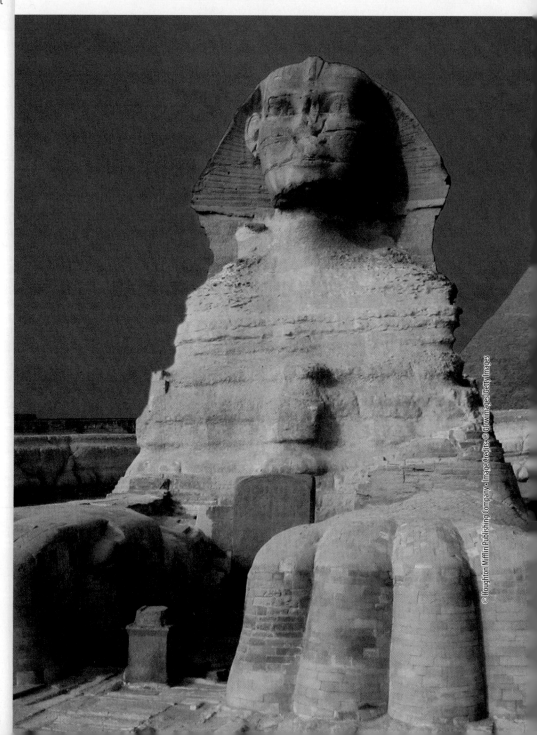

CHECK YOUR UNDERSTANDING

Answer these questions about "The Second Coming" before moving on to the next selection.

1   What situation is suggested by the phrase <u>the center cannot hold</u> in line 3?

   A Repressive government

   B Political disagreement

   C Artistic freedom

   D Descent into chaos

2   Why does the speaker say in line 10 that the Second Coming is at hand?

   F Religious leaders have announced it.

   G The world is full of turmoil.

   H He had a vision of Christ's rebirth.

   J He feels hopeful about the future.

3   Which of the following phrases is ironic in the context of the poem?

   A *mere anarchy* (line 4)

   B *passionate intensity* (line 8)

   C *stony sleep* (line 19)

   D *rough beast* (line 21)

BACKGROUND

Fernando Pessoa *(1888–1935) was born in Lisbon, Portugal, but spent part of his childhood in South Africa where he attended an English school. After studying briefly at the University of Lisbon, he worked as a commercial translator while publishing literary criticism, poetry, and prose. Pessoa wrote in English as well as Portuguese. His work was not well known in his lifetime. After he died, thousands of unpublished manuscript pages were discovered, revealing the full extent of his achievement. Today Pessoa is considered one of the masters of modernist poetry.*

SYMBOLS? I'M SICK OF SYMBOLS

Poem by Fernando Pessoa

PREPARE TO COMPARE

As you read, pay attention to how Pessoa uses symbols and imagery to convey ideas in the poem.

© Houghton Mifflin Harcourt Publishing Company

Notice & Note

Use the side margins to notice and note signposts in the text.

UNDERSTAND SYMBOLISM

Annotate: Mark the symbols mentioned in lines 5–7.

Analyze: What idea does the speaker express in his elaboration of these symbols in lines 8–16?

Symbols? I'm sick of symbols . . .
Some people tell me that everything is symbols.
They're telling me nothing.

What symbols? Dreams . . .
5 Let the sun be a symbol, fine . . .
Let the moon be a symbol, fine . . .
Let the earth be a symbol, fine . . .
But who notices the sun except when the rain stops
And it breaks through the clouds and points behind its back
10 To the blue of the sky?
And who notices the moon except to admire
Not it but the beautiful light it radiates?
And who notices the very earth we tread?
We say earth and think of fields, trees and hills,
15 Unwittingly diminishing it,
For the sea is also earth.
Okay, let all of this be symbols.
But what's the symbol—not the sun, not the moon, not the earth—
In this premature sunset amid the fading blue

20 With the sun caught in expiring tatters of clouds
   And the moon already mystically present at the other end of the sky
   As the last remnant of daylight
   Gilds the head of the seamstress who hesitates at the corner
   Where she used to linger (she lives nearby) with the boyfriend who
        left her?
25 Symbols? I don't want symbols.
   All I want—poor frail and forlorn creature! —
   Is for the boyfriend to go back to the seamstress.

CHECK YOUR UNDERSTANDING

Answer these questions before moving on to the **Analyze the Texts** section on the following page.

1 In lines 8–10, the speaker describes —

   A the abstract idea of the sun

   B the sun as a symbol of hope

   C how the sun appears after a rainfall

   D the beauty of a sunset

2 What idea does the speaker convey in line 16 when he says the sea is also earth?

   F Symbolic language is often too vague.

   G The sea and the earth are both symbols.

   H Seawater is often mixed with earth.

   J Rising seas are diminishing the earth.

3 Why does the seamstress hesitate at the corner?

   A She is waiting for the boyfriend to join her.

   B She used to spend time there with her boyfriend.

   C She doesn't want to walk home in the dark.

   D She doesn't want to walk back to work.

ANALYZE THE TEXTS

Support your responses with evidence from the texts. ▤ NOTEBOOK

1. **Interpret** In lines 7–8 of "The Second Coming," what does the speaker mean when he says, "The best lack all conviction, while the worst / Are full of passionate intensity"?

2. **Analyze** What is ironic about the image that comes to the speaker's mind after he declares, "Surely the Second Coming is at hand"?

3. **Connect** What does the sphinx-like image in lines 13–22 of "The Second Coming" symbolize? How might this symbol be related to historical events around the time Yeats wrote this poem, such as the Russian Revolution or World War I?

4. **Analyze** Reread lines 5–7 and 8–16 of "Symbols? I'm Sick of Symbols." How does Pessoa change the poem's rhythm when he goes from mentioning common symbols to describing more detailed experiences?

5. **Draw Conclusions** In "Symbols? I'm Sick of Symbols," what does the speaker value in the image of the seamstress that he doesn't find in symbols such as the sun, the moon, and the earth?

RESEARCH

RESEARCH TIP
Remember that when you do research, you need to keep track of where you find information. For print sources, make a note of the title, author, publisher, publication date, and page number. For online sources, make a note of the website, URL, article title, author, and access date.

Objects and images gain symbolic meaning over time. With a small group, research the history behind these familiar symbols.

SYMBOL	HISTORY
the Statue of Liberty	
the skull and crossbones symbol	
the Bluetooth symbol	

Extend With your group, discuss the difference between familiar symbols, such as the ones in the chart, and the symbols in "The Second Coming," which take on meaning from their context in the poem.

CREATE AND PRESENT

Write a Response to Literature How do the poems connect to your own experiences and thoughts about symbolism? Capture your thoughts and feelings by freewriting about the use of symbols in poems. Then, use ideas from your writing to decide what feelings and emotions you want to convey in a dramatic reading of one of the poems.

- ❏ Set a time limit of 10–15 minutes for your writing.
- ❏ Write without stopping to check spelling or grammar.
- ❏ At the end of your time limit, read what you wrote and underline all the ideas you would like to convey in a dramatic poetry reading.
- ❏ If your freewriting doesn't yield any useful ideas, try another session.

Give a Dramatic Reading Work with a partner to create a dramatic reading of one of the poems.

- ❏ Begin by discussing the impact of the poet's word choices.
- ❏ Practice reading each line of your chosen poem in a way that conveys your personal connection to the poem's meaning.
- ❏ Consider how you will accompany the words with movements or gestures.
- ❏ Take turns rehearsing with a partner, giving and receiving feedback.
- ❏ Present your dramatic reading to the class, using appropriate volume, phrasing, and expression.

Go to the **Writing Studio: Writing as a Process** for help.

Go to **Giving a Presentation: Delivering Your Presentation** in the **Speaking and Listening Studio** for help.

RESPOND TO THE ESSENTIAL QUESTION

 What is the power of symbols?

Gather Information Review your annotations and notes on "The Second Coming" and "Symbols? I'm Sick of Symbols." Then, add relevant details to your Response Log. As you determine which information to include, think about:

- how you've used symbols to express yourself
- how symbols help you understand difficult concepts
- how symbols can express double meanings

ACADEMIC VOCABULARY

As you write and discuss what you learned from the poems, be sure to use the Academic Vocabulary words. Check off each of the words that you use.

- ❏ **arbitrary**
- ❏ **controversy**
- ❏ **convince**
- ❏ **denote**
- ❏ **undergo**

Collaborate & Compare

COMPARE THEMES

Symbols play an important role in both "The Second Coming" and "Symbols? I'm Sick of Symbols." However, the poems are quite different from each other. Yeats uses symbols to express a grand vision, while Pessoa works on a much more modest scale to make a point about symbolism. Compare how the two authors develop their themes. As you consider the themes of the poems, think about:

- key statements made by the speaker or any characters in the poem
- central images that play important symbolic roles or evoke the theme
- tone, or the overall mood or feeling of the poem

In a small group, identify similarities and differences between the two poems. Record your thoughts in the chart.

THE SECOND COMING
Poem by William Butler Yeats

SYMBOLS? I'M SICK OF SYMBOLS
Poem by Fernando Pessoa

	"THE SECOND COMING"	"SYMBOLS? I'M SICK OF SYMBOLS"
Key Statements		
Central Images, Symbols		
Tone		

ANALYZE THE TEXTS

Discuss these questions in your group.

1. **Compare** What similarities and differences do you see in how the two poets use imagery and symbols?

2. **Analyze** What is the overall tone of each poem? How does the tone reflect the poem's topic?

3. **Evaluate** Which poet expresses ideas more clearly? How might this relate to their different approaches to symbolism?

4. **Critique** Yeats's speaker expresses a prophetic view of history, while Pessoa's speaker gets emotional about something he observes on a street corner. Which poem is more likely to appeal to readers today? Explain.

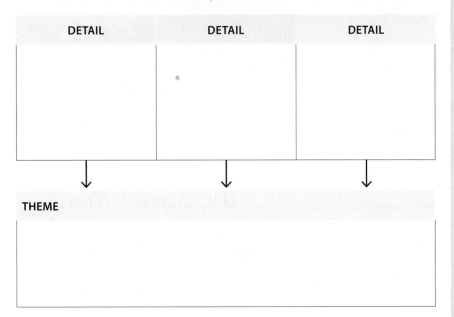

COLLABORATE AND PRESENT

Now your group can continue exploring the ideas in these texts by identifying and comparing their themes. Follow these steps:

1. **Decide on the most important details.** With your group, review the chart you created to identify the most important details, including symbols, from each poem. Identify points you agree on, and resolve disagreements through discussion, basing your decisions on evidence from the texts.

2. **Create theme statements.** State a theme for each poem, using complete sentences. Remember, it is up to you and your group to infer the themes based on details. You can use a chart like the one shown here to determine the theme of each poem.

Go to **Giving a Presentation** in the **Speaking and Listening Studio** for more help.

DETAIL	DETAIL	DETAIL

THEME

3. **Compare and contrast themes.** With your group, discuss similarities and differences in the themes of the poems. Listen actively to the members of your group, take notes, and ask the group to clarify any points you do not understand. Identify points of agreement or disagreement before you present your ideas.

4. **Present your ideas to the class.** Now it is time to present your ideas. State your conclusions about the themes of the poems. Cite text evidence from the poems to support your ideas. Discuss points of similarity and difference in the themes. You may adapt the charts you created or use other visuals to help convey your ideas to the class.

SPEECH

BUDGET 2016: GEORGE OSBORNE'S SPEECH

by **George Osborne**

pages 771–772

COMPARE ARGUMENTS

As you read George Osborne's speech, pay attention to the techniques he uses to influence his audience. Also pay attention to the way he uses evidence to build the case for the plan he puts forward. Notice how the information in the speech is presented, and ask whether it appeals to logic or emotion. After you read both selections, you will collaborate with a group on a final project.

 ESSENTIAL QUESTION:

When should the government interfere in our decisions?

EDITORIAL

WILL THE SUGAR TAX STOP CHILDHOOD OBESITY?

by **Chris Hall**

pages 781–783

Budget 2016: George Osborne's Speech

QUICK START

Think about a time when you had to convince someone to give you permission to do or buy something. Jot down techniques you used to get what you wanted. Share with a classmate how successful you were.

EVALUATE PERSUASIVE TECHNIQUES

George Osborne delivered the speech you are about to read to members of Britain's Parliament, but it was also broadcast on television to all British citizens. His goal was to persuade both of these audiences about the merits of his government's taxing and spending policies, including a tax on sugar. **Persuasive techniques** are the methods used to influence others. Writers use these techniques to enhance their arguments and communicate more effectively with an **audience,** or the specific people to whom an argument is addressed. As you read, evaluate how well Osborne uses the following kinds of appeals:

- **Logical appeals** are arguments that use facts and evidence to support a position, appealing to an audience's reasoning or intellect.

- **Ethical appeals** invoke shared values and principles. They call upon the audience's sense of right and wrong.

- **Emotional appeals** are intended to arouse strong feelings in an audience, such as pity or fear.

ANALYZE INDUCTIVE REASONING

Inductive reasoning is a method of argument in which a writer presents evidence about an issue or problem and then draws a conclusion from the evidence. This conclusion presents the writer's belief about how to resolve the issue or problem. When you analyze an inductive argument, it is important to think critically because writers sometimes introduce **logical fallacies,** or errors in logic or reasoning.

As you read and analyze the argument put forth in Osborne's speech, focus on answering these questions:

Is the evidence provided thorough?	Determine whether Osborne has provided sufficient evidence to support his conclusion.
Is the evidence valid and relevant?	Determine whether Osborne presents facts that can be verified with reputable sources.
Does the conclusion follow logically from the evidence?	Determine whether the facts and evidence provided by Osborne lead logically to the conclusion he has presented.

GENRE ELEMENTS: SPEECH
- is a talk or public address presented to an audience
- may have one or more purposes, such as to entertain, to explain, or to persuade
- may conclude with a call to action
- may be recorded or transcribed for later reading and analysis

CRITICAL VOCABULARY

incentive	levy	implementation	compulsory

To see how many Critical Vocabulary words you already know, use them to complete the sentences.

1. It is a requirement that you attend school until a certain age. This is called _____ education.

2. The government can increase its revenue with a new _____ on services that are not currently being taxed.

3. Many times the government will provide a(n) _____, such as a tax rebate, so companies will invest in the production of energy-saving products.

4. New laws voted on by the Congress may take several years for the _____ to be fully realized.

LANGUAGE CONVENTIONS

Relative Pronouns and Relative Clauses Relative pronouns connect relative, or adjective, clauses to the words they modify in a sentence. Relative pronouns include *that*, *which*, *who*, *whom*, and *whose*. The noun or pronoun that a relative clause modifies is the antecedent of the relative pronoun.

> **George Osborne, <u>who</u> served as Chancellor of Exchequer, delivered a speech about a new tax on sugary drinks.**

In this sentence, *who* is the relative pronoun and *who served as Chancellor of Exchequer* is the relative clause. *George Osborne* is the antecedent of the relative pronoun.

ANNOTATION MODEL

NOTICE & NOTE

As you read, make note of how the author uses facts, statistics, and other kinds of evidence to support his argument. The model shows how one reader annotated the beginning of the speech.

Mr. Deputy Speaker, you <u>cannot have a long-term plan for the country unless you have a long-term plan for our children's health care.</u> Here are the facts we know.

- Five-year-old children are <u>consuming their body weight in sugar every year.</u>

- Experts predict that within a generation, <u>over half of all boys and 70% of girls could be overweight or obese.</u>

This is a logical appeal: children's health issues affect the nation's future.

These surprising facts all relate to children's health.

BACKGROUND

George Osborne *(b. 1971) served as chief financial minister of the United Kingdom as Chancellor of Exchequer from 2010 to 2016. His responsibilities included controlling public spending and raising money through taxation or borrowing. He delivered a speech about the government's budget plan to the House of Commons on March 1, 2016. In this speech, he announced that a new tax on sugar in soft drinks would take effect in 2018.*

BUDGET 2016: GEORGE OSBORNE'S SPEECH

Speech by George Osborne

PREPARE TO COMPARE

As you read Osborne's speech, think about the methods he uses to persuade his audience. Paying attention to how Osborne presents his message will allow you to compare his argument to that of Chris Hall, the author of the next selection.

1   Mr. Deputy Speaker, you cannot have a long term plan for the country unless you have a long term plan for our children's health care. Here are the facts we know.
   - Five-year-old children are consuming their body weight in sugar every year.
   - Experts predict that within a generation, over half of all boys and 70% of girls could be overweight or obese.

2   Here's another fact that we all know. Obesity drives disease. It increases the risk of cancer, diabetes and heart disease—and it costs our economy £27 billion a year; that's more than half the entire NHS[1] paybill.

3   And here's another truth we all know. One of the biggest contributors to childhood obesity is sugary drinks. A can of cola typically has nine teaspoons of sugar in it. Some popular

---

[1] **NHS:** National Health Service (United Kingdom).

Notice & Note

Use the side margins to notice and note signposts in the text.

> **NUMBERS AND STATS**

Notice & Note: Mark the statistics Osborne includes in paragraph 1.

Evaluate: How effective are these statistics as a way to introduce the topic?

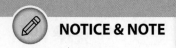

EVALUATE PERSUASIVE TECHNIQUES

Annotate: Mark phrases in paragraph 4 that suggest Osborne is making an ethical appeal.

Analyze: How does mentioning the steps the soft drink industry is taking strengthen Osborne's argument?

incentive
(ĭn-sĕn´tĭv) *n.* something, such as the fear of punishment or the expectation of reward, that induces action or motivates effort.

levy
(lĕv´ē) *n.* a tax or fine imposed on a person or business.

implementation
(ĭm-plə-mən-tā´shən) *n.* the process of putting into practical effect; carry out.

LANGUAGE CONVENTIONS

Annotate: Mark the relative clause in paragraph 7.

Analyze: What is the antecedent of the relative clause?

ANALYZE INDUCTIVE REASONING

Annotate: Mark sentences in paragraphs 8 and 9 that summarize the actions that Parliament wants to take to make children healthier and the results they expect to see.

Analyze: Can you find any logical fallacies in Osborne's argument for his plan to fight childhood obesity?

compulsory
(kəm-pŭl´sə-rē) *adj.* obligatory; required.

drinks have as many as 13. That can be more than double a child's recommended added sugar intake.

4   Let me give credit where credit is due. Many in the soft drinks industry recognize there's a problem and have started to reformulate their products. . . . So industry can act, and with the right **incentives** I'm sure it will.

5   Mr Deputy Speaker, I am not prepared to look back at my time here in this Parliament, doing this job and say to my children's generation: I'm sorry. We knew there was a problem with sugary drinks. We knew it caused disease. But we ducked the difficult decisions and we did nothing.

6   So today I can announce that we will introduce a new sugar **levy** on the soft drinks industry. Let me explain how it will work. It will be levied on the companies. It will be introduced in two years' time to give companies plenty of space to change their product mix. It will be assessed on the volume of the sugar-sweetened drinks they produce or import. There will be two bands—one for total sugar content above 5 grams per 100 millilitres; a second, higher band for the most sugary drinks with more than 8 grams per 100 millilitres. Pure fruit juices and milk-based drinks will be excluded, and we'll ensure the smallest producers are kept out of scope. We will of course consult with Parliament on **implementation**.

7   We're introducing the levy on the industry which means they can reduce the sugar content of their products—as many already do. It means they can promote low-sugar or no sugar brands—as many already are. They can take these perfectly reasonable steps to help with children's health. Of course, some may choose to pass the price onto consumers and that will be their decision, and this would have an impact on consumption too. We understand that tax affects behavior. So let's tax the things we want to reduce, not the things we want to encourage.

8   The OBR[2] estimate that this levy will raise £520 million. And this is tied directly to the second thing we're going to do today to help children's health and wellbeing. We're going to use the money from this new levy to double the amount of funding we dedicate to sport in every primary school. And for secondary schools we're going to fund longer school days for those that want to offer their pupils a wider range of activities, including extra sport. It will be voluntary for schools. **Compulsory** for the pupils. There will be enough resources for a quarter of secondary schools to take part—but that's just a start. . . .

9   A determination to improve the health of our children. A new levy on excessive sugar in soft drinks. The money used to double sport in our schools. A Britain fit for the future. We're not afraid to put the next generation first.

_____

[2] **OBR:** Office for Budget Responsibility (United Kingdom).

CHECK YOUR UNDERSTANDING

Answer these questions before moving on to the **Analyze the Text** section on the following page.

1 Read this sentence from the speech.

We're going to use the money from this new levy to double the amount of funding we dedicate to sport in every primary school.

Which persuasive technique is used in the sentence?

A A logical appeal

B A legislative appeal

C An ethical appeal

D An emotional appeal

2 At the beginning of paragraphs 1, 2, and 3, the author most likely repeats the phrases facts we know and truth we know in order to make —

F himself appear trustworthy to the audience

G logical connections between the evidence he presents

H an emotional appeal

J a bandwagon appeal

3 Which one of the questions below should be asked *first* to effectively analyze Osborne's reasoning that a tax on sugary drinks will make children healthier?

A How true are the three facts that he states are already known?

B How many schools want to implement programs that promote sports?

C What are the other causes of childhood obesity?

D How much will people pay for sugary drinks?

RESPOND

ANALYZE THE TEXT

Support your responses with evidence from the text. NOTEBOOK

1. **Analyze** In what ways does Osborne effectively use persuasive techniques?

2. **Identify** What conclusion does Osborne draw based on the evidence he presents?

3. **Critique** Does Osborne provide adequate support for his argument?

4. **Evaluate** Osborne's speech has two audiences—the Parliament and the British people. How successful is he in addressing both of them?

5. **Notice & Note** In paragraph 6, what is the effect of providing the numbers to explain the two bands of sugar content in sweetened drinks?

RESEARCH

© Houghton Mifflin Harcourt Publishing Company

RESEARCH TIP

Start your research by accessing your state government's website. Then, expand your search by going to your county website. Sites that end in *.gov* are websites that are managed by a government agency. However, *.com* websites may also be helpful.

The national government, states, and counties levy taxes on goods and services to generate money. Research to discover the purpose of the following taxes and at which level of government they are collected. Use the empty rows in the chart to add additional taxes that you might find in your research.

TAX	PURPOSE	LEVEL (NATION/STATE/COUNTY)
Income Tax		
State Tax		
Property Tax		
Gasoline Tax		
Capital Gains Tax		
Inheritance Tax		
Sales Tax		
Business Profit Tax		

Extend Many people believe they are taxed too much. Others think we need more taxes so the government can fund more programs to help keep people safe and healthy. Consider the taxes above and what you learned from your research to determine which taxes you think are the most important and which ones are the least important.

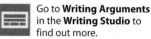

CREATE AND DEBATE

Develop a Persuasive Argument With a small group, decide on a tax you want to support or eliminate. Divide the group into two teams, each taking a *For* or *Against* stance. Both sides should take the following steps:

❏ Determine the facts that can be used to support your stance. This will be the basis for your logical appeal.

❏ Determine how the tax benefits the community or has had negative consequences. Choose words that elicit strong emotions to develop your emotional appeal.

❏ Develop your ethical appeal by explaining how the tax is the "right thing to do" or how the tax is "unfair and imbalanced."

❏ Write down your argument statements that you will use to persuade others to agree with your argument. Organize them in order so you can present a cohesive presentation.

❏ Be sure to anticipate the other side's argument so you can make counterarguments.

Debate Set up a time to meet in front of the class to hold a debate. Each person on the team should take part in presenting a statement using at least one kind of persuasive technique.

❏ Set up debate rules to define how both sides will present their arguments.

❏ Both sides should have the opportunity to make counterarguments.

Go to **Writing Arguments** in the **Writing Studio** to find out more.

 Go to **Analyzing and Evaluating Presentations** in the **Speaking and Listening Studio** to learn more.

RESPOND TO THE ESSENTIAL QUESTION

? When should the government interfere with our decisions?

Gather Information Review your annotations and notes on "Budget 2016: George Osborne's Speech." Then, add relevant details to your Response Log. As you determine which information to include, think about:

- the types of persuasive techniques that the author uses
- whether his reasoning is valid, logical, and stands on a firm premise
- what you have learned from your research and discussions

UNIT 6
RESPONSE LOG

? Essential Question	Details from Texts
What makes people feel insecure?	
Why is it hard to resist social pressure?	
What is the power of symbols?	
When should the government interfere in our decisions?	

R6 Student Resources

ACADEMIC VOCABULARY

As you write and discuss what you learned from the speech, be sure to use the Academic Vocabulary words. Check off each of the words that you use.

❏ **arbitrary**

❏ **controversy**

❏ **convince**

❏ **denote**

❏ **undergo**

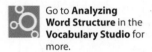

Go to **Analyzing Word Structure** in the **Vocabulary Studio** for more.

CRITICAL VOCABULARY

Practice and Apply Write the Critical Vocabulary word that has the same or similar meaning as the given word.

1. reward

2. mandatory

3. tax

4. enactment

VOCABULARY STRATEGY:
Related Words

Often you can use related words to figure out the meaning of an unfamiliar word. For example, you might not know the meaning of *compulsory.* However, if you are familiar with the related word *compel,* which means "to force or require," you could guess that *compulsory* describes something that is required.

Practice and Apply Use the related word in parentheses to help you determine the meaning of each boldfaced word. Check your work by consulting a dictionary.

1. (discreet) Some people may consider calling children overweight to be an **indiscretion.**

2. (impede) Members of Parliament who disagree with Osborne might be an **impediment** to passing a sugar tax.

3. (consume) Obesity in children has been blamed on **consumption** of sugary drinks.

4. (suppose) Osborne's **presupposition** for his proposal is that sugary drinks are the main cause of childhood obesity.

5. (exclude) Osborne's proposal has **exclusionary** measures for milk and fruit juices.

LANGUAGE CONVENTIONS:
Relative Pronouns and Relative Clauses

Good writers look for opportunities to combine short, choppy sentences into longer ones. This helps to connect ideas and vary sentence structure. One way to combine sentences is to use relative pronouns and relative clauses. **Relative pronouns** are used to help identify or provide more information about the person or thing that is being discussed. The noun or pronoun that a relative clause modifies is the **antecedent** of the relative pronoun. The chart shows the relative pronouns and explains how to use them.

Go to **The Adjective Clause** in the **Grammar Studio** for more on relative pronouns and clauses.

RELATIVE PRONOUN(S)	USED TO MODIFY
who, whom	people
which	things
that, whose	people or things

Read these sentences:

> **The tax is intended to help reduce the amount of sugar in popular drinks.**

> **The tax will be implemented two years from now.**

Now read the sentence below, which combines the first two sentences into one by using a relative pronoun.

> **The tax, (which) will be implemented two years from now, is intended to help reduce the amount of sugar in popular drinks.**

In the sentence above, *which* is used because the antecedent of the relative pronoun is a thing. The relative pronoun *which* begins a **relative clause** that describes the tax. This clause can also be called an adjective clause.

Practice and Apply Complete the table below. First, identify the antecedent. Then, use a relative clause to combine each pair of sentences. Circle the relative pronoun and underline the relative clause in your combined sentence.

SENTENCES	COMBINED SENTENCE
1. The speaker gave a speech about sugar tax. 2. The speaker answered questions that followed.	
1. The soft drink companies were aware of the problem. 2. The soft drink companies began to reduce the amount of sugar in their products.	
1. The schools sought extra funding from the government. 2. The schools agreed to lengthen school days.	

© Houghton Mifflin Harcourt Publishing Company

EDITORIAL

WILL THE SUGAR TAX STOP CHILDHOOD OBESITY?

by **Chris Hall**

pages 781–783

COMPARE ARGUMENTS

Now that you've read "Budget 2016: George Osborne's Speech," read an argument that takes a position opposing the one set forth in the speech. As you read, note the primary argument made by the writer and how he develops his argument with evidence and reasoning. Also notice whether the evidence ever causes you to question your own opinion on this matter. After you read both selections, you will collaborate with a small group on a final project.

 ESSENTIAL QUESTION:

When should the government interfere in our decisions?

SPEECH

BUDGET 2016: GEORGE OSBORNE'S SPEECH

by **George Osborne**

pages 771–772

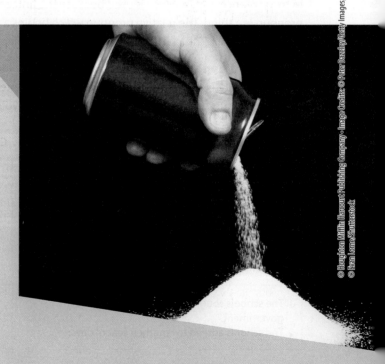

© Houghton Mifflin Harcourt Publishing Company • Image Credits: © Peter Dazeley/Getty Images; © Evan Lorne/Shutterstock

Will the Sugar Tax Stop Childhood Obesity?

QUICK START

Think about a problem or issue in your school or community. What was one proposed solution? Did the solution effectively solve the problem or issue? What solution would you have proposed? Discuss your ideas with a partner.

EVALUATE ARGUMENTS

A strong argument clearly states a **claim,** or position on an issue, and has key ideas to back up that claim. It also provides sufficient evidence to support the claim and key ideas. **Evidence** may include facts, examples, statistics, and expert opinions.

In his editorial, Chris Hall makes an argument about the effectiveness of using a sugar tax on certain beverages to combat childhood obesity. As you read, use the questions below to help you evaluate the strength of his argument.

- **Claim:** Is Hall's claim about sugary drinks and the effectiveness of taxation credible and supported by sound reasons and evidence?
- **Reasoning:** Is Hall's argument based on logic? Does he introduce any logical fallacies or errors in presenting his conclusions? For example, does he make any generalizations that are too broad?
- **Evidence:** Are the facts, examples, and other details included in the editorial valid, authoritative, relevant, and sufficient?

EVALUATE COUNTERARGUMENTS

An effective argument anticipates opposing viewpoints and provides counterarguments to challenge or disprove them. A **counterargument** is an argument made to oppose another argument. In structuring a counterargument, a writer often acknowledges an opposing viewpoint or claim and then states or implies the counterargument which refutes that viewpoint, supporting it with facts and evidence.

OPPOSING VIEW	HALL'S COUNTERARGUMENT	HALL'S FACTS AND EVIDENCE
Increased consumption of sugar-sweetened beverages is impacting rising rates of obesity and type 2 diabetes.	Sugar-sweetened beverage consumption is rising, but it is not the root of the obesity and type 2 diabetes problem.	Less than 2% of weight gain is caused by sugary drinks.

As you read the editorial, note the counterarguments Hall presents, paying attention to the quality of the facts and evidence that support them.

GENRE ELEMENTS: EDITORIAL

- states an opinion rather than being objective
- appears in a dedicated editorial/opinion section of a newspaper or broadcast
- presents the ideas of the news staff or is submitted by an independent writer
- may note opposing viewpoints and provide counterarguments to disprove them

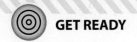

CRITICAL VOCABULARY

| theorize | attribute | demonize | consumption |

To preview the Critical Vocabulary words, use context clues and your knowledge of word roots and suffixes to fill in the correct word for each sentence.

1. I know you do not agree with them, but there is no need to _____ them at every opportunity.

2. My _____ of fresh fruit increases in the summer when my favorite kinds of fruit are in season.

3. I _____ my success in school to my good teachers and study habits.

4. Historians can _____, but nobody knows for sure what Shakespeare was doing during his "lost years."

LANGUAGE CONVENTIONS

Rhetorical Questions In this lesson, you will learn how writers use **rhetorical questions** to enhance arguments and effectively convey ideas. As you read "Will the Sugar Tax Stop Childhood Obesity?" watch for questions that the author uses to get the reader to think critically about and get emotionally involved in the topic of discussion.

ANNOTATION MODEL

NOTICE & NOTE

As you read, note how the author develops his argument. In the model, you can see one reader's notes about how the author introduces his argument.

With the release of the United Kingdom's 2016 budget, it seems everyone is talking about the sugar tax. Over the last few days I've read several opinions on whether this is a good idea and ultimately, whether it will help to halt the obesity crisis—the million dollar question!

The writer sets himself up as an authority on the topic, but he has gotten his knowledge from reading opinions. Is his argument based on solid facts, or on the opinions of others?

The writer prepares the reader for an argument against the sugar tax by questioning whether it is a "good idea" and pointing out the high stakes involved: public health and large amounts of money.

© Houghton Mifflin Harcourt Publishing Company

BACKGROUND

Chris Hall is a personal trainer based in Oxford, England. As part of his stated mission, Hall feels compelled to keep up to date with the latest research on health, nutrition, and exercise. He writes articles about health-related issues for a fitness blog and for major news websites.

WILL THE SUGAR TAX STOP CHILDHOOD OBESITY?

Editorial by Chris Hall

PREPARE TO COMPARE

As you read, pay attention to the argument that the author is making. Note any details that support his argument or errors in logic that undermine his argument. Paying attention to how he presents his message and employs reasoning will allow you to compare his argument to that of George Osborne, the author of the first selection.

1   With the release of the United Kingdom's 2016 budget, it seems everyone is talking about the sugar tax. Over the last few days I've read several opinions on whether this is a good idea and ultimately, whether it will help to halt the obesity crisis—the million dollar question!

2   The Government's new tax on sugary drinks will be split into two bands: the first for total sugar above 5g per 100ml, and the second for when total sugar exceeds 8g per 100ml. To give you some context, a typical cola contains 10.6g of sugar per 100ml, while typical orange juice has 8g.

3   The tax won't be placed on pure fruit juices or milk based drinks. But in an effort to drive down childhood obesity, is this the right approach?

4   There's no denying it: our consumption of sugar-sweetened beverages (SSBs) has risen in recent decades, and there is

Notice & Note

Use the side margins to notice and note signposts in the text.

LANGUAGE CONVENTIONS

Annotate: Mark the rhetorical question in paragraph 3.

Analyze: How does the author use this rhetorical question to develop his argument?

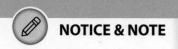
evidence to suggest that this increase is having an impact on obesity and the rising number of cases of type 2 diabetes. But sugary drinks alone are not the root of the problem.

5   The number of articles, statements and scientific studies linking sugary drinks to weight gain makes it easy to point the finger, and come to the conclusion that sugary drinks should be eliminated. In theory, this makes a lot of sense, but when you compare the theoretical data with the observed data, you can see that the actual weight gain associated with sugary drinks is in fact ten times less than was originally **theorized,** and actually, less than 2% of weight gain can be **attributed** to drinking sugary drinks!

6   It's only in the last ten years or so that sugar has been **demonized** for our increasing waistlines. Interestingly, our total **consumption** of sugar in the UK has actually fallen by 20 per cent in the last 30 years! In fact, it is our eating patterns as a whole that are to blame. If you look at the most recent data on calorie consumption, we are both eating more (approximately 445 calories more) but also moving less than we were 40 years ago.

7   Interestingly out of the 445 extra calories we're now consuming, less than 10 percent are from sweeteners/sugar; that's only 45 calories! The remaining calories can be blamed on our increased consumption of refined grains such as french fries, potatoes, crisps[1] and baked goods, along with fats and oils.

8   Now, placing a tax on sugary drinks does indicate that the Government is realizing the extent of the obesity crisis and starting to do something about it. But let's be honest, the price isn't going to increase so dramatically that it will force those who buy them to find a healthier alternative. In fact, a lot of the 'healthier' alternatives are probably going to have just the same impact (if not worse!) than if you were to choose a sugary drink.

9   Milkshakes, flavored waters and off-the-shelf cold coffees can contain nearly as much sugar, if not more, than your average can of soda and they tend to be higher in calories! In fact, if you compare a standard 471ml bottle of chocolate milkshake to a can of cola you'll find the milkshake has an extra 203 calories. Yet these drinks are exempt from the tax!

10   If we are serious about tackling childhood obesity, then we must not be naive enough as to think that pushing up the cost of fizzy drinks is going to have a noticeable impact. It is more important to focus on the issue of over-eating in general, and reducing our consumption of delicious but unhealthy foods such as refined grains and fatty foods.

11   It's also crucially important that we remain active and encourage our children to put the digital tablet down, get up off the sofa and out into the fresh air. Only then do I believe we'll stand a fighting chance of tackling the obesity crisis. . . .

---

[1] **crisps:** a British term for potato chips.

theorize
(thē´ə-rīz, thîr´īz) *v.* to formulate theories or a theory; speculate.

attribute
(ə-trĭb´yōŏt) *v.* to regard as arising from a particular cause or source; ascribe.

demonize
(dē´mə-nīz) *v.* to represent as evil or diabolic.

consumption
(kən-sŭmp´shən) *n.* an amount consumed.

EVALUATE COUNTERARGUMENTS

Annotate: Mark evidence in paragraphs 8–9 that contradicts the opposing view that increased prices will force people to drink healthier beverages.

Analyze: What counterargument does Hall make to refute the government's view?

EVALUATE ARGUMENTS

Annotate: In paragraphs 10–11, mark the author's recommendations for combating the obesity crisis.

Evaluate: Which claim or recommendation is best supported by the evidence the author presents? Cite examples from the article to support your answer.

12   Any move to tackle the obesity crisis must be praised, but the issue is much more deeply rooted in our lifestyles than what we drink. Any serious attempt to tackle the crisis must face up to this fact, and make real efforts to encourage change.

CHECK YOUR UNDERSTANDING

Answer these questions before moving on to the **Analyze the Text** section on the following page.

1 Which sentence best describes the author's opinion of the sugar tax?

  A The sugar tax is not a useful response to the obesity crisis.

  B The sugar tax will cause a substantial decrease in purchases of sugar-sweetened beverages.

  C The sugar tax will motivate British people to be more active.

  D The sugar tax does not address the main causes of increased obesity rates in Britain.

2 Which of the following would the author of the editorial most likely support?

  F A sugar tax that is higher than the one proposed

  G A public health campaign to educate citizens on nutritious food choices

  H A tax on all beverages with sugar, including milkshakes and fruit juice

  J A public health campaign to educate citizens on how sugar consumption causes weight gain

3 Read this sentence from the editorial.

  It's only in the last ten years or so that sugar has been demonized for our increasing waistlines.

  This sentence shows that the author believes —

  A the size of the average person's waistline has increased during the past ten years because of sugar consumption

  B overconsumption of sugar for the past ten years is primarily responsible for the country's current obesity crisis

  C scientists have found solid evidence linking obesity to sugar consumption during the past ten years

  D people have put too much emphasis on the role of sugar in the obesity crisis during the past ten years

ANALYZE THE TEXT

Support your responses with evidence from the text. NOTEBOOK

1. **Summarize** In your own words, describe the argument the author makes about the sugar tax. Explain why he feels the tax will or will not be effective.

2. **Analyze** Consider the most likely source of the opposing viewpoints that the author addresses with his counterarguments—George Osborne's speech. Why does the author most likely choose to structure parts of his editorial using counterarguments?

3. **Infer** How does the author of the editorial view sugar-sweetened beverages?

4. **Evaluate** How well does the author develop his argument? Does it contain any errors in logic that undermine the argument?

5. **Critique** Identify an aspect of the author's argument that is weak or lacks support. How could the author strengthen that part of the argument?

RESEARCH

RESEARCH TIP

When you are looking for credible and up-to-date information on a recent or developing news story, be sure to evaluate the type of sources you find. Although opinion pieces, editorials, and blog posts can contain valuable information and give the reader insight into multiple sides of a topic, they may not always cite the most accurate or up-to-date information, and may only present information that supports the author's point of view or argument.

When Hall wrote the editorial "Will the Sugar Tax Stop Childhood Obesity?" the tax had not yet been implemented. Conduct research to locate the most recent information about how the tax works and what effects it may have had in the United Kingdom. Use the chart to record the results of your research.

IMPLEMENTATION DATE	
AMOUNT OF THE TAX	
HEALTH EFFECTS OF THE TAX	
TOTAL EARNINGS FROM THE TAX	

CREATE AND DISCUSS

Evaluate an Argument Write a three-paragraph opinion essay in which you evaluate the author's argument and use of counterarguments in "Will the Sugar Tax Stop Childhood Obesity?" Consider reviewing your notes and annotations in the text before you begin.

❏ Introduce your essay by identifying the author's primary argument and indicating your evaluation of the argument.

❏ Then, explain your evaluation of the author's argument. Include details about how the author develops specific lines of reasoning and counterarguments.

❏ In your final paragraph, sum up your evaluation of the author's argument and offer praise or constructive criticism as necessary.

Discuss In a small group, discuss your opinions about the author's arguments in "Will the Sugar Tax Stop Childhood Obesity?" Are they logical, convincing, and well supported, or illogical, unconvincing, and poorly supported? Are all parts of the argument developed equally?

❏ Review the editorial with your group to identify the main arguments and counterarguments the author uses.

❏ Then, discuss your individual evaluations of those arguments and counterarguments. As you discuss, listen closely and ask each other questions to help clarify when ideas are unclear.

❏ Finally, end the discussion by identifying similarities, differences, and/or common themes in the evaluations of each member of your group.

Go to **Writing Arguments: Persuasive Techniques** in the **Writing Studio** to find out more.

Go to **Participating in Collaborative Discussions** in the **Speaking and Listening Studio** for more.

RESPOND TO THE ESSENTIAL QUESTION

? When should the government interfere in our decisions?

Gather Information Review your annotations and notes on "Will the Sugar Tax Stop Childhood Obesity?" Then, add relevant details to your Response Log. As you determine which information to include, think about:

• the role government influence plays in everyday life
• what kinds of decisions should always be left in the hands of individuals
• who gets to determine what is the "common good"

ACADEMIC VOCABULARY

As you write and discuss what you learned from the editorial, be sure to use the Academic Vocabulary words. Check off each of the words that you use.

❏ **arbitrary**

❏ **controversy**

❏ **convince**

❏ **denote**

❏ **undergo**

UNIT 6
RESPONSE LOG

Use this Response Log to record information from the texts that relates to or comments on the **Essential Questions** in Unit 6.

? Essential Question	Details from Texts
What makes people feel insecure?	
Why is it hard to resist social pressure?	
What is the power of symbols?	
When should the government interfere in our decisions?	

R6   Student Resources

WORD BANK

theorize
attribute
demonize
consumption

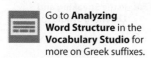

Go to **Analyzing Word Structure** in the **Vocabulary Studio** for more on Greek suffixes.

CRITICAL VOCABULARY

Practice and Apply With a partner, discuss and then write down an answer to each of the following questions. Then, work together to write a sentence for each vocabulary word.

1. Which vocabulary word goes with *blame* and *credit*? Why?

2. Which vocabulary word goes with *hypothesis*? Why?

3. Which vocabulary word goes with *use*? Why?

4. Which vocabulary word goes with *negative*? Why?

VOCABULARY STRATEGY:
The Greek Suffix *-ize*

The Greek suffix *-ize* has several related meanings. A few of its meanings are listed below:

- to cause to be or become
- to cause to conform to or resemble
- to treat as
- to perform, engage in, or produce

Understanding the different meanings of the suffix *-ize* can help you determine the meaning of a word when you encounter it. Take a look at an example from "Will the Sugar Tax Stop Childhood Obesity?" below.

> **It's only in the last ten years or so that sugar has been <u>demonized</u> for our increasing waistlines.**

In the word *demonize*, the suffix *-ize* means "to treat as." Hall suggests that opponents of sugar are representing it as something evil or diabolic.

Practice and Apply Determine which meaning of the Greek suffix *-ize* helps you best understand the meaning of these words. Write your own definition of the word, incorporating the meaning of the Greek suffix.

1. agonize

2. colonize

3. familiarize

4. satirize

5. standardize

LANGUAGE CONVENTIONS:
Rhetorical Questions

A **rhetorical question** is a question to which no answer is expected. Rhetorical questions are often used to emphasize meaning and evoke an emotional or thoughtful response in the reader. Writers and speakers also use them to suggest that their claims are so obvious everyone should agree with them. Employed appropriately, rhetorical questions can enhance an argument.

In "Will the Sugar Tax Stop Childhood Obesity?" Hall uses a rhetorical question in the third paragraph:

> **The tax won't be placed on pure fruit juices or milk based drinks. But in an effort to drive down childhood obesity, is this the right approach?**

Hall does not expect his readers to have a ready answer for the question. Rather, he uses the question to make readers think critically about both the claim of those who promote the sugar tax and about his own claim that the tax will not have the desired effect.

By starting the question with the word *but*, he first signals to the reader he is going to introduce a new idea that is at odds with what he just described. Then, he uses the strong phrase *drive down* to emphasize the idea that firm action and struggle will be necessary to combat childhood obesity. Finally, he uses the emotionally charged word *right*, which encourages the reader to consider the question in ethical terms of right and wrong.

Practice and Apply Reread your evaluation of Hall's argument, looking for places where you could use rhetorical questions to strengthen your position. Rewrite one of your paragraphs so it includes a rhetorical question.

BUDGET 2016: GEORGE OSBORNE'S SPEECH
Speech by George Osborne

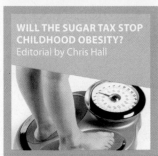

WILL THE SUGAR TAX STOP CHILDHOOD OBESITY?
Editorial by Chris Hall

Collaborate & Compare

COMPARE ARGUMENTS

When you read just one argument, you primarily learn about only one point of view on a topic, even though the opposing point of view is usually acknowledged. Reading at least two arguments provides a more well-rounded and thorough understanding of the topic. When you compare two opposing arguments on the same topic, you can synthesize the information, taking into account all of the evidence provided by both arguments, as you evaluate each author's claim and determine your own opinion.

In a small group, complete the graphic organizer. Use the information you gather to decide whether you believe that a sugar tax will help reduce obesity in children.

OSBORNE'S CONCLUSION	HALL'S CONCLUSION

MY CONCLUSION

ANALYZE THE TEXTS

Discuss these questions in your group.

1. **Analyze** Which elements of the arguments offered by each author are most in conflict? How might the conflict affect readers?

2. **Compare** Both authors believe that people's behaviors need to change. How do their views on the best way to change behavior differ?

3. **Synthesize** Which part of Osborne's plan would Hall be most likely to support?

4. **Evaluate** Which author's argument do you find more effective and why?

RESEARCH AND SHARE

Now your group can continue exploring the ideas in these texts by collaborating on research to present a public policy proposal for reducing obesity. Follow these steps:

Go to **Participating in Collaborative Discussions** in the **Speaking and Listening Studio** to learn more.

1. **Develop Questions** In your group, brainstorm questions that you will need to research answers for in order to create your public policy proposal. Determine the most important questions and reach agreement on which group member will research each question. If you have more questions than group members, combine related questions before making research assignments.

2. **Gather Information** As you begin to research your question(s), make sure that the sources you consult are relevant, reliable, and credible. Although some overlap may be unavoidable, try to research only your own question(s) and not those of other group members so that each person has a meaningful share in the research process.

3. **Share Research** Once each group member has completed his or her research, discuss your findings as a group and take notes about the answer to each research question. You can use a table like the one below to track your group's research.

RESEARCH QUESTION	ANSWER

4. **Collaborate and Create** Now that your group has researched questions related to reducing obesity, it is time to develop your public policy. Discuss the findings as a group, and try to reach an agreement on a public policy addressing obesity that is supported by facts and evidence from your research. Working together and using your notes, draft a paragraph that details your public policy proposal. Be sure to explain your reasoning and back up your ideas with evidence.

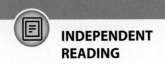
Reader's Choice

? ESSENTIAL QUESTIONS

Review the four Essential Questions for this unit on page 691.

Setting a Purpose   Select one or more of these options from your eBook to continue your exploration of the Essential Questions.

- Read the descriptions to see which text grabs your interest.
- Think about which genres you enjoy reading.

Notice & Note

In this unit, you practiced noticing and noting the signposts and asking big questions about nonfiction. As you read independently, these signposts and others will aid your understanding. Below are the anchor questions to ask when you read literature and nonfiction.

Reading Literature: Stories, Poems, and Plays	
Signpost	**Key Question**
Contrasts and Contradictions	Why did the character act that way?
Aha Moment	How might this change things?
Tough Questions	What does this make me wonder about?
Words of the Wiser	What's the lesson for the character?
Again and Again	Why might the author keep bringing this up?
Memory Moment	Why is this memory important?

Reading Nonfiction: Essays, Articles, and Arguments	
Signpost	**Key Question(s)**
Big Questions	What surprised me? What did the author think I already knew? What challenged, changed, or confirmed what I already knew?
Contrasts and Contradictions	What is the difference, and why does it matter?
Extreme or Absolute Language	Why did the author use this language?
Numbers and Stats	Why did the author use these numbers or amounts?
Quoted Words	Why was this person quoted or cited, and what did this add?
Word Gaps	Do I know this word from someplace else? Does it seem like technical talk for this topic? Do clues in the sentence help me understand the word?

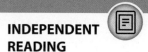

You can preview these texts in Unit 6 of your eBook.

Then, check off the text or texts that you select to read on your own.

SHORT STORY

Araby
James Joyce

Can a poor schoolboy hope to impress a girl with a small gift?

SPEECH

Professions for Women
Virginia Woolf

Woolf relates two strategies she has used to confront obstacles which all women face.

POEM

Do Not Go Gentle into That Good Night
Dylan Thomas

A son pleads with his dying father to resist death and hold on to life for as long as possible.

POEM

Digging
Seamus Heaney

Can a son fulfill his own life's purpose while taking a completely different path from his father?

SHORT STORY

Marriage Is a Private Affair
Chinua Achebe

Nnaemeka married for love, offending his father. Can he bridge the rift he created by choosing his own path?

Collaborate and Share With a partner, discuss what you learned from at least one of your independent readings.

- Give a brief synopsis or summary of the text.

- Describe any signposts that you noticed in the text and explain what they revealed to you.

- Describe what you most enjoyed or found most challenging about the text. Give specific examples.

- Decide if you would recommend the text to others. Why or why not?

Go to the **Reading Studio** for more resources on **Notice & Note.**

Write an Argument

Go to the **Writing Studio** for help writing arguments.

This unit focuses on modern and contemporary literature. Responding to the devastation of two world wars and the loss of the once-powerful British Empire, British writers struggled to carve out a role for themselves in their new and different world. For this writing task, you will write an argument about a social or political issue in your community, such as school choice or homelessness. You can use both George Osborne's speech given to the House of Commons and Chris Hall's editorial as mentor texts to write your own argument.

As you write your argument, you can use the notes from your Response Log, which you filled out after reading the texts in this unit.

Writing Prompt

Read the information in the box below.

This is the topic or context for your argument.

> Think about various issues facing your own community—such as conservation efforts, homelessness, taxes, or unemployment. Consider the role of the government and what responsibilities they have to individuals and communities.

Think carefully about the following Essential Question.

How might this Essential Question relate to your argument?

> When should the government interfere in our decisions?

Choose an issue that you care about or that means something to you.

Write an argument about a social or political issue facing your community and the government's role in helping to solve this issue.

Be sure to—

Review these points as you write and again when you finish. Make any needed changes.

- ❑ clearly state a claim, or thesis statement, about the issue you chose
- ❑ develop your argument with key ideas, supported by relevant evidence
- ❑ address opposing claims with legitimate counterarguments
- ❑ establish logical relationships between all of the elements of your argument
- ❑ use specific rhetorical devices to support your claim and counterarguments
- ❑ write a conclusion that summarizes your argument
- ❑ maintain a formal tone through the use of Standard English

1 Plan

Before you begin to write, plan your argument using the chart below. Think of two or three political or social issues that interest you—homelessness, school choice, conservation—then, choose one about which you will make a claim. Think about the government's role, as opposed to the responsibility of individual citizens on this issue. Make a list of key questions about your topic to help focus your research. Then, gather facts and evidence from reliable sources online, and talk to informed members of your community. Consider both sides of the argument carefully and use any background reading or class discussions to generate key ideas to help develop your claim, or thesis statement.

Argument Planning Chart	
Topic	
Questions to consider	
Ideas from background reading	
Ideas from class discussions	
Claim	

Background Reading Review the notes you have taken in your Response Log that relate to the question, "When should the government interfere in our decisions?" Texts in this unit provide background reading that will help you formulate your argument.

Go to **Writing Arguments: What is a Claim?** for help planning your argument.

Notice & Note
From Reading to Writing

As you plan your argument, apply what you've learned about signposts to your own writing. Remember that writers use common features, called signposts, to help convey their message to readers.

Think how you can incorporate **Numbers and Stats** into your argument.

Go to the **Reading Studio** for more resources on **Notice & Note.**

Use the notes from your Response Log as you plan your argument.

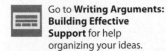

Go to **Writing Arguments: Building Effective Support** for help organizing your ideas.

Organize Your Ideas After completing the planning chart, you should have a claim on which to base your argument. Use this chart to organize key ideas in support of your claim. Anticipate any opposing arguments and develop counterarguments. Think about how you might use rhetorical devices in supporting your claim and developing counterarguments.

Claim:		
Key ideas	**Opposing arguments**	**Counterarguments**

2 Develop a Draft

You may prefer to draft your argument online.

Once you have completed your planning activities, you will be ready to begin drafting your argument. Refer to your planning and organizational charts, as well as any notes you took as you studied the texts in this unit. These will provide a plan for you to follow as you write. Using a laptop or computer makes it easier to make changes or move sentences around later when you are ready to revise your first draft.

Use the Mentor Texts

Author's Craft

In supporting your claim, it's important to use strong, reliable, and relevant evidence. Specific details such as facts, examples, statistics, and quotations from experts contribute to a logical and effective argument. Note how George Osborne uses clear, reliable facts and statistics that are directly related to his claim and that will likely catch his listeners' attention.

> Children are consuming their body weight in sugar every year.
>
> Experts predict that within a generation over half of all boys, and 70% of girls could be overweight or obese.
>
> . . . Obesity drives disease. . . . cancer, diabetes and heart disease . . . One of the biggest contributors to childhood obesity is sugary drinks.
>
> A can of cola typically has nine teaspoons of sugar in it.

Osborne's serious and surprising details draw his listeners in and help them to understand his point of view. His use of statistics helps give weight to his argument that excessive sugar is harmful to children's health.

Apply What You've Learned As you search for evidence to support your claim, look for interesting facts, statistics, and examples that might surprise your reader. Be sure to use enough detail to make a convincing argument.

Genre Characteristics

An effective counterargument acknowledges the opposition with a respectful tone. In his editorial, Chris Hall recognizes the validity of the opposing view before presenting specific evidence to refute the claim about the advantage of taxing sugary drinks.

> There's no denying it: our consumption of sugar sweetened beverages (SSBs) has risen in recent decades, and there is evidence to suggest that this increase is having an impact on obesity and the rising number of cases of type 2 diabetes. But sugary drinks alone are not the root of the problem.

Hall agrees that there is a problem with sugar consumption and then acknowledges the valid evidence offered by the opposing view. Note the transition sentence at the end of the paragraph. This shows he will present a counterclaim.

Apply What You've Learned Maintain a formal tone when you are making a counterargument. Begin by respectfully presenting the opposition view of a particular point. Then, transition smoothly into your counterargument.

WRITING TASK

③ Revise

Go to **Writing Arguments: Formal Style** for help revising your argument.

On Your Own Once you have written your draft, you'll want to go back and look for ways to improve your argument. As you reread and revise, think about whether you have achieved your purpose. The Revision Chart will help you focus on specific elements to make your writing stronger.

Revision Guide		
Ask Yourself	**Tips**	**Revision Techniques**
1. Did I make a claim that states my position clearly?	**Highlight** your thesis statement.	If necessary, **add** a sentence or two to clarify your claim. **Add** an interesting example or related quotation to hook your reader.
2. Did I back up my claim with key ideas, supported by facts and evidence?	**Highlight** your key ideas and **underline** supporting facts and evidence.	**Read** your thesis statement aloud, followed by your key ideas. Does your argument make sense so far? **Add** more support if you can.
3. Are opposing claims addressed with well-supported counterarguments?	**Ask** a classmate to challenge your claim.	**Elaborate** by adding opposing claims and counterarguments to refute them, as needed.
4. Did I transition smoothly between ideas, paragraphs, and sentences?	**Underline** transitional words and phrases.	**Clarify** the relationship between the claim and key ideas and evidence by adding transitions.
5. Did I use rhetorical devices effectively?	**Highlight** any rhetorical devices.	**Add** appropriate rhetorical devices, such as repetition or rhetorical questions, to support and emphasize your claim and counterarguments.
6. Does my conclusion effectively restate my claim?	**Underline** your conclusion.	**Add** a statement that summarizes your claim.

ACADEMIC VOCABULARY
As you conduct your **peer review,** be sure to use these words.

❏ **arbitrary**

❏ **controversy**

❏ **convince**

❏ **denote**

❏ **undergo**

With a Partner Once you and your partner have worked through the Revision Guide on your own, exchange arguments and evaluate each other's draft in a **peer review.** Focus on providing revision suggestions for at least three of the items mentioned in the chart. Explain why you think your partner's draft should be revised and what your specific suggestions are. When receiving feedback from your partner, listen attentively and ask questions to make sure you fully understand the revision suggestions.

4 Edit

Now that you've revised the content of your argument, it's time to improve the finer points of your draft. Edit for the proper use of Standard English conventions and make sure to correct any misspellings or grammatical errors.

! Go to **Sentence Structure** in the **Grammar Studio** to learn more.

Language Conventions

Vary Syntax for Effect Vary the **syntax,** or word order, of your sentences for more effective writing. When you use the same sentence patterns repeatedly, your writing becomes boring and your readers tend to lose interest. As you edit your argument, try the following strategies:

- To create a smooth flow, **vary sentence structure** by combining shorter sentences into compound or complex sentences.
- **Vary sentence lengths** within paragraphs to emphasize certain ideas.

The chart includes specific examples of the authors' uses of both strategies.

Strategy	Osborne	Hall
Vary sentence structure by combining shorter sentences into compound or complex sentences.	Pure fruit juices and milk-based drinks will be excluded, and we'll ensure the smallest producers are kept out of· scope.	In theory, this makes a lot of sense, but when you compare the theoretical data with the observed data, you can see that the actual weight gain associated with sugary drinks is in fact ten times less than was originally theorized . . .
Vary sentence lengths within paragraphs. (Osborne: short—long) (Hall: long—short)	Obesity drives disease. It increases the risk of cancer, diabetes and heart disease—and it costs our economy £27 billion a year; that's more than half the entire NHS paybill.	Milkshakes, flavored waters and off-the-shelf cold coffees can contain nearly as much sugar as, if not more than, your average can of soda, and they tend to be higher in calories! . . . Yet these drinks are exempt from the tax!

5 Publish

Finalize your argument and choose a way to share it with your audience. Consider these options:

- Submit your argument as a letter to the editor of your local newspaper.
- Post your argument on an online news forum.

Use the scoring guide to evaluate your argument.

Writing Task Scoring Guide: Argument		
Organization/Progression	**Development of Ideas and Evidence**	**Use of Language and Conventions**
4 • Organization is appropriate to the purpose. • Claim is stated clearly, with all ideas strongly related to the claim. • Key ideas and evidence are organized consistently and logically with meaningful transitions.	• Introduction is memorable and persuasive; the claim states a position on a substantive topic. • Key ideas support the claim. • Opposing views are anticipated and addressed effectively. • Argument is supported by a variety of rhetorical devices. • Conclusion summarizes the claim.	• Writing reflects purposeful, precise word choice and maintains formal, respectful tone. • Sentences are varied. • Writing shows a consistent command of spelling, capitalization, punctuation, grammar, and usage conventions.
3 • For the most part, structure is appropriate and effective. • Claim is stated clearly, with most ideas related to the claim. Minor lapses in focus. • Organization of key ideas and evidence is confusing in a few places, and a few more transitions are needed.	• Introduction needs more to hook the reader; the claim states a position on an issue. • Key ideas support the claim but could be more convincing. • Counterarguments need further development. • Rhetorical devices do not directly support the argument. • Conclusion restates the claim.	• For the most part, writing reflects specific word choice. Style is informal in a few places and the tone defensive at times. • Sentences are reasonably varied. • Writing shows adequate command of spelling, capitalization, punctuation, grammar, and usage conventions, with few errors.
2 • Organization is evident but not always appropriate. • Irrelevant information is included or many ideas are not strongly connected to the claim. • Progression is not always logical; weak transitions, wordiness, or repetition affect the flow.	• The introduction is ordinary; the claim lacks clarity. • Key ideas are not always relevant. • Opposing views are anticipated but not addressed logically. • No clear relationship between rhetorical devices and argument. • The conclusion includes an incomplete summary of claim.	• Writing uses general or imprecise word choice, with little awareness of appropriate tone. • Sentences are often awkward, with little variation. • Writing shows only a partial command of spelling, capitalization, punctuation, grammar, and usage conventions, with some distracting errors.
1 • Organization is inappropriate to the purpose or no pattern is followed. • Claim is missing, unclear, or illogical; writing may include extraneous information or abrupt shifts between ideas. • Progression is weak; repetition, wordiness, and lack of transitions result in random or illogical presentation.	• The introduction is missing. • Significant support and evidence are missing. • Counterclaims are neither anticipated nor addressed. • Rhetorical devices are not included. • The conclusion is missing.	• Writing is vague, with limited word choice and a disrespectful tone. • Awkward sentences, fragments, and run-on sentences make the writing hard to follow. • Writing shows little or no command of spelling, capitalization, punctuation, grammar, and usage, with serious and persistent errors.

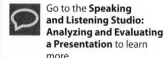

Debate an Issue

You will now adapt your argument for a debate with your classmates. You also will listen to other debate teams and prepare to critique their presentations.

Go to the **Speaking and Listening Studio: Analyzing and Evaluating a Presentation** to learn more.

① **Adapt Your Argument for a Debate**

Review your written argument, and use the chart below to guide you as you adapt it and plan for a debate. Note that one team will argue for your claim, and the other will argue against it.

Plan the Debate		
Identify two debate teams with two or three members each. Team 1: _____ _____ Team 2: _____ _____	Appoint a moderator to introduce the debate and the speakers and to keep everyone on task. Moderator: _____	Assign debate roles to each member: 1. Introduce team's argument: _____ 2. Refute opposing team: _____ 3. Present summary and closing statement: _____

Prepare Briefs	Prepare Rebuttals
Identify your claim:	Identify the opposing claim:
List key ideas and evidence that support your claim:	Identify weaknesses in the opposing claim and possible counterarguments:
Summarize your argument in a closing statement:	

As you work to improve your presentations, be sure to follow discussion rules:

❑ **listen closely to each other**

❑ **don't interrupt**

❑ **stay on topic**

❑ **ask helpful, relevant questions**

❑ **provide clear, thoughtful, and direct answers**

② Practice with Your Team

Once you've prepared your materials, work with your team to improve the presentation of your claim, key ideas, and evidence. Also practice rebuttals. Practice listening and responding respectfully.

Practice Effective Verbal and Nonverbal Techniques

❑ **Voice** Enunciate your words clearly and speak slowly and loudly enough so that everyone can hear you. Use your voice to show enthusiasm and emphasis.

❑ **Eye Contact** Try to let your eyes rest on each member of the audience at least once.

❑ **Facial Expression** Smile, frown, or raise an eyebrow to show your feelings or to emphasize points.

❑ **Gestures** Use natural gestures to add meaning and interest to your presentation.

Provide and Consider Advice for Improvement

As you and your team practice, take notes and provide helpful advice to each other. Consider ways to revise your presentation to make sure your points are clear and logically sequenced.

③ Hold the Debate

Set up the classroom for a formal debate, with the team members facing the audience. Follow the format below:

❑ **Pro Speaker 1:** Present claim and supporting evidence for the "pro," or supportive, side of the argument. —5 minutes

❑ **Con Speaker 2:** Ask probing questions that will prompt the other team to address flaws in the argument. —3 minutes

❑ **Pro Speaker 2:** Respond to the questions posed by the opposing team and provide counterarguments. —3 minutes

❑ **Con Speaker 1:** Present the claim and supporting evidence for the "con," or opposed, side of the argument. —5 minutes

❑ **Pro Speaker 2:** Ask probing questions that will prompt the other team to address flaws in the argument. —3 minutes

❑ **Con Speaker 2:** Respond to the questions posed by the opposing team and provide counterarguments. —3 minutes

❑ **Pro Speaker 3:** Summarize the claim and evidence for the "pro" side and explain why your claim is more valid. —3 minutes

❑ **Con Speaker 3:** Summarize the claim and evidence for the "con" side and explain why your claim is more valid. —3 minutes

Reflect on the Unit

By completing your argument, you have created a writing product that pulls together and expresses your thoughts about the reading you have done in this unit. Now is a good time to reflect on what you have learned.

Reflect on the Essential Questions

- Review the four Essential Questions on page 691. How have your answers to these questions changed in response to the texts you've read in this unit?

- What are some examples from the texts you've read that show how people relate to society?

Reflect on Your Reading

- Which selections were the most interesting or surprising to you?

- From which selection did you learn the most about how people relate to society?

Reflect on the Writing Task

- What difficulties did you encounter while working on your argument? How might you avoid them next time?

- What part of the argument was the easiest to write? The hardest to write? Why?

- What improvements did you make to your argument as you were revising?

UNIT 6 SELECTIONS
- "A Cup of Tea"
- "The Love Song of J. Alfred Prufrock"
- "Shooting an Elephant"
- "My Daughter the Racist"
- "The Second Coming"
- "Symbols? I'm Sick of Symbols"
- "Budget 2016: George Osborne's Speech"
- "Will the Sugar Tax Stop Childhood Obesity?"

RESOURCES

HMH *INTO LITERATURE* STUDIOS

For more instruction and practice, visit the HMH *Into Literature* Studios.

 Reading Studio

 Writing Studio

 Speaking & Listening Studio

 Grammar Studio

 Vocabulary Studio

UNIT 1
RESPONSE LOG

? Essential Question	Details from Texts
What makes someone a hero?	
What is true chivalry?	
Can we control our fate?	
What happens when a society unravels?	

UNIT 2
RESPONSE LOG

? Essential Question	Details from Texts
What can drive someone to seek revenge?	
How does time affect our feelings?	
What's the difference between love and passion?	
How do you defy expectations?	

UNIT 3
RESPONSE LOG

? **Essential Question**	**Details from Texts**
How can satire change people's behavior?	
What is your most memorable experience?	
What keeps women from achieving equality with men?	
Why are plagues so horrifying?	

UNIT 4
RESPONSE LOG

? Essential Question	Details from Texts
What can nature offer us?	
How do you define beauty?	
How can science go wrong?	
What shapes your outlook on life?	

UNIT 5
RESPONSE LOG

? Essential Question	Details from Texts
What is a true benefactor?	
How do you view the world?	
What brings out cruelty in people?	
What invention has had the greatest impact on your life?	

UNIT 6
RESPONSE LOG

? Essential Question	Details from Texts
What makes people feel insecure?	
Why is it hard to resist social pressure?	
What is the power of symbols?	
When should the government interfere in our decisions?	

Using a Glossary

A glossary is an alphabetical list of vocabulary words. Use a glossary just as you would a dictionary—to determine the meanings, parts of speech, pronunciation, and syllabification of words. (Some technical, foreign, and more obscure words in this book are defined for you in the footnotes that accompany many of the selections.)

Many words in the English language have more than one meaning. This glossary gives the meanings that apply to the words as they are used in the selections in this book.

The following abbreviations are used to identify parts of speech of words:

adj. adjective   *adv.* adverb   *n.* noun   *v.* verb

Each word's pronunciation is given in parentheses. A guide to the pronunciation symbols appears in the Pronunciation Key below. The stress marks in the Pronunciation Key are used to indicate the force given to each syllable in a word. They can also help you determine where words are divided into syllables.

For more information about the words in this glossary or for information about words not listed here, consult a dictionary.

Pronunciation Key

Symbol	Examples	Symbol	Examples	Symbol	Examples
ă	pat	m	mum	ûr	urge, term, firm, word, heard
ā	pay	n	no, sudden* (sud´n)	v	valve
ä	father	ng	thing	w	with
âr	care	ŏ	pot	y	yes
b	bib	ō	toe	z	zebra, xylem
ch	church	ô	caught, paw	zh	vision, pleasure, garage
d	deed, milled	oi	noise	ə	about, item, edible, gallop, circus
ĕ	pet	o͝o	took	ər	butter
ē	bee	o͞o	boot		
f	fife, phase, rough	o͝or	lure	**Sounds in Foreign Words**	
g	gag	ôr	core	KH	German ich, ach; Scottish loch
h	hat	ou	out	N	French, bon (bôn)
hw	which	p	pop	œ	French feu, œuf; German schön
ĭ	pit	r	roar	ü	French tu; German über
ī	pie, by	s	sauce		
îr	pier	sh	ship, dish		
j	judge	t	tight, stopped		
k	kick, cat, pique	th	thin		
l	lid, needle* (nēd´l)	*th*	this		
		ŭ	cut		

*In English the consonants *l* and *n* often constitute complete syllables by themselves.

Stress Marks

The relative emphasis with which the syllables of a word or phrase are spoken, called stress, is indicated in three different ways. The strongest, or primary, stress is marked with a bold mark (´). An intermediate, or secondary, level of stress is marked with a similar but lighter mark (´). The weakest stress is unmarked. Words of one syllable show no stress mark.

GLOSSARY OF ACADEMIC VOCABULARY

abandon (ə-băn´dən) *v.* to withdraw one's support or help, especially in spite of duty, allegiance, or responsibility.

ambiguous (ăm-bĭg´yoō-əs) *adj.* open to more than one interpretation.

anticipate (ăn-tĭs´ə-pāt) *v.* to see as a probable occurrence; expect.

appreciate (ə-prē´shē-āt) *v. tr.* to recognize the quality, significance, or magnitude of.

arbitrary (är´bĭ-trĕr-ē) *adj.* determined by chance, whim, or impulse, and not by necessity, reason, or principle.

collapse (kə-lăps´) *v.* to break down or fall apart suddenly and cease to function.

conceive (kən-sēv´) *v.* to understand or form in the mind; to devise.

confine (kən-fīn´) *v.* to keep within bounds; restrict.

conform (kən-fôrm´) *v.* to be similar to or match something or someone; to act or be in accord or agreement.

controversy (kŏn´trə-vûr-sē) *n.* public disagreement, argument.

convince (kən-vĭns´) *v.* persuade or lead to agreement by means of argument.

denote (dĭ-nōt´) *v.* to serve as a symbol for the meaning of; signify.

depress (dĭ-prĕs´) *v.* to cause to be sad or dejected.

displace (dĭs-plās´) *v.* to move, shift, or force from the usual place or position.

drama (drä´mə) *n.* a prose or verse composition intended to be acted out.

encounter (ĕn-koun´tər) *n.* to confront in battle or competition.

exploit (ĭk-sploit´) *v.* to take advantage of; to use for selfish or unethical purposes.

insight (ĭn´sīt) *n.* the ability to discern the true nature of a situation.

integrity (ĭn-tĕg´rĭ-tē) *n.* the quality of being ethically or morally upright.

intensity (ĭn-tĕn´sĭ-tē) *n.* a high degree of concentration, power, or force.

invoke (ĭn-vōk´) *v.* to call on for assistance, support, or inspiration.

military (mĭl´ĭ-tĕr-ē) *n.* the armed forces of a nation considered collectively; *adj.* of, related to, or characteristic of members of the armed forces.

persist (pər-sĭst´) *v.* to hold firmly to a purpose or task in spite of obstacles.

radical (răd´ĭ-kəl) *adj.* departing markedly from the usual or customary; extreme or drastic.

reluctance (rĭ-lŭk´təns) *n.* the state of being reluctant; unwillingness.

subordinate (sə-bôr´dn-ĭt) *adj.* subject to the authority or control of another.

undergo (ŭn-dər-gō´) *v.* to experience or be subjected to.

violate (vī´ə-lāt) *tr. v.* to disregard or act in a manner that does not conform to (a law or promise, for example).

visual (vĭzh´oō-əl) *adj.* seen or able to be seen by the eye; visible.

widespread (wīd´sprĕd´) *adj.* occurring or accepted widely.

GLOSSARY OF CRITICAL VOCABULARY

abate (ə-bāt´) *v.* to reduce in amount, degree, or intensity; lessen.

abrogate (ăb´rə-gāt) *v.* to revoke or nullify.

abyss (ə-bĭs´) *n.* an immeasurably deep chasm, depth, or void.

accolade (ăk´ə-lād, -läd) *n.* a special acknowledgement; an award.

affairs (ə-fârz´) *n.* personal business.

affliction (ə-flĭk´shən) *n.* something that causes suffering or pain.

aghast (ə-găst´) *adj.* struck by shock, terror, or amazement.

algorithm (ăl´gə-rĭth-əm) *n.* a finite set of unambiguous instructions that, given some set of initial conditions, can be performed in a prescribed sequence to achieve a certain goal and that has a recognizable set of end conditions.

anecdote (ăn´ĭk-dōt) *n.* a short account of an interesting or humorous incident.

appraise (ə-prāz´) *tr. v.* 1. to estimate the price or value of: appraise a diamond; appraise real estate. 2. to make a considered judgment about.

ardor (är´dər) *n.* intensity of emotion, especially strong desire, enthusiasm, or devotion.

artifice (är´tə-fĭs) *n.* cleverness or ingenuity in making or doing something.

attribute (ə-trĭb´yoot) *v.* to regard as arising from a particular cause or source; ascribe.

aversion (ə-vûr´zhən) *n.* a fixed, intense dislike; repugnance.

autonomy (ô-tŏn´ə-mē) *n.* the condition or quality of being autonomous; independence.

bailiff (bā´lĭf) *n.* an overseer of an estate; a steward.

baleful (bāl´fəl) *adj.* harmful or malignant in intent or effect.

balmy (bä´mē) *adj.* mild and pleasant.

bequeath (bĭ-kwēth´, -kwēth´) *tr. v.* to pass (something) on to another; hand down.

bereft (bĭ-rĕft´) *adj.* 1. deprived of something. 2. lacking something needed or expected.

brazen (brā´zən) *adj.* unrestrained by a sense of shame; rudely bold.

brooding (broo´dĭng) *adj.* thinking about something moodily.

cacophony (kə-kŏf´ə-nē) *n.* jarring, discordant sound; dissonance.

calamity (kə-lăm´ĭ-tē) *n.* an event that brings terrible loss, lasting distress, or severe affliction; a disaster.

chafe (chāf) *v. intr.* to cause irritation by rubbing or friction: The high collar chafed against my neck.

chow (chou) *n.* food; victuals.

collateral (kə-lăt´ər-əl) *adj.* concomitant or accompanying.

commence (kə-mĕns´) *v.* to begin or start.

commend (kə-mĕnd´) *tr. v.* to commit to the care of another; entrust.

compulsory (kəm-pŭl´sə-rē) *adj.* obligatory; required.

condone (kən-dōn´) *v.* to overlook, forgive, or disregard (an offense) without protest or censure.

congenial (kən-jēn´yəl) *adj.* agreeable, sympathetic.

consumption (kən-sŭmp´shən) *n.* an amount consumed.

cowed (koud) *tr. v.* to frighten or subdue with threats or a show of force.

GLOSSARY OF CRITICAL VOCABULARY

curate (kyŏŏr´āt) *tr. v.* to gather and present to the public.

demonize (dē´mə-nīz) *v.* to represent as evil or diabolic.

deprivation (dĕp-rə-vā´shən) *n.* the condition of being deprived; lacking the basic necessities or comforts of life.

despotic (dĭ-spŏt´ĭk) *adj.* of or relating to a person who wields power oppressively, or a tyrant.

discourse (dĭs´kôrs) *n.* verbal exchange or conversation.

dismay (dĭs-mā´) *v.* to upset or distress.

dissimulation (dĭ-sĭm´yə-lā-shən) *n.* deceit or pretense.

dogged (dô´gĭd, dŏg´ĭd) *adj.* stubbornly persevering; tenacious.

domain (dō-mān´) *n.* a sphere of activity, influence, or knowledge.

dominion (də-mĭn´yən) *n.* rule or power to rule; mastery.

double entendre (dûb´əl än-tän´drə) *n.* an expression having a double meaning.

emulation (ĕm´yə-lā-shən) *n.* competitive imitation.

encumbrance (ĕn-kŭm´brəns) *n.* a burden or impediment.

engagement (ĕn-gāj´mənt) *n.* a promise or agreement to be at a particular place at a particular time.

entail (ĕn-tāl´) *v.* involve as a consequence.

ersatz (ĕr´zäts, ĕr-zäts´) *adj.* being a usually inferior imitation or substitute; artificial.

eschew (ĕ-shōō´, ĕs-chōō´) *tr. v.* to avoid using, accepting, participating in, or partaking of.

esprit de corps (ĕ-sprē´ də kôr´) *n.* a spirit of devotion and loyalty among group members.

evanescent (ĕv-ə-nĕs´ənt) *adj.* vanishing or likely to vanish like vapor.

exorbitant (ĭg-zôr´bĭ-tənt) *adj.* beyond what is reasonable or customary, especially in cost or price.

expound (ĭk-spound´) *v.* to explain in detail; elucidate.

extract (ĭk-străkt´) *v.* to draw or pull out, often with great force or effort.

extremist (ĭk-strē´mĭst) *adj.* advocating or resorting to measures beyond the norm, especially in politics.

feeble (fē´bəl) *adj.* lacking strength.

finite (fī´nīt) *adj.* having bounds; limited.

flotsam (flŏt´səm) *n.* discarded or unimportant things.

forebear (fôr´bâr) *n.* a person from whom one is descended; an ancestor.

forge (fôrj) *v.* to form (metal, for example) by heating in a forge and beating or hammering into shape.

garish (gâr´ĭsh, găr´-) *adj.* overly bright or ornamented, especially in a vulgar or tasteless way; gaudy.

genre (zhän´rə) *n.* a category within an art form, based on style or subject.

gilded (gĭl´dĭd) *adj.* covered with or having the appearance of being covered with a thin layer of gold.

guile (gīl) *n.* clever trickery; deceit.

hierarchy (hī´ə-rär-kē) *n.* a ranking of status within a group.

huddle (hŭd´l) *v.* to crowd together, as from cold or fear.

ignoble (ĭg-nō´bəl) *adj.* not noble in quality, character, or purpose; base or dishonorable.

immersion (ĭ-mûr´zhən, -shən) *n.* the act or instance of engaging in something wholly or deeply.

impeccably (ĭm-pĕk´ə-blē) *adv.* in accordance with having no flaws; perfectly.

imperialism (ĭm-pîr´ē-ə-lĭz-əm) *n.* the extension of a nation's authority by territorial acquisition or by the establishment of economic and political dominance over other nations.

implementation (ĭm-plə-mən-tā´shən) *n.* the process of putting into practical effect; carry out.

inanimate (ĭn-ăn´ə-mĭt) *adj.* not having the qualities associated with active, living organisms.

inarticulate (ĭn-är-tĭkʹyə-lĭt) *adj.* uttered without the use of normal words or syllables; incomprehensible as speech or language.

incentive (ĭn-sĕnʹtĭv) *n.* something, such as the fear of punishment or the expectation of reward, that induces action or motivates effort.

inculcate (ĭn-kŭlʹkāt, ĭnʹkŭl-) *v.* to impress (something) upon the mind of another by frequent instruction or repetition; instill.

incumbent (ĭn-kŭmʹbənt) *adj.* required as a duty or an obligation.

inducement (ĭn-do͞osʹmənt, -dyo͞osʹ-) *n.* an incentive.

infantry (ĭnʹfən-trē) *n.* the branch of an army made up of units trained to fight on foot.

infuse (ĭn-fyo͞ozʹ) *v.* to fill or cause to be filled with something.

inoculate (ĭ-nŏkʹyə-lāt) *v.* to safeguard as if by inoculation; to protect.

labyrinth (lăbʹə-rĭnth) *n.* an intricate structure of interconnecting passages through which it is difficult to find one's way; a maze.

levy (lĕvʹē) *v.* to impose (a tax or fine, for example) on someone.

listless (lĭstʹlĭs) *adj.* lacking energy or disinclined to exert effort; lethargic: felt tired and listless.

loathsome (lōthʹsəm) *adj.* causing loathing; abhorrent.

loftily (loftʹĭ-ly) *adv.* arrogantly; haughtily.

luddite (lŭdʹīt) *n.* one who opposes technical or technological change.

malady (mălʹə-dē) *n.* a disease, disorder, or ailment.

manacle (mănʹə-kəl) *v.* to restrain the action or progress of something or someone.

mandatory (mănʹdə-tôr-ē) *adj.* required or commanded by authority; obligatory.

meme (mēm) *n.* a unit of cultural information, such as a cultural practice or idea, that is transmitted verbally or by repeated action from one mind to another.

mire (mīr) *v.* to hinder, entrap, or entangle.

misdeed (mĭs-dēdʹ) *n.* a wrong or illegal deed; a wrongdoing.

misogyny (mĭ-sŏjʹə-nē) *n.* hatred or mistrust of women.

monetize (mŏnʹĭ-tīz, mŭnʹ-) *tr. v.* to convert into a source of income.

morose (mə-rōsʹ, mô-) *adj.* sullen or gloomy.

odious (ōʹdē-əs) *adj.* extremely unpleasant; repulsive.

ominous (ŏmʹə-nəs) *adj.* menacing; threatening.

pension (pĕnʹshən) *n.* a sum of money paid regularly as a retirement benefit.

pervasive (pər-vāʹsĭv,-zĭv) *adj.* having the quality or tendency to pervade or permeate.

plateau (plă-tōʹ) *intr. v.* to reach a stable level; level off.

plight (plīt) *n.* a situation, especially a bad or unfortunate one.

posit (pŏzʹĭt) *tr. v.* to assume or put forward, as for consideration or the basis of argument.

preamble (prēʹăm-bəl, prē-ămʹ-) *n.* a preliminary statement.

precipice (prĕsʹə-pĭs) *n.* an overhanging or extremely steep mass of rock; the brink of a dangerous or disastrous situation.

prerogative (prĭ-rŏgʹə-tĭv) *n.* an exclusive right or privilege held by a person or group, especially a hereditary or official right.

prescient (prĕshʹənt) *adj.* of or relating to prescience— which means knowledge of actions or events before they occur.

presentable (prĭ-zĕnʹtə-bəl) *adj.* fit for introduction to others.

prodigious (prə-dĭjʹəs) *adj.* enormous.

prognosis (prŏg-nōʹsĭs) *n.* a prediction of the probable course and outcome of a disease.

promiscuously (prə-mĭsʹkyo͞o-əs-lə) *adv.* lacking standards of selection; acting without careful judgment; indiscriminate.

GLOSSARY OF CRITICAL VOCABULARY

prostrate (pros′trāt) *adj.* lying face down, as in submission or adoration.

pyrrhic victory (pĭr′ĭk vĭk′tə-rē) *n.* a victory that is offset by staggering losses.

quell (kwĕl) *tr. v.* to pacify; quiet.

ransack (răn′săk) *tr. v.* to go through (a place) stealing valuables and causing disarray.

realm (rĕlm) *n.* kingdom.

rebuke (rĭ-byo͞ok′) *tr. v.* to criticize (someone) sharply; reprimand.

recoil (rĭ-koil′) *v.* to shrink back, as in fear or repugnance.

redress (rĭ-drĕs′) *n.* repayment for a wrong or an injury.

repine (rĭ-pīn′) *v.* to be discontented; complain or fret.

rotation (rō-tā′shən) *n.* regular and uniform variation in a sequence or series.

ruddy (rŭd′ē) *adj.* having a healthy reddish glow.

rudiment (ro͞o′də-mənt) *n.* fundamental element, principle, or skill.

salutation (săl-yə-tā′shən) *n.* a polite expression of greeting or goodwill.

satire (săt′īr) *n.* a literary work in which human foolishness or vice is attacked through irony, derision, or wit.

scorn (skôrn) *n.* contempt or disdain.

scrounge (skrounj) *v. intr.* to obtain by salvaging or foraging; round up.

scrupulous (skro͞o′pyə-ləs) *adj.* conscientious and exact; having scruples.

sea change (sē chānj) *n.* a marked transformation.

self-possessed (sĕlf-pə-zĕst′) *adj.* having calm and self-assured command of one's faculties, feelings, and behavior.

senility (sĭ′nĭl-ĭ-tē) *n.* relating to or having diminished cognitive function, as when memory is impaired, because of old age.

sentient (sĕn′shənt) *adj.* having sense perception; conscious.

smart (smärt) *v.* to suffer acutely, as from mental distress, wounded feelings, or remorse.

sovereignty (sŏv′ər-ĭn-tē, sŏv′rĭn-) *n.* complete independence and self-government.

spoof (spo͞of) *n.* a satirical imitation; a parody or send-up.

succinct (sək-sĭngkt′) *adj.* characterized by clear, precise expression in few words; concise and terse.

summon (sŭm′ən) *v.* to bring into existence or readiness.

superficial (so͞o-pər-fĭsh′əl) *adj.* apparent rather than actual or substantial; shallow.

supplant (sə-plănt′) *tr. v.* to take the place of or substitute for (another).

sustenance (sŭs′tə-nəns) *n.* something, especially food, that sustains life or health.

tactfully (tăkt′fəl-lə) *adv.* considerately and discreetly.

theorize (thē′ə-rīz, thîr′īz) *v.* to formulate theories or a theory; speculate.

treachery (trĕch′ə-rē) *n.* an act of betrayal.

trinket (trĭng′kĭt) *n.* a small ornament, such as a piece of jewelry.

tumult (to͞o′mŭlt) *n.* a state of agitation of the mind or emotions.

undaunted (ŭn-dôn′tĭd, -dän′-) *adj.* not discouraged or disheartened; resolutely courageous.

underpin (ŭn-dər-pĭn′) *tr. v.* to give support or substance to.

usurp (yo͞o-sûrp′) *v.* to seize unlawfully by force.

Utopian (yo͞o-tō′pē-ən) *adj.* excellent or ideal but impracticable; visionary.

valor (văl′ər) *n.* courage, bravery.

veracity (və-răs′ĭ-tē) *n.* conformity to fact or truth; accuracy.

verandah (və-răn′də) *n.* a porch or balcony.

vexation (vĕk-sā´shən) *n.* a source of irritation or annoyance.

vigilance (vĭj´ə-ləns) *n.* alert watchfulness.

vile (vīl) *adj.* unpleasant or objectionable.

vindication (vĭn-dĭ-kā´shən) *n.* justification.

virtue (vûr´chōō) *n. Archaic* chastity, especially in a woman.

visitation (vĭz-ĭ-tā´shən) *n.* a.gathering of people in remembrance of a deceased person.

vogue (vōg) *adj.* the prevailing fashion, practice, or style.

wail (wāl) *v.* to make a long, loud, high-pitched cry, as in grief, sorrow, or fear.

writ (rĭt) *n.* a written order issued by a court, commanding the party to whom it is addressed to perform or cease performing a specified act.

INDEX OF SKILLS

INDEX OF TITLES AND AUTHORS

ACKNOWLEDGMENTS

Excerpts from *Beowulf* translated by Seamus Heaney. Translation copyright © 2000 by Seamus Heaney. Reprinted by permission of W. W. Norton & Company, Inc., and Faber & Faber Ltd.

Excerpt from "Budget 2016: George Osborne's Speech" by George Osborne from www.gov.uk. Contains Parliamentary information licensed under the Open Parliament License v3.0.

"Chivalry" from *Smoke and Mirrors* by Neil Gaiman. Text copyright © 1998 by Neil Gaiman. Reprinted by permission of Writers House, LLC.

"Confession" from *Borderless Bodies* by Linh Dinh. Text copyright © 2005 by Linh Dinh. Reprinted by permission of Linh Dinh.

"A Cup of Tea" from *The Short Stories of Katherine Mansfield* by Katherine Mansfield. Text copyright © 1923 by Penguin Random House LLC, renewed by J. Middleton Murry. Reprinted by permission of Alfred A. Knopf, an imprint of the Knopf Doubleday Publishing Group, a division of Penguin Random House LLC. All rights reserved. Any third-party use of this material, outside of this publication, is prohibited. Interested parties must apply directly to Penguin Random House LLC for permission.

"Education Protects Women from Abuse" by Olga Khazan as first published in *The Atlantic Magazine*, May 14, 2014. Text copyright © 2014 by The Atlantic Media Co. Reprinted by permission of Tribune Content Agency, LLC. All rights reserved. Distributed by Tribune Content Agency, LLC.

"For Army Infantry's 1st Women, Heavy Packs and the Weight of History" by Dave Phillips from *The New York Times*, May 27, 2017. Text copyright © 2017 by *The New York Times*. Reprinted by permission of PARS International Corps on behalf of *The New York Times*. All rights reserved. Protected by the Copyright Laws of the United States. Any printing, copying, redistribution, or retransmission of this content without express written permission is prohibited. www.nytimes.com

Excerpt from "Frankenstein: Giving Voice to the Monster" by Langdon Winner from www.langdonwinner.com, July 7, 2017. Text copyright © 2017 by Langdon Winner. Reprinted by permission of Langdon Winner.

Excerpt from "Hamlet's Dull Revenge" by René Girard from *Stanford Literature Review 1*, Fall 1984. Text copyright © 1984 by René Girard. Reprinted by permission of Martha Girard.

Excerpt from *Inferno: A Doctor's Ebola Story* by Steven Hatch. Text copyright © 2017 by Steven Hatch. Reprinted by permission of St. Martin's Press and Blackstone Publishing.

Excerpt from *Le Morte D'Arthur: King Arthur and the Legends of the Round Table* by Sir Thomas Malory, a new rendition by Keith Baines. Text copyright © 1962 by Keith Baines. Text copyright renewed © 1990 by Francesca Evans. Any third-party use of this material, outside of this publication, is prohibited. Interested parties must apply directly to Penguin Random House LLC for permission. Reprinted by permission of New American Library, an imprint of Penguin Publishing Group, a division of Penguin Random House LLC. All rights reserved.

"Loneliness" from *Second Childhood* by Fanny Howe. Text copyright © 2014 by Fanny Howe. Reprinted by permission of The Permissions Company, Inc., on behalf of Graywolf Press. www.graywolfpress.org

"The Love Song of J. Alfred Prufrock" from *Collected Poems 1909–1962* by T.S. Eliot. Text copyright © 1930, 1940, 1941, 1942, 1943, 1958, 1962, 1963 by T.S. Eliot, renewed 1970 by Esme Valerie Eliot. Reprinted by permission of Faber and Faber Ltd.

"My Daughter the Racist" from *Mr. Fox* by Helen Oyeyemi. Text copyright © 2011 by Helen Oyeyemi. Any third-party use of this material, outside of this publication, is prohibited. Interested parties must apply directly to Penguin Random House LLC for permission. Reprinted by permission of Riverhead, an imprint of Penguin Publishing Group, a division of Penguin Random House LLC, Penguin Canada, a division of Penguin Random House Canada Limited, and Wylie Agency LLC. All rights reserved.

"My Syrian Diary: Parts 1–3" by Marah from www.NewsDeeply.com. Text copyright © 2014 by Syria Deeply. Reprinted by permission of News Deeply, Inc.

Excerpt from *The Pastons: A Family in the War of the Roses* edited by Richard Barber. Text copyright © 1981 by Richard Barber. Reprinted by permission of Boydell & Brewer Ltd.

Quote from *A Dance with Dragons: A Song of Ice and Fire: Book Five* by George R. R. Martin. Text copyright © 2011 by George R. R. Martin. Any third-party use of this material, outside this publication, is prohibited. Interested parties must apply directly to Penguin Random House LLC for permission. Reprinted by permission of Bantam Books, an imprint of Random House, a division of Penguin Random House LLC and HarperCollins Publishers Ltd. All rights reserved.

From "Derek Walcott, the Art of Poetry No. 37," an interview by Edward Hirsch, originally published in *The Paris Review,* Issue 101, Winter 1986. Text copyright © The Paris Review, Inc. Reprinted by permission of Wylie Agency LLC.

"Satire is dying - the internet is killing it" by Arwa Mahdawi from www.theguardian.com, August 19, 2014. Text copyright © 2014 by The Guardian News & Media Ltd. Reprinted by permission of The Guardian News & Media Ltd.

"The Second Coming" from *The Collected Works of W. B. Yeats, Volume I: The Poems, Revised* by W. B. Yeats, edited by Richard J. Finneran. Text copyright 1924 by The Macmillan Company, renewed 1952 by Bertha Georgie Yeats. Reprinted by permission of Scribner, a division of Simon & Schuster, Inc. All rights reserved.

"Shooting an Elephant" from *Shooting an Elephant and Other Essays* by George Orwell. Text copyright © 1950 by Sonig Brownell, renewed © 1978 by Sonig, Pitt-Rivers. Reprinted by permission of Houghton Mifflin Harcourt Publishing Company, Penguin Books Ltd., and Bill Hamilton as the Literary Executor of the Estate of the Late Sonia Brownell Orwell. All rights reserved.

"Song of a Thatched Hut Damaged in Autumn Wind" by Du Fu, translated by Tony Barnstone and Chou Ping from *The Anchor Book of Chinese Poetry: From Ancient to Contemporary, the Full 3000-Year Tradition* edited by Tony Barnstone and Chou Ping. Text copyright © 2005 by Tony Barnstone and Chou Ping. Reprinted by permission of Penguin Random House LLC. All rights reserved. Any third-party use of this material, outside of this publication, is prohibited. Interested parties must apply directly to Penguin Random House LLC for permission.

"Symbols? I'm Sick of Symbols" by Fernando Pessoa from *Fernando Pessoa & Co.: Selected Poems*, edited and translated by Richard Zenith. Translation copyright © 1998 by Richard Zenith. Reprinted by permission of Grove Atlantic, Inc.

"Poem III" from *Twenty-One Love Poems* (retitled from "Part III") from *Collected Poems: 1950-2012* by Adrienne Rich. Text copyright © 1978 by Adrienne Rich, renewed © 2016 by the Adrienne Rich Literary Trust. Reprinted by permission of W. W. Norton & Company and The Frances Goldin Literary Agency.

"The Victorians Had the Same Concerns About Technology as We Do" by Melissa Dickson from www.theconversation.com, June 21, 2016. Text copyright © 2016 by Melissa Dickson. Reprinted by permission of Melissa Dickson.

"The Wanderer" from *Poems and Prose from the Old English* translated by Burton Raffel. Text copyright © 1997 by Yale University Press. Reprinted by permission of Yale University Press.

Excerpt from "The Wife of Bath's Tale" from *The Canterbury Tales* by Geoffrey Chaucer, translated by Nevill Coghill. Translation copyright © 1951 by Nevill Coghill, renewed 1958, 1960, 1975, 1977 by Nevill Coghill. Reprinted by permission of Penguin Books Ltd. and Curtis Brown Group Ltd, London on behalf of the Estate of Nevill Coghill. All rights reserved.

Excerpt from "Will the Sugar Tax Stop Childhood Obesity?" by Chris Hall from the HuffPost blog, March 22, 2016. Text copyright © 2016 by Chris Hall. Reprinted by permission of Chris Hall.